Craftsbury
sculling center

www.craftsbury.com
stay@craftsbury.com
802.586.7767

PO Box 31, 535 Lost Nation Road, Craftsbury Common,
Vermont 05827

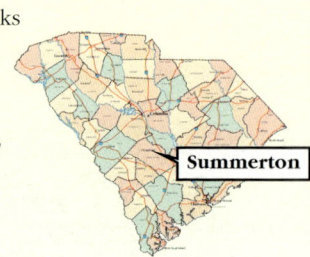

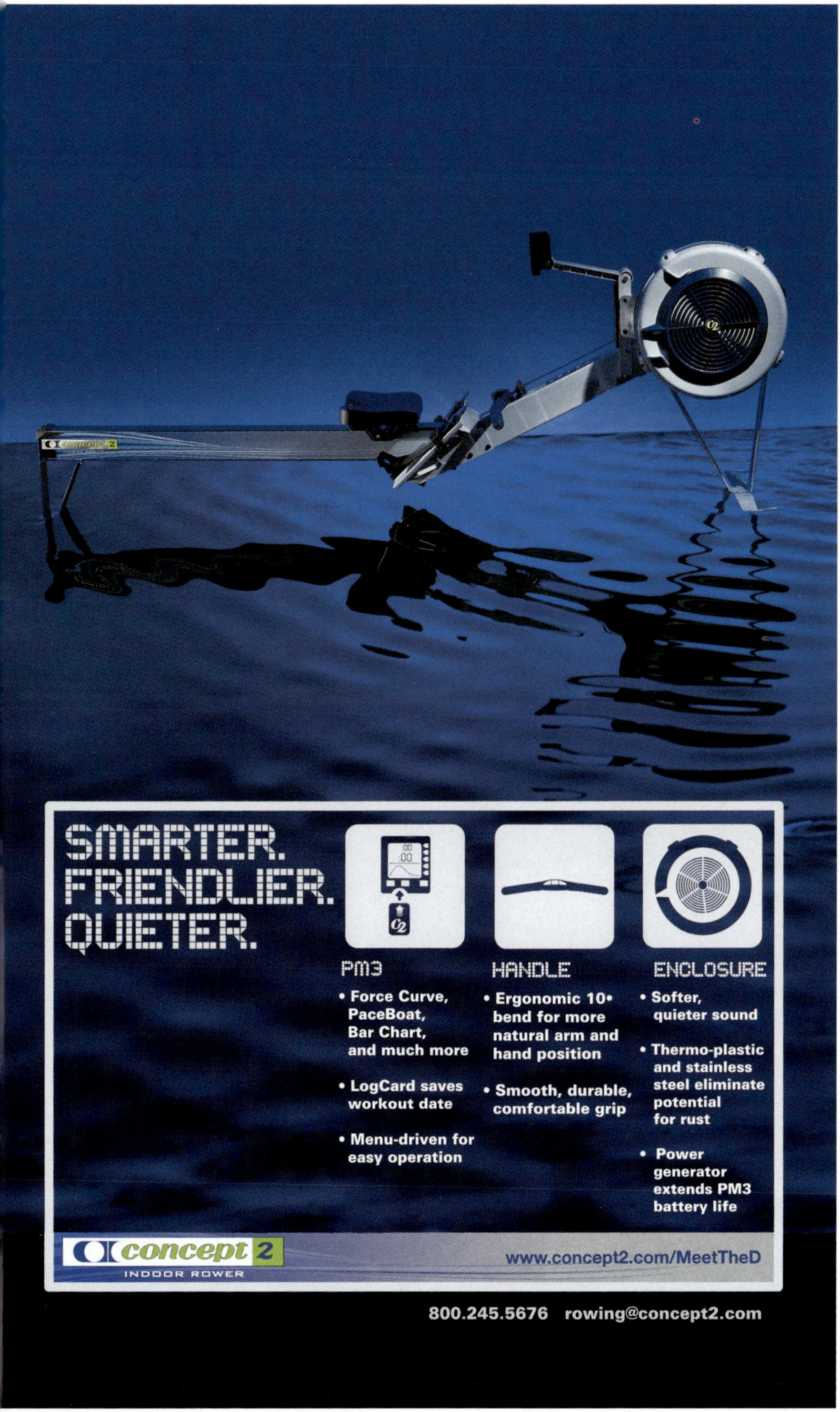

SMARTER.
FRIENDLIER.
QUIETER.
PM3
• Force Curve, PaceBoat, Bar Chart, and much more
• LogCard saves workout date
• Menu-driven for easy operation
HANDLE
• Ergonomic 10• bend for more natural arm and hand position
• Smooth, durable, comfortable grip
ENCLOSURE
• Softer, quieter sound
• Thermo-plastic and stainless steel eliminate potential for rust
• Power generator extends PM3 battery life
concept 2
INDOOR ROWER
www.concept2.com/MeetTheD
800.245.5676 rowing@concept2.com

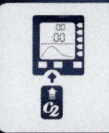

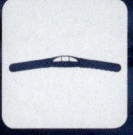

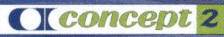

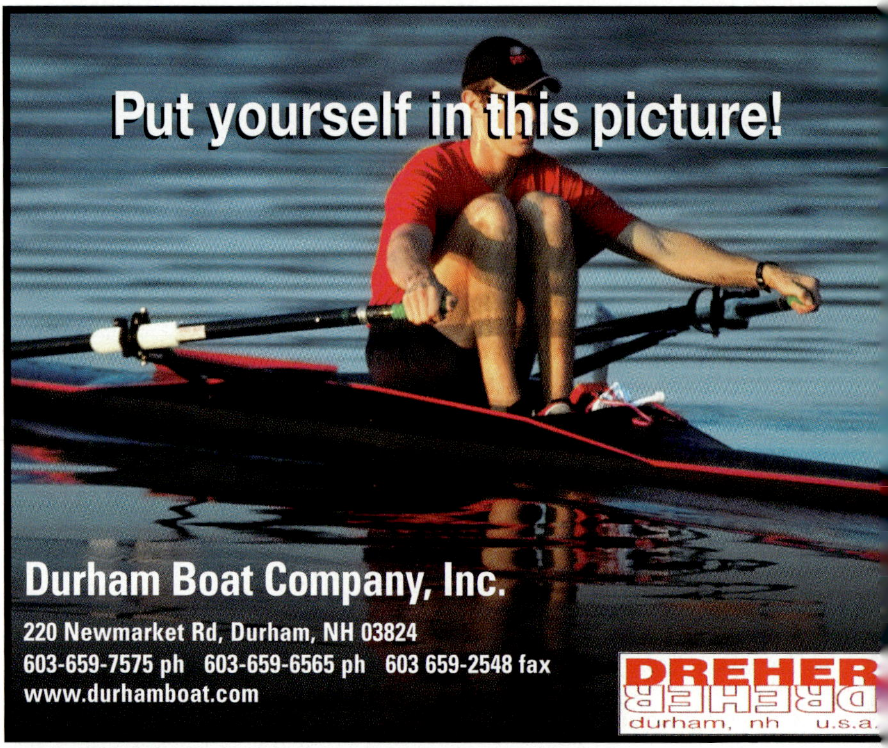
Put yourself in this picture!
Durham Boat Company, Inc.
220 Newmarket Rd, Durham, NH 03824
603-659-7575 ph 603-659-6565 ph 603 659-2548 fax
www.durhamboat.com
DREHER
durham, nh u.s.a.

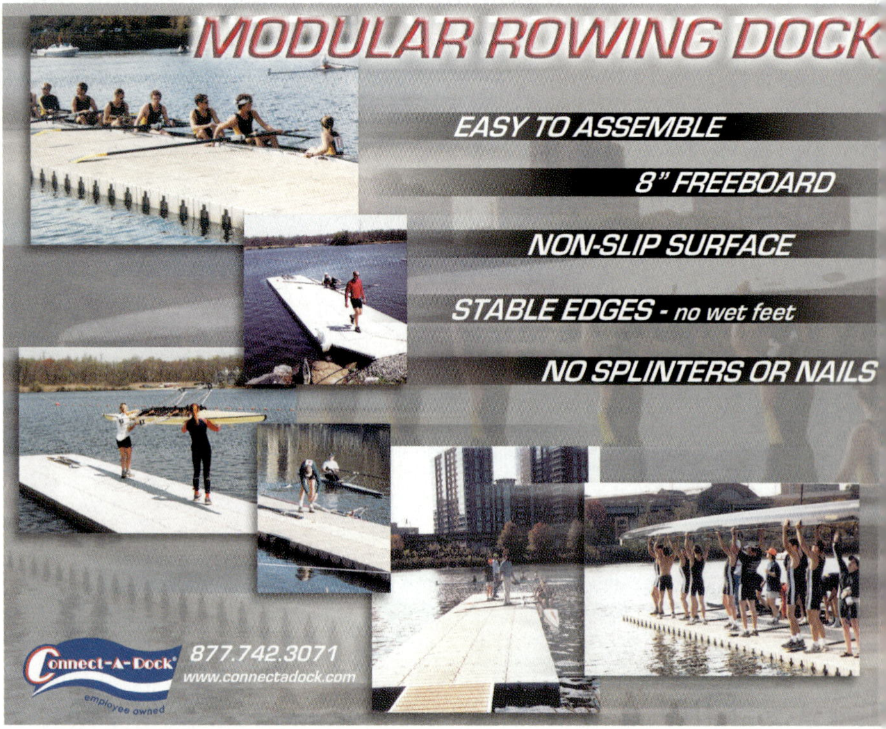
MODULAR ROWING DOCK
EASY TO ASSEMBLE
8" FREEBOARD
NON-SLIP SURFACE
STABLE EDGES - no wet feet
NO SPLINTERS OR NAILS
Connect-A-Dock
employee owned
877.742.3071
www.connectadock.com

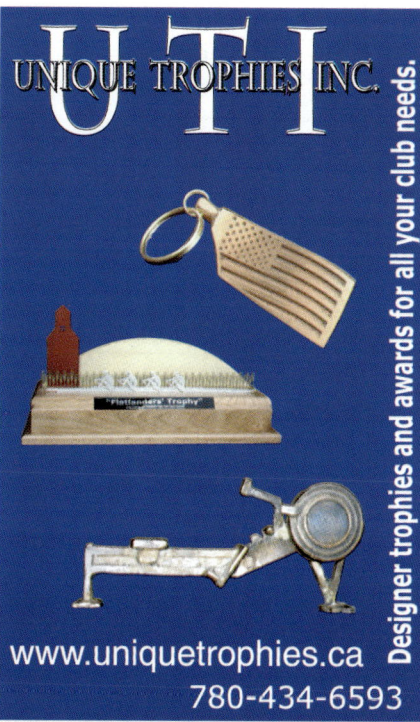

National ★ Federations

ALB Albania

ALG Algeria

ANG Angola

ARG Argentina

ARM Armenia

AUS Australia

AUT Austria

AZE Azerbaijan

BAN Bangladesh

BAR Barbados

BEL Belgium

BLR Belarus

BRA Brazil

BRN Bahrain

BUL Bulgaria

BUR Burkina Faso

CAN Canada

CAY Cayman Islands

CHI Chile

CHN China

CIV Ivory Coast

CMR Cameroon

COL Colombia

CRC Costa Rica

CRO Croatia

CUB Cuba

CYP Cyprus

CZE Czech Republic

DEN Denmark

DOM Dominican Republic

ECU Ecuador

EGY Egypt

ESA El Salvador

ESP Spain

EST Estonia

FIN Finland

FRA France

GBR Great Britain

GEO Georgia

GER Germany

GIB Gibraltar

GRE Greece

GUA Guatemala

HKG Hong Kong

HON Honduras

HUN Hungary

INA Indonesia

IND India

IRL Ireland

IRQ Iraq

ISL Iceland

ISR Israel

ITA Italy

JPN Japan

KAZ Kazakhstan

KEN Kenya

KGZ Kyrgyzstan

KOR Korea

KUW Kuwait

LAT Latvia

National ★ Federations

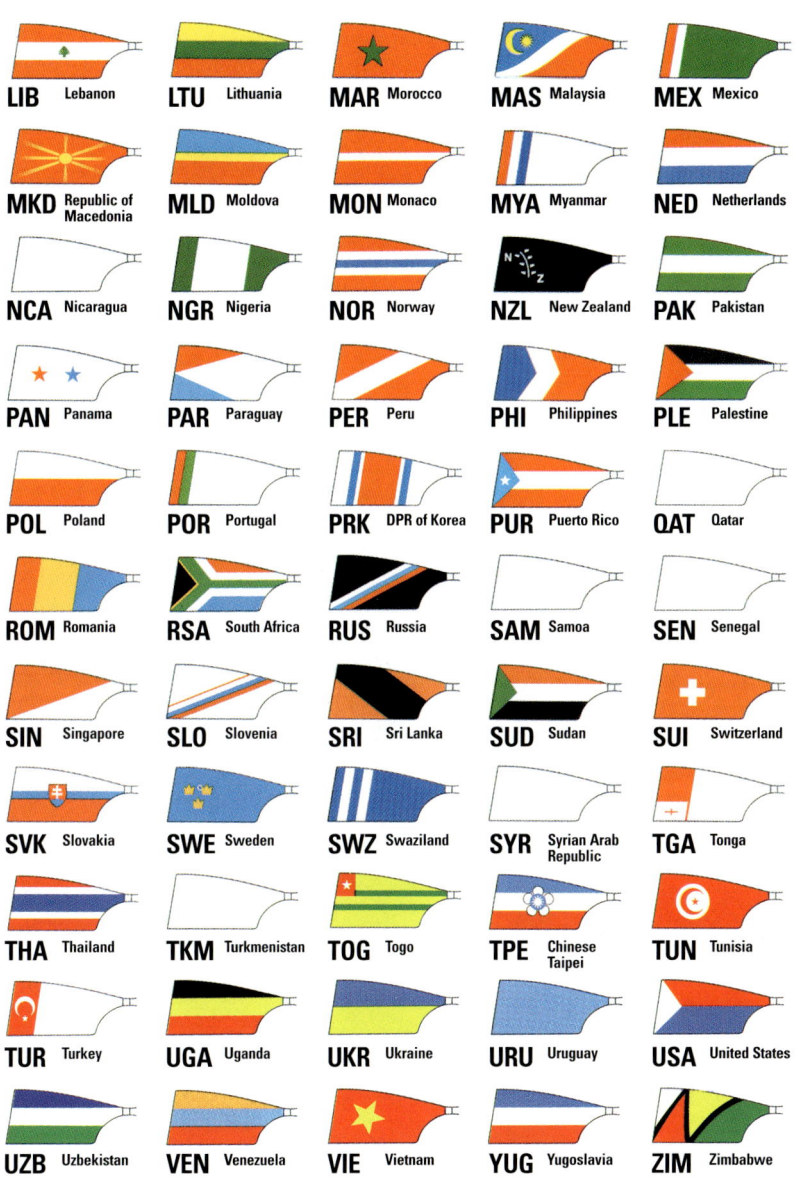

LIB Lebanon	**LTU** Lithuania	**MAR** Morocco	**MAS** Malaysia	**MEX** Mexico
MKD Republic of Macedonia	**MLD** Moldova	**MON** Monaco	**MYA** Myanmar	**NED** Netherlands
NCA Nicaragua	**NGR** Nigeria	**NOR** Norway	**NZL** New Zealand	**PAK** Pakistan
PAN Panama	**PAR** Paraguay	**PER** Peru	**PHI** Philippines	**PLE** Palestine
POL Poland	**POR** Portugal	**PRK** DPR of Korea	**PUR** Puerto Rico	**QAT** Qatar
ROM Romania	**RSA** South Africa	**RUS** Russia	**SAM** Samoa	**SEN** Senegal
SIN Singapore	**SLO** Slovenia	**SRI** Sri Lanka	**SUD** Sudan	**SUI** Switzerland
SVK Slovakia	**SWE** Sweden	**SWZ** Swaziland	**SYR** Syrian Arab Republic	**TGA** Tonga
THA Thailand	**TKM** Turkmenistan	**TOG** Togo	**TPE** Chinese Taipei	**TUN** Tunisia
TUR Turkey	**UGA** Uganda	**UKR** Ukraine	**URU** Uruguay	**USA** United States
UZB Uzbekistan	**VEN** Venezuela	**VIE** Vietnam	**YUG** Yugoslavia	**ZIM** Zimbabwe

Oars provided compliments of FISA, www.fisa.org

FIRST THE BOOK, NOW THE DATABASE

ROWER'S ALMANAC DATABASE

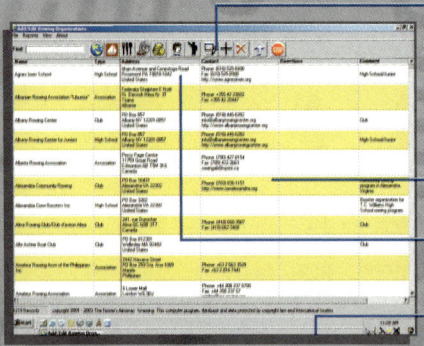

Features

- Detailed program information on thousands of rowing organizations around the world
- Thousands of coach and contact telephones, emails and addresses

Functions

- Select and export records automatically into excel spreadsheets
- Use to create targeted emails and mailings

ROWER'S ALMANAC CONTACT MANAGER

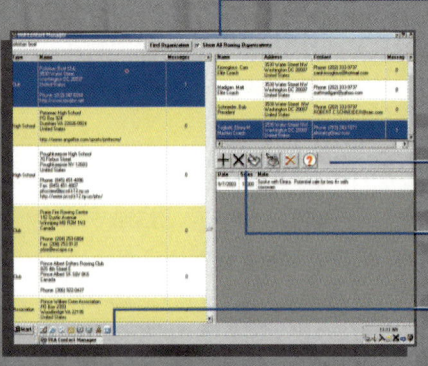

Features

- Works with The Rower's Almanac Database to record, edit and update sales and potential sales contacts
- Easily tracks and manages sales and contact information for your business

Functions

- Select and export records automatically into excel spreadsheets
- Use to communicate and manage client relationships

VISIT WWW.ROWERSALMANAC.COM
FOR MORE INFORMATION.

2004 ★ 2005
Rower's Almanac

The Official Guidebook
to Rowing Around the World

The Rower's Almanac, Inc.
Washington, D.C.

www.rowersalmanac.com

Publisher
Karen Solem

International
Elmira Togliatti

Editorial
Marlene Royle
Carmen Marquez

Art/Design
Aleksandr Gembinski — Layout
Joel Rogers — Cover Photo

Contributors

Luke Agnini	Kevin Luecke	Eli Szabo
Debbie Arenberg	Masters Rowing Association	Susan Urbas
Ellen Braithwaite	Scott Meade	Susan Varga
Karyn Crouthamel	Bill Miller	Steve Wells
Kathleen DiGiacomo	Mark Miller	Liz Wray
Louisa Edgerly	Demie Moore	Renee Wunderli
FISA	Pattie Pinkerton	Urs Wunderli
Richard Gonci	Elaine Roden	Rachel Yates
Doug Kidder	Giyora Saar	
Susan Lillestol	Shirwin Smith	

Contributing Federations

Argentina	Ireland	Portugal
Bulgaria	Israel	Romania
Canada	Kenya	Russia
Chile	Lithuania	South Africa
Estonia	Monaco	Uganda
France	New Zealand	United Kingdom
Germany	Palestine	United States
Hungary	Peru	
Iceland	Poland	

The Rower's Almanac, Inc.

9902 Parkwood Drive Bethesda, MD 20814, United States
Tel: (301) 520-8066   Fax: (703) 812-8199
info@rowersalmanac.com | www.rowersalmanac.com

International Standard Book Number: 0-96513-275-7

The Rower's Almanac may be accessed on the Internet at www.rowersalmanac.com

Printed in Canada.

From the Publisher . . .

I AM A LUCKY PERSON. My husband, who has never rowed a stroke in his life (with the exception of the time I forced him in one of those virtually un-flippable ocean-going learn-to-row boats) puts up with all the spare time I devote to this sport. For example, last summer, I insisted on toting twenty extra Almanacs along with us on our seven-country three-week honeymoon. My plan was to contact rowing clubs along the way and handout Almanacs to those rowers I met. Arriving at our first destination, I discovered how heavy each Almanac was. It was not a travel-friendly book! Our latest edition has been better designed for travel — it's lighter and smaller. It also has about 40% more information packed into a neat, concise layout.

Another discovery I made on our trip was that the book really works! What I mean by that is over the years, I have heard from people who have rowed on the Nile, and other exotic places thanks to contact information provided in the book. Last summer, I was able to test it myself: I took a single out at the Cairns Rowing Club in Cairns, Australia, and I met rowers in Hong Kong and toured their boathouse.

Some other really interesting features in this edition include contributions from twenty-five National Governing Bodies describing the history of the sport in their country, famous personalities, and rowing-related sites of interest. These contributions come from five different continents including Africa, Europe, the Middle East, and North and South America.

This edition also contains some wonderful stories on open water and touring rows ranging from the coast of Maine, to Jackson Hole, WY to the wild Missouri River in Montana, to the urban San Francisco Bay. When I read about following the Lewis & Clark Trail down the Missouri, I was ready to pack my bags and leave the next day.

Our Rower-Friendly Dining section contains some funny and witty recommendations of "rower-friendly" restaurants all over the U.S. and Canada. All of these restaurants are considered the crème de la crème of "post-practice chow fests", as one rower remarks. When I read about the biscuits from The Flying Biscuit Café in Atlanta, GA being described as "sublime works of culinary art", I simply had to find out for myself. And, it's true!

And finally, for those of you in the market for a racing, open water or recreational boat, you must peruse our new Buyer's Guide starting on page 405. This section also features some of the top Rowing Schools and Camps in North America.

I hope you enjoy this edition of The Rower's Almanac. If you have any travel stories or adventures, or find any of this information useful in your travel plans, please write me. I'd love to hear from you!

Sincerely,

Karen Solem
karen@rowersalmanac.com

In Memory of Kari Osterhaug

On January 5, 2003, at the age of 31, Karin Ingrid Osterhaug was killed suddenly and unexpectedly. She was expecting her first child in March.

A recent profile in Washington Wildlands Magazine called her a "passionate conservationist, capable scientist, dedicated athlete, helpful colleague, caring friend…a strong, joyful spirit with a ready smile and a contagious laugh."

Kari was born and raised in the Seattle area, the youngest of five children. She earned a degree in zoology at the University of Washington, where she also lettered in crew all four years and was co-captain her senior year. After graduation she worked as a field researcher for several years, including a six-month project in the jungles of Panama for the Smithsonian. She married Tom Gergen, a fellow zoology student, in 1999. A course in wetlands management at the University of Washington led to a position as Environmental Scientist with King County, Department of Natural Resources. "Kari's passion and love of nature were reflected in her work" said a colleague. Always willing to go the extra mile, she discovered a large bog in eastern King County and was instrumental in saving it from imminent development. She was also active in masters rowing and swimming programs.

Memorial donations are suggested to the Nature Conservancy of Washington, 217 Pine Street, Suite 1100, Seattle, WA 98101.

★ Table of Contents ★

Cairns Rowing Club member wading in to launch pair. Pictured in background is the marina for the Cairns fishing industry.
Photo courtesy of Digital Future Photography

Rowing Outside the Lanes ★ A Guide to Open Water

By Doug Kidder

Open water rowing gives access to scenic water that is otherwise inaccessible with flat-water boats. Analogous to mountain biking where one has a chance to get "off the roads" into beautiful countryside, open water rowing lets the rower "row outside the lanes."

From racing in demanding open water events like the twenty-two mile Blackburn Challenge and thirty-five mile Catalina Crossing, camping and rowing in Jackson Hole or Missouri, or simply enjoying a row in the Bay of Maine, all are accessible to anyone who has the equipment, experience, and desire.

I came to this sport late in life. I learned to row in college and continued rowing in flat-water races as a master. It was not an either/or choice; I used my road bike, my mountain bike, my flat-water single and my open water single. I loved blasting off the starting line for one thousand meters in a quad and I also loved feeling the bow of my boat lifting out of the water under the Golden Gate Bridge.

As in flat-water racing, open water racing has its list of champions; men and women who have a real mastery with the stroke and equipment. Scullers who can maintain a 2:10 per 500-meters pace in a double through three to five-foot waves while staying on course. People who can pack a boat and take off into the wilds of Alaska for a month of camping. These champions usually are not big rangy men. Two of the best open water rowers I know are one hundred ten-pound masters women.

The article that follows is a compilation of rows from around the country. Open water rowers that I know write about their favorite rows. These rows will inspire you to try them yourself. Contact information is included to help you find your way "outside the lanes."

Puget Sound
Gull Harbor ★ Hope Island

Steve Wells

Joel Rogers, in his excellent book Watertrail, sets the stage:

"Budd Inlet is one of six inlets that carve the shores of southernmost Puget Sound. They are as narrow as the low, forested peninsulas separating them, north south trending, gouged and elongated by the Pleistocene glaciers. Here is the quiet part of the Sound, where the wind has to work its way between overhanging alders to touch the water..."

The Gull Harbor — Hope Island row offers either a half-day or overnight trip option. The overnight option begins in Olympia at the southern tip of Puget Sound, passes the undeveloped shoreline of Priest Point Park, includes the pristine estuary at Gull Harbor, crosses the ship channel in Dana Passage and turns at the campground of Hope Island State Park for the return to Olympia. The half-day option includes an exploration of Gull Harbor, whose entire shoreline is protected by conservation easements, a visit to Boston Harbor for refreshments and then a return to Olympia along either shoreline of Budd Inlet.

Boats are launched from the docks belonging to Olympia Area Rowing located at the Port of Olympia's Swantown Marina. This is a public access dock, and no fees are charged. Vehicles may be parked in the Visitor's lot, and the Port provides 24-hour security.

Hope Island State Park is accessible only by boat. It is one of the registered campgrounds on the Cascadia Marine Trail. Details about the Marine Trail as well as the park and its campground are posted at www.wwta.org/trails/southsound.html. Hope Island is located in the middle of often-strong currents flowing into Squaxin Passage from four inlets, so trip preparation and timing should include consideration of tide charts.

Copyright Michael Lampi Courtesy of SoundRowers

Gull Harbor is three miles north of the put-in at Swantown. The entrance to the harbor is protected by a gravel spit, which at low-tide is notoriously shallow. Once over the bar, the harbor deepens. This is a quiet place offering refuge to rafts of ducks, kingfishers, herons, and harbor seals. The state has

provided generous grants to acquire conservation easements here to protect habitat for endangered salmon. The shoreline remains in private ownership, so boaters cannot pull out on the beach, but the calm and peacefulness of this haven are remarkable.

Copyright Michael Lampi courtesy of SoundRowers

Past the public beach at Burfoot County Park is the marina and boat launch at Boston Harbor, about 6 miles north of Olympia. There's a grocery store at the marina where one may buy the standard refreshments available anywhere but, in addition, the store sells fresh salmon and shellfish for your dinner on Hope Island. They also rent kayaks and Alden shells. If you opt for the half-day row, this is where you turn and head back to Swantown.

Directions: Take exit 105B from I-5 at Olympia. Proceed north on Plum Street, following signs to Port of Olympia. After six lights, turn left at Tom's Outboard onto Marine Drive. Follow signs to Swantown Marina. Park in the visitor's parking lot. Boats may be launched from the dock of Olympia Area Rowing club located on the breakwater north of the boat launch ramps.

Contacts: Steve Wells at Evergreen Rowing LLC in Olympia. Telephone is (360) 357-6588 and email is steve@evergreenrowing.com.

Washington State Parks information is available at www.parks.wa.gov.

A really helpful website is at www.soundrowers.org.

Copyright Michael Lampi courtesy of SoundRowers

Maine
Debbie Arenberg

Maine Island Trail: A 325-mile-long waterway for small boats extending from Casco Bay to Machias. Designed specifically for self-propelled watercraft and small sailboats and motorboats, the Trail winds its way along the coast over protected salt rivers and quiet bays, around magnificent and exposed capes, and among islands large and small. It takes advantage of the existence of small, state-owned islands along most of the route, using them as overnight stopovers where one can camp in a wilderness setting. Other islands, including many privately owned ones, are also in the Trail system.

The best way to learn more about this amazing trail is to contact the Maine Island Trail Association (MITA.) The mission of MITA is "to establish a model of thoughtful use and volunteer stewardship for the Maine islands that will assure their conservation in a natural state while providing an exceptional recreational asset that is maintained and cared for by the people who use it." If you join MITA, you get access to the privately-owned islands as well as a 300-page Stewardship Handbook which includes chapters on cruising guidelines, access information, island descriptions, in-depth technical articles and educational essays on the local floral and fauna.

Suggested reading in addition to the guidebook is "Hot Showers", written by Lee Bumstead. This book is a guide to Maine coast lodgings for rowers, kayakers and sailors. Lee also begins her recommended travels in the Casco Bay region and takes rowers Downeast to Lubec. Her guide gives specifics from available parking to launching hints (tide, etc), recommended inns and B&B's, chart excerpts, wheel chair access, and much more.

Contacts: To join M.I.T.A .- www.mita.org or contact the Maine Island Trail Association offices at: POB Box C, Rockland, Maine 04841, islands@ime.net, (207) 596-7796 or the Portland, Maine office at (207) 761-8225, mita@ime.net. Individual memberships start at $65 per person.

Order Hot Showers from Audenreed Press at (888) 315-0582 9AM-5PM EST, or online at www.biddle-audenreed.com at $18.95 plus $2 S&H.

Piscataqua River to Pepperell Cove, Kittery Point: Most tourists funnel into the state of Maine near the coast via the tall I-95 bridge that passes over the Piscataqua River. (Accent on the 2nd of four syllables!) This unsuspecting body of water forms the boundary that separates Maine from New Hampshire and is the mouth of a water network that flows from the southern seacoast to the sea via the Great Bay, and the Oyster, Salmon Falls, Squamscott, Cocheco, and the Bellemy Rivers. All rivers are accessible directly or very nearly from many launch sites located in both Maine and NH. The Piscataqua River is tidal and is prone to swift currents, especially through the

Portsmouth, NH area, so do your homework and check local navigational and tidal charts before attempting this row.

The Piscataqua River empties out into Portsmouth Harbor (NH side) and Pepperell Cove (the Maine side). Rowers can launch from either the Great Common Park in Newcastle, NH or Fort Foster (WWII) Park in Kittery Point, ME to experience a variety of protected saltwater rowing cruises.

My favorite row is to launch at Fort Foster, cross the harbor mouth, enter Little Harbor, pass the historic Wentworth By The Sea Hotel, circle around the island of New Castle, NH and back to Fort Foster, for a round trip of approximately 7 miles. You can extend your trip by turning into one of the many creeks or coves along the course. The view of the harbor from both locations is spectacular and includes Ft. McClary (Revolutionary War), the Whaleback Light, passing ferries to the Isles of Shoals, working lobster boats, rocky coastline, excellent swimming beaches, harbor seals, puffins, and a myriad of water fowl.

Contacts: Alden Rowing Shells, Eliot, ME (800) 477-1507 (rent shells) or Portsmouth Visitor Information at (603) 436-1118 (NH) or Kittery Chamber (207) 439-7545 (ME).

San Francisco Bay

Shirwin Smith and Ellen Braithwaite

Home is San Francisco Bay — specifically the waters off Sausalito and out into the main San Francisco Bay. Twenty years ago those waters both thrilled and terrified me — the rough water could be so rough, and it would seem sometimes to come up for no reason at all. Twenty years and a lot of learning later, the same waters still have the power to thrill, but terror has mellowed into paying attention and in some cases,

choosing another direction to row, or even, staying on shore with breakfast.

Why is San Francisco Bay my favorite spot? Some part of this has to be attributed to watching the sport grow on the scrappy northern Sausalito shoreline, but there are many more reasons:

1. Variety of conditions, even on a single row.

You can start on flat water, fly through a wicked tide rip with foot and a half to two foot standing waves, hit chop driven by an 18-20 knot breeze, go back into shiny flat water and finish with a downwind run to the boathouse under wind-driven fog. This is all within a 4 to 8 mile row. Or, the same day, you could choose a different direction and row over no more than rippled water the whole time you're out.

2. Variety of vistas.

We've got islands — natural islands, islands with prisons, islands covered with birds, islands with lighthouses. We've got mountains — no Rockies, but mountains nonetheless. We've got hills that change from glowing green to gold. We've got a big city in one direction and a national park with all its open space in another. You can row just off an urban shoreline, or off a shore of a state park with rocky headlands and wildflowers on the bluffs above. There's more, but you get the idea.

3. Lots of folks who love the sport, but plenty of room for all.

To me, open water is precious because you don't have to "stay in your lane". For me, living in an urban area, open space and the ability to enjoy it in solitude are precious gifts. But when you want to be with others who love it all like you do, you have that, too.

Where: Richardson Bay (arm of San Francisco Bay off Sausalito)

Jay Graham Photography — All Rights Reserved

How: Launch from the beach at Schoonmaker Point Marina, or from Open Water Rowing Center (within the marina), but call first. 415-332-1091

What: You need a true open water shell — hard-decked, with small volume cockpit and self-bailer. And bring a lifevest to have in the shell — the USCG approved small blow up vests are fine, but make sure they're manual or the auto-inflate feature may blow parts off your shell if you have it tucked behind the footstretcher!

Suggested rows all starting at Open Water Rowing:

Short: NM (approx) along the Sausalito shoreline to Yellow Bluff and return

Medium: 8.5 NM around Angel Island or around Alcatraz. Be ready for the possibility of wild water. Experienced open water scullers only

Longer: 12.4 NM Through Raccoon Strait, out to and around Red Rock and return. Experienced open water scullers only

More: 16.2 NM Through Raccoon Strait, out to and around East Brother Light and return. Experienced open water scullers only.

Contacts: Open Water Rowing, Sausalito, CA 415-332-1091, www.owrc.com, owrc@owrc.com

Florida
Urs and Renee Wunderli

Florida has an abundance of public access to lakes, canals, bays, ocean and the Gulf of Mexico. Starting in the northern part of the state is the famous Suwannee River.

The Suwannee begins in the Okefenokee Swamp in Southern Georgia, and winds it's way through 206 miles of age old cypress trees and beautiful pines that line the river banks and high bluffs, before emptying into the Gulf of Mexico near Cedar Key, FL. The river teems with wildlife such as exotic birds, otters, turtles and yes, the occasional Florida Gator. There are campsites along the way, as well as accommodations for the non-camper. Not all of the river is navigable by rowing, only a stones throw wide as the locals say, but with the maps a row tour can be planned with ease.

Maps of the river, launch areas and campsites are available from the Suwannee River Water Management District (www.srwmd.state.fl.us or 386.362.1001).

Further south are the islands of Captiva and Sanibel. The canals and mangroves are endless. In the canals the waters are generally calm, therefore, a narrow rowing shell can manage without fighting wind and waves. Accommodations on the islands are usually small resorts and cottages or B &

B's, many with water access. Day trips can be planned and for the more adventurous a row out into the Gulf of Mexico.

The Captiva/Sanibel Chamber of Commerce (www-sanibel-captiva.org or 239-472-1080) is the best source for information on accommodations and maps of the islands.

If one has the time and is inclined to a longer row, a row across the state can be accomplished through Lake Okeechobee and the Okeechobee Waterway. To begin a row across the state, boats can be launched from Shepards Park in Stuart, FL. The row from Stuart to Fort Myers, FL is 155 miles, which takes approximately one week. There are marinas, restaurants and campsites along the way, as well as, locks to negotiate and the proverbial Florida Gator. Neither locks nor gators have caused distress to those who have "rowed the state". The park rangers, water patrol and lockmasters have all proven to be agreeable to seeing rowers on their waterway.

The furthest point south for rowing or anything else in the US is Key West. Boyd's Camp Ground has been the site of the annual Keys Row, although some prefer the comfort of a real bed after a day of rowing. Always on Presidents Day week-end and always rowing fun with everything from Assay life guard boats to rec/racing shells. This past year there were even the "odd" kayakers. It is primarily a rower's event. The weather has cooperated for the most part. This past year one stop on the row was at a defunct submarine dry dock. They are now filled with water, excellent for snorkeling and diving.

These are only a mere sampling of rowing opportunities in Florida. There are rowing waters for every boat and every rower, regardless of boat type or rowing skills. Most rowing shells can be outfitted for touring with basic kayak hatches and tie downs. We have carried as much as 150 lbs of water plus rower and personal gear on a recreational rowing shell.

Contacts: More information on rowing in Florida is available by calling Urs Wunderli at 888.767.8827 or 941.387.7773.

Jackson Hole
Mark Miller

This country is of a nature best described as awesome and breathtaking. The row is actually three rows, minimum, that you should experience if you are to make such a trip with an open water boat. They are Jenny Lake, Jackson Lake and the first section of the Snake River (roughly in order of challenge).

The first, Jenny Lake, is about 3,000 meters north to south. Jenny Lake is right at the foot of the Grand Tetons, so the water is at about 6,400' and the slope up and out at the southwest shore goes right up to 13,770'.

Rowing at this altitude requires some care and preparation. When we were there in late June, the air was 46 degrees but it can be 80. All the water up there is really cold so take special care and with a range like the Tetons at your side things can change very fast so over prepared. In addition, Jenny Lake is supposed to be wakeless, but the Park Service vendor that operates the shuttle boats that take hikers to the Hidden Falls trail can kick up a swell (not to mention the wind swell if things kick up.)

Stop at the Jenny Lake visitor desk first to ask where to launch, because it is not out of that parking area, but further south on the other side of the lake outlet.

Next, for some more distance is Jackson Lake, which is 20 miles long and is dominated again by the range, Mt. Moran in particular. Launch from the Colter Bay Marina (free for shells and canoes), and start with the protected bays and islands in that area and venture out from there.

The weather patterns on Jackson Lake are similar to those on Jenny Lake. After we had just gotten off the water we witnessed a squall of snow and wind come in over the course of 3 minutes. All the fishing motor craft fled the lake for harbor. So, if you range out keep close to shore and keep your crossings short.

Finally, although it's a little unorthodox, the best row is the first section of the Snake River putting in below the dam of Lake Jackson and taking out at the Pacific Creek takeout. It is about a 5 mile row with the option of taking the still water oxbow for extra scenery. I did this row three times: once alone late in the afternoon in my 2x touring wherry to scout it out, once with my 7yr old son pulling out at sunset, and then again at about 10am the next day with my wife.

The current is significant, the water is shallow (perhaps 4 to 6 feet for most of it) and it will only take you 50 minutes if rowed most of the way. However, it is so beautiful you're unlikely to row the entire distance.

The same mountains dominate the scenery and there are tons of Osprey crashing in just off your bow; port then starboard! The ospreys are so close that you can actually tell if it is a Cut Throat or a Rainbow as they fly past with the fish in talons.

In addition to the Ospreys, there are White Pelicans, Great Blue Herons, Beavers (smacking their tails in display), River Otters, Moose (watch out for those they swim pretty fast), Canada Geese, assorted ducks and Elk. In the afternoon we were the only boat with just two fly-fishermen on the bank. The next day we shared the river with three sea kayaks, two drift boats and some white water rafts putting in at the takeout. A word of caution is that you should have river skills and experience since, depending on the flow out of the dam, there are two modest riffles, one about a mile after put in and one right at takeout. You can scout the takeout on foot (since you need to see where you will be leaving your car and hitching back to the launch area, if you are alone). This one was a little shallow and if you don't hit the "tongue" just right you may drag your fin so have the plastic short one in. Again your boating skills must be very very good and prior river experience important.

Contacts: You will need a National Park Boat Permit, $10. Go on line to www.nps.gov/grte to read more and view the great images plus go to the Boating page for full details. June-Sept are the dates and stay at the cabins at Colter Bay Village, great food in the cafe there with reasonable prices, check for the best deals June or Sept. at www.gtlc.com

Mark Miller at Rowest/RARC 505.988.7191 rowest@myexcel.com

Montana

Urs and Renee Wunderli

Rowing the Upper and Wild Missouri River — Following the Path of Lewis & Clark: We were introduced to the idea of rowing the Missouri, by Don and Sylvia Hollaran from Madison, WI. A few years ago Don and Sylvia spent 2 weeks on the upper Missouri floating the river and exploring the many sites along the 155 miles stretch. We realized that it must be very possible and an extraordinary experience to row the river, as Lewis and Clark did with their Corps of Discovery in 1804. We discussed it, planned and did it, in August of 2001.

Setting up for the row

Preparation is crucial for a journey of this sort. Renee launched herself in to the research of local contacts in Montana. We read Stephen Ambrose's book "Undaunted Courage", buried ourselves in research and created long lists of necessary equipment and gear.

We counted on 5 days of rowing (that was all the time we could allow ourselves for this trip) for 155 miles, 31 miles per day. Deducting 7 miles per day for the river's flow of about 1-1.5 miles/hour, calculating about 24 miles per day was positively feasible.

Next, was preparing psychologically for a camping trip on this remote part of the Missouri. While both being good distance rowers, the camping part we had to start from scratch. Buying things from T=tent to P=porto potty (collapsible) and 17 gallons of bottled water for drinking, cooking and showers. One rule of the Upper and Wild Missouri River is "pack in and pack out". We needed to be fully self supportive for 5 days.

We rowed a pair of single sculls for this trip: a twin-hulled Virus Kataram and a modified Virus Turbo II Classic (Polyethylene) sliding seat. From a Virus rower we learned how to convert two Wall-Mart 5$ aluminum lawn chairs into a robust platform across the hulls of the Kataram to tie down gear and dry bags. On the Turbo II Classic we installed a large oval hatch (L16"W8") that provided for water storage in the hull.

The next important issue was food. Planning what to take and how. We found that we needed a mixture of dried and fresh foods, all pre-packed to meal size portions. We ate very well. The morning cowboy coffee tasted better than **bucks. With pre-installed cleats on both boats we tied down our dry bags containing everything for the 5 days. Preparing and packing was half the fun. Research well done.

Kataram ultimate stability

Securing autos and trailer to have in place at the end of the row, in James Kipp State Park, was an undertaking by itself. With the help of friends we created our own shuttle service driving over 450 miles of dirt roads and back to Fort Benton before launching the boats. Local canoe outfitters do offer a shuttle service for a fee.

Fully loaded Turbo II

Rowing a river requires navigational skills "in reverse". It was practical to have the Turbo II in the lead, hitting the occasional "under water" rock was not a problem for the poly boat. The upper Missouri, on certain stretches, in August, is only 2-3 feet deep, with rocks just barely covered by water.

The scenery of the Upper Missouri is spectacular. Many sites along the river are full of Wild West great history. There is hardly a mile without some significance, some connection to a great story of the past. In this respect, one can appreciate "rowing" a scenic area. The vista never ends, until the river takes another turn.

Other than the few canoeists on the river we encountered only two locals in the entire stretch of 155 miles.

The Park Authorities in Montana provide spartan, yet very clean campsites. Some with latrines, fire rings and lean-tos incase of "weather". We pitched our tent in places where 200 years ago the delegation of the Corps of Discovery camped and hunted. Spectacular rock forma-

tions, such as, Steamboat Rock, Citadel and the legendary White Cliffs were seen all along the way. We visited the former settlements of many homesteaders from the late 1800's and walked the grounds of famous outlaw hideouts. The Upper Missouri is row touring at it's best!

Breath taking scenery on the Missouri

Useful information for packing:

- Enough water to prevent dehydration (extremely important)
- Insect repellent (recommended by a James Kipp ranger, equal parts water and vanilla extract)
- Comfortable water shoes
- Sunscreen and hat
- Rowing gloves
- Rain gear
- Sufficient garbage bags

Contacts: Fort Benton Chamber of Commerce and Visitors Center 406.622.3864. www.fortbenton.com (go to members for all local contacts) RUM International, Inc. 941.387.7773 info@rowvirusboats.com

Most Traveled Cities in the United States
by Masters Rowing Association and The Rower's Almanac

Masters rowers are a dynamic group who lead busy lives, and careers that take them all over the country. With the opportunity to travel comes the opportunity to see what rowing is like in a different city, and take in some sites, time willing. In cooperation with Masters Rowing Association, The Rower's Almanac has compiled a list of the Most Traveled Cities in the United States. We have included an overview of each city's "rowing scene", a list of clubs that allow guest rowers, and a list of rower-friendly restaurants, hotels, and sites of interest. All information was collected and compiled by rowers local to each area, and provides some excellent tips and insight into what rowing is like in each of these cities. The information presented herein is not necessarily comprehensive, and may not be entirely accurate, as we cannot verify every piece of information.

If you have any travel tips, travel stories, travel rows, or restaurants and hotels to recommend, we'd love to hear about them. You can email The Rower's Almanac at info@rowersalmanac.com, or Masters Rowing Association at mra@mastersrowing.org. You can also check our website, www.rowersalmanac.com, to search for rowing clubs around the world and related hotel, restaurant and travel information.

AUSTIN

Austin's Town Lake is arguably the perfect spot to row. The 6 miles of water is dammed at both ends, so there is no strong current. The weather is mild throughout the year, so rowing never stops; in fact the winter is the preferred time to row among local rowers, and spring breakers. There are no motor-boats or jet skis allowed (except for coaches' launches), so no need to worry about getting waked.

Rowing Dock is a privately owned, privately managed rowing club and boat rental facility located on the west end of Town Lake. Here the water is calm and the lush banks create a serene atmosphere. It is easy to get to from MoPac or downtown, and it offers a large parking lot. Rowing Dock is open a dock attendant is on duty all year during busy hours to help patrons with boats. With proof of skill and current membership in any recognized club, out of town rowers can rent the recreational single sculling boat. Other patrons may rent from a selection of single, double or triple kayaks or quad water cycles. Check the website or call for hours.

Austin Rowing Club is a non-profit run by an elected board. It hosts the two major regattas in Austin each year. They offer sweep rowing and sculling. ARC is located in downtown Austin near the Four Season Hotel; if you get the timing of your row right, you could enjoy the nightly bat flight from Congress Bridge, which can be seen from ARC.

CLUBS ALLOWING GUEST ROWING

Austin Rowing Club
Town Lake Rowing Center Boathouse
74 Trinity Street
Austin, TX 78767-1741
Contact: Meghan Ackley, Executive Dir.
Tel: (512) 477-7168
Email: exdir@austinrowing.org
http://www.austinrowing.org

Rowing Dock
2418 Stratford Drive
Austin, TX 78703
mailing address:
P.O. Box 685162
Austin, TX 78768
Contact: Rachel Yates Thomas
Tel: (512) 459-0999
Email: Rachel@rowingdock.com
http://www.rowingdock.com

ROWER-FRIENDLY RESTAURANTS

Chango's Taqueria
3023 Guadalupe Street
Austin, TX 78705

Magnolia Café and Magnolia Cafe South
2304 Lake Austin Boulevard
Austin, TX 78703
1920 South Congress Avenue
Austin, TX 78704

Castle Hill Café
1101 West 5th Street
Austin, TX 78703

Shady Grove
1624 Barton Springs Road
Austin, TX 78704

HOTELS

Hotel San Jose
1316 South Congress
Austin, TX 78704
(512) 444-7342
1-800-547-8897
www.sanjosehotel.com

Hyatt Regency Austin
208 Barton Springs
Austin, TX 78704
(512) 477-1234
www.austin.hyatt.com

SITES OF INTEREST

- World's largest urban bat population under Congress Bridge; nightly flights spring, summer, early fall
- 4 miles of Waterfront hike and bike trails around Town Lake
- Bob Bullock Texas State History Museum & IMAX Theatre
- Shopping SOCO and the Drag
- SOCO first Thursday (evening shopping, festival-feel)
- LBJ Library
- State Capitol and grounds

MAJOR REGATTAS

Fall: Pumpkin Head Regatta; October
Spring: Heart of Texas Regatta; March

BOSTON

Boston and Cambridge are rife with rowing history. Nine boathouses line the Charles River. Four belong to clubs: Union, Riverside, Cambridge, and Community Rowing. Five belong to colleges: MIT, Boston University, Harvard, Radcliffe, and Northeastern. Guest rowing can be difficult depending upon which club you contact as some clubs require sponsorship from a member. Cygnet Rowing Club, with two boathouse locations, offers hourly rentals of single sculls.

Dividing Boston and Cambridge, the Charles River is an elegantly serpentine aquatic ribbon that varies in width from about 200 meters to more than a kilometer. During warm weather, and even not so warm weather, it is alive with all manner of rowing craft, sailboats, kayaks, "duck" boats, excursion boats, and powered pleasure craft. The round-trip distance from the Science Museum to Watertown and back is about seventeen miles. On the average morning the entire length of the river is rowable, although the chop tends to kick up below the Boston University (BU) bridge after nine a.m. Almost all the college programs have agreed to use wakeless launches, which has maintained the generally flat conditions, and only on impossibly windy days (or winter, when the river freezes) is the entire river unrowable. The scenery along the way ranges from intensely urban to quietly suburban. The river is bordered by Memorial Drive on the north bank, and Storrow Drive on the south, and a bike path runs the entire length of the river on both banks.

CLUBS ALLOWING GUEST ROWING

Cambridge Boat Club
7 Meadow Way
Cambridge, MA 02138
Contact: Carmen Garufo
Tel: (617) 354-9696
Email: jglcmg@channel1.com
http://www.cambridge-boat-club.org

Community Rowing Inc. of Boston
PO Box 382604
Cambridge, MA 02238-2604
Contact: Alyson Magian
Tel: (617) 964-2455
Email: office@communityrowing.org
http://www.communityrowing.org

Cygnet Rowing Club
6 Ballord Place
Cambridge, MA 02139
Contact: Richard Gonci
Tel: (617) 251-6612
Email: richard@neoscape.com
http://www.ski-paddle.com

Riverside Boat Club
769 Memorial Drive
Cambridge, MA 2139
Tel: (617) 492-1869
Email: secretary@riversideboatclub.com
http://www.riversideboatclub.com

ROWER-FRIENDLY RESTAURANTS

Border Cafe
32 Church Street
Cambridge, MA 02138-3730
Tel: (617) 864-6100

Brew Moon
115 Stuart Street
Boston, MA 02116-5609
Tel: (617) 742-5225

Carberry's Bakery & Coffee House
74 Prospect Street
Cambridge, MA 02139-2503
Tel: (617) 576-3530

Fire and Ice
50 Church Street
Cambridge, MA 02138-3726
Tel: (617) 547-9007

Henry's Diner
270 Western Avenue
Allston, MA 02134-1034
Tel: (617) 783-5844

International House of Pancakes
1850 Soldier's Field Road
Brighton, MA 02135-1113
Tel: (617) 787-0533

HOTELS

Boston has literally dozens of hotels and B&B's with a wide range of room rates and amenities. A visit to www.hotels.com will provide a good overview.

SITES OF INTEREST

Boathouses dot both shores from the Lower Basin out to Watertown. Faneuil Hall Marketplace and Quincy Market are hugely popular settings for dining and shopping. Whale watch excursions leave from the inner harbor throughout the day, as to harbor island excursions. Jacques Cousteau once proclaimed that Boston Harbor is the most beautiful harbor in the world as one enters from the sea.

The Freedom Trail brings history alive for millions every year, while the "duck" boat tours unite the experience of river and city. The Museum of Fine Arts, Fenway Park (home of the Red Sox), the Boston Public Library, and the Hatch Shell (riverside outdoor performances of all kinds) are just a sampling of rewarding outings awaiting the curious traveler.

MAJOR REGATTAS

Fall: Head of the Charles
Summer: Cromwell Cup
Spring: Riverside Sprints

CHICAGO

Visitors to Chicago are often surprised to discover how very beautiful this city is — with its sparkling lakefront, world-class architecture, and incredible cultural attractions. For rowers, an additional source of amazement is the experience of rowing on the Chicago River in the very heart of a great American metropolis.

Chicago's three rowing clubs are situated at different points along the "Y" shape of the River. The Chicago River Rowing & Paddling Center's boathouse is located at the base of the "Y", at the mouth of the River where it meets Lake Michigan. This downtown portion of the River, the Main Branch, runs East to West right through the business district and a panorama of famous buildings. Chicagoans walking to work hail to the rowers below from the many bridges that span this segment of the River. The other two sites — the Chicago Rowing Center's site on the South Branch, and Lincoln Park Boat Club's site on the North Branch, are located in industrial areas that evoke the "City of Big Shoulders" image. In any case, the water is as smooth and endless as the vistas are compelling.

CLUBS ALLOWING GUEST ROWING

Chicago River Rowing & Paddling Center
P.O. Box 811190
Chicago, IL 60681-1190
Contact: Susan Urbas
Tel: (312) 458-0810
Email: chicagoriverrowing@yahoo.com
http://www.chicagorowing.org

Chicago Rowing Center/ South Chicago Rowing Center
c/o Harrison Trading Company
601 South LaSalle Street 2nd Floor
Chicago, IL 60605
Contact: Michael O'Gorman
Tel: (312) 593-8040
Email: chicagorowingcenter@yahoo.com
http://www.rowchicago.org

Lincoln Park Boat Club
4510 North Greenview
Chicago, IL 60640
Tel: (773) 549-2628
Email: rowing@lpbc.net
http://www.lpbc.net

ROWER-FRIENDLY RESTAURANTS

West Egg Cafe
620 N. Fairbanks Ct.
Chicago, IL
(312) 280-8366

Wishbone Restaurant
1001 W. Washington Street
Chicago, IL
(312) 850-2663

HOTELS

Comfort Inn & Suites Downtown
15 E. Ohio Street
Chicago, IL
(312) 894-0900

Fairmont Hotel of Chicago
200 N. Columbus Drive
Chicago, IL
(312) 565-8000

Hotel Monaco
225 N. Wabash St.
Chicago, IL
(312) 960-8500

Hyatt Regency
151 E. Wacker Drive
Chicago, IL
(312) 552-2000

Sheraton Chicago Hotel & Towers
301 E. North Water St.
Chicago, IL
(312) 464-1000

Swissotel Chicago
323 E. Wacker Drive
Chicago, IL
(312) 565-0565

SITES OF INTEREST

The Chicago River Rowing & Paddling Center is within easy walking distance of Grant Park and Monroe Harbor, DuSable Harbor & Park, Millennium Park, Meigs Field, the Chicago Symphony, The Art Institute of Chicago, the Field Museum of Natural History, the Shedd Aquarium, the Oak Street Beach, Navy Pier, and the downtown Business and Theatre Districts. The Lincoln Park Boat Club is within walking distance of the Lincoln Park Zoo.

MAJOR REGATTAS

Fall: Chicago Chase
Summer: Chicago Sprints
Spring: Iron Oars Marathon

LOS ANGELES

Sunny Los Angeles offers a lot of great things for rowers, with the best being the opportunity to row year-round. There are very few days each year when weather keeps you from getting a great workout.

Los Angeles rowers have the good fortune to row in the largest man-made small boat harbor in the world, a place called Marina del Rey. The Marina's waters are well protected, making it possible to row on flat water most mornings. A three-mile head race is hosted by the California Yacht Club every fall, which is one loop around the Marina.

Beyond rowing, there are tons of tourist attractions and outdoor adventures to be had in Los Angeles, with countless hotels and restaurants near the water (and near LAX, which is just minutes from Marina del Rey).

CLUBS ALLOWING GUEST ROWING

Lions Rowing Club
13669 Fiji Way
Los Angeles, CA 90292
Contact: Sara-Mai Conway, Patrick Kelly
Email: SConway@lmu.edu

Tel: (310) 338-7624
http://www.jdenuno.com/Rowing/lmu.htm

Los Angeles Rowing Club
13428 Maxella Avenue #358
Marina del Rey CA 90292
Contact: Susan Varga
Email: susan@larowing.com
http://www.larowing.com

ROWER-FRIENDLY RESTAURANTS

Noah's Bagels
546 Washington Boulevard
Marina del Rey, CA
Tel: (310) 574-1155

Joni's Juice Joint
548 Washington Boulevard
Marina del Rey, CA
Tel: (310) 574-2660

C&O Trattoria
31 Washington Boulevard
Venice, CA
Tel: (310) 823-9491

Baja Cantina Restaurant
311 Washington Boulevard
Marina del Rey, CA
Tel: (310) 821-2252

Tony P's
4445 Admiralty Way
Marina del Rey, CA
Tel: (310) 823-4534

Cafe Del Rey
4451 Admiralty Way
Marina del Rey, CA
(310) 823-6395

Shanghai Reds
13813 Fiji Way
Marina del Rey, CA
Tel: (310) 823-4522

HOTELS

Marina Beach Marriott Resort
4100 Admiralty Way
Marina del Rey, CA
Tel: (310) 301-3000

Marina International Hotel
4200 Admiralty Way
Marina del Rey, CA
Tel: (310) 301-2000

Ritz Carlton Marina del Rey
4375 Admiralty Way
Marina del Rey, CA
Tel: (310) 823-1700

Hyatt Hotels & Resorts
4676 Admiralty Way # 525
Marina del Rey, CA
Tel: (310) 301-2626

SITES OF INTEREST

Westside/close to rowing: Venice Beach, Fisherman's Village on Fiji Way, Santa Monica Pier, 3rd St Promenade in Santa Monica, Manhattan Beach, hiking in the Santa Monica Mountains, bike riding/skating on the 26-mile-long bike path along the Pacific Ocean

Further inland: Beverly Hills, Hollywood Walk of Fame, Universal Studios Citywalk and Studio Tour, Getty Museum, Los Angeles County Museum of Art, La Brea Tar Pits, Griffith Observatory, Griffith Park, Old Town Pasadena

MAJOR REGATTAS

Fall: Head of the Marina, November
Summer: Regatta del Sol, June

MIAMI

Rowing in Miami Beach is a unique experience. The sheltered waterways of Indian Creek provide the perfect setting for training, just a few steps away from affordable oceanfront hotels. Guests are welcome and can rent by the hour provided they have sculling experience. For winter training, Miami Beach is the place to be. Escape to the warm waters of Biscayne Bay and enjoy the scenic views of tropical islands with palm trees and spectacular sunsets. While rowing at sunrise, expect to be accompanied by some playful dolphins, which are often seen within a few yards of our dock. Miles of flat water, year round rowing and a stunning location are the reasons people call Miami Beach a rower's paradise.

CLUBS ALLOWING GUEST ROWING

Miami Beach Rowing Club
6500 Indian Creek Drive
Miami Beach, FL 33141
Tel: (305) 861-8876
Email: miamibeachrowing@bellsouth.net
http://www.rowmiamibeach.com

Miami Rowing & Watersports Center Inc.
3832 Shipping Avenue
3601 Rickenbacker Causeway
Virginia Key, FL 33149
Tel: (305) 582-4373
http://www.mrc.org

ROWER-FRIENDLY RESTAURANTS

Brickell Emporium
1100 Brickell Plaza
Miami, FL 33131

New York Bagel Deli
6546 Collins Ave
Miami Beach, Fl 33141

HOTELS

Comfort Inn Oceanfront
6261 Collins Ave
Miami Beach Fl 33140
A visiting crew favorite just a few blocks from the Watersports Center. Basic and superior rooms & efficiencies are available. On the ocean with pool & snack bar. Contract rates available through the Center.

SITES OF INTEREST

The Center is within walking distance of many restaurants from Norman's, a local sports bar to small and delicious ethnic eateries. On the weekends, the Normandy Village Farmers Market sells delicious smoothies as well as fresh fruits, vegetables and many other items. Only ten minutes away is the vibrant South Beach Art Deco District for shopping, dining, movies and nightlife.

MAJOR REGATTAS

Fall: Head of the Indian Creek
Spring: Miami Beach Winter Sprints

PHILADELPHIA

Philadelphia was one of America's original rowing cities. It is host to the infamous Boathouse Row and is home to hundreds of oarsmen/women. On any given day of the week, you can find numerous boats ranging from club rowers to high schoolers to collegiate rowers. Philadelphia is host to dozens of regattas each year, including the Dad Vail Regatta, the Stotesbury Cup Regatta, the Independence Day Regatta and the Head of the Schuylkill. Rowing in Philadelphia is truly an experience you could feel in very few cities across the USA.

CLUBS ALLOWING GUEST ROWING

There are no rowing clubs in Philadelphia that will allow guest rowing without being sponsored by a member. Most rowing clubs in Philly will allow guest rowing with a member.

ROWER-FRIENDLY RESTAURANTS

LeBUS
4266 Main Street
Phidelphia, PA 19127
Tel: (215) 487-2663

Jack's Firehouse
2130 Fairmount Ave
Philadelphia, PA 19130
Tel: (215) 232-9000

London Grill
2301 Fairmount Ave
Philadelphia, PA 19130
Tel: (215) 978-4545

Pete's Pizza & Restaurant
2320 Fairmount Avenue
Philadelphia, PA 19130-2519
Tel: (215) 765-3040

HOTELS

Best Western
501 N. 22nd St., Philadelphia, PA
Tel: (215) 568-8300

Holiday Inn-City Line
4100 Presidential Boulevard
Philadelphia, PA

Adams Mark-Philadelphia
City Ave/Monument Plaza
Tel: (215) 581-2100

Comfort Inn
100 Columbus Boulevard
Philadelphia, PA
Tel: (215) 627-7900

SITES OF INTEREST

Philadelphia is filled with a wide range of historical sites, Museums and interactive institutes. One of the most famous is the Philadelphia Art Museum. The stairway leading up to it is the exact one that Rocky ran up in the movie Rocky. There is also the Franklin Institute, which has a variety of activities as well as an IMAX theatre. The Philadelphia Zoo is only five minutes from Boathouse Row. And you can't visit Philadelphia, the home of Independence, without visiting the Liberty Bell.

MAJOR REGATTAS

Fall: Head of the Schuylkill
Summer: Independence Day Regatta
Spring: Dad Vail Regatta

SAN DIEGO

Rowing in San Diego is pretty much situated on Mission Bay, located about six miles north of the San Diego Airport, and flanked by Mission Beach and Pacific Beach. The area abounds with restaurants, beach and bay boardwalks, and hotels. San Diego Rowing Club is located in Mission Beach, with ZLAC Rowing Club located in Pacific Beach. In general, due to water-skiers, most rowing is done in the early hours, or at dusk, but there is plenty of water, and ever-changing scenery, with bird sanctuaries, Sea World pens and the local marine life.

CLUBS ALLOWING GUEST ROWING

San Diego Rowing Club
1220 El Carmel Place
San Diego, CA 92109
Contact: Captain Tim Watenpaugh
Tel: (858) 488-1893
Email: twatenpaugh@san.rr.com
http://www.sdrc-row.org

ZLAC
1111 Pacific Beach Drive
San Diego, CA 92109
Tel: 858 274 7826
Email: masters@zlac.com
http://www.zlac.com

ROWER-FRIENDLY RESTAURANTS

Bangkok Thai & Vegetarian Cuisine
4656 Mission Boulevard
San Diego, CA 92109
Tel: (858) 581-1100

Gringo's
4474 Mission Boulevard
San Diego, CA 92109-3920
Tel: (858) 490-2877

Kono's Café
704 Garnet Avenue
San Diego, CA 92109
Tel: (619) 483-1669

Lotsa Pasta
Garnet Avenue (in Von's Shopping Center)
San Diego 92109
Tel: (619) 581-6777

Broken Yolk
1851 Garnet Avenue
San Diego 92109
Tel: (858) 270-9655

Nick's at the Beach
809 Thomas Avenue
San Diego CA 92109
Tel: (858) 270-1730

El Indio's
3695 India Street
San Diego, CA
Tel: (619) 299-0333

HOTELS

Bahia
998 West Mission Bay Drive
(858) 488-0551

Catamaran Resort
3999 Mission Boulevard
(858) 488-1081

Dana Inn
1710 West Mission Bay Drive
619 222-6440

Best Western Blue Sea Lodge
707 Pacific Beach Drive
Tel: (858) 488-4700

SITES OF INTEREST

San Diego has it all, and most of it within a few miles of the airport and the rowing clubs, beginning with Seaworld (local crews train past the shows and the penguins), Belmont Park (with an original wooden roller coaster, swimming pool and amusement park rides, right on the beach) and Old Town (a historical area specializing in specialty stores and restaurants TIP, do lunch, evening waits can be a drag if you are really hungry); Balboa Park has museums, restaurants and the world famous San Diego Zoo, or you can head north to the Birch Aquarium by the UCSD campus. Further a field you can go to the Wild Animal Park, or Legoland (north about 40 minutes) or south to Tijuana, Mexico (20 minutes by car, 30 minutes by San Diego Trolley). You can find outlet shopping by Legoland or the last USA exit in San Ysidro (GREAT buys from all the major athletic shoe companies, plus Levi and the usual suspects). Interested in human wildlife? Check out Garnet Street in Pacific Beach, or the Gaslamp District downtown.

MAJOR REGATTAS

Fall: San Diego Fall Classic, Row for the Cure
Spring: San Diego Crew Classic

SEATTLE

Rowing in Seattle is rather mystical. Rowers often start their day by launching while looking at the top of Mount Rainier, and seeing the reflection of dawn breaking over the city skyline all in one glance. Then there is plenty of water to choose from, all of which has a different flavor and feel. One direction can take rowers up a shipping canal toward the Puget Sound (the Locks) where there are barges, huge ships and fishing vessels along the shore. Rowing in Lake Union offers the opportunity to see the awesome Seattle city skyline. Turn north from Lake Union and Portage Bay is home to many houseboats bobbing up and down on the water. The Montlake Cut, or "the cut" as it is known, connects Puget Sound via the Locks to Lake Washington. Once through the cut, Husky rowers generally populate this area. Rowing in Lake Washington offers spectacular views of the Olympic Mountain ranges and Mt Rainier.

Rowers can go out every day of the year. Inclement weather is few and far between, though a constant soft drizzle in the winter is common. When the sun is out, it is arguably one of the most spectacular urban rowing landscapes.

CLUBS ALLOWING GUEST ROWING

Cascade Rowing
3320 Fuhrman Ave East
Seattle, WA 98102
Tel: (206) 328-0778
http://www.cascadewomen.com/

Conibear Rowing Club
3800 Lake Washington Boulevard
Seattle, WA 98118
Contact: Liz Baker
Tel: (206) 386-1913
Email: mount.baker@ci.seattle.wa.us
http://www.conibearrowing.org

Lake Union Crew
11 East Allison Street
Seattle, WA 98102
Contact: Rome Ventura
Tel: (206) 860-4199
Email: raventura@aol.com
http://www.lakeunioncrew.com

Lake Washington Rowing Club
910 N. Northlake Way
Seattle, WA 98103
Contact: Karyn Freer
Tel: (206) 547-1583
Email: lwrcmanager@yahoo.com
http://www.lakewashingtonrowing.com

Moss Bay Rowing and Kayaking Center
1001 Fairview Avenue North #1900
Seattle, WA 98109
Contact: Jim Clark
Tel: (206) 682-0455
Email: mossbay@earthlink.net
http://www.mossbay.net

Pocock Rowing Center
3320 Fuhrman Avenue East
Seattle, WA 98102
Contact: Colby
Tel: (206) 328-7272
Email: pocockrow@mindspring.com
http://www.pocockrowing.org/

ROWER-FRIENDLY RESTAURANTS

Fred Hutchinson Cafeteria
1901 Fairview Avenue North
Seattle, WA 98109

Louisa's Bakery & Cafe
2379 Eastlake Ave East
Seattle, WA 98102-3305
Tel: (206) 325-0081

Mae's Phinney Ridge Cafe
6412 Phinney Avenue North
Seattle, WA 98103

Nickerson Street Saloon
318 Nickerson
Seattle, WA 98109
Tel: (206) 284-8819

Still Life In Fremont Coffeehouse
709 N. 35th
Seattle, WA 98103
Tel: (206) 547-9850

The Long Shoreman's Daughter
3508 Fremont Place N
Seattle, WA 98103-8623
Tel: (206) 633-5169

Torrefazione Italia
701 N. 34th Street
Seattle, WA 98103
Tel: (206) 545-2721

Dad Watsons Restaurant and Brewery (McMenamins)
3601 Fremont Ave. N
Seattle, WA 98103
Tel: (206) 632-6505

The Red Door Ale House
3401 Evanston Avenue N.
Seattle WA 98103
Tel: (206) 547-7521

HOTELS

Courtyard Seattle Downtown/Lake Union
925 Westlake Avenue North
Seattle, WA 98109
Tel: (206) 213-0100

Residence Inn Downtown/Lake Union
800 Fairview Avenue North
Seattle, WA 98109
Tel: (206) 624-6000

SITES OF INTEREST

Seattle is comprised of twenty-six neighborhoods all of which have their own character and charm. Fremont, near Lake Washington Rowing Club, is a funky/artsy neighborhood full of unique boutiques, restaurants and pubs. In Fremont, you can visit the infamous Troll that overtook a VW BUG that lives underneath the Aurora Bridge or the rocket ship that is stuck on a building or the statue of People Waiting for the Bus.

A few miles from Fremont is another neighborhood called Ballard. In Ballard, it's still possible to hear Swedish and Norwegian being spoken on the streets. Ballard traditionally housed Seattle's fishing industry, which was dominated by Scandinavian immigrants. If you want fresh-caught fish from the market, this is the place to go.

North of the University District is the Greenlake neighborhood. This hugely popular lake has a walking/biking/rollerblading path around the whole lake (about 3 miles). The north side of Greenlake has some wonderful coffee shops and a great chowder house.

Capitol Hill is the gay/lesbian/artsy part of Seattle. It is known for its nightlife and houses a trendy strip of nightclubs. The best cup of coffee in Seattle can also be had on Capitol Hill, at Espresso Vivace.

The downtown Seattle area boasts one of the most famous open-air markets: Pike Place. This market is known for its flying fish, crafts, food, pastries and shopping. Virtually anywhere you go in Seattle, you'll find something totally different and unique.

MAJOR REGATTAS

Fall: Head of the Lake Regatta
Spring: Opening Day Regatta

WASHINGTON, D.C.

Rowing in the nation's capital dates back to the early 1800's. The oldest boat club in Washington, D.C., Potomac Boat Club (circa 1869), is well over one-hundred and thirty years old. Thompson's Boat Center, a public facility located a half-mile down river from Potomac Boat Club hosts the majority of the high school and collegiate rowing programs in the area. At Thompson's Boat Center, individuals can rent single sculls by the hour, providing they can prove they have sculling experience. Capital Rowing Club, located next to the Navy Yard, in southeast D.C., rows on the Anacostia River, and also offers opportunities for guest rowing. Perhaps the best thing about rowing in D.C. is being able to see many of the monuments from the shoreline such as the Washington Monument, the Lincoln Memorial, and Arlington Cemetery to name a few.

CLUBS ALLOWING GUEST ROWING

Capital Rowing Club
1115 O Street, SE
Washington, DC 20036
Contact: Sarah Dunham
Tel: (202) 289-6666
Email: membership@capitalrowing.org
http://www.capitalrowing.org

D.C. Strokes Rowing Club
PO Box 53019
Washington, DC 20009
Contact: J. Doug, President
Tel: (202) 232-1071
Email: president@dcstrokes.org
http://www.dcstrokes.org

Potomac Boat Club
3530 Water Street
Washington, DC 20007
Contact: Bob Schneider, President
Tel: (202) 347-6084
http://www.rowpbc.net

Thompson Boat Center
2900 Virginia Avenue N.W.
Washington, DC 20037
Contact: Emmanuel Caudron, Manager
Tel: (202) 333-9543
Email: tbc@guestservices.com
http://www.guestservices.com/tbc

ROWER-FRIENDLY RESTAURANTS

Booeymonger
3265 Prospect Street
Washington, DC 20007

Common Grounds Coffee and Tea House
3211 Wilson Boulevard
Arlington, VA 22201

Faccia Luna
2400 Wisconsin Avenue, NW
Washington, DC 20007-1800

The Georgetown Bagelry
3245 M Street, N.W.
Washington, DC 20007-3616

The Tombs
1226 36th Street, N.W.
Washington, DC 20007-2627

HOTELS

Marriott-Key Bridge
1401 Lee Highway
Arlington, VA 22209
Tel: (703) 524-6400

Sheraton National Hotel Arlington
Columbia Pike & Washington Boulevard
900 South Orme Street
Arlington, Virginia 22204
Tel: (703) 521-1900

Days Inn
2000 Jefferson Davis Highway
Arlington, VA
Tel: (703) 920-8600

SITES OF INTEREST

Obviously the tourist attractions are numerous in Washington, DC, but a couple of sites near Potomac Boat Club and Thompson's Boat Center include the Iwo Jima Memorial and Arlington Cemetery, the National Cathedral, a plethora of monuments on and around the Smithsonian, and walking and shopping in historic Georgetown, Dupont Circle and Adams Morgan. If you're in the neighborhood of Capital Rowing Club, a nice place to visit on the weekends is the Eastern Market, an open-air crafts and foods market that has been in existence for over 100 years. It's directly across the street from the Eastern Market metro stop.

A nice place to have lunch or dinner right on the Potomac River is Tony & Joe's or Sequoia's at the Washington Harbor in Georgetown. In fair weather, these restaurants are packed on the weekend, and are great places for people watching.

MAJOR REGATTAS

Fall: Head of the Potomac, September
Summer: Crabfeast Regatta, July
Spring: Oxford-Cambridge alumni regatta

Sculling in the Shadows of Byzantium

By Louisa Edgerley

A recreational rower in Istanbul could find himself empathising with the Ancient Mariner, for there is "water, water everywhere" but not an easy way to row. Istanbul sits astride the fabled Bosporus Straits, which link the Black Sea with the Sea of Marmara and eventually the Aegean and Mediterranean Seas. Another body of water called the Golden Horn meets the Bosporus at the edge of the Sea of Marmara. Here, the Ottoman palace Topkapi sits on a point of land overlooking both waterways. Massive oil tankers and container ships travel up and down the dangerous strait, along with numerous local ferryboats, fishing boats and private yachts.

Rowing in these waters dates back to ancient times when galleys powered by a combination of oars and wind plied up and down the coasts carrying trade goods and occasionally soldiers. Today, the modern sport of rowing has a number of adherents in Turkey, with several clubs located in and around Istanbul. Although the Bosporus is too treacherous, with swift currents and heavy traffic, the Golden Horn offers calmer water and fewer dangerous large ships. Three clubs, Besiktas, Denizcilik and Bosporus University currently train on the Golden Horn. Other clubs, such as Galatasaray and Fenerbace have chosen to locate on small lakes outside the city, either to the west or the east. None of these clubs is open to the public and all maintain a

Bosporus Strait, Turkey

backdrop for an early-morning workout. Further up the waterway, one might even spot a flock of sheep grazing in a park along the edge of the water. The municipality of Istanbul has taken huge strides in cleaning up the pollution that had turned the waterway into a cesspool. Fish are returning, and the water is cleaner than it has been in decades. While boathouse conditions on the Golden Horn can be quite primitive and few accommodations are provided for female athletes, the experience is worth the effort. The rowers can be quite welcoming and one immediately feels at home among others pursuing the same passion, which helps to make up for the lack of facilities.

semi-professional status that severely restricts their ability to attract new athletes to the sport. To anyone familiar with international soccer, the names of the rowing clubs will immediately ring a bell. Most rowing clubs are affiliated with the major sports clubs in Istanbul, and the revenues from the world-famous soccer teams belonging to those same clubs subsidize much of their budget. Rowers are generally paid a small stipend by the club and train and compete under the direction of the club coach. For most, the goal is to try for the Turkish National Team.

The concept of a paid boathouse membership or renting rack space is almost completely unknown in Turkey. Some universities have rowing clubs, but these are, of course, restricted to students of those universities. Once graduated, rowers who wish to continue in the sport must find a club willing to add them to the roster and sponsor their competitive license. Because most graduates need to concentrate on finding full-time work, they must drop out of the sport entirely given the lack of recreational clubs.

As with most things in Turkey, with the right connections one can manage to get out on the water for a day or two. For those lucky enough to get the opportunity, rowing on the Golden Horn can be a beautiful experience. The architecture of Istanbul and the famous Galata Bridge provides a dramatic

Rowing at Galatasary, one finds a large and fully equipped boathouse with full indoor training facilities and large locker rooms. Both men and women train here on the weekends they live in the boathouse. The water, a small lake about forty-five minutes outside the city centre, is unfortunately quite polluted from nearby sewage outflows, but once away from shore the smell is not so bad. The history of Galatasaray rowing is depicted in photographs on the walls and in the pride that the athletes take in their club. They travel to regional and international competitions, including the Balkan championships where they face Bulgaria, the regional powerhouse in rowing. Galatasaray boats have also competed at Henley Royal Regatta and the CRASH-B Sprints.

Fenerbace also has a training facility outside Istanbul, theirs on the Asian side of the Bosporus. They have the best equipment of any team in Istanbul, and their heavyweight men's eight recently competed in the Head of the Charles Regatta in Boston. As in soccer, the rivalry between Galatasaray and Fenerbace is strong, and the two clubs usually dominate the rest of the field at the Turkish rowing championships.

There is one place, on the island of Heybeli, where individual rowers can rent a shell to take out. This is ocean rowing, on the waters of the Sea of Marmara, and the best time of day is shortly before sunrise. The stretch of water between Heybeli and another island, Burgaz, is the usual training area for those hardy souls who venture out.

The establishment of a boat club open to the public, where recreational rowers could enjoy their sport and the public could learn would vastly improve rowing in Turkey and in Istanbul in particular. Istanbul is a beautiful location and is potentially a wonderful place to row.

Do Boats Float Higher on the Great Salt Lake?

By The Rower's Almanac

Nowhere else on earth is there such active rowing happening on such salty water. Second in size to the Dead Sea (and we haven't found evidence of rowing there), the Great Salt Lake has salinity five times that of ocean water. The lake is a remnant of one of two ice-age lakes, which filled the Great Basin 25,000 years ago. One of them, Lake Bonneville in present day Utah, was named after the surveyor who mapped it. Over 75 miles long and 45 miles wide, the lake's surface area has varied dramatically over the years. In 1963, the lake covered only 950 square miles. In 1986, the lake covered about 3,300 square miles. Today, it covers about 1,700 square miles. Mountain water runoff and rainfall contribute to the lake's inflow. Evaporation is the lake's only outflow.

Great Salt Lake rowers launch from the marina.

Rowing and sailing have played a role on the Great Salt Lake since the 1880's. In 1888, the Salt Lake Boat Club hosted a large regatta that brought single scull, double scull and four man boats from Chicago, St. Louis, Moline and St. Paul. The regatta drew 55,000 people to its shore. Records show the population of Salt Lake City at that time to be only 30,000. Rowing made a comeback at "The Lake" when Wendy Whitney formed the Salt Lake Sculling Club in the early 1990's. Today, two clubs, Bonneville Rowing and Great Salt Lake Rowing, make their home and row out of the Great Salt Lake Marina.

A rower works her way toward one of the marker buoys that provides orientation on the Great Salt Lake. Stansbury Island pictured in the background.

Launching from the boathouse, rowers go down a narrow channel passing the sailboat docks, out the mouth of the marina into the lake. Because the lake is very shallow, averaging thirteen to fifteen feet, there are few, if any powerboats, and miles and miles of water. Heading in a westerly direction, Black Rock, is about one mile from the Marina. About seven miles beyond Black Rock is Antelope Island, a large island that looms above the almost endless expanse of water. There are over three-hundred bison (buffalo) on Antelope Island. A managed herd, they roam over a portion of this State Park.

Saltair Pavilion after it was rebuilt in 1925.

Heading one and a half miles in an easterly direction from the Marina is Saltair Pavillion. In Victorian days, Saltair Pavilion housed a palace, social activities, and a train running alongside the water. Rebuilt after a fire in 1925, today, it hosts concerts.

While the landscape is stark, there are mountain ranges surrounding much of the lake which change color during the seasons, from a grassy sage, to brown, to winter white. The lake is fed by run-off from the mountains, and supports a host of bird species including migrating birds, sea gulls, pelicans and a Pink Flamingo the rowers have named "Floyd." On many evenings the western sky fills with stunning color at sunset — great for an evening row.

The high concentration of salt dictates that rowers be especially prudent about equipment maintenance. Boats must be washed down after every practice because the salt can do extensive damage to the equipment. The salt can literally crystallize all over the boat, rendering into a "salty paste", as one rower describes it. This equipment maintenance extends not only to the boat, but also to the oars and any other equipment that accompanies a rower on his or her excursion.

The high concentration of salt also does another peculiar thing. It causes boats to float higher on the lake. Buoyancy, caused by the difference in density between the water and an object floating in it is noticeable on the ocean. It is even more noticeable on the Great Salt Lake, whose density has ranged from 5% to 27% (beyond which water cannot hold more salt). The density of the water varies, of course, upon the level of the lake. When the lake is low, it's highly dense and visa versa. The water is so salty that a person floats on the surface very easily — like a cork.

The extent of the buoyancy is remarkable, and can affect rigging, technique and a host of details that fresh-water rowers don't even have to consider. But all this does not deter the rowers of the Great Salt Lake. They laugh at the brine flies — and watch the brine shrimp (the mascot of Great Salt Lake Rowing) — and welcome rowers from anywhere who'd enjoy a row with the saltiest rowers in the world.

To learn more about rowing on the Great Salt Lake visit: www.gslr.org. Thanks to the following sources for information and resources: http://www.gslr.org, and http://www.gslyc.org. Photos courtesy of Demie Moore.

Pictured in foreground is a native Tahitian boat. In the background is the island of Moorea, part of French Polynesia. Photo courtesy of Digital Future Photography.

Rower-Friendly Dining

Rowers are generally easy to please in terms of food: if it's there, it won't be for very long. While some rowers prefer quantity, others prefer quality, and this list has a good selection of both. For the vegetarians among us, we have included restaurants that at least have enough variety for special preferences. Since rowers do more before breakfast than most people do all day, there is a heavy emphasis on the breakfast spots.

We are always looking for more recommendations. If you know of a unique restaurant, deli or cafe that is frequented by rowers, please tell us about it. We define a "rower-friendly" restaurant as the following: (1) serves sufficiently large quantities of food; (2) provides an atmosphere where lycra is considered acceptable; (3) may be characterized by some unique rowing theme; or, (4) just serves darn good coffee!

Email your restaurant suggestions to info@rowersalmanac.com. A special thanks to the Greasy Spoon Index (http://www.forr.org) and to all those who contributed their restaurant recommendations and witty remarks.

Restaurants are listed alphabetically by City Name.

AIKEN, SC

NEW MOON CAFE
116 Laurens Street
Aiken, SC 29801

Tel: (803) 643-7088

Description: When the National Sculling Center was located in Augusta, GA, scullers happened upon this little gem, an oasis of good coffee and pastries, in an otherwise stiflingly hot southern town. New Moon is 30 miles from downtown Augusta, and a couple miles from the 2000 meter course in Aiken.

Recommendation: Fabulous coffee and pastries, sandwiches and sundries, an eclectic music collection, and sometimes even a computer with web access make this cafe a must-experience for people passing through or spending time in the area.

Rowing Club: Augusta Rowing Club

OLIVE OILS
232 Chesterfield Street Aiken, SC 29801

Tel: (803) 649-3726

Description: This place is ALWAYS packed! Great pastas and sauces. Elegant ambience. Aiken, SC is a great dining experience: a laid back atmosphere, warm sultry weather, and fabulous food. You'll have to try it yourself to believe it!

Rowing Club: Augusta Rowing Club

UP YOUR ALLEY
222 The Alley
Aiken, SC 29801

Tel: (803) 649-2603

Description: Serving continental cuisine and seafood, this restaurant is located in a happening alley that is always buzzing with crowds and entertainment.

Rowing Club: Augusta Rowing Club

ALBANY, NY

MISS ALBANY DINER
893 Broadway
Albany, NY 12207

Tel: (518) 465-9148

Description: Scenes from the movie Ironweed with Jack Nicholson were filmed here. UK rowers will be happy to see that they have bangers and crumpets on the menu.

Rowing Club: Albany Rowing Center

ALEXANDRIA, VA

MISHA'S COFFEE ROASTER COFFEEHOUSE
102 S. Patrick Street
Alexandria, VA 22302

Tel: (703) 548-4089

Description: A beatnik coffeehouse right in the heart of upscale Old Town Alexandria. They know their coffee so anything you order will be outstanding. Most people bring their dogs and hang out while sipping their java.

Recommendation: Route 66 Blend Coffee, Pumpkin Muffins and Spinch-n-Feta Croissants.

Rowing Club: Alexandria Community Rowing

PERKS COFFEE SHOP
822 N. Fairfax Street
Alexandria, VA 22314

Tel: (703) 706-5886

Description: Coffee joint with some baked goods. Owner memorizes names like crazy. Outside seating.

Rowing Club: Alexandria Community Rowing

ROYAL RESTAURANT
734 N. St. Asaph Street
Alexandria, VA 22314

Tel: (703) 548-1616

Description: This place is for Elvis lovers: pictures, juke box and a fifties booth and counter room. A great place to put on the carbohydrates you took off on the erg at the boathouse only an hour before chowing down on a stack of pancakes, eggs and bacon.

Recommendation: Buffet.

Rowing Club: Alexandria Community Rowing

ALLSTON, MA

HENRY'S DINER
270 Western Avenue Allston, MA 02134-1034

Tel: (617) 783-5844

Description: Otherwise known as Chez Henri by the denizens of Riverside Boat Club. Breakfast is your best bet. Convenient to the Harvard and Radcliffe boathouse, easy biking distance to Riverside and Northeastern.

Recommendation: Breakfast

Rowing Club: Riverside Boat Club, and other Boston area rowing clubs.

ANN ARBOR, MI

NORTHSIDE GRILL
1015 Broadway
Ann Arbor, MI 48105

Tel: (734) 995-0965

Description: Breakfast & Lunch: Specializing in breakfast sandwiches.

Recommendation: Try the Pontiac Trail — two eggs, bacon, lettuce, tomato on grilled multi-grain bread.

Rowing Club: Ann Arbor Rowing Club, Michigan Rowing Association, University of Michigan

ANNAPOLIS, MD

CHICK AND RUTH'S
165 Main Street
Annapolis, MD 21401

Tel: (410) 269-6737

Description: Oldest restaurant in Annapolis — 24/7 diner in downtown Annapolis. Frequented by Naval Academy students.

Recommendation: Try the milk shakes with real Hersey's ice cream and the kosher hot dogs.

Rowing Club: Annapolis Rowing Club, United States Naval Academy

CITY DOCK CAFE
18 Market Street
Annapolis, MD 21401-2606

Tel: (410) 269-0969

Description: Rowers gather here in the mornings after early AM workouts.

Rowing Club: Annapolis Rowing Club, United States Naval Academy

ARLINGTON, VA

COMMON GROUNDS COFFEE AND TEA HOUSE
3211 Wilson Boulevard
Arlington, VA 22201

Tel: (703) 312-0427

Description: A Seattle-style coffee house located in progressive Arlington, VA, about three miles from Potomac Boat Club. They serve great coffee, muffins and sandwiches, in a relaxed casual atmosphere.

Recommendation: Try a foamy cappuccino along with a mouth-watering sour cream poppy seed muffin.

Rowing Club: Potomac Boat Club, and Washington, DC area rowing clubs.

ASHLAND, OR

THE WILD GOOSE CAFE & BAR
2365 Ashland Street Ashland, OR 97520

Tel: (541) 488-4103

Description: Funky coffee shop.

Recommendation: Great breakfasts!

Rowing Club: Ashland Rowing Club

ATLANTA, GA

NUEVO LAREDO CANTINA
1495 Chattahoochee Ave
Atlanta, GA 30318

Tel: (404) 352-9009

Description: A Mexican restaurant voted best Mexican food in Atlanta for the past four years. Great food, cheap prices, and can handle big groups in sweaty rowing gear.

Recommendation: Lunch/Dinner

Rowing Club: Atlanta Rowing Club

OLD SPAGETTI FACTORY
249 Ponce de Leon Ave NE, Atlanta, GA 30308

Tel: (404) 872-2841

Description: A nation-wide restaurant chain where your team can get a lot of pre-race food for a "little green". This Old Spaghetti Factory is located just 1 mile from Georgia Tech campus.

Rowing Club: Atlanta Rowing Club, Georgia Tech

ATLANTA, GA

THE FLYING BISCUIT CAFE
1655 McLendon NE Ave
Atlanta, GA 30307

Tel: (404) 687-8888

Description: Co-owned by one of the Indigo Girls, in the tattoo-artist/funky part of town — excellent bakery, good coffee, and the biscuits are sublime works of culinary art. Highly recommended for breakfast or sunday brunch, although the wait can be long, (just get a coffee and muffin at the bakery while you wait), the food and the atmosphere are worth it. Large, sunny rooms, and an eclectic and interesting clientele.

Recommendation: Breakfast/Brunch, and their famous biscuits.

Rowing Club: Atlanta Rowing Club

AUGUSTA, GA

NACHO MAMA'S
Broad Street
Augusta, GA 30901

Description: This place serves up wraps and other Tex-Mex cuisine in a casual atmosphere. They have a pool table upstairs and it serves as a great place to hang out on a hot, Augusta southern evening.

Recommendation: Bahia wrap, large selection of micro brew beer.

Rowing Club: Augusta Rowing Club

THE PIZZA JOINT
1032 Broad Street
Augusta, GA 30901

Tel: (706) 774-0037

Description: The best homemade pizzas and calzones in a town where Italian is considered ethnic. (Not open on Mondays.)

Recommendation: Lunch/Dinner

Rowing Club: Augusta Rowing Club

THE WHISTLE STOP
573 Greene Street
Augusta, GA 30901

Tel: (706) 724-8224

Description: On the corner of 5th and Greene, next to the tracks running through downtown Augusta. The main draw for the hungry and competitive rower is not the excitement of watching the trains roll by only 6 feet away, but their "eat 3, get 'em for free" pancake offer. These cakes are $1.25 each and the size of a plate: beware of the post carbo-induced coma after chowing on these puppies! (Don't forget, as in most of the South, The Whistle Stop is closed on Sundays!)

Recommendation: Breakfast

Rowing Club: Augusta Rowing Club

AUSTIN, TX

CHANGO'S TAQUERIA
3023 Guadalupe Street Austin, TX 78705

Tel: (512) 480-8226

Description: For the professional burrito lover in you. Connoisseurs claim Chango's and Freebirds (below) would put anything from the North to shame.

Rowing Club: Austin Rowing Club

FREEBIRDS WORLD BURRITO
1000 East 41st Street Austin, TX 78751

Tel: (512) 451-5514

Description: For the professional burrito lover in you.

Rowing Club: Austin Rowing Club

MAGNOLIA CAFE
2304 Lake Austin Boulevard Austin, TX 78703

Tel: (512) 478-8645

MAGNOLIA CAFE SOUTH
1920 South Congress Ave Austin, TX 78704

Tel: (512) 445-0000

Description: Breakfast in Texas!!! The Magnolia comes with an enthusiastic review from a Northern transplant to Austin. Austin has become a popular place to train, especially in the winter months. The Migas "an egg and tortilla breakfast thing" come with a "must try!"

Rowing Club: Austin Rowing Club

BALTIMORE, MD

NO WAY JOSE CAFE
38 East Cross Street Baltimore, MD 21202

Tel: (410) 752-2837

Description: Great mexican restaurant with fantastic staff.

Recommendation: RED ENCHILADA: Three corn tortillas stuffed with beef braised in red wine and spices, topped w/ a rich ancho chili sauce and cheddar cheese, baked to perfection and served with beans and rice

BEYOGLU ISTANBUL, TURKEY

FORZATO
Istiklal Caddesi Postacilar Sokak, No:5, Beyoglu Istanbul, Turkey

Tel: + 90 (212) 251 56 26

Description: Run by a Turkish rower from Galatasarae RC who loves rowing and Italian food. Forzato means "rowing slave" in Italian. Forzato serves very good Italian food and the entire cafe is very attractively decorated with rowing memorabilia from Turkey, Europe, and Canada.

BOSTON, MA

BREW MOON
115 Stuart Street Boston, MA 02116-5609

Tel: (617) 742-5225

Description: A microbrewery located downtown in the Theater District. A good place to celebrate after the Charles.

Recommendation: Lunch/Dinner

BRIGHTON, MA

INTERNATIONAL HOUSE OF PANCAKES
1850 Soldier's Field Road Brighton, MA 02135-1113

Tel: (617) 787-0533

Description: A favorite place for Youth Programs at CRI.

BUFFALO, NY

PANO'S RESTAURANT
1081 Elmwood Avenue Buffalo, NY 14222-1225

Tel: (716) 886-9081

Description: All day breakfast, open on Sunday.

Recommendation: $3.99 Steak and eggs are a must have!

Rowing Club: West Side Rowing Club of Buffalo

CAMBRIDGE, MA

BORDER CAFE
32 Church Street Cambridge, MA 02138-3730

Tel: (617) 864-6100

Description: Crowded, but a HUGE menu with everything Mexican you could want. Signature margaritas should not be consumed before any major regattas, but ought to be afterwards.

Recommendation: Dinner/Lunch

CARBERRY'S BAKERY & COFFEE HOUSE

74 Prospect Street
Cambridge, MA 02139-2503

Tel: (617) 576-3530

Description: The big plus about Carberry's is the parking and bike racks out front. Check out the picture of the 1996 Silver medal men's quad near the side door. Excellent coffee (French roast would wake the dead and make them dance!), and pastries are equally noteworthy.

Recommendation: Breakfast

FIRE AND ICE

50 Church Street Cambridge, MA 02138-3726

Tel: (617) 547-9007

Description: Located next to the Border on Church St "an improvisational grill" allows you to chose from a wide selection of meats, veggies, and sauces to create your own meal. Great for the vegetarian who hangs out with carnivores.

Recommendation: Lunch/Dinner

CINCINNATI, OH

LA ROSA'S

2411-15-17 Boudinot Avenue
Cincinnati, OH 45238-3418

Description: To-die-for-pizza!

Rowing Club: Cincinnati Rowing Club

MONTGOMERY INN/ THE BOATHOUSE

925 Eastern Avenue
Cincinnati, OH 45202-1631

Tel: (513) 721-7427

Description: Great barbeque & view of the river.

Recommendation: Lunch/Dinner

Rowing Club: Cincinnati Rowing Club

CLEVELAND, OH

BIG EGG RESTAURANT

5107 Detroit Avenue
Cleveland, OH 44102

Tel: (216) 961-8000

Description: Open 24/7 with 24 hour breakfast.

Recommendation: Sundays... gotta go with an omelet with hash browns with cheese (never the same cheese twice).

Rowing Club: Western Reserve Rowing Association

CORALVILLE, IA

OLD COUNTRY BUFFET

Coral Ridge Avenue Coralville, IA 52241

Tel: (319) 625-2360

Description: Buffet-style food. Good for large parties.

Rowing Club: University of Iowa, River Rats Rowing

COSTA MESA, CA

BACK BAY ROWING & RUNNING CLUB

3333 Bristol Street
Costa Mesa, CA 92626

Tel: (714) 641-0118

Description: Hearty classics and an award-winning salad bar, served in a boathouse setting. A selection to satisfy everyone, with meals and the friendliest service, all at reasonable prices. The Restaurant's setting includes oars, many pictures of different crew teams.

Rowing Club: Newport Aquatic Center, Orange Coast College

DALLAS, TX

CLUB SCHMITZ

9661 Denton Drive
Dallas, TX 75220-5703

Tel: (214) 350-3607

Description: Family bar and grill around the corner from the Dallas Rowing Club.

DEPERE, WI

SUE ANNE'S BAGELS

124 N. Broadway
DePere, WI 54115

Tel: (920) 983-1170

Description: Bagels of every type you can imagine. They were voted the favorite regatta food by members of USRA in the early 90's. Both Sue and her husband Bob, owners, were rowers at the University of Wisconsin, Madison.

Recommendation: Everything is good, try the lox on an onion bagel.

Rowing Club: La Baie Verte Rowing Club

FAIRHAVEN, MA

MORGAN'S RESTAURANT

58 Washington Street
Fairhaven, MA 02719

Tel: (508) 997-4443

Description: Breakfast and Lunch. Home-made foods. Known for the largest variety of signature omlettes and accommodating the "healthy-option" person (from low-fat to no-fat items).

Recommendation: Home-made "low-fat, 5-star cornbread. Whipped rasberry butter. Homemade house juice. AKA: Nectar of the gods!

Rowing Club: Whaling City Rowing Club

GLENVILLE, NY

MANHATTEN BAGEL
133 Saratoga Road Glenville,
NY 12302

Description: A favorite after morning practice stop 5-10 minutes from the Aqueduct Rowing Club.

HANOVER, NH

LOU'S RESTAURANT
30 South Main Street
Hanover, NH 03755

Tel: (603) 643-3321

Description: Big and hearty breakfasts are served all day here at this diner-style restaurant just off the green at Dartmouth College. Poplar with students, athletes, full-time residents and tourists.

Recommendation: Everything on the menu is good! Their baked goods are fabulous. Try the french toast made with their famous cruellers.

Rowing Club: Hanover Rowing Club, Dresden Rowing Club, Dartmouth College

HUNTINGTON, NY

CANTERBURY ALES
314 New York Avenue
Huntington, NY 11743

Tel: (631) 549-4404

Description: Bar & Restaurant near the Sagamore Rowing Assn Huntington Boathouse.

Recommendation: Excellent Choice of Beers with pub food.

KEY BISCAYNE, FL

THE DONUT GALLERY
83 Harbor Drive
Key Biscayne, FL 33149

Tel: (305) 361-9985

Description: Ask for the "Ted Special" It's not on the menu. It's a glorified egg McMuffin with Cuban attitude (dos huevos). Mop it up with your toast. Belly up to the counter and you might be sitting next to 70's Watergate icon Bebe Rebozo. (The old-timers know exactly who he is).

Recommendation: Breakfast

KNOXVILLE, TN

THE TENNESSEE GRILL
900 Neyland Drive
Knoxville, TN 37902

Tel: (865) 862-8657

Description: Serving lunch, dinner and Sunday brunch. Great view of the river, located on top of the Lady Vols Boathouse.

Recommendation: Try the chicken salad or steak platters.

Rowing Club: University of Tennessee at Knoxville

LONG BEACH, CA

CASA SANCHEZ NO 3
1801 East Pacific Coast Hwy
Long Beach, CA 90806

Tel: (562) 599-5774

Description: Casa Sanchez is a great Mexican take out place in Long Beach. There are a few tables inside and out. It offers authentic Sonora style food and is pretty inexpensive. There is no rowing theme, but it plays a part in all of Brad Lewis's books. If you're a coach, plan your southern California recruiting trips around a visit to Casa Sanchez.

Rowing Club: Long Beach Rowing Association

THE POTHOLDER
Broadway and Euclid
Long Beach, CA

Description: This Long Beach restaurant serves a breakfast burrito, (home fries included) that is to die for. Lycra on customers is fine; the waitresses often sport lycra shorts and halter tops. There are rowing pictures on the wall, including a Long Beach State women's eight.

Rowing Club: Long Beach Rowing Association

MAYS LANDING, NJ

SUGAR HILL SUBS AND DELI
5445 Mays Landing-Somers Point Road Route 559
Mays Landing, NJ 08330

Description: A family run business since 1983.

Rowing Club: Atlantic Country Rowing Association

MIAMI, FL

BRICKELL EMPORIUM
1100 Brickell Plaza
Miami, FL 33131

Tel: (305) 377-3354

Description: Superior French toast, fresh-from-the-oven bagels, fresh-squeezed orange juice, huge omlettes. A Miami Rowing Club hangout.

Recommendation: Breakfast.

Rowing Club: Miami Rowing & Watersports Center

MILTON, PA

GOOD WIL'S RESTAURANT
RR 1 Box 419
Milton, PA 17847-9741

Tel: (570) 523-6406

Description: Does all day breakfast and is open on Sundays. This place is a-w-e-s-o-m-e awesome. The kind of diner where the OJ costs just as much as an entré. The only requirement: get a chocolate shake with every meal (a crew requirement, that is). A great meal for a great price.

Rowing Club: Bucknell University

NANTUCKET, MA

JARED COFFEE HOUSE
29 Broad Street
Nantucket, MA 02554

Description: Located near Nantucket Rowing Association. Best breakfast on the Island and best-kept secret: (The "J.C."). Don't wear your grubby rowing trou with the track grit all over 'em to THIS breakfast. It's easily the best value in town for the location, amount and quality of the food, atmosphere, and service. The J.C. is at the top of Broad Street where it meets Center Street.

Recommendation: Breakfast.

NEW ORLEANS, LA

THE BLUE BIRD CAFE
3625 Prytania Street
New Orleans, LA 70115

Tel: (504) 895-7166

Description: A rower writes: "Rower-friendly restaurant in a not-so-rower-friendly city. I went to the Blue Bird Cafe in the Garden District of town and believe you me, there SHOULD have been rowers there. Bottomless cups of coffee, super-friendly service and the best blueberry buckwheat pancakes from here to Kingdom Come, I found a home away from home!"

NORWALK, CT

JIMMY'S MEDITERRANEAN DELI
65 Van Zant Street
Norwalk, CT 06855

Tel: (203) 838-7340

Description: Good, quick food when you're in a hurry to get to work after a row.

Recommendation: Try the breakfast sandwich and coffee.

Rowing Club: Norwalk River Rowing Association

OAK RIDGE, TN

BIG ED'S PIZZA
101 Broadway Avenue
Oak Ridge, TN 37830

Tel: (865) 482-4885

Description: Pizza Parlor that is "extremely" rower friendly.

Recommendation: Pizza

Rowing Club: Oak Ridge Rowing Association, Clinton Rowing Club

PANERA BREAD
371 S. Illinois Avenue
Oak Ridge, TN 37830

Tel: (865) 220-5699

Description: Bakery — Cafe

Recommendation: Large variety of bagels and breads. Also serves soups and salads.

Rowing Club: Oak Ridge Rowing Association, Clinton Rowing Club

ORLANDO, FL

WINTER PARK DINER
1700 Fairbanks Avenue,
Orlando, FL 32789

Tel: (407) 644-2343

Description: Popular post-practice stop serving breakfasts.

Recommendation: Try the omlettes!

Rowing Club: Orlando Rowing Club

OYSTER BAY, NY

CANTERBURY ALES OYSTER BAR & GRILL
46 Audrey Avenue
Oyster Bay, NY 11771

Tel: (516) 922-3614

Description: Full Restaurant & Bar near the Sagamore Rowing Assn Oyster Bay Boathouse.

Recommendation: Excellent Choice of Beers. Oysters!

TABBY'S BURGER HOUSE
28 Audrey Avenue
Oyster Bay, NY 11771

Tel: (516) 624-7781

Description: Diner Style Food.

Recommendation: Best Burgers!

Rowing Club: Sagamore Rowing Association

PALM BEACH, FL

BREAKERS HOTEL
1 South County Road
Palm Beach, FL 33480

Tel: (561) 655-6611

Description: Near the Palm Beach Rowing Association. Best breakfast on the east coast: A swanky five star kind of place. You don't have to get all dressed up anymore for THIS chow-fest. But don't wear spandex. Huge buffet. Unbelievable dining room. Dine like a Vanderbilt, eat like Jethro Bodine.

Recommendation: Breakfast

PHILADELPHIA, PA

DOWN HOME DINER
12th and Filbert Streets
Philadelphia, PA 19102

Tel: (215) 627-1955

Description: Located in the center of Philadelphia, the Down Home Diner can be crowded, particularly on

Saturdays and Sundays after about 10 a.m. Fortunately this is slightly later than the rower's typical breakfast hours, so it's worth the trouble to get there and find a place to park. Serving large helpings of traditional diner food, from pancakes to meat loaf.

FLOWER SHOP CAFE
2501 Meredith Street,
Philadelphia, PA 19130

Tel: (215) 232-1076

Description: This is located in the Fairmount area, close to Boathouse Row. Your upscale breakfast with unique omlette combinations and organic waffles. All the ingrediants are fresh and everything tastes great. Good for a Sunday treat. They serve excellent lunch, too.

LEBUS
4266 Main Street Philadelphia, PA 19127-1609

Tel: (215) 487-2663

Description: Le Bus serves up terrific omlettes, pancakes, vegetarian chili, pasta and fish to name a few. For Sunday morning brunch, park yourself at their spacious bar, order a Bloody Mary and indulge in some fluffy french toast. Located in Manayunk, LeBus neighbors a plethora of boutiques and unique stores — one of Philadelphia's best shopping and eating destinations.

Recommendation:
Brunch/Lunch/Dinner

NEIGHBORHOOD DINER
Fairmount Neighborhood of Philly, Philadelphia, PA

Description: A hangout for Fairmount RC Since 1997, you'll see many of the same faces in here every day. Real vermont and pennsylvania maple syrup. Only 100% butter

no margarine allowed. They have many vegatarian dishes and soups, great home-made veggie burgers, fritattas, salads and BYOB.

Recommendation: The macaroni and cheese is the cheesiest. Won best of Philly for Mac-n-Cheese — Try it with Sam's homemade ketchup. Also Won Best of Philly Brunch.

PETE'S PIZZA & RESTAURANT
2320 Fairmount Avenue
Philadelphia, PA 19130-2519

Tel: (215) 765-3040

Description: Pete's is a breakfast place by morning and an Italian neighborhood pizza joint by day. A Philadelphia classic, this place is teeming with rowers on any given morning. If you want to run into someone you haven't seen in years, it would most likely happen at Pete's. Perfect for late-morning post practice gluttony, because you can get breakfast and lunch at one sitting.

Recommendation: Try the "Coach's Special," creamed chipped beef on toast!

PITTSBURGH, PA

JO JOSEPH RESTAURANT
110 24th Street
Pittsburgh, PA 15222

Tel: (412) 461-0280

Description: In Pittsburgh, a favorite post-row breakfast spot is Jo-Jo's Restaurant. This is one of the good old short-order joints. It's not far from the river. Bottomless coffee, huge omeletes, great home fries and fresh Italian bread toast.

PORTLAND, OR

THE ORIGINAL STEAK AND HOTCAKE HOUSE
1002 SE Powell Boulevard
Portland, OR 97202-2534

Tel: (503) 236-7402

Description: Breakfast served all day, seven days a week.

Recommendation: The greatest hotcakes ever, bar none. Rich, creamy, buttery and so much more. The best deal: an omelet with a side of hotcakes. A tip: underestimate, you'll get filled up faster than you ever have before, so go easy!

Rowing Club: Station L Rowing Club

PROVIDENCE, RI

LOUIS RESTAURANT
286 Brook Street Providence, RI 02906-1109

Tel: (401) 861-5255

Description: Large, filling servings. An ideal spot for post-practice and post-Saturday nights. Located next to Brown University campus.

Recommendation:
Breakfast/Lunch/Dinner

RED BANK, NJ

BASIL T'S
183 Riverside Avenue
Red Bank, NJ 07701

Tel: (732) 849-5990

Description: This ain't just another Italian restaurant. A hop, skip and a jump away from Navesink River Rowing Club, you will have an unbelievable pasta experience at Basil T's. Fresh, homemade pasta, seafood and pizza among many other delectable dishes. They also brew their own beer!

Recommendation: Lunch/Dinner

Rowing Club: Navesink River Rowing Club

ROSWELL, GA

CICI'S PIZZA
10516 Alpharetta Hwy
Roswell, GA 30076-1429

Tel: (770) 645-1550

Description: Pizza joint.

Recommendation: A favorite of Georgia Tech rowers with a $2.99 all-you-can-eat pizza buffet. Also located within a mile and a half of the Atlanta RC and Head of the Chattahoochee Race Course.

Rowing Club: Atlanta Rowing Club, Georgia Tech

SALT LAKE CITY, UT

BACI TRATTORIA
134 West Pierpoint Avenue
Salt Lake City, UT 84117

Tel: (801) 328-1500

Description: Located in downtown Salt Lake City, this Italian restaurant combines ambience and exquisite food in a fresh and open setting. High ceilings, southwest decor.

Recommendation: Dinner: Try the seared halibut or Atlantic salmon. The spinach and gorgonzola stuffed pasta is exquisite. Flourless chocolate cake or chocolate layered mousse for dessert!

Rowing Club: Great Salt Lake Rowing

LEMON GRASS THAI CUISINE
327 West 200 South
Salt Lake City, UT 84101

Description: Authentic Thai cuisine in the heartland of America. The menu offers thai barbecue, curry dishes, fried rice and noodles and chef specials daily.

Recommendation: Dinner/Lunch: One of the curry dishes or pad thai.

Rowing Club: Great Salt Lake Rowing

SAN DIEGO, CA

GRINGO'S
4474 Mission Boulevard
San Diego, CA 92109-3920

Tel: (858) 490-2877

Rowing Club: Mission Bay Rowing Association

KARINYA THAI & VEGETARIAN CUISINE
4475 Mission Boulevard San Diego, CA 92109-3966

Tel: (858) 270-5050

Rowing Club: Mission Bay Rowing Association

KONO'S CAFE
704 Garnet Avenue
San Diego, CA 92109

Tel: (619) 483-1669

Description: Located in Pacific Beach along the boardwalk, Kono's is a favorite breakfast spot for rowers, serving huge breakfast burritos all day long.

Recommendation: Breakfast burritos served all day.

Rowing Club: Mission Bay Rowing Association

SAN FRANCISCO, CA

THE RAMP RESTAURANT
855 Terry Francois Blvd
San Francisco, CA 94107

Tel: (415) 621-2378

Rowing Club: Embarcadero Rowing Club

SCHENECTADY, NY

LUIGI'S
1125 Barrett Street
Schenectady, NY 12305

Tel: (518) 382-5429

Description: Great home-made Italian food.

Recommendation: Get the Chicken Ricotta.

Rowing Club: Aqueduct Rowing Club

SEATTLE, WA

FRED HUTCHINSON CAFETERIA
1901 Fairview Avenue North
Seattle, WA 98109

Description: Research Center Cafeteria and Coffee Shop.

Recommendation: Fresh salads and fruit, great coffee

LOUISA'S BAKERY & CAFE
2379 Eastlake Ave East
Seattle, WA 98102-3305

Tel: (206) 325-0081

Description: Popular with the floating Lake Union Crew Boathouse and Pocock Rowing Foundation, Louisa's serves delicious and healthy sandwiches, soups and homemade baked goods.

MAE'S PHINNEY RIDGE CAFE
6412 Phinney Avenue North
Seattle, WA 98103

Description: Open on Sundays. The best classic American brunch foods. Plus some great milk shakes if you can handle it. After a hard weekend workout it's a must with the whole boat.

NICKERSON STREET SALOON
318 Nickerson,
Seattle, WA 98109

Tel: (206) 284-8819

Description: Bar/Restaurant

Recommendation: All the food is good, and great Microbrews on tap!

STILL LIFE IN FREMONT COFFEEHOUSE
709 N. 35th
Seattle, WA 98103

Tel: (206) 547-9850

Description: Located in Fremont, a casual cafe that serves amazing food, coffee and desserts.

Recommendation: Try everything! Some favorites include the fruit and yogurt, hot oatmeal and gourmet sandwiches.

THE LONG SHOREMAN'S DAUGHTER
3508 Fremont Place N Seattle, WA 98103-8623

Tel: (206) 633-5169

Description: Located in Fremont, a short walk from Lake Washington Rowing Club, The Long Shoreman's Daughter serves up delicious omlettes, pancakes and homefries as well as lunch and dinner.

Recommendation: Breakfast/Lunch/Dinner

TORREFAZIONE ITALIA
701 N. 34th Street,
Seattle, WA 98103

Tel: (206) 545-2721

Description: Coffee house near Lake Washington Rowing Club.

SHAMOKIN DAM, PA

TEDD'S LANDING
Intersection of US Rts 11 & 15
Shamokin Dam, PA 17876

Tel: (570) 743-1591

Description: Owned by the Skotedis family, and located in the heart of Pennsylvania where the North and West branches of the Susquehanna River join, Tedd's offers a variety of well-prepared, fresh seafood as part of their full menu.

Recommendation: Seafood of course... especially the crabcakes! Also, homemade desserts that call to you as you approach... don't miss the Baklava!

Rowing Club: Central Pennsylvania Rowing Association, Bucknell University, Susquehanna University

SOMERVILLE, MA

SOUND BITES
708 Broadway
Somerville, MA 02144

Tel: (617) 623-8338

Description: A short drive from Riverside, Cambridge or CRI. Excellent food!! A favorite of Tuft's students, so arrive early on weekend mornings, to beat out the hungover students for a table.

Recommendation: Everything's great. If you get waffles/pancakes, order "w/fruit"...you'll get an amazing assortment of fresh yummy fruit piled high. Eggs Benedict and home fries can't be beat! Portions proper for rowers!

ST. CATHARINES, ON

SPICE OF LIFE CAFE
12 Lock Street
Hogan's Alley Port Dalhousie,
St. Catharines, ON L2N 5B5
Canada

Tel: (905) 937-9027

Description: Vegan, vegetarian and selected meat dishes prepared with unbelievably fresh and wholesome ingredients. Every dish is to die for!

Recommendation: Everything!

Rowing Club: While at the CSSRA or the Canadian Henley Regatta.

SPICY THAI RESTAURANT
208 Church Street
St. Catharines, ON Canada

Tel: (905) 687-6981

Description: Fresh healthy delicious Thai food!

Recommendation: Lunch/dinner. Fresh healthy and most delicious Asian food in town! Voted best every year and it's non-smoking! Vegetarian version available as well.

THE BRONX, NY

PETE'S CAFE
570 E Fordham Road
The Bronx, NY 10458

Tel: (718) 733-7416

Description: Open on Sundays. Breakfast specials before 11 am.

Rowing Club: Fordham University

WASHINGTON, DC

BOOEYMONGER
3265 Prospect Street
Washington, DC 20007

Description: A favorite among Georgetown University students and Potomac Boat Club rowers, this little deli offers great breakfasts, sandwiches and bagels. Get your Washington Post and read the latest political scandals over breakfast. Located right off of "M" Street

Recommendation: Sandwiches: Booey Wrap and the Pita Pan. Try their chocolate-chocolate cake and the cinnamon coffee.

Rowing Club: Potomac Boat Club, Thompson's Boat Center and other D.C. area clubs.

FACCIA LUNA
2400 Wisconsin Avenue NW
Washington, DC 20007-1800

Tel: (202) 337-3132

Description: Thin-crust pizzas that melt in your mouth, italian entrees, fast service, interesting beer selection. Also a location in Arlington, VA on Wilson Boulevard (Clarendon).

Recommendation: White pizza with pesto and ricotta cheese. Mussels for an appetizer.

Rowing Club: Potomac Boat Club, Thompson's Boat Center and other D.C. area clubs.

THE GEORGETOWN BAGELRY
3245 M Street, NW
Washington, DC 20007-3616

Tel: (202) 965-1011

Description: The place to go for bagels, The Georgetown Bagelry serves freshly made bagels, pizza, muffins and more. The chocolate chip muffins are a must! However, there are a limited amount of stools (no tables) so plan to eat and run.

Recommendation: Miami Burger, Pizza, and Chocolate Chip Muffins. Tip: Go across the street to Dean & Deluca for coffee.

Rowing Club: Potomac Boat Club, Thompson's Boat Center and other D.C. area clubs.

THE TOMBS
1226 36th Street, NW
Washington, DC 20007-2627

Tel: (202) 337-6668

Description: A Georgetown student hangout, this restaurant/bar has a "rowing" theme, with a plethora of Georgetown crew photos, mounted oars etc. American cuisine, and a great ambience.

Rowing Club: Potomac Boat Club, Thompson's Boat Center and other D.C. area clubs.

WATERTOWN, MA

ARSENAL DINER
356 Arsenal Street
Watertown, MA 02472-2892

Tel: (617) 926-8371

Description: A popular breakfast place for the Riverside bunch.

Recommendation: Breakfast

VICTOR'S VILLAGE COUNTRY KITCHEN
214 North Beacon Street
Watertown, MA 02472

Tel: (617) 926-4975

Description: Rower-friendly diner, great breakfast grub, no-nonsense

Recommendation: Omelettes — look like they're made from about 10 eggs each!

Rowing Club: Community Rowing Inc.

WESTPORT, CT

THE RIVERVIEW
521 Riverside Avenue
Westport, CT 06880

Tel: (203) 227-3399

WHITEHALL, PA

BUCA DI BEPPO
714 Grape Street Whitehall,
PA 18052-5207

Tel: (610) 264-3389

Description: Italian

Recommendation: All dishes are very large and tasty.

Rowing Club: Lehigh University

WILMINGTON, DE

BERNIE'S TAVERN
10 E. 2nd Street
Wilmington, DE 19801-2512

Tel: (302) 656-8795

Description: Like a Cheers, real informal and comfortable, this is a favorite for Wilmington

Rowing Club rowers. Serves sandwiches, soups, seafood, burgers & fries.

Recommendation: Lunch/Dinner

MARKETPLACE (ON THE RIVERFRONT)
1 S. Market Street
Wilmington, DE 19801-5003

Description: Right on the riverfront walk near the train station, the marketplace has coffee and is "the spot" for post-practice coffee and snack.

Rowing Club: Wilmington Rowing Club

WOODBRIDGE, VA

CHESAPEAKE BAGEL BAKERY
8420 Old Keene Mill Road
Woodbridge, VA 22152

Tel: (703) 451-4788

Description: A favorite post-practice hangout among the Woodbridge HS rowers, the Chesapeake Bagel Bakery serves fresh bagels, muffins and sandwiches. Located near the Occoquan Reservoir, site of Head of the Occoquan, Occoquan Sprints and NOVAs.

Recommendation: Pre-race snack, post-race chow-down.

WORCESTER, MA

REGATTA DELI & SANDWICH SHOPPE
28 Lake Avenue
Worcester, MA 01604

Tel: (508) 756-6916

Description: In Worcester, MA on Lake Avenue (down the street from Quinsigamond Regatta Point) is an AWESOME deli. The sandwiches are huge and delcious and they have cool rowing memorabilia.

Rowers from the Haifa Rowing Club on the Kishon River. Photo courtesy of Giyora Saar.

Country Key for Olympic Medals 1900-2000

ARG — ARGENTINA	EUN — UNITED TEAM EX-USSR	NZL — NEW ZEALAND
AUS — AUSTRALIA	FIN — FINLAND	POL — POLAND
AUT — AUSTRIA	FRA — FRANCE	ROM — ROMANIA
BEL — BELGIUM	FRG — FORMER REP. OF GERMANY	RUS — RUSSIA
BLR — BELARUS	GBR — GREAT BRITAIN	SLO — SLOVENIA
BUL — BULGARIA	GDR — GERMAN DEM.REPUBLIC	SUI — SWITZERLAND
CAN — CANADA	GER — GERMANY	SWE — SWEDEN
CHN — CHINA	HUN — HUNGARY	TCH — CZECHSLOVAKIA
CRO — CROATIA	ITA — ITALY	URS — SOVIET UNION
DEN — DENMARK	LTU — LITHUANIA	USA — UNITED STATES
ESP — SPAIN	NED — NETHERLANDS	YUG — YUGOSLAVIA
EUA — UNITED TEAM OF GERMANY	NOR — NORWAY	

Olympic Medals 1900–2000

1900 ★ Paris

MEN'S SINGLE SCULLS (M1X)

Gold	FRA	Barrelet, Henri
Silver	FRA	Gaudin, André
Bronze	GBR	Ashe, Saint-George

MEN'S PAIR WITH COXSWAIN (M2+)

Gold	NED/FRA	Brandt, Francois Antoine; Brockmann, Hermanus Gerardus; Klein, Roelof
Silver	FRA	Waleff; Martinet, Louis; Unknown Cox; Barreur Inconnu
Bronze	FRA	Deltour, Carlos; Paoli, Raoul; Vedrenne, Antoine Erneste

MEN'S FOUR WITH COXSWAIN (M4+)

Gold	FRA	Delchambre, Emile; Cau, Jean; Bouckaert, Henri; Hazebrouck, Henri;
	GER	Gossler, Oscar; Katzenstein, Walther; Tietgens, Waldemar; Gossler, Gustav Ludwig; Gossler, Carl Heinrich
Silver	FRA	Lumpp, Georges; Perrin, Charles; Soubeyran, Daniel; Wegelin, Emile
	NED	Brockmann, Hermanus Gerardus; Hiebendaai, Coenraad Christiaan; Lotsy, Gerhard Oswald; Lotsy, Paulus Jan; Terwogt, Johannes Hester Lambertus
Bronze	GER	Felle, Ernst; Fickeisen, Otto; Kröwerath, Franz; Lehle, Carl; Wilker, Hermann
	GER	Carstens, Wilhelm; Körner, Julius; Möller, Adolf; Moths, Gustav; Rüster, Hugo

MEN'S EIGHT (M8+)

Gold	USA	Abell, Louis; Debaecke, Harry; Carr, William; Exley, John; Geiger, John; Hedley, Edward; Juvenal, James; Lockwood, Roscoe; Marsh, Edward
Silver	BEL	Bruggeman, Prospère; De Bisschop, Jules; De Cock, Oscar; De Somville, Oscar Charles; Hemelsoet, Maurice; Odberg, Frank; Van Crombrugghe, Marcel Lucien; Van Landeghem, Alfred; Verdonck, Maurice
Bronze	NED	Brandt, Francois Antoine; Brockmann, Hermanus Gerardus; Klein, Roelof; Leegstra, Ruud Gerbens; Middelberg, Walter; Offerhaus, Hendrik Kare; Thijssen, Walter; Tromp, Henricus; Van Dijk, Johannes Wilhelmus Maria

1904 ★ St. Louis

MEN'S SINGLE SCULLS (M1X)

Gold	USA	Greer, Frank
Silver	USA	Juvenal, James
Bronze	USA	Titus, Constance

MEN'S DOUBLE SCULLS

Gold	USA	Mulcahy, John J.F.; Varley, William
Silver	USA	Hoben, John Grey; McLoughlin, James
Bronze	USA	Ravanack, Joseph; Wells, John

MEN'S FOUR WITHOUT COXSWAIN (M4-)

Gold	USA	Dietz, George; Erker, August; Nasse, Albert; Stockhoff, Arthur
Silver	USA	Aman, Charles; Begley, Michael; Fromanack, Martin; Suerig, Frederick
Bronze	USA	Dunimerth, Frank; Freitag, John; Helm, Louis G.; Voerg, Gustav

MEN'S EIGHT (M8+)

Gold	USA	Armstrong, Charles E; Cresser, Frederick; Exley, John; Flanigan, James; Gleason, Micahel D.; Lott, Harry Hunter; Schell, Frank Reaner
Silver	CAN	Bailey, Arthur B.; Boyd, Philip Ewing; Loudon, Thomas Richardson; Mackenzie, Donald; Reiffenstein, George Patrick; Rice, William; Strange, George M.; Wadsworth, William; Wright, Joseph George

1908 ★ London

MEN'S SINGLE SCULLS (M1X)

Gold	GBR	Blackstaffe, Harry Thomas
Silver	GBR	Mcculloch, Alexander
Bronze	GER	Von Gaza, Bernhard
Bronze	HUN	Leviczky, Károly

MEN'S PAIR WITHOUT COXSWAIN (M2-)

Gold	GBR	Fenning, John Reginald Keith; Thomson, Gordon Lindsay
Silver	GBR	Fairbairn, George Eric; Verdon, Philip
Bronze	GER	Düskow, Willi; Stahnke, Martin
Bronze	CAN	Jackes, Norman B.; Toms, Fred P.

MEN'S FOUR WITHOUT COXSWAIN (M4-)

Gold	GBR	Cudmore, Collier Robert; Gillan, James Angus; Mackinnon, Duncan; Somers-Smith, John Robert
Silver	GBR	Barker, Harold Ross; Fenning, John Reginald Keith; Filleul, Philip Rowland; Thomson, Gordon Lindsay

MEN'S EIGHT (M8+)

Gold	GBR	Bucknall, Henry Cresswell; Burnell, Charles Desborough; Etherington-Smith, Raymond Broadley; Gladstone, Albert Charles; Johnstone, Banner Carruthers; Kelly, Frederick Septimus; Maclagan, Gilchrist Stanley; Nickalls, Guy O.; Sanderson, Ronald Harcour
Silver	BEL	De Somville, Oscar Charles; Mijs, Georges; Morimont, Marcel; Orban, Rémy; Poma, Rodolphe; Taelman, Oscar; Van Landeghem, Alfred; Veirman, Polydore; Vergucht, François
Bronze	GBR	Boyle, Richard Frederick; Burn, John Southerden; Carver, Oswald Armitage; Goldsmith, Henry Mills; Jerwood, Frank Harold; Kitching, Harold Edward; Powell, Eric Walter; Stuart, Douglas Cecil Rees; Williams, Edward Gordon
Bronze	CAN	Balfour, Gordon Bruce; Gale, Becher Robert; Kertland, Douglas Edwin; Lewis, Walter Aiken; Riddy, Charles; Robertson, Irvine Geale; Taylor, Geoffrey; Thomson, Julius A.; Wright, Joseph George

1912 ★ Stockholm

MEN'S SINGLE SCULLS (M1X)

Gold	GBR	Kinnear, William Duthie
Silver	BEL	Veirman, Polydore
Bronze	CAN	Butler, Everard Burnside
Bronze	n/a	Kusik, Mikhaïl Maksimilian

MEN'S FOUR WITHOUT COXSWAIN (M4-)

Gold	DEN	Allert, Ejlert Arild Emil; Hansen, Jörgen Christian; Hartman, Poul Richard; Möller, Carl Martin August; Petersen, Carl Frederik
Silver	SWE	Bruhn-Möller, William; Brunkman, Conrad; Dahlbäck, Herman; Rosvall, Ture; Wilkens, Wilhelm
Bronze	NOR	Björnstad, Olaf; Herseth, Magnus; Holter, Reidar Durie; Höyer, Claus; Olstad, Frithiof

MEN'S FOUR WITH COXSWAIN (M4+)

Gold	GER	Arnheiter, Albert; Fickeisen, Otto; Fickeisen, Rudolf; Leister, Karl; Wilker, Hermann
Silver	GBR	Beresford, Julius; Carr, Geoffrey; Logan, Herbert Bruce; Rought, Charles Gardner; Vernon, Karl
Bronze	DEN	Bisgaard, Erik; Clemmensen, Eigil; Frandsen, Rasmus Peter; Simonsen, Mikael; Thymann, Poul

1912 ★ Stockholm (continued)

MEN'S EIGHT (M8+)

Gold	GBR	Burgess, Edgar Richard; Fleming, Philip; Garton, Arthur Stanley; Gillan, James Angus; Horsfall, Ewart Douglas; Kirby, Alister Graham; Swann, Sidney Ernest; Wells, Henry Bensley; Wormald, Leslie Graham
Silver	GBR	Bourne, Robert Croft; Burdekin, Beaufort; Fison, William Guy; Gillespie, Thomas Cunningham; Littlejohn, Charles William Berry; Parker, William Lorenzo; Pitman, Frederick Archibald Hugo; Walker, John Drummond; Wiggins, Arthur Frederick Reginald
Bronze	GER	Bartholomae, Fritz; Bartholomae, Willi; Broeske, Max; Dehn, Werner; Liebing, Otto; Mathiae, Hans; Reichelt, Rudolf; Runge, Kurt; Vetter, Max

1920 ★ Antwerp

MEN'S SINGLE SCULLS (M1X)

Gold	USA	Kelly, John Brendan
Silver	GBR	Beresford, Jack
Bronze	NZL	Hadfield D'arcy, D. Clarence

MEN'S DOUBLE SCULLS (M2X)

Gold	USA	Costello, Paul Vincent; Kelly, John Brendan
Silver	ITA	Annoni, Pietro; Dones, Erminio
Bronze	FRA	Giran, Gaston; Ple, Alfred

MEN'S PAIR WITH COXSWAIN (M2+)

Gold	ITA	De Filip, Guido; Olgeni, Ercole; Scatturin, Giovanni
Silver	FRA	Barberolle, Ernest; Bouton, Maurice; Poix, Gabriel
Bronze	SUI	Candeveau, Edouard; Felber, Alfred; Piaget, Paul

MEN'S FOUR WITH COXSWAIN (M4+)

Gold	SUI	Brüderlin, Willy; Rudolf, Max; Rudolf, Paul; Staub, Paul; Walter, Hans
Silver	USA	Clark, Sherman Rockwell; Federschmidt, Erich; Federschmidt, Franz; Klose, Carl Otto; Myers, Kenneth
Bronze	NOR	Gulbrandsen, Per; Hagen, Thoralf; Klem, Theodor; Larsen, Henry; Var, Birger

MEN'S EIGHT (M8+)

Gold	USA	Clark, Sherman Rockwell; Gallagher, Vincent Joseph; Graves, Edwin Darius; Jacomini, Virgil Victor; Johnston, Donald Hendric; Jordan, William Conrad; King, Clyde Whitlock; Moore, Edward Peerman; Sandborn, Allen Ream
Silver	GBR	Campbell, John Alan; Earl, Sebastian; Horsfall, Ewart Douglas; James, Walter; Johnstone, Robin Talbot; Lucas, Richard Saville; Nickalls, Guy Oliver Jr.; Shove, Ralph Samuel; Swann, Sidney Ernest
Bronze	NOR	Ellingsen, Haakon; Hagen, Thoralf; Michelsen, Thore; Mortensen, Arne; Nag, Karl; Nag, Theodor; Nilsen, Adolf; Olsen, Conrad; Tollefsen, Tollef

1924 ★ Paris

MEN'S SINGLE SCULLS (M1X)

Gold	GBR	Beresford, Jack
Silver	USA	Gilmore, Williams E.Garrett
Bronze	SUI	Schneider, Josef

MEN'S DOUBLE SCULLS (M2X)

Gold	USA	Costello, Paul Vincent; Kelly, John Brendan
Silver	FRA	Detton, Marc P.; Stock, Jean-Pierre
Bronze	SUI	Bosshard, Rudolf; Thoma, Heinrich

MEN'S PAIR WITHOUT COXSWAIN (M2-)

Gold	NED	Beijnen, Antonie Christiaan; Rösingh, Wilhelm
Silver	FRA	Bouton, Maurice; Piot, Georges

MEN'S PAIR WITH COXSWAIN (M2+)

Gold	SUI	Candeveau, Edouard; Felber, Alfred; Lachapelle, Emil
Silver	ITA	Olgeni, Ercole; Scatturin, Giovanni; Sopracordevole, Gino
Bronze	USA	Butler, Leon; Wilson, Harold; Jennings, Edward Francis

MEN'S FOUR WITHOUT COXSWAIN (M4-)

Gold	GBR	Eley, Charles; Macnabb, James; Morrisson, Robert; Sanders, Terence
Silver	CAN	Black, Archibald; Mackay, George; Mariacher, A.; Wood, William
Bronze	SUI	Albrecht, Emile; Probst, Alfred; Sigg, Eugen; Walter, Hans

MEN'S FOUR WITH COXSWAIN (M4+)

Gold	SUI	Albrecht, Emile; Lossli, Walter; Probst, Alfred; Sigg, Eugen; Walther, Hans
Silver	FRA	Barberolle, Ernest; Constant, Eugène; Gressier, Louis A.; Lecointe, Georges; Talleux, Raymond
Bronze	USA	Gerhardt, Robert; Jelinek, Sidney; Kennedy, John; Mitchell, Edward; Welsford, Henry

MEN'S EIGHT (M8+)

Gold	USA	Carpentier, Leonard; Kingsbury, Howard; Lindley, Allen; Miller, John; Rockefeller, James; Sheffield, Frederick; Spock, Benjamin; Stoddard, Laurence; Wilson, Alfred
Silver	CAN	Bell, Arthur; Campbell, Ivor; Hunter, Robert; Langford, William; Little, Harold; Smith, John; Snyder, Warren; Taylor, Norman; Wallace, William
Bronze	ITA	Cattalinich, Antonio; Cattalinich, Francesco; Cattalinich, Simeone; Crivelli, Giuseppe; Gallasso, Latino; Gliubich, Vittorio; Ivanov, Pietro; Sorich, Bruno; Toniatti, Carlo

1928 ★ Amsterdam

MEN'S SINGLE SCULLS (M1X)

Gold	AUS	Pearce, Henry Robert
Silver	USA	Myers, Kenneth
Bronze	GBR	Collet, Theodore David Anthony

MEN'S DOUBLE SCULLS (M2X)

Gold	USA	Costello, Paul Vincent; McIlvaine, Charles Joseph
Silver	CAN	Guest, John Schofield; Wright Jr., Joseph William
Bronze	AUT	Flessl, Viktor; Losert, Leo

1928 ★ Amsterdam (continued)

MEN'S PAIR WITHOUT COXSWAIN (M2-)
Gold   GER   Möschter, Kurt; Müller, Bruno
Silver   GBR   Nisbet, Robert Archibald; O'Brien, Terence Noel
Bronze   USA   McDowell, Paul L.; Schmitt, John Victor

MEN'S PAIR WITH COXSWAIN (M2+)
Gold   SUI   Bourquin, Hans; Schöchlin, Hans W.; Schöchlin, Karl F.
Silver   FRA   Marcelle, Armand; Marcelle, Edouard; Préaux, Henri
Bronze   BEL   Anthony, Georges; De Coninck, François; Flament, Léon

MEN'S FOUR WITHOUT COXSWAIN (M4-)
Gold   GBR   Beesly, Richard; Bevan, Edward Vaughan; Lander, John Gerard Heath;
                Warriner, Michael Henry
Silver   USA   Bayer, Ernest Henry; Healis, George; Karle, Charles G.; Miller, William G.
Bronze   ITA   Bonade, Umberto; Freschi, Pietro; Gennari, Paolo; Rossi, Cesare

MEN'S FOUR WITH COXSWAIN (M4+)
Gold   ITA   D, Giliante; Delise, Giovanni; Perentin, Valerio; Petronio, Renato; Vittori, Nicolo
Silver   SUI   Bösch, Fritz; Bucher, Otto; Haas, Ernst; Meyer, Joseph; Schwegler, Karl
Bronze   POL   Birkholz, Leszek Leon; Bronikowski, Franciszek; Drewek, Boleslaw;
                Jankowski, Edmund; Ormanowski, Bernard

MEN'S EIGHT (M8+)
Gold   USA   Blessing, Donald F.; Brinck, John Manning; Caldwell, Hubert Aspinwall;
                Dally, William Morris; Donlon, Peter Dwight; Frederick, Francis Harland;
                Stalder, Marvin Frederick; Thompson, William G.; Workman, James Theodore
Silver   GBR   Badcock, John Charles; Beresford, Jack; Gollan, Donald Herbert Louis;
                Hamilton, James Hamish; Killick, G. Cecil; Lane, Harold Mansfield;
                Nickalls, Guy Oliver Jr.; Sulley, Arthur Lindsay; West, Harold E.
Bronze   CAN   Donnelly, John Henry; Fiddes, Frank James; Hand, John L.;
                Hedges, Frederick Charles; Meech, Athol Charles; Murdoch, Jack L.;
                Norris, Charles Edgar; Richardson, Herbert Trenchard; Ross, William M.

1932 ★ Los Angeles

MEN'S SINGLE SCULLS (M1X)
Gold   AUS   Pearce, Robert Henry
Silver   USA   Miller, William G.
Bronze   URU   Douglas, Guillermo

MEN'S DOUBLE SCULLS (M2X)
Gold   USA   Gilmore, Williams E.Garrett; Myers, Kenneth
Silver   GER   Boetzelen, Gerhard; Buhtz, Herbert
Bronze   CAN   De Mille, Noel; Pratt, Charles E.

MEN'S PAIR WITHOUT COXSWAIN (M2-)
Gold   GBR   Clive, Lewis; Edwards, Hugh
Silver   NZL   Stiles, Cyril Alec; Thompson, Fred Houghton
Bronze   POL   Budzinski, Henryk; Krenz-Mikolajczak, Janusz

MEN'S PAIR WITH COXSWAIN (M2+)
Gold   USA   Jennings, Edward Francis; Kieffer, Charles M.; Schauers, Joseph Anthony
Silver   POL   Braun, Jerzy; Skolimowski, Jerzy; Slazak, Janusz
Bronze   FRA   Brunet, Pierre; Brusa, Anselme; Giriat, Andre

1932 ★ Los Angeles (continued)

MEN'S FOUR WITHOUT COXSWAIN (M4-)
Gold   GBR   Badcock, John Charles; Beresford, Jack; Edwards, Hugh; George, Rowland David
Silver   GER   Aletter, Karl; Flinsch, Walter; Gaber, Ernst; Maier, Hans
Bronze   ITA   Cossu, Francesco; D, Giliante; Ghiardello, Antonio; Provenzani Garzoni, Antonio

MEN'S FOUR WITH COXSWAIN (M4+)
Gold   GER   Eller, Hans; Hoeck, Horst; Meyer, Walter; Neumann, Karl-Heinz; Spremberg, Joachim
Silver   GER   Divora, Riccardo; Parovel, Bruno; Plazzer, Giovanni; Scher, Giorgio; Vattovaz, Bruno
Bronze   POL   Braun, Jerzy; Kobylinski, Edward; Skolimowski, Jerzy; Slazak, Janusz; Urban, Stanislaw

MEN'S EIGHT (M8+)
Gold   USA   Blair, James Howard; Chandler, Charles; Dunlap, David Coombs; Graham, Norris James; Gregg, Duncan Smith; Hall, Winslow William; Jastram, Burton Albert; Salisbury, Edwin Lyle; Tower, Harold
Silver   ITA   Balleri, Mario; Barbieri, Renato; Barsotti, Dino; Bracci, Renato; Cioni, Vittorio; Del Bimbo, Guglielmo; Garzelli, Enrico; Milani, Cesare; Vestrini, Roberto
Bronze   CAN   Boal, Donald G.; Eastwood, Earl; Fry, Harry Britain; Harris, Joseph John; Liddell, Cedric Haswell; Mac Donald, George Leslie; Stanyar, Stanley; Taylor, Albert; Thoburn, William

1936 ★ Berlin

MEN'S SINGLE SCULLS (M1X)
Gold   GER   Schäfer, Gustav
Silver   AUT   Hasenöhrl, Josef
Bronze   USA   Barrow, Daniel Hubert Jr.

MEN'S DOUBLE SCULLS (M2X)
Gold   GBR   Beresford, Jack; Southwood, Leslie Frank
Silver   GER   Kaidel, Willi; Pirsch, Joachim
Bronze   POL   Ustupski, Jersy; Verey, Roger

MEN'S PAIR WITHOUT COXSWAIN (M2-)
Gold   GER   Eichhorn, Willi; Strauss, Hugo
Silver   DEN   Larsen, Harry Julius; Olsen, Peter Richard
Bronze   ARG   Curatella, Julio Pedro; Podesta, Horacio

MEN'S PAIR WITH COXSWAIN (M2+)
Gold   GER   Adamski, Herbert; Arend, Dietrich; Gustmann, Gerhard
Silver   ITA   Bergamo, Almiro; Negrini, Luciano; Santin, Guido
Bronze   FRA   Fourcade, Marceau; Tapie, Georges; Vandernotte, Noël

MEN'S FOUR WITHOUT COXSWAIN (M4-)
Gold   GER   Eckstein, Rudolf; Karl, Martin; Menne, Wilhelm; Rom, Anton
Silver   GBR   Barrett, Alan John; Bristow, Thomas Richard Mart.; Jackson, Peter Herbert; Sturrock, John Duncan
Bronze   SUI   Betschart, Hermann; Homberger, Alexander; Homberger, Hans; Schmid, Karl

1936 ★ Berlin (continued)

MEN'S FOUR WITH COXSWAIN (M4+)
Gold   GER Bauer, Fritz; Gaber, Ernst; Maier, Hans; Söllner, Paul; Volle, Walter
Silver   SUI Betschart, Hermann; Homberger, Alexander;
                Homberger, Hans; Schmid, Karl; Spring, Rolf
Bronze FRA Chauvigne, Marcel; Cosmat, Jean Marcel; Vandernotte, Fernand;
                Vandernotte, Marcel; Vandernotte, Noël

MEN'S EIGHT (M8+)
Gold   USA Adam, Gordon Belgum; Day, Charles Ward; Hume, Donald Bruce;
                Hunt, George Elwood Jr.; Mcmillin, James Burge; Moch, Robert Gaston;
                Morris, Herbert Roger; Rantz, Joseph Harry; White, John Galbraith
Silver   ITA Barsotti, Dino; Bartolini, Enzo; Checcacci, Mario; Del Bimbo, Guglielmo;
                Garzelli, Enrico; Grossi, Oreste; Milani, Cesare; Quaglierini, Ottorino;
                Secchi, Dante
Bronze GER Hannemann, Hans-Joachim; Kaufmann, Heinz; Kuschke, Hans;
                Loeckle, Werner; Mahlow, Wilhelm; Radach, Helmut; Rieck, Alfred;
                Schmidt, Herbert; Völs, Gerd

1948 ★ London

MEN'S SINGLE SCULLS (M1X)
Gold   AUS Wood, Merwyn Thomas
Silver   URU Risso, Eduardo G.
Bronze ITA Catasta, Romolo

MEN'S DOUBLE SCULLS (M2X)
Gold   GBR Burnell, Richard Desborough; Bushnell, Bertram Herbert Th.
Silver   DEN Larsen, Aage Ernst; Parsner, Ebbe Vestermann
Bronze URU Jones, William; Rodriguez, Juan A.

MEN'S PAIR WITHOUT COXSWAIN (M2-)
Gold   GBR Laurie, William; Wilson, John
Silver   SUI Kalt, Hans; Kalt, Josef
Bronze ITA Boni, Bruno; Fanetti, Felice

MEN'S PAIR WITH COXSWAIN (M2+)
Gold   DEN Andersen, Carl-Ebbe; Henriksen, Tage; Pedersen, Finn
Silver   ITA Radi, Alberto; Steffe, Giovanni; Tarlao, Aldo
Bronze HUN Szendey, Antal; Zimonyi, Robert; Zsitnik Sr., Bela

MEN'S FOUR WITHOUT COXSWAIN (M4-)
Gold   ITA Faggi, Francesco; Invernizzi, Giovanni; Moioli, Giuseppe; Morille, Elio
Silver   DEN Halkjaer, Helge; Hansen, Aksel Bonde; Larsen, Ib Storm;
                Schröder, Helge Muxoll
Bronze USA Gates, Gregory Crozier; Griffing, Stuart Lane;
                Kingsbury, Frederick John IV; Perew, Roben Strahan

MEN'S FOUR WITH COXSWAIN (M4+)
Gold   USA Westlund, Warren DeHaven; Giovanelli, Gordon Stephen;
                Martin, Robert Doud; Morgan, Allan Jerome; Will, Robert Ide
Silver   SUI Knecht, Emile A.; Moccand, Andre; Reichling, Rudolf;
                Schriever, Erich; Stebler, Pierre Armand
Bronze DEN Knudsen, Harry Madsen; Larsen, Erik Christian; Larsen, Henry Christian;
                Nielsen, Börge Daniel Raahauge; Olsen, Jörgen Ib

1948 ★ London (continued)

MEN'S EIGHT (M8+)
Gold	USA	Ahlgren, George Lewis; Brown, David Preston; Butler, Lloyd Lemarr; Hardy, James Herbert; Purchase, Ralph Kenneth; Smith, Justus Ketcham; Stack, John Charles; Turner, David Lindsay; Turner, Ian Gordon
Silver	GBR	Barton, Christopher Bertram; Bircher, Ernest Augustus Paul; Dearlove, Jack G.; Lapage, Michael Clement; Lloyd, Charles Brian Murray; Massey, Paul Mackintosh O.; Mellows, Alfred Paul; Meyrick, David John Charlton; Richardson, Guy Colquhoun
Bronze	NOR	Gran Olsen/Grangard, Halfdan; Hansen, Hans Egil; Kraakenes, Harald; Kraakenes, Thorstein; Lepsoë, Kristoffer; Monssen, Carl Henrik; Monssen, Sigurd; Naess, Leif; Pedersen, Thor

Helsinki ★ 1952

MEN'S SINGLE SCULLS (M1X)
Gold	URS	Tyukalov, Yuri
Silver	AUS	Wood, Merwyn Thomas
Bronze	POL	Kocerka, Teodor

MEN'S DOUBLE SCULLS (M2X)
Gold	ARG	Cappozzo, Tranquilo; Guerrero, Eduardo
Silver	URS	Emchuk, Igor; Zhilin, Georgi
Bronze	URU	Rodriguez, Juan A.; Seijas, Miguel

MEN'S PAIR WITHOUT COXSWAIN (M2-)
Gold	USA	Logg, Charles Paul Jr.; Price, Thomas Steele
Silver	BEL	Baetens, Robert Frederik; Knuysen, Michel Jules L.
Bronze	SUI	Kalt, Hans; Schmid, Kurt

MEN'S PAIR WITH COXSWAIN (M2+)
Gold	FRA	Malivoire, Bernard Robert; Mercier, Gaston Antoine; Salles, Raymond Julien
Silver	GER	Heinhold, Helmut; Manchen, Heinz Joachim; Noll, Helmut
Bronze	DEN	Frantzen, Jörgen Nagel; Petersen, Svend Ove; Svendsen, Poul Verner

MEN'S FOUR WITHOUT COXSWAIN (M4-)
Gold	YUG	Bonacic, Duje; Segvic, Petar; Trojanovic, Mate; Valenta, Velimir
Silver	FRA	Blondiaux, Pierre Auguste; Bouissou, Marc Emile; Gautier, Roger; Guissart, Jacques Jean
Bronze	FIN	Lommi, Oiva; Lommi, Veikko Kristian; Nevalainen, Lauri Armas; Wahlsten, Kauko Wilhelm

MEN'S FOUR WITH COXSWAIN (M4+)
Gold	CZE	Havlis, Jiri; Jindra, Jan; Koranda, Miroslav; Lusk, Stanislav; Mejta Sr., Karel
Silver	SUI	Bianchi, Enrico; Ess, Emile; Leiser, Walter; Scheller, Heinrich; Weidmann, Karl
Bronze	USA	Leanderson, Matthew Fillip; Lovested, Carl Martin; Rossi, Albert; Ulbrickson, Alvin Edmund; Wahlstrom, Richard Wayne

MEN'S EIGHT (M8+)
Gold	USA	Detweiler, Robert Milan; Dunbar, James Ralph; Fields, William Beauford; Frye, Wayne Thomas; Manning, Charles David; Murphy, Richard Frederick; Proctor, Henry Arthur; Shakespeare, Franklin Bradford; Stevens, Edward Glenister
Silver	URS	Amiragov, Slava; Borisov, Igor; Brago, Yevgeni; Gissen, Leonid; Komarov, Aleksei; Kryukov, Vladimir; Polyakov, Igor; Rodimushkin, Vladimir; Samsonov, Yevgeni
Bronze	AUS	Anderson, David Rollo; Cayzer, Phillip Arthur; Chapman, Ernest William; Chessell, Thomas Edmund; Finlay, Merwyn David; Greenwood, Nimrod; Pain, Edward Oscar; Tinning, Robert Noel; Williamson, Geoffrey

Melbourne/Stockholm ★ 1956

MEN'S SINGLE SCULLS (M1X)
Gold	AUS	Ivanov, Vyacheslav
Silver	AUS	Mackenzie, Stuart A.
Bronze	USA	Kelly, John Brenden Jr.

MEN'S DOUBLE SCULLS (M2X)
Gold	URS	Berkutov, Aleksandr; Tyukalov, Yuri
Silver	USA	Costello, Bernard Patrick Jr.; Gardiner, James Arthur
Bronze	AUS	Riley, Murray Stewart; Wood, Merwyn Thomas

MEN'S PAIR WITHOUT COXSWAIN (M2-)
Gold	USA	Fifer, James Thomas; Hecht, Duvall Young
Silver	URS	Buldakov, Igor; Ivanov, Viktor
Bronze	AUT	Kloimstein, Josef; Sageder, Alfred

MEN'S PAIR WITH COXSWAIN (M2+)
Gold	USA	Ayrault, Arthur Delancey Jr.; Findlay, Conrad Francis; Seiffert, Armin Kurt
Silver	EUR	Arndt, Horst; Borkowsky, Rainer; Von Groddeck, Karl-Heinrich
Bronze	URS	Emchuk, Igor; Petrov, Vladimir; Zhilin, Georgi

MEN'S FOUR WITHOUT COXSWAIN (M4-)
Gold	CAN	Mac Kinnon, Archibald A.; Loomer, Lorne Kenneth; D'Hondt, Ignace Walter; Arnold, Donald John
Silver	USA	Welchli, John Richard; McKinley, John Dickinson; McKinley, Arthur Frank; Mcintosh, James Stewart
Bronze	FRA	Delacour, Yves; Guillabert, Guy; Guissart, Rene Jacques; Mercier, Gaston Antoine

MEN'S FOUR WITH COXSWAIN (M4+)
Gold	ITA	Sgheiz, Romano; Stefanoni, Ivo; Trincavelli, Franco; Vanzin, Angelo; Winkler, Alberto
Silver	SWE	Aronsson, Ivar; Eriksson, Gösta; Göransson, Bertil; Gunnarsson, Evert; Larsson, Olle
Bronze	FIN	Hänninen, Kauko Antero; Lehtelä, Veli Veikko; Niemi, Matti Juhani; Pitkänen, Toimi Johannes; Poutanen, Reino Richard

MEN'S EIGHT (M8+)
Gold	USA	Charlton, Thomas Jackson Jr.; Becklean, William Russell; Beer, Donald Andrew E.; Cooke, John Patrick; Esselstyn, Caldwell Blackman; Grimes, Charles Livingston; Morey, Robert Willis Jr.; Wailes, Richard Donald; Wight, David Henry
Silver	CAN	Helliwell, David Leedom; Kueber, Philip Thomas; Mcclure, Richard Neil; Mcdonald, Douglas John; Mckerlich, William Arthur M.; Ogawa, Carlton Susumi; Pretty, Donald Wayne; West, Lawrence Kingsley; Wilson, Robert Andrew
Bronze	AUS	Aikman, Michael Hirst; Benfield, Angus Fred; Boykett, David Herbert; Doyle, Brian John; Hewitt, Harold Neil; Howden, James Guthrie; Howell, Walter Neville; Manton, Garth O.V.; Monger, Adrian Calero

1960 ★ Rome

MEN'S SINGLE SCULLS (M1X)
Gold	URS	Ivanov, Vyacheslav
Silver	EUA	Hill, Achim
Bronze	POL	Kocerka, Teodor

MEN'S DOUBLE SCULLS (M2X)
Gold	CZE	Kozak, Vaclav; Schmidt, Pavel
Silver	URS	Berkutov, Aleksandr; Tyukalov, Yuri
Bronze	SUI	Hürlimann, Ernst; Larcher, Rolf

MEN'S PAIR WITHOUT COXSWAIN (M2-)
Gold	URS	Boreiko, Valentin; Golovanov, Oleg
Silver	AUT	Kloimstein, Josef; Sageder, Alfred
Bronze	FIN	Lehtelä, Veli Veikko; Pitkänen, Toimi Johannes

MEN'S PAIR WITH COXSWAIN (M2+)
Gold	EUA	Knubel, Bernhard; Renneberg, Karl Heinz; Zerta, Klaus
Silver	URS	Bogdanavichus, Antanas; Yukna, Zigmas; Rudakov, Igor
Bronze	USA	Draeger, Richard Arthur; Findlay, Conrad Francis; Mitchell, Henry Kent II

MEN'S FOUR WITHOUT COXSWAIN (M4-)
Gold	USA	Ayrault, Arthur Delancey Jr.; Nash, Theodore Allison; Sayre, John Anthony; Wailes, Richard Donald
Silver	ITA	Baraglia, Tullio; Bosatta, Renato; Crosta, Giancarlo; Galante, Giuseppe
Bronze	URS	Akhremchik, Igor; Bachurov, Yuri; Morkovkin, Valentin; Tarabrin, Anatoli

MEN'S FOUR WITH COXSWAIN (M4+)
Gold	EUA	Cintl, Gerd; Effertz, Horst; Litz, Jürgen; Riemann, Klaus; Obst, Michael
Silver	FRA	Dumontois, Robert; Martin, Claude Auguste; Morel, Jacques; Nosbaum, Guy Fernand; Klein, Jean
Bronze	ITA	Balatti, Fulvio; Sgheiz, Romano; Trincavelli, Franco; Zucchi, Giovanni; Stefanoni, Ivo

MEN'S EIGHT (M8+)
Gold	EUA	Bittner, Klaus; Hopp, Karl Heinz; Lenk, Hans; Padge, Willi; Rulffs, Manfred; Schepke, Frank; Schepke, Kraft; Schröder, Walter; Von Groddeck, Karl-Heinrich
Silver	CAN	Arnold, Donald John; D'hondt, Ignace Walter; Kuhn, Nelson; Lecky, John; Loomer, Lorne Kenneth; Mckerlich, William Arthur M.; Mac Kinnon, Archibald A.; Merwyn, Glenn; Biln, Sohen
Bronze	CZE	Janousek, Bohumil; Jindra, Jan; Lundak, Jiri; Lusk, Stanislav; Pavkovic, Vaclav; Pojezny, Ludek; Sveda, Jan; Ventus, Josef; Konicek, Miroslav

1964 ★ Tokyo

MEN'S SINGLE SCULLS (M1X)
Gold	URS	Ivanov, Vyacheslav
Silver	EUA	Hill, Achim
Bronze	SUI	Kottmann, Gottfried

MEN'S DOUBLE SCULLS (M2X)
Gold	URS	Tyurin, Oleg; Dubrovsky, Boris
Silver	USA	Cromwell, Seymour Legrand Ii; Storm, James Eugene
Bronze	CZE	Andrs, Vladimir; Hofman, Pavel

1964 ★ Tokyo (continued)

MEN'S PAIR WITHOUT COXSWAIN (M2-)
Gold	CAN	Hungerford, George William; Jackson, Roger Charles
Silver	NED	Blaisse, Steven Joseph; Veenemans, Ernest Willem
Bronze	EUA	Schwan, Michael; Hottenrott, Wolfgang

MEN'S PAIR WITH COXSWAIN (M2+)
Gold	USA	Ferry, Edward Payson; Findlay, Conrad Francis; Mitchell, Henry Kent II
Silver	FRA	Morel, Georges; Morel, Jacques; Derouy, Jean-Claude
Bronze	NED	Bos, Jan Justus; Rouwe, Herman Jan; Hartsuiker, Frederik Klaas Jan

MEN'S FOUR WITHOUT COXSWAIN (M4-)
Gold	DEN	Hansen, John Orsted; Haslov, Björn Borgen; Petersen, Erik; Helmudt, Kurt
Silver	GBR	Russell, John Michael; Wardell-Yerburgh, Hugh Arthur; Barry, William Louis; James, John Jesse
Bronze	USA	Picard, Geoffrey William; Lyon, Richard Avery; Mittet, Theodore Peder; Nash, Theodore Allison

MEN'S FOUR WITH COXSWAIN (M4+)
Gold	EUA	Neusel, Peter; Britting, Bernhard; Werner, Joachim; Hirschfelder, Egbert; Oelke, Jürgen
Silver	ITA	Bosatta, Renato; Trivini, Emilio; Galante, Giuseppe; De Pedrina, Franco; Spinola, Giovanni
Bronze	NED	Mullink, Alex Gerhard; Van De Graaff, Jan; Van De Graaff, Frederik Robbert; Van De Graaf, Robert; Klumperbeek, Marius Pieter Louis

MEN'S EIGHT (M8+)
Gold	USA	Amlong, Joseph Brian; Amlong, Thomas Kennedy; Budd, Harold Boyce Jr.; Clark, Emory Wendell Ii; Cwiklinski, Stanley Francis; Foley, Hugh Miller; Knecht, William Joseph; Stowe, William Arthur; Zimonyi, Robert
Silver	URS	Aeffke, Klaus; Bittner, Klaus; Von Groddeck, Karl-Heinrich; Wallbrecht, Hans-Jürgen; Behrens, Klaus; Schroeder, Jürgen; Plagemann, Jürgen; Meyer, Horst; Ahrens, Thomas
Bronze	CZE	Cermak, Petr; Lundak, Jiri; Mrvik, Jan; Tocek, Julius; Ventus, Josef; Pojezny, Ludek; Janousek, Bohumil; Novy, Richard; Konicek, Miroslav

1968 ★ Mexico City

MEN'S SINGLE SCULLS (M1X)
Gold	NED	Wienese, Henri-Jan
Silver	FRG	Meissner, Jochen
Bronze	ARG	Demiddi, Alberto

MEN'S DOUBLE SCULLS (M2X)
Gold	URS	Sass, Anatoli; Timoshinin, Aleksandr
Silver	NED	Droog, Henricus Antonius; Van Dis, Leendert Frans
Bronze	USA	Maher, William Patrick; Nunn, John Hamann

MEN'S PAIR WITHOUT COXSWAIN (M2-)
Gold	GDR	Bothe, Heinz-Jürgen; Lucke, Jörg
Silver	USA	Hough, Lawrence Alan; Johnson, Philip Anthony
Bronze	DEN	Christiansen, Peter Fich; Larsen, Ib Ivan

1968 ★ Mexico City (continued)

MEN'S PAIR WITH COXSWAIN (M2+)
Gold   ITA   Baran, Primo; Cipolla, Bruno; Sambo, Renzo
Silver   NED   Rijnders, Roderick Falesca Rene; Suselbeek, Herman Johan; Van Nes, Hadriaan
Bronze DEN   Jorgensen, Harry; Krab, Jorn; Krab, Preben

MEN'S FOUR WITHOUT COXSWAIN (M4-)
Gold   GDR   Forberger, Frank; Grahn, Dieter; Rühle, Frank; Schubert, Dieter
Silver   HUN   Csermely, Jozsef; Melios, Zoltan; Melis, Antal; Sarlos, György
Bronze ITA   Bosatta, Renato; Baraglia, Tullio; Conti-Manzini, Pier Angelo; Albini, Abramo

MEN'S FOUR WITH COXSWAIN (M4+)
Gold   NZL   Cole, Warren Joseph; Collinge, Ross Hounsell; Dickie, Simon Charles; Joyce, Richard John; Storey, Dudley Leonard
Silver   GDR   Gelpke, Manfred; Göhler, Roland; Jakob, Klaus; Kremtz, Peter; Semetzky, Dieter
Bronze SUI   Bolliger, Peter; Fröhlich, Gottlieb; Grob, Jakob; Oswald, Denis; Waser, Hugo

MEN'S EIGHT (M8+)
Gold   FRG   Henning, Rüdiger; Hirschfelder, Egbert; Hottenrott, Wolfgang; Meyer, Horst; Ott, Nikolaus; Schreyer, Dirk; Siebert, Jörg; Tiersch, Günther; Ulbricht, Lutz
Silver   AUS   Dickson, Peter; Douglas, David; Duval, Alfred W.; Fazio, Joseph; Grover, Alan Geoffrey; Morgan, Michael Dennis; Pearce, Gary Malcolm; Ranch, John; Shirlaw, Robert Alan
Bronze URS   Bogdanavichus, Antanas; Briedis, Vitautas Julius; Kravchuk, Valentin; Lorentson, Yuri; Martishkin, Aleksandr; Sterlik, Vladimir; Suslin, Viktor; Yagelavichus, Yozanas; Yukna, Zigmas

1972 ★ Munich

MEN'S SINGLE SCULLS (M1X)
Gold   URS   Malishev, Yuri
Silver   ARG   Demiddi, Alberto
Bronze GDR   Güldenpfennig, Wolfgang

MEN'S DOUBLE SCULLS (M2X)
Gold   URS   Korshikov, Gennadi; Timoshinin, Aleksandr
Silver   NOR   Hansen, Frank; Thögersem, Svein Th.
Bronze GDR   Böhmer, Joachim; Schmied, Hans-Ulrich

MEN'S PAIR WITHOUT COXSWAIN (M2-)
Gold   GDR   Brietzke, Siegfried; Mager, Wolfgang
Silver   SUI   Bachmann, Alfred; Fischer, Heinrich
Bronze NED   Luynenburg, Roelof Johan; Stokvis, Rudolf (Ruud)

MEN'S PAIR WITH COXSWAIN (M2+)
Gold   GDR   Gunkel, Wolfgang; Lucke, Jörg; Neubert, Klaus-Dieter
Silver   CZE   Petricek, Vladimir; Svojanovsky, Oldrich; Svojanovsky, Pavel
Bronze ROM   Ceapura, Petre; Lovrenschi, Ladislau; Tudor, Stefan

MEN'S FOUR WITHOUT COXSWAIN (M4-)
Gold   GDR   Forberger, Frank; Grahn, Dieter; Rühle, Frank; Schubert, Dieter
Silver   NZL   Collinge, Ross Hounsell; Mills, Noel; Storey, Dudley Leonard; Tonks, Richard
Bronze FRG   Ehrig, Joachim Werner; Funnekötter, Peter; Held, Franz; Plottke, Wolfgang

1972 ★ Munich (continued)

MEN'S FOUR WITH COXSWAIN (M4+)
Gold   FRG   Auer, Gerhard; Benter, Uwe; Berger, Peter; Bierl, Alois; Färber, Hans-Johann
Silver   GDR   Gust, Reinhard; Jobst, Rolf; Ludwig, Klaus-Dieter; Martens, Eckhard; Zander, Dietrich
Bronze   CZE   Janos, Vladimir; Marecek, Otakar; Neffe, Karel; Petricek, Vladimir; Provaznik, Frantisek

MEN'S EIGHT (M8+)
Gold   NZL   Coker, Trevor; Dickie, Simon Charles; Earl, Athol; Hunter, John Andrew; Hurt, Anthony; Joyce, Richard John; Robertson, Gary; Veldman, Gerard Wybo; Wilson, Lindsay
Silver   USA   Clapp, Eugene Howard IV; Hobbs, Franklin Warren IV; Hobbs, William Barton Rogers; Hoffman, Paul; Livingston, John Cleve; Livingston, Michael Kent; Mickelson, Timothy Carl; Raymond, Peter Harlow; Terry, Lawrence Jr.
Bronze   GDR   Borzym, Hans-Joachim; Dimke, Harold; Landvoigt, Bernd; Landvoigt, Jörg; Mederow, Heinrich; Schmorde, Manfred; Schneider, Manfred; Schreiber, Hartmut; Schwarz, Dietmar

1976 ★ Montreal

MEN'S SINGLE SCULLS (M1X)
Gold   FIN   Karppinen, Pertti
Silver   FRG   Kolbe, Peter-Michael
Bronze   GDR   Dreifke, Joachim

WOMEN'S SINGLE SCULLS (W1X)
Gold   GDR   Scheiblich, Christine
Silver   USA   Lind, Joan Louise
Bronze   URS   Antonova, Elena

MEN'S DOUBLE SCULLS (M2X)
Gold   NOR   Hansen, Alf John; Hansen, Frank
Silver   GBR   Baillieu, Christopher; Hart, Michael John
Bronze   GDR   Bertow, Jürgen; Schmied, Hans-Ulrich

WOMEN'S DOUBLE SCULLS (W2X)
Gold   BUL   Otzetova, Svetla; Yordanova, Zdravka
Silver   GDR   Boesler, Petra; Jahn, Sabine
Bronze   URS   Kaminskaite, Leonora; Ramoshkene, Genovate

MEN'S PAIR WITHOUT COXSWAIN (M2-)
Gold   GDR   Landvoigt, Bernd; Landvoigt, Jörg
Silver   USA   Coffey, Calvin Thomas; Staines, Michael Laurence
Bronze   FIN   Strauss, Thomas; Vanroye, Peter

WOMEN'S PAIR WITHOUT COXSWAIN (W2-)
Gold   BUL   Gruitcheva-Kubatova, Stoyanka; Kelbetcheva-Barbulova, Siika
Silver   GDR   Dähne, Sabine; Noack, Angelika
Bronze   FRG   Eckbauer-Baumann, Edith; Einöder-Straube, Thea

1976 ★ Montreal (continued)

MEN'S PAIR WITH COXSWAIN (M2+)
Gold   GDR   Jährling, Harald; Spohr, Georg; Ulrich, Friedrich-Wilhelm
Silver   URS   Bekhterev, Dmitri; Lorentson, Yuri; Shurkalov, Yuri
Bronze   CZE   Svojanovsky, Oldrich; Svojanovsky, Pavel; Vebr, Ludvik

MEN'S QUADRUPLE SCULLS (M4X)
Gold   GDR   Bussert, Karl-Heinz; Güldenpfennig, Wolfgang; Reiche, Rüdiger; Wolfgramm, Michael
Silver   URS   Butkus, Vitautas; Duleev, Evgeni; Lazdenieks, Aivar; Yakimov, Yuri
Bronze   CZE   Hellebrand, Jaroslav; Lacina, Vladek; Pecka, Zdenek; Vochoska, Vaclav

WOMEN'S QUADRUPLE SCULLS (W4X)
Gold   GDR   Borchmann, Anke; Lau, Jutta; Poley, Viola; Weigelt-Buhr, Liane; Zobelt, Roswietha
Silver   URS   Aleksandrova-Popova, Larisa; Bryunina, Mira; Chernyshova, Nadezhda; Ermolaeva, Galina; Kondrashina, Anna
Bronze   ROM   Afrasiloaia, Felicia; Giurca, Elena; Lazar, Elisabeta; Micsa-Macoviciuc, Maria; Tudoran, Ioana

MEN'S FOUR WITHOUT COXSWAIN (M4-)
Gold   GDR   Brietzke, Siegfried; Decker, Andreas; Mager, Wolfgang; Semmler, Stefan
Silver   NOR   Andreassen, Rolf; Bergodd, Arne; Nafstad, Ole Sverre; Tveter, Finn Ivar
Bronze   URS   Arnemann, Raul; Dolinin, Valeri; Gasan-Dzhalalov, Anushavan; Kuznetsov, Nikolai

MEN'S FOUR WITH COXSWAIN (M4+)
Gold   URS   Eshinov, Vladimir; Ivanov, Nikolai; Klepikov, Aleksandr; Kuznetsov, Mikhail; Lukyanov, Aleksandr
Silver   GDR   Diessner, Ullrich; Diessner, Walter; Kunze, Rüdiger; Schulz, Andreas; Thomas, Johannes
Bronze   FRG   Färber, Hans-Johann; Fricke, Siegfried; Kubail, Ralph; Niehusen, Peter; Wenzel, Hartmut

WOMEN'S FOUR WITH COXSWAIN (W4+)
Gold   GDR   Hess, Sabine; Kurth, Andrea; Lohs-Kuhn, Gabriele; Metze, Karin; Schwede, Bianka
Silver   BUL   Georgieva, Kapka; Gurova, Ginka; Modeva, Mariika; Vasseva, Liliana; Yordanova, Reni
Bronze   URS   Krokhina, Lyudmila; Krylova, Lidiya; Mishenina, Galina; Pasokha, Anna; Sevostyanova, Nadezhda

MEN'S EIGHT (M8+)
Gold   GDR   Baumgart, Bernd; Danielowski, Karl-Heinz; Döhn, Gottfried; Karnatz, Ulrich; Klatt, Werner; Kostulski, Roland; Lück, Hans-Joachim; Prudöhl, Karl-Heinz; Wendisch, Dieter
Silver   GBR   Clark, Richard James Scott; Crooks, Timothy John; Lester, Richard C.; Matheson, Hugh Patrick; Maxwell, David Lindsay; Robertson, Leonard David; Smallbone, Frederick John; Sweeney, Patrick John; Yallop, John C.
Bronze   NZL   Coker, Trevor; Dickie, Simon Charles; Digman, Peter; Earl, Athol; Hurt, Anthony; Mclean, Alexander; Rodger, David; Sutherland, Ivan; Wilson, Lindsay

WOMEN'S EIGHT (W8+)
Gold   GDR   Ahrenholz, Brigitte; Ebert, Henrietta; Goretzki, Viola; Kallies, Monika; Knetsch-Köpke, Christiane; Lehmann, Helma; Müller, Irina; Richter, Ilona; Wilke, Marina
Silver   URS   Guzenko, Olga; Kolkova, Olga; Kozenkova, Klavdiya; Pugovskaya, Olga; Roshchina, Nadezhda; Rozgon, Nadezhda; Talalaeva, Lyubov; Tarakanova, Nelli; Zubko, Elena
Bronze   USA   Brown, Carol Page; Defrantz, Anita Luceete; Graves, Carolyn Brand; Greig, Marion; Mccarthy, Margaret Ann; Ricketson, Gail Susan; Silliman, Lynn; Warner, Anne Elizabeth; Zoch, Jacqueline Jean

1980 ★ Moscow

MEN'S SINGLE SCULLS (M1X)
Gold   FIN   Karppinen, Pertti
Silver URS   Yakusha, Vasili
Bronze GDR   Kersten, Peter

WOMEN'S SINGLE SCULLS (W1X)
Gold   ROM   Toma, Sanda
Silver URS   Makhina, Antonina
Bronze GDR   Schröter, Martina

MEN'S DOUBLE SCULLS (M2X)
Gold   GDR   Dreifke, Joachim; Kröppelien, Klaus
Silver YUG   Pancic, Zoran; Stanulov, Milorad
Bronze CZE   Pecka, Zdenek; Vochoska, Vaclav

WOMEN'S DOUBLE SCULLS (W2X)
Gold   URS   Aleksandrova-Popova, Larisa; Khloptseva, Elena
Silver GDR   Linse, Cornelia; Westphal, Heidi
Bronze ROM   Homeghi-Bularda, Olga; Rosca-Rasila, Valeria

MEN'S PAIR WITHOUT COXSWAIN (M2-)
Gold   GDR   Landvoigt, Bernd; Landvoigt, Jörg
Silver URS   Pimenov, Yuri; Pimenov, Nikolai
Bronze GBR   Carmichael, Malcolm; Wiggin, Charles

WOMEN'S PAIR WITHOUT COXSWAIN (W2-)
Gold   GDR   Klier, Cornelia; Steindorf, Ute
Silver POL   Dluzewska, Malgorzata; Koscianska, Czeslawa
Bronze BUL   Gruitcheva-Kubatova, Stoyanka; Kelbetcheva-Barbulova, Siika

MEN'S PAIR WITH COXSWAIN (M2+)
Gold   GDR   Jährling, Harald; Spohr, Georg; Ulrich, Friedrich-Wilhelm
Silver URS   Kriuchkin, Gennadi; Lukyanov, Aleksandr; Pereverzev, Viktor
Bronze YUG   Celent, Zlatko; Mrduljas, Dusko; Reic, Josip

MEN'S QUADRUPLE SCULLS (M4X)
Gold   GDR   Bunk, Karsten; Dundr, Frank; Heppner, Uwe; Winter, Martin
Silver URS   Barbakov, Evgeni; Dovgan, Nikolai; Kleshnev, Valeri; Shapochka, Yuri
Bronze BUL   Dobrev, Bogdan; Nikolov, Mintcho; Petrov, Liubomir; Rusev, Ivo

WOMEN'S QUADRUPLE SCULLS (W4X)
Gold   GDR   Lau, Jutta; Ploch, Jutta; Reinhard, Sybille; Weigelt-Buhr, Liane; Zobelt, Roswietha
Silver URS   Cheremisina, Nina; Liubimova, Nadezhda; Matievskaia, Elena; Pustovit, Antonina; Vasilchenko, Olga
Bronze BUL   Bakova, Anka; Boncheva, Rumeliana; Georgieva, Stanka; Nakova, Dolores; Serbezova, Mariana

MEN'S FOUR WITHOUT COXSWAIN (M4-)
Gold   GDR   Thiele, Jürgen; Decker, Andreas; Semmler, Stefan; Brietzke, Siegfried
Silver URS   Dolinin, Valeri; Eliseev, Vitali; Kamkin, Aleksei; Kulagin, Aleksandr
Bronze GBR   Beattie, John; Cross, Martin; Mcnuff, Ian; Townsend, David

MEN'S FOUR WITH COXSWAIN (M4+)
Gold   GDR   Diessner, Ullrich; Diessner, Walter; Döhn, Gottfried; Gregor, Andreas; Wendisch, Dieter
Silver URS   Berzinsh, Yuris; Garonskis, Artur; Krishianis, Dimant; Krishianis, Dzintars; Tikmers, Zhorzh
Bronze POL   Kubiak, Ryszard; Nowak, Grzegorz; Stadniuk, Ryszard; Stellak, Grzegorz; Tomasiak, Adam

1980 ★ Moscow (continued)

WOMEN'S FOUR WITH COXSWAIN (W4+)

Gold   GDR   Fröhlich, Silvia; Kapheim, Ramona; Noack, Angelika; Saalfeld, Romy; Wenzel, Kirsten

Silver   BUL   Filipova, Nadezhda; Gurova, Ginka; Modeva, Mariika; Todorova, Rita; Velinova, Iskra

Bronze   URS   Cheremisina, Nina; Fadeeva, Maria; Semenova, Svetlana; Sovetnikova, Galina; Studneva, Marina

MEN'S EIGHT (M8+)

Gold   GDR   Doberschütz, Jens; Dühring, Uwe; Friedrich, Jörg; Höing, Bernd; Karnatz, Ulrich; Kons, Ulrich; Koppe, Hans-Peter; Krauss, Bernd; Ludwig, Klaus-Dieter

Silver   GBR   Clay, Henry; Justice, Andrew; Mahoney, Chris; McDougall, Duncan; McGowan, Malkolm; Moynihan, Colin; Pritchard, John; Stanhope, Richard; Whitwell, Allan

Bronze   URS   Dmitrienko, Grigori; Kokoshin, Viktor; Lugin, Andrei; Maistrenko, Igor; Mantsevich, Aleksandr; Normantas, Ionas; Pintskus, Ionas; Tishchenko, Andrei; Tkachenko, Aleksandr

WOMEN'S EIGHT (W8+)

Gold   GDR   Boesler, Martina; Knetsch-Köpke, Christiane; Lohs-Kuhn, Gabriele; Metze, Karin; Neisser, Kersten; Richter, Ilona; Sandig, Marita; Schütz, Birgit; Wilke, Marina

Silver   URS   Frolova, Nina; Paziun, Maria; Pivovarova, Olga; Preobrazhenskaia, Nina; Prishchepa, Nadezhda; Stetsenko, Tatiana; Tereshina, Elena; Umanets, Nina; Zhulina, Valentina

Bronze   ROM   Aposteanu, Angelica; Bondar, Elena; Bucur, Florica; Constantinescu, Maria; Dobritoiu, Elena; Frintu, Rodica; Iliuta, Ana; Puscatu-Arba, Rodica; Zagoni, Marlena

1984 ★ Los Angeles

MEN'S SINGLE SCULLS (M1X)

Gold   FIN   Karppinen, Pertti
Silver   FRG   Kolbe, Peter-Michael
Bronze   CAN   Mills, Robert

WOMEN'S SINGLE SCULLS (W1X)

Gold   ROM   Rosca-Rasila, Valeria
Silver   USA   Geer, Charlotte Mosher
Bronze   BEL   Haesebrouck, Ann

MEN'S DOUBLE SCULLS (M2X)

Gold   USA   Enquist, Paul N.; Lewis, Bradley Alan
Silver   BEL   Crois, Dirk; Deloof, Pierre Marie
Bronze   YUG   Pancic, Zoran; Stanulov, Milorad

WOMEN'S DOUBLE SCULLS (W2X)

Gold   ROM   Lipa, Elisabeta; Popescu, Marioara
Silver   NED   Hellemans, Greet; Hellemans, Nicolette
Bronze   CAN   Laumann, Daniele; Laumann, Silken Suzette

1984 ★ Los Angeles (continued)

MEN'S PAIR WITHOUT COXSWAIN (M2-)
Gold   ROM   Iosub, Petru; Toma, Valer
Silver   ESP   Climent Huerta, Fernando; Lasurtegui Berridi, Luis Maria
Bronze   NOR   Grepperud, Hans Magnus; Loken, Sverre Bertrand

WOMEN'S PAIR WITHOUT COXSWAIN (W2-)
Gold   ROM   Oprea-Horvat, Elena; Puscatu-Arba, Rodica
Silver   CAN   Craig, Elizabeth; Smith, Patricia
Bronze   FRG   Becker, Ellen; Volkner, Iris

MEN'S PAIR WITH COXSWAIN (M2+)
Gold   ITA   Abbagnale, Carmine; Abbagnale, Giuseppe; Di Capua, Giuseppe
Silver   ROM   Popescu, Dimitru; Raducanu, Dumitru; Tomoiaga, Vasile
Bronze   USA   Espeseth, Robert Douglas, Jr.; Herland, Douglas John; Still, Kevin Raymond

MEN'S QUADRUPLE SCULLS (M4X)
Gold   FRG   Dursch, Michael; Hedderich, Albert; Hormann, Raimund; Wiedenmann, Dieter
Silver   AUS   Gullock, Gary; Lovrich, Anthony; Mclaren, Timothy; Reedy, Paul
Bronze   CAN   Ford, Bruce; Hamilton, Douglas; Hughes, Michael; Monckton, Philip

WOMEN'S QUADRUPLE SCULLS (W4X)
Gold   ROM   Badea, Ioana; Corban, Sofia; Oancia, Ecaterina;
            Sorohan-Minea, Anisoara; Taran, Titie
Silver   USA   Gilder, Virginia Marie; Lind, Joan Louise; Marden, Anne R.; Rickon, Kelly Anne;
            Rohde, Lisa Diane
Bronze   DEN   Eriksen, Hanne Mandsfeldt; Hanel, Birgitte; Koefoed, Inger Charlotte;
            Rasmussen, Bodil Steen; Sorensen, Jette Hejli

MEN'S FOUR WITHOUT COXSWAIN (M4-)
Gold   NZL   O'Connell, Leslie; O'Brian, Shane; Robertson, Conrad; Trask, Keith
Silver   USA   Clark, David Robert; Forney, Alan Michael; Smith, Jonathan S.; Stekl, Philip William
Bronze   DEN   Christiansen, Erik; Jessen, Michael; Nielsen, Lars; Rasmussen, Per

MEN'S FOUR WITH COXSWAIN (M4+)
Gold   GBR   Budgett, Richard Gordon M.; Cross, Martin; Ellison, Adrian Charles;
            Holmes, Andrew John; Redgrave, Steven
Silver   USA   Bach, Michael; Ives, Edward Ashley; Kiefer, Thomas Nisbit;
            Springer, Gregory T.; Stillings, John Stuart
Bronze   NZL   Hollister, Brett; Lawton, Kevin; Mabbott, Barrie; Symon, Donald; Tong, Ross

WOMEN'S FOUR WITH COXSWAIN (W4+)
Gold   ROM   Apostol, Chira; Homeghi-Bularda, Olga; Ioja, Viorica;
            Lavric, Florica; Tanasa-Fricioiu, Maria
Silver   CAN   Armbrust, Barbara; Brain, Marilyn; Schneider, Angela;
            Thompson, Lesley Allison; Tregunno, Jane
Bronze   ROM   Brancourt-Pollock, Karen; Chapman-Popa, Susan; Foster, Margot;
            Grey-Gardner, Robyn; Lee, Susan

MEN'S EIGHT (M8+)
Gold   CAN   Crawford, Dean; Evans, Marc; Evans, Michael; Horm, Blair; Main, Gerald Grant;
            Mcmahon, Robert Brian; Neufeld, Kevin; Steele, Paul; Turner, Patrick
Silver   USA   Borchert, Earl Frederick; Clapp, Charles Elmer Iii.; Darling, Thomas Ward;
            Ibbetson, Bruce Bernard; Jaugstetter, Robert C.; Lubsen, Walter Harry Jr.;
            Penny, Christopher Gore; Sudduth, Andrew Hancock; Terwilliger, John Richard
Bronze   AUS   Battersby, James; Edmunds, Ian; Evans, Stephen; Hefer, Clyde; Muller, Craig;
            Patten, Samuel; Popa, Ion; Thredgold, Gavin; Willoughby, Timothy

1984 ★ Los Angeles (continued)

WOMEN'S EIGHT (W8+)

Gold	USA	Beard, Elizabeth Ann; Bower, Caroll Ann; Flanagan, Jeanne Ann; Graves, Carolyn Brand; Keeler, Kathryn Elliott; Metcalf, Harriet Morris; Norelius, Kristine Lee; O'Steen, Shyril; Thorssness, Kristen Joy
Silver	ROM	Armasescu, Mihaela; Balan-Snep, Doina Lilian; Chelariu-Bazon, Adriana; Diaconescu, Camelia; Ioja, Viorica; Mihaly, Aneta; Plesca, Aurora; Sauca, Lucia; Trasca, Marioara
Bronze	NED	Cornet, Lynda; Hellemans, Greet; Hellemans, Nicolette; Laurijsen, Martha; Neelissen, Catalien; Quist, Anne-Marie; Vaandrager, Willemientje; Van Drogenbroek, Marieke; Van Ettekoven, Harriet

Seoul ★ 1988

MEN'S SINGLE SCULLS (M1X)

Gold	GDR	Lange, Thomas
Silver	FRG	Kolbe, Peter-Michael
Bronze	NZL	Verdonk, Eric Franciscus

WOMEN'S SINGLE SCULLS (W1X)

Gold	GDR	Behrendt, Jutta
Silver	USA	Marden, Anne R.
Bronze	BUL	Georgieva, Magdalena

MEN'S DOUBLE SCULLS (M2X)

Gold	NED	Florijn, Ronald; Rienks, Nico
Silver	SUI	Bodenmann, Ueli; Schwerzmann, Beat
Bronze	URS	Marchenko, Aleksandr; Yakusha, Vasili

WOMEN'S DOUBLE SCULLS (W2X)

Gold	GDR	Schröter, Martina; Peter, Birgit
Silver	ROM	Cochelea, Veronica; Lipa, Elisabeta
Bronze	BUL	Madina, Stefka; Ninova, Violeta

MEN'S PAIR WITHOUT COXSWAIN (M2-)

Gold	GBR	Holmes, Andrew John; Redgrave, Steven
Silver	ROM	Dobre, Danut; Neagu, Dragos
Bronze	YUG	Mujkic, Sadik; Preseren, Bojan

WOMEN'S PAIR WITHOUT COXSWAIN (W2-)

Gold	ROM	Homeghi-Bularda, Olga; Puscatu-Arba, Rodica
Silver	BUL	Berberova, Lalka Stoyanova; Stoyanova, Radka
Bronze	NZL	Hannen, Lynley; Payne, Nicola

MEN'S PAIR WITH COXSWAIN (M2+)

Gold	ITA	Abbagnale, Carmine; Abbagnale, Giuseppe; Di Capua, Giuseppe
Silver	GDR	Kirchhoff, Detlef; Rensch, Rene; Streit, Mario
Bronze	GBR	Holmes, Andrew John; Redgrave, Steven; Sweeney, Patrick John

MEN'S QUADRUPLE SCULLS (M4X)

Gold	ITA	Abbagnale, Agostino; Farina, Gianluca; Poli, Piero; Tizzano, Davide
Silver	NOR	Bjönness, Lars; Hansen, Alf John; Thorsen, Rolf Bernt; Vinje, Vetle
Bronze	GDR	Bogs, Steffen; Habermann, Heiko; Koppen, Jens; Zühlke, Steffen

Seoul ★ 1988 (continued)

WOMEN'S QUADRUPLE SCULLS (W4X)

Gold	GDR	Förster, Kerstin; Mundt, Kristina; Schramm, Beate; Sorgers, Jana
Silver	URS	Dumcheva, Antonina; Frolova, Inna; Kalimbet, Irina; Maziy, Svetlana
Bronze	ROM	Cochelea, Veronica; Dobre, Anisoara; Lipa, Elisabeta; Sorohan-Minea, Anisoara

MEN'S FOUR WITHOUT COXSWAIN (M4-)

Gold	GDR	Brudel, Ralf; Förster, Olaf; Greiner, Thomas; Schröder, Roland
Silver	USA	Bohrer, Thomas Robert; Kennelly, Richard; Krmpotich, David Mattthew; Rodriguez, Raoul Pedro, Jr.
Bronze	FRG	Grabow, Guido; Grabow, Volker; Kesslau, Norbert; Puttlitz, Jörg

MEN'S FOUR WITH COXSWAIN (M4+)

Gold	GDR	Eichwurzel, Bernd; Klawonn, Frank; Niesecke, Bernd; Reiher, Hendrik; Schmeling, Karsten
Silver	ROM	Lovrenschi, Ladislau; Popescu, Dimitru; Robu, Valentin; Snep, Ioan Gabor; Tomoiaga, Vasile
Bronze	NZL	Bird, Andrew; Johnston, Gregory; Keys, George; White, Christopher S.; Wright, Ian Andrew

WOMEN'S FOUR WITH COXSWAIN (W4+)

Gold	GDR	Walther, Martina; Doberschütz, Gerlinde; Hornig, Carola; Siech, Birte; Rose, Sylvia
Silver	CHN	Zhang, Xiang-Hua; Hu, Ya-Dong; Yang, Xiao; Zhou, Shouying; Li, Rong-Hua
Bronze	ROM	Trasca, Marioara; Necula, Veronica; Anitas, Herta; Balan-Snep, Doina Lilian; Oancia, Ecaterina

MEN'S EIGHT (M8+)

Gold	FRG	Domain, Thomas; Eichholz, Armin; Klein, Manfred Willi; Männig, Wolfgang; Mellinghaus, Matthias; Möllenkamp, Thomas; Rabe, Bahne; Schultz, Eckhardt; Wessling, Ansgar
Silver	URS	But, Veniamin; Komarov, Nikolai; Tikhanov, Vasili; Dumchev, Aleksandr; Gurkovsky, Pavel; Diduk, Viktor; Omelyanovich, Viktor; Vasiliev, Andrei; Lukyanov, Aleksandr
Bronze	USA	Bauer, Seth David; Burden, William Douglas; Mclaughlin, Jeffrey Dean; Nordell, Peter W.; Patton, Edward Bickford; Pescatore, John A.; Rusher, John Dunbar, Iv; Smith, Jonathan S.; Teti, Michael Francis

WOMEN'S EIGHT (W8+)

Gold	GDR	Balthasar, Ramona; Haacker, Kathrin; Kluge, Anja; Neunast, Daniela; Schrör, Beatrix; Stange, Uta; Strauch, Annegret; Wild-Wagner, Ute; Zeidler, Judith
Silver	ROM	Anitas, Herta; Armasescu, Mihaela; Balan-Snep, Doina Lilian; Chelariu-Bazon, Adriana; Homeghi-Bularda, Olga; Necula, Veronica; Oancia, Ecaterina; Puscatu-Arba, Rodica; Trasca, Marioara
Bronze	CHN	Han, Ya-Qin; He, Yanwen; Hu, Ya-Dong; Li, Rong-Hua; Yang, Xiao; Zhang, Xiang-Hua; Zhang, Ya-Li; Zhou, Shouying; Zhou, Xiu-Hua

Barcelona ★ 1992

MEN'S SINGLE SCULLS (M1X)
Gold	GER	Lange, Thomas
Silver	CZE	Chalupa, Vaclav
Bronze	POL	Broniewski, Kajetan

WOMEN'S SINGLE SCULLS (W1X)
Gold	ROM	Lipa, Elisabeta
Silver	BEL	Bredael, Annelies
Bronze	CAN	Laumann, Silken Suzette

MEN'S DOUBLE SCULLS (M2X)
Gold	AUS	Antonie, Peter; Hawkins, Stephen Mark
Silver	AUT	Jonke, Arnold; Zerbst, Christoph
Bronze	NED	Rienks, Nico; Zwolle, Hendrik Jan

WOMEN'S DOUBLE SCULLS (W2X)
Gold	GER	Boron, Kathrin; Köppen, Kerstin
Silver	ROM	Cochelea, Veronica; Lipa, Elisabeta
Bronze	CHN	Gu, Xiaoli; Lu, Huali

MEN'S PAIR WITHOUT COXSWAIN (M2-)
Gold	GBR	Pinsent, Matthew Clive; Redgrave, Steven
Silver	GER	Ettingshausen, Colin; Höltzenbein, Peter
Bronze	SLO	Cop, Iztok; Zvegelj, Denis

WOMEN'S PAIR WITHOUT COXSWAIN (W2-)
Gold	CAN	Heddle, Kathleen; McBean, Marnie Elizabeth
Silver	GER	Schwerzmann, Ingeburg; Werremeier, Stefani
Bronze	USA	Maxwell Pierson, Stephanie; Seaton, Anna B.

MEN'S PAIR WITH COXSWAIN (M2+)
Gold	GBR	Herbert, Garry Gerard Paul; Searle, Gregory Mark Pascol; Searle, Jonathan William
Silver	ITA	Abbagnale, Carmine; Abbagnale, Giuseppe; Di Capua, Giuseppe
Bronze	ROM	Popescu, Dimitrie; Raducanu, Dumitru; Taga, Nicolaie

MEN'S QUADRUPLE SCULLS (M4X)
Gold	GER	Hajek, Andreas; Steinbach, Michael; Volkert, Stephan; Willms, Andre
Silver	NOR	Bjönness, Lars; Sätersdal, Per Albert; Thorsen, Rolf Bernt; Undset, Kjetil
Bronze	ITA	Corona, Alessandro; Farina, Gianluca; Galtarossa, Rossano; Soffici, Filippo

WOMEN'S QUADRUPLE SCULLS (W4X)
Gold	GER	Müller, Kerstin; Mundt, Kristina; Peter, Birgit; Schmidt, Sybille
Silver	ROM	Burcica, Constanta; Cochelea, Veronica; Dobre, Anisoara; Ignat, Doina
Bronze	EUR	Khloptseva, Elena; Khodotovich, Ekaterina; Ustyuzhanina, Tatiana; Zelikovitch, Antonina

MEN'S FOUR WITHOUT COXSWAIN (M4-)
Gold	AUS	Cooper, Andrew; Green, Nicholas; McKay, Michael Scott; Tomkins, James
Silver	USA	Bohrer, Thomas Robert; Burden, William Douglas; Manning, Patrick Francis Jr.; McLaughlin, Jeffrey Dean
Bronze	SLO	Jansa, Milan; Klemencic, Janez; Mirjanic, Saso; Mujkic, Sadik

WOMEN'S FOUR WITHOUT COXSWAIN (M4-)
Gold	CAN	Barnes, Jennifer Kirsten; Monroe, Jessica; Taylor, Brenda Susan; Worthington, Kay Frances
Silver	USA	Donohoe, Shelagh; Eckert, Cynthia L.; Feeney, Carol; Fuller, Amy
Silver	GER	Frank, Antje; Hohn, Annette; Mehl, Gabriele; Siech, Birte

Barcelona ★ 1992 (continued)

MEN'S FOUR WITH COXSWAIN (M4+)

Gold	ROM	Popescu, Dimitrie; Raducanu, Dumitru; Ruican, Iulica; Taga, Nicolaie; Talapan, Viorel
Silver	GER	Brudel, Ralf; Finger, Karsten; Kellner, Uwe Jörg; Peters, Thoralf; Reiher, Hendrik
Bronze	POL	Cieslak, Michal; Jankowski, Wojciech; Lasicki, Maciej; Streich, Jacek; Tomiak, Tomasz

MEN'S EIGHT (M8+)

Gold	CAN	Barber, Darren; Crosby, Andrew; Forgeron, Michael Joseph; Marland, Robert Davies; Paul, Terence Michael; Porter, Derek; Rascher, Michael G.; Robertson, Bruce; Wallace, John William
Silver	ROM	Dobre, Danut; Gheorghe, Marin; Marin, Claudiu Gabriel; Mastacan, Vasile Ionel; Nastase, Vasile Dorel; Robu, Valentin; Ruican, Iulica; Talapan, Viorel; Vizitiu, Ioan Iulian
Bronze	GER	Baar, Roland; Eichholz, Armin; Kirchhoff, Detlef; Klein, Manfred Willi; Rabe, Bahne; Richter, Frank Joerg; Sennewald, Hans; Streppelhoff, Thorsten; Wessling, Ansgar

WOMEN'S EIGHT (W8+)

Gold	CAN	Barnes, Jennifer Kirsten; Crawford, Shannon; Delehanty, Megan Catherine; Heddle, Kathleen; Mcbean, Marnie Elizabeth; Monroe, Jessica; Taylor, Brenda Susan; Thompson, Lesley Allison; Worthington, Kay Frances
Silver	ROM	Bazon, Adriana; Bulie, Iulia; Georgescu, Elena; Lepadatu, Victoria; Neculai, Viorica; Olteanu, Ioana; Padurariu, Maria; Robu, Doina; Snep, Doina Liliana
Bronze	GER	Dördelmann, Sylvia; Haacker, Kathrin; Harzendorf, Christiane; Neunast, Daniela; Petersmann, Cerstin; Pyritz, Dana; Strauch, Annegret; Schell, Ute; Zeidler, Judith

1996 ★ Atlanta

MEN'S SINGLE SCULLS (M1X)

Gold	SUI	Mueller, Xeno
Silver	CAN	Porter, Derek
Bronze	GER	Lange, Thomas

WOMEN'S SINGLE SCULLS (W1X)

Gold	BLR	Khodotovich, Ekaterina
Silver	CAN	Laumann, Silken Suzette
Bronze	DEN	Hansen, Trine

LIGHTWEIGHT MEN'S DOUBLE SCULLS (LM2X)

Gold	SUI	Gier, Michael; Gier, Markus
Silver	NED	Aardewijn, Pepijn; Van Der Linden, Maarten
Bronze	AUS	Edwards, Anthony; Hick, Bruce

LIGHTWEIGHT WOMEN'S DOUBLE SCULLS (LW2X)

Gold	ROM	Burcica, Constanta; Macoviciuc, Camelia
Silver	USA	Bell, Teresa Z.; Burns, Lindsay
Bronze	AUS	Joyce, Rebecca; Lee, Virginia

MEN'S DOUBLE SCULLS (M2X)

Gold	ITA	Abbagnale, Agostino; Tizzano, Davide
Silver	NOR	Stoerseth, Steffen; Undset, Kjetil
Bronze	FRA	Barathay, Samuel; Kowal, Frederic

1996 ★ Atlanta (continued)

WOMEN'S DOUBLE SCULLS (W2X)
Gold	CAN	Heddle, Kathleen; McBean, Marnie Elizabeth
Silver	CHN	Cao, Mianying; Zhang, Xiuyun
Bronze	NED	Eijs, Irene; Van Nes, Eeke

MEN'S PAIR WITHOUT COXSWAIN (M2-)
Gold	GBR	Pinsent, Matthew Clive; Redgrave, Steven
Silver	AUS	Scott, Robert Geoffrey; Weightman, David
Bronze	FRA	Andrieux, Michel; Rolland, Jean Christophe

WOMEN'S PAIR WITHOUT COXSWAIN (W2-)
Gold	AUS	Slatter, Kate Elizabeth; Still, Megan Leanne
Silver	USA	Kraft, Karen; Schwen, Missy
Bronze	FRA	Cortin, Helene; Gosse, Christine

MEN'S QUADRUPLE SCULLS (M4x)
Gold	GER	Hajek, Andreas; Steiner, Andre; Volkert, Stephan; Willms, Andre
Silver	USA	Gailes, Jason; Jamieson, Brian; Mueller, Eric; Young, Tim
Bronze	AUS	Free, Duncan; Hanson, Boden Joseph; Hooker, Janusz; Snook, Ronald

WOMEN'S QUADRUPLE SCULLS (W4X)
Gold	GER	Boron, Kathrin; Köppen, Kerstin; Rutschow, Katrin; Sorgers, Jana
Silver	UKR	Frolova, Inna; Maziy, Svetlana; Miftakhutdinova, Diana; Ronzhina, Olena
Bronze	CAN	Biesenthal, Laryssa; Heddle, Kathleen; Mcbean, Marnie; O'Grady, Diane

LIGHTWEIGHT MEN'S FOUR WITHOUT COXSWAIN (LM4-)
Gold	DEN	Ebbesen, Eskild; Feddersen, Victor; Henriksen, Niels; Poulsen, Thomas
Silver	CAN	Boyes, Dave; Hassett, Gavin; Lay, Jeffrey; Peaker, Brian
Bronze	USA	Carlucci, William; Collins, David; Pfaendtner, Jeff; Schneider, Marc

MEN'S FOUR WITHOUT COXSWAIN (M4-)
Gold	AUS	Ginn, Drew; Green, Nicholas; McKay, Michael Scott; Tomkins, James
Silver	FRA	Bosquet, Gilles; Fauche, Daniel; Moncelet, Olivier; Vecten, Bertrand
Bronze	GBR	Foster, Tim James; Obholzer, Rupert John; Searle, Gregory Mark Pascol; Searle, Jonathan William

MEN'S EIGHT (M8+)
Gold	NED	Bartman, Michiel; Duyster, Jeroen; Florijn, Ronald; Maasdijk, Koos; Rienks, Nico; Simon, Diederik; Van Der Zwan, Niels; Van Steenis, Niels; Zwolle, Hendrik Jan
Silver	GER	Baar, Roland; Huhn, Wolfram; Kirchhoff, Detlef; Kleinschmidt, Mark; Richter, Frank; Streppelhoff, Thorsten; Thiede, Peter; Viefers, Ulrich; Weber, Marc
Bronze	RUS	Aksyonov, Nikolay; Chermashentsev, Anton; Glukhov, Andrey; Lukyanov, Aleksandr; Matveyev, Sergey; Melnikov, Pavel; Monchenko, Roman; Rozinkevich, Dmitriy; Volodenkov, Vladimir

WOMEN'S EIGHT (W8+)
Gold	ROM	Cochelea, Veronica; Gafencu, Liliana; Georgescu, Elena; Ignat, Doina; Lipa, Elisabeta; Olteanu, Ioana; Popescu, Marioara; Spircu, Doina; Tanase, Anca
Silver	CAN	Korn, Alison; Luke, Theresa; Maunder, Maria; McDermid, Heather; Monroe, Jessica; Robinson, Emma; Thompson, Lesley Allison; Tsang, Tosha; Van Der Kamp, Anna
Bronze	BLR	Davydenko, Tamara; Lavrinenko, Natalya; Mikulich, Yelena; Pankina, Aleksandra; Pavlovich, Yaroslava; Skrabatun, Valentina; Stasyuk, Natalia; Volchek, Natalya; Znak, Marina;

2000 ★ Sydney

MEN'S SINGLE SCULLS (M1X)
Gold   NZL   Waddell, Robert
Silver   SUI   Mueller, Xeno
Bronze GER   Hacker, Marcel

WOMEN'S SINGLE SCULLS (W1X)
Gold   BLR   Khodotovich, Ekaterina
Silver   BUL   Neykova, Rumyana
Bronze GER   Rutschow, Katrin

LIGHTWEIGHT MEN'S DOUBLE SCULLS (M2X)
Gold   POL   Kucharski, Tomasz; Sycz, Robert
Silver   ITA   Luini, Elia; Pettinari, Leonardo
Bronze FRA   Chapelle, Thibaud; Touron, Pascal

LIGHTWEIGHT WOMEN'S DOUBLE SCULLS (W2X)
Gold   ROM   Burcica, Constanta; Tamas, Angela
Silver   GER   Blasberg, Claudia; Viehoff, Valerie
Bronze USA   Collins, Christine; Garner, Sarah m

MEN'S DOUBLE SCULLS (M2X)
Gold   SLO   Cop, Iztok; Spik, Luka
Silver   NOR   Tufte, Olaf; Bekken, Fredrik
Bronze ITA   Calabrese, Giovanni

WOMEN'S DOUBLE SCULLS (W2X)
Gold   GER   Boron, Kathrin; Thieme, Jana
Silver   NED   Van Dishoeck, Pieta; Van Nes, Eeke
Bronze LTU   Poplavskaja, Kristina; Sakickiene, Birute

MEN'S PAIR WITHOUT COXSWAIN (M2-)
Gold   FRA   Andrieux, Michel; Rolland, Jean Christophe
Silver   USA   Bea, Sebastian; Murphy, Edward
Bronze AUS   Tomkins, James; Long, Matthew

WOMEN'S PAIR WITHOUT COXSWAIN (W2-)
Gold   ROM   Damian, Georgeta; Ignat, Doina
Silver   AUS   Slatter, Kate Elizabeth; Taylor, Rachael
Bronze USA   Kraft, Karen; Ryan, Melissa

MEN'S QUADRUPLE SCULLS (M4X)
Gold   ITA   Abbagnale, Agostino; Galtarossa, Rossano; Raineri, Simone; Sartori, Alessio
Silver   NED   Bartman, Michiel; Lippits, Dirk; Simon, Diederik; Verberne, Jochem
Bronze GER   Geisler, Marco; Hajek, Andreas; Volkert, Stephan; Willms, Andre

WOMEN'S QUADRUPLE SCULLS (W4X)
Gold   GER   Evers, Meike; Kowalski, Kerstin; Kowalski, Manja; Lutze, Manuela
Silver   GBR   Batten, Guin; Lindsay, Gillian Anne; Grainger, Katherine; Batten, Miriam
Bronze RUS   Dorodnova, Oksana; Fedotova, Irina; Levina, Ioulia; Merk, Larisa li

LIGHTWEIGHT MEN'S FOUR WITHOUT COXSWAIN (M4-)
Gold   FRA   Bette, Jean-Christophe; Dorfmann, Xavier; Hocde, Yves; Porchier, Laurent
Silver   AUS   Balmforth, Darren; Burgess, Simon; Edwards, Anthony; Richards, Robert
Bronze DEN   Ebbesen, Eskild; Ebert, Thomas; Feddersen, Victor; Madsen, Soren

2000 ★ Sydney (continued)

MEN'S FOUR WITHOUT COXSWAIN (M4-)

Gold   GBR   Cracknell, James; Foster, Tim James; Pinsent, Matthew Clive; Redgrave, Steven
Silver   ITA   Carboncini, Lorenzo; Dei Rossi, Riccardo; Molea, Walter; Mornati, Carlo
Bronze   AUS   Andrieux, Michel; Dodwell, Ben Philip; Hanson, Boden Joseph;
Stewart, Geoffrey; Stewart, James

MEN'S EIGHT (M8+)

Gold   GBR   Attrill, Louis; Dennis, Simon; Douglas, Rowley; Grubor, Luka; Hunt-Davis, Ben;
Lindsay, Andrew; Scarlett, Fred; Trapmore, Steve; West, Kieran
Silver   AUS   Burke, Daniel; Fernandez, Jaime; Gordon, Alastair; Hayman, Brett; Jahrling,
Robert;

Mckay, Michael Scott; Porzig, Nicholas; Ryan, Christian; Welch, Stuart
Bronze   CRO   Francetic, Igor; Frankovic, Tihomir; Smoljanovic, Tomislav; Skelin, Niksa; Skelin,
Sinisa;

Culjak, Kresimir; Boraska, Igor; Vujevic, Branimir; Petrisko, Silvijo

WOMEN'S EIGHT (W8+)

Gold   ROM   Cochelea, Veronica; Damian, Georgeta; Dumitrache, Maria Magdalena;
Gafencu, Liliana; Georgescu, Elena; Ignat, Doina; Lipa, Elisabeta;
Olteanu, Ioana; Susanu, Viorica
Silver   NED   Appeldoorn, Tessa; Beek Ter, Carin; Meijer, Elien; Penninx, Nelleke;
Quik, Martijntje; Van Dishoeck, Pieta; Van Nes, Eeke; Venema, Anneke;
Westerhof, Marieke
Bronze   CAN   Alexander, Buffy; Biesenthal, Laryssa; Davis, Heather; Korn, Alison;
Luke, Theresa; McDermid, Heather; Robinson, Emma; Thompson, Lesley Allison;
Urbaniak, Dorota

Visit our website, www.rowersalmanac.com/olympic,
for statistical analysis on top medal winners of the 20th Century.

Country Profiles and World Clubs ★ A to Z

Albania

NATIONAL FEDERATION

Albanian Rowing Association "Liburnia"
Federata Shqiptare E Notit
Rr. Dervish Hima Nr. 31
Tirana, Albania
Tel: +355 42 23682
Fax: +355 42 28447

Algeria

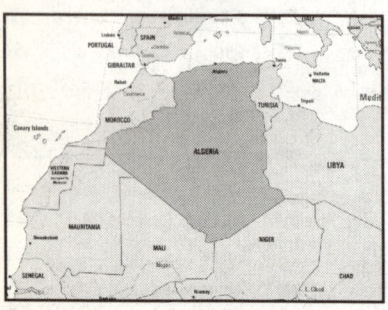

NATIONAL FEDERATION

Federation Algerienne des Societes d'Aviron
CNOS AOS — Cite Olympique Mohamed Boudiaf
BP 88 El Biar
Alger, Algeria
Tel: +213 2192 2034
Email: fasac-rowing@hotmail.com

Angola

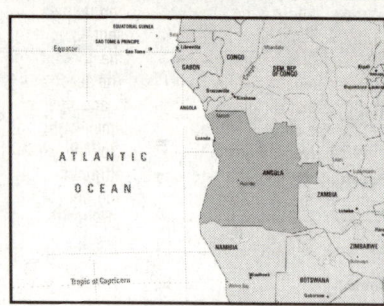

NATIONAL FEDERATION

Federacao Angolana de Canoageme Remo
Caixa Postal 832
Luanda, Angola
Tel: +244 235 4896
Fax: +244 235 4896
Email: lotus@netangola.com

Argentina

HISTORY

Argentina's rowing history was strongly influenced by modern European rowing that began in the 1800's. The earliest boats in Argentina were imported from England in 1856. Evidence dating from 1870 mentions the christening of the rowing boat Lalas; the first boat to race the distance between Tigre and Buenos Aires in an astonishing record time of 2 hours and 50 minutes. This event marked the beginning of a period of great popularity among rowing enthusiasts and the creation of rowing clubs in Argentina.

The first official rowing regatta in Argentina was held on the Rio Lujan, February 12, 1871. The event became so popular with rowing fans as well as the general public that in December of 1873 Argentina's President, Domingo F. Sarmiento, officially opened the regatta.

Between 1873 and 1890 rowing clubs quickly sprouted up throughout the country. The Buenos Aires Rowing Club was the first club to open its doors in 1873. On September 21, 1893, representatives from the most prominent clubs at that time formed the Union de Regatas del Rio de la Plata. The association was responsible for the organization and development of the sport in addition to the administration of regattas. Over the next few years, as rowing gained in popularity and the association attracted more members, the Union de Regatas del Rio de la Plata became what is known today as the Argentine Rowing Association.

REGIONS

Buenos Aires: Buenos Aires, Cap Fed, Tigre, Barbadero, San Nicolas, San Fernando, Zarate, Ensenada
Avg. temp: Summer (December-February) 18-30°C; Fall (March-May) 13-27°C; Winter (June-August) 4-16°C; Spring (September-November) 10-26°C.

Mendoza
Avg. temp: Winter (June-August) 2-17°C; Spring (September-November) 6-29°C; Summer (December-February) 17-33°C; Fall (March-May) 6-27°C;

Cordoba
Avg. temp: Winter (June-August) 4-19°C; Spring (September-November) 8-27°C; Summer (December-February) 14-30°C; Fall (March-May) 8-27°C.

Santa Fe: Rosario, Santa Fe, Avellaneda
Avg. temp: Winter (June-August) 5-20°C; Spring (September-November) 8-24°C; Summer (December-February) 16-31°C; Fall (March-May) 8-27°C.

Misiones: Posadeas
Avg. temp: Winter (June-August) 11-22°C; Spring (September-November) 14-30°C; Summer 21-32°C; Fall (March-May) 14-31°C.

PERSONALITIES

Alberto Demiddi: The most accomplished and highly decorated rower in Argentina, Demiddi was a 3-time Olympian representing Argentina in Tokyo-1964, Mexico City- 1968 and Munich-1972. Demiddi won the Diamond Sculls at the Royal Henley Regatta in 1971.

NATIONAL FEDERATION

Asociacion Argentina de Remo
Avenida Rivadavia 717
Buenos Aires, 1002
Argentina
Tel: +54 114 343 9321
Fax: +54 114 343 9321
Email: asocargremo@lnea.com.ar

CLUBS

Buenos Aires Rowing Club
Gral. Mitre 226 — Tigre (1648)
Buenos Aires, Argentina
Contact: Arq. José M. Gassó
Tel: +54 4749-0549 / +54 4749-0046/0096

Campana Boat Club
Casilla de correo 3 — Campana (2804)
Buenos Aires
Contact: Dr. Miguel Dell' Acqua
Tel: +54 (03489) 422101

Club Canottieri Italiani
Gral. Mitre 74 — Tigre (1648)
Buenos Aires, Argentina
Contact: Dr. Hugo Leber
Tel: +54 4749-0084

Club de Activ. Acuaticas Atlantis
Formosa 46.300 (7600)
Mar del Plata, Argentina
Contact: Sr. Alberto Blanca
Tel: +54 (0223) 4726903
Fax: +54 4893549 fax

Club de Regatas América
Lavalle 167 — Tigre (1648)
Buenos Aires, Argentina
Contact: Sr. Alfio Pulvirenti
Tel: +54 4749-0320

Club de Regatas Baradero
Av. Alte. Brown s/nº — Baradero (2942)
Buenos Aires, Argentina
Contact: Sr. Enrique Bernardi
Tel: +54 (02329) 480353

Club de Regatas Bariloche
Campichuelo 967 — S. C. de Bariloche (8499)
Río Negro, Argentina
Contact: Sr. Miguel Labay
Tel: +54 (02944) 424790

Club de Regatas Chascomús
Av. España y Moreno — Chascomús (7130)
Buenos Aires, Argentina
Contact: Sr. Emilio O. Seillant
Tel: +54 (02241) 422286

Club de Regatas Concordia
Casilla de correo 48 — Concordia (3200)
Entre Ríos, Argentina
Contact: Sr. Hector Andres Rousset
Tel: +54 (0345) 4212663

Club de Regatas Corrientes
Parque Mitre — Corrientes (3400)
Corrientes, Argentina
Contact: Sr. Eduardo Tassano
Tel: +54 (03783) 424602

Club de Regatas de Avellaneda
Rosetti y Güifra — Avellaneda (1870)
Buenos Aires, Argentina
Contact: Sr. Osvaldo Zona
Tel: +54 4201-7844

Club de Regatas Hispano Argentino
Paseo Victorica 50/80 — Tigre (1648)
Buenos Aires, Argentina
Contact: Sr. Juan Guzmán
Tel: +54 4749-0201

Club de Regatas La Marina
Paseo Victorica y Colón — Tigre (1648)
Buenos Aires, Argentina
Contact: Sr. Miguel A. Carrere
Tel: +54 4728-0076
Fax: +54 4728-5076

Club de Regatas La Plata
Aº Doña Flora y Río Santiago — Ensenada (1925)
Buenos Aires, Argentina
Contact: Sr. Jorge Oscar Gutierrez
Tel: +54 (0221) 4691628

Club de Regatas Rosario
J.B.Cordiviola 1268 — Rosario (2000)
Santa Fe, Argentina
Contact: Sr. Oscar Martinez
Tel: +54 (0341) 4399281

Club de Regatas San Nicolás
Av. J. M. de Rosas 100 — San Nicolás (2900)
Buenos Aires, Argentina
Contact: Sr. Jose Carrera
Tel: +54 (03461) 422109

Club de Regatas Santa Fe
Av. Alem 3288 — Santa Fe (3000)
Santa Fe, Argentina
Contact: Sr. Enrique Stringhini
Tel: +54 (0342) 4528627

Club de Remeros Alberdi
Puccio 150 — Rosario (2000)
Contact: Sr. Hugo Menendez
Tel: +54 (0341) 4550092

Club de Remo Teutonia
Casilla de correo 31 — Victoria (1644)
Buenos Aires, Argentina
Contact: Sr. Roberto Speiser
Tel: +54 4728-2447
Fax: +54 4728-7447

Club Mendoza de Regatas
Casilla de correo 170 — Mendoza (5500)
Mendoza, Argentina
Contact: Dr. José E. Nazar
Tel: +54 (0261) 4288192

Club Náutico El Timón
Av. Flandes s/n — Villa Flandria (6706)
Buenos Aires, Argentina
Contact: Sr. Miguel A. Mauri
Tel: +54 (02323) 497268

Club Náutico Ensenada
San Martín y Aº Doña Flora — Ensenada (1925)
Buenos Aires, Argentina
Contact: Sr. Roberto Orioli
Tel: +54 (0221) 4691698

Club Náutico Hacoaj
Estado de Israel 4156 — Capital Federal (1185)
Buenos Aires, Argentina
Contact: Sr. Juan Ofman
Tel: +54 4863-2121 862-3643
Fax: +54 4749-4693/0520

Club Náutico Mar del Plata
Espigón "C" - Mar del Plata (7600)
Buenos Aires, Argentina
Contact: Sr. Jaime Alemany Pallés
Tel: +54 (0223) 4800323

Club Nautico Rio Parana Corrientes
Buenos Aires 1260 planta alta — (3400)
Corrientes, Argentina
Tel: +54 (03787) 421315

Club Náutico Universidad del Salvador
Viamonte 1856 — Capital Federal (1058)
Buenos Aires, Argentina
Contact: Dr. Enrique A. Betta
Tel: +54 4813-9630/1408

Club Náutico Villa Constitución
Bvard. Seguí y San Luis — V. Constitución (2919)
Santa Fe, Argentina
Contact: Sr. Adolfo Bustos
Tel: +54 (03400) 474004

Club Náutico Zárate
Rivadavia y Río Paraná — Zárate (2800)
Buenos Aires, Argentina
Contact: Sr. Juan Carlos Berns
Tel: +54 (03487) 424659

Club San Clemente del Tuyu
Calle 1 Nº 2338 (7105)
San Clemente del Tuyu, Argentina
Contact: Sr. Isidro Diaz
Tel: +54 (02252) 421147

Club San Fernando
Sarmiento y Escalada — San Fernando (1646)
Buenos Aires, Argentina
Contact: Sr. Alejandro Farina
Tel: +54 4744-0647/3717

Club Suizo de Buenos Aires
Rodríguez Peña 254 — Capital Federal (1020)
Buenos Aires, Argentina
Contact: Sr. Juan Walter
Tel: +54 4371-9977

Escuela de Prefectura Naval
A. del Valle y Rivadavia — Zárate (2800)
Buenos Aires, Argentina
Contact: Prefecto Mayor Hector Omar Valles
Tel: +54 (03487) 422846
Fax: +54 423989

Escuela Municipal de Remo (EMDER)
Juan B. Juto y Dorrego (7600)
Mar del Plata, Argentina
Contact: Sr. Norberto Alonso
Tel: +54 (0223) 4819120/22

Escuela Naval Militar
Río Santiago — La Plata (1900)
Buenos Aires, Argentina
Contact: Capitan de Navio Carlos Mazzoni
Tel: +54 (0221) 4680330/32

L´Aviron Club de Regatas
Lavalle 945 — Tigre (1648)
Buenos Aires, Argentina
Contact: Sr. Nicolas N. Sade
Tel: +54 4749-0322

Nahuel Rowing Club
Lavalle 235 — Tigre (1648)
Buenos Aires, Argentina
Contact: Sr. Alejandro Maritano
Tel: +54 4749-0387

Nautico Escobar Country Club
Casilla de correo Nº 159 — Escobar (1625)
Argentina
Contact: Sr. Guillermo Waddle
Tel: +54 (03488) 480298

Paraná Rowing Club
Av. Costanera s/nº — Paraná (3100)
Entre Ríos, Argentina
Contact: Sr. Jaime Barba
Tel: +54 (0343) 4312048

Rosario Rowing Club
Av. Colombres 1798 — Rosario (2000)
Santa Fe, Argentina
Contact: Sr. Hugo Angel Galloni
Tel: +54 (0341) 4552219

Rowing Club Argentino
Paseo Victorica 316 — Tigre (1648)
Buenos Aires, Argentina
Contact: Sr. Ricardo J. Burgio
Tel: +54 4749-0100

Tigre Boat Club
Paseo Victorica 156 — Tigre (1648)
Buenos Aires, Argentina
Contact: Sr. Juan A. Graham
Tel: +54 4749-0071

Tiro Federal Gualeguaychú
Bvard. De Leon y Luis Palma
Gualeguaychu (2820)
E. Rios, Argentina
Tel: +54 03446 422672

Universidad Nacional de Cuyo
Av. Champagnat s/n — Mendoza (5500)
Mendoza, Argentina
Contact: Prof. Daniel Yenaropulos
Tel: +54 (0261) 4494091

Armenia

NATIONAL FEDERATION
Armenian National Federation of Rowing
Apt 4
8a Kanaker GES Str
Yerevan, 375021
Armenia
Email: samslena@yahoo.com

Australia

NATIONAL FEDERATION

Rowing Australia
PO Box 4216
Penrith, 2750
Australia
Tel: +61 247 294 500
Fax: +61 247 294 511
Email: rowing@rowingaustralia.com.au
www.rowingaustralia.com.au

CLUBS (BY REGION)

AUSTRALIAN CAPITAL TERRITORY (ACT)

Australian Capital Territory RA
PO Box 3079, Manuka ACT 2603
Tel: +61 02 6282 0639
Fax: +61 02 6282 0610
Email: actra@rowingact.org.au
www.rowingact.org.au

Australian Defence Force Academy
Northcott Drive
Campbell ACT 2600
Australia
Tel: +61 02 6268 8111
Black Mountain Rowing Club
Email: davidb@pi.csiro.au

Canberra Girls Grammar School RA
Senior School
Melbourne Ave, Deakin ACT 2600
Junior School
Grey St, Deakin ACT 2600
Australia
Tel: +61 02 6202 6400
Fax: +61 02 6273 1505
Email: enrolments@cggs.act.edu.au

Canberra Grammar School Rowing Association
Australia
Tel: +61 (02) 6260 9837
Email: catherine.borger@cgs.act.edu.au

Capital Lakes Rowing Club
Australia
Tel: +61 62396501
Email: butt279@ozemail.com.au

Canberra Rowing Club
PO Box E24
Kingston ACT 2604
Australia
BH: Yarralumla Bay
Alexandrina Drive
Yarralumla, ACT

Daramalan College Rowing Club
Email: daramalan@geocities.com
www.geocities.com/daramalan

Lake Tuggeranong Rowing Club
email: bekmo47@hotmail.com

Radford College Rowing Club
College Street
Bruce ACT 2617
Australia
Tel: +61 (02) 6162 6200
Fax: +61 (02) 6162 6263

NEW SOUTH WALES

New South Wales Rowing Association
P.O. Box 722, Glebe NSW 2037
Australia
Tel: +61 2 9552 1263
Fax: +61 2 9660 4178
Email: office@rowingnsw.asn.au
www.rowingnsw.asn.au

SYDNEY METROPOLITAN AREA

Balmain Rowing Club
P.O. Box 15, Balmain 2041
Australia
BH: Lower White St, Balmain
Australia
Tel: +61 9810 3400
www.balmainrowingclub.com

Drummoyne Rowing Club
P.O. Box 19, Drummoyne 2047
BH: Henley Marine Drive, Drummoyne
Australia
Tel: +61 9719 1522
www.drummoynerowingclub.com.au

Leichhardt Rowing Club
P.O. Box 3, Leichhardt 2040
BH: Lower Glover St, Leichhardt
Australia
Tel: +61 9810 6001

Mosman Rowing Club
P.O. Box 283, MOSMAN 2088
Australia
Tel: +61 9953 7966
BH: Pearl Bay, The Spit
Tel: +61 9969 6121
www.mosmanrowers.com

Nepean Rowing Club
P.O. Box 27, Penrith 2750
Australia
Tel: +61 4731 2255
BH: Bruce Neale Drive, Penrith
www.nepeanrowingclub.org.au

North Shore Rowing Club
P.O. Box 49, Lane Cove 2066
Australia
Tel: +61 9427 4693
BH: Aquatic Park, Longueville
www.users.tpg.com.au/nsrc

Penrith Rowing Club
BH: School Boatshed
Bruce Neale Drive
Australia

St George Rowing Club
P.O. Box 57, Rockdale 2216
Australia
Tel: +61 9567 1489
BH: Verona Range, COMO
Tel: +61 9589 1823
www.stgeorgerowing.com.au

Sydney Rowing Club
P.O. Box 45, Five Dock 2046
Australia
Tel: +61 9712 1199
BH: 613 Great North Road, Abbotsford
Tel: +61 9712 3296
www.sydneyrowingclub.com.au

Sydney University Boat Club
Women's BH: Ferry Road, Glebe
Australia
Tel: +61 9566 2476
www.usyd.edu.au/su/suwsa
Email: j.rodrigues@susu.usyd.edu.au
Men's BH: Linley Res
Burns Bay Rd, Linley Point
Tel: +61 9418 6259
www.susport.com

Sydney Womens MLC Rowing Club
P.O. Box 10, Five Dock 2046
BH: Battersea Park, Abbotsford

UTS Rowing Club
P.O. Box 3210, Broadway 2007
BH: Dobroyd Pde, Haberfield
Australia
Tel: +61 9797 9523
www.geocities.com/Colosseum/Dugout/6817/

Univ of NSW Rowing Club
BH: Tarban Creek, Gladesville
www.unswrc.com

REGIONAL CLUBS

Illawarra Rowing Club
Email: bob_rowlan@uow.edu.au

Shoalhaven Rowing Club
P.O. Box 888, Nowra 2541
Riverview Rd, Nr Bridge, Nowra

Northern Rivers Rowing Association
Grafton Rowing Club
P.O. Box 308, Grafton 2460
Email: graftonrowing@hotmail.com
graftonrowing.cjb.net

Iluka Rowing Club
P.O. Box 50
Iluka 2466

Lismore Rowing Club
P.O. Box 466
Lismore 2480

Lower Clarence Rowing Club
P.O. Box 139
Maclean 2463

Murwillumbah Rowing Club
P.O. Box 846, Murwillumbah 2484
Email: nanuwun@better.net.au
www.community.better.net.au/rowing/

South Grafton Rowing Club
SGHS, Tyson Street
STH Grafton

Tweed Heads Rowing & Aquatic Club
P.O. Box 1150
Tweed Heads 2485

Central District Rowing Association
Armidale Rowing Club
Malpas Dam, Guyra

City Rowers Rowing Club
P.O. Box 255, Mayfield 2304

Endeavour Rowing Club
Hunter Valley Grammar Boatshed
Berry Park

Hunter Rowing Club
P.O. Box 600, Charlestown 2290
hunterrowing.itgo.com

Manning River Rowing Club
Endeavour Place, Taree

Newcastle Rowing Club
Merewether Street
Newcastle 2300

Port Macquarie Rowing Club
P.O. Box 462
Port Macquarie 2444

University of Newcastle Boat Club
c/o The Sports Union
Newcastle University
Callaghan 2308

Upper Hunter Rowing Club
Lake Glenbawn
Scone

GPS SCHOOLS

Hon. Convenor
College St, Darlinghurst 2010
Australia
Tel: +61 9332 5800
Email: jk@sydgram.nsw.edu.au
www.aagps.nsw.edu.au/

Newington College
200 Stanmore Road
Stanmore 2048
Australia
Tel: +61 9560 5355
Email: rgraham@newingtoncollege.nsw.edu.au
www.newingtoncollege.nsw.edu.au
BH: 14 Checkley Street
Abbotsford 2046
Australia
Tel: +61 9713 1343

Saint Ignatius' College
Riverview, Lane Cove 2066
Australia
Tel: +61 9882 8329
BH: Riverview, Lane Cove 2066
Tel: +61 9882 8498
Email: arybak@riverview.nsw.edu.au
www.riverview.nsw.edu.au

Saint Joseph's College
Mark Street, Hunter's Hill 2110
Australia
Tel: +61 9816 1044
BH: 6 Joly Parade
Hunter's Hill 2210
Tel: +61 9817 1929
Email: jgray@joeys.org
www.joeys.org

Shore School
P.O. Box 1221
North Sydney 2059
Australia
Tel: +61 9923 2277
BH: 896 Wharf Road
Gladesville 2111
Email: rshirlaw@shore.nsw.edu.au
www.shore.nsw.edu.au

Sydney Boys High School
Moore Park, Surry Hills 2010
Australia
Tel: +61 9361 6910
BH: 3 Teviot Avenue
Abbotsford 2046
Tel: +61 9713 7880
www.sbhs.nsw.edu.au

Sydney Grammar School
College Street
Darlinghurst 2010
Australia
Tel: +61 9332 5800
BH: 73 Wharf Road
Gladesville 2111
Tel: +61 9817 3616
Email: rimh@sydgram.nsw.edu.au
www.sydgram.nsw.edu.au

The Kings School
P.O. Box 1parramatta 2124
Australia
Tel: +61 9683 8555
BH: 33 Pellisier Road
Putney
Tel: +61 9808 1315
Email: ppc@kings.edu.au
www.kings.edu.au

The Scots College
Victoria Road, Bellevue Hill 2023
Australia
Tel: +61 9327 7986
BH: 3 Delmar Parade
Gladesville 2111
Tel: +61 9391 7600
Email: g.marks@tsc.nsw.edu.au
www.tsc.nsw.edu.au

CHS SCHOOLS

Sydney Boys High School
Moore Park Road
Surry Hills 2010
Australia
Tel: +61 9361 6910

Ballina High School
Burnet Street
Ballina 2478
Australia
Tel: +61 6686 2133

Barrenjoey High School
Coonanga Road
Avalon 2107
Australia
Tel: +61 9918 8811

Belmont High School
PO Box 2345
Gateshead MDC 2290
Australia
Tel: +61 4945 0600

Blaxland High School
Coughlan Road
Blaxland 2774

Bomaderry High School
Cambewarra Road
Bomaderry 2541
Australia
Tel: +61 4421 0699

Caringbah High School
111-129 Willarong Road
Caringbah
Australia
Tel: +61 9524 3859

Chatham High School
Davis Street
Taree 2430
Australia
Tel: +61 6552 2588

Cheltenham Girls High School
The Promenade
Cheltenham 2119
Australia
Tel: +61 9876 4566

Crestwood High School
Chapel Lane
Baulkham Hills 2153
Australia
Tel: +61 9639 7422

Endeavour Sports High School
The Boulevarde
Caringbah 2229
Australia
Tel: +61 9524 0615

Engadine High School
Waratah Road
Engadine 2233
Australia
Tel: +61 9520 0411

Erskine Park High School
Swallow Drive
Erskine Park 2759
Australia
Tel: +61 9834 3536

Fort St High School
Parramatta Road
Petersham 2049
Australia
Tel: +61 9569 4355

Glebe High School
Taylor Street
Glebe 2037
Australia
Tel: +61 9660 5688

Gloucester High School
Ravenshaw Street
Gloucester 2422
Australia
Tel: +61 6558 1605

Grafton High School
Mary Street
Grafton 2460
Australia
Tel: +61 6642 3355

Gymea Technology High School
Princes Highway
Gymea 2227
Australia
Tel: +61 9521 3244

Heathcote High School
Wilson Parade
Heathcote 2233
Australia
Tel: +61 9520 9582

Hunter School of Performing Arts
Lambton Road
Broadmeadow 2292
Australia
Tel: +61 4952 3355

Irrawang High School
Mount Hall Road
Raymond Terrace 2324
Australia
Tel: +61 4987 4687

Jamison High School
Evan Street
South Penrith 2750
Australia
Tel: +61 4731 6150
4721 2502

Kiera Technology High School
Lysaught Street
Fairy Meadow 2519
Australia
Tel: +61 4229 4644

Killara High School
Koola Avenue
Killara 2071
Australia
Tel: +61 9498 3299

Killarney Heights High School
Starkey Street
Killarney Heights 2087
Australia
Tel: +61 9451 7005

Kingswood High School
P.O. Box 3365
Kingswood 2747
Australia
Tel: +61 4736 1201

Kirrawee High School
21-29 Hunter Street
Kirrawee 2232
Australia
Tel: +61 9521 2099

Kotara High School
Lexington Parade
Adamstown 2289
Australia
Tel: +61 4943 3281

Lambton High School
Young Street
Lambton 2299
Australia
Tel: +61 4952 3977

Leichhardt High School
210 Balmain Road
Leichhardt 2040
Australia
Tel: +61 9560 2355

MacKellar Girls High School
Campbell Pde & Quirk Sts
Manly Vale 2093
Australia
Tel: +61 9949 2083

Maclean High School
Woombah Street
MaClean 2463
Australia
Tel: +61 6645 2244
www.maclean.nsw.edu.au

Merewether High School
Chatham Road
Broadmeadow 2292
Australia
Tel: +61 4969 3855

Muirfield Technology High School
Barclay Road
North Rocks 2150
Australia
Tel: +61 98722244

Murwillumbah High School
River Street
Murwillumbah 2484
Australia
Tel: +61 6672 1566

Nepean High School
Great Western Highway
Emu Plains 2750
Australia
Tel: +61 4735 5600

Newcastle High School
Parkway Avenue
Hamilton 2303
Australia
Tel: +61 4969 3177

North Sydney Boys High School
Falcon Street
Crows Nest 2065
Australia
Tel: +61 9952 6666
Email: pbutcher@westpac.com.au

North Sydney Girls High School
Pacific Highway
Crows Nest 2065
Australia
Tel: +61 9922 6666
Email: pbutcher@westpac.com.au

Nowra Technology High School
Moss Street
Nowra 2541
Australia
Tel: +61 4421 4977

Penshurst Girls High School
2 Austral Street
Penshurst 2222
Australia
Tel: +61 9580 3141

Pittwater High School
Mona Street
Mona Vale 2103
Australia
Tel: +61 99994035

Port Hacking High School
Kingsway
Miranda 2228
Australia
Tel: +61 9524 8816

Port Macquarie High School
Burrawan Street
Port Macquarie 2444
Australia
Tel: +61 6583 1844

Queanbeyanhigh School
Agnes Avenue
Queanbeyan 2620
Australia
Tel: +61 6297 2088

Riverside Girls High School
Huntley's Point Road
Gladesville 2111
Australia
Tel: +61 9816 4264

Shoalhaven High School
Park Road
South Nowra 2541
Australia
Tel: +61 4421 8022

South Grafton High School
P.O. Box 170
South Grafton 2461
Australia
Tel: +61 6642 1466

Southern Cross High School
Chickiba Drive
Ballina East 2478
Australia
Tel: +61 6686 0503

St Clair High School
Endeavour Avenue
St Clair 2759
Australia
Tel: +61 9670 6700

St George Girls High School
Victoria Rd, Kogarah 2217
Australia
Tel: +61 9587 3996

St Marys Senior High School
Kalang Avenue
St Marys 2760
Australia
Tel: +61 9623 8333

Strathfield Girls Languages High School
Albert Road
Strathfield 2135
Australia
Tel: +61 9746 6990

Sydney Boys High School
Moore Park Road
Surry Hills 2010
Australia
Tel: +61 93616910

Sydney Girls High School
Cleveland Street
Surry Hills 2010
Australia
Tel: +61 93312336
Email: czamagias@sghs.nsw.edu.au

Sydney Technical High School
Forest Road
Bexley 2207
Australia
Tel: +61 9581 5899

Taree High School
Albert Street
Taree 2430
Australia
Tel: +61 6552 1166

Terrigal High School
Chanes Kay Drive
Terrigal 2260
Australia
Tel: +61 4384 4677

Tweed River High School
Heffron Street
Tweed Heads South 2486
Australia
Tel: +61 7552 43007

Warners Bay High School
King Road
Warners Bay 2282
Australia
Tel: +61 4954 9488

Westport High School
Widderson Street
Port Macquarie 2444
Australia
Tel: +61 6583 6400

Westfields Sports High School
Hamilton Road
Fairfield West 2065
Australia
Tel: +61 96043333

Whitebridge High School
Lonus Avenue
Whitebridge 2290
Australia
Tel: +61 4943 3966

Willoughby Girls High School
Mowbray Road
Willoughby 2068
Australia
Tel: +61 9958 4141

Wingham High School
Rowley St
Wingham 2429
Australia
Tel: +61 6553 5488

Wollumbin High School
P.O. Box 101
Murwillumbah 2484
Australia
Tel: +61 6672 5121, 6672 6056

Woolooware High School
Woolooware Road
Woolooware 2230
Australia
Tel: +61 9523 6752

INDEPENDENT SCHOOLS

Ascham
188 New South Head Road
Edgecliff 2027
Australia
Tel: +61 9327 3100
BH: Sydney R.C.
613 Great North Rd, Abbotsford
Tel: +61 9712 3296

Catherine McCauley College
Victoria Street, Grafton 2460
Australia
Tel: +61 6643 1434
BH: Grafton R.C.
P.O. Box 308, Grafton 2460

Cranbrook
5 Victoria Rd
Bellevue Hill 2023
Australia
Tel: +61 9327 6864
BH: S.U.B.C.
Linley Res, Burns Bay Rd
Linley Point
Tel: +61 9418 6259
Email: pslavin@cranbrook.nsw.edu.au
www.cranbrookschool.com.au

Hunter Valley Grammar
Norfolk Street
Ashtonfield 2323
Australia
Tel: +61 4934 2444
BH: Duckenfield Rd, Berry Park
www.hvgs.nsw.edu.au

Kincross Wolaroi School
Locked Bag 4, Orange, 2800

Loreto College Normanhurst
Pennant Hills Rd
Normanhurst 2076
Australia
Tel: +61 9487 3488
BH: St Joseph's College
Joly Pde, Hunters Hill
Email: mo'halloran@loretonh.nsw.edu.au
www.loretonh.nsw.edu.au

Loreto College Kirribilli
85 Carabella St
Kirribilli 2061
Australia
Tel: +61 9957 4722
www.loreto.nsw.edu.au

MLC School
Rowley Street
Burwood 2134
Australia
Tel: +61 9747 1266
BH: Syd. Womens MLC
Battersea Park, Abbotsford 2046
Email: wcaldwell@mlcsyd.nsw.edu.au
www.mlcsyd.nsw.edu.au

Newcastle Grammar School
P.O. Box 680
Newcastle 2300
Australia
Tel: +61 4929 5811
Email: boys@ngs.nsw.edu.au
www.ngs.nsw.edu.au

Pymble Ladies College
Avon Road, Pymble 2073
Australia
Tel: +61 9855 7671
BH: Leichhardt R.C.
Glover Street, Leichhardt
Email: gshrosbee@pymblelc.nsw.edu.au
www.pymblelc.nsw.edu.au

PLC Sydney
Boundary Street
Croydon 2132
Australia
Tel: +61 9704 5666
BH: Drummoyne R.C.
Henley Marine Drive
Drummoyne
Email: jclarke@plc.nsw.edu.au
www.plc.nsw.edu.au

Queenwood
44 Mandalong Rd
Mosman 2088
Australia
Tel: +61 9960 2911
BH: Pearl Bay, The Spit
Tel: +61 9969 6121
www.queenwood.nsw.edu.au

Roseville College
27 Bancroft Ave
Roseville 2069
Australia
Tel: +61 9419 3277
BH: North Shore R.C.
Mary Street, Longueville 2066
www.roseville.nsw.edu.au

SCEGS Darlinghurst
215 Forbes St
Darlinghurst 2010
Australia
Tel: +61 9332 1133
BH: UNI NSW R.C.
Tarban Creek, Huntley Point
www.sceggs.nsw.edu.au

SCEGS Redlands
272 Military Rd
Cremorne 2090
Australia
Tel: +61 9909 3133
BH: Macquarie UNI R.C.
Tambourine Bay, Lane Cove
Email: arowley@redlands.nsw.edu.au
www.redlands.nsw.edu.au

St Joseph's High School
Hay Street
Port Macquarie 2444
Australia
Tel: +61 6581 0867
Email: tmorgan@lism.catholic.edu.au

St Paul's Grammar
Locked Bag 16
Penrith 2751
Australia
Tel: +61 4777 4888
BH: Don Croot Boatshed
Bruce Neale Drive, Penrith
Email: rowing@stpauls.nsw.edu.au
www.stpauls.nsw.edu.au/

QUEENSLAND

Queensland Rowing Association
CNR Riverside Drive and Jane Streets
West End, Brisbane
P.O. Box 575, South Brisbane
QLD 4101, Australia
Tel: +61 (7) 38462711
Fax: +61 (7) 38462188
Email: rowqld@rowingqld.asn.au
www.rowingqld.asn.au

Brisbane & GPS Rowing Club
Contact: Warwick Agnew
Australia
Tel: +61 (07) 33997018
Email: warwick.agnew@treasury.qld.gov.au

Bundaberg Rowing Club
Contact: Bruce & LynMcCarthy
Australia
Tel: +61 (07) 41518088
Fax: +61 (07) 41518616
Email: bundytools@bigpond.com

Cairns Rowing Club
Contact: Tania Crossley
Australia
Tel: +61 (07) 40504033
Email: tcmermaid@hotmail.com

Commercial Rowing Club
Contact: PennyDixon
Australia
Tel: +61 (07) 32354910
Fax: +61 (07) 32258436
Email: penny.dixon@publicworks.qld.gov.au

Coomera Watersports Club
Contact: GrantPforr
Australia
Tel: +61 0419701942

Dragons Rowing Club
Contact: MarilynSlawson
Fax: +61 (07) 33539174
Email: cslawson@bigpond.net.au

GCRASRA
Contact: CarlaWhite
Australia
Tel: +61 (07) 55915990
Email: meljules@bigpond.net.au

Grammarians Rowing Club
Contact: KenBuckly
Australia
Tel: +61 (07) 49226910
Email: kajabi@dingoblue.net.au

Innisfail Rowing Club
Contact: TonyTermine
Australia
Tel: +61 (07) 40611485
Email: term5@bigpond.com.au

Leichhardt Rowing Club
Contact: FrankHick
Australia
Tel: +61 (07) 49223402

Mackay Rowing Club
Contact: DavidHouston
Australia
Tel: +61 0418735310
Fax: +61 (07) 49533955
Email: hesmky@bigpond.net.au

Murwillumbah Rowing Club
Contact: GordonLee
Australia
Tel: +61 (02) 66724859
Fax: +61 (02) 66725383
Email: gordonplee@hotmail.com

Noosa Rowing Club
Contact: StephanMulenberg
Australia
Tel: +61 (07) 54498602
Fax: +61 (07) 54741109
Email: stephanyouthrow@hotmail.com

Pine Rivers Rowing Club
Contact: Keith&VirginiaWatts
Australia
Tel: +61 (07) 32852226

Redlegs Rowing Club
Contact: MelodieDowney
Australia
Tel: +61 738912988
Email: philandmel@powerup.com.au

Sunshine Coast Rowing Club
Contact: IanBuscombe
Australia
Tel: +61 (07) 54431490
Fax: +61 (07) 54432940
Email: ian@rbw.com.au

Surfers Paradise Rowing Club
Contact: CarlaWhite
Australia
Tel: +61 (07) 55321055
Email: meljules@bigpond.net.au

The College Rowing Club
Contact: AnthonyPatterson
Australia
Tel: +61 (07) 38719832
Fax: +61 (07) 38719666
Email: sport@kings.uq.edu.au

Toowong Rowing Club
Contact: KerryO'Rourke
Australia
Tel: +61 (07) 32268070

Townsville & JCU
Contact: DinahHansman
Australia
Tel: +61 (07) 47725775
Email: wild@beyond.net.au

Tweed Heads Rowing Club
Contact: GarryAnnand
Australia
Tel: +61 (07) 55246968
Fax: +61 (07) 55234981
Email: gazandann@optusnet.com.au

UQBC
Contact: TonyGeorge
Australia
Tel: +61 (07) 32246129
Email: tony.george@projectservices.qld.gov.au

Vintage Vikings
Contact: JoyFerris
Australia
Tel: +61 (07) 33496651
Email: ferrisjoy@hotmail.com

Wide Bay Rowing Club
Contact: JimMcCawley
Australia
Tel: +61 (07) 41212940
Fax: +61 (07) 41235318
Email: jmccawley@maryborough.net

SOUTH AUSTRALIA

South Australia Rowing Association
100 Military Rd
West Lakes Shore
SA 5020, Australia
Tel: +61 (08) 82423288
Fax: +61 (08) 82423162
Email: secretary@rowingsa.asn.au
www.rowingsa.asn.au

Adelaide High School
West Terrace
Adelaide, SA 5000
Australia
Tel: +61 82127827
Fax: +61 82319373
BH: Victoria Drive
Torrens Lake
Adelaide, SA 5000
Email: jralph@adelaidehs.sa.edu.au
www.adelaidehs.sa.edu.au

Adelaide Rowing Club
GPO Box 1228
Adelaide, SA 5001
Australia
Tel: +61 82316572
BH: Festival Drive
Torrens Lake
Adelaide, SA 5000
Email: captain@adelaide_rowing_club.com.au
www.adelaide_rowing_club.com.au

Adelaide University Boat Club
c/o Adelaide Uni Sports Assoc.
University of Adelaide, SA 5005
Australia
Tel: +61 83035403
Fax: +61 82321300
BH: War Memorial Drive
Torrens Lake, Adelaide, SA 5000
Email: wfargher@hotmail.com
www.smug.adelaide.edu/~aubc

Berri Rowing Club
PO Box 205
Berri, SA 5343
Australia
Tel: +61 85823410
Fax: +61 85821571
Email: berrirowingclub@hotmail.com
BH: Draper Street
Berri, SA 5343

Christian Brothers College
GPO Box 2707
Adelaide, SA 5001
Australia
Tel: +61 84004200
Fax: +61 84004299
BH: War Memorial Drive
Torrens Lake
Adelaide, SA 5000
Email: tvanruth@cbc.sa.edu.au
www.cbc.sa.edu.au

Mannum Rowing Club
PO Box100
Mannum, SA 5238
Tel/Fax: +61 85698037
BH: River Lane
Mannum, SA 5238

Murray Bridge Boat Club
PO Box72
Murray Bridge, SA 5253
BH: Sturt Reserve
Murray Bridge, SA 5253
Email: cmcrae@lm.net.au

Norwood-Morialta High School
505 The Parade
Magill, SA 5072
Australia
Tel: +61 83640455
Fax: +61 83378397
BH: Festival Drive
Torrens Lake
Adelaide, SA 5000
Email: rkuchel@nmhs.sa.edu.au
www.nmhs.sa.edu.au

Pembroke School
342 The Parade
Kensington Park, SA 5068
Australia
Tel: +61 83326111
Fax: +61 83640291
BH: Festival Drive
Torrens Lake
Adelaide, SA 5000
Email: rodelleway@ozemail.com.au
www.pembroke.sa.edu.au

Port Adelaide Rowing Club
PO Box 70
Port Adelaide, SA 5015
Australia
Tel: +61 84498660
Fax: +61 83416976
Email: port_adel_ rowing_club@bigpond.com
BH: Snowden's Beach
Port Adelaide, SA 5015
Email: jjanonis@iprimus.com.au

Port Pirie Rowing Club
BH: 20 Mary Elie Street
Port Pirie, SA 5540
Email: mmalcolm@pprdb.com.au

Prince Alfred College
PO Box 571
Kent Town, SA 5071
Australia
Tel: +61 83341200
Fax: +61 83630702
Email: croberts@pac.edu.au
www.pac.edu.au

Pulteney Grammar School
190 SouthTerrace
Adelaide, SA 5000
Australia
Tel: +61 82165555
Fax: +61 82165588
Email: bholloway@staff.pulteney.sa.edu.au
www.pulteney.sa.edu.au

Renmark Rowing Club
PO Box 1517
Renmark, SA 5341
BH: Rowing Club Lane
Renmark, SA 5341
Email: lilm@stjoren.pp.catholic.edu.au

Riverside Rowing Club
PO Box 477
Tynte Street
North Adelaide, SA 5006
Australia
Tel: +61 82126838
Fax: +61 82126199
Email: riverside@chariot.net.au
www.riversiderowing.asn.au

Scotch College
Carruth Road
Mitcham, SA 5062
Australia
Tel: +61 82744333
Fax: +61 82744344
Email: barnabyeaton@hotmail.com
www.scotch.sa.edu.au

SienaCollege
176 Crittenden Road
Findon, SA 5023
Australia
Tel: +61 84459666
Fax: +61 84456034
Email: erezes@lawguard.com.au
www.siena.adl.catholic.edu.au

St Peter's College
St Peters, SA 5069
Australia
Tel: +61 83623451
Fax: +61 83632239
www.stpeters.sa.edu.au

Tailem Bend Rowing Club
PO Box 139
Tailem Bend, SA 5260
Fax: +61 85727772
Email: capes@lm.net.au

Torrens Rowing Club
GPO Box 512
Adelaide, SA 5001
Australia
Tel: +61 82234428
Email: jandctonkin@hotmail.com
www.torrensrc.mtx.net

Unley High School
Kitchener Street
Netherby, SA 5062
Australia
Tel: +61 82721455
Fax: +61 83733031
www.uhs.sa.edu.au
Email: kmagee@uhs.sa.edu.au

Walford School
PO Box 430
Unley, SA 5061
Australia
Tel: +61 82726555
Fax: +61 82720313
Email: perryqa@ozemail.com.au
www.walford.asn.au

Wilderness School
PO Box 93
Walkerville, SA 5081
Australia
Tel: +61 83446688
Fax: +61 83442094
Email: sperry@wilderness.com.au
www.wilderness.com.au

VICTORIA

Rowing Victoria
Level 1, 1A Bowen Crescent
Melbourne 3004
Australia
Tel: +61 (3) 9820 6374
Fax: +61 (3) 9820 6394
office@rowingvictoria.asn.au
www.rowingvictoria.asn.au

Banks Rowing Club
Princes Bridge
Melbourne VIC, 3004
PO Box 4181
Richmond East VIC, 3121
Australia
Tel: +61 9654 7182
Email: banksrowing@hotmail.com

Corio Bay Rowing Club
G.P.O. Box 420
Geelong VIC
Australia 3220
BH: Barwon Tce
Geelong South.
Tel: +61 (03) 5221 5106

Essendon Rowing Club
48 The Boulevard
Moonee Ponds, Victoria
Australia 3039
Tel: +61 3 9370 1973
Email: info@essrc.com

Hawthorn Rowing Club
Email: ghirst@bigpond.net.au
www.hawthornrc.inter.net.au/

Melbourne University Boat Club
Email: mubc@mubc.asn.au

Melbourne Rowing Club
Boat House Drive, Melbourne, 3004
Australia
Tel: +61 9654 7754
Email: members@melbournerowing.com.au

Mercantile Rowing Club
Boathouse 5, Boathouse Drive
Melbourne VIC 3004
Australia
Tel/Fax: +61 3 9650 3044
Email mercantile.rowing@bigpond.com

Mildura Rowing Club
Email: ntink@telstra.com
www.mildurarowingclub.org.au/MRC.html

Queer Rowing Assn of Vic Inc — Melbourne Argonauts
PO Box 2036, Richmond South,
Victoria, 3121, Australia
Email: queerrowing@melbourneargonauts.com

Richmond Rowing Club
Boathouse Drive
Melbourne
Victoria 3004
Australia
Tel: +61 (03) 9654-8982
Email: learntorow@richmondrowing.com.au
www.richmondrowing.com.au

Yarra Yarra Rowing Club
Australia
Tel: +61 03 9654 7969
Email: captain@yyrc.com.au
www.yyrc.com.au/

YWCA Rowing Centre
Cnr Lakeside Drive & Queens Road,
(Ground floor Power House Function Centre)
Albert Park Lake, Melbourne 3004
Australia
Tel: +61 03 9529 8596
Fax: +61 03 9592 2147
Email: ywrowing@hotmail.com

TASMANIA

Tasmanian Rowing Council
c/o Administration Manager
PO Box 595 Devenport
TAS 7310
Email: dolbelranj@bigpond.com.au
www.rowingtas.asn.au

Buckingham Rowing Club
GPO Box 1093
Hobart, TAS 7001
Australia

Derwent Mercantile Collegiate Rowing Club
PO Box 222
Sandy Bay, TAS 7005
Australia

The Friends School
PO Box 42
North Hobart, TAS 7002
Australia

Glenorchy Rowing Club
47 Catherine Street
Berriedale, TAS 7011
Australia

Huon Rowing Club
PO Box 145
Huonville, Tas 7109
Australia

Lindisfarne Rowing Club
PO Box 73
Lindisfarne, TAS 7015
Australia

Mersey Rowing Club
PO Box 253
Devonport, TAS 7310
Australia

New Norfolk Rowing Club
PO Box 338
New Norfolk, Tas 7140
Australia

North Esk Rowing Club
PO Box 64
Launceston, Tas 7250
Australia

Reeconian Rowing Club
PO Box 94
Devonport, 7310
Australia

Sandy Bay Rowing Club
PO Box 50
Sandy Bay, TAS 7005
Australia

Tasmania University Boat Club (TUBC)
64 York Street
Sandy Bay, TAS 7005
Australia

Tamar Rowing Club
PO Box 631
Launceston, TAS 7250
Australia

Ulverstone Rowing Club
PO Box 126
Ulverstone, Tas 7315
Australia

WESTERN AUSTRALIA

Rowing WA
The Esplanade
Mount Pleasant WA
Australia
Tel: +61 +61(09) 93643905
Fax: +61 +61(09) 93643908
Email:rowingwa@iinet.net.au
www.rowingwa.asn.au

Albany Rowing Club
PO Box 5089
Albany, W.A.6332

ANA Rowing Club
PO Box 6
Bayswater, WA 6053
Australia
Email: john@orna.com.au
www.anarowingclub.org.au/

Bunbury Rowing Club
PO Box 151
Bunbury WA 6230
Australia
BH: Clubhouse, Queens Gardens
Tel: +61 9721 3788
Email: stuart.brown@wapl.com.au

Collie River Rowing Club
55 Atkinson Street
Collie, WA 6225
Australia
BH: Minninup Pool
Minninup Road
Tel: +61 9734 7332
Fax: +61 9734 4505

Curtin University Rowing Club
31 Alsace Street
Manning 6152
Carine, WA 6020
Australia
www.curtin.edu.au/

ECU-Perth Rowing Club
PO Box 1020
Applecross W.A. 6153
Australia

Esperance Rowing Club
PO Box 398
Esperance, W.A. 6450
Australia

Fremantle Rowing Club
PO Box 557
Preston Point, Fremantle
East Fremantle, W.A. 6160
Australia
Tel/Fax: +61 9319 8222
BH: Riverside Road

Greenough Rowing Club
PO Box 332
Geraldton, W.A. 6531
Australia
Tel: +61 9965 2403
Email craig-joss@modnet.com.au

Murdoch University Rowing Club
PO Box 876A
Mt. Pleasant 6153
Canning Bridge, W.A. 6153
Australia
Tel: +61 93108252
Email: pear@iinet.net.au

Swan River Rowing Club
P.O. Box 823
Mt. Pleasant 6153
Australia
Tel/Fax: +61 9316 8812
www.srrc.org.au/

University Boat Club
c/o UWA Sports
Nedlands W.A. 6907
Australia
Tel/Fax: +61 9389 6375
Email: uwabc-committee@yahoogroups.com
www.uwarowing.org.au/

West Australian Rowing Club
PO Box 6772
East Perth, WA 6892
Australia
Tel: +61 9325 6525
Fax: +61 9325 4627
BH: Riverside Drive
www.warowingclub.org/

Austria

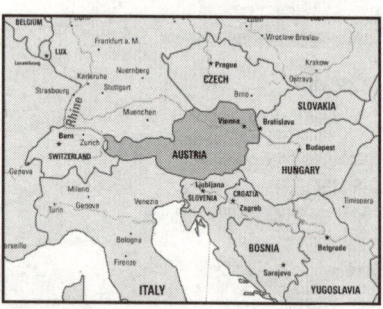

NATIONAL FEDERATION

Oesterreichischer Ruderverband
Blattgasse 4
Wien, 1030
Austria
Tel: +43 1 712 0878
Fax: +43 1 712 08784
Email: orv@asn.or.at
www.rudern.at

CLUBS (BY REGION)

WIEN

Wiener Ruderverband
Liesneckgasse 6/1
1210 Wien
Austria
Tel: +43 01/272 35 50
Fax: +43 01/272 35 50-4
Email: weba@concept2.at

Wiener Ruderclub Argonauten
Untere Alte Donau 21
1220 Wien
Austria
Tel: +43 01/ 283 59 11
Email: argowien@gmx.at
http://www.argowien.at

Wiener Ruderverein "Austria"
Kuchelauer Hafenstrasse 4
1190 Wien
Austria
Tel: +43 (0) 1 370 54 27
Email: hahn.apae@aon.at

Wiener Ruderclub Donaubund
Dampfschiffhaufen 14
1220 Wien
Austria
Tel: +43 0676-3194253
Email: christian.rutka@aon.at

Wiener Ruderverein Donauhort
Brigittenauer Sporn
1200 Wien
Austria
Email: guuu@gmx.net
http://www.donauhort.at/

Wiener Ruderklub Donau
Florian Berndlgasse 16 (Zufahrt)
1222 Wien
Austria
Tel: +43 01/ 203 62 32
Fax: +43 01/ 489 18 87
Email: wrk.donau@chello.at
http://www.wrkdonau.at.tt

Ruderverein Ellida
Florian Berndl-Gasse 10
(Untere Alte Donau 7)
1220 Wien
Austria
Tel: +43 01/ 220 89 50

Ruderverein Friesen
An der Unteren Alten Donau 47
1220 Wien
Austria
Tel: +43 01/ 204 71 71
http://www.rv-friesen.at

Erster Wiener Ruderclub "LIA"
Arminenstrasse 2
1220 Wien
Austria
Tel: +43 01/ 203 63 67
Email: info@lia.at
www.lia.at

Wiener-Ruder-Club Pirat
Am Kaisermühlendamm 92
1220 Wien
Austria
Tel: +43 01/ 263 34 17

Ruderverein STAW
Moissigasse 21
1223 Wien
Austria
Tel: +43 01/ 263 36 36
mail@ruderverein.at
http://www.ruderverein.at

NIEDERÖSTERREICH

Niederösterreichischer Ruderverband
Niederösterreichischer Ruderverband
p.A. Alfons Breitmeyer/Präsident
Heimkehrergasse 28
A-1100 Wien
Austria

Korneuburger Ruderverein Alemannia
Donaustraße 70
2100 Korneuburg
Austria
Tel: +43 02262/ 62 316
Email: Fuchsko@via.at
http://www.ruderverein-alemannia.at/

Ruderverein Nibelungen
Nibelungenlände 10
A-3400 Klosterneuburg
Austria
Email: obmann.nibelungen@aon.at
http://go.to/rvnibelungen

Ruderverein Normannen
Normannengasse 2
3400 Klosterneuburg
Austria
Tel: +43 02243/ 21 888
Email: kol@haaswaffel.at

Union Ruderverein Pöchlarn
Regensburger Strasse 16
3380 Pöchlarn
Austria
Email: Andreas.Trauner@Quarzwerke.at

Ruder-Union-Melk
Am Räcking 2
3390 Melk
Austria

Erster Wassersportverein Orth/Donau
Fadenbachstraße 6
2304 Orth a.d.Donau
Austria
Tel: +43 02212/ 31 57
Fax: +43 02212/ 29 63

Steiner Ruder-Club
Donaulände
Stein an der Donau
Austria
Tel: +43 (0) 2732 86501-25
Fax: +43 (0) 2732 74980
Email: steiner.rc@aon.at
http://members.aon.at/steiner.rc/

Tullner Ruderverein
Kronauer Strasse 8
3430 Tulln
Austria
Email: r_hauck@everyday.com
http://www.trv.at/

Wasser Sport Union Wachau Dürnstein
Postfach 1
3601 Dürnstein
Austria
Email: office@wsw.at
http://www.wsw.at/

Österreichische Sportunion Wallsee
Mag. Herbert Pallinger
Nr. 74
3313 Wallsee
Austria

OBERÖSTERREICH

Oberösterr. Landesruderverband
Postfach 299
4010 Linz
Austria

E.K.u. Ruderverein Donau Linz
Heilhamerweg 2
4040 Linz
Austria
Tel: +43 0732/ 73 62 50
Email: ssageder@hotmail.com
http://donaulinz.virtualave.net/

Gmundner Ruderverein
Dr. Franz Thomas-Straße 15
A — 4810 Gmunden
Austria
Tel: +43 0043/7612/64880
Email: gmundner.ruderverein@aon.at
www.gmundner-ruderverein.at

Linzer Ruderverein "ISTER"
Im Winterhafen 19
4020 Linz
Austria
Tel: +43 0732/ 77 48 88
Fax: +43 0732/ 380481 11
Email: ransmayr@ransmayr.at
www.ister.at

Ruderclub Mondsee
Seebadstraße
(zwischen Seebad und Segelschule)
5310 Mondsee
Austria
Email: fritschf@ping.at

Wassersportverein Ottensheim
Rodlstrasse 21
4100 Ottensheim
Austria
Email: wsv@ottensheim.at
wsv.ottensheim.at/RUDERN/ruder_index.htm

Racing Club Linz
Am Winterhafen 27
4020 Linz
Austria

Ruderverein Seewalchen
Promenade
4863 Seewalchen
Austria

Ruderverein Steyr 1888
Rennbahnweg
4400 Steyr
Austria
Tel: +43 07252/ 850 50

Ruderclub Wels
Prielstrasse 2
A-4600 Wels
Austria
Email: office@ruderclub.wels.or.at
http://www.ruderclub.wels.or.at

Ruderverein Wiking Linz
Wilheringerstraße 10
4048 Puchenau
Austria
Tel: +43 0732 / 221066
Email: ruderverein.wikinglinz@liwest.at
http://www.geocities.com/rv_wiking/

Österreichischer Zillensportverband
Jedleseer Straße 79/10/12
1210 Wien
Austria

BURGENLAND

Bgld. Ruderclub Breitenbrunn
Seebad
7091 Breitenbrunn
Austria

STEIERMARK

Erster Steirischer Ruderclub Ausseerland
Schachensiedlung
8993 Grundlsee
Austria
Email: ruderclub@utanet.at
http://www.8ung.at/ruderclub

KÄRNTEN

Klagenfurter Ruderverein "Albatros"
Friedlstrand 11
9020 Klagenfurt
Austria
Tel: +43 0463/ 246 221
Email: willy.koska@wkk.or.at
http://www.rv-albatros.at

Ruderverein Nautilus v. 1878
Friedlstrand 21
9020 Klagenfurt
Austria
Tel: +43 0463/21232
Email: Nautilus@connect.to
http://soulweb.com/nautilus

SALZBURG

Salzburger Ruderklub "MOEVE"
Rupertiweg 13
5201 Seekirchen
Austria
Tel: +43 662 88969 4116
Fax: +43 662 88969 84
Email: salzburger-ruderklub@free.pages.at
http://free.pages.at/salzburger-ruderklub/

Ruder Club Wolfgangsee
Mondseestr.14
5340 St. Gilgen
Austria
Tel: +43 06227/2416
Fax: +43 06227/241618
Email: noppi@sport2000.at

VORARLBERG

Ruderverein Wiking Bregenz
Strandweg 40
A-6900 Bregenz
Austria
Tel: +43 05574/ 78066
Fax: +43 05574/ 86836
Email: rv-wiking@vol.at
http://www.rv-wiking.at

Azerbaijan

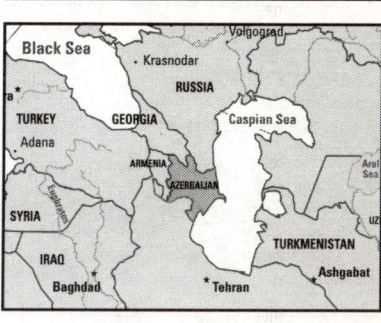

NATIONAL FEDERATION

Azerbaijan Rowing Federation
c/o National Olympic Committee of Azerbaijan Republic
21 Yousif Saforov Str
Baki, 370025
Azerbaijan
Tel: +994 12 901323
Fax: +994 12 930485

Bahrain

NATIONAL FEDERATION

Bahrain Maritime Sports Association
PO Box 11622
Manama
Bahrain
Tel: +973 310 252
Fax: +973 310 252

Bangladesh

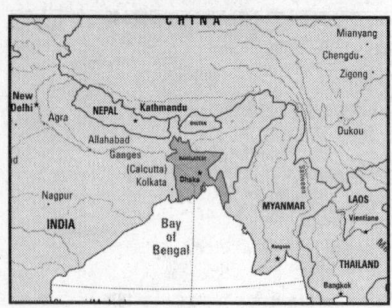

NATIONAL FEDERATION

Bangaldesh Rowing Federation
Bangabandhu National Stadium
Gate 3 - 2nd Floor
Dhaka, 1000
Bangladesh
Tel: +880 2 831 79 11

Barbados

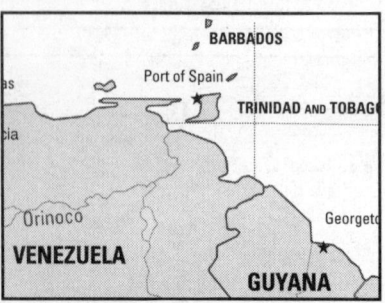

NATIONAL FEDERATION

Barbados Yachting Association
PO Box 40
Bridgetown
Barbados
Tel: (246) 435-6548
Fax: (246) 435-6939

Belarus

NATIONAL FEDERATION

Belarusian Rowing Federation
Surganova Str. 2
Minsk, 220012
Belarus
Tel: +375 172 39 88 61
Fax: +375 172 66 46 14
Email: Haiduk_valeri@tut.by

CLUBS

Dinamo Rowing Club
25 Artema str.
Gomel, Belarus
Tel: +375 232 442462

Dinamo Rowing Club
23 Daumana str.
Minsk, Belarus
Tel: +375 172 345804

Gomel Town Rowing Club
25 Artema str.
Gomel, Belarus
Tel: +375 232 559088

Gomselmash Rowing Club
49 Kosmonavtov Ave.
Gomel, Belarus
Tel: +375 232 548931

Lakokraska Rrowing Club
3 Kirova Str.
Lida, Grodno Region
Belarus
Tel: +375 1561 23309

Minsk City Rowing Club
3a Naberezhnaya Str.
Minsk, Belarus
Tel: +375 172 269065

Mogilev Town Rowing Club
1a Bolshaya Chausskaya Str.
Mogilev, Belarus
Tel: +375 222 444474

Pinsk Town Rowing Club
22 Pankovoi Str.
Pinsk, Brest Region
Belarus
Tel: +375 271 58735

Polotsk Town Rowing Club
10A Streletskaya Str.
Polotsk, Vitebsk Region
Belarus
Tel: +375 2144 45362

Spartak Rowing Club
2 1/1 Krasnoflotskaya str.
Brest, Belarus
Tel: +375 162 54514

Spartak Rowing Club
Zavodskaya Str.
Mogilev, Belarus
Tel: +375 222 253729

Sport Rowing Club
2 Poselok Maliavki Str.
Minsk, Belarus
Tel: +375 172 498135

Zenit Rowing Club
26 Chapaeva Str.
Vileika, Minsk Region
Belarus

Belgium

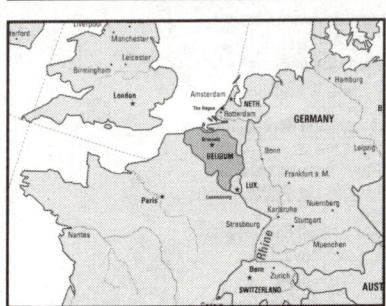

NATIONAL FEDERATION

Belgium Rowing Federation
84/61, quai de la Boverie
4020 Liège
Belgium
Tel: +32 04/342 10 75
Fax: +32 04/342 10 75
Email: riverm@skynet.be

CLUBS (BY REGION)

BRUSSELS

Royal Sport Nautique de Brussels asbl 1865
170, chaussée de Vilvorde
1120 Brussels
Belgium
Tel: +32 02/268 12 36
Fax: +32 02/268 12 36

Union Nautique de Brussels asbl 1874
172, chaussée de Vilvorde
1120 Brussels
Belgium
Tel: +32 02/268 12 37

Cercle des Régates de Brussels asbl 1878
65, quai de Veeweyde
1070 Brussels
Belgium
Tel: +32 02/523 04 78
Email: roger.polspoel@belgacom.be

Sport Nautique Universitaire de Brussels asbl 1911
65, quai de Veeweyde
1070 Brussels
Belgium
Tel: +32 02/523 04 78

HENEGOUWEN

Royal Club Nautique de Tournai asbl 1908
Chemin de Halage
7640 Maubray
Belgium
Tel: +32 069/22 70 81

Club d'Aviron "Les 3Y" asbl 1973
Chemin de Halage
7640 Maubray
Belgium
Tel: +32 069/22 70 81

LUIK

Royal Sport Nautique de le Meuse asbl 1860
3, rue de la Marlette
7180 Seneffe
Belgium
Tel: +32 02/384 05 35

Union Nautique de Liège asbl 1873
2, parc de la Boverie
4020 Liege
Belgium
Tel: +32 04/343 80 31
Fax: +32 04/343 80 31

Royal Cercle Athlétique des Etudiants asbl 1968
Section RCAE-ULG Aviron, 1
parc de la Boverie
4020 Liege
Belgium
Tel: +32 04/226 23 11

NAMEN

Royal Club Nautique Sambre et Meuse asbl 1862
11, chemin des Pruniers 11
5100 Wepion
Belgium
Tel: +32 081/46 11 30

Royal Cercle Nautique Dinantais asbl 1865
25, quai J.B.Culot
5500 Dinant
Belgium
Tel: +32 082/22 42 39

Brazil

NATIONAL FEDERATION

Confederaçao Brasileira de Remo
Estádio de Remo da Lagoa
Av. Borges de Medeiros 1424
Rio de Janeiro, 22470-000
Brazil
Tel: +55 21 2294 3342
Fax: +55 21 2294 3342
Email: cbr_remo@infolink.com.br
www.cbr-remo.com.br

CLUBS (BY REGION)

BAHIA

Esporte Clube Vitória
Av. Otávio Mangabeira, 3.900
Jardim Armação
Salvador, 41.750-970
Brazil
Tel: +55 (71) 362-0394
Fax: +55 (71) 362-0394
Email: vitoria@ecvitoria.com.br
www.ecvitoria.com.br

Clube de Regatas Itapagipe
Praça General Justo, 05
Ribeira
Salvador, 40.420-270
Brazil
Tel: +55 (71) 316-1073
Fax: +55 (71) 316-9480

Esporte Clube Santa Cruz
Av. Mem de Sá, 62
Ribeira
Salvador, 40.420-250
Brazil
Tel: +55 (71) 341-2956
Fax: +55 (71) 341-2956

Clube de Natação E Regatas São Salvador
Av. Mem de Sá, 16
Ribeira
Salvador, 40420-240
Brazil
Tel: +55 (71) 314-2507
Fax: +55 (71) 331-2789
Email: saosalvador@bol.com.br
saosalvador.cjb.net

AMAZONAS

Associação Atlética Ifilt
Rua Dona Libania, 300
Centro
Manaus, 69000-000
Brazil
Tel: +55 (92) 234-1676

BRASILIA

Academia de Remo Cadu
Distrito Federal
Brazil
Tel: +55 (61) 233-3689

Clube Naval de Brasília
Sces Trecho 2 Lotes 6a/6b
Brasília
Distrito Federal, 70.200-000
Brazil
Tel: +55 (61) 321-4332
Fax: +55 (61) 322-9430

Minas Brasília Tênis Clube
Setor de Clubes Esportivos Norte
Lote 3a/3b Bloco MBTC
Brasília
Distrito Federal, 70.800-200
Brazil
Tel: +55 (61) 347-9559
Fax: +55 (61) 347-4761

Associação Atlética Banco de Brasília
Sces Trecho 1 Conjunto 3
Brasília
Distrito Federal, 71000-000
Brazil
Tel: +55 (61) 244-1642
Fax: +55 (61) 242-2628

Associação Atlética Banco do Brasil
Sces Trecho 2 Lotes 5/8
Brasília
Distrito Federal, 70.200-000
Brazil
Tel: +55 (61) 223-0078
Fax: +55 (61) 223-0897

ESPIRITO SANTO

Clube de Natação E Regatas "Álvares Cabral"
Av. Marechal Mascarenhas de Moraes, 2.100
Bento Ferreira
Vitória
Espírito Santo, 29.052-120
Brazil
Tel: +55 (27) 3324-0101
Fax: +55 (27) 3324-0101

Clube de Regatas Saldanha da Gama
Av. Mar. Mascarenhas de Moraes S/Nº
Forte São João
Vitória
Espírito Santo, 29010-330
Brazil
Tel: +55 (27) 3222-8435
Fax: +55 (27) 3222-8220

Clube Náutico Brasil
Av. Santo Antônio, 111
Santo Antonio
Vitória
Espírito Santo, 29.025-000
Brazil
Tel: +55 (27) 3223-6796

Associação Desportiva Ferroviária do Vale do Rio Doce
Vitória
Espírito Santo
Brazil
Tel: +55 (27) 3226-1109

PARÁ

Clube do Remo
Av. Nazaré, 962
Belém
Pará, 66.035-170
Brazil
Tel: +55 (91) 225-1542
Fax: +55 (91) 225-1542

Paysandú Sport Club
Av. Nazaré, 404
Belém
Pará, 66.035-170
Brazil
Tel: +55 (91) 241-9367
Fax: +55 (91) 241-9367

Tuna Luso Brasileira
Av. Almirante Barroso, 4110
Belém
Pará, 66.610-000
Brazil
Tel: +55 (91) 231-6415/5624/0999
Fax: +55 (91) 231-6416

PARANÁ

Clube de Regatas Y-Guaçu de Remo
Galpão de Remo do Parque Náutico do Iguaçu
Boqueirão, Curitiba
Paraná
Brazil
Tel: +55 (41) 344-9114
Fax: +55 (41) 283-1162

Clube de Natação E Regatas Comandante Santa Rita
Rua Benjamin Constant, Nº 05
Centro Histórico
Paranaguá
Paraná, 83203-190
Brazil
Tel: +55 (41) 252-5252
Email: singlebras@lg.com.br

Base Nautica de Tres Lagoas
Av: João Ricieri Maran, S/N.
Foz do Iguaçu
Paraná
Brazil
Tel: +55 (45) 526-7677
Fax: +55 (45) 523-4223

Distrito Administrativo de Cachoeira do Espírito Santo
R Cel. Emilio Gomes, 731
Prainha da Cachoeira
Ribeirão Claro
Paraná, 86.410-000
Brazil
Tel: +55 (43) 536-1144
Fax: +55 (43) 536-1222

Base Náutica de Santa Helena
Av: Paraná, 1921
Paraná, 85.892-000
Brazil
Tel: +55 (045) 9974-8951
Fax: +55 (45) 268-1138

Parque Náutico do Iguaçu
Curitiba, Paraná
Brazil
Tel: +55 (41) 344-9114

PERNAMBUCO

Clube Náutico Capibaribe
Av. Conselheiro Rosa E Silva, 1086
Recife
Pernambuco, 52050-020
Brazil
Tel: +55 (81) 473-8900
Fax: +55 (81) 473-8900

Sport Clube do Recife
Praça da Bandeira, S/Nº
Madalena
Recife
Pernambuco, 50.750-221
Brazil
Tel: +55 (81) 227-1213
Fax: +55 (81) 227-1213

Clube Esportivo Almirante Barroso
Av. Conselheiro Rosa E Silva, 1086
Aflitos, Recife
Pernambuco, 52050-000
Brazil
Tel: +55 (81) 222-2452

RIO DE JANEIRO

Clube de Regatas Piraquê
Av. Borges de Medeiros, 1424 - Box 7
Rio de Janeiro, 22.470-000
Brazil
Tel: +55 (21) 2512-0980
Email: crpiraque@olimpo.cm.br
webspace.com.br/crpiraque

Grêmio Náutico Marapendi
Av. Prefeito Dulcídio Cardoso, 400
Barra da Tijuca
Rio de Janeiro
Brazil
Tel: +55 (21) 2509-8782

Clube de Regatas Guanabara
Av. Repórter Nestor Moreira, 42
Botafogo
Rio de Janeiro, 22.290-210
Brazil
Tel: +55 (21) 2295-2597
Fax: +55 (21) 2275-1796

Clube de Regatas do Flamengo
Av. Borges de Medeiros
Rio de Janeiro, 22.430-040\
Brazil
Tel: +55 (21) 2529-0100
Fax: +55 (21) 2529-0111
flamengo.com.br

Club de Regatas Vasco da Gama
R. General Almério de Moura, 131
São Cristóvão
Rio de Janeiro, 20.921-060
Brazil
Tel: +55 (21) 2580-7373
Fax: +55 (21) 2580-0488
Email: crvgremo@infolink.com.br
www.crvasco.com.br

Grêmio de Vela Escola Naval
Av. Almirante Silvio de Noronha
S/Nº - Ilha de Villegagnon
Castelo
Rio de Janeiro, 20021-010
Brazil
Tel: +55 (21) 2292-1252
Fax: +55 (21) 2240-7828

Botafogo de Futebol E Regatas
Av. Venceslau Brás, 72
Botafogo
Rio de Janeiro, 22.290-140
Brazil
Tel: +55 (21) 2543-7272
Fax: +55 (21) 2543-8387
Email: sede@botafogofr.com.br

Clube de Natação E Regatas Campista
Av. XV de Novembro, 25 A 29
Centro
Campos dos Goytacazes
Rio de Janeiro, 28010-550
Brazil
Tel: +55 (24) 722-3629
Fax: +55 (24) 722-3629
Email: mlemos@rol.com.br

Yacht Club Lagoa de Cima
Rua dr. Sampaio, 39
Caju
Campos dos Goytacazes
Rio de Janeiro, 28050-210
Brazil
Tel: +55 (022) 2732-9340
Fax: +55 (022) 2734-3007
Email: lagoayacht@ig.com.br

RIO GRANDE DO NORTE

Sport Club de Natal
R. Chile, 70
Ribeira
Natal, 59.012-250
Brazil
Tel: +55 (84) 221-6259
Fax: +55 (84) 221-6259

ABC Futebol Clube
Av. Senador Salgado Filho, 1535
Tirol, Natal
Rio Grande do Norte, 59.016-000
Brazil
Tel: +55 (84) 222-0949

América Futebol Clube (América de Natal)
Av. Rodrigues Alves, 950
Tirol, Natal
Rio Grande do Norte, 59.020-200
Brazil
Tel: +55 (84) 212-1301
Fax: +55 (84) 212-2352

CENTRO NÁUTICO POTENGI
R. Chile, 38
Ribeira, Natal
Rio Grande do Norte, 59.012-250
Brazil
Tel: +55 (84) 221-3145
Fax: +55 (84) 221-3145

Clube de Regatas Vasco da Gama - Porto Alegre
Av. Mauá, 8590
Navegantes
Porto Alegre
Rio Grande do Sul, 90.230-270
Brazil
Tel: +55 (51) 3342-1631
Fax: +55 (51) 3342-1631

Clube Náutico Gaúcho
R. Bento Martins, 2
Pelotas
Rio Grande do Sul
Brazil
Tel: +55 (51) 3322-4867

Clube de Regatas Almirante Barroso
Av. João Moreira Maciel, 580
Porto Alegre
Rio Grande do Sul, 90250-680
Brazil
Tel: +55 (051) 3342-2762
Fax: +55 (051) 224-7886

Grêmio Náutico Tamandaré
Rio Grande do Sul
Brazil

Grêmio Foot-Ball Porto Alegrense
Largo dos Campeões, Nº 1
Porto Alegre
Rio Grande do Sul, 90.880-440
Brazil
Tel: +55 (51) 223-9188
Fax: +55 (51) 223-9383

SAO PAULO

Clube Esperia
Av. Santos Dumont, 1313
São Paulo, 02.012-010
Brazil
Tel: +55 (11) 6221-2344
Fax: +55 (11) 6221-7563
Email: atendimento@esperia.com.br
www.esperia.com.br

Clube de Regatas Bandeirante
Estrada Luiz Pasteur, 230
Embú
São Paulo, 06.835-080
Brazil
Fax: +55 (11) 4785-2768

Sport Club Corinthians Paulista
R. São Jorge, 777
Parque São Jorge
São Paulo, 03.087-000
Brazil
Tel: +55 (11) 6942-9633
Fax: +55 (11) 6941-3417

Centro de Práticas Esportivas da Univ de São Paulo
Praça 02 - Prof. Rubião Meira,
61- Cidade Universitária
Butantã
São Paulo, 05.508-900
Brazil
Tel: +55 (11) 818-3555
Fax: +55 (11) 814-2278
Email: cepeusp@org.usp.br
www.usp.br/cepe

Clube de Regatas Vasco da Gama - Sp
Av. Almirante Saldanha da Gama 33/35
São Paulo, 11.030-400
Brazil
Tel: +55 (11) 3236-2810
Fax: +55 (11) 3236-2810
Email: crvascodagamabr@yahoo.com.br

Club Athlético Paulistano
Rua Honduras, 1400
São Paulo, 01428-900
Brazil
Tel: +55 (11) 3065-2000
Fax: +55 (11) 3065-2000

Clube Atlético Ypiranga
Rua do Manifesto, 475
São Paulo, 04209-000
Brazil
Tel: +55 (11) 273-9922
Fax: +55 (11) 272-2956

SANTA CATARINA

Clube Náutico Francisco Martinelli
Parque Náutico Aterro Baía Sul
Centro, Florianópolis
Santa Catarina, 88.010-280
Brazil
Tel: +55 (48) 222-7792
Fax: +55 (48) 222-7792
www.martinellihp.kit.net

Clube de Regatas Aldo Luz
Rua Osni João Vieira, 21 - 3º Andar Sala 317
Campinas, São José
Santa Catarina, 88101-270
Brazil
Tel: +55 (48) 2224-9140
Fax: +55 (48) 2241-2233

Clube Náutico Riachuelo
Av. Antônio Pereira Oliveira Neto S/Nº - Garagem 1
Centro, Florianópolis
Santa Catarina, 88.010-280
Brazil
Tel: +55 (48) 223-5157

Clube Náutico América
Rua 15 de Novembro, 74
Centro, Blumenau
Santa Catarina, 89.010-000
Brazil
Tel: +55 (47) 376-6613

SERGIPE
Cotinguiba Esporte Clube
Av. Augusto Maynard, 13
São José, Aracajú
Sergipe, 49.015-380
Brazil
Tel: +55 (79) 214-6267
Fax: +55 (79) 214-6267

Bulgaria

HISTORY

Although the history of rowing in Bulgaria can be traced back to the mid-seventh century, the sport became popular after the end of the 500-year period of Ottoman rule. In the late nineteenth century, rowing became part of the formal training of the Bulgarian Navy and the first rowing competition was held between students of the Naval Academy. This marked the beginning of competitive rowing in Bulgaria.

With the founding of athletic clubs in Varna, Russe, and Veliko Turnovo from 1889-1892, and navy athletic leagues from 1920-1924, the popularity of rowing spread rapidly over Bulgaria making it a favorite sport.

On August 19, 1924, in the seaside town of Bourgas, the first official national regatta triggering an interest in rowing took place. The end of World War II was the start of an official national championship. Bulgaria became a member of FISA in 1955 and a year later Bulgarian rowers made their debut at the European Championships in Bled with remarkable performances in the men's pair with coxswain and men's single. Bulgarian rowing gained international recognition at the 1967 European Championships in Vichy, France with victories in women's quadruple sculls with coxswain and the men's double sculls.

Although rowing in Bulgaria has had to undergo significant changes due to the economic and political changes in early 1990's, it continues to be a leading power in the international arena. Rowing in Bulgaria enjoys tremendous popularity and is equally appreciated by men and women. Every year scouts recruit many teenagers giving them the opportunity to develop their talent with the help of highly qualified coaches and excellent training facilities.

REGIONS

Twenty-eight regions make up Bulgaria. The most prominent rowing centers are in Sofia, Plovdiv, Russe and Varna. Due to the mild continental climate, rowing is possible from March through November with the exception of regions at high elevation.

PERSONALITIES

Svetla Otzetova and Zdravka Yordanova: Olympic gold medallists in 1972 and World Championship bronze medallists in 1980 in the women's double sculls.

Magdalena Georgieva: World Champion in 1987 and 1988 Olympic bronze medallist in the women's single scull.

Siya Kelbecheva and Stoyanka Gruicheva: Olympic Champions in the women's pair in 1976 and 1980.

Violeta Nonova and Stefka Madina: World Champions in 1987 and 1988 Olympic bronze medallists in the women's double sculls.

Vassil Radev: 1987 World Champion in the men's double sculls.

Today, Bulgaria is proud to be represented by some of the strongest scullers in the world: Rumyana Neikova (W1x), Victoria Dimitrova (LW1x) and Ivo Yanakiev (M1x).

Did You Know ?

Plovdiv, Bulgaria has one of the most modern rowing facilities in the world. The Olympic, man-made rowing canal hosts numerous national and international events.

NATIONAL FEDERATION

Bulgarian Rowing Federation
75 "Vasil Levski" Boulevard
Sofia, 1040
Bulgaria
Contact: Mitko Kolev
Tel: +359 2 981 6577
Fax: +359 2 981 5728
Email: rowing_bg@abv.bg

CLUBS

Bulgarian Rowing Federation
75 Vasil Levsky Blvd
1040 Sofia, Bulgaria
contact: Mitko Kolev, President
Tel/Fax: +359-2-981 6577
Email: rowing@bgnet.bg

Academic Rowing Club
L.C. Geo Milev Bl. 3-A
1330, Sofia
Bulgaria

Academic Plovdiv Rowing Club
BL. 524, entrance A, app.3
1000, Sofia
Bulgaria

Black Sea Rowing Club
Nr.9, Nikoloa Vaptzarov Str.
9000, Varna
Bulgaria

CSKA Rowing Club
l.c. Drouzhba 1, bl.37, entrance E, app.20
1592, Sofia
Bulgaria

Electron Rowing Club
2116, Pravetz
Bulgaria

Hebros Rowing Club
Sporten complexGrebna baza, Kulata
4003, Plovdiv
Bulgaria
Tel: +359 32 65 08 58
Fax: +359 32 65 08 18
Email: teamc@plov.omega.bg
www.grebane.hit.bg

Levski Rowing Club
Nr. 21,11th August Str.
1000, Sofia
Bulgaria

Locomotiv Rowing Club
Nr.13-a, Petko D. Petkov Str.
7000, Rouse
Bulgaria

Lukoil Rowing Club
L.C.Bratia Miladinovi Bl. 56
Entrance B, App. 9
8000 Bourgas
Bulgaria

NSA - V. Boianov Rowing Club
Nr. 59shipchenski Prohod, Bl. 262 - A
Entrance B, App.42
1111 Sofia
Bulgaria

Spartac Rowing Club
Nr. 52, Benkovski Str., entrance B, app.19
5800, Sofia
Bulgaria

Trakia Rowing Club
Nr. 21, Makedonia Str.
4000, Plovdiv
Bulgaria

Vaptzarov Rowing Club
Nr. 6, Ribarska Str.
8130, Sozopol
Bulgaria

Burkina Faso

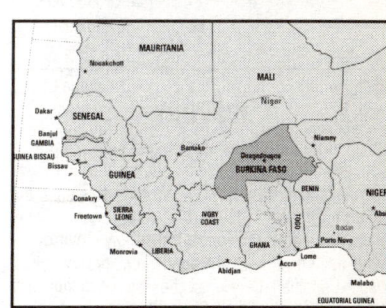

NATIONAL FEDERATION

Burkina Rowing Federation
BP 2714
Ouagadougou
Burkina Faso
Tel: +226 35 92 92
Fax: +226 35 92 92
Email: horizonfm@fasonet.bf

Cameroon

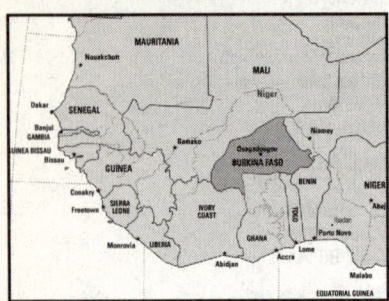

NATIONAL FEDERATION

Fédération Camerounaise des Sports Nautiques
B.P. 4434
Douala
Cameroon
Tel: +237 427703

Canada

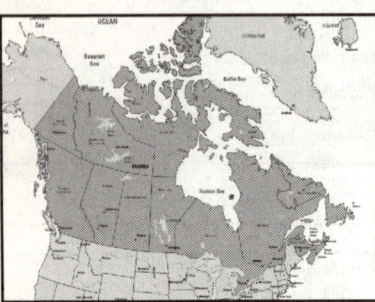

HISTORY

Long before Canadians participated in the Olympics, Canada's professional scullers dominated the international scene. Ned Hanlan, World Champion in the single scull from 1880 to 1884, was a small sinewy man whose ability to out-perform many larger opponents gained admiration around the world. His coach, also a Canadian, developed the original sliding seat. A long list of prominent Canadian scullers followed Hanlan, including Jake Gaudaur and Lou Scholes.

Until recently, amateur rowing has maintained a relatively low profile. Canada's success at the 1984 Olympics increased interest in the sport and resulted in the introduction of learn-to-row and recreational rowing programs at many clubs. These programs have enjoyed a great deal of success over the years as more people have become captivated by the sport.

Recent outstanding performances of Silken Laumann, Marnie McBean, Kathleen Heddle, the Canadian rowing team's gold medals in the men's and women's eights at the 1992 Olympic Games, has done a great deal to increase awareness and create excitement for the sport.

INTERNET LINKS
www.rowingcanada.org
www.rowbc.org
www.rowontario.ca
www.rowmanitoba.ca
www.avironquebec.ca
www.henleyregatta.ca

REGIONS

Canada has ten provinces, nine of which have club rowing programs and provincial associations. British Columbia has the mildest climate and therefore the longest rowing season. In most other regions, rowing is mainly confined to the spring, summer and fall seasons.

Did You Know ?

Marnie McBean has won World or Olympic medals in every boat class open to heavyweight women. She and her rowing partner, Kathleen Heddle, were the first Canadians to win three gold medals at summer Olympic Games; two in 1992 and one in 1996.

NATIONAL FEDERATION

Rowing Canada
NOTC Venture PO Box 17 000
STN Forces
Victoria, BC V9A 7N2
Canada
Tel: (250) 361-4222
Fax: (250) 361-4211
Email: comm@rowingcanada.org
www.rowingcanada.org

CLUBS

Alma Rowing Club/Club d'Aviron Alma
241 rue Durocher
Alma, QC G8B 3T7
Canada
Tel: (418) 668-3507
Fax: (418) 662-3468

Argonaut Rowing Club
1225 Lakeshore Boulevard West
Toronto, ON M6K 3C1
Canada
Tel: (416) 532-2803
Fax: (416) 532-2804
Email: info@argonautrowingclub.com
http://www.argonautrowingclub.com/

Barrie Rowing Club
PO Box 21071
Barrie, ON L4M 6J7
Canada
Tel: (705) 739-0874

Bayside Rowing Club
#405 - 1071 King Street W.
Toronto, ON M6K 3K2
Canada
Tel: (416) 345-9175

Boucherville Rowing Club
330 D'Avaugour
Boucherville, QC J4B 1A3
Canada
Tel: (450) 670-0730 poste 476
Email: serge_cote@csmv.qc.ca

Brockville Rowing Club
PO Box 112
Brockville, ON K6V 5T7
Canada
Tel: (613) 342-4849

Burnaby Lake Rowing Club
640 St Georges Avenue
North Vancouver, BC V7L 4S4
Canada
Tel: (604) 984-6014
Fax: (604) 984-6019

Burnstown Rowing Club
Arnprior, ON
Canada
Tel: (613) 623-7939

Bytown Boat Club
11 Morris Street
Ottawa, ON K1H 6V3
Canada
Tel: (613) 235-4105

Calgary Rowing Club
PO Box 36117
6449 Crowchild Terrace SW
Calgary, AB T3E 7C6
Canada
Tel: (403) 249-2880

Cambridge Rowing Club
31- 130 Cedar Street
PO Box 211
Cambridge, ON N1S 1A5
Canada
Tel: (519) 658-9963

Chambly Rowing Club/Club d'Aviron Chambly
Laurent Perreault
Chambly, QC J3B 7Z9
Canada
Tel: (450) 447-9054

Club Richelieu
165 Bessette
Iberville, QC J2X 2N3
Canada
Tel: (514) 994-0157

Crocus Coulee Rowing Society
Box 923
Hanna, AB T0J 1P0
Canada
Tel: (403) 854-5197

Delta Deas Rowing Club
PO Box 1084
Delta, BC V4M 3T2
Canada
Tel: (604) 946-3074

Durham Rowing Club
PO Box 62131
Oshawa, ON L1K 1K0
Canada
Tel: (905) 259-ROWW
Email: row@durham.net
http://www.durhamrowing.on.ca

Eagle Boat Club
715 Cordova Bay Road
Victoria, BC V8Y 1P7
Canada
Tel: (604) 658-4942
Email: eagleboatclub@primus.ca

Edmonton Rowing Club
Box 52002 Garneau Stn.
Edmonton, AB T6G 2T5
Canada
Tel: (403) 484-6946

Fort McMurray Rowing Club
PO Box 5931
Fort McMurray, AB T9H 4V9
Canada
Tel: (403) 791-4594

Fraser Valley Rowing Club
39000 Quadling Rd
Abbortsford, BC V3G 2T3
Canada
Tel: (604) 823-6580

Fredericton Rowing Club
Woodstock Road
Fredericton, NB
Canada
Tel: (506) 453-9428
http://www.f2000p.org/fredericton

Georgian Bay Rowing Club
PO Box 815
Midland, ON L4R 4P4
Canada
Tel: (705) 527-1995

Gorge Rowing and Paddling Centre
2940 Jutland Road
Victoria, BC V8T 5K6
Canada
Tel: (250) 380-4669
http://www.f2000p.org/gorge

Halifax Rowing Club
PO Box 62
Founder's Square
Halifax, NS B3J 3J7
Canada
Tel: (902) 423-0323

Hanlan Boat Club
98 Teddington Park
Toronto, ON M4N 2C8
Canada
Tel: (416) 483-4510

Humber Valley Rowing Club
General Delivery
Pasadena, NF A0L 1K0
Canada
Fax: (709) 634-4474
Email: humbervalleyrowingclub@yahoo.com
http://www.humberrowing.8m.com/

James Bay Athletic Association
C/O Deb Taylor - Treasurer
1525 Regents Place
Victoria, BC V8S 1Y5
Canada
Email: JBAA_RC@hotmail.com

Kamloops Rowing Club
PO Box 1353
Kamloops, BC V2C 6L7
Canada
Tel: (250) 828-2110

Kennebecasis Rowing Club
RPO 21
2055 Rothesay Road
Renforth, NB E2H 2K0
Canada
Tel: (506) 847-5803
Email: rowkrc@nb.sympatico.ca
www.geocities.com/kvhs/sports/rowing.htm

Kenora Rowing Club
PO Box 264
Kenora, ON P9N 3X3
Canada
Tel: (807) 548-6183

Kingston Rowing Club
PO Box 1016
Kingston, OR K7L 4X8
Canada
Tel: (613) 542-4767

Labrador West Rowing Association
828 D'aigle Cres.
Labrador City, NF A2V 2E4
Canada
Tel: (709) 944-3109
Fax: (709) 944-7151

Lachine Rowing Club
2901 bld St. Joseph
Lachine, QC J7A 3N2
Canada
Tel: (514) 637-4110
Fax: (514) 938-7750
Email: chauss@ca.ibm.com
http://www.avironlachine.ca

Lake Louise Rowing Club
Box 344
Lake Louise, AB T0L 1E0
Canada
Tel: (403) 522-2192
Email: lakelouiserc@hotmail.com

Lake Windermere Rowing Club
29B Black Forest Heights
Invermere, BC V0A 1K0
Canada
Tel: (250) 342-6172

LaSalle Rowing Club
40 Laurier Drive
LaSalle, ON N9J 3L4
Canada
Email: rowlasalle@altavista.com
http://members.tripod.ca/lasallerowing

Laval Rowing Club
3781 Boul. Levesque
Laval, QC H7L 1G5
Canada
Tel: (514) 697-3751

Leander Boat Club
LCD1 PO BOX 1034
Hamilton, ON L8N 3R4
Canada
Tel: (905) 527-7377

London Rowing Club
PO Box 8088
Subst. 41
London, ON N6G 2B0
Canada
Tel: (519) 472-1980

London Rowing Society
155 Commissioners Road E
London, ON N6C 2S9
Canada
Tel: (519) 661-2087

Maple Bay Rowing Club
6735 Beaumont Avenue
Duncan, BC V9L 5X4
Canada
Tel: (250) 748-7231

Mic Mac Aquatic Club
192 Prince Albert Road
Dartmouth, NS B2Y 3Z5
Canada
Tel: (902) 464-9480

Montreal Rowing Club
Bassin Olympique Circuit Gilles Villeneuve
Parc Jean Drapeau
Montreal, QC H3C 1A9
Canada
Tel: (514) 861-8959

Muskoka Rowing Club
Box 784
Bracebridge, ON P1L 1V1
Canada
Tel: (705) 645-4614

Nanaimo Rowing Club
4295 Victoria Avenue
PO Box 946 Stn. A
Nanaimo, BC V9R 5N2
Canada
Tel: (250) 754-7746

Nelson Rowing Club
1802 Ft. Sheppard Drive
Nelson, BC V1L 5P5
Canada
Tel: (250) 352-2652

New Edinburgh Rowing Club (Ottawa)
PO Box 74088/CP74088
Ottawa, ON K1M 2H9
Canada
Tel: (613) 722-1197

North Shore Rowing Club
766 Huntington Crescent
Deep Cove, BC V7G 1M3
Canada
Tel: (604) 929-6316

North Star Rowing Club
5 Erin Drive
Dartmouth, NS B2W 2B9
Canada
Tel: (902) 434-5896

Norway House White Caps
PO Box 307
Norway House, MB R0B 1B0
Canada
Tel: (204) 359-4551

Orillia Rowing Club
PO Box 981
Orillia, ON L3V 6K8
Canada
Tel: (705) 325-4039

Ottawa Rowing Club
PO Box 1457 Stn. B
Ottawa, ON K1P 5P9
Canada
Tel: (613) 241-1120

Ottawa Valley Rowing Club
50 Seymour Street
Arnprior, ON K7S 1R3
Canada
Tel: (613) 623-8648

Owen Sound Rowing Club
ON, Canada
Tel: (519) 376-5325

Peterborough Rowing Club
PO Box 1403
Peterborough, ON K9J 7H6
Canada
Tel: (705) 748-0462

Pinawa Sailing & Rowing Club
Box 591
Willis Drive
Pinawa, MB R0R 1L0
Canada
Tel: (204) 753-2492

Prarie Fire Rowing Centre
192 Oustic Avenue
Winnipeg, MB R2M 1N3
Canada
Tel: (204) 253-6804
Fax: (204) 253-9131
Email: pfire@escape.ca

Prince Albert Drifters Rowing Club
825 4th Street E
Prince Albert, SK S6V 0K6
Canada
Tel: (306) 922-0427

Queen's University Rowing
Physical Education Centre
Kingston, ON K7L 3N6
Canada
Tel: (613) 542-4767

Quinte Rowing Club
35 Keegan Parkway
Belleville, ON K8N 5R1
Canada
Tel: (613) 969-0171

Radisson Rowing Club d'Aviron
170 chemin de la Riviere
Wakefield, QC J0X 3G0
Canada
Tel: (819) 459-3860

RCS Netherwood Rowing Club
Rothesay, NB E0G 2W0
Canada
Tel: (506) 847-8224

Regina Rowing Club
PO Box 1246
Stn. Main
Regina, SK S4P 3B8
Canada
Tel: (306) 777-0632

Ridley Graduate Boat Club
5 Swan Drive
St. Catharines, ON L2T 2C2
Canada
Tel: (905) 646-4734

Rowing Boat Club
1367 West Broadway #314
Vancouver, BC V6H 4A9
Canada
Tel: (604) 737-3064

Rowing Newfoundland
PO Box 50536 SS3
Street Johns, NF A1B 4M2
Canada
Tel: (709) 753-8515

Saint John River Rowing Club
46 Pitt Street
Saint John, NB E2L 2V5
Canada
Tel: (506) 657-5278

Saskatoon Rowing Club
PO Box 8817
Saskatoon, SK S7K 6S6
Canada
Tel: (306) 653-2977

Shawnigan Lake Rowing Club
1975 Renfrew Road
Shawnigan Lake, BC V0R 2W0
Canada
Tel: (250) 743-5516

Silver Lake Rowing Club
65 Leslie Avenue
Port Dover, ON N0A 1N2
Canada
Tel: (519) 583-9997
Email: brinkman@execulink.com
http://web.kwic.com/jdover

Societe du Parc des Iles
Bassin olympique Ile Notre Dame
Montreal, QC H3C 1A9
Canada
Tel: (514) 872-3327
Fax: (514) 872-3329

South Niagara Rowing Club
PO Box 33
Welland, ON L3B 5N9
Canada
Tel: (905) 734-7815

St. Catharines Rowing Club
Lakeport PO Box 28010
St. Catharines, ON L2N 7P8
Canada
Email: rowscrc@niagara.com
http://www.niagara.com/~rowscrc

St. John's Rowing Club
PO Box 28054
St. John's, NF A1B 4J8
Canada
Tel: (709) 576-0082

Sudbury Rowing Club
1935 Paris Street Plaza 69
PO Box 21006
Sudbury, ON P3E 6G6
Canada
Tel: (705) 670-1201

Thunder Bay Rowing Club
1 Dock Street
Box 20030
Thunder Bay, ON P7E 6P2
Canada
Tel: (807) 622-1044

Tillsonburg Rowing Club
PO Box 303
Tillsonburg, ON N4G 4H8
Canada
Tel: (519) 842-6543

Vancouver Rowing Club
PO Box 5206
North Vancouver, BC V6B 4B3
Canada
Tel: (604) 687-3400

Vermilion Lakeland Rowing Club
PO Box 3354
Vermilion, AB T9X 2B3
Canada
Tel: (780) 853-6291
Email: dhaverslew@hotmail.com

Victoria City Rowing Club
5100 Pat Bay Highway
Victoria, BC V8Y 1S7
Canada
Tel: (250) 658-5331
Email: vcrc@telus.net
http://www.vcrc.bc.ca

Waterloo Rowing Club
170 University W. #12-203
Waterloo, ON N2L 3E9
Canada
Email: madison@golden.net
http://www.geocities.com/kwrow

Western Rowing Club (Middlesex)
4212 Hamilton Road
Dorchester, ON N0L 1G3
Canada
Tel: (519) 453-1288

Winnipeg Rowing Club
Box 54
287 Tache Avenue
Winnipeg, MB R2H 3B8
Canada
Tel: (204) 237-1690

Woodstock Rowing Club
PO Box 20102
Woodstock, ON N4S 8X8
Canada
Tel: (519) 421-0556

Yorkton Rowing Club
PO Box 333
Yorkton, SK S3N 2W1
Canada
Tel: (306) 783-9332

UNIVERSITIES AND COLLEGES

Brock University Rowing Club
Faculty of Phys Ed & Rec
St. Catharines, ON L2S 3A1
Canada
Tel: (905) 688-5550 x4105

Dalhousie University
Dalplex South Street
Halifax, NS B3H 3J5
Canada
Tel: (902) 494-2079
Email: rowing@is2.dal.ca
http://www.dal.ca/

McGill Rowing Club
Sir Arthur Currie Gym
475 Pine Avenue West
Montreal, QC H2W 1S4
Canada

Ridley College Rowing Club
PO Box 3013
St. Catharines, ON L2R 7C3
Canada
Tel: (905) 684-8193

Royal Roads University Rowing Centre
c/o West Coast Rowing
Victoria, BC V9B 1L1
Canada
Tel: (250) 727-0966

Trent University Rowing
1600 West Bank Drive
Department of Athletics - Rowing
Peterborough, ON K9J 7B8
Canada
Tel: (705) 748-1011
http://www.trentu.ca/rowing

University of Alberta Rowing Club
PO Box 18 Students Union Bldg.
Edmonton, AK T6G 2J7
Canada
Tel: (780) 988-3350

University of British Columbia
Department of Athletis - Rowing
272-6081 University Boulevard
Vancouver, BC V6T 1Z1
Canada
Tel: (604) 737-4338
http://www.f2000p.org/thunderbird

University of Calgary
c/o Campus Recreation
Calgary, AB T2N 1N4
Canada
Tel: (403) 220-8018
Email: rowing@ucalgary.ca
http://www.ucalgary.ca/~rowing

University of Toronto
c/o Dept. of Athletics
55 Harbord Street
Toronto, ON M5S 2W6
Canada

University of Victoria
PO Box 3015
Victoria, BC V8W 3P1
Canada
Tel: (250) 658-4293

Vancouver College Rowing Club
5400 Cartier Street
Vancouver, BC V6M 3A5
Canada
Tel: (604) 261-4285

HIGH SCHOOLS AND JUNIORS

Brentwood College School
PO Box 1000
Mill Bay, BC V0R 2P0
Canada
Tel: (250) 743-5521

Collingwood School Rowing Club
70 Morven Drive
West Vancouver, BC V7S 1B2
Canada
Tel: (604) 921-8360

Greater Victoria Youth Rowing Society
7278 Chatwell Drive
Saanichton, BC V8M 1M8
Canada
Tel: (250) 652-9481

St. Mary's High School
200 Whitney Ave
Hamilton, ONT L8S 2G7
Canada
Tel: (905) 527-0214 x439
Email: crew01_coach@yahoo.com

Cayman Islands

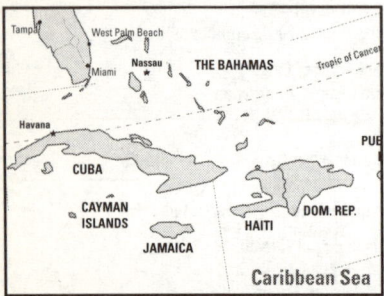

NATIONAL FEDERATION

Rowing Association of Cayman Islands
PO Box 1778 GT
Grand Cayman
Cayman Islands
Tel: (345) 9450 916
Fax: (345) 9452 972
Email: douglas@calder.com

Chile

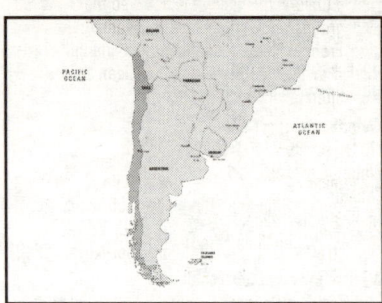

HISTORY

Rowing in Chile has strong ties with European clubs. Europeans residing in Chile during the late nineteenth century established many of the first organizations. The initial draw to the sport was for both social and health reasons, though an interest in competition soon followed. The first rowing club, Sport Club Phoenix, was founded in the city of Valdivia in 1880. Two years later, three more clubs opened their doors. In 1888, Rowing Club Centenario and Rowing Club Arturo Prat were founded. Both of these clubs quickly became known for their popular social competitions on the Calle-Calle River.

Expatriate European communities in Chile were the champions of the sport for many years. The German community established Club Deusche Ruders Verein, later changed to Club Neptune, in 1895. In 1896, the British Rowing Club was created and then a few years later the Iberian Rowing Club and the Italian Rowing Society. Informal racing, though fiercely competitive, began in the 1890's. By the turn of the century, the need for a national rowing body was clear-if only to mediate between the British, German, Italian and Spanish clubs! The National Rowing Association of Chile was started in 1904.

It seems that 50 years passed before a major annual competition began. As the story goes, in 1948 the local authorities of the city of Valparaiso wanted to create a memorable celebration on the anniversary of the independence of Chile. Mayor Admiral don Manuel Blanco Encalada is credited with suggesting the organization of an annual rowing regatta to happen together with Independence Day festivities.

The Valparaiso daily newspaper, Mercury, announced the event in September 1948 and invited all interested enthusiasts to register for the race. Local clubs and teams of sailors from visiting navy ships enthusiastically accepted. To stimulate interest and increase the level of competition, the organizers announced a grand prize of forty dollars for the winner and thirty dollars for the runner-up — not a small sum in Chile at this time. It is believed that ultimately eight groups fielded teams for the event. Alas, the visiting French Navy team won this inaugural race though in the years to follow, Chilean teams have most often taken home the gold.

REGIONS

Valparaiso
Avg. temp: Summer (December-February) 15C to 25°C; Fall (March-May) 10C to 18°C; Winter (June-August) 6C to 15°C; Spring (September-November) 8C to 20°C.

Concepcion
Avg. temp: Summer (December-February) 15C to 26°C; Fall (March-May) 8C to 21°C; Winter (June-August) 4C to 12°C; Spring (September-November) 6C to 17°C.

Valdivia
Avg. temp: Summer (December-February) 12C to 25°C; Fall (March-May) 8C to 20°C; Winter (June-August) 0C to10°C; Spring (September-November) 7C to 19°C.

Puerto Montt
Avg. temp: Summer (December-February) 12C to 23°C; Fall (March-May) 10C to16°C; Winter (June-August) 2C to11°C; Spring (September-November) 7C to 15°C.

NATIONAL FEDERATION

Federación Chilena De Remo Amateur
Vicuna Mackenna 44
Correo 22 — Casilla 74
Santiago de Chile
Chile
Tel: +56 2222-0052
Fax: +56 2220-0052
Email: federemo@entelchile.net

China

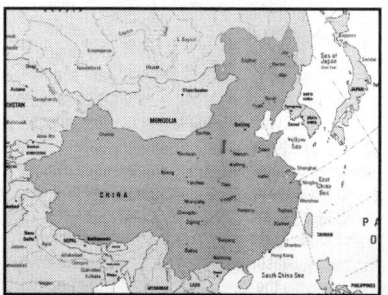

NATIONAL FEDERATION

Association d'Aviron de la R.P. de Chine
9 Rue Tiyuguan
Beijing, 100763
China
Tel: +86 10 6711 3690
Fax: +86 10 6711 2793

Colombia

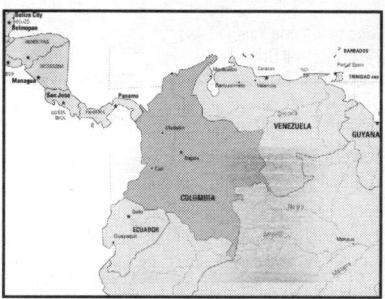

NATIONAL FEDERATION

Federacion Colombiana de Remo
Calle 28 No. 25 18
Santa Fé de Bogotá D.C.
Colombia
Tel: +57 1 287 7963
Fax: +57 1 245 9231

Costa Rica

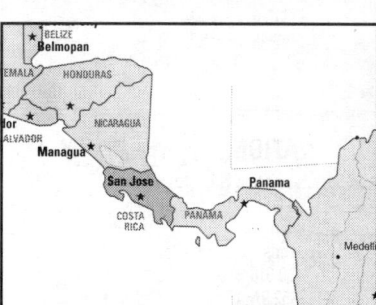

NATIONAL FEDERATION

Asociacion Costaricense de Remo y Canotaje
PO Box 41, 1200 Pavas
San Josè, Costa Rica
Tel: (506) 233 6455
Fax: (506) 255 4354
Email: rgallo@riostropicales.com

Croatia

NATIONAL FEDERATION

Croatian Rowing Federation
TRG Sportova 11
Zagreb, 10 000
Croatia
Tel: +385 1 36 50 547
Fax: +385 1 30 91 119
Email: hvs@zg.tel.hr

Cuba

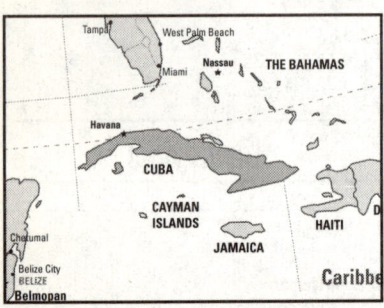

NATIONAL FEDERATION

Federation Amateur Cubana de Remo
Calle 13 No 601
Zona Postal 4
Ciudad de la Habana
Cuba
Tel: (537) 403 581(156)

Cyprus

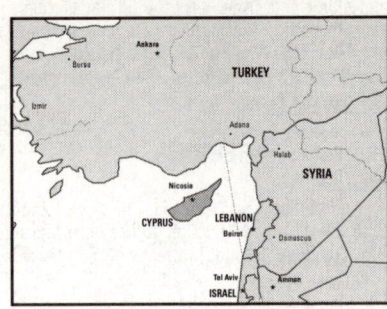

NATIONAL FEDERATION

Cyprus Rowing Association
PO Box 56639
Limassol, Cyprus
Tel: +357 25 806 457
Fax: +357 25 305 023

Czech Republic

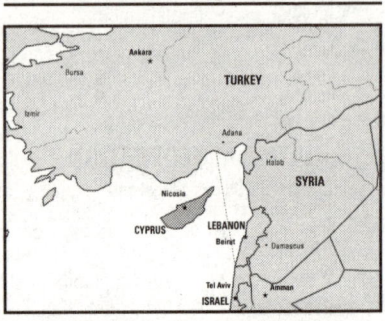

NATIONAL FEDERATION

Czech Rowing Association
Athleticka 100/2
Praha 6, 160 17
Czech Republic
Tel: +420 233 017 415
Email: info@ceskeveslovani.cz
www.ceskeveslovani.cz

CLUBS

Veslarsky klub Blesk
Veslarsky ostrov 62
147 00 Praha 4 — Podoli
Czech Republic
Tel: +420 241 431 012
http://www.vkblesk.cz/

Bohemians Praha
Modranska 51/1107
147 00 Praha 4 — Podoli
Czech Republic
Tel: +420 244 463 767-6
http://www.bohemianstj.cz/veslovani/

Veslarsky klub Slavia
lodenice klubu — Nabrezni 87
150 00 Praha 5
Czech Republic
Tel: +420 0254 4717
http://www.vkslavia.cz/

Veslarsky klub Smichov
Strakonicka 17 nouz.
150 00 Praha 5 — Smichov
Czech Republic
Tel/Fax +420 257 317 629
http://sweb.cz/vksmichov

Cesky veslarsky klub Praha
Veslarsky ostrov 59
147 00 Praha 4 — Podoli
Czech Republic
Fax +420 241430580
Email: blecha@bal.cz
http://cvkpraha.wz.cz/

ASC — Dukla Praha
Pod Juliskou 1
160 44 Praha 6
Czech Republic
Tel: +420 251 632 377

VK Vajgar
Veslarska lodenice,
377 01 Jindrichuv Hradec
Czech Republic
Tel: +420 0331-22586
http://vkvajgar.unas.cz/

TJ Vodni stavby Tabor
BydlinskZho ul. 2867
390 02 Tabor
Czech Republic
Tel: +420 0361-257805
Email: jmladek@osoud.tab.justice.cz

Jiskra Trebon
Hlinik 1006 / II
379 01 Trebon
Czech Republic
Tel: +420 0333-2815

CAC — Cesky atletic club
lodenice Pod lipou,
413 01 Roudnice nad Labem
Czech Republic

Slavoj Litomerice
Strelecky ostrov 3
412 01 Litomerice
Czech Republic
Tel: +420 0416-3683

Chemicka Usti nad Labem
Veslarsky oddil TJ Chemicka
Prazska 64
400 01 Usti nad Labem
Czech Republic
Tel: +420 047 — 520 18 30

Slavia SCE Decin
Polabi 7
405 01 Decin
Czech Republic
Tel: +420 0412-25773

Veslarsky klub Ohre
V Benatkach 1765
440 01 Louny
Czech Republic
Tel: +420 0395-2891
http://www.fcilouny.cz/vko.htm

SEPAP Steti
Litomericka 411
411 08 Steti
Czech Republic

Spartak Boletice n.L.
veslarsky oddil
407 11 Boletice n.L.
Czech Republic

Klub veslaru melnickych
Rybare 743
276 01 Melnik
Czech Republic
Tel: +420 0206-622759
http://sweb.cz/kvm1881

Spolana Neratovice
277 11 Neratovice
Czech Republic
Tel: +420 026-662667
http://tjspolanaveslari.webzdarma.cz/

VK Slovan Lysa n. L.
veslarska lodenice
289 22 Lysa nad Labem
Czech Republic

Klub Veslovani Kondor Brandys nad Labem
Skroupova 704
250 01 Brandys nad Labem
Czech Republic
http://sweb.cz/kvkondor/

CVK Pardubice
Cihelna 73
530 03 Pardubice
Czech Republic
Tel: +420 040-44933
http://cvk.webzdarma.cz/

Lokomotiva Nymburk
veslarsky oddil
288 01 Nymburk
Czech Republic

Cesky veslarsky klub
se sidlem v Brne, Veslarska 179
602 00 Brno
Czech Republic
Email: cvkbrno@tiscali.cz
http://home.tiscali.cz/cvkbrno/

Lodni sporty Brno
Veslarska 177
600 00 Brno
Czech Republic
Tel: +420 05-462100223
http://lsbrno.webpark.cz/

Slovacky veslarsky klub Breclav
Haskova 2760, PS BOX 21
690 03 Breclav
Czech Republic

Veslarsky klub Olomouc
tr. 17. listopadu 10
772 00 Olomouc
Czech Republic
Tel: +420 068-26267
http://www.sweb.cz/vkolomouc/

Veslarsky klub Prerov
Bezrucova 770
750 00 Prerov
Czech Republic
Tel: +420 0607-809182
Email: veslo@prerpv.net
http://veslo.prerov.net/

Oddil veslovani VSB-TU Ostrava
Vysokoskolsky sportovni klub
VSB-Technicka univerzita Ostrava, oddil veslovani
Tr.17.listopadu 15, Ostrava Poruba, 708 33
Czech Republic
Tel: +420 069 / 699 3506
http://www.volny.cz/veslarivsbtuo

VK Perun
Na Nahonu 30
Ostrava-Privoz 702 00
Czech Republic
Tel: +420 069 / 212615 a 223177
http://mujweb.cz/sport/perunostrava/

Jiskra Otrokovice
veslarsky oddil
765 01 Otrokovice
Czech Republic
http://veslari.hogan.cz/

Fatra Slavia Napajedla
Na Kapli 673
763 61 Napajedla
Czech Republic

VK Moravia
Tyrsovo nam. 440
686 01 UherskZ Hradiste
Czech Republic
Tel: +420 0632-3018

VK Hodonin
PS 155, Legionaru 2132
695 01 Hodonin
Czech Republic
Tel: +420 0628-21915

Lokomotiva Beroun
Tyrsova 85, PS 110
Beroun 25, 266 80
Czech Republic
Tel: +420 311-744143
Fax +420 311-744253

KVM Melnik
Czech Republic
Email: kvm1881@seznam.cz
http://sweb.cz/KVM1881

Denmark

NATIONAL FEDERATION

Dansk Forening for Rosport
Skovalleen 38A
Postboks 74
Bagsvaerd, 2880
Denmark
Tel: +45 44 440 633
Fax: +45 44 440 449
Email: dffr@roning.dk
www.roning.dk

CLUBS (BY REGION)

GREATER COPENHAGEN

Amager Ro-og Kajakklub
Islands Brygge 66A
2300 København S
Denmark

Bagsværd Roklub
Skovalleen 38 B
2880 Bagsværd
Denmark
Email: post@bagsvaerdroklub.dk
www.bagsvaerdroklub.dk

B&Ws Roklub
Langelinie
Lystbådehavnen
2100 København Ø.
Denmark

Danske Studenters Roklub
Strandvænget 55
2100 København Ø.
Denmark
Email: formand@dsr-online.dk
www.dsr-online.dk/

DFDS Roklub
Langelinie Lystbådehavn
2100 København Ø
Denmark

Dragør Roklub
Gl. Havn
Tolderhuset
2791 Dragør
Denmark

Hellerup Dameroklub
Strandparksvej 40
2900 Hellerup
Denmark
www.hdr.dk

Hellerup Roklub
Hellerup Havn
Strandparksvej 38
2900 Hellerup
Denmark
www.hellerup-roklub.dk/

Holte Roklub
Frederikslundsvej
2840 Holte
Denmark
Email: holte-roklub@email.dk

Hvidovre Roklub
Hvidovre Strandvej 29
2650 Hvidovre
Denmark
www.hvidovreroklub.dk

Ishøj Roklub
Tangloppen 1
2635 Ishøj
Denmark
Email: ishoj-roklub@ishoj-roklub.dk
www.ishoj-roklub.dk

Københavns Roklub
Tømmergravsgade 13
2450 København SV
Denmark
www.koebenhavnsroklub.dk/

Lyngby Dameroklub
Chr. Winthersvej 24
2800 Kgs. Lyngby
Denmark
Email: lyngbydame@roklub.net
www.lyngbydame.roklub.net

Lyngby Roklub
Rustenborgvej 19 A
2800 Lyngby
Denmark
www.lyngbyroklub.dk

Roforeningen KVIK
Strandvænget 53
2100 København Ø
Denmark
Email: roforeningen@mail.tele.dk
www.roforeningen.dk

Roklubben Furesø
Furesøbad
Fiskebæk
3500 Værløse
Denmark
Email:
www.fureso.dk/

Roklubben Gefion
Strandvænget 47
2100 København Ø
Denmark
Email: roklubben.gefion@tdcadsl.dk
http://home19.inet.tele.dk/roklubben-gefion/

Roklubben SAS
Islands Brygge 66 B
2300 København S
Denmark
http://sasklub.dk/roklub/

Roklubben Skjold
Strandvænget 51
2100 København Ø
Denmark
http://www.roklubbenskjold.dk/

Roklubben Øresund
Amager Strandvej 413
2770 Kastrup
Denmark

Rungsted Roklub
Rungsted Strandvej 120
2960 Rungsted Kyst
Denmark
Email: post@rungsted-roklub.dk
www.rungsted-roklub.dk

Rønne Roklub
Remisevej 16
3700 Rønne
Denmark
www.roenneroklub.dk/

Skovshoved Roklub
Skovshoved Havn 3
2920 Charlottenlund
Denmark
www.skovshoved.dk

ISLAND OF SEELAND

Birkerød Roklub
Plantagevej 82
3460 Birkerød
Denmark
Email: gorm@praefke.dk
garm.adm.ku.dk/br

Brøndby Roklub
Svingelstien 10
2660 Brøndby
Denmark
http://welcome.to/BR

Fredensborg Roklub
Sørupvej 6
2480 Fredensborg
Denmark
www.fredensborgroklub.dk

Frederikssund Roklub
Kalvøen
3600 Frederikssund
Denmark
www.frederikssund-roklub.dk

Frederiksværk Ro- og Kajaklub
Havnelinien 14
3300 Frederiksværk
Denmark
Email: info@frv-roklub.dk
frv-rokub.dk

Gilleleje Ro- og Kajakklub
Østmolen 7
Gilleleje Havn
3250 Gilleleje
Denmark

Greve Roklub
Havnevej 20 B
Mosede Havn
2670 Greve
Denmark
hjem.get2net.dk/greveroklub/

Helsingør Roklub
Færgevej 1
3000 Helsingør
Denmark
http://www.roklubben.dk/

Holbæk Roklub
Kalundborgvej 58 A
4300 Holbæk
Denmark
Email: post@holbaek-roklub.dk
holbaek-roklub.dk

Humlebæk Roklub
Havnevej 9
3050 Humlebæk
Denmark

Hundested Roklub
Strandlodden 14
3390 Hundested
Denmark

Kalundborg Roklub
Radiovej 5
4400 Kalundborg
Denmark

Karlebo Roklub
Nivå Strand Park 7
Nivå Havn
2990 Nivå
Denmark
http://www.karleboroklub.dk/

Korsør Roklub
Lilleøvej
4220 Korsør
Denmark

Køge Roklub
Sdr. Molevej 19
4600 Køge
Denmark

Lindenborg Roklub
Borrevejle Idrætscenter
Borrevejlevej 26 — Gevninge
4000 Roskilde
Denmark

Nykøbing Sjælland Roklub
Nykøbing S. Havn
Korvetvej 10
4500 Nykøbing Sj.
Denmark
Email: nykobing-sj-roklub@mail.tele.dk

Næstved Roklub
Kanalvej 18
4700 Næstved
Denmark
www.naestvedroklub.dk

Præstø Roklub
Fjordstien 7
4720 Præstø
Denmark
Email: tove.hjorth@mail.tele.dk

Ringsted Roklub
Ejlstrupvej 160
4100 Ringsted
Denmark

Roklubben Stevns
Fiskerihavnen 13
4673 Rødvig Stevns
Denmark

Roklubben Viking
Frederiksvej 16
4654 Fakse Ladeplads
Denmark

Roskilde Roklub
Havnevej 47 B
4000 Roskilde
Denmark

Skelskør Roklub
Gammelgade 13
4230 Skælskør
Denmark

Sorø Roklub
Frederiksvej 33
4180 Sorø
Denmark

Tissø Roklub
Søvejen 14
4490 Jerslev — Sjælland
Denmark
Email: lis@bayclan.com

Vordingborg Roklub
Nordhavnsvej 56
4760 Vordingborg
Denmark
Email: vo-roklub@vo-roklub.dk
www.vo-roklub.dk

LOLLAND-FALSTER

Bandholm Roklub
Havnepladsen 1
4941 Bandholm
Denmark

Maribo Roklub
Bangshavevej 27
4930 Maribo
Denmark
www.mariboroklub.dk

Nakskov Roklub
Sydkajen 21
Færgelandet
4900 Nakskov
Denmark

N.S. Roklub
Strandpromenaden
4900 Nakskov
Denmark

Nykøbing F. Roklub
Codan Plads
4800 Nykøbing F.
Denmark

Nysted Roklub
Strandvejen 4
4880 Nysted
Denmark

Roforeningen Fjorden
Oreby Havn
4990 Sakskøbing
Denmark

Saxkjøbing Roklub
Havnegade 6
4990 Sakskøbing
Denmark

Stege Roklub
Fiskervej v/Havnen
4780 Stege
Denmark

Stubbekøbing Roklub
Vestergade 32 C
4850 Stubbekøbing
Denmark

FYN

Assens Roklub
Næsvej 30
5610 Assens
Denmark

Bogense Ro- og Kajakklub
Østre Havnevej 41
5400 Bogense
Denmark
Email: humleand@worldonline.dk

Faaborg Roklub
Færgevej 19
5600 Fåborg
Denmark
Email: jerl@odense.dk
faaborg-roklub.dk

Kerteminde Roklub
Odensevej 48
5300 Kerteminde
Denmark

Marstal Sejlklub Roafdeling
Lystbådehavnen
5960 Marstal
Denmark

Middelfart Roklub
Kongebrovej 66
5500 Middelfart
Denmark

Munkebo Sejl- og Roklub
Syvstjernen 28
5330 Munkebo
Denmark

Nyborg Roklub
Havnepromenaden 6
5800 Nyborg
Denmark

Odense Roklub
Kanalvej 160
5000 Odense C
Denmark
Email: kasserer@odense-roklub.dk
odense-roklub.dk

Rudkøbing Roklub
Skudehavnen 2
5900 Rudkøbing
Denmark

Svendborg Roklub
Østre Havnevej 20
5700 Svendborg
Denmark

Føns Søsportsklub
Rosnæsbrovej 12
5580 Nr. Aaby
Denmark

Strib Ro- og Kajakklub
Strandvejen
Strib
5500 Middelfart
Denmark

JUTLAND SOUTH

Aabenraa Roklub
Strandvej 5
6200 Aabenraa
Denmark

Aarhus Roklub
Hjortholmvej 2 B
Lystbådehavnen
8000 Århus C
Denmark
Email: bestyrelse@aarhusroklub.dk
www.aarhusroklub.dk

Aarhus Studenter Roklub
Fiskerivej 7
Fiskerihavnen
8000 Århus C
Denmark
Email: asr@asr.dk
www.asr.dk

Augustenborg Roklub
Augustenborg Skov
6440 Augustenborg
Denmark
www.augustenborg-roklub.dk

Esbjerg Roklub
Fiskerihavnsgade 23
6700 Esbjerg
Denmark

Fanø Roklub
Strandslippe 1
Nordby
6720 Fanø
Denmark

Flensborg Roklub
Am Ostseebad 35
Flensborg Nord
D 24939 Flensborg
Denmark
www.flensborg-roklub.de.

Fredericia Dameroklub
Østerstrand
v/Sygehuset
7000 Fredericia
Denmark

Fredericia Roklub
Østre Strand
7000 Fredericia
Denmark

Graasten Roklub
Toldbodgade 20 — Havnen
6300 Gråsten
Denmark

Grindsted Roklub
Jyllandsgade 51
7200 Grindsted
Denmark

Haderslev Roklub
Klosteret 33
6100 Haderslev
Denmark

HEI Rosport
Egå Marina
8250 Egå
Denmark
www.hei-rosport.dk

Horsens Roklub
Langelinie 12
8700 Horsens
Denmark
www.horsensrklub.dk

Høruphav Ro- og Kajakklub
Høruphav
6470 Sydals
Denmark

Jels Roklub
Søvej 5 A
Jels
6630 Rødding
Denmark

Kolding Dameroklub
Gl. Strandvej 3
6000 Kolding
Denmark

Kolding Roklub
Gl. Strandvej 1
6000 Kolding
Denmark
Email: js@kolding-bynet.dk
www.koldingroklub.dk

Kollund Roklub
Molevej 27
Kollund
6340 Kruså
Denmark

Nordborg Roklub
Hesnæsvej 2
Dyvig
6430 Nordborg
Denmark

Nordslesvigsk Roklub
Denmark

Odder Roklub
Rylevej 85 A — Saksild Strand
Boks 214
8300 Odder
Denmark

Ribe Roklub
Erik Menvedsvej 16
6760 Ribe
Denmark
Email: mail@riberoklub.dk
www.riberoklub.dk

Risskov Roklub
Fortevej 107
8240 Risskov
Denmark
Email: risskov_roklub@hotmail.com
hjem.get2net.dk/risskovroklub/

Roklubben ARA
Fiskerivej
8000 Århus C
Denmark
Email: roklubbenara@sport.dk
www.roklubbenara.dk

Ry Roklub
Siimtoften 15
8680 Ry
Denmark
Email: info@ry-roklub.dk
www.ry-roklub.dk

Samsø Roklub
Langør 27
8305 Samsø
Denmark

Silkeborg Roklub
Åhavevej 1 B
8600 Silkeborg
Denmark

Skanderborg Roklub
Sølystvej 4
8660 Skanderborg
Denmark
www.skanderborg-roklub.dk

Slesvig Roklub
Am Luisenbad 6
D 24837 Slesvig
Denmark
Email: slesvig-roklub@foni.net
www.slesvig-roklub.dk

Solbjerg Søsport
Solbjerg Søsport
Søvangsvej 1 A
8355 Solbjerg
Denmark

Sønderborg Roklub
Verdens Ende 2
6400 Sønderborg
Denmark
Email: bestyrelse@sonderboerg-roklub.dk
www.sonderborg-roklub.dk

Tange Roklub
Tangesøvej 19
Tange
8850 Bjerringbro
Denmark

Tønder Roklub
Nyholmvej
6270 Tønder
Denmark

Varde Roklub
Dr. Margrethesvej 17
6800 Varde
Denmark
Email: bestyrelsen@varderoklub.dk
www.varderoklub.dk

Vejle Roklub
Svineryggen
7100 Vejle
Denmark
www.vejleroklub.dk

JUTLAND NORTH

Aalborg Dame Roklub
Søsportsvej 12
9000 Aalborg
Denmark
Email: aalborg-dame-roklub@get2net.dk
hjem.get2net.dk/adr

Aalborg Roklub
Søsportsvej 8
9000 Aalborg
Denmark

Ebeltoft Ro- og Kajakklub
Vestervej 15
8400 Ebeltoft
Denmark
www.roiebeltoft.dk

Frederikshavn Roklub
Ndr. Strandvej 58
9900 Frederikshavn
Denmark

Fur Bådelaug
Sunde
7884 Fur
Denmark

Gjøl Roklub
Havnen Gjøl
9440 Åbybro
Denmark

Grenaa Roklub
Fiskerikajerne 18
8500 Grenaa
Denmark

Hadsund Roklub
Thygeslundvej 9
9560 Hadsund
Denmark
Email: kej@midtnord.dk
hadsundroklub.dk

Hals Roklub
Lodsvej 23
9370 Hals
Denmark

Herning Roklub
Skivevej 4
7451 Sunds
Denmark

Hobro Ro- Kano og Kajakklub
Nordre Kajgade 13-15
9500 Hobro
Denmark

Holstebro Roklub
Søvej 6
7500 Holstebro
Denmark

Lemvig Roklub
Strandvejen 24
7620 Lemvig
Denmark

Løgstør Roklub
Kanalvejen 29
9670 Løgstør
Denmark

Nibe Roklub
Mindet
Aalborgvej 1
9240 Nibe
Denmark

Nykøbing Mors Roklub
Øroddevej/Østerstrand
7900 Nykøbing M.
Denmark

Randers Roklub
Fjordgade 20
8900 Randers
Denmark

Ringkøbing Roklub
Vester Strandbjerg 29
6950 Ringkøbing
Denmark
www.ringkoebingroklub.dk

Roklubben Ægir
Søsportsvej 4
9000 Aalborg
Denmark
Email: roklubben.aegir@mail.tele.dk
www.roklubben-aegir.dk

Skive Roklub
Strandvejen 22
7800 Skive
Denmark

Struer Roklub
Fjordvejen 10 B
7600 Struer
Denmark
Email: formand@struerroklub.dk

Sæby Roklub
Havnen 1
9300 Sæby
Denmark
Email: post@saebyroklub.dk
www.saebyroklub.dk

Thisted Roklub
Simmons Bakke 21
7700 Thisted
Denmark

Vestervig Roklub
Havnevej 3
Agger
7770 Vestervig
Denmark

Viborg Roklub
Erik Menveds Vej 28-30
8800 Viborg
Denmark

Dominican Republic

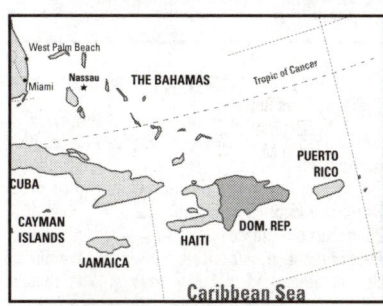

NATIONAL FEDERATION
Federaciön Dominicana de Remo
Av. Espana #120 Edif
H-8 3er Piso apto. 4 Proyecto Villa Duarte
Santo Domingo D.N.
Dominican Republic
Tel: (809) 593 2208
Fax: (809) 326 4297

Ecuador

NATIONAL FEDERATION
Federcacion Ecautoriana De Remo
Av. de Las Américas
Explanada del Estadio Modelo
PO Box 09 014567
Guayaquil, Ecuador
Tel: +593 4 395222
Fax: +593 4 283025

Egypt

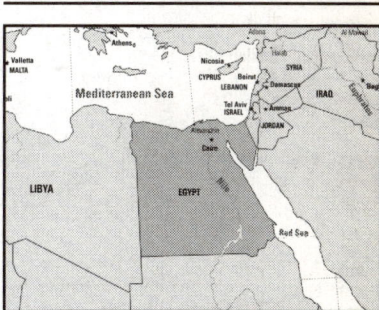

NATIONAL FEDERATION
Egyptian Rowing and Canoe Federation
3 El Shawarabi St.
Kasr El Nil
Cairo, Egypt
Tel: +20 2 392 5498
Fax: +20 2 393 4350
Email: egyrcfed@starnet.com.eg

CLUBS
Al-Ahley Bank Rowing Club
Complex of Rowing Club
El-Nozaha Airport
Alexandria, Egypt

Army Forces Rowing Club
111 El-Nil St.
Dokki, Giza
Egypt

Cairo University RC
114 El-Nil St.
Dokki, Giza
Egypt

El-Kahraba RC
8 Abou El-Feda St.
Zamalek, Cairo
Egypt

El-Massery RC
115 El-Nil St.
Dokki, Giza
Egypt

El-Yacht El-Massery Club
Complex of Rowing Club
El-Nozaha Airport, Alexandria
Egypt

Greek Rowing Club
112, El-Nil St.
Dokki, Giza
Egypt

Police Rowing Club
111 El-Nil St.
Dokki, Giza, Egypt
Suez Canal Authority Club (Ismailia)
Suez Canal Authority, Ismailia
El-Nady El-Ame
Egypt

Suez Canal Authority Club (Port-Said)
Suez Canal Authority RC
PO Box 16
Port Said, Port Fouad
Egypt

El Salvador

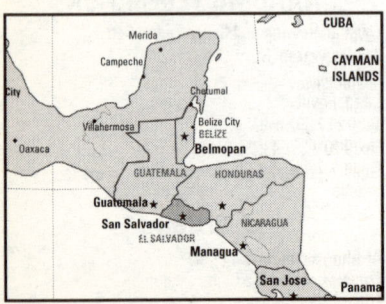

NATIONAL FEDERATION

Federacion Salvadorena de Remo y Canotaje
3 Calle Poniente
3898 Col. Escalon
San Salvador
El Salvador
Tel: (503) 260-6216
Fax: (503) 260-5840
Email: epalomo@sal.gbm.net

Estonia

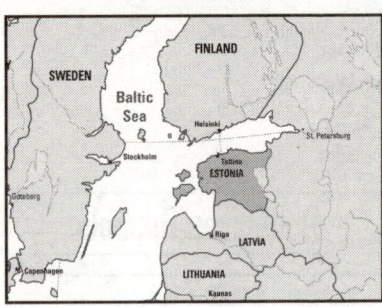

HISTORY

A young German businessman who founded a rowing club in 1875 brought rowing to Estonia. The earliest known boats also came from Germany. The history of Estonian rowing can be divided into three main eras. The first was from 1875 until World War I in 1914. During this time, there were two rowing clubs- one in Tartu and one in Parnu. This represented the beginning of structured club-level rowing with regular training and the purchasing of rowing equipment. Estonian, Latvian, and Russian clubs also started to organize open regattas to promote rowing. At the Stockholm Olympics, Mart Kusick, was the first Estonian rower, then a member of the Russian team, to win a bronze medal.

The second period was from 1916-1940, between World War I and II. The country's third rowing club was established in Tallin in 1930. Rowing became increasingly popular in Estonia; year-round training was planned, junior and women rowers flocked to the sport, and as a result of the growing interest in competition, events became better organized. The first Estonian national rower participated in the Berlin Olympics in 1936.

The conclusion of World War II in 1948 represents the beginning of the third period of Estonia's rowing history when training resumed at the club in Parnu. In 1949, the first Estonian championships were held in regular boats and in 1950, the first championships in academic boats. A FISA-B category 2000-meter rowing course was built in Estonia in 1974. New clubs were formed in Narva, 1975, and Viljandi, 1981. The number of people involved in rowing continued to grow as coaches recruited athletes, programs were added to sport schools and special rowing schools were formed. In 1976, Estonian athlete, Raul Arnemann wins the first Olympic medal as a member of coxless four. Juri Jaanson became the first World Champion and World Cup winner in the men's single sculls in 1990.

The Estonian Rowing Federation rejoined FISA in 1991, which allowed Estonia to send athletes to international regattas. Rowing in the nineties in Estonia had difficulties due to the change in government and the financing of clubs. Currently, the Estonian rowing system is functioning well with the senior team having good support through the Bejing Olympics. Junior rowers are able to training and study at the same time, cooperation is being developed with scientists from local universities, and some international regattas have been organized. To date there are over eight rowing clubs in Estonia.

REGIONS

North Estonia
Counties: Harjumaa, Ida Virumaa, Lääne Virumaa. Sites of interest: North coast of Estonia, Rowin Club Tallinn, Harku regatta (July).

Central Estonia
Counties: Raplamaa, Järvamaa, Jõgevamaa. Sites of Interest: Manors in Järvamaa

West Estonia
Counties: Hiiumaa, Saaremaa, Läänemaa, Pärnumaa. Sites of interest: Western islands of Estonia, Rowing Clubs "Kalev" and "Pärnu", Estonian Rowing Championships (August).

South Estonia
Counties: Viljandimaa, Tartumaa, Valgamaa, Põlvamaa, Võrumaa. **Sites of interest**: South Estonian landscape, The University of Tartu and Agricultural University boat race in eights (May), "The Boatman of Viljandi" Regatta (July), the Fall Regatta in Eights (October) since 1957. **Average temperature**: Winter: -3 to -7°C, Spring: 4 to 6°C, Summer: 15 to 16°C, Autumn: 5 to 8°C.

PERSONALITIES

Arnold Ebrok: Rebuilt rowing as a sport after World War II. He was the head of the sport committee in Pärnu, as well as, a rowing trainer and referee.

Mihkel Leppik: A legendary trainer, Leppik, has worked in the field since 1951. His athletes have won several medals in both the World and European Championships. He is currently one of the trainers for the Estonian national team.

Raul Arnemann: The only Estonian rower to win a medal at the 1976 Olympic Games in Montreal. He stroked the Soviet Union coxless four. Arnemann also won a silver medal in the Junior World Championships in 1971. He currently works as a forester administrating a 12-hectare farm.

Juri Jaanson: Born in 1965, Jaanson has been Estonia's best rower for 17 years. He won his first World Cup in the single sculls in 1990 and became the World Champion in singles the same year. He has also earned a bronze medal in 1989 and silver medal in the 1995 World Championships. Jaanson is still training seriously preparing for his fifth Olympics in Athens.

Did You Know ?

About 10,000 spectators watch the University of Tartu and Agricultural University boat race and a rubberboat race in Tartu every year — The highest number of spectators for a single sports event in Estonia.

NATIONAL FEDERATION

Estonian Rowing Association
Regati Puiestee 1
11911, Tallinn
Estonia
Tel: +372 6398 675
Fax: +372 6398 653
Email: estonianrowing@hot.ee
www.sport.ee/era

CLUBS

Pärnu Rowing Club
Rääma 27, 80039 Pärnu
Estonia
Tel: +372 4443797

Kalev Rowing Centre, Pärnu
Suur- Joe 50B, 80042 Pärnu
Estonia
Tel: +372 4432456
Contact: Matti Killing
Email: matti@estpak.ee

Energia Rowing Centre, Narva
Voidu 4, 20609 Narva
Estonia
Tel: +372 3573504
Email: spordikoolenergia@neti.ee
Boathouse: Joe 1, 20609 Narva

SAK Tartu
Lutsu 2, 51006 Tartu
Estonia
Tel: +372 7406563
Email: saktartu@online.ee
Boathouse: Ranna tee 3, 51013 Tartu
Tel: +372 7352415

Rowing Club "Aht"
Ranna tee 1, 51013 Tartu
Estonia
Tel: +372 7433468

University of Tartu Rowing Centre
Ranna tee 1, 51013 Tartu
Estonia
Tel: +372 7433468

Viljandi Rowing Centre
Ranna pst. 3, 71003 Viljandi
Estonia
Boathouse: Ranna pst. 6, 71003 Viljandi

Tallinna SK
Tatari 6
10116 Tallinn
Tel: +372 5014012

Harku Rowing Centre
Soudebaasi tee 21
13517 Tallinn
Estonia
Tel: +372 6574864

Rowing Club "Aeron"
Reiu Spordibaas
80046 Paikuse vald
Pärnumaa
Estonia
Tel: +372 4455206

Finland

NATIONAL FEDERATION

Finnish Rowing Association
Kotipolku 2
Imatra, 55120
Finland
Tel: +358 5 431 7224
Fax: +358 5 431 7226
Email: aira.varis@suomensoutuliitto.fi
www.suomensoutuliitto.fi

CLUBS (BY REGION)

ETELÄ-SUOMEN LÄÄNI

Akademiska Roddklubben rf, Helsinki
Maija Erkolahti p. 050-3842550
Poutamäentie 12 A 10
00360 Helsinki
Finland
Email: maija.erkolahti@valio.fi
www.ark-rowing.fi

Anjalankosken Soutajat ry, Anjalankoski
Hannu Liekola p. 044-5756466
Kymenrannantie 31
46800 Anjalankoski
Finland
Email: www.anjalankoskensoutajat.net

Ekenäs Roddare rf, Ekenäs
Bernt Degerlund p. 019-2462950
Hangövägen 455
10600 Ekenäs
Finland
Email: bernt.degerlund@inet.fi

Esbo Idrottsförening rf, Espoo
Zita Svanhström-Gammals p. 050-5440848
PB 54, 02611 Espoo
Finland
Email: zitagammals@hotmail.com
www.esboif.net/rodd

Helsingin Soutuklubi ry, Helsinki
Tero Heikkilä p. 050-3534595
Kousatie 17 B 4
00430 Helsinki
Finland
Email: tero.heikkila@helsinki.fi

Helsingin Soutupiiri ry, Helsinki
Anna-Riikka Mahlamäki p. 040-5778307
Salpausseläntie 9 A 18
00710 Helsinki
Finland
Email: anna.mahlamäki@helsinki.fi

Hämeenlinnan Latu ry, Hämeenlinna
Jorma Warvas p.040-5864308
Honkalankatu 2 B 4
13210 Hämeenlinna
Finland
Email: jorma.warvas@mail.htk.fi

Hämeenlinnan Soutajat ry, Turenki
Livinus Ven p. 040-7099830
Kantomäenkuja 3
14200 Turenki
Finland
Email: tiina.ven@kiipula.fi
www.hameenlinnansoutajat.com

Iitin Soutajat ry, Kausala
Anne Lundgren p.040-7336982
Pohjanmäentie 12
47520 Iitti
Finland
Email: anne.lundgren@novogroup.com

Imatran Kahvakopla ry, Imatra
Mika Saarela p.040-5110229
Mertatie 1-3 A
56120 Salosaari
Finland
Email: mika.saarela@storaenso.com

Joutsenon Kullervo ry, Joutseno
Pentti Miettinen p. 040-7317220
Reitkallintie 126, 49480 Summa

Kannonkosken Kiho ry, Kannonkoski
Jatta Halmiala p. 040-7637521
Sininintie 2006 D
43300 Kannonkoski
Finland

Kaukaan Lylyn Soutajat ry, Lappeenranta
Tarja Kostiainen p. 020-4154210
UPM-Kymmene Oyj Kaukas
53200 Lappeenranta
Finland
Email: tarja.kostiainen@upm-kymmene.com

Keravan Urheilijat ry, Kerava
Aimo Kurki p. 050-5344146
Heinätie 5 A 1
01350 Vantaa
Finland
Email: aimo.kurki@vantaa.fi

Lappeenrannan Soutajat ry, Lappeenranta
Ari Posti, p. 050-5432300
Karhumäenkatu 4
53850 Lappeenranta
Finland
Email: ari.posti@pp.inet.fi
yhdistykset.etela-karjala.fi/soutajat

Saimaan Norpat Urheilusukellusseura ry, Lappeenranta
Esa Melanen p.0500-938075
Henrikinkatu 12
53200 Lappeenranta
Finland

Lohjan Järvipäivät ry, Kirkniemi
Tuula Laine p.019-341737
Vanhansahantie 13 A 4
08800 Kirkniemi
Finland
Email: tuula.laine@pp3.inet.fi
www.lohjanjarvipaivat.lohja.fi

Lohjan Seudun Soutajat ry, Virkkala
Stig-Olof Westerholm p. 0400-216876
Imatrantie 2
08700 Virkkala
Finland
Email: sonanne@surfeu.fi

Lohjan Teho ry, Lohja
Aarne Aalto p. 040-5769491
Patruunankuja 7 C 28
08200 Lohja
Finland

Mommilanjärven soutelu ry, Helsinki
Markku Juhola p.0400-444714
Töölönkatu 26 C 47
00260 Helsinki
Finland
Email: markku.juhola@tamro.com

Nesteen Soutajat ry, Porvoo
Janne Masalin p. 040-8254760
Sirkkalankatu 9 as 3
20500 Turku
Finland
Email: janne.masalin@fidelionordic.com
www.nesteensoutajat.net

Orimattilan Jymy ry, Orimattila
Matti Kuoppala p. 0500-359183
Pajulinnuntie 13
16300 Orimattila
Finland
Email: matti.kuoppala@phnet.fi

Parikkalan Urheilijat ry, Parikkala
Pekka Anttonen p. 040-5909580
Kirjolankatu 7 B 6
59100 Parikkala
Finland

Rowing Club Saimaa ry, Lappeenranta
Ari Mykkänen p. 0500-849259, f. 05-4190464
Ainonkatu 28 as 15
53130 Lappeenranta
Finland
Email: ari.mykkanen@quicknet.inet.fi

Soutumiehet ry, Espoo
Seppo Ketonen p. 040-5472149
Joupinmäenrinne 4 B 29
02760 Espoo
Finland
Email: seppo.ketonen@majorblue.fi

Soutu ja Kuntoseura Joutele ry, Helsinki
Esa Lumme p. 040-5683297
Angervontie 11
04260 Kerava
Finland
Email: esa.lumme@metso.com

Sunilan Sisu ry, Sunila
Ilkka Laasonen p. 050-5617512
Alvar Aallonkatu 9
48900 Sunila
Finland

Soutu Team Albatrossi ry, Kotka
Veli-Antti Kaukinen p. 050-5616451
Tallikivenkuja 4 as 3
49490 Neuvoton
Finland
Email: veliantti.kaukinen@kotka.poliisi.fi
www.soututeam-albatrossi.tk

Taipalsaaren Kisa ry, Lappeenranta
Matti Hulkkonen p. 050-5160412
Hanhijärventie 139
53100 Lappeenranta
Finland
Email: taurama@wwnet.fi

Taipalsaaren Veikot ry, Saimaanharju
Hannu Olkkonen p. 0400-656945
Ruutanantie 18
54915 Saimaanharju
Finland

Tuuloksen Säkiä ry, Tuulos
Juhani Jokiranta p. 050-5285214
Kangastie 5
14820 Tuulos
Finland
Email: jokijussi@hotmail.com

Vesikansan Urheilijat -78 ry, Paimela
Unto Mälkönen p. 03-7873274
Pykälistö 66
17120 Paimela
Finland
Email: unto@malkonen.com

Voiton Soutajat ry, Taavetti
Voitto Pesu p. 050-3090506
Vallitie 41
54500 Taavetti
Finland
Email: eero.kettunen@osuuspankki.fi

Vuoksen Soutajat ry, Imatra
Veikko Sinisalo p.0400-832268
Kotipolku 2
55120 Imatra
Finland
Email: sinisalo@finnrowing.inet.fi
www.vuoksensoutajat.fi

Ylioppilassoutajat ry, Vantaa
Kalevi Raitio p. 040-7400074
Sinisiiventie 24 C
01490 Vantaa
Finland
Email: kalevi.raitio@kolumbus.fi

LÄNSI-SUOMEN LÄÄNI

Halikon kirkkoveneyhdistys ry, Halikko
Erkki Laine p. 050-4135720
Majurintie 4
25250 Märynummi
Finland
Email: erkki.laine@halikko.salonseutu.fi

Ikaalisten Soutajat ry, Ikaalinen
Vesa Keso p. 050-5188671
Tapiolankatu 2
39500 Ikaalinen
Finland
Email: vkeso@saunalahti.fi

Iso-Mustajärven Urheilijat ry, Tampere
Pekka Petäjäniemi p. 0400-238167
Pohjajärventie 13 C
33430 Vuorentausta
Finland
Email: pekka.petajaniemi@tieliikelaitos.fi

Joutsan Veneseura ry, Joutsa
Heikki Partanen p. 040-7789539
Huttulankuja 5
19650 Joutsa
Finland
Email: heikki.partanen@pp.inet.fi
www.joutsa.fi/veneseura

Jämsänjoen Soutuveikot ry, Jämsänkoski
Ari Järvinen p. 040-5148347
Lammenkuja 18
42300 Jämsänkoski
Finland
Email: ari.x.jarvinen@upm-kymmene.com

Kalmarin Soutajat ry, Pirkkala
Jorma Haapsaari p. 040-7216983
Killontorintie 18 B
33950 Pirkkala
Finland
Email: jorma.haapsaari@kalmarind.com

Kannuksen Team Eskopuu ry, Kannus
Alpo Vuorenmaa p. 050-3643466
Valtakatu 23 A
69100 Kannus
Finland
Email: alpo.vuorenmaa@luukku.com

Karhun Soutajat, Pori
Pekka Lehtonen p. 0400-860705
Väinönraitti 3 i 65
28330 Pori
Finland
Email: pekka.lehtonen@satabaana.net

Voimistelu ja Urheiluseura Kuhmoisten Kumu ry
Juha Kankkunen p. 041-4516560
Peippokuja 6
17800 Kuhmoinen
Finland
Email: juha.kankkunen@evo.hamk.fi

Kensu ry, Jyväskylä
Jorma Harjula p. 014-3388700
Kaakkoiskaari 4
40530 Jyväskylä
Finland
Email: jorma.harjula@kolumbus.fi

Keurusselän Pursiseura ry, Keuruu
Merja Niemelä p. 0400-187112
Valkeisentie 48
42700 Keuruu
Finland
Email: merja_niemela@jippii.fi

Kuntoseura Homenokat ry, Äänekoski
Sisko Kinnunen p.040-7335361
Saarijärventie 44 D A
44170 Äänekoski
Finland
Email: risto.kinnunen@pp.inet.fi

Kymön Nestessä Soutajat ry, Kymönkoski
Kauko Ikäheimonen p. 040-5824167
Valkeisentie 8 B
44640 Kymönkoski
Finland
Email: tarja.ikaheimonen@pp.inet.fi

Kyyjärven Kyky ry, Kyyjärvi
Jarmo Lautanen p. 0400-218365
Eetunkuja 4
43700 Kyyjärvi
Finland
Email: esa.kyronlahti@betset.fi

Muroleen kylät ry, Murole
Heimo Moisio p. 0500-330129
Muroleenkanavantie 96
34410 Murole
Finland

Nesteen Soutajat ry, Naantali
Juha Helenius p. 02-2463003
Luhakatu 14 A 4
20660 Littoinen
Finland
Email: juha.helenius@turkuamk.fi

Nokian Veneilijät ry, Nokia
Kalevi Viitanen p. 03-3414433 tai 0500-929585
Ilkantie 7 C 28
37100 Nokia
Finland

Pargas Roddklubb rf, Parainen
Tomas Söderblom p. 040-7484721
Pajbackavägen 2/4
21600 Pargas
Finland
Email: tomas.soderblom@wartsila.com

Parkanon Urheilijat ry, Parkano
Erkki Niemenmaa p. 0400-726016
Luomanperäntie 120
39700 Parkano
Finland
Email: marja.makiviinikko@tiki.inet.fi

Pirkan Soutu ry, Tampere
Onerva Rekola p. 03-31261450
Sarvijaakonkatu 32
33540 Tampere
Finland
Email: pirkankierros@pirkankierros.hlu.fi
www.pirkankierros.hlu.fi

Ruoveden Pirkat, Ruovesi
Pentti Lehto p. 03-4762472
Kaartotie 3
34600 Ruovesi
Finland

Suomenselän Soutajat ry, Jyväskylä
Seija Laaksonen p. 050-5642596
Hovilantie 230 V
43640 Humppi
Finland

Takon Soutajat ry, Tampere
Toimisto p. 03-2132105
Hatanpäänkatu 6
33900 Tampere
Finland
Email: takonsoutajat@koti.soon.fi
sivut.koti.soon.fi/takonsoutajat

Turun Akateemiset Soutajat ry, Turku
Matti Sankinen p. 040-5959399
Piispankatu 10
20500 Turku
Finland
Email: matti.sankinen@utu.fi

Turun Soutajat ry, Turku
Keijo Aaltonen p. 040-5204892
Pampinkatu 10
20900 Turku
Finland
Email: laura.aaltonen@pp1.inet.fi

Valkeakosken Vesiveikot ry, Valkeakoski
Lasse Jääskeläinen p. 0400-987592
Kasurisentie 10-12 b
37630 Valkeakoski
Finland
Email: lasse.jaaskelainen@upm-kymmene.com

Vihtavuoren Pamaus ry, Leppävesi
Ilkka Riikonen p.014-3779555
Susikuja 5
41310 Leppävesi
Finland
Email: ilkka.riikonen@kemira.com

Virtain Urheilijat ry, Virrat
Paula Räty p. 050-5867350
Virtaintie 15
34800 Virrat
Finland
Email: virtu.virtainurheilijat.fi

ITÄ-SUOMEN LÄÄNI

Airoteam ry, Niemisjärvi
Seppo Marttinen p. 0400-515820
Kulmatie 12
41490 Niemisjärvi
Finland
Email: jpikka@cc.jyu.fi
cc.jyu.fi/~jpikka/airoteam

Enonkosken Kohina ry, Enonkoski
Kirsi Malmstedt p. 040-7778710
Kelkkamäentie 126
58160 Karvila
Finland
Email: kirsi.malmstedt@mikkeli.fi

Future Club ry, Onttola
Toivo Turunen p. 0400-375070
Alakoskentie 2
80510 Onttola
Finland
Email: toivo.turunen@vauhtispeed.fi

Hullun Hirven Soutajat ry, Mikkeli
Sari Karhu
Tykkimiehenkatu 12
50100 Mikkeli
Finland

Itä-Suomen Soutuklubi ry, Luikonlahti
Pertti Tuomikoski p. 0400-697469
Laiturintie 22
73670 Luikonlahti
Finland

Järvi-Suomen Soutajat ry, Rahula
Heimo Karjalainen p. 040-5071792
Kummaniementie 1 A
51720 Rahula
Finland

Karelia-Soutu ry, Liperi
Raimo Piiroinen p. 013-6865304 tai 0400-678799
PL 20
83101 Liperi
Finland
Email: raimo.piiroinen@liperi.fi

Kostonsoutajat, Huutokoski
Esko Kotivuori p.040-5042900
Paronraitti 30
79600 Joroinen
Finland
Email: esko.kotivuori@pp.inet.fi

Lieksan Loiske ry, Lieksa
Pentti Tapanen p. 050-5749118
Pärekoski 8
81720 Lieksa
Finland
Email: pentti.tapanen@pp.inet.fi

Lohikosken Kisaveikot ry, Lohikoski
Jeri Hämäläinen p. 0500-805803
Kaarretie 20
58700 Sulkava
Finland

Mikkelin Soutajat ry, Mikkeli
Pentti Iivanainen p. 015-172823 tai 044-0400702
Saukonkuja3
50190 Mikkeli
Finland
Email: mikkelinsoutajat.tripod.com
pentti.iivanainen@dnainternet.net

Puumalan Soutu-Team ry, Puumala
Asko Löppönen p. 0500-256233
Kokkopellonkuja 2
52200 Puumala
Finland
Email: asko.lopponen@pp.inet.fi

Rantasalmen Urheilijat ry, Rantasalmi
Jaakko Laukka
Huhtatie 4, 58900 Rantasalmi

Savonlinnan Soutu ry, Savonlinna
Pauli Mehtonen p. 040-834049
Apajatie 27
57600 Savonlinna
Finland
Email: kaisa.mehtonen@ita-savo.fi

Soinilansalmen kyläyhdistys ry, Leppävirta
Keijo Vepsäläinen p. 040-5081063
Kivimäentie
79100 Leppävirta
Finland
Email: keijo vepsalainen@fwfin.fwc.com

Sulkava-Seura ry, Sulkava
Jukka Simpanen p. 0400-656106
PL 45
58701 Sulkava
Finland
Email: jukka.simpanen@suursoudut.net
www.suursoudut.net

Sulkavan Tarmo, Sulkava
Oiva Väisänen p. 015-471377
Pistotie 3
58700 Sulkava
Finland

Sulkavan Urheilijat -41 ry, Sulkava
Essi Virta p. 050-3033736
Itäpäijänteentie 63
40320 Jyväskylä
Finland
Email: emvirta@st.jyu.fi

Virranviemät ry, Leppävirta
Riitta Minkkinen p. 040-5260971
Kauppilanmäentie 1
79100 Leppävirta
Finland
Email: riitta.minkkinen@leppavirta.fi

OULUN LÄÄNI

Kainuun Liikunta ry, Kainuu
Hannu Tikkanen p. 050-5421033
Kauppakatu 21 3.krs
87100 Kajaani
Finland
Email: hannu.tikkanen@kainuunliikunta.fi

Kuusamon Soutajat ry, Kuusamo
Ilkka Karvonen p. 040-7599185
Siulakaarre 5
93600 Kuusamo
Finland
Email: ilkka.karvonen@kuusamo.fi

LC-Oulunsalo ry, Oulunsalo
Jarkko Marttila p. 0400-683277
Pahajärventie
90460 Oulunsalo
Finland

Oulun Kilpaveljet ry, Oulu
Pertti Törmi p. 050-5553315
Hiekkakiventie 2 B 4
90240 Oulu
Finland
Email: pentti.tormi@mail.suomi.net
www.tervasoutu.fi

LAPIN LÄÄNI

Rovaniemen Kirkkovenesoutajat ry, Rovaniemi
Jani Laine p. 050-3876669
Valtatie 6-8 B 16
90500 Oulu
Finland
Email: jani.laine@mail.suomi.net

France

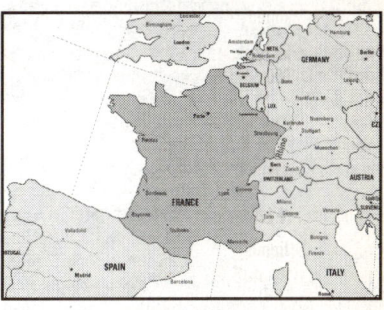

HISTORY

Modern rowing in France can trace its origins to the rowing known as canotage. Canotage, the French equivalent of the word for English pleasure rowing, began on the Seine River in Paris and spread rapidly throughout France at the beginning of the nineteenth century. It is estimated that there were over 2,000 boats in the Paris area by the 1830's. The French so much enjoyed their weekend boating tours and the social events that accompanied these outings to the Paris outskirts, that it became trendy for all social classes. Through the 1800's, French artists included views of rowing and boating in their depictions of French social gatherings. Given the distances involved, was natural that the French were among the first to hold head races as the winner secured the best picnic area and restaurant table. The first rowing race was organized in 1834 on the canals in Paris.

Before football, cycling and motor racing, rowing was the derrigure pastime. By the 1840's rowing had become one of France's first public sports attracting many spectators with prizes and betting. The Paris newspapers promoted the sport by announcing matches between crews and reporting on the most popular teams. At the same time, modern competitive rowing began to take shape. French high society did not appreciate what they perceived as the loose morals of the pleasure rowers. Soon society-sponsored clubs were created to exclusively support racing and disciplined rowing. It is these clubs that began to transform the cantonage boats into the sleek racing shells we recognize today. Sadly, as these clubs began to champion the sport, women were forbidden in boats though they were allowed in the grandstands. The Societe des Regates Parisiennes (the Society of Parisian Regattas) was created in 1853. Over the next fifteen years at least thirty clubs were established in Paris and the larger cities. One of the first international rowing events was held at the Paris World Exposition in 1867 where crews from England, Belgium, Germany and Canada were represented. The French clubs became regular participants in all international regattas from that time forward. A unique event provided the next major catalyst to the development of rowing in France. After the Franco-Prussian war of 1870, the new French republic sought to shape-up French youth through the encouragement of sports. Fifty more clubs opened their doors between 1872 and 1882. Many of these athletic clubs often included several different sports such as fencing, gymnastics, tennis and cycling.

During this time rowing became one of the most popular sports in France, but the multitude of clubs also gave rise to infighting between the leading clubs. Many cities saw their clubs uniting to form regional federations; each with their own rules, boat types and competitive categories. Many vain attempts were made to create a national federation as it appeared impossible to achieve consensus between the regional organizations, particularly on the issue of prize money. In 1890, the leading three regional bodies finally decided on a diplomatic truce and the national federation was created. The establishment of the French Federation of Rowing Clubs facilitated the organization of the first national championship.

Even though some French clubs were still hesitant to join the French Rowing Federation, France was among the founding members of the International Rowing Federation, FISA, in 1892. Soon after, the European Championships were created to address the need for an international competition for those continental rowers who could not compete in the Royal Henley Regatta in England because of the regulations on amateurism. In 1899, the French Rowing Federation adopted new rules to promote amateurs and more French rowers began to appear at this now, historic regatta.

The French clubs, rather than universities, have been the champions of the sport of rowing in France. The model of club rowing as a system that could produce world champions was proven with the famous successes of Frenchman, Gaston Delapane. Delapane won over fifty important races including the European Championship in the single scull on four occasions before 1914.

Through the years France has maintained its position as a leading rowing nation. France has been the host to numerous international competitions including the European Championships, the World Cup and two Olympics.

PERSONALITIES

Henri Barrelet: The first French Olympic champion in the single scull at the Paris Games in 1900.

Jean Sepheriades: The first French winner of the Diamond Sculls at the Royal Henley Regatta in 1946.

Did You Know ?

France, Belgium, Italy and Switzerland founded the International Rowing Federation, FISA in 1892 and the first publication dedicated to rowing, L'Aviron was published in 1886.

NATIONAL FEDERATION

Fédération Française des Sociétés d'Aviron
17 Boulevard de la Marne
Nogent Sur Marne Cedex, 94736
France
Tel: +33 1 4514 2640
Fax: +33 1 4875 7875
Email: ffsa@avironfrance.asso.fr
www.avironfrance.asso.fr

CLUBS (BY CITY)

Sport Nautique d'Abbeville
105-107, chemin des Canotiers
80100, Abbeville
France
Tel: +33 03 22 24 48 59

Aviron Agathois
Base d'Aviron — Bois de Boulogne
Route de Bessan
34300, Agde
France
Tel: +33 04 67 94 47 40

Aviron Agenais
rue Jean Laffore
47000, Agen
France
Tel: +33 05 53 68 28 74

Entente Nautique d'Aix-Les-Bains Aviron
22, rue Daniel Rops
73100, Aix les Bains
France
Tel: +33 04 79 88 12 07
Email: entente.nautique.aix@free.fr
aviron.aix.les.bains.free.fr/

Societe Nautique d'Ajaccio
Base Nautique Saint Joseph
20000, Ajaccio
France
Tel: +33 04 95 22 14 04

Aviron Club Albigeois
Canavieres le Bas
81000, Albi
France
Tel: +33 05 63 54 37 12
Email: albi.aviron@free.fr
albi.aviron.free.fr/

Societe Nautique d'Almayrac
Barrage de la Roucarie
81190, Almayrac
France
Tel: +33 05 63 36 71 07

Sport Nautique d'Amiens
2, boulevard du Cange
B.P. 1624
80000, Amiens
France
Tel: +33 03 22 92 11 02
Email: snamiens@wanadoo.fr
assoc.wanadoo.fr/snamiens/

Association le Coudey
Base Nautique
Port Ostreicole
33510, Andernos
France
Tel: +33 05 56 26 10 14

Association David Allegre
cabane 55, quai Lahillon
port ostréicole
33510, Andernos les Bains
France
Tel: +33 05 56 82 47 14
Email: pinassottes@multimania.com
pinassottes.multimania.com/

Cercle d'Aviron du Confluent
57, rue des Robaresses
78570, Andresy
France

Angers Nautique
11, rue Larrey
49100, Angers
France
Tel: +33 02 41 48 23 61
Email: angers_nautique@yahoo.fr
www.chez.com/angersnautique

Association Ibaialde
6, promenade du Prince Impérial
64600, Anglet
France
Tel: +33 05 59 52 13 30
Email: ibaialde@wanadoo.fr

Club Nautique d'Angouleme
Ile de Bourgines
Centre Nautique
16000, Angouleme
France
Tel: +33 05 45 95 88 01
Email: aviron-angouleme@fr.st
www.aviron-angouleme.fr.st

Cercle Nautique d'Annecy
avenue des Maquisats
Base Nautique
74000, Annecy
France
Tel: +33 04 50 45 74 67
Email: cnannecy@wanadoo.fr

Club des Sports Annecy le Vieux
29, avenue du Petit Port
74940, Annecy Le Vieux
France
Tel: +33 04 50 27 77 69

Aviron Arcachonnais
Quai de Goslär
Port de Plaisance
33120, Arcachon
France
Tel: +33 05 56 83 82 40

Club Olympique Multisports d'argenteuil Aviron
30, rue Carnot
95100, Argenteuil
France
Tel: +33 01 39 47 31 31
www.chez.com/comaaviron/

Club Leo Lagrange d'armentieres
Foyer Brossolette
avenue Pierre Brossolette
59280, Armentieres
France
Tel: +33 03 20 77 09 40
Email: aviron2@hotmail.com
www.cyberleo-armentières.org/

Ars Scull Aviron
route de la Prée Z.A.
17590, Ars En Re
France
Tel: +33 05 46 29 41 57

Club Aviron Arvieu Pareloup
Plage d'Arvieu
Cite de Pareloup
12120, Arvieu
France
Email: jeanmarie.allier@wanadoo.fr

Association Intercommunale d'animation
Base de loisirs
63120, Aubusson d'auvergne
France
Tel: +33 04 73 53 56 02
Email: lac-d'aubusson@wanadoo.fr

Aviron Club Auscitain
Salle E. Vila
rue du 8 mai 1945
32000, Auch
France
Tel: +33 05 62 63 60 68
Email: president@auch-aviron.com
www.auch-aviron.com/

Aviron Club d'auray
26, quai Franklin
Port de Saint Goustan
56400, Auray
France

Societe Nautique d'avignon
Ile de la Barthelasse
84000, Avignon
France
Tel: +33 04 90 82 02 54

Ass. Nautique Fontainebleau-Avon
16, avenue de Valvin
ou rue du Port de Valvin
77210, Avon
France
Tel: +33 01 60 72 06 64
Email: anfa-aviron@wanadoo.fr

Aviron Club du Bassin de Thau
Centre Nautique Municipal
34540, Balaruc les Bains
France
Tel: +33 04 67 46 11 34
Email: a.mantion@libertysurf.com

Club d'Aviron de Mer Barneville-Carteret
Promenade Abbé Lebouteiller
50270, Barneville Carteret
France
Tel: +33 02 33 04 67 36
Email: cambc@ifrance.com
www.legoupil.fr/

Cercle Nautique d'indre
cale du bac
44610, Basse Indre
France
Tel: +33 02 40 85 05 37
Email: olivier_cottineau@yahoo.fr
site.voila.fr/cni

La Yole Hamoise
Mairie de Basse-Ham
33, rue de la Forêt
57970, Basse-Ham
France
Tel: +33 03 82 51 95 54
layolehamoise.free.fr

Societe Nautique de Bayonne
1, avenue du Capitaine Resplandy
Garage de Mousserolles
64100, Bayonne
France
Tel: +33 05 59 59 02 39
Email: sn.bayonne@wanadoo.fr

Aviron Bayonnais
Garage de la Nive
rue Owen Roe
64100, Bayonne
France
Tel: +33 05 59 63 33 15
Email: aviron-bayonnais@wanadoo.fr
www.aviron-bayonnais.asso.fr

Aviron de Beaucaire
Centre Nautique et de Loisirs
Champ de Foire
30300, Beaucaire
France
Tel: +33 04 66 59 18 28

Beaumont Aviron
Z.A. St Roch
Rue de l'Ancienne Cimenterie
95260, Beaumont sur Oise
France

Club Nautique de Belbeuf
Base Nautique de Belbeuf
8, route de Paris
76240, Belbeuf
France
Tel: +33 02 35 02 03 33
Email: aviron@normandnet.fr
perso.normandnet.fr/aviron/

Aviron Mjc Bellegarde
Base Nautique Arlod
01200, Bellegarde
France
Tel: +33 04 50 48 08 91
Email:

Aviron Belle-Islois
Place de l'Eglise Sauzon
56360, Belle-Isle En Mer
France
Tel: +33 02 91 31 64 71

Belleville 55 Aviron
Mairie de Belleville
55430, Belleville sur Meuse
France
Tel: +33 03 29 84 36 87

Sport Nautique de Bergerac
18, promenade Pierre Loti
24100, Bergerac
France
Tel: +33 05 53 57 85 02
Email: aviron.snbergerac@wanadoo.fr

Sport Nautique Bisontin
2, avenue de Chardonnet
Section Aviron
25000, Besancon
France
Tel: +33 03 81 53 89 40

Aviron Club Biterrois
base Nautique
Avenue de Serignan
34500, Beziers
France
Tel: +33 04 67 49 33 29
Email: ac.biterrois@libertysurf.fr

Societe Gymnastique de Blere Aviron
bse nautique de Bléré
rue de la Grange
37150, Blere
France
Tel: +33 02 47 30 30 55

Bouillac Aviron Club
Les Cambous
12300, Bouillac
France
Tel: +33 05 65 63 20 31

Athletique Club Boulogne Billancourt
129, rue de Bellevue
92100, Boulogne Billancourt
France
Tel: +33 01 46 05 92 84
Email: acbbaviron@free.fr
acbbaviron.free.fr/

Aviron Boulonnais
Stade Nautique de la Liane
boulevard Chanzy
62200, Boulogne sur Mer
France
Tel: +33 03 21 87 31 46
Email: aviron.boulonnais@free.fr
aviron.boulonnais.free.fr

Aviron Club de Bourges
chemin du Grand Mazières
Val d'Auron
18000, Bourges
France
Tel: +33 02 48 67 94 46
Email: aviron.bourges@free.fr
aviron.bourges.free.fr/

Bressols Aviron Club
Base Nautique
chemin de la Rive
82710, Bressols
France
Tel: +33 05 63 02 14 08
Email: bressolsavironclub@chez.com
www.chez.com/bressolsavironclub/

Aviron Brestois
Centre Nautique Municipal du Moulin Blanc
29200, Brest
France
Tel: +33 02 98 04 26 32
Email: brest.aviron@free.fr
brest.aviron.free.fr

Yole Club Brest-Iroise
Centre Nautique du Moulin Blanc
29200, Brest
France
Tel: +33 02 98 34 64 64

Emulation Nautique de Bordeaux
Centre Nautique de Bordeaux-Lac
boulevard du Parc des Expositions
33520, Bruges
France
Tel: +33 05 56 50 70 60
Email: enbaviron@wanadoo.fr

Val d'oise Aviron
63, rue des Iles
95430, Butry sur Oise
France
Tel: +33 01 34 73 19 51
Email: voaviron@free.fr

Societe Nautique de Caderousse
Ile de la Piboulette
84860, Caderousse
France
Tel: +33 04 90 51 92 87

Aviron Cadurcien
quai de Regourd
46000, Cahors
France
Tel: +33 05 65 35 44 95

Aviron Club Lyon-Caluire
Maison Eclusière
quai Clemenceau
69300, Caluire
France
Tel: +33 04 78 30 01 41
Email: aviron_CNLC@hotmail.com
cnlc.ifrance.com/

Cercle de L'aviron de Lyon
12, quai Clemenceau
69300, Caluire
France
Tel: +33 04 78 29 35 94
Email: info@cercle-aviron-lyon.com
www.cercle-aviron-lyon.com/

Aviron Union Nautique de Lyon
59, quai Georges Clémenceau
69300, Caluire
France
Tel: +33 04 78 23 21 92
Email: infos@aunlyon.com
www.aunlyon.com

Union Nautique de Cambrai
rue Lucien Sampaix
digue du Canal
59400, Cambrai
France
Tel: +33 03 27 70 38 43

Rowing Club Cannes-Mandelieu
boulevard de la Mer
Base Patrice Auger
06210, Cannes Mandelieu
France
Tel: +33 04 93 49 71 34
Email: rccm@laposte.net
www.rccm.fr.st/

Cercle Nautique de Canteleu-Croisset
46, quai Gustave Flaubert
76380, Canteleu
France
Tel: +33 02 35 36 61 29

Club d'Aviron Carantecois
plage de Kelenn
29660, Carantec
France
Tel: +33 02 98 67 01 12

Club Omnisport de Carnon
Club Aviron
Mauguio Carnon
34280, Carnon
France
Tel: +33 04 67 68 49 73
Email: aviron.carnon@free.fr
aviron.carnon.free.fr/

O.M.A. Jeunes de Carpentras
Hôtel de Ville
B.P. 264
84208, Carpentras Cedex
France

Club Nautique des Salettes
port de Salettes
83320, Carqueirane
France
Tel: +33 04 94 58 75 08

A.S. Aviron de La Martinique
Port de Case Pilote
97222, Case Pilote
France

Association Sportive Culturelle et Nautique "La Fregate"
Port de pêche de Case Pilote
97222, Case Pilote
France
Tel: +33 05 96 78 70 27

Cercle Nautique de Cassis Section Aviron
quai des Moulins
13260, Cassis
France
Tel: +33 04 42 01 79 04
Email: cn.cassis@wanadoo.fr
www.port-cassis.com

Cercle Nautique de Grenade et Castelnau d'estretefonds
Chemin du Canal
31620, Castelnau d'estretefonds
France
Tel: +33 05 61 35 10 34

Rowing Club de Castillon
quai André Duranton
33350, Castillon La Bataille
France
Tel: +33 05 57 40 23 68
Email: rccastillon@multimania.com
www.multimania.com/rccastillon/

Club Nautique Caudebecquais
Section Aviron
route de Villequier
76490, Caudebec En Caux
France
Tel: +33 02 35 96 99 66

Armagnac Aviron Club
Base de l'Uby
32150, Cazaubon
France
Tel: +33 05 62 09 53 92

Aviron des Deux Lacs
Mairie de Celles sur Plaine
88110, Celles sur Plaine
France
Tel: +33 03 29 41 18 60

Club d'Aviron de L'essec
1, avenue Bernard Hirsch
BP 105
95021, Cergy Pontoise Cedex
France
Tel: +33 01 30 30 53 90
Email: clubavironessec@caramail.com

Cercle de L'aviron de Chalon
Base nautique
rue d'Amsterdam
71100, Chalon sur Saone
France
Tel: +33 03 85 41 30 04
Email: cac.chalon@libertysurf.fr
www.chez.com/cercleavironchalon/

Les Pelles Chalonnaises
rue du Canal Louis XII
51000, Chalons En Champagne
France
Tel: +33 03 26 64 46 37

Red Star Club Champigny
02, quai Gallieni
94500, Champigny sur Marne
France
Tel: +33 01 48 81 30 09
Email: avironchampigny@free.fr
avironchampigny.free.fr/

Cn de Charleville Mezieres
Base Nautique Jean Delautre
rue des Paquis
08000, Charleville Mezieres
France
Tel: +33 03 24 33 91 71

Club Nautique de Chateau-Gontier
Aviron
Halage de Mirwault
53200, Chateau Gontier
France
Tel: +33 02 43 07 97 24
Email: philippeclaudie.ledoux@tiscali.fr
www.geocities.com/aviron53/

Aviron Chateau Thierry 02
2, avenue d'Essômes
02400, Chateau Thierry
France
Tel: +33 03 23 83 47 83
aviron-chateau-thierry-02.club@laposte.net

Aviron Chateaulinois
Quai Robert Alba
Ancienne usine LARZUL
29150, Chateaulin
France
Tel: +33 02 98 86 33 25
Email: aviron.chateaulinois@wanadoo.fr
perso.wanadoo.fr/aviron.chateaulinois/index.htm

Societe Nautique de Chatellerault
1, rue Henri Boucher
86100, Chatellerault
France
Tel: +33 05 49 21 01 97

Sport Nautique Romanais Peageois
Le Martinet
Route de Grenoble
26300, Chatuzange Le Goubet
France
Tel: +33 04 75 70 32 53
Email: snrp@wanadoo.fr
perso.wanadoo.fr/thierry.gravelot/aviron/snrp.html

Aviron Pontissalien — Lac Saint Point
Base Nautique du Chaudron
25160, Chaudron
France
Tel: +33 06 84 43 94 91

Aviron Club du Bocage
La Petite Grassière
85250, Chavagnes-En-Paillers
France
Tel: +33 02 51 42 24 78 / 06 87 28 23 56

Leman Aviron Club
Centre Nautique de Touges
2555, rue du Port
74140, Chens sur Leman
France
Tel: +33 06 82 92 60 92

Cherbourg Club Aviron de Mer
Plage Napoléon
50100, Cherbourg
France
Tel: +33 02 33 01 77 39
Email: remy.alnet@wanadoo.fr
ccam.ifrance.com

Aviron Sport Choletais
Centre Nautique
Port de Ribou
49300, Cholet
France
Tel: +33 02 41 71 28 27

Aviron Clairacais
Maubourguet
Quai de la République
47320, Clairac
France
Tel: +33 05 53 88 90 82

Club Nautique Clamecycois
314 Bis Cité Saint Roch
58500, Clamecy
France
Tel: +33 03 86 27 98 45
Email: avironclamecy@aol.fr

Cognac Yacht Rowing Club
27, rue Jean Bart
16100, Cognac
France
Tel: +33 05 45 82 02 66
Email: C.Y.R.C.@wanadoo.fr
www.aviron-cognac.com

Club Omnisport et Culturel de Combleux
Mairie de Combleux
45800, Combleux
France
Tel: +33 02 38 55 11 13

Club d'Aviron de Sainte Marine
rue Ar Pussou, Sainte Marine
Base Nautique de Kerobistin
29120, Combrit
France

Aviron Commercy
route d'Euville
55200, Commercy
France
Tel: +33 03 29 91 57 50

Sport Nautique Compiegnois
2, cours Guynemer
60200, Compiegne
France
Tel: +33 03 44 40 28 13
Email: aviron-compiegne@wanadoo.fr
www.aviron-compiegne.com/

Aviron de Mer Concarnois
Complexe sportif du Porzou
29900, Concarneau
France
Tel: +33 02 98 51 13 50

Societe Nautique de Condrieu
Chemin du Moulin
69420, Condrieu
France
Tel: +33 04 74 59 80 72

Association Sportive de Corbeil- Essonnes
71, quai Maurice Riquiez
91100, Corbeil Essonnes
France
Tel: +33 01 60 75 51 52
Email: aviron.corbeil@wanadoo.fr
www.multimania.com/avironcorbeil

Elan Nautique Coudekerquois-Section Aviron
centre Nautique "Pascal Leys"
113, rue des Forts
59210, Coudekerque Branche
France
Tel: +33 03 28 61 06 80

Societe Nautique de La Basse Seine
26, quai du Président Paul Doumer
92400, Courbevoie
France
Tel: +33 01 43 33 03 47
Email: club@basseseine.net
www.basseseine.net

Etoile Nautique de L'oise
7, rue de l'Ile
60100, Creil
France
Tel: +33 03 44 25 20 71
Email: enocreil.aviron@worldonline.fr
www.chez.com/stef123/

Sauveteurs et Aviron Decinois
Rue de la Fraternité
Pont de Décines
69150, Decines-Charpieu
France
Tel: +33 04 78 49 18 19

Aviron Decizois
Chemin des Olympiades
58300, Decize
France

Club Nautique Dieppois
chemin de la Rivière
cours de Dakar
76200, Dieppe
France
Tel: +33 02 35 84 27 55

Aviron Dijonnais
Base Nautique du Lac Kir
21000, Dijon
France
Tel: +33 03 80 45 27 89

Club Nautique Divonne les Bains
BP 48
01220, Divonne
France
Tel: +33 04 50 20 06 40
Email: cndivonne@tiscali.fr
club-nautique-divonne.chez.tiscali.fr

Aviron Club Dolois
Centre de Rencontre
Pierre Mendes-France — CRISSEY
39100, Dole
France
Tel: +33 03 84 82 14 24
Email: rthereau@club-internet.fr
perso.club-internet.fr/rthereau/

Club Nautique de Doussard
Bout du lac
B.P. 36
74210, Doussard
France
Tel: +33 04 50 44 81 45

Societe Nautique de La Haute Seine
49, avenue Libert
91210, Draveil
France
Tel: +33 01 69 42 36 13
Email: snhs@free.fr
snhs.free.fr

Sporting Dunkerquois
56, rue des Scieries
59640, Dunkerque
France
Tel: +33 03 28 25 26 69

Club d'Aviron d'embrun
Abri des Rameurs
Plan d'eau d'Embrun
05200, Embrun
France
Tel: +33 04 92 43 46 13

Societe Nautique d'enghien
22 bis, boulevard du Lac
95880, Enghien les Bains
France
Tel: +33 01 34 17 31 53
Email: sn.enghien@free.fr

Societe Nautique d'epernay
1, quai de l'Ile Belon
51200, Epernay
France
Tel: +33 03 26 54 90 47

Aviron Club d'epinal
Maison des Sports
12, rue du Général Leclerc
88000, Epinal
France
Tel: +33 03 29 30 77 32
Email:

Club Nautique Esparron de Verdon
Base Nautique
04800, Esparron de Verdon
France
Tel: +33 04 92 77 15 25
Email: cneu@club-internet.fr
perso.club-internet.fr

Ass.Dep.de Plein Air de Belfort
Base Nautique du Malsaucy
90350, Evette Salbert
France
Tel: +33 03 84 29 21 84
Email:

Club Aviron Evian
Centre Paul Arrandel
10, avenue de Noailles
74500, Evian les Bains
France
Tel: +33 04 50 75 12 07
www.cur-archamps.fr/mjc-evian/sport.htm

Aviron d'evry Sca 2000
chemin de Halage
parking de la Gare
91000, Evry
France
Tel: +33 01 64 97 05 15

Excenevex — Skiff
Le Moulin
74140, Excevenex
France
Tel: +33 041 05 72 85 64
Email:

Association Voile et Plein Air
Centre Nautique de l'Etang de Boulet
La Bijouterie
35440, Feins
France
Tel: +33 02 99 69 70 69
Email: centre.nautique.avpa@wanadoo.fr
assoc.wanadoo.fr/avpa/

Aviron du Bocage
30, chemin du Bocage
31150, Fenouillet
France
Tel: +33 05 62 75 22 10
Email: aviron.bocage@free.fr
aviron.bocage.free.fr/

Club Nautique de Fille sur Sarthe
6, rue du Pont
72210, Fille sur Sarthe
France
Tel: +33 02 43 87 15 78
Email: mat.zim@wanadoo.fr

Csl Flize Aviron
20, rue Baccarat
8160, Flize
France
Tel: +33 03 24 53 58 76
Email: flizeaviron@aol.com

Rowing Club de L'argens
Villa Marie
Camp Marin RN 98
83600, Frejus
France
Tel: +33 04 94 53 54 86

Aviron Bassin d'elbeuf
2, rue de la Belle Aurore
76410, Freneuse
France
Tel: +33 02 35 77 38 55

Association Sportive de Libourne
Section Aviron
Centre Nautique
33126, Fronsac
France
Tel: +33 05 57 51 25 97

Club Nautique du Migron Aviron
route des Carris
Le Migron
44320, Frossay
France
Tel: +33 02 40 39 79 52

Associaton Sportive Gerardmer
Union Nautique Droite du Lac
4, chemin des Myrtilles
88400, Gerardmer
France
Tel: +33 03 29 60 02 09/87 53

Aviron Giennois
quai de Nice
45500, Gien
France

Cercle d'Aviron du Der Chantecoq
Bassin Sud Lac du Der
51290, Giffaumont
France

Club Nautique Givetois
Hôtel de Ville
place Carnot
8600, Givet
France

Societe Havraise de L'Aviron
avenue Charles de Gaulle
Pont VIII
76700, Gonfreville L'Orcher
France
Tel: +33 02 35 47 62 21
Email: avironlehavre@wanadoo.fr

Aviron Granvillais
Centre Régional de Nautisme de Granville
boulevard des Amiraux
50400, Granville
France
Tel: +33 02 33 91 22 60

Gravelines Union Sportive Aviron
Chemin du Guindal
Saint Georges sur L'Aa
59820, Gravelines
France
Tel: +33 03 28 23 36 03

Sports Nautiques Gray-Saone Club Aviron
route d'Essertey
70100, Gray
France
Tel: +33 03 84 64 81 73
avirongray.multimania.com

Aviron Grenoblois
37, quai Jongkind
38000, Grenoble
France
Tel: +33 04 76 42 77 86, +33 04 76 63 11 23
Email: aviron.grenoblois@altavista.net
www.aviron-grenoblois.com/

Association Sportive de Fontaine Aviron
172, avenue des Martyrs
38000, Grenoble
France
Tel: +33 04 76 43 35 30
Email: asf.aviron@wanadoo.fr
perso.wanadoo.fr/fontaine.aviron/

Com Merger Aviron
Ce Schneider Electric Grenoble
quai Paul Louis Merlin
38050, Grenoble Cedex
France
Tel: +33 04 76 57 60 60

Aviron Club Grisollais
430, chemin du Canal
82170, Grisolles
France
Tel: +33 05 63 67 39 11

Scull Club Halluinois
Port de Plaisance d'Halluin-Menen
59250, Halluin
France

Aviron Meulan les Mureaux — Hardricourt
2, promenade du Bac
78250, Hardricourt
France
Tel: +33 01 34 74 28 55
ammh.asso.fr

Cercle Nautique Haubourdinois
91, rue Léo Lagrange
59320, Haubourdin
France
Tel: +33 03 20 07 02 09

Endaika
rue des Orangers
64700, Hendaye
France
Tel: +33 05 59 48 06 07

Aviron Hennebontais
47, rue Eric Tabarly
56700, Hennebont
France
Tel: +33 02 97 36 43 71
Email: aviron.hennebontais@wanadoo.fr
aviron-hennebontais.fr.st/

Club Herouvillais d'Aviron de Riviere et de Mer
Base Nautique
Domaine de Beauregard
14200, Herouville Saint Clair
France
Tel: +33 02 31 43 73 46

Cercle de L'aviron de Lamothe
Plan d'eau Lac de Lamothe
33125, Hosteins
France
Tel: +33 05 56 25 74 46

Ass. Sportive des Ptt d'hyeres
Complexe Sportif Jean Berteau l'Auguade
83400, Hyeres
France
Tel: +33 04 94 66 37 70

Istres Sports Aviron
chemin du Castellan
13800, Istres
France
Tel: +33 04 42 55 51 52
Email: isaviron@aol.com

Association Nautique Omnisport Istreenne
Istrium du Sport
C.E.C. les Heures Claires
13800, Istres
France
Tel: +33 04 42 56 16 50

Aviron Jarnacais
20, quai de l'Orangerie
16200, Jarnac
France
Tel: +33 05 45 81 27 84
Email: pbraastad@duquai.com

Union Sportive de Joigny Aviron
Ancienne baignade de Joigny Lemail
89300, Joigny
France
Tel: +33 03 86 91 42 33

Association Sportive de La Police de Paris
100, quai de Polangis
94340, Joinville Le Pont
France
Tel: +33 01 48 83 21 97
Email: aspp.aviron@free.fr
aspp.aviron.free.fr/

Union Sportive Metropolitaine des Transports Parisiens
150, quai de Polangis
94340, Joinville Le Pont
France
Tel: +33 6 07 63 93 10
Email: pierrebusolini@softhome.net
usmtaviron.free.fr

Aviron Marne et Joinville
97, quai de la Marne
94340, Joinville Le Pont
France
Tel: +33 0148 89 33 22

Aviron Blesois
Levée des Tuileries Prolongée
41260, La Chaussee Saint Victor
France
Tel: +33 02 54 74 76 50

Societe Nautique Aviron de La Ciotat
avenue Wilson
Nouveau Port de Plaisance
13600, La Ciotat
France
Tel: +33 04 42 71 67 82
Email: s.n.c@free.fr

C.A. La Ferte Sous Jouarre
quai des Anglais Prolongé
embouchure du Petit Morin
77260, La Ferte Sous Jouarre
France
Tel: +33 06 60 53 95 58
Email: j.colinet@libertysurf.fr

Aviron Club du Ponant — La Grande Motte
Plaine des Jeux
BP 71
34280, La Grande Motte
France
Tel: +33 04 67 56 24 47
Email: acpgrandemotte@multimania.com
acpgrandemotte.multimania.com

Nautic Club Medeen
BP 26
13220, La Mede
France
Tel: +33 04 42 81 14 22

Aviron et Sauveteurs Reolais
11, route d'Aillas le Rouergue
33190, La Reole
France
Tel: +33 05 56 71 29 36
Email: aviron.reolais@libertysurf.fr
asr.homepageclub.org/

Aviron 85 Laroche sur Yon
La Benetière
Plan d'eau Moulin Papon
85000, La Roche sur Yon
France
Tel: +33 02 51 05 13 70
Email: aviron85@voila.fr
www.aviron85.fr.st

Aviron Seynois
Base Nautique Municipale de Saint Elme
avenue de la Jetée
83500, La Seyne sur Mer
France
Tel: +33 04 94 06 47 49
Email: aviron.seynois@laposte.net
aviron.seynois.free.fr

Club d'Aviron du Sud Gresivaudan
Promenade des Tufières
38840, La Sone
France
Tel: +33 04 76 64 44 61
Email: avironlasone@fr.st
www.avironlasone.fr.st

Societe Nautique de Lagny Aviron
131, quai de la Gourdine
77400, Lagny sur Marne
France
Tel: +33 01 64 30 04 67

Ass. des Sports de Lez Douai
route d'Arras
Club Nautique
59552, Lambres Lez Douai
France
Tel: +33 03 27 96 82 50

Asce "Le Flambeau" Sect. Aviron
Baie de Blachon
97129, Lamentin
France

Sport Nautique Langonnais
8, avenue Elie Samson
33210, Langon
France
Email: sport.nautique.langonnais@wanadoo.fr
perso.wanadoo.fr/sport.nautique.langon/

Cercle Nautique de Dinan
16, rue du Four
22100, Lanvallay
France
Tel: +33 02 96 85 14 03

Base Departementale de Voile et d'Aviron de Lavalette
Base de Voile et d'Aviron de Lavalette
43200, Lapte
France
Tel: +33 04 71 59 38 06
Email: bvlavalette@wanadoo.fr

Club des Sports Nautiques de Brive
Base Nautique de la Ville de Brive
Port Lissac
19600, Larche
France
Tel: +33 05 55 85 42 93
Email: csnbrive@club-internet.fr
www.csn-brive.com

Club d'Aviron de Mer de La Rochelle
avenue de la Capitainerie
Môle centrale — Les Minimes
17000, Larochelle
France
Tel: +33 05 46 28 94 20

Club Nautique de Laval
181, rue de la Filature
53000, Laval
France
Tel: +33 02 43 56 08 65

Societe Nautique Le Bono
Mairie
56400, Le Bono
France
Tel: +33 02 97 57 86 86

Cn Chambery Le Bourget
711, boulevard du Lac
73370, Le Bourget du Lac
France
Tel: +33 04 79 25 26 98
Email: cncbaviron@aol.com

Cercle d'Aviron Oleronais
Base nautique du Chateau d'Oléron
Le port du Chateau
17480, Le Chateau d'oleron
France
Tel: +33 05 46 47 73 57

Aviron Grau du Roi
Zone technique du Grau du Roi
impasse des Berges du Vidourles BP 71
30240, Le Grau du Roi
France
Tel: +33 04 66 51 50 08
Email: aviron.gdr@wanadoo.fr

Union Sportive du Mans
180 bis, avenue François Chancel
72000, Le Mans
France
Tel: +33 02 43 24 41 93
Email: jarry@forestmaine.com

Cercle des Rameurs Mansonniens et Mesnilois
Madame JARRET secretaire
8, chemin de l'ile Laborde
78600, Le Mesnil Le Roi
France
Tel: +33 01 39 62 32 13
Email: usml@libertysurf.fr

Aviron de Rance
3, rue des Chênes
35870, Le Minihic-Sur-Rance
France
Tel: +33 02 99 88 61 90

Aviron Club du Palais
Base Nautique
87410, Le Palais sur Vienne
France
Tel: +33 05 55 35 88 52

Societe Nautique du Perreux
7-10, quai de l'Argonne
94170, Le Perreux sur Marne
France
Tel: +33 01 48 71 39 08
Email: aviron.snp@free.fr
aviron.snp.free.fr

Club Nautique de Nogent
Ile aux Loups
face au 33, quai d'Artois
94170, Le Perreux sur Marne
France
Tel: +33 01 48 72 40 32

Club Nautique de Claouey
avenue du port
place Eric Tabarly
33950, Lege Cap Ferret
France
Tel: +33 05 56 60 73 15

Aviron Club du Verdon
Margaridon
83630, Les Salles sur Verdon
France
Tel: +33 04 94 84 22 33
Email: aviron.club.verdon@wanadoo.fr
www.aviron-verdon.com/

Sport Nautique du C.H.Libourne
Hôpital Garderose
70, rue des Réaux
33505, Libourne
France
Tel: +33 05 57 25 01 98
Email: sn.ch.libourne@wanadoo.fr

Liginiac Aviron Club
Le Maury
Centre Touristique du Maury
19160, Liginiac
France
Tel: +33 05 55 95 91 17
Email: liginiacavironclub@voila.fr

Rowing Club
15, boulevard Marcel Paul
93450, L'ile Saint Denis
France
Tel: +33 01 42 43 61 95
Email: rowing@club-internet.fr
perso.club-internet.fr/rowing/

Union Nautique de Lille
38, avenue Marx Dormoy
BP 86
59006, Lille Cedex
France
Tel: +33 03 20 92 10 98
Email: unlille@mail.dotcom.fr
unlille.zoy.org

Club Nautique de Limoges
Base Nautique de la ville de Limoges
10, rue Victor Duruy — Port du Naveix
87000, Limoges
France
Tel: +33 05 55 33 13 79
www.cnlimoges.fr.st

Societe Nautique Loire sur Rhone
Bassin du Prin
69700, Loire sur Rhone
France
Tel: +33 04 72 49 21 21

Centre Nautique de Lorient
quai Eric Tabarly
56100, Lorient
France
Tel: +33 02 97 84 81 30
Email: bienvenue@cnlorient.com
www.cnlorient.com

Aviron du Scorff
rue Amiral Favereau
56100, Lorient
France
Tel: +33 02 97 84 04 96

Patronage Laique de Lorient — Aviron du Ter
Base Nautique du Ter
Bd Guillerot
56100, Lorient
France
Tel: +33 02 97 83 69 64

Societe des Regates Maconnaises
Centre Paul Bert
389, avenue Maréchal de Lattre de Tassigny
71000, Macon
France
Tel: +33 03 85 38 00 67

Aviron Club de Manosque
Lac des Vaunades
04100, Manosque
France

Association Sportive Mantaise
Stade Nautique du Val Fourrée
boulevard Albert Camu prolongé
78200, Mantes La Jolie
France
Tel: +33 01 30 94 56 31
Email: aviron.asm@tiscali.fr
aviron.asm.chez.tiscali.fr/

Avimar Club de Voile Marandais
Le Bout des Barques
17230, Marans
France
Tel: +33 05 46 01 05 49

C.M.S. Aviron Marignane
Gymnase Saint Pierre
13700, Marignane
France
Tel: +33 04 42 88 17 58

Aviron Marmandais
26, Terrasse des Capucins
47200, Marmande
France
Tel: +33 05 53 20 66 99

Rowing Club Marseille
34, boulevard Charles Livon
13007, Marseille
France
Tel: +33 04 91 52 27 15
Email: rcmarseille@wanadoo.fr

Cercle de L'aviron de Marseille
1, plage de l'Estaque
13016, Marseille
France
Tel: +33 04 91 46 00 66
Email: aviron.marseille@libertysurf.fr
www.office-sports-mrs.asso.fr/top_club/cam

Asptt Marseille Section Aviron
Maison de la Mer
Port de la Pointe Rouge
13008, Marseille
France
Tel: +33 04 91 16 35 90
Email: asptt.marseille@wanadoo.fr
www.asptt-marseille.org

Martigues Aviron Club
7, quai Sainte Anne
13500, Martigues
France
Tel: +33 04 42 07 31 20
Email: martigues.aviron@wanadoo.fr
martigues.aviron.free.fr

Cercle Nautique de Meaux
quai Jacques Prévert prolongé
77100, Meaux
France
Tel: +33 01 64 33 46 28
Email: cnmeaux@free.fr

Cercle Nautique de Melun
48, quai du Maréchal Joffre
77000, Melun
France
Tel: +33 01 64 37 07 83

Sporting Club Aviron de Menton
promenade de la Mer
06500, Menton
France
Tel: +33 06 74 83 13 38
Email: scam_online@hotmail.com

Societe des Regates Messines
2, quai des Régates
57000, Metz
France
Tel: +33 03 87 66 86 03
Email: srmetzaviron@wanadoo.fr

Ass. Pour Le Developpement du Sport et des Loisirs de Sechemailles
Base de Loisirs de Séchemailles
19250, Meymac
France
Tel: +33 05 55 94 24 06

Aviron Majolan
avenue du Carreau
69330, Meyzieu
France
Tel: +33 04 78 31 77 49
Email: infos@avironmajolan.com
www.avironmajolan.com

Club International des Regates Aviron de Meze
52, rue de la Méditerranée
34140, Meze
France
Tel: +33 04 67 18 12 67
Email: toledopiza@ifrance.com
aviron-meze.ifrance.com/

Aviron Mimizan
Centre Nautique Jacques Martin
Quartier Woolsack
40200, Mimizan
France
Tel: +33 05 58 82 41 82
Email: aviron@nautic-sejour.org
www.nautic-sejour.org/

Association Nautique de Moissac
quartier Delbessou
294, chemin de la Rhode
82200, Moissac
France
Tel: +33 05 63 04 43 39

Societe Nautique de Monaco
3, avenue J.F. Kennedy
98000, Monaco
France
Tel: +33 377 92 16 03 03

Societe Nautique de Caen et du Calvados
4, rue de La Rochelle
14120, Mondeville
France
Tel: +33 02 31 93 36 14

Aviron Club Montargis Gatinais
16, chemin de la Baignade
45200, Montargis
France
Tel: +33 02 38 98 42 84
Email: aviron.montargis@free.fr

Union Nautique Montalbanaise
11, avenue de Toulouse
82000, Montauban
France
Tel: +33 05 63 63 01 06
Email: unm@oreka.com
www.multimania.com/UNM

Aviron Saint Cassien
base nautique Saint-Cassien
Lieu-dit "Biançon"
83440, Montauroux Le Lac
France
Tel: +33 04 94 39 88 64
Email: aviron.saint-cassien@wanadoo.fr
perso.wanadoo.fr/aviron.saint-cassien/

Club Nautique de Libos-Fumel
1, avenue de Fumel
47500, Montayral
France
Tel: +33 05 53 71 50 23

Club Montluconnais d'Aviron
rue Chabot d'Allier
03100, Montlucon
France

Aviron Club du Lac du Laragou
Plaine de la Soulade
31380, Montpitol
France
Tel: +33 05 61 84 47 60

Club Aviron de Montsoreau
avenue de la Loire
49730, Montsoreau
France
Tel: +33 02 41 38 10 16

Club d'Aviron Moulinois
Hangard Plaine des Champins
3000, Moulins
France

Sport Nautique de Nancy
75, boulevard d'Austrasie
54000, Nancy
France
Tel: +33 03 83 32 18 79
www.nancyaviron.com

Cercle Aviron de Nantes
20, avenue d'Alsace
44000, Nantes
France
Tel: +33 02 40 50 67 45
02 40 93 06 87
Email: c.a.n.@wanadoo.fr
www.canantes.org

Club Aviron Leo Lagrange Nantes
L'Eraudière
9, chemin de Belle Ile
44300, Nantes
France
Tel: +33 02 40 93 07 59
Email: club@cll-aviron.org

Universite de Nantes Aviron
Base Nautique
2, rue de la Houssinière
44072, Nantes Cedex 03
France
Tel: +33 02 51 12 58 81
Email: una@una.asso.fr
www.una.asso.fr

Aviron Club de Nantua
Route de la Cluse
RN 84
01130, Nantua
France
Tel: +33 04 74 75 26 19

Association Narbonaise Omnisports
Ecluse de Mandirac
11100, Narbonne
France

Cercle Nautique de France
Ile du Pont
92200, Neuilly sur Seine
France
Tel: +33 01 47 22 61 74
Email: cnf@compaqnet.fr

Truyere Aventure
résidence Le Belvédère
15260, Neuveglise-Lanau
France
Email: truyere@aol.com
www.sports-vancances.com

Club Nautique de Nice
50, boulevard Franck Pilatte
Bassin de la Tour Rouge
06300, Nice
France
Tel: +33 04 93 89 39 78
Email: clubnautiquenice@wanadoo.fr

Niort Aviron Club
Base Nautique de Noron
79000, Niort
France
Tel: +33 05 49 79 01 93
Email: niortaviron@chez.com
www.chez.com/niortaviron/nac.htm

Societe d'encouragement du Sport Nautique
Ile des Loups
face au 01 quai du Port
94130, Nogent sur Marne
France
Tel: +33 01 43 24 38 06
www.rowing-encou.com

Cercle d'Aviron Nogentais
Chemin Villiers aux Choux
10400, Nogent sur Seine
France
Tel: +33 03 25 21 42 93
aviron-nogentais.fr.st/

Nort Athletic Club Nautique
13, place du Bassin
44390, Nort sur Erdre
France
Tel: +33 02 40 72 20 18

Aviron Club du Lac d'aiguebelette
Base de Bouvent
73470, Novalaise
France
Tel: +33 04 79 36 02 90

Aviron Club d'orleans-Olivet
Centre Nautique Marcel Baratta
2575, route de la Source
45072, Orleans Cedex
France
Tel: +33 02 38 63 38 73
Email: avironorleans@netcourrier.com
aviron-orleans-olivet.org

Groupement Nautique des Estuaires Treger-Goelo
Roz-Glaz
22500, Paimpol
France

L'aviron du Lac Bleu
Le Calatrin
38850, Paladru
France
Tel: +33 06 03 01 53 70

Club d'Aviron de Montpellier
Les Cabanes de L'Arnel
34250, Palavas Les Flots
France
Tel: +33 04 67 50 92 40
Email: aviron.montpellier@free.fr
aviron.montpellier.free.fr/

Aviron de Mer de Perros-Guirec
Hangard Poidevin
Cale du Linkin
22700, Perros-Guirec
France

Canot Club des Gaves de Peyrehorade
Port de Plaisance
Route d'Hastingues
40300, Peyrehorade
France
Tel: +33 05 58 73 00 18

Aviron Club de Tournemine
Base Nautique
22270, Pledeliac
France
Tel: +33 02 96 34 18 38
Email: tournemine@chez.com
chez.com/tournemine

Aviron Club du Gouet-Ploufragan
Base de Loisir
le Pont Noir
22440, Ploufragan
France
Tel: +33 02 96 78 93 72
Email: avirongouet@mullimania.com

Ass. Aviron de Mer "Ar Rederien Mor"
Port du Tinduff
29470, Plougastel Daoulas
France
Tel: +33 02 98 04 29 87
www.multimania.com.rederienmor

Aviron de Mer de Plougonvelin
Centre nautique
boulevard de la Mer
29217, Plougonvelin
France
Tel: +33 02 98 48 22 20
aviron.plougonvelin.free.fr

Club d'Aviron de Paluden
cale de Treiz Coz
29880, Plouguerneau
France
Tel: +33 02 98 04 53 07
Email: clubavironpaluden@minitel.net

Centre Nautique Aviron Canoe Kayak Plouhinec
anse de Poulgoazec
29780, Plouhinec
France
Tel: +33 02 98 74 90 35

Societe Nautique de Pont A Mousson
Tour de Prague
Ile d'Esch
54700, Pont A Mousson
France
Tel: +33 03 83 81 37 31

Cercle Nautique de La Haute Moselle
Rue Aristide Briand
54550, Pont Saint Vincent
France
Email: CNHM-aviron@ifrance.com
cnhm.ifrance.com/

Pontch'aviron
Centre Social René Cassin
21, Rue Laurent Gayet
38530, Pontcharra
France
Tel: +33 04 76 97 79 79

Club Nautique de Pornic
Base Nautique de la Noëveillard
BP 1201
44210, Pornic
France
Tel: +33 02 40 82 34 72
Email: cnpornic@wanadoo.fr
www.asso.ffv/cn.pornic

Rowing Club de Port Marly
12 bis, rue de Paris
78560, Port Marly
France
Tel: +33 01 39 58 58 19

Club Nautique Foyen
allée Paul Ducou
Port Sainte Foy et Ponchapt
33220, Port-Sainte-Foy
France
Tel: +33 05 53 24 70 40

Club d'Aviron de L'odet
Base Nautique de Locmaria
1, rue du Chanoine Moreau
29000, Quimper
France
Tel: +33 02 98 90 64 16
Email: jean-michel.sempere@wanadoo.fr

Club Nautique de Trevoux
Section Aviron — Base de Chamalan
4, rue de la Plage
69650, Quincieux
France
Tel: +33 04 74 08 86 37
Email: CNT1@libertysurf.fr

Port Sud Aviron Ramonville
allée des Sportifs
31520, Ramonville Saint Agne
France
Tel: +33 05 62 17 24 03
Email: aviron.ramonville@free.fr

Regates Remoises
2, rue Clovis Chezel
51100, Reims
France
Tel: +33 03 26 50 19 34

Cercle Nautique Remois
11, rue Saint Charles
51100, Reims
France
Tel: +33 03 28 87 54 20
cn.remois.free.fr/

Societe des Regates Rennaises
Centre Nautique de la Plaine de Baud
35 F, rue Jean Marie Huchet
35000, Rennes
France
Tel: +33 02 99 36 65 75
Email: regates.rennaises@wanadoo.fr

Rennes Etudiants Club Aviron
Base Nautique Municipale de Rennes
plaine de Baud
35000, Rennes
France
Email: recaviron@yahoo.fr
www.recaviron.fr.tc

Rowing Club de Mulhouse
51, rue de la Navigation
68400, Riedisheim
France
Tel: +33 03 89 61 94 65
Email: p.suhr@nmg.fr
perso.worldonline.fr/rcm/

U.S. de Ris-Orangis Aviron
chemin de la Sous Station
91130, Ris Orangis
France
Tel: +33 01 69 06 33 94
Email: usroaviron@free.fr
usroaviron.free.fr/

Aviron Roanne — Le Coteau
Ile du Transvaal
42300, Roanne
France
Tel: +33 04 77 67 08 82

A.S. Roanne Aviron
Base Nautique du Port
Au Linquet Quai de l'ile
42300, Roanne
France
Tel: +33 04 77 71 22 97

Aviron Romanais Peageois R.C.B.I
Base Nautique Fénestrier
rue Paul Joud
26100, Romans sur Isere
France
Tel: +33 04 75 70 34 48

Club Nautique et Athletique de Rouen
20, rue de l'Industrie
Ile Lacroix
76000, Rouen
France
Tel: +33 02 35 71 41 79
Email: CNAR.aviron@libertysurf.fr

Sable Nautique Aviron
8, rue de Breil
72300, Sable sur Sarthe
France
Tel: +33 02 43 92 34 41

Varenne Plein Air Aviron
Base de la Varenne
76510, Saint Aubin Le Cauf
France
Tel: +33 02 35 85 69 05

Ass. Omnisports Nautique Eure et Seine
6, impasse des Lilas
27430, Saint Etienne du Vauvray
France
Tel: +33 02 32 61 01 84
Email: f.simian@libertysurf.fr
www.aones-aviron.com/

Amitie Plein — Air Saint Fargeau
Hangar Amitie Plein — Air
Lac du Bourdon
89170, Saint Fargeau
France

Aviron Club de Saint Gilles
Port de Saint Gilles
30800, Saint Gilles
France
Tel: +33 04 66 87 27 31

Societe Nautique de Saumur
Base Nautique Claude Baroux
route de Gennes
49400, Saint Hilaire Saint Florent
France
Tel: +33 02 41 50 64 66

Ur-Yoko
Garage Nautique
route de Chantaco
64500, Saint Jean de Luz
France
Tel: +33 05 59 51 08 88
Email: uryoko@wanadoo.fr
perso.wanadoo.fr/uryoko/

Societe Nautique Troyenne
1, avenue Auguste Terrenoire
10800, Saint Julien les Villas
France
Tel: +33 03 25 75 49 16
Email: avirontroyes@wanadoo.fr
perso.wanadoo.fr/avirontroyes/

Surf School Saint Malo
2, avenue de la Hoguette
35400, Saint Malo
France
Tel: +33 02 99 40 07 47

Societe Nautique de La Baie de Saint Malo
Cale du Naye
35400, Saint Malo
France
Tel: +33 02 99 20 22 95
Email: snbsm.saintmalo@wanadoo.fr

Bonneval Aviron du Loir
Chemin des Prés
28800, Saint Martin du Pean
France
Tel: +33 02 37 47 30 55

Schelcher Club Aviron Saint-Maur
35, quai de Bonneuil
94100, Saint Maur des Fosses
France
Tel: +33 01 48 83 65 51
www.schelcher-aviron-club-saint-maur.asso.fr

Club Nautique Saint Mihielois
rue des Avioths
55300, Saint Mihiel
France
Tel: +33 03 29 89 00 81
Email: aviron-st-mihiel@voila.fr

Saint-Nazaire O.S. Aviron
Base Jean Beauvilain
Chemin du Bois Joalland
44600, Saint Nazaire
France
Tel: +33 02 40 00 80 88
Email: snos-aviron@wanadoo.fr

Societe d'Aviron de Redon et Vilaine
La Digue
rue de la vilaine
44460, Saint Nicolas de Redon
France
Tel: +33 02 99 72 75 44
Email: aviron.redon@wanadoo.fr

Aviron Audomarois
allée des Marronniers
62500, Saint Omer
France
Tel: +33 03 21 98 39 36

Societe Nautique de L'oise
23, quai de l'Ecluse
95310, Saint Ouen L'aumone
France
Tel: +33 01 34 64 47 74
Email: sno.aviron@infonie.fr
perso.infonie.fr/sno.aviron/

Aviron Stephanois
U.S. Vigie Mouette
Le Pochet
42240, Saint Paul En Cornillon
France
Tel: +33 04 77 35 71 31

Association Sportive "Les Avirons du Precheur"
quartier Charmeuse Précheur
97250, Saint Pierre
France

Saint Pierre de Boeuf Limony Aviron
Les Graviers
42410, Saint Pierre de Boeuf
France

Groupement des Clubs d'Aviron du Nord Caraïbe
quartier Sainte Philomène
97250, Saint Pierre Martinique
France
Tel: +33 05 96 31 32 75

Yole Club Saint Politain
La Baie Pempoul
Centre Nautique
29250, Saint Pol de Leon
France
Tel: +33 02 98 19 15 08
Email: roudautd@aol.com

Aviron Saint Quentinois
avenue Léo Lagrange
B.P. 740
02314, Saint Quentin Cedex
France
Tel: +33 03 23 64 33 44

Aviron Club de Vienne et Saint Romain En Gal
chemin Guichard
Ile Baslet
69560, Saint Romain En Gal
France
Tel: +33 04 37 02 06 75

Us de Saint Tropez (Aviron)
Ecole de Voile
Baie des Canoubiers
83990, Saint Tropez
France
Tel: +33 04 94 97 73 07

Cercle Nautique de Saint Vit
Moulin du Pré
25410, Saint Vit
France
Tel: +33 03 81 87 40 40

Association Voile et Nautisme 04
Base Nautique
route du Lac
04500, Sainte Croix du Verdon
France
Tel: +33 04 92 77 76 51

Aviron Saint Livradais
Saint-Martin
47110, Sainte Livrade sur Lot
France
Tel: +33 05 53 01 17 01

Club d'Avirons Maximois
08, avenue Raoul Nordling
plage de la Croisette
83120, Sainte Maxime
France
Tel: +33 04 94 49 34 86

Club d'Aviron Saintais
6, rue de Courbiac
17100, Saintes
France
Tel: +33 05 46 74 01 66
Email: averdure@caramail.com
avironsaintais.free.fr

Societe Nautique de Sauvetage de Saint-Fons
Maison de l'eau
rue Pierre Semard
69100, Saint-Fons
France
Tel: +33 04 72 89 53 35

Rowing et Kayak Club de Sarreguemines
avenue de la Blies
57200, Sarreguemines
France
Tel: +33 03 87 89 59 34

Aviron Club de Sassenage Isere
Base Inter — Communale
de Noyarey — Sassenage
38360, Sassenage
France
Tel: +33 04 76 27 48 63

Asc Frappez des Ailes de Schoelcher
Bord de Mer Fond Lahaye
97233, Schoelcher
France

Aviron Club 233
Fond Lahaye Bord de Mer
97233, Schoelcher
France
Tel: +33 05 96 91 22 90

Aviron Sedanais
promenade Corne de Soissons
08200, Sedan
France
Tel: +33 03 24 27 07 15
Email: aviron.sedanais@wanadoo.fr

Club Nautique du Haut Segala
Lac du Tolerrme
46210, Senaillac Latronquiere
France
Tel: +33 05 65 40 32 87

Club de Voile-Aviron de Sens
Quai Boffrand
Pointe Sud de l'Ile de l'Yonne
89100, Sens
France

Aviron Setois
54, quai des Moulins
34200, Sete
France
Tel: +33 04 67 43 68 29

Val de Seine Nautique
2, grande rue
92310, Sèvres
France
Tel: +33 01 45 39 56 01
Email: jean-alex.brunelle@wanadoo.fr

Aviron de Sevrier, Rive Gauche
429, route des Mongets BP 30
74320, Sevrier
France
Tel: +33 04 50 52 61 77
Email: sevrier.avi@infonie.fr
perso.infornie.fr/avironsevrier

Aviron Club de Six-Fours
Base Nautique — Corniche des Iles
Le Brusc
83140, Six-Fours les Plages
France
Tel: +33 04 94 34 15 85

Societe Nautique Soissonnaise
2, avenue du Mail
02200, Soissons
France
Tel: +33 03 23 59 72 75

Cercle Nautique de Soisy sur Seine
rue du Port Soisy
91450, Soisy sur Seine
France
Tel: +33 01 64 85 06 11

Aviron Club Soustonnais
Centre sportif de l'Isle Verte
40140, Soustons
France
Tel: +33 05 58 41 37 87

Societe d'Aviron de Stenay
Mairie de Stenay
Au boulodrome chemin de Meuse
55700, Stenay
France
Tel: +33 03 29 80 30 31

Rowing Club de Strasbourg
2, rue de Saales
67000, Strasbourg
France
Tel: +33 03 88 22 55 77
Email: info@rowing-club.com
www.rowing-club.com

Aviron Strasbourg 1881
22, rue du Général Uhrich
67000, Strasbourg
France
Tel: +33 03 88 35 68 89
Email: aviron.as-1881@wanadoo.fr

Cercle de L'aviron de Strasbourg
Ile Weiler
Quai Jean-Pierre Mayno
67100, Strasbourg
France
Tel: +33 03 88 30 48 74

Rowing Club de Suce sur Erdre
Complexe Sportis et de Loisirs
La Papinière
44240, Suce sur Erdre
France
Tel: +33 02 40 25 66 69
Email: rowing.club.suceen@wanadoo.fr
perso.wanadoo.fr/rowing.club.suceen

Sports Nautiques Tain-Tournon
Base Nautique RN 7
BP 8
26600, Tain L'hermitage
France
Tel: +33 04 75 08 44 88

Cercle Nautique de Talloires
Plage de Talloires
74290, Talloires
France
Tel: +33 04 50 60 79 92

Club Nautique de Ploermel-Taupont
Le lac au Duc
56800, Taupont
France
Tel: +33 02 97 74 14 51
Email: clubnautiqueploermel@wanadoo.fr

Chablais Aviron Thonon
Base Nautique des Clerges
74200, Thonon les Bains
France
Tel: +33 04 50 70 23 52
Email: avironthonon@wanadoo.fr
www.avironthonon.com

Club Nautique Creusotin
Base nautique
La Grande Motte
71210, Torcy
France
Tel: +33 03 85 80 41 31
Email: cnc.comm@wanadoo.fr
hhp://www.chez.com/cncreusotin

Club Sportif des Andelys
Résidence du Lac de Tosny
27700, Tosny
France
Email: andre.giriat@wanadoo.fr
perso.wanadoo.fr/andre.giriat/

Union Sportive de Toul Aviron
Maison de l'Aviron
1683 avenue du Général Bigeard
54200, Toul
France
Tel: +33 03 83 63 17 62

Aviron Toulonnais
quai des Pêcheurs
83000, Toulon
France
Tel: +33 04 94 41 19 90
Email: jpprod.2010@worldonline.fr
www.avirontoulonnais.fr.st/

Emulation Nautique de Toulouse
allée Alfred Maysonnié
31400, Toulouse
France
Tel: +33 05 61 52 86 79

Aviron Toulousain
allée Fernand Jourdan
Parc Toulousain
31400, Toulouse
France
Tel: +33 05 61 52 71 02
Email: aviron.toulousain@wanadoo.fr
www.aviron-toulousain.com

Toulouse Aviron Sports et Loisirs
Ecluse de Lalande
Impasse de la Glacière Ouest
31200, Toulouse
France
Tel: +33 05 61 13 19 37
Email: tasl@free.fr
tasl.free.fr/

Toulouse Pierre Paul Riquet
allée Mayssonniée
31000, Toulouse
France
Tel: +33 05 61 84 90 79
Email: atppr@wanadoo.fr
perso.wanadoo.fr/beauselle/ATPPRmain.html

Toulouse Universite Club
Base Nautique André Dandine
allée Fernand Jourdant
31400, Toulouse
France
Tel: +33 05 61 53 40 78
Email: club.tucaviron@free.fr

Tours Aviron Club
avenue de Florence
37000, Tours
France
Tel: +33 02 47 44 30 44

Cercle Olympique Tours Sud Aviron
Stade des Fontaines
place Degas
37200, Tours
France
Tel: +33 02 47 27 52 67
Email: cots.aviron@wanadoo.fr
perso.micro-video.fr/jaudebert/cots/

Tregunc Aviron
Centre de Porz Halen
Route de Pouldohan
29910, Tregunc
France
Tel: +33 06 83 53 62 17

Aviron Valentinois
Base Nautique de l'Eperviere
26000, Valence
France
Tel: +33 04 75 81 61 08
Email: jean.meurillon@bus.ctav.com

Valenciennes Universite Club
Le Mont Houy
59313, Valenciennes Cedex 9
France
Tel: +33 03 27 51 12 45
Email: vuc@univ-valenciennes.fr
www.univ-valenciennes.fr/vuc

Cercle de L'aviron de Vannes
42, rue du Commerce
56000, Vannes
France
Tel: +33 02 97 47 55 03
Email: vanaviron@aol.com
www.chez.com/avironvannes/index.html

Cercle Nautique Verdunois
Ensemble Sportif Jean Herbemont
allée Chanteraine
55100, Verdun
France
Tel: +33 03 29 86 49 74

Emulation Nautique de Vernon
Base des Tourelles
rue Orgereau
27200, Vernon
France

Cercle Nautique de Versailles
La Petite Venise
Parc du Chateau
78000, Versailles
France
Tel: +33 01 30 21 10 96
www.cnv.dyndns.org

Club de L'aviron de Vichy
3 — 5, avenue de la Croix Saint-Martin
03200, Vichy
France
Tel: +33 04 70 32 36 52
Email: info@clubavironvichy.asso.fr
www.clubavironvichy.asso.fr

Sports Nautiques Villefranchois
La Darse
22, chemin du Lazaret
06230, Villefranche sur Mer
France

Aviron Union Nautique de Villefranche
Port de Beauregard
69400, Villefranche sur Saone
France
Tel: +33 04 74 68 02 12
Email: unv@laposte.com
unv.free.fr

Association Sportive Villemurienne
rue Pierre Marchet
31340, Villemur sur Tarn
France
Tel: +33 05 61 09 97 46

Aviron 66
Base nautique
Lac de villeneuve de la Raho
66180, Villeneuve de La Raho
France
Tel: +33 06 82 36 68 26
Email: aviron66@wanadoo.fr

Aviron Villeneuvois
Centre Nautique
Quai d'Alsace
47300, Villeneuve sur Lot
France
Tel: +33 05 53 49 18 27

Aviron Club de Villennes — Poissy
chemin des Pêcheurs
Port de la Mourée
78250, Villennes
France
Tel: +33 01 39 65 45 78
Email: avironvillennes@multimania.com
www.multimania.com/avironvillennes/

Ass. Nautique des Communes du Pays de Vitre
BP 80 102
35501, Vitre Cedex
France
Tel: +33 02 99 76 74 46
perso.wanadoo.fr/ancpv

Vitrolles Sport Aviron
Parc
Les Vignettes — Bt E 15
13127, Vitrolles
France
Tel: +33 04 42 89 24 91

Un Viviers Montelimar Pierrelatte
Section Aviron
Port de Plaisance
07220, Viviers sur Rhone
France
Tel: +33 04 75 52 82 15

Aviron Club de Colmar
Base du Geiskopf
68600, Vogelgrun
France
Email: avironcolmar@free.fr

Aviron Plaisir Passion
avenue du Rhône
73170, Yenne
France
Email: aviron.app@free.fr
aviron.app.free.fr/

Georgia

NATIONAL FEDERATION

Rowing Federation of the Republic of Georgia
2 Sanapiro Street
Tbilisi, 380005
Georgia
Tel: +995 32 932 037
Fax: +995 32 22 7004
Email: Ktp@geo.net.ge

Germany

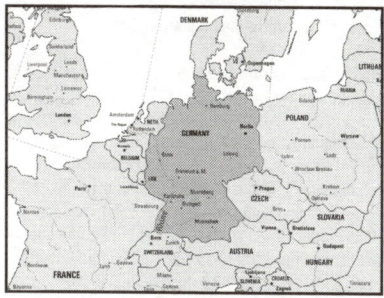

HISTORY

Exported from Great Britain, rowing came to Germany in the early 1800's with the first German rowing club founded in Hamburg in 1836 by British rowers living there. Over the next half century, a large number of rowing clubs were started all over the country culminating with the creation of the German Rowing Association, Deutscher Ruderverband or DRV in March 1883 with thirty-four rowing clubs and one thousand one hundred sixty six members. The regatta scene then was dominated by racing in pairs, fours, single sculls and eights, with single scullers held in the highest regard among athletes and spectators. Until 1905 the German Championships were conducted in this class only.

Around 1884, women started to enter the German rowing scene. By 1892, every fourth rower was a woman and the first women's rowing club was founded in 1901. In 1919, women had their first regatta with competitions in rowing style. The first speed races for women were introduced in 1921 over 1000-meters. The first German Championships in this category were held in 1937 although the style competitions remained part of the German regatta program until 1969. The first German championships for youth were held in 1937 and lightweight rowing races were introduced in 1925.

Racing dominated the rowing scene until the start of the twentieth century. Since then, rowing in Germany is not only about competing in racing shells, but is also a leisure sport practiced in gig-boats. More and more

clubs developed a strong interest for the leisure-rowing scene, wanderrudern, with trips being organized on Germany's splendid waterways. Long distance tours and gig-races were also introduced to the regatta schedules. Today, almost every club offers rowing to both interest groups.

During the two World Wars, the German rowing scene suffered a harsh blow with many of the clubhouses built over the last 100 years, as well as, the majority of the boats being destroyed. The first post-war regatta took place in 1946. This period then saw German rowing split into two, following the division of the country into East and West. From 1965-1991, there were two German rowing teams and rowing associations, DRV & DRSV. With the fall of the Berlin wall in November 1989, German rowing was reunited. In 1991, the two German rowing teams that each had successfully competed on the international rowing scene for over thirty years became one team again.

Today, the German Rowing Association, DRV, has the largest membership within FISA and is one of the most successful rowing countries in the world. In fact, since 2000, the DRV is the most successful rowing association in the world. The DRV is the oldest sports association in Germany and ranks at the top as one of the strongest sport associations in the country.

Rowing is enjoyed all over Germany by every age group from children to adults, as well as, masters rowers; living up to its marketing slogan "Rowing, a sport for everybody aged 8-80".

INTERNET LINKS
www.rudern.de
www.rudern1.de
www.werow.com

REGIONS

There are 16 federal states in Germany, though they are not precisely divided. Rowing is possible in most regions on rivers, lakes artificial regatta courses, canals or the sea.

Northern / North-East Germany
The lowlands in the north of Germany stretch from the Netherlands to Poland, skimming southern Denmark where it bridges the North and Baltic seas, including the federal states of Lower-Saxony, the Hanse Cities Bremen and Hamburg, Schleswig-Holstein, Mecklenburg-West Pomerania, Berlin and Brandenburg

Middle-West / Middle-East Germany
There is a rather industrialized central belt that cinches Belgium and Luxembourg to the Czech Republic's western prong. (North-Rhine Westfalia to the West, to the East Saxony and Saxony-Anhalt). In addition, the middle part of Germany is dominated by the rivers

Rhine and Main long crucial for inland shipping, that power through the troughs and gorges which cut through the Central Uplands and wine-dominated regions (Hesse, Rhineland-Palatinate, Saarland, Thuringia)

Southern Germany
To the south, the Danube River drains the Bavarian highlands from the Black Forest, near the French and Swiss borders, to Munich. The southern reaches of the Bavarian Alps give way to Austria. Federal states: Bavaria, Baden-Wuerttemberg]

Germany has a predominantly temperate climate. Average summer temperatures range from 20C to 30C (68F to 86F). The average winter temperature is 0C (32F). The German climate is variable, so it is best to be prepared for all types of weather throughout the year. The most reliable weather is from May to October, which coincides with the main regatta season.

ROWING SITES OF INTEREST
There are a large variety of major regattas, as well as, long distance tours happening throughout the year in almost every part of Germany; check the calendars at www.rudern.de or www.werow.com for detailed information on events and dates:

Berlin: Berlin-Grünau, Olympic Regatta Course from 1936, "Across Berlin" — Berlin long distance regatta in the fall;
City of Brandenburg: host course of the 2005 Junior World Championships.
Potsdam: Women's sculling trainings center
Hamburg: Several regattas, e.g., speedrows: sprint regatta in spring April/May.
Cologne: Fühlingen regatta course, host course of the World Championships 1997
Duisburg: International Wedau-Regatta 22./23. May 2004
Essen: Baldeney-Lake, host lake to the international Hügelregatta every 2nd year.
Dortmund: home and trainings center to the German sweep rowing team and the "Deutschlandachter"
Dresden: Elbe-Pokal, long distance regatta, end of October.
Munich: Olympic regatta course of 1972, usually hosts one World Cup regatta each season (end of June), applicant city for the World Championships 2007.
Starnberg: Lake Starnberg, "rose-island eight", long distance regatta, October
Ratzeburg: Rowing academy, sculling training center
Rendsburg: Canal-Cup, first weekend in October, international long distance national team eights races (e.g. finalists world championships)
Mecklenburg-West Pomerania: Coast of Mecklenburg-West Pomerania, e.g. Stralsund: sea water rowing on the baltic sea

PERSONALITIES
Willy Empacher: Founder of the world-famous German rowing boat building company. In 1923, Willy Empacher, a trained master boat builder and chief master of the guild, started his first boatyard in Königsberg, East Prussia at the age of 21. In 1947, he started a new business at Eberbach on the Neckar River, which grew to become one of the world's most successful rowing shell builders. To date, more than five hundred medals have been won in Empacher boats and roughly sixty percent of the participants in World Championships and Olympic Games row boats crafted by Empacher, including the majority of the members of the German national team.

Karl Adam: Rowing professor and coach who was already a legend when still alive, Karl Adam, 1912-1976, had a major impact on one of the most successful eras in German rowing history that starting at the end of the 1950's. Adam is considered a great innovator of training techniques and methods that impacted the development of rowing known in the rowing world as the Ratzeburger style. In the 1960's, Karl Adam's world-champion crews from Ratzeburg pioneered advances such as speed play, interval training, shovel-shaped oars, and bucket rigging, which puts the #4 and #5 oars on the starboard side of the boat.

Jörg and Bernd Landvoigt: The famous German twins, born in 1951 from the Potsdamer Rudergesellschaft, formerly Dynamo Potsdam, who made rowing history and dominated the international rowing scene in the pair for over two decades. Their record of success is legendary in the rowing world with one hundred seventy nine victories in one hundred eighty races: three Olympic medals, gold in 1976 and 1980, bronze in 1972, plus six world championship titles.

Peter-Michael Kolbe: German sculling legend that was world champion in the single in 1975, 1978, 1981, 1983 and 1986. Though he was considered the best sculler in the world for five years, he was never able to win an Olympic gold medal. At three Olympic Games he won the silver medal; in 1976 and 1984 he came second against his Finnish rival Pertii Karppinnen, and in 1988 he placed second against the next German sculling legend, Thomas Lange, then still racing for the GDR. Lange went on to become Olympic champion again in 1992 and the bronze medallist in 1996.

Kathrin Boron: Born in 1969, Kathrin Boron's current title is that of the world's best female sculler — with three Olympic gold medals: Sydney 2002-women's double sculls, Atlanta 1996- women's quadruple sculls, Barcelona 1992- women's double sculls and eight world championship titles: women's double sculls 1990,1991,1997,1999, 2001 and women's quadruple sculls 1989,1997, 1998.

Did You Know ?

The Der Hamburger Ruder Club, DHRC, is not only the oldest rowing club in Germany, but the oldest on the European continent. At the top of prominent Hamburg rowing history, the Allgemeiner Alster Club, AAC, founded in 1844, is the second oldest regatta association in the world after the Henley Royal Regatta, 1842.

NATIONAL FEDERATION

Deutscher Ruderverband E.V.
Maschstrasse 20
30169, Hannover
Germany
Tel: +49 511 980 940
Fax: +49 511 980 9425
Email: info@rudern.de
www.rudern.de

CLUBS (BY CITY)

Ruder-Club Aken e.V.
Köthener Chausee 8
6385, Aken
Germany

Alt Ruppiner Ruderclub 1928 e.V.
Heimburgerstr. 121
16827, Alt Ruppin
Germany

Ruderverein Rhenus e.V. Andernach
Karolingerstr. 19
56626, Andernach
Germany

Anklamer Ruderklub e.V.
Hamburger Ring 27
17389, Anklam
Germany

Ruder-Club Aschaffenburg von 1898 e.V.
Postfach 100 349
63703, Aschaffenburg
Germany

Yacht- und Ruderclub Attendorn e.V.
Waldenburger Bucht 26
57439, Attendorn-Waldenburg
Germany

Ruderverein ARGO Aurich e.V.
Hilgenbusch 33
26605, Aurich
Germany

Bacharacher Ruder-Verein 1884 e.V.
Blücherstr. 94
55422, Bacharach
Germany

Wassersportverein Twistesee e.V. 1972
Fürstenallee 27
34454, Bad Arolsen
Germany

Ruderverein Bad Ems e.V.
Postfach 16 25
56124, Bad Ems
Germany

Hersfelder Ruderverein 1977 e.V.
von-Harnack-Str. 7
36251, Bad Hersfeld
Germany

Wassersportverein Honnef e.V.
Postfach 18 23
53588, Bad Honnef
Germany

Creuznacher Ruderverein 1876 e.V.
Magister Faust-Gasse 18 — 20
55545, Bad Kreuznach
Germany

Ruder- und Kanu-Verein Bad Kreuznach 1950 e.V.
Karl-Kuhn-Str. 8
55543, Bad Kreuznach
Germany

Ruderclub Bad Säckingen e.V.
Bündtenstr. 20
79713, Bad Säckingen
Germany

Frankfurter Ruder-Verein von 1865 e.V.
Frankfurter Str. 98 b
61118, Bad Vilbel
Germany

Ruderverein Waldsee 1900 e.V.
St.-Blasius-Weg 3
88339, Bad Waldsee
Germany

Ruderverein Bad Wimpfen e.V.
Postfach 2 22
74201, Bad Wimpfen
Germany

Bamberger Rudergesellschaft von 1884 e.V.
Postfach 110 141
96029, Bamberg
Germany

Ruder-Club 'Welle' Bardowickvon 1894 e.V.
Postfach 53
21355, Bardowick
Germany

Schulruderzentrum Kassel e.V.
Mainweg 13
34225, Baunatal
Germany

Ruderclub Beeskow 1920 e.V.
Markt 5-6
15848, Beeskow
Germany

Wassersportverein Belau e.V.
Dorfstr. 56
24601, Belau
Germany

Wurzener Rudervereinigung 'Schwarz-Gelb' e.V.
Am Schwarzwasser
4828, Bennewitz
Germany

Verein für Leibesübungen Bergen 94 e.V. Abt. Rudern
Karlstr. 4
18528, Bergen
Germany

Ruder-Club Preußen e.V.
Händelstr. 15
51427, Bergisch Gladbach
Germany

Akademische Ruder-Gesellschaft zu Berlin e.V.
Haeselerstr. 25d
14050, Berlin
Germany

RR des Akademischen Turnvereins zu Berlin e.V.
Wolframstr. 5
12105, Berlin
Germany

Ruder-Union Arkona Berlin 1879 e.V.
Wintersteinstr. 23
10587, Berlin
Germany

Berliner Ruderklub 'Astoria' e.V.
Grunewaldstr. 46
10825, Berlin
Germany

Berliner Ruderklub Brandenburgia e.V.
Wattstr. 9
13629, Berlin
Germany

Berliner Ruder-Club e.V.
Bismarckstr.4
14109, Berlin
Germany

Berliner Ruder-Gesellschaft e.V.
Otto-Suhr-Allee 43
10585, Berlin
Germany

Rudervereinigung Berlin von 1878 e.V.
Brandensteinweg 2
13595, Berlin
Germany

Sport-Vereinigung Dresdenia Berlin e.V.
Alt-Pichelsdorf 11
13595, Berlin
Germany

Spandauer Ruder-Club 'Friesen' e.V.
Mahnkopfweg 6, 8, 10
13595, Berlin
Germany

Rudervereinigung Hellas-Titania Berlin e.V.
Ilsensteinweg 3b
14129, Berlin
Germany

Berliner Ruder-Club Hevella e.V.
Stieffring 2
13627, Berlin
Germany

Märkischer Wassersport e.V.
Bootshausweg 5
13599, Berlin
Germany

Berliner Ruderclub 'Phönix' e.V.
Topeliusweg 3 b
14089, Berlin
Germany

Pichelsberger Rudergesellschaft 1914 e.V.
Am Havelufer 13
14089, Berlin
Germany

Postsportverein Berlin e.V.
Argentinische Allee 181
14169, Berlin
Germany

Ruderverein 'Preußen' e.V.
Klemkestr. 84c
13409, Berlin
Germany

Potsdamer Ruder-Club Germania e.V.
Am Großen Wannsee 46
14109, Berlin
Germany

Ruder-Club 'Saffonia 08' e.V.
Bänschstr. 74
10247, Berlin
Germany

Ruder-Club Tegel 1886 e.V.
Urbanstr. 66
10967, Berlin
Germany

Ruder-Club Tegelort e.V.
Grimbartsteig 60
13503, Berlin
Germany

Ruderverein 'Vorwärts' Berlin e.V.
Conradstr. 1
14109, Berlin
Germany

Ruderriege TV Waidmannslust e.V.
Sandgrasweg 12
13509, Berlin
Germany

Frauen-Ruder-Club Wannsee e.V.
Marmaraweg 20
12109, Berlin
Germany

Ruderklub am Wannsee e.V.
Scabellstr. 8
14109, Berlin
Germany

Berliner Ruder-Club 'Welle-Poseidon' e.V.
Am Großen Wannsee 46 A
14109, Berlin
Germany

Rudergesellschaft West e.V.
Solmsstr. 13
10961, Berlin
Germany

Rudergesellschaft Wiking Berlin e.V.
Haarlemer Str. 45 e
12359, Berlin
Germany

Die Ruder-Union Marathon von 1980 e.V.
Schönwalder Allee 63
13587, Berlin
Germany

Versehrten-Wassersport-Gemeinschaft e.V.
Havelchaussee 115
14055, Berlin
Germany

Märkischer Ruderverein e.V.
Hektorstr. 7
10711, Berlin
Germany

Berliner-Ruder-Club 'Ägir' e.V.
Spreestr. 1
12587, Berlin
Germany

Eisenbahnsportverein Schmöckwitz e.V. Abt. Rudern
Imkerweg 26
12527, Berlin
Germany

Richtershorner Ruderverein e.V.
Sportpromenade 17
12527, Berlin
Germany

Ruder-Club Rahnsdorf Luftfahrt e.V.
Püttbergeweg 40 A
12589, Berlin
Germany

Ruder-Gemeinschaft Grünau e.V.
Regattastr. 247
12527, Berlin
Germany

Rudergemeinschaft Rotation Berlin e.V.
Sportpromenade 23
12527, Berlin
Germany

Ruderverein Empor e.V.
Regattastr. 251
12527, Berlin
Germany

Sport-Club Berlin e.V. Abt. Rudern
Nixenstr. 2
12459, Berlin
Germany

Sportclub Berlin-Grünau e.V. Abteilung Rudern
Sportpromenade 3
12527, Berlin
Germany

Ruderverein Sparta Klein Köris e.V.
Ludwig-Richter-Str. 5
12435, Berlin
Germany

Cottbusser Rudersportverein im PSV Cottbus 90 e.V.
Teikeweg 13
12109, Berlin
Germany

Ruderclub Kleinmachnow-Stahnsdorf-Teltow e.V.
Geisenheimer Str. 18
14197, Berlin
Germany

Ruderverein Collegia 1895 e.V.
Am Südpark 73
13595, Berlin
Germany

Ruder-Riege der Turngemeinde in Berlin 1848 e.V.
Columbiadamm 111
10965, Berlin
Germany

Akademischer Ruder Club zu Berlin e.V.
Brandensteinweg 5
13595, Berlin
Germany

Friedrichshagener Ruderverein e.V.
Am Lupinenfeld 86
12623, Berlin-Hellersdorf
Germany

SG NARVA Berlin e.V. Abt. Rudern
Rudower Str. 50
12557, Berlin-Köpenick
Germany

Treptower Rudergemeinschaft e.V.
Elli-Voigt-Str. 5
10367, Berlin-Lichtenberg
Germany

Rathenower Ruder-Club Wiking e.V.
Siegfriedstr. 17
10365, Berlin-Lichtenberg
Germany

Sportverein Energie Berlin e.V. Abt. Rudern
Schwarzwurzelstr. 46
12689, Berlin-Marzahn
Germany

Ruderverein Wasserfreunde Erkner e.V.
Grimaustr. 80
12439, Berlin-Niederschöneweide
Germany

Spree-Ruder-Club Köpenick e.V.
Buchholzer Str. 86
13156, Berlin-Niederschönhausen
Germany

Bernburger Ruderclub e.V.
Neuborner Str. 35
6406, Bernburg
Germany

Bernkasteler Ruderverein 1874 e.V.
Postfach 13 53
54463, Bernkastel-Kues
Germany

Ruder-Club Holzminden e.V.
Sollingbreite 28
37639, Bevern
Germany

Binger Rudergesellschaft 1911 e.V.
Postfach 13 13
55383, Bingen
Germany

Rudergesellschaft Linden- Dahlhausen e.V.
Postfach 50 03 29
44873, Bochum
Germany

Ruderverein Bodenwerder von 1922 e.V.
Postfach 12 28
37616, Bodenwerder
Germany

Akademischer Ruderclub Rhenus Sportheim e.V.
Postfach 17 02 41
53028, Bonn
Germany

Wassersportverein Godesberg 1909/11 e.V.
Rheinstr. 80
53179, Bonn
Germany

Bonner Ruder-Gesellschaft e.V.
Postfach 7128
53071, Bonn
Germany

Bonner Ruder-Verein 1882 e.V.
Grubenstr. 8
53179, Bonn
Germany

Akademischer Ruderclub Rhenus
Postfach 17 02 41
53028, Bonn
Germany

Ruderclub Germania Boppard e.V.
Postafch 1515
56154, Boppard
Germany

Kölner Rudergesellschaft 1891 e.V.
Weimarer Str. 58
53332, Bornheim
Germany

Rudergemeinschaft Bottrop e.V.
Görkenstr. 34c
46242, Bottrop
Germany

Erlebnisruderverein Saarlouis
Zur Schafbrücke 6
66359, Bous
Germany

TSV Bramsche e.V. Ruderabteilung
Leuschnerstr. 17
49565, Bramsche
Germany

Ruder-Club Plaue (Havel) e.V.
Am Havelgut 2 a
14774, Brandenburg
Germany

Ruder-Club Havel Brandenburg e.V.
Hammerstr. 5
14776, Brandenburg
Germany

Brandenburger Sport- und Ruderklub 1883 e.V.
Krakauer Str. 14
14776, Brandenburg
Germany

Ruder-Klub "Normannia" e.V.
Maschplatz 15
38114, Braunschweig
Germany

Ruderverein 'Meteor' Chemnitz 1903 e.V.
Dorfstr. 23
9577, Braunsdorf
Germany

Breisacher Ruderverein e.V.
Rheinuferstr. 14
79206, Breisach
Germany

Bremer Ruderclub 'Hansa' (1879/83) e.V.
Werderstr. 64
28199, Bremen
Germany

Bremer Ruderverein von 1882 e.V.
Werderstr. 60
28199, Bremen
Germany

Post-Sportverein Bremen e.V. Ruderabteilung
Werderstr. 66
28199, Bremen
Germany

Vegesacker Ruderverein e.V.
Postfach 710 409
28764, Bremen
Germany

Bremerhavener Ruderverein von 1889 e.V.
Stresemannstr. 51
27576, Bremerhaven
Germany

Ruderabteilung von 1962 TSV Bremervörde
Buchenstr. 14
27432, Bremervörde
Germany

Hanauer Ruderclub Hassia e.V.
Bonhoefferstr. 16a
63486, Bruchköbel
Germany

Wassersportfreunde Burg e.V. 1924
Mauerstr. 28
39288, Burg
Germany

Straubinger Ruderclub von 1881 e.V.
Postfach 0115
94301, BZ Straubing
Germany

Ruderverein Rauxel e.V.
Wartburgstr. 283a
44577, Castrop-Rauxel
Germany

Celler Ruderverein e.V.
Postfach 1567
29205, Celle
Germany

Ruderclub Ernestinum-Hölty Celle e.V.
Grupenstr. 7
29221, Celle
Germany

Hermann Billung Celle e.V.
Postfach 13 45
29203, Celle
Germany

Cochemer Rudergesellschaft e.V.
Birkenstr. 8
56812, Cochem
Germany

Ruder-Club 'Neptun' e.V.
Postfach 11 12 17
64227, Darmstadt
Germany

Darmstädter Schwimm- und Wassersport-Club 1912 e.V.
Viktoriaplatz 4
64293, Darmstadt
Germany

Ruderverein Datteln von 1928 e.V.
Hafenstr. 133
45711, Datteln
Germany

Deggendorfer Ruder-Verein 1876 e.V.
Pferdemarkt 18
94469, Deggendorf
Germany

Rudervereinigung Dessau e.V.
Saalestr. 46
6846, Dessau
Germany

SG Diepholz von 1870 e.V. Ruderabteilung
Postfach 12 11
49342, Diepholz
Germany

Ruderverein Dorsten e.V.
Gelsenkirchener Str. 37
46282, Dorsten
Germany

Ruder-Club 'Hansa' von 1898 e.V.
Westerholz 87
44147, Dortmund
Germany

Dresdner Ruder-Club 1902 e.V.
Hamburger Str. 74
1157, Dresden
Germany

Laubegaster Ruderverein Dresden e.V.
Neuberinstr. 9
1279, Dresden
Germany

Dresdner Ruderverein e.V.
Tolkewitzer Str. 45
1277, Dresden
Germany

USV Technische Universität Dresden e.V.
1067, Dresden
Germany

Duisburger Ruderverein e.V. (1897/1910)
Postfach 21 02 05
47024, Duisburg
Germany

Homberger Ruderklub 'Germania' e.V.
Rheinanlagen 13
47198, Duisburg
Germany

Ruderclub 'Borussia' Rheinhausen e.V.
Düsseldorfer Str. 141
47239, Duisburg
Germany

Ruder-Gesellschaft Benrath e.V.
Postfach 18 03 39
40570, Düsseldorf
Germany

Ruderclub Germania Düsseldorf 1904 e.V.
Postfach 250 107
40093, Düsseldorf
Germany

Düsseldorfer Ruderverein 1880 e.V.
Kronprinzenstr. 131
40217, Düsseldorf
Germany

WSV Düsseldorf Rudergesellschaft von 1893 e.V.
Rotterdamer Str. 40
40474, Düsseldorf
Germany

Rudergesellschaft Eberbach 1899 e.V.
Rockenauer Str. 1
69412, Eberbach
Germany

Eckernförder Ruderclub von 1924 e.V.
Petersberg 9
24340, Eckernförde
Germany

Ruder Club Turbine Grünau e.V.
Bruno-H.-Bürgel Allee 27
15732, Eichwalde
Germany

Ruderclub Eilenburg e.V.
Fridrichshöhe 22
4838, Eilenburg
Germany

Ruderverein Fürstenberg/O. 1910 e.V.
Am Trockendock 4
15890, Eisenhüttenstadt
Germany

Elmshorner Ruder-Club von 1909 e.V.
Falkenweg28
25337, Elmshorn
Germany

Ruderverein Eltville 1919 e.V.
Postfach 14 17
65334, Eltville
Germany

Ruderverein 'Weser' von 1885 e.V.
Am Hanlah 49
31008, Elze
Germany

Emder Ruderverein e.V.
Postfach 14 07
26694, Emden
Germany

Clever Ruder Club e.V.
Lobither Str. 12
46446, Emmerich
Germany

Ruderverein Erlangen e.V. 1911
Habichtstr. 12
91056, Erlangen
Germany

Erlanger Wanderrudergesellschaft Franken e.V.
Goethestr. 54
91054, Erlangen
Germany

Eschweger Ruderverein e.V.
Neissestr. 2
37269, Eschwege
Germany

Ruderklub am Baldeneysee e.V.
Postfach 23 02 80
45070, Essen
Germany

Ruderriege ETUF Essen e.V.
Freiherr-vom-Stein-Str. 204a
45133, Essen
Germany

Essen-Werdener Ruder-Club von 1896 e.V.
Forstmannstr. 56
45239, Essen
Germany

Steeler Ruder-Verein e.V. 1904
Grendtor 40
45276, Essen
Germany

Kettwiger Rudergesellschaft e.V.
Postfach 185 624
45206, Essen
Germany

Ruderriege TVK Essen 1877 e.V.
Kampmannbrücke 1
45257, Essen
Germany

Ruderverein Esslingen e.V.
Seitenstraße 28
73734, Esslingen a.N.
Germany

Germania Ruderverein Eutin e.V.
Heinrich-Lüth-Weg 12
23701, Eutin
Germany

Ruderklub Flensburg e.V.
Am Ostseebad 8
24939, Flensburg
Germany

Flörsheimer Ruderverein 08 e.V.
Riedstr. 53
65439, Flörsheim
Germany

Frankenthaler Ruderverein von 1895 e.V.
Postfach 13 31
67203, Frankenthal
Germany

Frankfurter Ruder-Club von 1882 e.V.
Lehmgasse 11
15230, Frankfurt
Germany

Frankfurter Rudergesellschaft 'Borussia' 1896 e.V.
Mainwasenweg 31
60599, Frankfurt
Germany

Frankfurter Ruder-Club 'Fechenheim' 1887 e.V.
Postfach 610 228
60344, Frankfurt
Germany

Frauen-Ruderverein 'Freiweg' e.V. Frankfurt
Kelsterbacher Str. 10
60528, Frankfurt
Germany

Frankfurter Ruder-Club Griesheim 1906 e.V.
Schwarzerlenweg 77a
65933, Frankfurt
Germany

Ruder-Club Nassovia Höchst 1881 e.V.
Mainzer Landstr. 791
65934, Frankfurt
Germany

Frankfurter Rudergesellschaft Nied 1921 e.V.
Mainzer Landstr. 793
65934, Frankfurt
Germany

Ruderverbindung Rheno- Franconia e.V.
Schadowstr. 8
60596, Frankfurt
Germany

Frankfurter Ruder-Club 1884 e.V.
Mainwasenweg 33
60553, Frankfurt
Germany

Frankfurter RG 'Sachsenhausen' von 1879 e.V.
Mainwasenweg 35
60599, Frankfurt
Germany

Frankfurter Rudersport-Verein Sachsenhausen 1898 e.V.
Postfach 700 322
60553, Frankfurt
Germany

Offenbacher Ruderverein 1874 e.V.
Starkenburger Str. 150
60386, Frankfurt
Germany

Offenbacher Rudergesellschaft "Undine" 1876 e.V.
Postfach 10 14 09
63014, Frankfurt
Germany

Sport- und Kulturgemeinschaft-Wassersportabteilung Frankfurt am Main e.V. (SKGF)
Mainfeldstr. 29
60528, Frankfurt
Germany

Frankfurter Rudergesellschaft 'Germania' 1869 e.V.
Schaumainkai 65
60596, Frankfurt/M.
Germany

Frankfurter Ruder-Gesellschaft Oberrad 1879 e.V.
Wiener Str. 125
60599, Frankfurt/Main
Germany

Sportverein Oderhort Frankfurt/Oder e.V.
Buschmühlenweg 172
15230, Frankfurt/O.
Germany

Ruderverein Friedrichshafen e.V.
Postfach 21 21
88011, Friedrichshafen
Germany

Friedrichstädter Rudergesellschaft e.V.
Am Stadtfeld 7
25840, Friedrichstadt
Germany

Rudergruppe Geesthacht von 1912 e.V.
Elbuferstr. 31
21502, Geesthacht
Germany

Wassersportverein Geisenheim 1912 e.V.
Blaubachstr. 11
65366, Geisenheim
Germany

Ruderverein Gelsenkirchen e.V.
Postfach 10 22 40
45822, Gelsenkirchen
Germany

Ruderverein Rhenania e.V.
Postfach 14 06
76714, Germersheim
Germany

Lauinger Ruder- und Surfclub "Donau" e.V.
Marktstr. 24
89537, Giengen
Germany

Gießener Ruder-Club 'Hassia' 1906 e.V.
Uferweg 14
35398, Gießen
Germany

Wassersportverein 'Hellas' 1920 e.V.
Wißmarerweg 125
35396, Gießen
Germany

Gießener Rudergesellschaft 1877 e.V.
Bootshausstr. 12
35390, Gießen
Germany

Rennrudergemeinschaft Mittellahn e.V.
In den Gärten 74
35398, Gießen
Germany

Ruderer-Vereinigung Nordharz e.V.
Postfach 23 65
38613, Goslar
Germany

Donau Ruder Club Deggendorf 2001 e.V.
Am Sonnenhang 19 b
94539, Grafling
Germany

Greifswalder Ruderclub 'Hilda' 1892 e.V.
H.-Hertz-Str. 9b
17489, Greifswald
Germany

Ruderclub Grenzach e.V.
Postfach 13 04
79631, Grenzach-Wyhlen
Germany

Rudergesellschaft Marktheidenfeld e.V.
Am Gehäg 18
97840, Hafenlohr
Germany

Rudergemeinschaft Bayern e.V.
Am Gehäg 18
97840, Hafenlohr
Germany

HRV Böllberg/ Nelson v. 1874 e.V. im SV Halle
Zur Rabeninsel 23
6128, Halle
Germany

HRC e.V. im Universitätssportverein Halle e.V.
Robert-Franz-Ring 14-15
6108, Halle
Germany

Ruder-Club Marl im VfB 1948/64 Hüls e.V.
Am Thiershof 40
45721, Haltern
Germany

Ruder-Club 'Allemannia von 1866'
An der Alster 47a
20099, Hamburg
Germany

Alster-Ruderverein Hanseat von 1925 e.V.
Kaemmererufer 30
22303, Hamburg
Germany

Ruder-Club Bergedorf e.V.
Postfach 800 152
21001, Hamburg
Germany

Biller Ruder-Club von 1883 e.V.
Karl-Strutz-Weg 58 B
22119, Hamburg
Germany

Der Hamburger und Germania Ruder Club e.V.
Alsterufer 21
20354, Hamburg
Germany

Ruder-Club 'Dresdenia' e.V.
Schäfersruh 4
22393, Hamburg
Germany

Ruder-Club Favorite Hammonia
Alsterufer 9
20354, Hamburg
Germany

Hammerdeicher Ruder-Verein von 1893 e.V.
Hammer Deich 132
20537, Hamburg
Germany

Ruder-Gesellschaft 'Hansa' e.V .
Schöne Aussicht 39
22605, Hamburg
Germany

Ruder-Club Süderelbe von 1892 e.V. Hamburg
Schweenssandhauptdeich 7
21079, Hamburg
Germany

Svg. Polizei Hamburg von 1920 e.V. WS-Abteilung
Isekai Ö12
20249, Hamburg
Germany

Ruder-Club 'Protesia' von 1907 e.V.
Eilbeker Weg 61 a
22089, Hamburg
Germany

RR des Sportvereins Rot-Gelb Hamburg von 1926 e.V.
Wellingsbütteler Landstraße 54
22337, Hamburg
Germany

Hamburger Ruderinnen-Club von 1925 e.V.
Krokusstieg 4
22297, Hamburg
Germany

Ruderverein an den Teichwiesen von 1965 e.V.
Durchschnitt 19
20146, Hamburg
Germany

Ruderverein Wandsbek e.V.
Sootweg 24
22175, Hamburg
Germany

Ruder-Club Hamburg e.V.
Arnold-Heise-Str. 16
20249, Hamburg
Germany

Wilhelmsburger Ruder Club von 1895 e.V.
Vogelhüttendeich 120
21107, Hamburg
Germany

Ruder-Vereinigung 'Bille' 1896 e.V.
Bahrenfelder Marktplatz 18
22761, Hamburg
Germany

Ruderclub Hamm von 1890 e.V.
Postfach 22 65
59012, Hamm
Germany

Ruderclub 'Möve' 1919 e.V.
Fasaneriestr. 8
63456, Hanau
Germany

Hanauer Rudergesellschaft 1879 e.V.
Antoniterstr. 10
63452, Hanau
Germany

Mündener Ruderverein e.V.
Postfach 14 16
34334, Hann Münden
Germany

Rudergemeinschaft "Angaria" e.V.
Weddigenufer 25
30167, Hannover
Germany

Deutscher Ruder-Club von 1884 e.V.
Roesebeckstr. 1
30449, Hannover
Germany

1. Frauen-Ruder-Club Hannover 1928 e.V.
Postfach 19 46
30019, Hannover
Germany

Hannoverscher Ruder-Club von 1880 e.V.
Postfach 25 23
30025, Hannover
Germany

Akademische Turnverbindung Hannover e.V.
Fischerstr. 21
30167, Hannover
Germany

Ruderriege Schaumburgia Bückeburg e.V.
Albert-Niemann-Str. 15
30171, Hannover
Germany

Ruderverein Linden von 1911 e.V.
Limmerstr. 134
30451, Hannover
Germany

Ruderverein Blankenstein-Ruhr e.V.
Postfach 30 01
45513, Hattingen
Germany

Hattinger Ruderverein e.V. 1923
Ruhrdeich 4
45525, Hattingen
Germany

Rudergesellschaft Heidelberg 1898 e.V.
Postfach 10 45 05
69035, Heidelberg
Germany

Heidelberger Ruderklub 1872 e.V.
Hauptstr. 91
69117, Heidelberg
Germany

Alte Herren RR am Gym.-Ruder-u. Leichtathletik-Verein e.V.
Neuenheimer Landstr. 16
69120, Heidelberg
Germany

Heilbronner Rudergesellschaft 'Schwaben' von 1879 e.V.
Postfach 20 11
74010, Heilbronn
Germany

Wasserfreunde Hemmoor e.V. Abt. Rudern
Bei den Eichbäumen 4
21745, Hemmoor
Germany

Ruderclub Oberhavel Hennigsdorf e.V.
Lindenring 40
16761, Hennigsdorf
Germany

Ruderverein 'Emscher' Wanne-Eickel-Herten e.V.
Am Westhafen 27
44653, Herne
Germany

Wassersportverein Herne 1920 e.V.
Gneisenaustr. 187
44628, Herne
Germany

TSV Herrsching e.V.
Madeleine-Ruoff-Str. 33
82211, Herrsching
Germany

Hildesheimer Ruder-Club e.V.
Beethovenstr. 16
31141, Hildesheim
Germany

Schwimmverein Hof 1911 e.V.
Theresienstein 4
95028, Hof/Saale
Germany

Ruderverein Höxter von 1898 e.V.
Postfach 100 326
37655, Höxter
Germany

Ruderverein Hoya von 1926 e.V.
Postfach 13 34
27316, Hoya
Germany

Hürther Rudergesellschaft e.V.
Schollsbrücke 24
50354, Hürth
Germany

Ruderverein Ingelheim 1920 e.V.
In der Rheingewann 44
55218, Ingelheim
Germany

Olympische Rennrudergemeinschaft Südwest
Am Landgraben 3
55218, Ingelheim
Germany

Donau-Ruder-Club Ingolstadt e.V.
Westliche Ringstr. 86
85049, Ingolstadt
Germany

Ruderclub Germania von 1929 e.V.
Am Westhang 64a
58640, Iserlohn
Germany

Wassersportverein Altwarmbüchen e.V.
Fuchsklint 42
30916, Isernhagen
Germany

Jenaer Kanu- und Ruderverein e.V.
Frongasse 10
7745, Jena
Germany

Karlsruher Rheinklub Alemannia e.V.
Werftstr. 8b
76189, Karlsruhe
Germany

Karlsruher Ruder-Verein Wiking von 1879 e.V.
Ludwig-Dill-Str. 16 b
76187, Karlsruhe
Germany

Ruder-Club Karlstadt 1928 e.V.
Postafch 12 12
97748, Karlstadt
Germany

Casseler Frauen- Ruder-Verein e.V.
Auedamm 35
34121, Kassel
Germany

Ruderverein Kurhessen- Cassel e.V.
Uhlenhorststr. 23 d
34132, Kassel
Germany

Rudergesellschaft Kassel 1927 e.V.
Auedamm 33
34121, Kassel
Germany

Ruder Club am Lech Kaufering e.V.
Heinestr. 21
86916, Kaufering
Germany

Rudergemeinschaft Sachsen 1993 e.V.
Alter Bahndamm 33
1723, Kesselsdorf
Germany

Akademischer Ruderverein e.V. Kiel
Düsternbrooker Weg 2
24105, Kiel
Germany

Erster Kieler Ruder-Club von 1862 e.V.
Düsternbrooker Weg 16
24105, Kiel
Germany

Rudergesellschaft Germania e.V. Kiel
Luisenweg 21
24105, Kiel
Germany

Ruderriege der ATV Ditmarsia Kiel
Lornsenstr. 1
24105, Kiel
Germany

Kitzinger Ruderverein 1897 e.V.
Kaiserstr. 27
97318, Kitzingen
Germany

Post-Sportverein Koblenz e.V.
Postfach 92 00
56065, Koblenz
Germany

Koblenzer Ruderclub Rhenania 1877/1921 e.V.
Am Moselstausee 16
56073, Koblenz
Germany

Ruder- u. Tennis-Klub GERMANIA e.V. Köln
Am Kielshof 29
51105, Köln
Germany

Mülheimer Wassersport e.V. Köln
Postfach 800 741
51007, Köln
Germany

Club für Wassersport Porz e.V. 1926
In der Rosenau 10a
51143, Köln
Germany

Telekom- Post- Sportgemeinschaft Köln e.V.
Hunsrückstr. 14
50739, Köln
Germany

Kölner Ruderverein von 1877 e.V.
Barbarastr. 47-49
50996, Köln
Germany

Ruderverein Schwarzer Adler e.V. Köln
An der Schanz 2
50735, Köln
Germany

Kölner Club für Wassersport e.V.
Oberländer Ufer
50968, Köln
Germany

Kölner-Ruder-Club Köln 71 e.V.
Herzog-Johann-Str. 1o
50769, Köln
Germany

TRV Rhenania Bingen 1897 e.V
Goffineweg 27
51069, Köln
Germany

Ruderclub Königs Wusterhausen e.V.
Fasanenstr. 34
15711, Königs Wusterhausen
Germany

Ruderverein 'Neptun' e.V. Konstanz
Fischenzstr. 18
78462, Konstanz
Germany

Ruder- u. Kanuverein Konz e.V.
Im Canet 6
54329, Konz
Germany

Rudersportverein Krakow am See e.V. von 1999
Plauer Chausee 17
18292, Krakow
Germany

Uerdinger Ruder-Club e.V.
Düsseldorfer Str. 47
47829, Krefeld
Germany

Crefelder Ruder-Club 1883 e.V.
Gneisenaustr. 26
47800, Krefeld
Germany

Storkower Ruder-Vereinigung 1919 e.V.
Siedlung Ost 29
15859, Kummersdorf
Germany

Rudergesellschaft Lahnstein 1922 e.V.
Postfach 13 24
56103, Lahnstein
Germany

Landshuter Ruderverein 1952 e.V.
Breslauer Str. 120
84028, Landshut
Germany

Ruder-Gesellschaft Lauenburg e.V.
Postafch 13 23
21472, Lauenburg
Germany

Lauffener Ruderclub 'Neckar' e.V. 1931
Hermann-Löns-Weg 4
74348, Lauffen
Germany

Ruder Club Leer e.V.
Bürgermeister-Diekmann-Str. 1
26789, Leer
Germany

Ruderverein Leer von 1903 e.V.
Postfach 1867
26789, Leer
Germany

SV Kloster Lehnin e.V. Sektion Rudern
Am Hasenkamp 5
14797, Lehnin
Germany

RV für das 'Große Freie' Lehrte/Sehnde e.V.
Iltener Str. 52
31275, Lehrte
Germany

Akademischer Ruderverein zu Leipzig e.V.
Moschelesstr. 17
4109, Leipzig
Germany

Ruderverein Triton 1893 e.V. Leipzig
Faradaystr, 7
4159, Leipzig
Germany

Rudergesellschaft Wiking Leipzig im SC DHfK e.V.
Friedrich-Ebert-Str. 130
4105, Leipzig
Germany

Dormagener Ruder-Gesellschaft 'Bayer' e.V.
Fr. Bayer Str. 10
51373, Leverkusen
Germany

RTHC Bayer Leverkusen Ruder-Abteilung
Knochenbergsweg
51373, Leverkusen
Germany

Limburger Club für Wassersport 1895/1907 e.V.
Postfach 13 05
65533, Limburg
Germany

Ruderclub Lindau (B) e.V.
Postfach 17 04
88107, Lindau
Germany

Lingener Rudergesellschaft e.V. von 1923
Georgstr. 34
49809, Lingen
Germany

Eisenbahn-Sportverein Lingen e.V.
Alte Josefstr. 44
49808, Lingen (Ems)
Germany

Lobensteiner Ruder-Verein 1932 e.V.
Graben 4
7356, Lobenstein
Germany

Post und Telekom Sportgemeinschaft Lübbecke e.V.
Postfach 1404
32294, Lübbecke
Germany

Lübecker Frauen-Ruder- Gesellschaft von 1907 e.V.
Hüxtertorallee 4
23564, Lübeck
Germany

Lübecker Frauen-Ruder- Klub e.V.
Galeonenweg 6
23558, Lübeck
Germany

Lübecker Rudergesellschaft von 1885 e.V.
Hüxtertoralle 4
23564, Lübeck
Germany

Lübecker Ruder-Klub e.V.
Charlottenstr. 33
23560, Lübeck
Germany

Ruderverein Lüdinghausen e.V.
Beethovenstr. 4
59348, Lüdinghausen
Germany

Ludwigshafener Ruderverein von 1878
Rheinuferstr. 4
67061, Ludwigshafen
Germany

Lüneburger Ruder-Club von 1875 e.V.
Klosterkamp 87
21337, Lüneburg
Germany

Rennrudergemeinschaft Lüneburg von 2000 e.V.
William-Watt-Str. 14
21339, Lüneburg
Germany

Ruderclub 'Wiking' e.V. Lüneburg
Postfach 2548
21315, Lüneburg
Germany

RRGem. Lüneburg
William-Watt-Str. 14
21339, Lüneburg
Germany

Ruderclub Magdeburg im Sportclub Magdeburg
Seilerweg 23
39114, Magdeburg
Germany

Universitätssportclub 'Otto von Guericke' Magdeburg e.V.
Schillerstr. 36
39108, Magdeburg
Germany

Rudervereinigung Alt Werder Magdeburg 1887 e.V.
Etgersleber Weg 25
39110, Magdeburg
Germany

Magdeburger Ruder-Club e.V.
Martin-Anderson-Nexö-Str. 22
39108, Magdeburg
Germany

EiSV Eintracht Mainz 1927 e.V. Ruderabteilung
Postfach 18 71
55008, Mainz
Germany

Mainzer Ruder-Gesellschaft 1898 e.V.
Postfach 30 46
55020, Mainz
Germany

Mainzer Ruder-Verein e.V.
Postfach 31 12
55021, Mainz
Germany

Weisenauer Ruderverein 1913 e.V.
Blussus-Str. 29
55130, Mainz
Germany

Kasteler Ruder- und Kanu- Gesellschaft 1880 e.V.
Wiesbadener Str. 19
55252, Mainz-Kastel
Germany

Mannheimer Ruder-Verein 'Amicitia' 1876 e.V.
Wallstadter Str. 66
68259, Mannheim
Germany

Mannheimer Rudergesellschaft Baden von 1880 e.V.
Feudenheimer Str. 2
68167, Mannheim
Germany

Mannheimer Ruder-Club von 1875 e.V.
Rheinpromenade 15
68163, Mannheim
Germany

Mannheimer Rudergesellschaft Rheinau 1909 e.V.
Schefflenzer Str. 6
68259, Mannheim
Germany

Volkstümlicher Wassersport Mannheim e.V.
Sandhofer-Str. 52-53
68305, Mannheim
Germany

Marbacher Ruderverein von 1920 e.V.
Postfach 12 57
71667, Marbach
Germany

Marburger Ruderverein von 1911 e.V.
Gießener Str. 1
35043, Marburg
Germany

Reit- und Sportverein Steinmühle e.V.
Steinmühlenweg 21
35043, Marburg
Germany

Meißner Ruderclub 'Neptun' 1882 e.V.
Siebeneichener Str. 39
1662, Meißen
Germany

Wassersportverein Meppen e.V.
Eschstr. 16
49716, Meppen
Germany

Merseburger Rudergesellschaft e.V.
Meuschauer Str. 7
6217, Merseburg
Germany

Ruderclub Meschede e.V.
Postfach 16 17
59856, Meschede
Germany

Miltenberger Ruder-Club von 1900 e.V.
Postfach 16 05
63886, Miltenberg
Germany

Mindener Ruder-Verein von 1905 e.V.
St. Ansgar Str. 2 B
32425, Minden
Germany

Bessel-Ruder-Club e.V.
Eickhof 23
32425, Minden
Germany

Herder-Ruder-Verein e.V.
Ackerstr. 4
32429, Minden
Germany

vorm. Möllner Turnerschaft v. 1884
Grambeker Weg 107F
23879, Mölln
Germany

Ruderverein Monheim e.V.
Postfach 10 05 51
40769, Monheim
Germany

Ruderclub Neptun Neckarelz e.V.
Postfach 16 46
74819, Mosbach
Germany

Ruder-Club Neumünster e.V.
An der L 318 Nr. 18
24582, Mühbrook
Germany

Sportverein Empor Mühlberg e.V.
Breitscheidstr. 8
4931, Mühlberg
Germany

Mühlheimer Ruderverein 1911 e.V.
Fährenstr. 38
63165, Mühlheim
Germany

Wassersportverein Mülheim-Ruhr e.V.
Postfach 102 107
45421, Mülheim
Germany

Ruderclub Mülheim a. d. Ruhr von 1977 e.V.
Leibnizstr. 9
45468, Mülheim
Germany

Renn-Ruder-Gemeinschaft Mülheim e.V.
Mendener Str. 74
45470, Mülheim
Germany

Mülheimer Ruder- Gesellschaft e.V.
Mendener Str. 74
45470, Mülheim/Ruhr
Germany

Akademischer Ruder-Club zu Münster e.V.
Rheinstr. 40
48145, Münster
Germany

Akademischer RV Westfalen Münster e.V.
Lütkenbecker Weg 2
48155, Münster
Germany

Ruderverein Münster von 1882 e.V.
Bennostr. 7
48155, Münster
Germany

RV Rot-Weiß Naumburg
Spechsart 38
6618, Naumburg
Germany

Neuruppiner Ruder-Club e.V.
Regattastr. 16
16816, Neuruppin
Germany

Neusser Ruderverein e.V.
Thywissenstraße 21
41464, Neuss
Germany

Wassersportverein 'Einheit' Neustrelitz e.V.
Zierker Straße 31
17235, Neustrelitz
Germany

Ulmer Ruder-Club 'Donau' e.V.
Bootshausstr. 7
89231, Neu-Ulm
Germany

Neuwieder Ruder-Gesellschaft 1883 e.V.
Postfach 1727
56507, Neuwied
Germany

Gymnasial-Turn-Ruder-Verein Neuwied 1882 e.V.
Zeisigpfad 7
56564, Neuwied
Germany

Rudergesellschaft Niederkassel von 1978 e.V.
Langgasse 87a
53859, Niederkassel
Germany

Ruder-Verein Nienburg e.V.
Postfach 16 49
31566, Nienburg
Germany

Norder Ruderclub e.V.
Fischerpfad 5
26506, Norden
Germany

Nordenhamer RC von 1908 e.V Nordenham
Wartfelder Str. 29
26954, Nordenham
Germany

Bootsclub Nordhorn e.V.
Zwinglistr. 11
48527, Nordhorn
Germany

Ruderverein Nürnberg von 1880 e.V.
Bayernstr. 136
90478, Nürnberg
Germany

Ruderclub Nürtingen e.V. 1921
Schellingstr. 20
72622, Nürtingen
Germany

Ruderverein Oberhausen e.V.
Konrad-Adenauer-Allee 75
46049, Oberhausen
Germany

Rudergesellschaft München 1972 e.V.
Postfach 12 36
85759, Oberschleißheim
Germany

Schleissheimer Ruderclub e.V.
Dachauer Str. 35
85764, Oberschleißheim
Germany

Interessengem. Offenbacher Rudervereine IGOR e.V.
Nordring 131
63067, Offenbach
Germany

WSV 1926 e.V. Offenbach am Main-Bürgel
Kettelerstr. 26
63075, Offenbach
Germany

Sportgemeinschaft 'Wiking' 1903 e.V.
Nordring 131
63067, Offenbach
Germany

Ruderverein Hellas Offenbach e.V.
Hafeninsel 26
63067, Offenbach
Germany

Oldenburger Ruderverein e.V.
Achterdiek 3
26131, Oldenburg
Germany

Postsportverein Oldenburg e.V. Ruderabteilung
Ohmstedter Esch 46
26125, Oldenburg
Germany

Ruder-Club Biggesee e.V.
Kurfürst-Heinrich-Str. 32
57462, Olpe
Germany

Osnabrücker Ruder-Verein e.V.
Glückaufstr. 16
49090, Osnabrück
Germany

Ruderclub Ratsgymnasium e.V. Osnabrück
Lammersstr. 10
49076, Osnabrück
Germany

Ruderclub Carolinum Osnabrück e.V.
Kleine Domsfreiheit 20
49076, Osnabrück
Germany

Ruder-Verein Osterholz-Scharmbeck von 1901 e.V.
Postfach 16 32
27703, Osterholz-Scharmbeck
Germany

TSV Otterndorf von 1862 e.V. Ruderabteilung
Knechtsand 5
21762, Otterndorf
Germany

Papenburger Ruderclub e.V.
Bgm.-Hettlage-Str. 18
26871, Papenburg
Germany

Passauer Ruderverein von 1874 e.V.
Bischof-Landersdorfer-Str. 39
94034, Passau
Germany

Pfullendorfer RC 2002 e.V.
Ochsensteige 30
88630, Pfullendorf
Germany

Pirnaer Ruderverein 1872 e.V.
An der Elbe 11
1796, Pirna
Germany

Plöner Ruderverein e.V.
Schlossgebiet 13
24306, Plön
Germany

Potsdamer Ruder-Gesellschaft e.V.
An der Pirschheide 28
14471, Potsdam
Germany

Preetzer Ruderclub e.V.
Breslauer Str. 13
24211, Preetz
Germany

Prenzlauer Sportverein 'Uckermark' e.V.
Ahornweg 9
17291, Prenzlau
Germany

Spiel- und Sportverein Planeta Radebeul e.V.
Geschwister-Scholl-Str. 15
1445, Radebeul
Germany

Ruder-Club Rastatt 1898 e.V.
Postfach 21 15
76437, Rastatt
Germany

Ratzeburger Ruderclub e.V.
Postfach 11 42
23901, Ratzeburg
Germany

Reeser Ruderverein 1905 e.V.
Postfach 13 08
46452, Rees
Germany

Regensburger Ruder-Klub von 1890 e.V.
Messerschmittstr. 2
93049, Regensburg
Germany

Regensburger Ruderverein von 1898 e.V.
Messerschmittstr. 2
93049, Regensburg
Germany

Ruder-Club 1881 e.V. Traben-Trarbach
Dorfstr. 25
56861, Reil
Germany

Reinfelder Rudergemeinschaft von 1963 e.V.
Theodor-Storm-Str. 2
23858, Reinfeld
Germany

Ruder-Gesellschaft Remagen e.V.
Karmeliterstr. 11
53424, Remagen
Germany

Wassersportverein Schifferclub Neckarrems e.V.
Postfach 13
71686, Remseck
Germany

Rvg. Kappeln im TSV Kappeln von 1876 e.V.
Bismarckstr. 9
24768, Rendsburg
Germany

Rendsburger Primaner Ruderclub von 1880
Graf-von-Stauffnberg-Str. 5
24768, Rendsburg
Germany

Rendsburger Ruderverein e.V.
Postfach 315
24755, Rendsburg
Germany

Verdener Ruderverein e.V.
An der Wölpe 21
27336, Rethem
Germany

Segeberger Ruderclub von 1926 e.V.
Bökenbusch 5
23847, Rethwisch
Germany

RHTC von 1901 Rheine e.V.
Sesenheimweg 30
48429, Rheine
Germany

FFS am Kopernikus-Gymnasium Rheine e.V.
Kopernikusstr. 61
48429, Rheine
Germany

Ruderclub Rheinfelden Baden e.V.
Zollstr. 5
79618, Rheinfelden
Germany

Ruderverein Rheinsberg 1910 e.V.
Rhinhöher Weg 1
16831, Rheinsberg
Germany

Ribnitzer Sportverein 1919 e.V. RA
Bahnhofstr. 03
18311, Ribnitz-Damgarten
Germany

Wasser-Sport- Verein Rinteln e.V.
Am Doktorsee 18
31737, Rinteln
Germany

Roßlauer Rudergesellschaft e.V.
Mühlenstraße 21
6862, Roßlau
Germany

Ruderclub Roßleben e.V.
Wendelsteinerstr. 9
6571, Roßleben
Germany

Olympischer Ruder-Club Rostock von 1956 e.V.
Postfach 10 20 63
18003, Rostock
Germany

Rostocker Ruder-Club von 1885 e.V
August-Bebel-Str. 1 b
18055, Rostock
Germany

HSG der Universität Rostock e.V. Ruderabteilung
Ulmenstr. 69
18057, Rostock
Germany

Rotenburger Ruderverein e.V.
Postfach 14 30
36190, Rotenburg
Germany

Rüdersdorfer Ruderverein Kalkberge e.V.
Seestraße 13
15562, Rüdersdorf
Germany

Rüsselsheimer Ruder-Klub 08 e.V.
Postfach 17 54
65407, Rüsselsheim
Germany

Ruderclub Saar e.V.
Hindenburgstr. 65
66119, Saarbrücken
Germany

Saarbrücker Rudergesellschaft Undine e.V.
Bismarckstr. 129
66121, Saarbrücken
Germany

Ruder Verein 'Saarbrücken e.V.
Hindenburgstr. 65
66119, Saarbrücken
Germany

Saarburger Ruderclub 1925 e.V.
Postfach 1312
54433, Saarburg
Germany

SV Alemannia 1919 Salzbergen e.V.
Am Bahndamm 12
48499, Salzbergen
Germany

Ruderclub am Salzgittersee e.V. v. 1968/98
Ulmenried 17
38226, Salzgitter
Germany

Sportvereinigung Scharnebeck e.V. Ruderabteilung
Meisterstr. 19
21379, Scharnebeck
Germany

Ruderclub Schieder am Emmerstausee von 1985 e.V.
Am Kronenbruch
32816, Schieder-Schwalenberg
Germany

Domschulruderclub Schleswig e.V.
Königstr. 37
24837, Schleswig
Germany

Schönebecker Sportclub e.V.
Am Gänsewinkel 16 b
39218, Schönebeck
Germany

Spiel- u. Sportvereinigung PCK 90 Schwedt e.V.
Breite Allee 3-9
16303, Schwedt
Germany

Ruderclub Schwedt e.V.
Regattastraße 2
16303, Schwedt
Germany

Schweinfurter Ruder-Club 'Franken' von 1882 e.V.
Postfach 14 44
97404, Schweinfurt
Germany

Schweriner Rudergesellschaft von 1874/75 e.V.
Franzosenweg 21
19061, Schwerin
Germany

Senftenberger Ruderverein e.V.
Antonienstr. 01
1968, Senftenberg
Germany

Siegburger Ruderverein 1910 e.V.
Hasenstr. 3
53721, Siegburg
Germany

Rudergesellschaft Speyer 1883 e.V.
Salierstr. 23
67346, Speyer
Germany

Wassersportverein Rheinfels St. Goar 1911/1924 e.V.
Ulmenhof 19
56329, St Goar
Germany

Münchener Ruder- und Segelverein 'Bayern' von 1910 e.V.
Seepromenade 2
82319, Starnberg
Germany

Tutzinger Ruderverein 1983 e.V.
Kirchplatz 6
82319, Starnberg
Germany

Münchener Ruder-Club von 1880 e.V.
Dampfschiffstr. 6
82319, Starnberg
Germany

Ruderclub Undine e.V.
Karl-Burg-Weg 9
78333, Stockach
Germany

Stralsunder Ruder-Club e.V.
Fr. Naumannstr. 5
18435, Stralsund
Germany

Stuttgart-Cannstatter Ruderclub von 1910 e.V.
Wagrainstr. 140
70378, Stuttgart
Germany

Behindertensport-Verein Stuttgart e.V. Ruderabteilung
Dreizlerstr. 3
70619, Stuttgart
Germany

Stuttgarter Rudergesellschaft von 1899 e.V.
Postfach 60 05 17
70327, Stuttgart
Germany

Ruderclub Sorpesee 1956 e.V.
Heckenweg 3 a
59846, Sundern
Germany

Tangermünder Ruderclub von 1906 e.V.
Ernst-Drong-Str. 5
39590, Tangermünde
Germany

Ruderverein am Tegernsee von 1949 e.V.
Schwaighofstr. 54
83684, Tegernsee
Germany

Ruderclub Titisee e.V.
Mozartstr. 19
79822, Titisee-Neustadt
Germany

Torgauer Ruderverein e.V.
Pestalozziweg 15
4860, Torgau
Germany

Rudergesellschaft Treis-Karden 1969 e.V.
Postfach 11 17
56251, Treis-Karden
Germany

Rudergesellschaft Trier 1883 e.V.
An der Jugendherberge 3
54292, Trier
Germany

Ruderverein 'Treviris 1921' e.V.
Luxemburger Str. 81
54290, Trier
Germany

Tübinger Ruderverein "Fidelia" 1877/1911 e.V.
Gartenstr. 180
72074, Tübingen
Germany

Überlinger Ruderclub 'Bodan' e.V.
Heinrich Emerich Str. 35
88662, Überlingen
Germany

Rennrudergemeinschaft Baden-Württemberg e.V.
Heinrich Emerich Str. 35
88662, Überlingen
Germany

Ruderclub Stolzenau von 1986 e.V.
Philosophenweg 32
31600, Uchte
Germany

Ruderverein Uelzen e.V.
Kl. Liedern Nr. 5
29525, Uelzen
Germany

Ruderclub Vilshofen 1913 e.V.
Am Flugplatz 5
94474, Vilshofen
Germany

Waginger Ruderverein e.V.
Ganghofer Str. 8
83329, Waging
Germany

Rudergesellschaft 'Ghibellinia' Waiblingen 1920 e.V.
Brunnweinbergstr. 16 a
71334, Waiblingen
Germany

Wassersport-Verein Waldshut e.V.
Postfach 19 08
79746, Waldshut-Tiengen
Germany

Ruderverein Waltrop von 1928 e.V.
Surenkamp 11
45731, Waltrop
Germany

Ruderverein Babensham von 1981 e.V.
Dr. Fritz-Huber-Str. 17
83512, Wasserburg
Germany

Weilburger Ruderverein 1905 e.V.
Zevenaar-Str. 3
35781, Weilburg
Germany

Weißenfelser Ruder-Verein 1884 e.V.
Jüdenstr. 41
06667, Weißenfels
Germany

Ruder-Klub Werder (H) 1918 e.V.
Werderwiesen 18
14542, Werder
Germany

Rudergesellschaft Wertheim von 1902 e.V.
Marktplatz 21
97877, Wertheim
Germany

Ruder- und Tennisgesellschaft Wesel e.V.
Am Yachthafen 7
46468, Wesel
Germany

Ruderclub 'Westfalen' Herdecke 1929 e.V.
Im Vogelsang 6
58300, Wetter
Germany

Sportgemeinschaft DEMAG e.V.
Königstr. 43
58300, Wetter
Germany

Rudergesellschaft Wetzlar 1880 e.V.
Inselstr. 10
35576, Wetzlar
Germany

Rudergesellschaft Wiesbaden- Biebrich 1888 e.V.
Postfach 12 05 04
65083, Wiesbaden
Germany

Wassersportverein Wildeshausen e.V.
Postfach 17 12
27784, Wildeshausen
Germany

Wilhelmshavener Ruderclub von 1909 e.V.
Postfach 26 06
26366, Wilhelmshaven
Germany

Ruderverein Bochum von 1920 e.V.
Dortmunder Str. 81
58453, Witten
Germany

Ruder-Club 'Mark' Wetter e.V.
Bellerslohstr. 10
58452, Witten
Germany

Ruder-Club Witten e.V.
Bodenborn 42
58452, Witten
Germany

Ruder-Club Wittenberg e.V.
Dresdener Str. 160
6886, Wittenberg
Germany

Wolfsburger Ruder-Club e.V.
Postfach 101 131
38410, Wolfsburg
Germany

Ruderverein Wolgast e.V.
Baustr. 47
17438, Wolgast
Germany

Wormser Ruderclub Blau-Weiß e.V.
Am Rhein 5
67547, Worms
Germany

Rudergesellschaft Worms 1883 e.V.
Kleiststr. 24
67551, Worms
Germany

Ruder- und Kanu-Club Wörth e.V.
Postfach 101 301
76730, Wörth
Germany

Wassersport-Verein Ennepetal e.V.
Zu den Dolinen 97
42279, Wuppertal
Germany

Akademischer Ruderclub Würzburg e.V.
Max-Dauthendey-str. 2
97072, Würzburg
Germany

Würzburger Ruderverein Bayern von 1875/1905 e.V.
Mergentheimer Str. 13
97082, Würzburg
Germany

Ruderverein Zell e.V. 1921
Postfach 12 09
56852, Zell
Germany

Ruder-Club Zellingen e.V.
Mainau 17
97225, Zellingen
Germany

Rudergesellschaft Zeltingen e.V.
Weingartenstr. 62
54492, Zeltingen
Germany

ESV Lok Zernsdorf e.V. Abt. Rudern
Senziger Weg 17
15758, Zernsdorf
Germany

Wassersportverein Königs Wusterhausen e.V.
Waldpromenade 101
15738, Zeuthen
Germany

Zschornewitzer RC v. 1954 e.V.
Goethehain 2
6791, Zschornewitz
Germany

Gibraltar

NATIONAL FEDERATION

Gibraltar Amateur Rowing Association
PO Box 113
Gibraltar
Tel: +350 45754
Fax: +350 45754
Email: gara@gibrowing.com

CLUBS

Calpe Rowing Club
6 Europort Road
Gibraltar
Tel: +350 72605
Fax: +350 50590

Mediterranean Rowing Club
4 Europort Road
Gibraltar
tel: +350 71357
fax: +350 40659
email: mrc@medrowing.com

Greece

NATIONAL FEDERATION

Hellenic Rowing Federation
22 Alex. Koumoundourou Street
18533, Pireaus
Greece
Tel: +30 10 411 8011
Fax: +30 10 411 8088
Email: ekofns1@aias.gr
www.kopilasia.gr

CLUBS

Omilos ereton
limani kanari- pasalimani
185 36 piraeus
Greece
+30 2104521424

N.O.N.F&PIREA
45, Tompazi Str
18537 Piraeus
Greece
+30 2104537648

N.A.S.
1, alex.koumoundourou 1
mikrolimano-18533 piraeus
Greece
+30 2104174395

N.O.thessalonikis
112, them.sofouli
551 31 thessaloniki
Greece
+30 2310 414521

I.O.thessalonikis
12 meg.alexandrou
546 43 thessaloniki
Greece
+30 2310 830939

N.O.B.A.
akti anavrou
38110 volos
Greece
+30 24210 20376 &31200

O.F.Qes/nikhs
10, leof.meg. alexandrou
546 42 thessaloniki
Greece
+30 2310 831 333

N.O.rodou
9 pl.kountourioti
85100 rhodes
Greece
+30 22410 23287 [23287]

O.S.F.P.
plateia alexandras
18534 piraeus
Greece
+30 2104190902-3

A.E.N.
poros troizinias
18020 poros
Greece
+30 2298022254/22662

N.A.O.Kerkyras
1. leof. dimokratias
491 00 corfu
Greece
+30 26610 30470

N.O.Ioanninon
10 kanari — limnopoula
454 45 ioannina
Greece
+30 2651038060

N.O.Kastorias
1. leof.souggaridou
521 00 kastoria
Greece
+30 24670 28956

N.O.Mutilinis
terma makri gialos
811 00 mutilini
Greece
+30 22510 20782

N.O.Katerinis
p.o.57 — 601 00 Katerini
Greece
+30 23510 61408

E.N.O.egiptioton
akrotiri agiou kosma
elliniko 16777
Greece
+30 2109818525/9858708

N.A.O.Kal. thes.
mikro emvolo-kalamaria
thessaloniki 551 10
Greece
+30 2310 454111-454533

N.A.O.salaminas
agiou nikolaou (enanti arith.12)
18900 salamina
Greece
+30 2104657006

N.O.giannitson
n.o.g.-p.o. box 101
giannitsa 581 00
Greece
+30 23820 26966

Oea-Nab
akti ag.konstantinou
382 22 volos
Greece
+30 24210 34633

N.O.irakliou
enetikos limhn irakliou-pob 27
713 02 iraklio kritis
Greece
+30 2810 280817

N.O.P.Trizinias
180 20 poros
+30 2298025834

K.O.ELLADOS
TQ175
16610 Glyfada
Greece
+30 2109612947

N.O.Mavrohoriou
mavrohori kastorias
52100 kastoria
Greece
+30 2467074624

K.O.Kastorias
2, tsakali
521 00 kastoria
Greece
+30 24670 82588

N.O.limnou
myrina limnou
81400 limnos
Greece
+30 2254024813

N.O.soudas
ethniko naftathlitiko kentro soudas (box 40)
732 00 souda
Greece
+30 28210 81120

N.A.S.panagioudas
tamvakelli despina
8 xenofontos — 811 00 mutilini
Greece
+30 22510 4270

D.N.O.Hgoum/tsas
17 gr. labraki
461 00 igoumenitsa
Greece
+30 2665022123 -28370

O.N.A.Trizinias
front.kartsoli dim.
180 20 poros trizinias
Greece
+30 22980 23960

N.O.Argostoliou
ilia zervou 16
281 00 argostoli
Greece
+30 26710 24145-22874

A.G.S.EPTANISON
mesolora 3
28100 kefalonia
Greece
+30 26710 24830

NATIONAL FEDERATION

Federación de Remo de Honduras
Jorge Marinakis Z.
Apartado Postal 287
San Pedro Sulaz
Honduras
Tel: (504) 233-4011
Fax: (504) 233-8006
Email: feh_reca@honduras.com

Guatemala

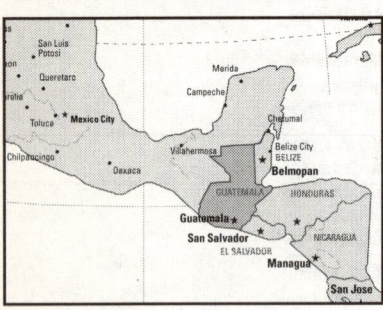

Guatemalan Rowing Federation
26 street 9-31 Zone 5
Palacio de los Deportes
C.A., FL
Guatemala
Tel: (502) 334 8458
Fax: (502) 334 8458
Email: federemo@terra.com.gt

Hong Kong - China

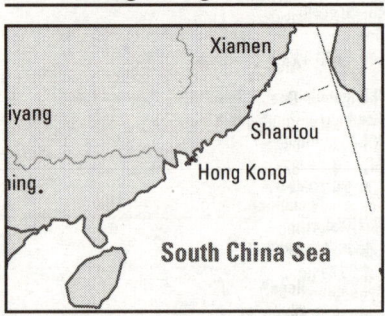

NATIONAL FEDERATION

Hong Kong China Rowing Association
Shatin Rowing Centre
27 Yuen Wo Road
Hong Kong
Hong Kong - China
Tel: +852 2 699 7271
Fax: +852 2 601 4477
Email: hkcra@rowing.org.hk
www.hkcra.org

CLUBS

Chong Heep Rowing Club — CHRC
Wong Wai Ming, Steven
Ip Chi Kin
Fax: +852 28324132
Email: chongheeprowingclub@yahoo.com

Lion Rock Rowing Club — LRRC
Tony Lau
Email: lrrc@mail.hongkong.com

Feather Rowing Club — FRC
Ng See Hung
Email: seehung@yahoo.com
Fax: +852 24151080

Sha Tin Sports Association — STSA
Stalle Wong
Keung Chung Wai
Fax: +852 26021966
Email: stsa@stsa.org.hk

Honduras

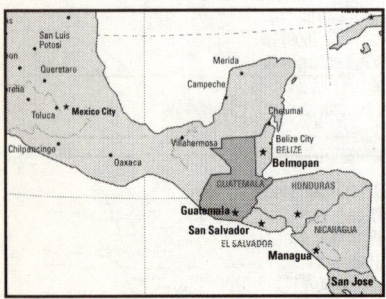

Lok Tsui Rowing Club — LTRC
Andrew Li
Cheung Siu Yin
Email: loktsui@doramail.com

Royal Hong Kong Yacht Club — RHKYC
Nicholas Southward
Email: nickjs@netvigater.com
Fax: +852 28167857

Sha Tin Baptist Rowing Club — STBRC
Kwok Tai Ming
Lo Yan Chak
Fax: +852 281057198
Email: tmkwok@hknet.com

SCHOOLS AND UNIVERSITIES

Fire Service Department Rowing Club — FSD
Jim Ka Keung
Email: jim-jim@i-cable
Fax: +852 23827402

Scout Association of Hong Kong — SAHK
Mak Yiu Chung
Fax: +852 23582177

Pui Ying College — PYC
Cheung Kwok Keung, John
Email: jc278ats@netvigater.com
Fax: +852 26020411

TWGHs Yow Kam Yuen College — YKY
Yuen Wai Shan
Fax: +852 26494688

HKCWC Fung Yiu King Memorial Secondary School — FYK
Chan Mei Yuk
Fax: +852 26421896

Island School Rowing Club — ISRC
Mr. B.J. Massingham
Fax: +852 28401673

South Island School — SIS
Ms Jayne Mathieson
Fax: +852 25538811

Hong Kong International School Rowing Club — HKIS
Mrs Duncan-Laird
Fax: +852 28139144

Sha Tin College — STC
Mr. Paul Tattam
Acc: Siew Po Li
Email: tattams@asiaonline.net

Chinese University of Hong Kong — CUHK
Amy Tung
Email: mongmongtungtung@hotmail.com

Chinese University of Hong Kong Alumni Rowing Club — CUHKA
Lee Kwan
Email: iambighead8@sinaman.com

University of Hong Kong — HKU
Chan Yui
Email: cykevin@hkusua.hku.hk

University of Hong Kong Alumni Rowing Club — HKUA
Cheng Chi Hong
Email: hong@graduate.hku.hk

Hong Kong Baptist University — HKBU
Ho Chi Kiu
Email: kiu312@sinaman.com
Fax: +852 23397896 (Attn: Rowing Club)

Hong Kong Polytechnic University — PolyU
Chung Wing Yee
Email: pharach24601@yahoo.com
Fax: +852 23333518 (Attn: Rowing Club)

City University of Hong Kong — CityU
Chan Man Yan
Tai Kin Yung
Fax: +852 27888066(Attn. Rowing Club)
Email: manyan2@sinaman.com

Hong Kong University of Science & Technology — HKUST
Cheng Ho Yin, Ewing
Email: su_row@ust.com
Fax: +852 23351728 (Attn: Rowing Club)

HKUST Alumni Rowing Team
Wong Ka Cheong
kcwong925@hotmail.com

Hong Kong Institute of Education — HKIEd
Tsang Hing Yin
Email: hy4523@hotmail.com

Metro water Sports Club MWSC
Maria Chan
So Tsan Wang
Email: maria@mtr.com.hk
Fax: +852 29937707

Shatin Government Sec. Sch. STGSS
Chan Yu Ho
Tel: +852 26091456

Hungary

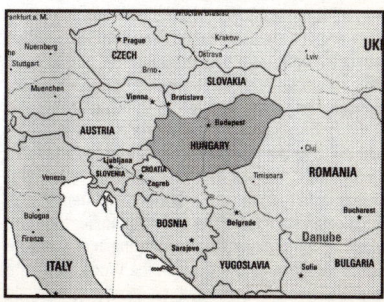

HISTORY

Hungary played an important role in the popularisation of rowing in Europe in the nineteenth century. On May 16, 1827, Count István Széchenyi rowed from Vienna to Bratislava; he covered the distance in 3 hours 52 minutes. The first Hungarian rowing race was held in Bratislava in 1863, and two years later the regatta between Margaret Island and Chain Bridge in Budapest attracted tens of thousands of spectators. In 1893, the Association of Hungarian Rowing Clubs was founded, and the following year the first rowing regatta for women was organised in Szeged.

Hungary was represented by an eight at the 1908 Olympic Games. The dynamic development of the rowing sport in Hungary brought results in the 1930's; Béla Szendey in the single sculls won the first gold medal for Hungary in the European Championships. For four consecutive years, 1932,1933,1934,1935, Hungary won the Glandaz Prize awarded to the most successful national team in the European Championships.

After World War II, at the London Olympics in 1848 the coxed pair of Béla Zsitnik, Antal Szendey, and Róbert Zimonyi, won the first Olympic medal for Hungary. A new era began when Pap Jen_né Kornélia Méray appeared on the scene. She won four European titles: 1958 at Poznan, 1959 at Macon, 1960 at London, and 1961 at Prague. Following her success, the women's crew of Mária Fekete, Mária Pekanovits, Ágnes Salamon, Zsuzsa Szappanos, cox: Margit Komornik, won the first gold medal in the quadruple sculls in 1965.

The best result was in Mexico City in the 1968 Olympic Games. The Hungarian four of Zoltán Melis, György Sarlós, József Csermely, and Antal Melis, became the silver medallists. In the 1970's, Mariann Ambrus, in the single sculls, won a silver medal in the World Championships in 1975 at Nottingham, and two bronze medals, 1977 at Amsterdam and 1978 at Hamilton. Katalin Sarlós won a bronze medal in the Worlds at Bled in 1989 after her.

Rowing in Hungary was in a difficult position in the post-war years. Because the socialist regime labelled rowing as a bourgeois sport, it had to cope with conservative support. Despite many difficulties, Hungary has produced some outstanding rowers and is trying to stay up with the world's rowing elite. The first result of the most recent era is Gergely Kokas's 1999 World Championships bronze medal in the lightweight men's single at St Catherines. Then, it was good omen that Tibor Peto and Ákos Haller took fifth place at the Sydney Olympics in the men's double sculls following a third place in the World Cup. Peto and Haller have continued on to win the World

Championships in 2001 and 2002, losing only once in the World Cup series. Recently, only three members of the improving Hungarian rowing team avoided the salmonella infection the hit the national squad just before the World Championships in Seville, 2002 affecting their ability to perform.

PERSONALITIES

Béla Zsitnik: Best result: 1948 London Olympic Games, Bronze medal in the Men's pair with coxswain. After resigning from active rowing he became secretary general of the Hungarian Rowing Federation.

Jenoné Pap (Kornélia Méray): Best results: Gold medallist at the European Championships: 1958 at Poznan, 1959 at Macon, 1960 at London, and 1961 at Prague. From 1960-1984 she was a journalist and correspondent for the National Sport newspaper. Now retired and she is the author of the novel Waters gave me freedom.

Zoltán Melis: Best results: Silver medal at the 1968 Mexico City Olympic Games in the men's four without coxswain; 33 times national champion. He has been the head coach of the Hungarian rowing team for 16 years and has also worked as the Head Coach in Egypt.

Mariann Ambrus: Best results: In the women's single scull, silver medallist at the 1975 World Championships and bronze medallist at the 1977 and 1978 World Championships. Her daughter, Zsófia Fekete, is a talented sculler.

Did You Know ?

There is only one rowing course in Hungary that meets international standards. It is in Szeged, named after count István Széchenyi. The most significant event so far held on this venue was the FISA World Rowing Junior Championships in 1989.

NATIONAL FEDERATION

Fédération d'Aviron Hongroise
Dozsa Gyorgy ut 1-3
Budapest, 1143
Hungary
Tel: +36 1 468 2478
Fax: +36 1 468 2479
Email: mesz@enternet.hu
www.mesz.org

CLUBS

Ászgárd Sport Klub
Kalocsai u. 40.
Budapest, 1141
Hungary
Contact: Szrapkó István
Tel: +36 20/9581622
Email: printpont@freemail.hu

Acélönto Sport Kör
Kinizsi u. 38.
Göd, 2132
Hungary
Contact: Fischer Géza
Tel: +36 312-7320
Boathouse: Kócsag csónakház SLV Római part

Bajai SpartacusVízügy SC
Bartok u. 4.
Baja, 6500
Hungary
Contact: Bartos Nándor
Tel: +36 79/323-438

Budapest Lido Szabadidosport Club
Hungary
Contact: Zimits Béláné
Tel: +36 20/9-169-472:

Budapesti Vízmo
Hungary
Contact: German Ottó
Tel: +36 284-0253
Boathouse: 1237 Bp., Vizisport u. 62.

Csepel Evezos Klub SE
Gubacsi hídfo
Budapest, 1213
Hungary
Contact: Melis Antal
Tel: +36 207-99-72

Csongrádi Vízügyi Sport Egylet
Vasút u. 90.
Csongrád, 6640
Hungary
Contact: Mucsi István
Tel: +36 63/483-859
Email: csvse@mailbox.hu

Danubius Nemzeti Hajós Egylet
Hajós Alfréd Sétány 2.
Budapest, Margitsziget, 1138
Hungary
Contact: Meszlarics Anita
Tel: +36 329-3142
Email: anitam@danubius.banknet.hu
Boathouse: Hajós Alfréd sétány 2

EGIS Gyógyszergyár Sport Kör
Keresztúri út 30-38.
Budapest, 1106
Hungary
Contact: Nemes Miklós
Tel: +36 265-5511

Esztergomi Evezosök Hajós Egylete
Prímás — Sziget Pf.:242
Esztergom, 2501
Hungary
Contact: Mármarosi Gyozo
Tel: +36 33/313-473
Email: esztehe@ax.hu

Ferencvárosi Evezos Club
Pf: 83.
Budapest, 1701
Hungary
Contact: Dr. Kokas Péter
Tel: +36 30/9-320-915
Email: kok6164@ello.hu
Boathouse: 1203 Bp. Vízisport u. 24.

Ganz Villamossági Evezos Klub
Királyok útja 166.
Budapest, 1039
Hungary
Contact: Halmi Béla
Tel: +36 240-2571, 3688-666
Boathouse: Budapest, 1039 Királyok útja 297.

Georgikon Diáksport Egyesület
Hungary

Gyori Spartacus Sport Egyesület
Verseny u.5.2/6.
Gyor, 9023
Hungary
Contact: Lánczi István
Tel: +36 96/420-314

Gyori Vízügy Sport Egyesület
Kálóczy tér 1-6.
Gyor, 9026
Hungary
Contact: Tóvári Péter
Tel: +36 96/437-460
Email: titkarsag@eduvizig.hu

Hajógyári Evezos Club
Torontál u. 27.
Budapest, 1145
Hungary
Contact: Sarkadi Nagy Imre
Tel: +36 220-4394
Email: gyongysorhaz@axelero.hu
Boathouse: 1138 Bp. Népsziget 1-3.

Kalocsai Sport Egyesület
Hungary
Contact: Rácz Pálné
Tel: +36 30/451-174

Külker Evezos Klub
Munyadi Mátyás u. 32.
Budapest, 1116
Hungary
Contact: Mihály Tibor
Tel: +36 264-9482
Email: kulkerek@kulkerek.hu
Boathouse: 1039 Bp. Szent János u. 7.

Magyar Nemzeti Bank Sport Kör
Hungary
Contact: Petho Zoltán
Email: bujdo_show@freemail.hu

Magyar Testgyakorlók Köre
Erzsébet krt. 24. 1. em.
Budapest, 1073
Hungary
Contact: Kozeschnik László
Tel: +36 361-2027
Email: Tompos@nfs.jozsef.kando.hu

Lri-Malev Sport Club
Nagyszalonta u. 25.
Budapest, 1185
Hungary
Contact: Varga Béla
Tel: +36 256-3783
Email: kistanya@matavnet.hu
Boathouse: Római Part 19

Mohácsi Torna Egylet
Kórház u. 11.
Mohács, 7700
Hungary
Contact: Schwoy Dezsoné
Tel: +36 30/238-8361
Email: mohacsviz@matavnet.hu
Boathouse: 7700 Mohács Felso Dunasor u.

Mosonmagyaróvári Vizisport Egyesület
Cseresznyés u. 35. Fsz:1.
Mosonmagyaróvár, 9200
Hungary
Contact: Nagy Gábor
Tel: +36 96/332-252
Email: wlasitsch@mail.datanet.hu
Boathouse: Karolina korház csónakháza Mosoni Duna partján

Moegyetemi Evezos Club
Vizisport u. 44.
Budapest, 1237
Hungary
Contact: Kovács Imre
Tel: +36 20/3815775
Email: mec@matavnet.hu
Boathouse: 1237 Bp., Vizisport u. 44.

Regatta Club Soroksár
Vizisport u. 44.
Budapest, 1238
Hungary
Contact: Kovács Imre
Tel: +36 20/3815775
Boathouse: 1238 Bp., Vizisport u. 44.

Szegedi Vizisport Egyesület
Stefánia út. 4.
Szeged, 6720
Hungary
Contact: Dani Zsolt
Tel: +36 20/9826-071
Email: danizsolt@freemail.hu
Boathouse: 6720 Szeged, Stefánia út. 4.

Tata Tóvárosi Vizisport Egylet
Május 1. u. 31.
Tata, 2890
Hungary
Contact: Domonkos Ágnes
Tel: +36 34/311-766
Email: Emho@suoftec.hu

Taurus Sport Club
Hungary
Contact: Renszer Mihály

Tisza Evezos Egylet
Városmajor út 59/G
Szolnok, 5000
Hungary
Contact: Molnár Dezso
Tel: +36 56/410-500
Email: oktogon@mail.externet.hu
Boathouse: Szolnok Szabadság tér 9.

Vác Városi Evezos Egylet
Pf: 402..
Vác, 2601
Hungary
Contact: Patay László
Tel: +36 27/319-015
Email: vvec@mail.digitel2002.hu

Velence tavi Vizisport Iskola és SZk
Tópart u. 17.
Agárd, 2481
Hungary
Contact: Csankó Tibor
Tel: +36 22/355-219
Email: vvsi@axelero.hu

Vízügyi Sport Club
Márvány u. 1/c
Budapest, 1012
Hungary
Contact: Wagner Mihály
Tel: +36 210-1090

Vizisport és Vitorlás Egyesület Balatonföldvár
Mátyás Király út 1.
Balatonföldvár, 8623
Hungary
Contact: Pásztor József
Tel: +36 30/9799401

Iceland

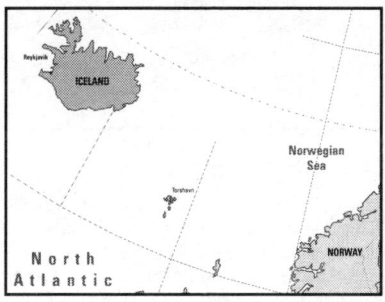

HISTORY

It is hard to say when rowing started in Iceland because there is little if any documented history. Between the 1930's and 1950's, a small team was training and competing at regattas in Denmark. It is, however, safe to say that the sport of rowing arrived in Iceland from Denmark.

Rowing in Iceland was reborn in the mid 1980's with the arrival of an ex-Italian Junior National Team rower who, working in conjunction with the Sport and Youth Council of Reykjavik and FISA, founded the Icelandic Rowing Association. With some gifts of boats from the Italian Federation, the Norwegian Federation, and the German Federation, the 20-athlete rowing club in Iceland, Brokey Rowing Club had its first boats out of which to row.

In 1995, an Icelandic junior girl won an international regatta in Denmark, the first significant international win for the Icelandic Rowing Association. Today, the Brokey club is still the only club in Iceland. Its motto is to "row, row, row and have a lot of fun!"

REGIONS

Southwest region of Iceland: Where Reykjavik is situated, is mostly windy all the year and the average temperature is -5C to 5C in the winter time. In summer the temperature is around 10C to 15°C; there can be a lot of rain.

Northwest region: Generally the same as the southwest part, but there is more snow in the winter time.

North region: Colder then southwest in the winter time, but the summer generally is much better; if there is sun and the wind blows from the south the temperature can go up to 30°C.

East Region: Similar to the North.

South Region: Very windy with a lot of rain and the average temperature is similar to the southwest part.

The best time of the year to visit Iceland is from the second half of May until the first half of July. Iceland, however, can have rapidly changing weather. Bad weather can happen in June, while August and September can have great weather.

PERSONALITIES

Leone Tinganelli: Founder of the modern Icelandic Rowing Association, and Brokey Rowing Club.

Anna Lára Steingrimsdottir: Placed twelfth at the 1995 Junior World Championships in Poland in the single scull and thirteenth in lightweight single scull in the 1996 World Championships in Scotland.

Ármann K. Jonsson: He was nineteenth in the lightweight single at the 1996 World Championships in Scotland and eighteenth in the lightweight single at the 1997 World Championships in France.

NATIONAL FEDERATION

Icelandic Rowing Association
Solheimar 7-104
Reykjavik, Iceland
Contact: Leone Tinganelli
Tel: +354 581 3995
Email: leone-sif@islandia.is

CLUBS

Brokey Rowing Club
Solheimar 7-104
Reykjavik, Iceland
Contact: Leone Tinganelli
Tel: +354 581 3995
Email: leone-sif@islandia.is

India

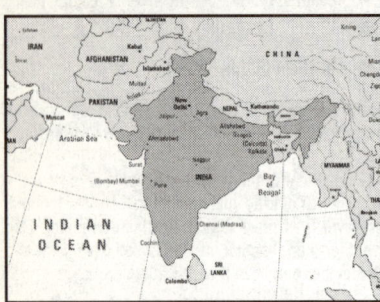

NATIONAL FEDERATION

Rowing Federation of India
33 17/2 Officers Colony
RK Puram
Secunderabad, 500056
India
Tel: +91 98480 28483
Fax: +91 98480 28483
Email: rowingindia@vsnl.net

Indonesia

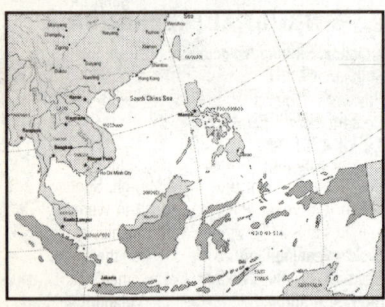

NATIONAL FEDERATION

Indonesian Rowing & Canoeing Association
Jalan Prapatan 38
Jakarta, 10410
Indonesia
Tel: +62 21 3862311
Fax: +62 21 3862312
Email: podsi@indosat.net.id

Ireland

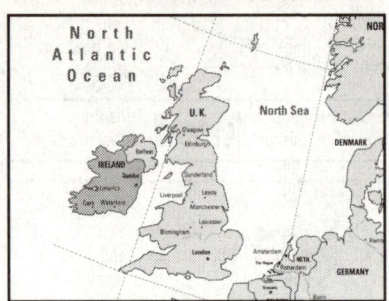

HISTORY

Competitive rowing in Ireland has existed since the 1830's. Rowing started first in the major ports and later at the main railheads because the transportation of boats was possible. In the earlier years it was easier for a Dublin crew to race in Liverpool, than in Galway or Limerick. The development of railways changed all that. More recently, club trailers and sectioned boats means that crews from any patch of water in Ireland can be ready to race at any other rowing center in Ireland in a few hours.

Dublin has always been the major center of Irish rowing with Dublin University Rowing and Dublin clubs in serious competition with each other. The rules of the Dublin Metropolitan Regatta, established in 1869, was a model for the entire country until the founding of the Irish Amateur Rowing Union in 1899. The other major centers were Derry, Coleraine, Belfast, Drogheda, Waterford, Cork, Limerick, Galway around the coast of Ireland and Athlone in the center of the country. The Irish Amateur Rowing Union created a men's eights championship in 1912. Since then more than thirty Irish championships have been added for men, women, seniors, intermediates, novices, and juniors in eights, fours, pairs, quads, doubles, and single sculls.

Irish crews have been racing at the Henley Royal Regatta in England since 1870, but in 1948 the Irish Amateur Rowing Union became affiliated with FISA sending it's first national crew to the Olympic regatta of that year. It should be noted that Ireland, in this context, meant the whole island of Ireland.

Since then, there has been remarkable progress by this small country on the international scene. Sean Drea, also well known on Boathouse Row in Philadelphia, won Ireland's first silver medal in the World Championships at Nottingham in 1975 in the men's single sculls. Gold medals followed in the men's lightweight single by Niall O'Toole at Vienna in

1991 and Sam Lynch at both the Lucerne 2001 and Seville 2002 World Championships. Women's lightweight single sculler, Sinead Jennings and the men's lightweight coxless pair also won the World Championships in Lucerne. The triple gold year of 2001 was an incredible achievement for Irish rowing.

Serious support is now going towards the new elite athletes in this sport, and a new national rowing center is being developed on Inniscarra Lake near Cork. At Blessington Lake in County Wicklow, the Dublin Metropolitan Regatta is creating its center for Leinster and Dublin. New clubs have sprung up in places like Skibbereen, Tullamore and Killarney to challenge the old historic centers, some of which have fallen on hard times. But each July the national championships will be battled out between the top Dublin clubs and their challengers from every corner of Ireland. And then, they'll join together to challenge the world.

INTERNET LINKS:
info@iaru.ie

REGIONS

Ireland as a whole has a very temperate climate, never very hot, never very cold, and never very predictable. It can rain a lot, but wind is the worst enemy of rowing in Ireland.

The Regatta season is from April to July, with Heads of the River earlier in the year.

Ulster: Includes the six counties that make up Northern Ireland, plus three counties that are part of the Republic of Ireland.

Rowing Centers:
Enniskillen: On Lough Erne: Portora BC & Enniskillen RC
Coleraine: On the river Bann: Bann RC and Coleraine AI
Portadown: On the upper Bann
Belfast: On the river Lagan: Belfast RC, Belfast BC, Queen's University, Lagan Scullers, Methodist College & RBAI Newry

Munster: The southern province

Rowing Centers:
Cork: On the river Lee: Cork BC, Shandon BC, Lee RC, UCC RC, Monkstown & Cork Harbour BC
Limerick: On the river Shannon: Limerick BC, Shannon RC; St Michael's RC; Athlunkard BC, University of Limerick
Waterford: On the river Suir: Waterford BC
Clonmel: On the river Suir: Clonmel RC
Fermoy: On the river Blackwater: Fermoy RC
Skibbereen: On the river Ilen: Skibbereen BC Bantry
Killarney: On the lakes of Killarney: Muckross RC,

Workmen's Club; Fossa RC
Cappoquin: On the river Blackwater: Cappoquin RC
Castleconnell: On the river Shannon: Castleconnell RC

Leinster: The eastern province.

Rowing Centers:
Dublin: On the Liffey: Dublin University, UCD, Neptune RC, Commercial RC, Garda Siochana BC, King's Hospital BC, Dublin Municipal RC
Carlow: On the river Barrow: Carlow RC
Tullamore: On the Grand Canal: Offaly RC
New Ross: On the river Barrow: New Ross RC

Connacht: The western province.

Rowing Centers:
Galway: On the river Corrib: Galway RC, Tribesmen RC, NUIG, St Joseph's RC, CR Colaiste Iognaid
Athlone: On the river Shannon: Athlone BC, Carrick-on-Shannon RC

PERSONALITIES

Sean Drea: Started rowing at Neptune Rowing Club in Dublin in 1966, and led Ireland into serious international rowing. Deciding to concentrate on sculling he went to London and then to Philadelphia seeking the coaching help he needed. He won all the major races in the United States and Europe several times, including the Diamond Sculls at Henley Royal Regatta three times. He gradually moved up the world rankings, missing the gold in Lucerne through illness in 1974, though taking the silver in Nottingham the following year. In 1976, in Montreal, he was fourth in the Olympics, Ireland's top Olympic placing in rowing to date.

Sinead Jennings: A native of Donegal, she changed from triathlon to sculling in Edinburgh, Scotland, and within two years she won bronze in women's lightweight sculls in the World Championships at Zagreb in 2000. A year later in Lucerne, she won the world championship. This was Ireland's first women's gold medal; the first of three gold medals for Ireland that year. In 2002, changing to the double sculls in anticipation for the Athens Olympics, she was dogged by injury all year though she remains Ireland's golden girl.

Vincent Rowan: Mr. Rowan or Mr. Rowing? Vincent dominated the administration of Irish rowing for over thirty years in the twentieth century. He was Hon. Secretary from 1923 to 1938, and then President from 1939 to 1953. He was a meticulous administrator, and he led Irish rowing through some difficult times, particularly World War II. He brought the Irish Amateur Rowing Union into FISA and Olympic participation in 1948.

Wally Stevens: Wally, a Neptune Rowing Club man, like Vincent Rowan, was spare man to the Irish Olympic eight in 1948. He rowed in Neptune's first Henley crew, and was a stalwart of the Dublin Metropolitan Regatta. He was deeply involved in the Metro move from Islandbridge to Blessington, and the determined to establish a modern, multi-lane course there for international rowing. He was Hon. Secretary of the Irish Amateur Rowing Union for fourteen years, from 1959 to 1972, and President for the following four years. He oversaw Sean Drea's progress to world medallist.

Did You Know ?

The Dublin Metropolitan Regatta was established in Ringsend in the port of Dublin in 1869; it has changed venues twice since then, moving first upstream to the non-tidal Liffey at Islandbridge, and then to Blessington in County Wicklow, still on the Liffey, to establish Ireland's first 2000-meter multi-lane course. Up to 2002, Metro had been staged 126 times, interrupted only by WW I, civil unrest in the early 1920's and insolvency in 1928-29. Crews from every part of Ireland, England, Scotland, Germany and the USA have won the top events.

NATIONAL FEDERATION

Irish Amateur Rowing Union Ltd.
House of Sport, Longmile Road
Walkinstown, Dublin 12
Ireland
Tel: +353 01 450 9831
Fax: +353 01 450 6830
Email: info@iaru.ie

CLUBS (BY CITY)
INCLUDES NORTHERN IRELAND CLUBS

Arklow Rowing Club
50 South Green
Arklow, Co.Wicklow
Ireland
Contact: Eddie McElheron
Email: eddiemcelheron@hotmail.com

Athlone Boat Club
3 Retreat Mews, Retreat Road
Athlone, Co. Westmeath
Ireland
Contact: Eamon Fahy
Tel: +353 0902 74805

Athy Rowing Club
Morningside, Celbridge Road
Leixlip, Co. Kildare
Ireland
Contact: John Cunniffe
Tel: +353 01 838 7911
Email: athyrowingclub@eircom.net

Lady Victoria Boat Club
17 Henryville Meadows
Ballyclare, County Antrim
BT39 9FY
Contact: James Cleland
Email: cleland_james@hotmail.com

Methodist College Rowing Club
Methodist College
1 Malone Road
Belfast, BT9 6BY
Contact: Neil Thompson
Tel: +353 028 9020 5205
Fax: +353 028 9020 5209
Email: tneilgthompson@aol.com

Queen's University Boat Club
79 Haypark Avenue
Belfast, BT7 3FE
Contact: Chris Wylie
Tel: +353 078 55599128
Email: w1303400@qub.ac.uk

Lagan Scullers
Alison Gilbert
28 Kingsway Avenue
Belfast, BT5 7DN
Tel: 0044 (0) 2890795465
Email: lscullers@hotmail.com

Queen's University Belfast Ladies Boat Club
15 Eglantine Gardens
Belfast, BT9 EZ
Contact: Alice Kendrick
Tel: +353 07734432706
Email: k1419401@qub.ac.uk

R.B.A.I. Boat Club
College Square East
Belfast, BT1 6DL
Contact: Neil McClements
Tel: +353 028 9024 0461
Email: nmc101@hotmail.com

Belfast Boat Club
Hay Island, Lockview Road
Belfast, BT9 5FH
Contact: Florence Gregg
Tel: +353 028 9066 5012
Email: f.gregg@qub.ac.uk

Belfast Rowing Club
17 Sallybush Road
Ballyrobert, Co. Antrim
BT36 4TS
Contact: Ms. Brenda Ewing
Tel: 0044 28 9084 9499
Fax: 0044 28 9084 9499
Email: brendaewing@yahoo.co.uk

Carlow Rowing Club
20 Avondale Drive
Hanover, Carlow
Contact: Barry Doogue
Tel: +353 0508 71198
Fax: +353 0508 71263
Email: barrydoogue@hotmail.com

Bann Rowing Club
86 Broomhill Park
Coleraine, Co. Derry.
BT51 3AN
Contact: Martin I. Clyde
Tel: +353 028 70340426

Coleraine Academic Institute Boat Club
Castlerock Road
Coleraine, Co. Derry
Ireland
Contact: Stephen Graham
Tel: +353 028 7034 4331
Fax: +353 028 7035 2632

North Coast Integrated College Rowing Club
6 Greenhill Road
Coleraine, Co. Derry
BT51 3JE
Contact: John Wilkinson
Tel: +353 028 70329026
Fax: +353 028 70329020
Email: johnfwilkinson@hotmail.com

University of Ulster Coleraine Rowing Club
c/o Clubs and Societies Office
UUC Students Union
Cromore Road, Coleraine
Co. Derry, BT52 1SA
Contact: Brendan Garvin
Tel: +44 7974138241
Email: uucrc@hotmail.com

Presentation College Rowing Club
Mardyke, Cork
Ireland
Contact: Hugh O'Brien
Tel: +353 021 4272743
 Fax: +353 021 4274137
Email: pbccork@iol.ie
www.pbc-cork.ie/rowing/

Bantry Rowing Club
Gurteenroe, Bantry
Co. Cork
Contact: Matt Murphy
Tel: +353 027 50504
Fax: +353 027 51988
Email: acireland@eircom.net

Monkstown & Cork Harbour Rowing Club
"The Orchard", The Demesne
Monkstown, Co. Cork
Ireland
Contact: Ms. Carla James
Tel: +353 021 480 2111
Fax: +353 021 427 3846
Email: carla.james@examiner.ie

Lee Rowing Club
35 Sidney Park
Welington Road
Cork
Ireland
Contact: Tom Walsh
Tel: +353 021 450 3549
Email: tomw@iol.ie

Lee Valley Rowing Club
Mount Deran, Templehill
Carrigrohane, Co. Cork
Ireland
Contact: Michael O'Callaghan
Tel: +353 021 490 2662
Fax: +353 021 427 1565
Email: mick.ocallaghan@ucc.ie

UCC Rowing Club
c/o P.E. Office, UCC
Mardyke Arena, Mardyke Walk
Cork
Ireland
Contact: PJ Kiely
Tel: +353 087 9696278
Email:uccrc@hotmail.com

Skibbereen Rowing Club
"Airdeall", Coronea
Co. Cork
Ireland
Contact: Bridie O'Donoghue
Tel: +353 280 23444

Fermoy Rowing Club
44 Patrick Street
Fermoy, Co. Cork
Ireland
Contact: Annette Barnes
Tel: +353 025 31324
Fax: +353 025 31324

Cork I.T. Rowing Club
Cork Institute of Technology
Bishopstown, Co. Cork
Ireland
Contact: Mr. Ronan Tinsley
Tel: +353 021 432682
Email: citrowing@hotmail.com
www27.brinkster.com/citrowing/

Cork Boat Club
88 Gate Lodge, Castle Road
Blackrock, Cork
Ireland
Contact: John McCarthy
Tel: +353 021 4321707
Fax: +353 021 4321708
Email: jfmccarthy@oceanfree.net

Shandon Boat Club
Torc, Rochestown Road
Cork, Ireland
Contact: Frank Coughlan
Tel: +353 021 436 3560
Email: frankc@musgrave.ie

Old Bones Boat Club
Boreenmanna Road
Cork, Ireland
Contact: Darren Desmond

City of Derry Boating Club
Ms. Teresa Duddy
34 Prehen Road
Derry
BT47 2NS
Tel: 0044 28 7135 1002
Contact: Declan Doherty
Email: declandoherty@dycw.co.uk

Defence Forces Rowing Association
Officer's Mess, McKee Barracks
Blackhorse Avenue
Dublin 7
Ireland
Contact: Capt. Mick Curran
Tel: +353 01 804 6181
Email: messec1@eircom.net

Garda Siochana Boat Club
Longmeadows, Islandbridge
Dublin 8
Ireland
Contact: Jonah Roche
Tel: +353 (01) 6770127
Email: boatclub@gardarowing.com
http://www.gardarowing.com/

King's Hospital Boat Club
The King's Hospital
Palmerstown
Dublin 20
Ireland
Tel: +353 01 626 5933
Fax: +353 01 623 0349
Email: khbc@irow.com

Dublin University Ladies Boat Club
c/o. DUCAC
House 27, Trinity College
Dublin 2
Ireland
Contact: Ms. Siobhan McGeever
Tel: +353 087 7487613
Email: smcgeever@hotmail.com

U.C.D. Boat Club
25 Roebuck Castle
Dublin 14
Ireland
Email: ucdbccommittee@hotmail.com

Dublin Municipal Rowing Centre
Longmeadows, Islandbridge
Dublin 8
Ireland
Tel: 01 611 9746

Commercial Rowing Club
31 St. Peter's Crescent
Walkinstown
Dublin 12
Ireland
Contact: Bill O'Gorman
Tel: +353 01 602 8243
Fax: +353 01 602 8525
Email: wcogorman@irishprisons.ie
http://www.commercialrowingclub.com/

Old Collegian's Boat Club
95 Meadow Mount, Churchtown
Dublin 16
Ireland
Contact: Ms. Carol-Ann Smith
Tel: +353 01 668 0288
Email: casmith@kavanagh.ie

The Bluecoat Club
The King's Hospital
Palmerstown
Dublin 20
Ireland
Contact: John Aiken
Tel: +353 01 626 5933
Fax: +353 01 623 0349
Email: bluecoat@irow.com

Tara Rowing Club
House of Sport, Longmile Road
Dublin 12
Ireland
Contact: James Bermingham
Tel: +353 01 450 9831
Fax +353 01 450 6830
Email: info@iaru.ie

Lady Elizabeth Boat Club
12 St. Helens Road
Booterstown
Co. Dublin
Ireland
Tel: +353 086 822 6502
Email: bsmyth@algoodbody.ie

Dublin University Boat Club
Contact: Stuart King, Captain
Tel: +353 087 7416993
Email: kingsf@tcd.ie

Neptune Rowing Club
Longmeadows
Islandbridge
Dublin 8
Ireland
Contact: Terence McEvoy
Tel: +353 01 661 2022
Fax: +353 01 662 8532
Email: terry.mcevoy@erha.ie
http://www.neptunerowingclub.com/

Enniskillen Rowing Club
11 The Willows, Tempo Road
Enniskillen, Co. Fermanagh
BT74 6HR
Contact: Brian O'Reilly

Enniskillen Rowing Club
11 The Willows
Tempo Road
Enniskillen
Ireland
Tel: +353 028 6632 4121
Fax: +353 028 6632 8622
Email: michken@tiscali.co.uk

Portora Boat Club
Portora Royal School
Enniskillen
Co. Fermanagh
BT74 7HA
Contact: Robert Northridge
Tel: +353 028 66322658
Fax: +353 028 66328668
Email: robhannort@aol.com

NUI Galway Boat Club
Freeport, Barna
Co. Galway
Ireland
Contact: Cormac Folan
Tel: +353 091 596989

St. Joseph's College Rowing Club
Nun's Island
Galway
Contact: Peadar S. O hIci
Tel: +353 091 565980
Fax: +353 091 565981
Email: ohici@eircom.net
http://www.bish.ie/rowing/

Galway Rowing Club
Woodquay, Galway
Ireland
Contact: Michael J. Gannon
Tel: +353 086 842 2986

Colaiste Iognaid Rowing Club
37 Churchfields
Lower Salthill
Galway
Contact: Neasa Folan
Secretary
Tel: +353 086-8054408
email:nfolan@nortelnetworks.com

Tribesmen Rowing Club
26 The Long Walk
Spanish Arch
Galway
Contact: Ms. Robin Winkels
Tel: +353 091 539 170
Email: rwkgalway@hotmail.com

Muckross Rowing Club
"Osprey", Muckross
Killarney, Co. Kerry
Contact: Ms. Clare Fogarty
Tel: +353 064 33213
Email: clarefog@hotmail.com

Callinafercy Pier Rowing Club
Callinafercy, Milltown
Co. Kerry
Contact: Ms. Elaine Harrington
Tel: +353 087 2967669

Fossa Rowing Club
"Douglasha", Crohane
Fossa, Killarney
Co. Kerry
Contact: Ms. Kathleen O'Sullivan
Tel: +353 064 32850
Email: fossarc@eircom.net.

Killorglin Rowing Club
Railway Terrace, School Road
Killorglin
Co. Kerry
Contact: Gerard Costello
Tel: +353 066 979 0668
http://www.geocities.com/killorglinrowingclub

Workmens Rowing Club
Riverside Drive, Killarney
Co. Kerry
Contact: Kieran Counihan

Ossory Rowing Club
The Race Course
Kells Road
Kilkenny

Graiguenamanagh Rowing Club
Tinnakeenly
Skeoughvasteen
Co. Kilkenny

Carrick-on-Shannon Rowing Club
95 Carysfort Park
Blackrock
Co. Dublin
Contact: Mark Kelly
Tel: +353 087 9791315
Email: mark@thewateredge.com

Athlunkard Boat Club
20 Belvedere Lawn
Fr. Russell Road
Limerick
Contact: Michael Kiely
Tel: +353 061 302 160

Limerick Boat Club
Wellesley Pier
Sarsfield Bridge
Limerick
Contact: Brian Sheppard
Tel: +353 086 270 4437
Email: limerickboatclub@eircom.net

Shannon Rowing Club
Sarsfield Bridge
Limerick
Contact: Ger O'Dowd
Tel: +353 061 415 150
Email: gerodl@eircom.net

University of Limerick Rowing Club
c/o Clubs & Societies Office
Student Union
Ireland
Tel: +353 8572 74663
Email: irow@ul.ie
rowing.csn.ul.ie

Castleconnell Boat Club
5 St. Flannan's Terrace
Castleconnell
Co. Limerick
Contact: Walter J. Healy
Tel: +353 061 310 286

St. Michael's Rowing Club
17 Grattan Court
Old Clare Street
Limerick
Tel: + 353 087 975 2742
Contact: Andy O'Sullivan
Tel: +353 061 326092

Lough Ree Rowing Club
Rathcline Road
Lanesborough
Co. Longford
Contact: Claire Brennan
Tel: +353 043 21211
Email: brennancha@eircom.net

Newry Rowing Club
1 The Woodlands
Lower Dromore Road
Warrenpoint
County Down
BT34 3WL
Contact: Sarah Sarsfield
Email: newryrc@hotmail.com

Offaly Rowing Club
Brocca, Screggan
Tullamore
Co. Offaly
Contact: Joan Grogan
Tel: +353 0506 41453
Fax: +353 0506 31752
Email: joangrogan@eircom.net

Portadown Boat Club
58C Killicomain Road
Portadown
Co. Armagh
BT63 5JH
Contact: Greg Forbes
Tel: +353 028 3889 2344
Fax: +353 028 3889 2333
Email: greg.forbes@dardni.gov.uk

Clonmel Rowing Club
20 Prior Park Cresent
Clonmel
Co. Tipperary
Contact: Nollag Dwyer
Tel: 058 42833 Ext 3359
Email: clonmelrowingclub@eircom.net

Cappoquin Rowing Club
Tourin
Cappoquin
Co. Waterford
Contact: Milo Murray
Tel: +353 058 54732

Waterford Boat Club
Canada Street
Waterford
Contact: Louvaine Purcell
Club: +353 051 858880

New Ross Boat Club
The Deep
Mountelliott
New Ross
Co. Wexford
Contact: Christopher Kelly
Tel: +353 051 388 171
Fax: +353 051 388 172
Email: newrossboatclub@eircom.net

Israel

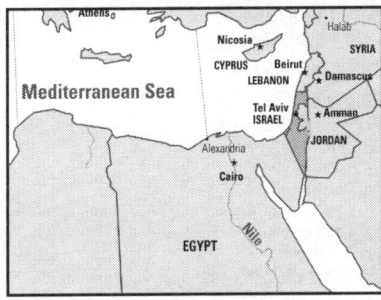

HISTORY

During the thirties, Jewish athletes fled Europe to the land of Israel, then a British mandate, when the Nazi party came to power in Germany. They were mainly university students and professors who had practiced rowing in Germany. They brought a few rowing boats with them to Israel. In 1934, a rowing club was established in the port city of Haifa (Haifa Rowing Club), shortly thereafter another in the city of Tel-Aviv and fifteen years later a third club was founded in Tiberias on the shore of the Sea of Galilee, also known as the Kineret. At the opening ceremony of the 1935 Maccabia Games — the Jewish Olympics that takes place every four years — an Israeli rowing team, consisting primarily of new immigrants participated.

From the day that the state of Israel was established in 1948, rowing was recognized as an Olympic sport. In 1995, rowing became an independent sport federation. There are four active rowing clubs in the country. Two clubs, the Tel-Aviv Rowing Club and Hapoel are located in the city of Tel-Aviv on the bank of the Yarkon River. The Haifa Rowing Club is located in the port city of Haifa, at the mouth of the Kishon River. The Tiberias Rowing Club is located in the city of Tiberias on the shore of the Sea of Galilee.

INTERNET LINKS
http://www.rowing.org.il

REGIONS

Tel- Aviv-Yaffo
Avg. temp: Winter: 10-18°C; Summer: 25-35C
Sites of interest: Yaffo (Jaffa) is one the most ancient cities in Israel and the oldest port in this part of the world. Yaffo is an interesting tourist attraction. Tel-Aviv, the first Hebrew city of the new era, established in 1906, is the business and cultural center of Israel. It is called the "city, which never stops". Tel-Aviv enjoys a beautiful 14-kilometer long sea front, with beaches, marinas and variety of water sports only thirty- minutes drive from Ben- Gurion International Airport. The best time for rowing is early in the morning and late in the afternoon.

Haifa
Avg. temp: Winter 10-18C summers 25-35C
Sites of interest: Haifa is an important port, built on the slopes of Mount Carmel. Haifa has been inhabited since the Bronze era. It is a beautiful city, rich with places of interest like the Bahai shrine and gardens, the German Colony, Druze villages and holy places like the church of "Stella Maris". Haifa has many beaches, a marina and variety of water sports. The best time for rowing is in the early morning and late afternoon.

Tiberias and the Kineret (The Sea of Galilee)
Avg. temp: Winter 14-20°C; Summer 28-35°C; Sites of interest: The Kineret is the lowest sweet water lake in the world at 208 meters below sea level. Situated in the Jordan valley, surrounded by breath taking scenery and historical places for Jews, Christians and Moslems; it is famous for Jesus' life and the miracles performed by him in this area. Tiberias is the largest town on the Sea of Galilee, an ancient town that was built in 18 A.D. and named after Tiberius Caesar. Tiberias is known for its hot springs. It is surrounded by numerous tourist attractions, including a variety of water sports. Rowing on the Kineret is very enjoyable and recommended in the early mornings and late afternoons.

Did You Know ?

The lowest place in the world where you can find a rowing club is on the Sea of Galilee at the Tiberias Rowing Club.

NATIONAL FEDERATION
Israeli Rowing Federation
P.O. Box 6101
61060, Tel-Aviv, Israel
Contact: Mr. Eli Szabo
Tel: +972-9-762 3264
Fax: +972-9-742 4955
Email: info@rowing.org.il
www.rowing.org.il

CLUBS

Haifa Rowing Club
Sport dock Kishon Harbour Haifa
35 A Carmel Street
Kiriat-Tivon 36081
Israel
Contact: Giyora Saar, Manager
Tel: +972 4 8376945
Fax: +972 4 8382529
Email: gsaar@netvision.net.il
www.haifarowing.up.co.il

Hapoel Rowing Club
Amnon Erez
Israel
Tel: +972 3 6048726
Fax: +972 3 6043617
Email: galsport65@hotmail.com

Tel Aviv Rowing Club
PO Box 6101
Tel Aviv 61060
Israel
Tel: +972 3 6051236

Tiberias Rowing Club
PO Box 178
Tiberias, 14223
Israel
Contact: Eytan Oved
Tel: +972 4 6734734
Fax: +972 4 6735736
Email: z_dar@zahav.net.il

Italy

NATIONAL FEDERATION

Federazione Italiana di Canottaggio
Viale Tiziano 70
Roma, 196
Italy
Tel: +39 06 368 58493
Fax: +39 06 368 58148
Email: segreteria@canottaggio.org
www.canottaggio.org

CLUBS (BY REGION)

PEIMONTE

S.C. Armida
10126 Torino
Parco del Valentino
Viale Virgilio, 45
Italy
Tel: +39 011/6699219

Circolo Amici del Fiume
10131 Torino
C.so Moncalieri, 18
Italy
Tel: +39 011/6604121
Email: info@amicidelfiume.it
www.amicidelfiume.it

S.C. Candia
10010 Candia Canavese
Via Lago
Italy
Tel: +39 011/9834692

S.C. Caprera
10131 Torino
C.so Moncalieri, 22
Italy
Tel: +39 011/6603816
Email: canottieri.caprera@libero.it
web.tiscalinet.it/canottiericaprera

S.C. Casale
15033 Casale Monferrato
Viale Lungo Po Gramsci, 14
Italy
Tel: +39 0142/53071

S.C. Cerea
10126 Torino
Parco del Valentino
Viale Virgilio, 61
Italy
Tel: +39 011/6699265
Fax: +39 011/6504330
Email: info@cerea.org
www.cerea.org

S.C. Esperia — Torino
10131 Torino
C.so Moncalieri, 2
Italy
Tel/Fax: +39 011/8193013
Email: fic.esperia@arpnet.it

Sisport Fiat
10133 Torino
C.so Moncalieri, 346/12
Italy
Tel: +39 011/66.19.801
Fax: +39 011/6614944

S.C. Lago D'orta
28028 Pettenasco
Via Per Agrano, 1 (c/o Sig. Antonio Soia)
Italy
Tel: +39 0323/888821

S.C. Pallanza
28922 Verbania Pallanza
Casella Postale 18 Agenzia Pallanza
Italy
Tel/Fax: +39 0323/502394
Email: info@canottieripallanza.it
www.canottieripallanza.it

S.C. Citta' Di Omegna
28026 Omegna
Lungolago Buozzi, 2
Italy
Tel/Fax: +39 0323/63821
Email: ccomegna@tiscalinet.it
web.tiscalinet.it/ccomegna/

S.C. Pallanza A Sedile Fisso
28048 Pallanza
Ghiardello — Via Zanitello, 9
(c/o Sig. Mario)
Italy
Tel: +39 0323/509384

Soc. Sp. Canottieri Ghiffa '83
28055 Ghiffa
C.so Risorgimento, 297
(c/o Sig. R. Malavasi)
Italy
Tel: +39 0323/59213

Associazione Amici del Remo
10133 Torino
C.so Moncalieri, 422
Italy
Tel: +39 0360/499478
Email: info@amicidelremo.it
www.amicidelremo.it/

Societa' Cannero Sportiva
28051 Cannero Riviera
Via Panoramica, 7 (c/o Sig. A. Guizzetti)
Italy
Tel: +39 0323/788078
Email: sportiva@geocities.com
www.geocities.com/colosseum/4443

S.C.Lesa
28040 Lesa
Via Davicini, 60 (c/o Sig. G.Martorio)
Italy
Tel: +39 0322/77126

Circolo S. Mauro
10099 San Mauro Torinese
Via XXV Aprile, 108 (c/o Sig. Pischiutta)

LOMBARDIA

S.C. Adda
20075 Lodi
Via N.Sauro, 16
Italy
Tel: +39 0371/67040-423421

S.C. Aurora
22020 Blevio
Via Caronti, 19
Tel: +39 031/419221

Canottieri Baldesio
26100 Cremona
Via Al Porto, 2
Italy
Tel/Fax: +39 0372/28716

S.C. Bissolati
26100 Cremona
Via Riglio, 12
Italy
Tel/Fax: +39 0372/463030

Unione Sportiva Bellagina
22021 Bellagio
Casella Postale
Italy
Tel/Fax: +39 031/950242
Email: usbellagio@mclink.it

Canottieri Cernobbio
22012 Cernobbio
Via P. Bernasconi, 1
Italy
Tel/Fax: +39 031/510784
Email: canottieri.cernobbio@tin.it

S.C. Plinio-Torno
22020 Torno
Via Rasina, 3/B
(c/o Sig. D. Tagliabue)
Italy
Tel: +39 0331/930488

S.C. Eridanea
26041 Casalmaggiore
Via Alzaia Loc. Torretta
Italy
Tel/Fax: +39 0375/200221
Email: c.eridanea@tin.it

S.C. Calde'
21010 Castelveccana
Via Monfalcone
Italy
Tel: +39 0332/520096-520900

Soc. Fraglia Vela Desenzano
25015 Desenzano Del Garda
Casella Postale, 35
Italy
Tel: +39 030/9143343

Ass. Canottieri Flora
26100 Cremona
Via Riglio,14
Italy
Tel: +39 0372/30529
Email: canottieriflora@libero.it
www.canottieriflora.it

Dopolav. Ferrov. Cremona
26100 Cremona
Via Bergamo, 19 — Sez. Canottieri
Italy
Tel: +39 0372/31453-25492

S.C. Garda
25087 Salo'
Via Canottieri, 1
Italy
Tel/Fax: +39 0365/43245

Ass. Sp. Can. Gavirate
21026 Gavirate
Via Cavour 2
Italy
Tel: +39 0332/744540
Email: davide.posteri@row-net.com
www.row-net.com/canottierigavirate

Canottieri Germignaga
21010 Germignaga
Via Bodmer, 16
Italy
Tel/Fax: +39 0332/511985
Email: canottierigermignaga@libero.it
digilander.iol.it/canottierigermignaga

S.C. La Sportiva
22025 Lezzeno
Loc. Chiesa, 5
Italy
Tel: +39 031/915230

S.C. Lario "G. Sinigaglia"
22100 Como
Viale Puecher, 6
Italy
Tel/Fax: +39 031/574720
Email: canottierilario@tiscalinet.it
www.canottierilario.it

S.C. Lecco
23900 Lecco
Via Nullo, 2 — Sez. Can.
Italy
Tel: +39 0341/364273

Can. Laveno
21014 Laveno Mombello
Via Labiena, 153
Italy
Tel: +39 0332/667825

S.C. Menaggio
22017 Menaggio
Lungo Lago Castelli, 7
Italy
Tel: +39 0344/32003
Fax: +39 32992

Ass. Sp. Can. "Aldo Meda"
22010 Cima
Cantiere C. Gobbi
Italy
Tel: +39 0344/61689

C.U.S. Milano
20090 Segrate
Via Circonvallazione Est, 11
Italy
Tel: +39 02/7021141
Fax: +39 02/7560633
Email: cusmilano@cusmilano.it
www.cusmilano.it/

S.C. Milano
20144 Milano
Alzaia Naviglio Grande, 160
Italy
Tel/Fax: +39 02/48951211

Ass. Can. Monate
21028 Travedona Monate
Via Binda, 2
Italy
Tel: +39 0332/977413
Fax: +39 977476
Email: canottierimonate@libero.it
www.row-net.com/canottierimonate/

S.C. Mincio
46100 Mantova
Via S.Maria Nuova, 15
Borgo Cittadella
Italy
Tel: +39 0376/391700-391719
Fax: +39 0376/391727
Email: info@canottierimincio.com
www.canottierimincio.com

Ass. Can. Moto Guzzi
23826 Mandello Del Lario
Casella Postale 162
Italy
Tel: +39 0341/732005
Fax: +39 733907
Email: guillo2000@subdimension.com

Canottieri Moltrasio
22010 Moltrasio
Via Bellini, 6
Italy
Tel/Fax: +39 031/290445
Email: info@canottierimoltrasio.com
www.canottierimoltrasio.com

S.C. Falco Della Rupe
22020 Nesso
Via Borgonuovo, 36
(c/o Sig. S. Vaccani)
Italy
Tel: +39 031/910464

S.C. Sebino
24065 Lovere
Via G. Paglia, 3
Italy
Tel/Fax: +39 035/983648
Email: canottieri.sebino@libero.it

C.U.S. Pavia
27100 Pavia
Via Bassi, 9/a
Italy
Tel: +39 0382/422134
Fax: +39 423556
BH: +39 0382/27422
Email: cuspaviacanottaggio@libero.it
cus.unipv.it/Ita/Tec/Canottaggio/index.html

Soc. Sp. Tritium
20056 Trezzo Sull'adda
Sez. Canottaggio
Via Alzaia dell'Adda
Italy
Tel/Fax: +39 02/9090188

Canottieri Revere
46036 Revere
Via Argine Po
Italy
Tel: +39 0386/46121

Canottieri Luino
21016 Luino
Via Lido, 4
Italy
Tel: +39 0332/560168
Email: canottieriluino@tiscalinet.it
web.tiscalinet.it/canottieri/

Soc. Can. Stella
22010 Laglio
Via Regina, 44
Italy

S.C. Somma
21019 Somma Lombardo
Via Fuser, 5
(c/o Polisportiva)
Italy
Tel: +39 0331/256259-0332

S.C. Varese
21100 Varese Schiranna
Via L.lago dei Canottieri, 21
Italy
Tel: +39 0332/310414
Fax: +39 0332/328406
Email: scvarese@tin.it
www.canottierivarese.com

Sporting Club Urio
22010 Carate Urio
Via Cavadino, 12
Italy
Tel: +39 031/400019

Canottieri Arolo
21038 Arolo Di Leggiuno
Via Milano, 36
(c/o A. Riva)
Italy
Tel: +39 0332/647223

Associazione Canottieri Pescate
23855 Pescate
Via Alzaia, 17
Italy
Tel: +39 0341/580049
Fax: 0341/207509

Nuova Can. Olona
20144 Milano
Via Alzaia Naviglio Grande, 146
Italy
Tel: +39 02/475415

Canottieri Eupili
22030 Eupilio
Via Ceresuola, 7
(c/o Sig. G.C. Vicini)
Italy
Tel: +39 031/655142

Associazione Idroscalo Club
(ex Circolo Kayak Canoa Canottaggio)
20090 Segrate
V.le Circonvallaz. Idroscalo, 29
Italy
Tel: +39 02/7560379
Fax: +39 02/7560364
Email: info@idroscaloclub.org
www.idroscaloclub.org

Circ. Can. Gruppo
Volontari Del Garda
25087 Salo'
Via Bezzecca, 8
Italy
Tel: +39 0365/520652

Soc. Can. Ispra
21027 Ispra
Via Mongini, 4
Italy
Tel: +39 0332/780725-780161

Societa' Sportiva Canottieri Corgeno
21029 Corgeno Di Vergiate
Via Campirolo, 25
Italy
Tel: +39 0331/964004
Email: davide.posteri@row-net.com
www.row-net.com/canottiericorgeno

A.C. Canottieri Mezzola Verceia
Via Nazionale, 92
23020 Verceia

Ass. Canottieri Pescate
Via Alzaia, 17 — 23855 Pescate (LC)
Italy
Tel: +39+39 3384584077
E-mail c.pescate@email.it
www.canottieripescate.sports-page.com

VENETO

C.N. Bardolino
37011 Bardolino
L.Lago Preite, 10
Italy
Tel/Fax: +39 045/7211488

S.C. Bucintoro
30100 Venezia
Casella Postale 164
Italy
Tel: +39 041/5222055-5205630
Email: admin@bucintoro.org
www.bucintoro.org

C.C. Diadora
30126 Venezia Lido
Via S.Gallo, 136/B
Italy
Tel: +39 041/5265742

Dopol. Ferrov. Treviso
31100 Treviso
Via Benzi, 86
Sez. Canottaggio
Italy
Tel: +39 0422/401540
Email: dlftreviso@dlf.it
dlftv.dadacasa.supereva.it/

Dopol. Ferrov. Venezia
30121 Venezia
Cannaregio 47
Sez. Canottaggio
Italy
Tel: +39 041/716995

Circolo Ospedalieri Treviso
31100 Treviso
Osp. S.M. Ca' Foncello
Italy
Tel: +39 0422/322456-322801

S.C. Padova
35142 Padova
Srada Polveriera
Loc. Voltabrusegana
Italy
Tel: +39 049/680857
Fax: +39 8804141

S.C. Mestre
30170 Mestre
Casella Postale 3131
Italy
Tel: +39 041/5317887-5312440
Email: scmestr@libero.it
www.canottierimestre.it

S.C. Querini
30122 Venezia
Via Castello, 6576/B
Italy
Tel: +39 041/5222039
Email: info@canottieriquerini.it
www.canottieriquerini.it

Canoa Team '70
37138 Verona
Via B. Longhena, 14
Italy
Tel: +39 045/567122

S.C. Sile
31100 Treviso
Via Tezzon, 7
Italy
Tel: +39 0422/545879-540658

Soc. Can. Treporti
30010 Venezia
Via L.Mare S. Felice
Loc. Treporti Sabbioni
Italy
Tel: +39 041/658457

Soc. Virtus Lagunare Murano
30141 Murano (Ve)
Ramo Da Mula 16
Italy

Ass. Can. Giudecca
30123 Venezia
Rio Ponte Lungo 259
Italy
Tel: +39 041/5287409

A.Sp. Can. Rovigo
45030 Villamarzana
Via 43 Martiri, 49

Can. Bardolino
37011 Bardolino
L.Lago Mirabello, 2
Italy
Tel: +39 0338/394327
Fax: +39 7211488

Soc. Nautica Can. Nettuno
34136 Trieste
V.le Miramare, 62
Italy
Tel: +39 040/410927

C.U.S. Trento
38100 Trento
Via Inama, 1
c/o Univ. Studi Trento
Facolta' Ec. E Comm.
Italy
Tel: +39 0461/981166
Fax: +39 236781

A.S. Padova Canottaggio
35142 Padova
Via Decorati al Valor Civile,2
Italy
Tel: +39 049/681300
Fax: +39 681558
Email: padovacanottaggio@libero.it

"Rari Nantes Patavium-1905"
35142 Padova
Via Decorati al Valor Civile,2
Italy
Tel: +39 049/687511

FRIULI-VENEZIA-GUILIA

Soc. Triestina Can. Adria
34123 Trieste
Pontile Istria, 2
Italy
Tel: +39 040/303803
Email: s_t_c_adria@tiscali.it

S.C. Ausonia
34073 Grado
Casella Postale 40
Italy
Tel: +39 0481/80305

Dopol. Ferrov. Trieste
34132 Trieste
P.za V.Veneto, 3
Italy
Tel: +39 040/36841
Email: canottieriDLFtrieste@hotmail.com

Canoa S.Giorgio
33058 S.Giorgio Di Nogaro
Via Famula
Italy
Tel: +39 0431/621157

Soc. Ginnastica Triestina
34123 Trieste
Pontile Istria, 6
Italy
Tel: +39 040/305239
Email: sgtnautica@libero.it
digilander.iol.it/sgtnautica

Circ. Marina Merc. "N.Sauro"
34136 Trieste
V.le Miramare, 40/A
Gruppo Canottieri
Italy
Tel: +39 040 412327
Fax: +39 040 4260077
Email: cmmnsauro@tcd.it
www.retecivica.trieste.it/cmmnsauro

Soc. Nautica "G.Pullino"
34015 Muggia
Via C. Battisti, 17
Italy
Tel/Fax: +39 040/272472
Email: snpullino@libero.it

Circ. Can. Saturnia
34136 Trieste
V.le Miramare, 36
Italy
Tel: +39 040/411042-414748
Fax: +39 040/44110
Email: saturniats@libero.it
digilander.libero.it/ccsaturniats

A.S. Nautilago
33010 Alessio Di Trasaghis
Casella Postale
Italy
Tel: +39 0432/981338

S.C. Timavo
34074 Monfalcone
Casella Postale 332
Monfalcone Centro
Italy
Tel/Fax: +39 0481/482797
Email: segreteria@canottieritimavo.it
www.canottieritimavo.it

Can. Trieste
34123 Trieste
Pontile Istria, 4
Italy
Tel: +39 040/306000

G.S.Vv.F."F. Ravalico"
34144 Trieste
Via d'Alviano, 15
Italy
Tel: +39 040/660061
Email: vvfravalico@triesterivista.it

C.U.S. Trieste
34127 Trieste
Via F. Severo, 152/A
Italy
Tel: +39 040/569629

EMILIA-ROMAGNA

Soc. Can. Brasimone
40137 Bologna
Via S.Ferrari, 15
(c/o Sig. L. Giagnorio)
Italy
Tel: +39 051/390574
Email: canottieribrasimone@libero.it
space.tin.it/clubnet/robdrusi/
Canottaggio/Brasimone.htm

S.C. Eridano Pimaspo
42016 Guastalla
Casella Postale 16
Italy
Tel: +39 0522/826350

S.C. Ferrara
44038 Pontelagoscuro
Via Ricostruzione, 121
Italy
Tel: +39 0532/461205

C.U.S. Ferinvest
44100 Ferrara
Via Gramicia, 41
Italy
Tel: +39 0532/750396
Fax: +39 0532/753308

S.C. Ravenna
48100 Ravenna
Casella Postale 123
Italy
Tel/Fax: +39 0544/560585
Email: canottierira@sira.it
www.canottieriravenna.it

S.C. Nino Bixio
29100 Piacenza
Via Nino Bixio, 24
Italy
Tel/Fax: +39 0523/335357

S.C. Vittorino Da Feltre
29100 Piacenza
Via del Pontiere, 29
Italy
Tel: +39 0523/385540-325380

LIGURIA

Lega Navale Italiana
16166 Genova Quinto A Mare
Via Majorana, 6/R
Sez. Canottaggio
Italy
Tel: +39 010/331863

S.C. Argus
16038 S.Margherita Ligure
Casella Postale 107
Italy
Tel/Fax: +39 0185/284484
Email: argus1910@libero.it

Circolo Nautico Al Mare
17021 Alassio
Porto Luca Ferrari, 142
Italy
Tel: +39 0182/42516

S.C. Elpis
16126 Genova
Via al Molo Giano
Italy
Tel: +39 010/2518720
Fax: +39 010/2532590
Email: scelpis@tin.it

Rowing Club Genovese
16126 Genova
Via al Molo Giano
Italy
Tel/Fax: +39 010/2461195

Lega Navale Italiana
16039 Sestri Levante
Via Portobello, 2
Italy
Tel: +39 0185/44810

Lega Navale Italiana
16043 Chiavari
Porto Turistico — Box 51
Italy
Tel: +39 0185/301769

S.C. Velocior "1883"
19121 La Spezia
Piazzale Dogana
Italy
Tel/Fax: +39 0187/731725
Email: velocior1883@libero.it
www.quasarbbs.com/velocior/

Gr.Sp.Mar. "G. Ingressi"
19024 Muggiano
Casella Postale 14
Italy

Circ. Ricr. Dipend.
Autorita' Portuale E
Soc. Di Servizi
Porto Di Genova
16154 Genova Sestri P.
Via Pionieri e Aviatori d'Italia
Sez. Nautica-Gruppo Can.
Italy
Tel: +39 010/6512425

S.C. Sampierdarenesi
16154 Genova Sestri P.
Via Cibrario Zona Aeroporto
Italy
Tel: +39 010/6513256
Fax: +39 6530323
Email: sampierdarenesi@libero.it
www.geocities.com/Colosseum/Court/9978

Can. Canoa Club
"Lago Di Osiglia"
17017 Millesimo
Via Piani Madonna, 127/II
(c/o M. Lovanio)
Italy
Tel: +39 019/565727

Ass. Can. Sanremo
18038 Sanremo
Via Matteotti, 107
c/o Centro Ariston
Italy
Tel: +39 0184/503690-507070

Ass. Can. S.Stefano Al Mare
18032 Sanremo
Str. Bussana Vecchia
(c/o Sig. A. Ramella)
Italy
Tel: +39 0184/514504

L.N.I. Sezione Sestri Ponente
16154 Genova
Via L. Cibrario
Italy
Tel: +39 010/6512654
Fax: +39 010/6599884
Email: gruppisportivi@leganavalegenovasestri.net
www.leganavalegenovasestri.net

Ass.Sp. Multedo 1930
16155 Genova Pegli
Via Ronchi, 13
Italy
Tel/Fax: +39 010/6987595
Email: multedo30@libero.it

Gruppo Sp. Speranza Pra'
16157 Genova Pra'
Via Pra' 54/r (lato mare)
Italy
Tel: +39 010/665325-662922

L.N.I. Sezione Savona
17100 Savona
Casella Postale 54
Italy
Tel: +39 019/854383
Email: leganavale@tnt.it
www.leganavale.savona.it

G.S. Canottieri Voltri
16158 Genova Voltri
P.Za Nicolo' Da Voltri
Italy
Tel: +39 010/6137252

Centro Imperiese
Promozione Sport
18100 Imperia
Via Artallo, 15
Italy
Tel: +39 0183/60361-61972

Societa' Sportiva Murcarolo
16166 Genova
Via A. Gianelli, 113/r
Italy
Tel: +39 010/3202127
Email: murcarolo@interfree.it
murcarolo.interfree.it/

Unione Sportiva Fezzanese
Via Paita, 1
19020 Fezzano

TOSCANI

C.S. Accademia Navale
57100 Livorno
Viale Italia, 72
Italy
Tel: +39 0586/238900
Fax: +39 238500

S.C. Arno — Il Fotoamatore
56122 Pisa
Via Bonaccorso da Padule 2
Porta a Mare
Italy
Tel: +39 050/28465
Fax: +39 41061

S.C. Berchielli
55049 Viareggio
Lungo Canale Est, 38
Italy
Tel: +39 0584/962793
Fax: +39 47197

Soc. Polisp. "P. D'aloja"
53043 Chiusi
Via delle Torri
(c/o Sig. A. Feri)
Italy
Tel: +39 0578/21410
Email: canottieri_daloja@hotmail.com
spazioinwind.libero.it/daloja

Circ. Naut. Foce Cecina
57023 Cecina Mare
Casella Postale 3
Italy
Tel: +39 0586/620602
Fax: +39 630765
Email: canottaggio@circolonauticofocececina.it
www.canottaggio.circolonauticofocececina.it

G.S. Can. "P. Cavallini"
56030 Calcinaia
Casella Postale 16
Italy
Tel: +39 0587/49180

Canottieri Comunali
50126 Firenze
L.Arno F. Ferrucci, 6
Italy
Tel: +39 055/6812151

S.C. Firenze
50122 Firenze
L.Arno A.M.L. de Medici, 8
Italy
Tel/Fax: +39 055/282130
Email: segreteria@canottierifirenze.it
www.canottierifirenze.it

S.C. Limite
50050 Limite Sull'arno
P.za C. Battisti, 6
Italy
Tel: +39 0571/578188
Email: canolimite@tin.it
space.tin.it/clubnet/bqfppu

Unione Can. Livornesi
57100 Livorno
Scali D'azeglio, 11
Italy
Tel: +39 0586/897060

C.U.S. Pisano
56100 Pisa
P.Za Dei Cavalieri, 6
Italy
Tel: +39 050/562326

C.C. Ombrone
58100 Grosseto
Via Venezia Giulia 12
(c/o Sig. G. Viti)
Italy
Tel: +39 0564/24581

S.C. Orbetello
58015 Orbetello
Idroscalo — V.Le Marconi
Italy
Tel: +39 0564/867638-867763

Can. Pontedera
56025 Pontedera
Via Bologna
Italy
Tel: +39 0587/52302
Fax: +39 54848

Circolo Can. Solvay
57013 Rosignano Solvay
Via Lillatro, 1
Italy
Tel: +39 0586/767360-763036

Gr. Sp. Vv. F. "G. Tomei"
57100 Livorno
Via dei Pelaghi, 200
Italy
Tel: +39 0586/859393
Fax: +39 852222
Email: vvftomei.rowing@tiscalinet.it
www.tomeirow.it

Ass. Can. Le Signe
50059 Signa
Via Argine Strada, 5
(c/o Pubbl. Assistenza)
Italy
Tel: +39 055/8732343

Ass. Can. "Renzo Giunti"
55054 Stiava Massarosa
Via Montramito, 12
Italy
Tel: +39 0584/922165

Canottieri Sodini Nilo
56100 Pisa
Via Delle Lenze, 292
Italy
Tel: +39 050/525422

Can. S.Miniato
50023 Impruneta
Via G. Rossa, 4
Italy
Tel: +39 055/209217
Fax: +39 209247

Ass. Sp. Can. "3 Comuni"-
Montescudaio
56040 Montescudaio
Strada Prov. Val Di Cecina, 31
Italy
Tel: +39 0336/9358296

Ass. Sp. Tirreno -
Can. Forte Dei Marmi
55042 Forte Dei Marmi
Via Viani, 6
Italy
Tel: +39 0584/752289
Fax: +39 752544

A.S.Can. Montenero
Sez. G. Bontempelli
57128 Livorno
Via Gozzer, 2
(c/o C. Gioli)
Italy
Tel: +39 0586/504143

Club Remiero Calcinaia
56030 Calcinaia
Via S. Ubaldesca T.
Italy
Tel: +39 0587/488212
Email: club.remiero@tiscali.it

Ass. Can. "L. Giacomelli"
56122 Pisa
Via Livornese, 214
Italy

Canottieri Marconcini
57128 Livorno
Via Antonio Pacinotti, 44
TeL. 0586/500633

Gr. Sp. Vv.F. "M. Billi"
56100 PISA
Via Matteotti, 2
Italy
Tel: +39 050/948111
Email: vvfpisarowing@libero.it
canottaggiovvfpisa.too.it/

MARCHE

S.C. Pesaro
61100 Pesaro
Calata Caio Duilio, 101
Italy
Tel: +39 0721/400010

Gr.Sp. Vv.F. "Maggi"
60100 Ancona
Via Miano, 50
(Com. Prov. VV.F.)
Italy
Tel: +39 071/280801
Fax: +39 202020
Email: gsmaggi@libero.it

S.E.F. "Stamura"
60100 Ancona
Via Mole Vanvitell.
Italy
Tel: +39 071/2075324
Fax: +39 52651

Gr.Sp. Vv.F. "N.Montesi
61100 Pesaro
Strada Adriatica, 92
(c/o Comando Vv.F.)
Italy
Tel: +39 0721/21201

A.S. Azzurra Plusport
62029 Tolentino
Via Zona Stichi S.N.C.
Italy
Tel: +39 0733/974500

ABRUZZO E MOLISSE

C. La Pescara
65100 Pescara
Spalti Del Re, 1
Italy
Tel: +39 085/28382

Gr.Can. L.N.I. Sez. Ortona
66026 Ortona Porto
Casella Postale
Italy
Tel: +39 085/9061042

Circolo Vela Termoli
Sez. Canoa E Canott.
86039 Termoli
Via Rivo Vivo, 31/A
Italy
Tel: +39 0875/84582

Ass. Can. Giulianova
64022 Giulianova
Via L.mare Zara, 19
Italy
Tel: +39 085/8005870

UMBRIA

C.C. Piediluco
05038 Piediluco
Loc. "Centro Nautico"
Vocabolo Quadri
Italy
Tel/Fax: +39 0744/368521
Email: c.c.piediluco@libero.it

S.C. Piediluco
05100 Terni
Casella Postale 141
Italy
Tel: +39 0744/368147

Circolo Can. Corlago
06059 Todi
Via Anzidei, 18
Italy
Tel: +39 075/8943195

Polisportiva Circolo
Lavoratori Terni S.R.L.
05100 Terni
Via L.A.Muratori, 3
Italy
Tel: +39 0744/407545

LAZIO

C.C. Aniene
00197 Roma
L.Re Acqua Acetosa, 119
Italy
Tel: +39 06/8079141

Circ. Can. Civitavecchia
00053 Civitavecchia
Casella Postale Aperta
Italy
Tel: +39 0766/502649
Email: civita@tin.it

A. Romana Canoa E Canott.
00199 Roma
Via Ponte Di Salario, 51
Italy
Tel: +39 06/86200955

Dop. Ferrov. Roma
00161 Roma
Via Bari, 22
Italy
Tel: +39 06/3208515
Fax: +39 06/32600000
www.canottieriferroviarioroma.it

Circolo Canott. Lazio
00196 Roma
L.Tevere Flaminio, 25
Italy
Tel/Fax: +39 06/3226853-3226801-3

Gr. Naut. Ff. Gg.
04016 Sabaudia
Sez. Canottaggio
P.za del Comune, 3
Italy
Tel/Fax: +39 0773/515066-518088

Gr.Sp. Ff.Oo. Canottaggio
04016 Sabaudia
Via Pr. Di Piemonte, 70
Italy
Tel/Fax: +39 0773/515331

1° Circ. Remiero Terracina
04019 Terracina
Viale Circe, 84
c/o Cusinato Claudio

Circ. Canottieri Roma
00196 Roma
L.Tevere Flaminio, 39
Italy
Tel: +39 06/3612921

Marina Militare Centro Sportivo Remiero
04016 Sabaudia
Via Pr. di Piemonte, 19
Italy
Tel: +39 0773/511570
Fax: +39 511558
Email: marisport@marina.difesa.it

Nettuno Yacht Club
00048 Marina Di Nettuno
Via A. Vespucci
Italy
Tel: +39 06/9806381-9800833

C.C. Tevere Remo
00186 Roma
L.Tevere in Augusta, 28
Italy
Tel: +39 06/8073875
Fax: +39 8076936
Email: segreteria@rcctevereremo.it
www.rcctevereremo.it

Circ. Can. Canoa Eur
00196 Roma
Via Flaminia, 287-Villino 27
(c/o Sig. E. Tonali)
Italy
Tel: +39 06/3227769

C.C. Tirrenia Todaro
00196 Roma
L.Tevere Flaminio, 61
Italy
Tel/Fax: +39 06/3610102
Email: canottieri.tirrenia@tin.it

Circ. Can. Gruppo Ina
00187 Roma
Via Sallustiana, 51
Italy
Tel: +39 06/47224311

Centro Sportivo Esercito
01100 Viterbo
Via Cimina, 4
c/o Sez. Can. Uff. Addestram.
Italy
Tel: +39 0761/234811-12-13

C.C. "Salvo D'acquisto
Medaglia D'oro Al Valor Militare"
00060 Formello
Loc. Castel de Ceveri
Italy
Tel: +39 06/9075052
Fax: +39 06/90409287
BH: +39 06/8887663
Email: cc.tiber@tin.it
www.cctiber.it

C.S. Corpo Forestale
Dello Stato
00187 Roma — Via Carducci, 5
Italy
Tel: +39 06/4881223
Fax: +39 48904210

Ass. Naut. Inps "M.Vandone"
00195 Roma
L.Tevere Delle Armi, 33
Italy
Tel: +39 06/3611246

C.C. Nettuno
00048 Nettuno
Via Velletri, 5
Italy
Tel: +39 06/9881297

Circ. Canott. Sabaudia
04016 Sabaudia
PO Box 53
Email: canottierisabaudia@genie.it
www.canottierisabaudia.cjb.net

Circ. Ministero Affari Esteri
00196 Roma
L.Re Acqua Acetosa, 42
Italy
Tel: +39 06/3962362

Ass.Sp. Mariner Canoa
Club Lazio
00144 Roma
Via S. Quasimodo, 30/3
Italy
Tel: +39 06/5014428-5913731

C.C. Lago Di Vico
01037 Ronciglione
Via Giulio Ii, 1 Pal.E
Italy
Tel: +39 0761/626221
Fax: +39 0761/652037

Moton. Fiume Sporting Club
00100 Roma
Via Salaria, 1541
Italy
Tel: +39 06/8889705

C.R.D.D. Marina Mil.-Roma
00196 Roma
P.zzale della Marina, 4
Italy
Tel: +39 06/36804229

Societa' Tennis Club Parioli
00199 Roma
Largo U. De Marpugo, 2
Italy
Tel: +39 06/86200882

Circolo Canottieri Azzurra Civitavecchia
Via Cant_, 12
00053 Civitavecchia
Italy
Tel: +39 0766/24909
Email: civazzurra@inwind.it

CAMPANIA

Circ. Canottieri Irno
84121 SALERNO
Via Porto, 41/43
Italy
Tel: +39 089/232893-224996-220841
Fax: +39 089/254125
Email: canottieri@canottieriirno.it
www.canottieriirno.it

C.R.V. Italia
80132 Napoli
Banchina S.Lucia, 21
Italy
Tel: +39 081/7646393
Fax: +39 7646232
Email: crvita@tin.it
www.crvitalia.it

Circolo Ilva
80124 Napoli
Sez. Canottaggio
Via Coroglio, 90
Italy
Tel: +39 081/7231111

Circ. Canott. Napoli
80121 Napoli
Molosiglio
Italy
Tel: +39 081/5512331-2-3
Fax: +39 5521162
Email: c.c.napoli@tin.it

Circ. Naut. Sapri
84073 Sapri
Contrada Pali
Italy
Tel: +39 0973/392115

Circ. Naut. Posillipo
80123 Napoli
Via Posillipo, 5
Italy
Tel: +39 081/5751377
Fax: +39 5757832

Circ. Naut. Stabia
80053 Castellam. Di Stabia
Via G.Bonito, 2
Italy
Tel/Fax: +39 081/8717187
Email: c.n.stabia@tiscali.it

Reale Yacht Club
Canottieri Savoia
80132 Napoli
Banchina S.Lucia, 13
Italy
Tel: +39 081/7646266
Fax: +39 7647445

Canott. Penisola
Sorrentina
80061 Massa Lubrense
Via C.Colombo, 18/A
Italy
Tel: +39 081/8789112

L.N.I. Sezione Agropoli
84043 Agropoli
P.Za Roma, 13
Italy
Tel: +39 0974/827205-828711

C.C. "A.Offredi"
84011 Amalfi
Casella Postale 57
Italy
Tel: +39 089/873268

S.C. Partenio
83013 Mercogliano (Va)
Via Cerreta, 4/A
Italy
Tel: +39 0825/788504

Associazione Sportiva Olimpica Salerno
84100 Salerno
Via Matteo Greco, 4
Tel: +39 089/794229

PUGLIA E BASILICATA

Gr. Sp. Avis-Barletta
70051 Barletta
Via Baccarini, 21
Italy
Tel: +39 0883/521686

C.U.S. Bari
70123 Bari
L.mare Starita, 1/B
Italy
Tel: +39 080/5341779
Fax: +39 5344865
Email: cusrowing@freemail.it
www.tno.it/cusbari/canot.htm

Marisport C.S.M.M.
Comar Brindisi
72100 Brindisi
Comando Marina Brindisi
Per Centro Sp. M.M.
Italy
Tel: +39 0831/593429-593348

Marisport C.S. Sott.Li
Taranto
74020 S.Vito (Ta)
Viale Jonio
Italy
Tel: +39 099/73391-320

Lega Navale Italiana
72011 Brindisi
L.re A.Vespucci
Italy
Tel: +39 0831/418824

C.C. Barion Sporting Club
70121 Bari
Molo S.Nicola, 5
Italy
Tel: +39 080/5232129-5247028
Email: canottieribarion@inwind.it
digilander.iol.it/davide978/barion.html

Canottieri Ilva
74100 Taranto
Via T. Livio, 7
(c/o Sig. C. Di Taranto)
Italy
Tel: +39 099/91944

C.C. Pro Monopoli
70043 Monopoli
Via Ricasoli, 123/A
(c/o Dr. S. Pugliese)
Italy
Tel: +39 080/9306655
Email: ccpromonopoli@yahoo.it
it.geocities.com/ccpromonopoli

Marisport C.S. Cincnay
2° Sez. Sportiva Ta
74100 Taranto
Staz. Sommergibili
c/o Arsenale M.M.
Italy
Tel: +39 099/7753035

Marisport Can. 3° Sez. Sp.
Sq. Navale Brindisi
72100 Brindisi
Comdinav Tre Brindisi
Italy
Tel: +39 0831/593475

G.S. Vv.F. "Carrino"
72100 Brindisi
Via Provinciale Per S.Vito 118
Italy
Tel: +39 0831/451680 (6 Linee Ric.Aut.)
Fax: 0831/451822

Lega Navale Italiana
73028 Otranto
Via Del Porto
Italy
Tel: +39 0836/81681

Circ. Della Vela Gallipoli
73014 Gallipoli
Casella Postale 29
Italy
Tel: +39 0833/263165

Lega Navale Italiana
70051 Barletta
V.Le C.Colombo (Zona Porto)
Italy
Tel: +39 0883/533354

A.S. Circ. Can. Lucani
85038 Senise
Via Fed. li Di Svezia, 15
Italy
Tel/Fax: +39 0973/686102

Circ. Naut. Barletta
70051 Barletta
Via V.Veneto, 40/F1
(c/o Sig. R. Rizzi)
Italy
Tel: +39 0883/534632

Circolo Canottieri Barletta
70051 Barletta
Via Andria, 49
cell. 3280253600

CALABRIA

Circ. Naut. Reggio
89100 Reggio Cal.
Via Vecchia Pentimele, 14
Italy
Tel: +39 0965/48749-48739

SICILIA

Can. Club Nuoto Augusta
96011 Augusta
Via Dessie', 26
(c/o Sig. M.Sergi)
Italy
Tel: +39 0931/975396

C.U.S. Catania
95125 Catania
V.le A.Doria, 6
Italy
Tel: +39 095/336327
Email: info@cuscatania.com
www.cuscatania.com

Circ. Can. Jonica
95126 Catania
V.le Artale Alagona, 2
Italy
Tel: +39 095/491145-491364

Lega Navale Italiana
96100 Siracusa
P.zale Lepanto, 24
Casa del Marinaio
Italy
Tel: +39 0931/69147

Marisport Can. Augusta
96011 Augusta-Comar
Augusta Per Centro Sp.
Italy
Tel: +39 0931/520549

S.C. Telimar
90149 Palermo
L.mare C.Colombo, 4977
Italy
Tel: +39 091/454419-6840433
Email: sport@telimar.it
www.telimar.it

S.C. Palermo
90133 Palermo
Molo Lupa-Cala
Italy
Tel: +39 091/328467-582650

C.U.S. Palermo
90145 Palermo
Via G.Paisiello, 31
(c/o Dr. P. Aprile)
Italy
Tel: +39 091/342752
Fax: +39 346464
Email: cuscanot-paolo@libero.it

Club Nautico Paradiso
98010 Messina
Via Consol. Pompea 221
Riviera Paradiso
Italy
Tel: +39 090/311772

S.C.Thalatta
98123 Messina
Via V.Emanuele Ii
Italy
Tel: +39 090/53643

Circ. Naut. Teocle
98035 Giardini Naxos
Casella Postale 25
Italy
Tel: +39 0942/51913

S.C. Trinacria
90141 Palermo
Via M.Stabile, 221
Italy
Tel: +39 091/332060
Email: fioresnc@libero.it

Soc. Can. Marsala
91025 Marsala
Casella Postale 140
Italy
Tel: +39 0923/953140
Fax: +39 716225
Email: canottierimarsala@tin.it
www.canottierimarsala.it

Circ. Velico Ribellino
96100 Siracusa
Via Sen. G.Moscuzza, 1
Italy
Tel: +39 0931/60480
Fax: +39 24381

Club Can. Cariddi
98168 Messina
Riviera Paradiso 153
Italy
Tel: +39 090/311975

Gr.Sp. "M.Montuori"
90141 Palermo
Via P.Paternostro, 43
Italy
Tel: +39 091/588173

A.C. Unione Siciliana
95131 Catania
Via Conte Di Torino, 78
Italy
Tel: +39 095/539050

C.U.S. Messina
98121 Messina
V.le Regina Elena, 125
Italy
Tel: +39 090/42575
Fax: +39 42576

Soc. Polisp. Piraineto
90134 Palermo
Vicolo Pantelleria, 8/4
(c/o Sig. F. Galioto)
Italy
Tel: +39 091/6882002

C.C. Ortigia
96100 Siracusa
Via Elorina, 95
Italy
Tel: +39 0931/24777

Ass. "Promosport"
90149 Palermo
Via Annibale, 2
(c/o Sig.Ra C. Calefati)
Italy

Club Nautico Messina
98164 Granatari
Torre Faro
Via Consolari Pompea, 41
Italy

Soc. Jomar Club Ct
95125 Catania
Via A. Gioeni, 11
Italy
Tel: +39 095/432922

Club Can. "R. Di Lauria"
90149 Palermo (Mondello Valdesi)
V.le delle Palme, 20
Italy
Tel: +39 091/6840924
Email: ccrl@neomedia.it
www.ccrl.it

"Furore-Centro Sp."
92028 Naro
Via Don A. Greco, 1
Italy
Tel: +39 0922/957200

Circ. Can. Peloro
98168 Messina
Via Riviera Paradiso, 161
Italy
Tel: +39 090/49485

Canottieri Aetna
95131 Catania
Via Conte Di Torino, 78
Italy
Tel: +39 095/539050

Polisp. Optimum
92026 Favara
Via S.Ambrogio, 41
Italy
Tel: +39 0922/415741

Circolo Di Canottaggio Diga San Giovanni
92028 Naro
Piazza Francesco Crispi, 21
Italy
Tel: +39 0922/956655

C.C. "G.Falcone"
90144 Palermo
Via dei Peloritani, 9
(c/o S. Barroni)
Italy
Tel: +39 091/6256650-586487
Fax: +39 091/6259163

SARDEGNA

C.U.S. Cagliari
091100 Cagliari
Casella Postale 459
Italy
Tel: +39 070/283764

C.C. "G. Sannio"
08013 Bosa
Casella Postale 39
Italy
Tel: +39 0785/373329

C.N. Oristano
09170 Oristano
Casella Postale
Italy
Tel: +39 0783/22027

S.C. Ichnusa
09125 Cagliari
Calata dei Trinitari, 14
Italy
Tel: +39 070/300226 — 301750
Email: info@canottieriichnusa.it
www.canottieriichnusa.it

Ass. Can. Olbia 84
07026 Olbia
Via Tamponi, 7/A
Italy
Tel: +39 0789/69322
Fax: +39 0781/67331

L.N.I. Sezione Cagliari
09125 Cagliari
Viale Colombo, 135
Italy
Tel: +39 070/300240

Associazione Canottieri Tula
07010 Tula
Via Angioj, 53
Italy
Tel: +39 079/718106
web.tiscalinet.it/canottieritula

C.S. M.M.-Marisardegna
La Maddalena
07024 La Maddalena
Marisardegna Centro Sportivo
Italy
Tel: +39 0789/792257

Polisportiva "Amici Del Remo"
09122 Cagliari
Via Dolcetta, 10 (c/o Sig. M. Mura)
Italy
Tel: +39 070/380610

Circolo Nautico Sorradile
09080 Sorradile
Via Grazia Deledda (c/o Medda)
Italy
Tel: +39 0783/69229

Associazione Polisportiva Boroneddu
09080 Boroneddu
Loc. S'ortu E S'olia
Italy
Tel: +39 0785/50191

Associazione Canottieri Cagliari
09100 Cagliari
Via Giardini, 149
Italy
Tel: +39 070/304439

Ivory Coast

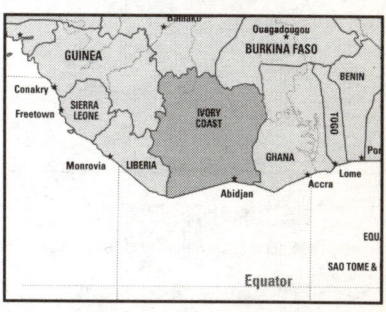

NATIONAL FEDERATION

Civfederation Ivoirienne d'Aviron
BP 6085
Abidjan, 1
Ivory Coast

Japan

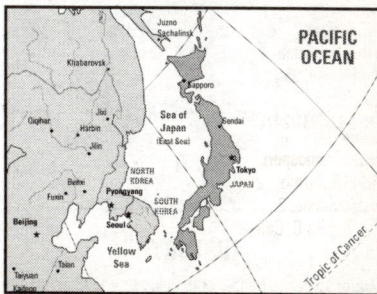

NATIONAL FEDERATION

Japan Rowing Association
C/O Kishi Memorial Hall
1-1-1 Jinnan — Shibuya-ku
Tokyo, 150-8050
Japan
Tel: +81 33 4812326
Fax: +81 33 4812327
Email: jara@japan-sports.or.jp
www.jara.or.jp/index.html

Kazakhstan

NATIONAL FEDERATION

Rowing Federation of the Republic of Kazakhstan
48 Abai Avenue
Alma Ata, 480072
Kazakhstan
Tel: +7 3272 420871
Fax: +7 3272 675088

Kenya

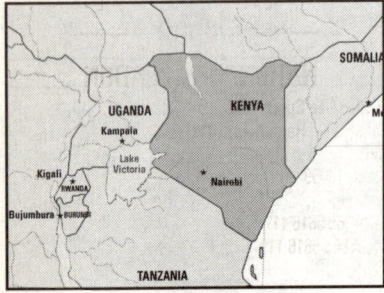

HISTORY

Modern Rowing has its origins in early 1933 when the Mombasa Rowing Club was founded on the Eastern shores of Mombasa Island by the English expatriate community. They enjoyed pleasure rowing and occasional competitions with the visiting naval companies and merchant ships that frequented the Kilindini Harbor. Later on, the club engaged in various competitions with the Kenyan navy and other friendly visitors who regularly called to port in Mombasa.

Mombasa Rowing Club always remained a small club in one corner of the harbor. It was more of a social club integrated with a rowing club. It was in the early nineties that the club was put under threat of eviction by a neighboring fishing industry. By 1992, the writing was on the wall and the rowing club came to a sad end when the fishing company forcefully took the land and the club was closed down. This was unfortunate, as much effort had been made by the members to avert the situation.

By 1993, rowing was restarted when Seifuddin Patwa and Alaisdair MacDonald formed the Kenya Rowing Association based at the nearby yacht club. Alaisdair previously rowed at Henley and is a member of the famous Leanders Club.

The Kenya Navy Rowing Club became the first club to take interest in competitive rowing. In 1995, Kenya became member of the International Rowing Federation. In 1997, the rowing club moved to a new site on the calm Tudor Creek on the western shore of Mombasa Island. FISA assisted the Kenya Rowing Association by donating some sculls and doubles. These boats have served well but a shortage of equipment is hampering the progress of rowing in other parts of the country.

Kenya sent its first international squad to the 4th African Rowing Championships in South Africa in March 2000 and followed up with participation in the 5th African Rowing Championships in Cairo Egypt in 2002. Indoor rowing and coastal rowing are being practiced in Mombasa as various competitions are organized.

In 2002, Kenya became affiliated with the International Canoe Federation becoming the Kenya Rowing and Canoe Federation. In 2002, Kenyan rowers received Solidarity Scholarships from the International Olympic Committee to train at The Australian Sports Institute in Canberra to prepare for the qualifications for the Athens 2004 Olympic Games, which would be the first time Kenya would be represented in rowing.

Starting in 2003, the Kenya Rowing and Canoe Federation and Kenya Tourist Board are undertaking a pilot project to promote Kenya as a winter training destination for rowing crews who wish to combine rowing training and some sightseeing. Kenya, in particular Mombasa, offers ideal rowing training on very long seawater creeks. Mombasa has a modern airport and international-standard accommodations.

For high-altitude training, Eldoret, a small town at approximately 2,000 meters offers great rowing at the nearby Lessos Dam. Eldoret is also home to Kenya's elite long distance runners, who train at the nearby IAAF training facility. Equipment and infrastructure for visiting crews is yet to be put in place but in due course all the necessary facilities will be available.

REGIONS

Kenya has eight provinces: Coastal, North Eastern, Eastern, Western, Nyanza Nairobi, and Rift Valley. The climate in Kenya varies from Alpine to Desert. The highest point is Mt. Kenya at over 5000 meters. Generally there are two rainy seasons in Kenya from April-May called long rains and October-November or short rains.

Avg. temp: Varies from about 10-40°C. Best time to visit: August-March when the climate is very favorable with very comfortable temperatures. Rowing can be done all year. Coastal Province where Mombasa and most of the rowing is situated is Kenya's only deep-water harbor. The climate here is favorable all year-round with average sunshine about 12 hours daily. Air temperature about 25C-33C and water temperature of about 25-29C all the year. Sites of Interest: The sites to see in Kenya are many and varied from the beaches of Coastal provinces and many national parks and reserves with a variety of flora and fauna. Kenya hosts the most varieties of birds in the world and the world-renowned Masai Mara national reserve. The Great Rift Valley of Africa and Lake Victoria, the second largest fresh water lake in the world and the source of the longest river in the world, the Nile River.

NATIONAL FEDERATION

Kenya Rowing & Canoe Association - National Authority
Tel: +254-722-421577
Tel/Fax: +254-41471429
Email: rowing@africaonline.co.ke
www.mombasaonline.com/kenyarowing

CLUBS

Mombasa Rowing Club
PO Box 90391
Mombasa, Kenya
Tel: +254-41-495598

Kenya Navy Rowing Club
PO Box 90350
Mombasa, Kenya
Tel: +254-41-451201/2/3/4/5/6

Kenya Ports Authority Rowing Club
PO Box 95009
Mombasa, Kenya
Tel: +254-41-312211

Krygyzstan

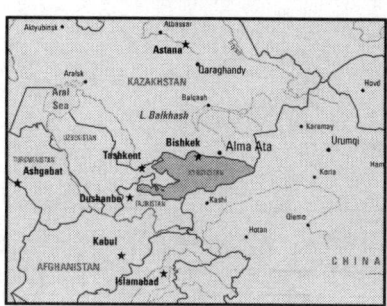

NATIONAL FEDERATION

Rowing Federation of Kyrgyzstan
503 Frunze Street
Blshkek
Kyrgyz Republic NOC
Krygyzstan
Tel: +3312 288 916
Fax: +3312 210 672

Kuwait

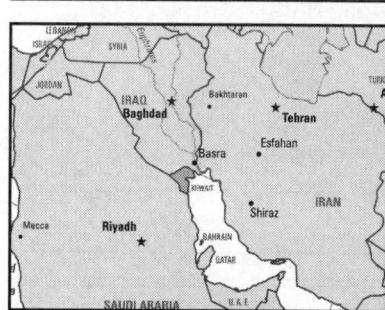

NATIONAL FEDERATION

Kuwait Sea Sports Club
Salmiya — Hamad El-Mubarak St.
5863
Safat, 13059
Kuwait
Tel: +965 5616 117
Fax: +965 5616 119

Latvia

NATIONAL FEDERATION

Latvian Rowing Federation
1 Augsiela St.
Riga LV, 1009
Latvia
Tel: +371 72 295748
Fax: +371 72 272613

Lebanon

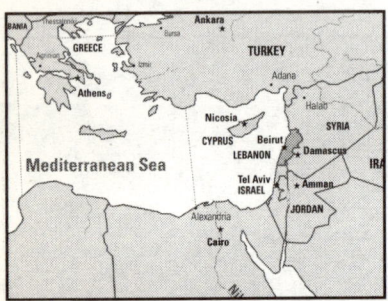

NATIONAL FEDERATION

Lebanese Rowing Federation
PO Box 135716
Chouran
Beirut, Lebanon
Tel: +961 1 300256
Fax: +961 1 310 449

Lithuania

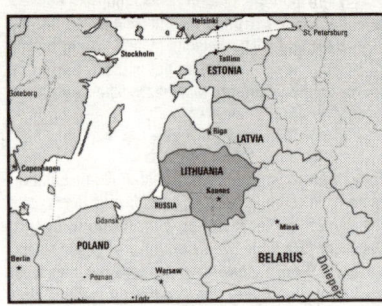

HISTORY

As the frozen world of the Lithuanian winter unlocks into a land of countless lakes and rivers, the rowing season once again begins and the country sees its enthusiasts taking to the water in a multitude of picturesque places on lakes near historic castles and on rivers winding through ancient forests. As a sport, rowing has old and deep traditions, first arriving in 1985 with German seamen in the post town of Klaipeda. Adopted by the local population, the "new" sport soon became popular across the entire country and within just a couple of decades had found its natural heartland and the beautiful lake Galve alongside Trakai Castle, now incorporated into a national park.

Founded over 600 years ago to defend the nation against invaders, the castle still stands proudly above the modern day battles; frequent competitions and regattas that are played out in its midst. In many ways, the history of rowing in Lithuania has been closely entwined with that of Trakai ever since those first boats touched the water at the turn of the nineteenth to twentieth centuries. Although clubs have spread to all the major centers of Lithuania, Trakai is, and has always served as Lithuania's showpiece of the sport. It was on this lake that the national competition was staged in 1928, that the first club was established in 1934, and where the first Olympic medallists trained. Since those early days, rowing has blossomed.

Lithuanian rowers now have over 130 medals to their credit from Olympic, World and European Championships; Trakai regularly hosts international regattas and, as of last year, now prides itself with the completion of the National Sport and Health Center. This center, dedicated to rowing, boasts a fully-equipped gym, a sport hall, newly installed rowing lanes equipped with an Albano system, boat storage and repair facilities. In addition, the complex also houses a modern hotel a variety of dinning possibili-

ties and both seminar and conference facilities.
At Trakai and across the country, rowing is becoming ever more popular season-by-season; more of our athletes represent our country as athletes and as judges within the FISA world.

INTERNET LINKS:
www.lif.lt

REGIONS

Avg. temp: 15-24°C. Best time to visit: Trakai, Lithuania is best in summer. May-October suggested for rowers, who want to row on the open water. Rowing indoors: November-April. Avg. temp: 5°C.

Did You Know ?

Lithuanian rowing city Trakai hosts the annual international rowing Amber Oars Sprint Regatta. Masters row 250 meters in mixed eight crews. You are invited!

PERSONALITIES

Antanas Bagdonavicius: The winner of the most Olympic medals in Lithuania not only among rowers but also in all disciplines. Born in 1938, he started to row when he was eighteen. Soon he won the title of Soviet champion and took this title ten times. Still rowing to this day, Antanas recently won a bronze at the Masters Games in Australia. Such is his dedication to the sport that Antanas has established a museum of his awards and medals in the sport and is instrumental in the development of the sport for youth.

Eugenijus and Ricardas Vaitkevicius: In the history of Lithuanian rowing, Eugenijus and Ricardas, were leading coaches. Both were national champions in their time, playing vital roles in the development of the sport. Eugenijus brought the national women's team to Olympic victory in Canada in 1976 and Ricardas achieved similar success with the men's team in the Mexico and Tokyo Olympics.

Vytautas Briedis: A very famous person, not because of many rowing awards, but as the man who is an organizer and the member of the many sport organizations. His entire life he has been faithful to rowing and sport. He now works as the Secretary General of the Lithuanian Rowing Federation.

NATIONAL FEDERATION

Lithuanian Rowing Federation
Zemaites 6
LT-2600, Vilnius
Lithuania
Tel: +370 5 213 3154
Fax: +370 5 213 3154
Email: lif@takas.lt
www.lif.lt

Macedonia

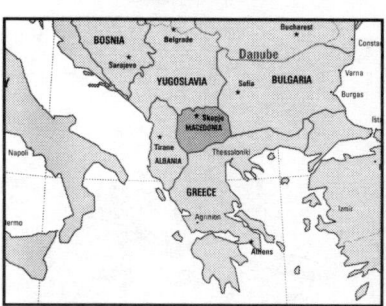

NATIONAL FEDERATION

Rowing Federation of Macedonia
26 Kosta Abras
Ohrid, 96000
Macedonia
Tel: +389 96 260362
Fax: +398 963 5538

Malaysia

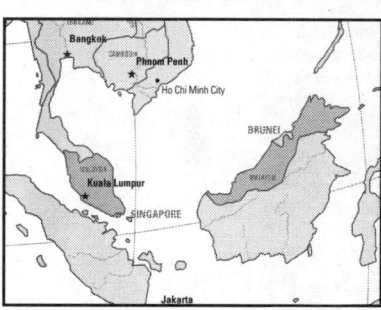

NATIONAL FEDERATION

Malaysian Rowing Association
c/o Unit Sukan
Universiti Teknologi Malaysia - Jalan Semarak
Kuala Lumpar, 54100
Malaysia
Tel: +60 32615 4223
Fax: +60 32615 4432
Email: perdama@hotmail.com

Mexico

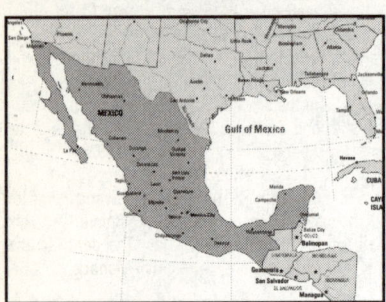

NATIONAL FEDERATION

Federación Mexicana De Remo
2a Cerrada De Pilares No 25 Col Las Aguilas
Deleg. Alvaro Obregon, 1710
Mexico
Tel: +52 5 6805055
Fax: +52 555 93 8025
Email: grupoct@df1.telmex.net.mx

CLUBS

Aleman de Regatas
Antares, A.C.
Calle Yucatan 21
Xochimilco 16000
Mexico D.F.
Mexico

Remo Canahutli
Pista Olimpica de Remo y
C. Virgilio Uribe
Mexico D.F. 16000
Mexico

Remo Espana
Callejon de Chicoco s/n
Xochimilco 016000
Mexico, D.F.
Mexico

Remo de Guardias Presidenciales
Pista Olimpica de Remo y
C. Virgilio Uribe
Mexicl D.F. 16000
Mexico

Remo de Instituto
Tecnologico de Monterrey
Pist a Olimpica de Remo y
C. Virgilio Uribe
Mexico D.F. 16000
Mexico

Remo de Michoacan
Injude Michoacan
Patzcuaro, Michoacan
Mexico

Remo del Instituto Politecnico Nacional
Pist Olimpice de Remo y
C. Virgilio Uribe
Mexico D.F. 16000
Mexico

Remo de la Secretaria de Marina
Pist Olimpica de Remo y
C. Virgilio Uribe
Mexico D.F. 16000
Mexico

Remo de Sinaioa
Injude Sinaloa
Mazatlan, Sinaloa
Mexico

Remo Lakeside
Privada de los Cedros 211
Col. Alcantarilla 01720
Mexico, D.F.
Mexico

Remo de la Universidad
Autonoma Metropolitana Xochimilco
Pista Olimpica de Remo y
C. Virgilio Uribe
Mexico D.F. 16000
Mexico
Tel: +52 7245326
www.geocities.com/remorana

Remo Xochimilco
Pista Olimpica de Remoy
C. Virgilio Uribe
Mexico D.F. 16000
Mexico

Moldova

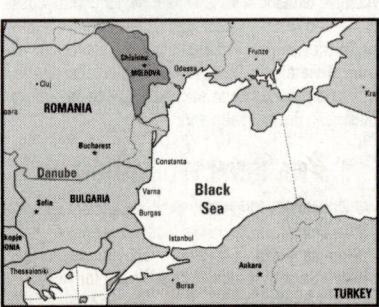

NATIONAL FEDERATION

Rowing Federation of the Republic of Moldova
73 Stefan cel Mare
Kishinev, 277001
Moldova
Tel: +373 227 7507
Fax: +373 227 7352

Monaco

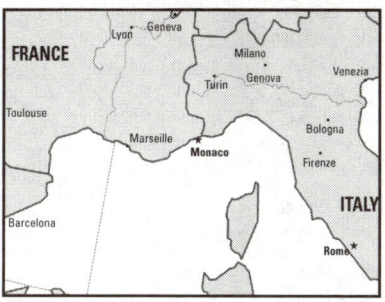

HISTORY

Since 1886, the small Principality of Monaco organized yacht regattas at the request of owners staying in the Riviera towns of Monte-Carlo, Nice, Cannes, and Marseille. Monaco currently has 32,000 inhabitants composed of 118 different nationalities. Following English example, rowing regattas became fashionable and were such a success that rowing is still one of the favourite sports of Monaco residents. It is common to see sea Yoles and Outriggers cross the beautiful Bay of Monaco heading for nearby Italy. Rowing is taught in school and many people discover the pleasure of rowing year round, especially in the wintertime, thanks to the mild climate.

REGIONS

Medium temperatures are around 10°C during the winter and 28°C in the summer. The Mediterranean is a beautiful sea and Monaco is the gateway to the Italian Riviera and to the interior of the French Riviera with lovely places such as Saint Paul de Vence and Grasse.

Did You Know ?

The Société des Régates is the most ancient sporting club in Monaco. Founded in 1888, it later became the prestigious Yacht Club of Monaco for sailing and became Société Nautique de Monaco for rowing in 1953. In Monaco, a floating berth of 352 meters has been built here for the first time in the world for pleasure yachts and big cruise ships.

PERSONALITIES

Gaston Delaplane: From 1905 to 1912, he was 8 times French Champion and 3 times European Champion.

John B. Kelly: In 1952, Kelly came to Monaco to train and get ready for the European Championships and he became the singles champion that year. He won the Diamond Sculls at Henley in 1947 and 1949. His father had been Olympic Champion in 1920.

Grace Kelly: John B. Kelly's sister, Grace came to Monaco in 1956; she married Prince Rainier and was a supporter of Société Nautique. The death of the princess saddened many people of Monaco.

NATIONAL FEDERATION

Fédération Monégasque du Sport Aviron
3 quai J.F.Kennedy, 98000 Monaco
Contact: Mr. Henri Doria, President
Tel: +377-92-160303

Morocco

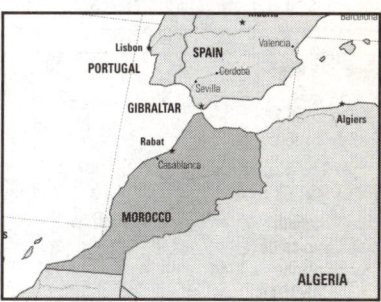

NATIONAL FEDERATION

Federation Royale Marocaine d'Aviron
B.P. 1386
Rabat RP
Morocco
Tel: +212 7 770248
Fax: +212 7 771332
Email: frmsa@caramail.com

Myanmar

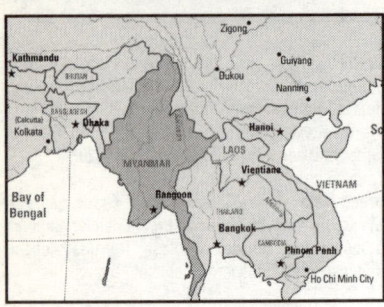

NATIONAL FEDERATION

Myanmar Rowing and Canoeing Federation
Inya Road University PO
Yangon, Mynamar
Tel: +95 1 514 986
Fax: +95 1 526 052

The Netherlands

NATIONAL FEDERATION

Koninklijke Nederlandsche Roeibond
Bosbaan 6
Amstelveen, 1182 AG
Netherlands
Tel: +31 20 646 2740
Fax: +31 20 646 3881
Email: info@knrb.nl
www.knrb.nl

CLUBS

GSR Aegir
Stockholmstraat 10
9723 BC, Groningen
The Netherlands
Tel: +31 050-3124666
Email: info@gsraegir.nl

RV Aeneas
Postbus 129
6040 AC, Roermond
The Netherlands
Tel: +31 0475-336751

RV Aengwirden
Buitenweg 69
8414 MB, Nieuwehorne
The Netherlands
Tel: +31 0513-541826

RV Alberdingk Thijm College
Postbus 700
1200 AS, Hilversum
The Netherlands
Tel: +31 035-6460088

Alkmaarsche R&ZV
Beverdam 1
1822 AA, Alkmaar
The Netherlands
Tel: +31 072-5614839
Email: nkingma@hetnet.nl

RV Alphen
Postbus 2011
2400 CA, Alphen Aan De Rijn
The Netherlands
Tel: +31 0172-492040

Amenophis Roeivereniging
p/a Schollevaarweg 1
3897 LA, Zeewolde
The Netherlands
Tel: +31 036-5222011
Email: j.kriek@chello.nl

H.S.R.V. Amphitrite
Postbus 253
2000 AG, Haarlem
The Netherlands
Email: amphitrite@hshaarlem.nl

R&ZV De Amstel
Hobbemakade 122
1071 XW, Amsterdam
The Netherlands
Tel: +31 020-6711631
Email: info@amstelroei.nl

Amsterdamsche Roeibond
Van Woustraat 143-I
1074 AJ, Amsterdam
The Netherlands
Tel: +31 020-6768541
Email: arbsecretariaat@passage.nl

TRV Amycus
Bellinckhofsdwarsweg 3
7604 PD, Almelo
The Netherlands
Tel: +31 0546-810136

WSR Argo
Grebbedijk 59
6702 PB, Wageningen
The Netherlands
Tel: +31 0317-420700
Email: wsr.argo@uni.student.wau.nl

ARV Aross
Lisztgaarde 1
5344 EA, Oss
The Netherlands
Tel: +31 0412-644487
Email: peter.mineur@xs4all.nl

A.L.S.R. Asopos de Vliet
Postbus 100
2300 AC, Leiden
The Netherlands
Tel: +31 071-5892897
Email: info@asopos.com

Asser Roeiclub
Postbus 786
9400 AT, Assen
The Netherlands
Tel: +31 0592-340977

RV Barendrecht
Klipper 75
2991 KL, Barendrecht
The Netherlands
Tel: +31
Email: edwilschut@planet.nl

ERV Beatrix
Jan Monicxgaarde 9
5671 EA, Nuenen
The Netherlands
Tel: +31 040-2815583
Email: ch.geukers@wxs.nl

RV Belos
Welleweg 81
3232 AV, Brielle
The Netherlands
Tel: +31 0181-414114
Email: broederstam@zonnet.nl

RV Breda
Bredaseweg 30
4844 CL, Terheijden
The Netherlands
Tel: +31 076-5933125
Email: steenman@tip.nl

RV Cadetten RZV Dudok van Heel
Kasteelplein 10
4811 XC, Breda
The Netherlands
Tel: +31 076-5273386

Comite voor Wherrywedstrijden
Churchilllaan 123-III
1078 DN, Amsterdam
The Netherlands
Tel: +31 020-6793433
Email: meulen113@zonnet.nl

HRV Cornelis Tromp
Vreelandseweg 56
1216 CH, Hilversum
The Netherlands
Tel: +31 035-6249433
Email: info@ctromp.nl

R&ZV Daventria
Postbus 85
7400 AB, Deventer
The Netherlands
Tel: +31 0570-618441
Email: rzvdaventria@hotmail.com

RV De Delftsche Sport
Oostplantsoen 140
2611 WN, Delft
The Netherlands
Tel: +31 015-2121433

RV De Drietand
Valeriusplein 15
1075 BJ, Amsterdam
The Netherlands
Tel: +31 020-6627790

RV De Honte
Postbus 396
4330 AJ, Middelburg
The Netherlands
Tel: +31 0118-628583

RV 't Diep
Kruisstraat 82
8375 BH, Oldemarkt
The Netherlands
Tel: +31 0561-452809

RV De Dragt
Marne 21
9204 BC, Drachten
The Netherlands
Tel: +31 0512-541472
Email: info@dedragt.nl

RV De Drie Provincien
Reeveld 2
5431 LJ, Cuijk
The Netherlands
Tel: +31 0485-330579
Email: klabbers53@zonnet.nl

BWSV de Eem
Postbus 531
3740 AM, Baarn
The Netherlands
Tel: +31 035-5413216

RV Epsilon
Franekerstraat 33
8913 AM, Leeuwarden
The Netherlands
Tel: +31 058-2155752

DRV Euros
Auke Vleerstraat 99
7547 AN, Enschede
The Netherlands
Tel: +31 053-4311625
Email: bestuur@drv-euros.nl

R&KV De Geeuw
Malta 1a
8601 GW, Sneek
The Netherlands
Tel: +31 0515-427523

Gorcumse R&ZV
Postbus 3004
4200 EA, Gorinchem
The Netherlands
Tel: +31 0183-632568
Email: gorcumse@zonnet.nl

R&ZV Gouda
Notaris d'Aumerielaan 35
2811 HS, Reeuwijk
The Netherlands
Tel: +31 0182-392280

Groninger Roeibond
Oude Ebbingestraat 6
9712 HH, Groningen
The Netherlands

AGSR Gyas
Postbus 1438
9701 BK, Groningen
The Netherlands
Tel: +31 050-5260390
Email: bestuur@gyas.nl

W.V. de Helling
Parklaan 213
4102 AG, Culemborg
The Netherlands
Tel: +31 0345-518352
Email: hhhoven@wxs.nl

RV Hemus
Postbus 1407
3800 BK, Amersfoort
The Netherlands
Tel: +31 033-4809288
Email: kt@arachnea.nl

RV de Hertog
Postbus 1623
5200 BR, Den Bosch
The Netherlands
Tel: +31 073-6213854
Email: secretaris@hertog.org

Holland Beker Wedstrijd Ver.
Diemerzeedijk 35
1095 KK, Amsterdam
The Netherlands
Email: marc.top@ovz.nl

Hollandia Roeiclub
Evert Cornelislaan 15
3533 SP, Utrecht
The Netherlands
Tel: +31 036-5303533

KAR&ZV de Hoop
Weesperzijde 1046A
1091 EH, Amsterdam
The Netherlands
Tel: +31 020-6657844
Email: karvhoop@xs4all.nl

KGRV de Hunze
Praediniussingel 32
9711 AG, Groningen
The Netherlands
Tel: +31 050-3122971
Email: hunze@hunze.net

KR&ZV de IJssel
Baan 22
8271 BE, Ijsselmuiden
The Netherlands
Tel: +31 038-4204870
Email: n.hendriks@huygens.nl

ZR&ZV Isala
p/a B. van Sytzamastraat 34
6971 ZB, Brummen
The Netherlands
Tel: +31 0575-564380

R&ZV Jason
Postbus 417
6800 AK, Arnhem
The Netherlands
Tel: +31 026-3615207

Kon. Holland Beker
The Netherlands

Kon.Ned. Studenten Roeibond
Eerste Jan Steenstraat 110-2
1072 NR, Amsterdam
The Netherlands
Tel: +31 020-4274758
Email: sp@knsrb.nl

Koninklijke Dordrechtsche R&ZV
Postbus 517
3300 AM, Dordrecht
The Netherlands
Tel: +31 078-6148550
Email: kdrzv@dordt.nl

Koninklijke NZ&RV
Postbus 30
1398 ZG, Muiden
The Netherlands
Tel: +31 0294-261540
Email: secretariaat@knzrv.nl

KPN Watersportbaan
Veenweg 28 b
9728 NM, Groningen
The Netherlands
Tel: +31 050-5263721
Email: bauman@hetnet.nl

RV de Krom
Postbus 309
3440 AH, Woerden
The Netherlands
Tel: +31 0348-413727

KZ&RV Hollandia
Kapelsteeg 9-11
3841 BJ, Harderwijk
The Netherlands
Tel: +31 0341-425185
Email: p.verbrugge@wxs.nl

RV de Laak
p/a Weissenbruchstraat 89
2596 GC, Den Haag
The Netherlands
Tel: +31 070-3859667
Email: secretaris@rvdelaak.nl

DSRV Laga
Nieuwelaan 53
2611 RR, Delft
The Netherlands
Tel: +31 015-2125266
Email: Laga@laga.nl

RV Leerdam
Lingedijk 27
4142 LD, Leerdam
The Netherlands
Tel: +31 0345-615115
Email: secretaris@rvleerdam.nl

LR&ZV die Leythe
Morsweg 148
2332 ER, Leiden
The Netherlands
Tel: +31 071-5760754
Email: secretaris@dieleythe.nl

KR&ZV de Maas
Postbus 23475
3001 KL, Rotterdam
The Netherlands
Tel: +31 010-4180845
Email: krzv@de-maas.nl

Maastrichtsche Watersport Club
Postbus 2200
6201 HA, Maastricht
The Netherlands
Tel: +31 043-3216195
Email: r.van.voorden@hetnet.nl

RV De Meije
Postbus 56
2420 AB, Nieuwkoop
The Netherlands
Email: irem@xs4all.nl

UR&KV Michiel de Ruyter
Amsteldijk-Zuid 253
1423 BZ, Uithoorn
The Netherlands
Tel: +31 0297-540499
Email: emden-merelle@planet.nl

RV Minerva
1e Jan Steenstraat 110-2
1072 NR, Amsterdam
The Netherlands
Tel: +31 020-4274758

R&ZV Naarden
Thierensweg 1
1411 EW, Naarden
The Netherlands
Tel: +31 035-6940452

RV Nautilus
Postbus 2535
3000 CM, Rotterdam
The Netherlands
Tel: +31 010-4138791
Email: rv.nautilus@worldmail.nl

Nederlandse Droogroeiveren.
Valkenburgseweg 11
2331 AA, Leiden
The Netherlands
Tel: +31 071-5722147

Nederlandse Studenten Roeifed.
Doddendaal 192
6511 DG, Nijmegen
The Netherlands
Tel: +31 024-3245883
Email: info@nsrf.nl

KZ&RV Neptunus
Aalgeer 6
9932 HM, Delfzijl
The Netherlands
Tel: +31 0596-626590

ASR Nereus
Amsteldijk 130a
1078 RT, Amsterdam
The Netherlands
Tel: +31 020-6797117
Email: bestuur@nereus.nl

Nijenrode rv Het Galjoen
Postbus 226
3620 AE, Breukelen
The Netherlands
Tel: +31 0346-291211

KSRV Njord
Morsweg 182-184
2332 ES, Leiden
The Netherlands
Tel: +31 071-5760776
Email: info@njord.nl

Noord Oostelijke Roeibond
Friesestraatweg 55 b
9718 NC, Groningen
The Netherlands
Email: i.delangen@wxs.nl

RSVU Okeanos
Bosbaan 2t-3
1182 AG, Amstelveen
The Netherlands
Tel: +31 020-6465818
Email: bestuur@okeanos.nl

AWSV Ondine, ASV S.H.E.L.L.
Postbus 38000
1030 BN, Amsterdam
The Netherlands
Tel: +31 020-6391702
Email: tim.t.nisbet@opc.shell.com

N.S.C.R.F OOCUZ
Morsweg 81
2332 EK, Leiden
The Netherlands
Tel: +31 071-5138879
Email: bestuur@oocuz.com

WSV Oostvoorne
Nachtegalenlaan 38
3233 BJ, Oostvoorne
The Netherlands
Tel: +31 0181-483846

A.U.S.R. Orca
Verlengde Hoogravenseweg 13
3525 BB, Utrecht
The Netherlands
Tel: +31 030-2890860
Email: bestuur@orcaroeien.nl

RV Ossa
Postbus 98
1700 AB, Heerhugowaard
The Netherlands
Tel: +31 072-5719823
Email: kosterjaba@cs.com

RV Pampus
Postbus 10329
1301 AH, Almere
The Netherlands
Tel: +31 036-5384352
Email: rvpampus@hotmail.com

AR&ZV Panta Rhei
Het Nieuwe Diep 8
1780 CA, Den Helder
The Netherlands
Tel: +31 0223-652424

NSRV Phocas
Postbus 31097
6503 CB, Nijmegen
The Netherlands
Tel: +31 024-3553105
Email: nsrvphocas@hotmail.com

RV Pontos
Postbus 1015
8200 BA, Lelystad
The Netherlands
Tel: +31 0320-257051
Email: w.bsmokers@freeler.nl

R&ZV Poseidon
Jan Vroegopsingel 4
1096 CN, Amsterdam
The Netherlands
Tel: +31 020-6941813
Email: bestuur@rzv-poseidon.nl

DSRV Proteus-Eretes
Postbus 322
2600 AH, Delft
The Netherlands
Tel: +31 015-2623720
Email: proteus-eretes@tudelft.nl

RV RIC
Korte Ouderkerkerdijk 32
1096 AC, Amsterdam
The Netherlands
Tel: +31 020-6656508

RV Rijnland
Oostvlietweg 63
2266 GN, Leidschendam
The Netherlands
Tel: +31 071-5610314

RV Rijnmond
Crooswijkse Bocht 100
3034 NC, Rotterdam
The Netherlands
Tel: +31 010-4129918
Email: roeiver.rijnmond@worldonline.nl

Roeibond Midden Nederland
Vermeerstraat 90
3817 DH, Amersfoort
The Netherlands
Tel: +31 033-4635456
Email: becappel@worldonline.nl

Roeicommissie WSV De Ank
Worpplein 15
7006 AM, Doetinchem
The Netherlands
Tel: +31 0314-362930

Roosendaalse Roeivereniging
Postbus 1805
4700 BV, Roosendaal
The Netherlands
Tel: +31 0165-512484
Email: secretaris@roosendaalserv.nl

RV RowDow
Jan van Galenstraat 62
4535 BX, Terneuzen
The Netherlands
Tel: +31 0115-620489
Email: kastel@zeelandnet.nl

RV Salland
Den Kaat 6
7707 PG, Balkbrug
The Netherlands
Tel: +31 0524-561115
Email: secretaris@salland-roeien.nl

MSRV Saurus
Postbus 175
6200 AD, Maastricht
The Netherlands
Tel: +31 043-3257140
Email: bestuur@msrvsaurus.com

GRV Scaldis
Hemstraat 5
4481 BL, Kloetinge
The Netherlands
Tel: +31 0113-213638

ARSRV Skadi
Noorderkanaalweg 20-22
3037 AV, Rotterdam
The Netherlands
Tel: +31 010-4656333
Email: secretaris@skadi.nl

AASRV Skoll
Jan Vroegopsingel 6
1096 CN, Amsterdam
The Netherlands
Tel: +31 020-6931599
Email: bestuur@skoll.nl

KR&ZV Het Spaarne
Marisplein 5
2102 AC, Heemstede
The Netherlands
Tel: +31 023-5285675

ST. Watersportbaan Tilburg
Hoge Wal 107
5053 AP, Goirle
The Netherlands
Email: mrdewit@home.nl

RV De Stern
Zuidelijk Sluiseiland 38
1975 AB, Ijmuiden
The Netherlands
Tel: +31 0255-517778

Stichting Roeivalidatie
Crooswijkse Bocht 100
3034 NC, Rotterdam
The Netherlands
Tel: +31 010-4123277
Email: info@roeivalidatie.nl

ESRV Theta
Kanaaldijk-Noord 13
5613 DH, Eindhoven
The Netherlands
Tel: +31 040-2438853
Email: secretaris@esrtheta.com

RV Thyro
Postbus 312
7500 AH, Enschede
The Netherlands
Email: info@wilmer.nl

Tilburgse Open roeivereniging
Postbus 10225
5000 JE, Tilburg
The Netherlands
Tel: +31 013-5352809
Email: keijzer@diamant-groep.nl

USRV Triton
Verlengde Hoogravenseweg 13
3525 BB, Utrecht
The Netherlands
Tel: +31 030-2889588
Email: bestuur@usrtriton.nl

TRV Tubantia
Postbus 19
7550 AA, Hengelo
The Netherlands
Tel: +31 074-2911318
Email: trvtubantia@freeler.nl

WSV Vada
Jachthaven 1
6702 DV, Wageningen
The Netherlands
Tel: +31 0317-415986
Email: wsv_vada@hotmail.com

Ver.Bevordering Watersp.Jonger
Leopoldlaan 33
1422 KD, Uithoorn
The Netherlands
Tel: +31 0297-565173

TSRV Vidar
Postbus 1085
5004 BB, Tilburg
The Netherlands
Tel: +31 013-5421282
Email: bestuur@tsr-vidar.nl, TSR-vidar@kub.nl

URV Viking
Verlengde Hoogravenseweg 13
3525 BB, Utrecht
The Netherlands
Tel: +31 030-2890870
Email: info@urvviking.nl, bestuur@urvviking.nl

Watersportvereniging Eeuwes
Doelenstraat 32
3271 TA, Mijnsheerenland
The Netherlands
Tel: +31 0186-603736
Email: info@eeuwes.nl

RV Weesp
Postbus 5264
1380 GG, Weesp
The Netherlands
Tel: +31 0294-419862

LRV Wetterwille
Poelruit 8
8935 RD, Leeuwarden
The Netherlands
Tel: +31 058-2880301
Email: secretariaat@wetterwille.demon.nl

PRV De Where
Postbus 257
1440 AG, Purmerend
The Netherlands
Tel: +31 0299-427098

RV Willem III
Jan Vroegopsingel 8
1096 CN, Amsterdam
The Netherlands
Tel: +31 020-6654230
Email: bestuur@willem3.nl

WRV De Zaan
Treilerstraat 105
1503 JE, Zaandam
The Netherlands
Tel: +31 075-6283297
Email: jkeppel@worldonline.nl

Zaanlandsche Zeilvereeniging
Suringarstraat 42
1504 HN, Zaandam
The Netherlands
Tel: +31 075-6164853
Email: zzvroeien@yahoo.co.uk

Het Zeilend Scheehout
Zuidlaarderweg 20
9756 CH, Glimmen
The Netherlands
Tel: +31 050-4061545
Email: p.lecoultre@zonnet.nl

Zuid Hollandse Roeibond
p/a Oude Vest 83
2312 XT, Leiden
The Netherlands

Zuidelijke Roeibond
Postbus 753
5000 AT, Tilburg
The Netherlands
Tel: +31 013-5456224
Email: M_Jongenotter@hotmail.com

J.G. van der Zwan
Calliopestraat 75
2511 GE, Den Haag
The Netherlands
Tel: +31 070-3656198
Email: mirjamenhans@zonnet.nl

Zwolsche R&ZV
Holtenbroekerdijk 100
8031 LJ, Zwolle
The Netherlands
Tel: +31 038-4542395
Email: webmaster@zrzv.nl

New Zealand

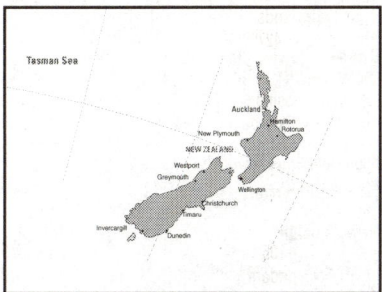

HISTORY

New Zealand's rowing history can be traced back to its colonial founding in the early nineteenth century. Trading and whaling combined with the abundance of harbors and beaches allowed various forms of oared rowing to flourish within a few short years. The earliest form of racing recorded was in whaleboats. These boats were broad beam and much wider than any rowing boats in use elsewhere at that time. They were powered by up to twelve oarsmen sitting two abreast. It was popular throughout the country and is considered the forerunner of the sport of rowing in New Zealand. Interestingly enough, it was the competitions between hotels, where most of the seafarers and whalers resided while on shore, that promoted the sport and led to the organization of the first competitions. Whaleboat racing became very popular involving high stakes. More conventional European rowing was present, though the whaleboat regattas remained the most popular through the 1860's and 1870's.

Canterbury Rowing Club, in Christchurch, was the first European-style rowing club to be founded between 1859 and 1861. Many other prestigious clubs were founded over the next twenty years. On March 16, 1887, instigated by William Fitzgerald of the Star Boat Club, the Wellington representatives of nine clubs formed the New Zealand Amateur Rowing Association. The first patron was Sir W.E.D. Jervois. Mr. J. O. James of Christchurch was the first president and A.G. Biss of Wellington was the secretary.

The founding clubs were Canterbury Rowing Club, Christchurch, 1861; Union Rowing Club, Christchurch, 1866; Star Boating Club, Wellington, 1867; Wanganui Rowing Club, Wanganui 1875; Union Boat Club, Wanganui, 1878; Wellington Rowing Club, Wellington, 1885; Napier Rowing Club, Hawkes Bay, 1886; Nelson Rowing Club, Nelson, 1886 and Whakaty Rowing Club, Nelson, 1886.

The popularity of rowing continued and by 1892 the original nine clubs had grown to thirty-four. By 1902, there were forty-five clubs in the association. Today there are seventy-four clubs, one hundred secondary schools and seven universities affiliated to the New Zealand Amateur Rowing Association. The National Rowing Association, as opposed to the amateur association, was formed in 1864. Today, the national office is located at Lake Karapiro, the venue of the 1978 World Championships and the current training base for New Zealand's elite rowing squad.

Rowing clubs are spread throughout the two islands and the rowing traveler can find a club in most provincial towns. Historical photographs taken by various rowing clubs show that women were involved in rowing as early as the 1920's. It wasn't until 1966 that New Zealand Rowing selected its first women's crew to compete in the Australian Women's Championships.

Unlike other countries, New Zealand does not have a major historical regatta such as Henley but focuses efforts on the annual National Championships and National Secondary School Championships. What New Zealand lacks in historical regattas it makes up for in trophy races. Two trophies are the Boss Rooster for the coxed four and the boys eights trophy the Maadi Cup at the New Zealand Secondary School Championships. The Boss Rooster started as a challenge between the crews of two sailing ships. As the story goes, after the first race the winning crew painted a tin cutout in the Port Chambers Club colors and nailed it to the mast of the losing crew's ship. The standing tradition is that the rooster must be painted in the winning clubs colors within an hour of winning the race and must be shouted at and enthusiastically welcomed with kegs of beer. The Maadi Cup was a trophy won by New Zealand servicemen on leave in Egypt during the World War II. This trophy was bought back and presented to New Zealand Rowing by surviving members of the winning crew. New Zealand Rowing subsequently decided this should be the trophy to foster youth rowing.

New Zealand's success on the international rowing arena began with D'Arcy Hadfield's bronze medal at the 1920 Olympic Games in Antwerp. New Zealand is famous today for fielding the reigning World and Olympic Champion in single scull, Rob Waddell, and the successful Ever-Swindell twins in the women's double scull.

REGIONS
South Island
Marlborough, Canterbury, Otago, Southland
Avg. temp: Summer (December-February) 13 to 24°C; Fall (March-May) 5 to 19°C; Winter (June-August) 3 to12°C; Spring (September-November) 8 to16°C;

North Island
Wanganui, Eastland, Bay of Plenty, Wellington
Avg. temp: Summer (December-February) 13 to 21°C;
Fall (March-May) 9 to 18°C; Winter (June-August) 7 to
12°C; Spring (September-November) 6 to17°C;

PERSONALITIES

D'Arcy Hadfield: New Zealand's first and only
Olympic competitor at the 1920 Games in Antwerp
who won the bronze medal in the men's single.

Rob Waddell: The reining World and Olympic
Champion and holder of the world record in indoor
rowing.

Did You Know ?

Rob Waddell has broken world records in one of the
most demanding sports of the Olympics, won the
world championship single sculls title for two consecutive years, won the indoor rowing title three
times and the Halberg Award for New Zealand
Sportsperson of the Year twice.

NATIONAL FEDERATION

Rowing New Zealand
PO Box 765
Cambridge, New Zealand
Tel: +64 7 823 4587
Fax: +64 7 823 4589
Email: info@rowingnz.org.nz
www.rowingnz.org.nz

CLUBS

Aramoho Wanganui Rowing Club
PO Box 5033
Wanganui
New Zealand

Auckland Grammar Rowing Club
PO Box 74069
Epsom Auckland
New Zealand

Auckland Rowing Club
PO Box 32-121
Devonport Auckland
New Zealand

Avon Rowing Club
PO Box 13-115
Christchurch
New Zealand

Awarua Boating Club
PO Box 13
Bluff
New Zealand

Bay of Plenty Coast Rowing Club
PO Box 13 027
Tauranga
New Zealand

Blenheim Rowing Club
C/- 135 Howick Road
Blenheim
New Zealand

Cambridge High School Rowing
Private Bag 882
Cambridge
New Zealand

Cambridge Rowing Club
PO Box 357
Cambridge
New Zealand

Canterbury Rowing Club
PO Box 22-479
Christchurch
New Zealand

Christs College Rowing Club
Private Bag 4900
Christchurch
New Zealand

Clifton Rowing Club
242 Inland North Road RD 43
Waitara
New Zealand

Counties-Manukau Rowing Club
PO Box 75-407
Manurewa Auckland
New Zealand

Cure Boating Club
PO Box 161
Kaiapoi
New Zealand

Dunstan Arm Rowing Club
PO Box 31
Alexandra
New Zealand

Eastern Bays Scullers Club
PO Box 12 101
Penrose Auckland
New Zealand

Gisborne Rowing Club
74B Main Road
Makaraka Gisborne
New Zealand

Golden Edge Nelson Rowing Club
PO Box 5006
Port Nelson
New Zealand

Hamilton Rowing Club
PO Box 724
Hamilton
New Zealand

Hauraki Plains Rowing Club
PO Box 82
Ngatea
New Zealand

Hawkes Bay Rowing Club
PO Box 17
Clive Hawkes Bay
New Zealand

Horowhenua Rowing Club
PO Box 163
Levin
New Zealand

Hutt Valley Rowing Club
PO Box 9577
Hutt Valley Wellington
New Zealand

Invercargill Rowing Club
PO Box 1138
Invercargill
New Zealand

Kings College Rowing Club
PO Box 22012
Otahuhu Auckland
New Zealand

Mercer Rowing Club
PO Box 690
Pukekohe
New Zealand

North End Rowing Club
PO Box 5537
Dunedin
New Zealand

North Shore Rowing Club
PO Box 33205
Takapuna Auckland
New Zealand

Oamaru Rowing Club
PO Box 118
Oamaru
New Zealand

Otago Rowing Club
PO Box 524
Dunedin
New Zealand

Otago University Rowing Club
C/- OUSA
PO Box 1436
Dunedin
New Zealand

Patterson's Realty
PO Box 302
Wanaka
New Zealand

Petone Rowing Club
PO Box 38-016
Petone Wellington
New Zealand

Picton Rowing Club
C/- Mr D Bugler
65 Milton Terrace
Picton
New Zealand

Porirua Rowing Club
2 Onepoto Road
Titahi Bay Porirua
New Zealand

Port Chalmers United Rowing Club
PO Box 45
Port Chalmers
New Zealand

Riverton Rowing Club
Gropers Bush RD 3
Riverton
New Zealand

Rotorua Rowing Club
PO Box 620
Rotorua
New Zealand

St Georges Rowing Club
PO Box 14-165
Panmure Auckland
New Zealand

St Kentigern College Rowing Club
PO Box 51-060
Pakuranga Auckland
New Zealand

St Pauls Collegiate Rowing Club
PO Box 12-337
Hamilton
New Zealand

Star Boating Club
PO Box 361
Wellington
New Zealand

Takapuna GS Rowing Club
PO Box 32-232
Devonport Auckland
New Zealand

Taupo Rowing Club
PO Box 292
Taupo
New Zealand

Tauranga Rowing Club
PO Box 13343
Tauranga
New Zealand

Te Awamutu Rowing Club
PO Box 187
Te Awamutu
New Zealand

Timaru Rowing Club
53 Rothwell Street
Timaru
New Zealand

Twizel Rowing Club
5 Huxley Place
Twizel
New Zealand

Union Boat Club
1c Taupo Quay
Wanganui
New Zealand

Union Rowing Club
PO Box 1839
Christchurch
New Zealand

Waihopai Rowing Club
PO Box 520
Invercargill
New Zealand

Waikato Diocesan School Rowing Club
PO Box 3051
Hamilton
New Zealand

Waikato Rowing Club
PO Box 1106
Hamilton
New Zealand

Wairau Rowing Club
C/- Mrs M Hegglun
PO Box 736
Blenheim
New Zealand

Waitemata Rowing Club
PO Box 79-107
Royal Heights
Auckland
New Zealand

Wakatipu Rowing Club
17 Golden Terrace
Queenstown
New Zealand

Wanganui Collegiate Rowing Club
Private Bag 3002
Wanganui
New Zealand

Wellington Rowing Club
PO Box 3273
Wellington
New Zealand

West End Rowing Club
PO Box 47-180
Ponsonby Auckland
New Zealand

Whakatane Rowing Club
PO Box 285
Whakatane
New Zealand

Whangarei Rowing Club
PO Box 145
Whangarei
New Zealand

Nicaragua

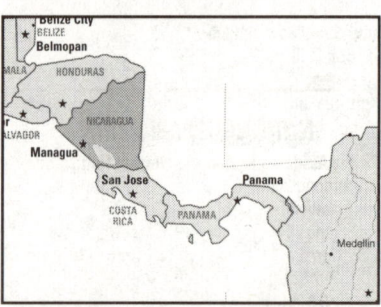

NATIONAL FEDERATION

Federación Nicaraguense de Remo
c/o Instituto Juventud y Deportes
Antigua Hacienda el Retiro - Apartado Postal #383
Managua, Nicaragua
Tel: (505) 266-3703
Fax: (505) 266-3704

Nigeria

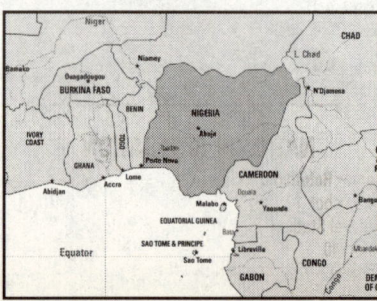

NATIONAL FEDERATION

Nigerian Amateur Rowing Association
c/o Nigeria Olympic Committee Nigerian National Stadium
P.O. Box 3156 - Marina
Lagos, Nigeria
Tel: +234 1 5450 105
Fax: +234 1 585 0530

North Korea

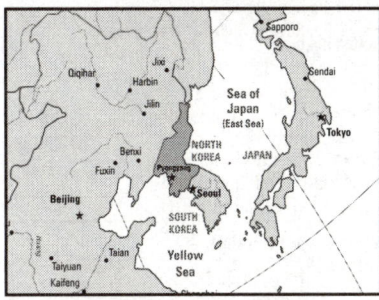

NATIONAL FEDERATION

Rowing Assoc. of the Dem. Republic of North Korea
Munsindong 2
Dongdaewon Dist
Pyongyang DPR
North Korea
Tel: +850 2 63998
Fax: +850 2 3814403

Norway

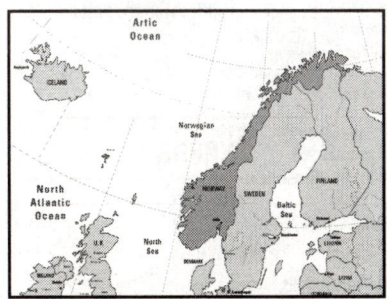

NATIONAL FEDERATION

Norges Roforbund
Servicebok 1
Ullevaal Stadion
Oslo, 840
Norway
Tel: +47 21 02 90 00
Fax: +47 21 02 98 41
Email: roing@nif.idrett.no
www.roing.no

CLUBS

Alvøen Roklubb
Postboks 90, Godvik
5882 Bergen
Norway
Contact: Tor Steen Johnsen
Tel: +47 55 17 84 82

Arbeidernes Roklubb
v/Gro Andersen
Frøyas vei 6
1412 Sofiemyr
Norway
Tel: +47 23 14 30 07
Fax: +47 23 14 34 50
Email: janhe-ho@frisurf.no

Gro Andersen
Frøyas vei 6
1412 Sofiemyr
Norway
Tel: +47 23 14 30 07
Email: janhe-ho@frisurf.no

Arendals Roklub
v/Per Jarle Brensdal
Barbugårdsvn. 47
4839 Arendal
Norway
Tel: +47 37 02 26 03
Fax: +47 37 02 42 58
Email: per.brensdal@c2i.net

Torleiv Moseid
Kystveien 55
4841 Arendal
Norway
Tel: +47 37 02 26 03
Email: Torleiv.Moseid@hia.no

Askøy Roklubb
Sæterstøl
5307 Ask
Norway
Tel: +47 90 20 98 18
Email: askoyroklubb@hotmail.com

Bergens Roklub
Harald Skjoldsveg 77
5236 Rådal
Norway
Tel: +47 55 13 46 50
Email: jankrohn@hotmail.com
www.bergens-roklub.no

Bærum Roklubb
Postboks 155
1313 Vøyenenga
Norway
Tel: +47 67 55 07 20
Fax: +47 67 55 07 21
Email: baerumro@online.no
www.baerum-roklubb.no

Christiania Roklub
Frognerstranda 2
0271 Oslo
Norway
Tel: +47 22 44 82 12
Fax: +47 22 44 17 27
Email: Styret@christiania-roklub.no
www.christiania-roklub.no/

Drammen Roklubb
Postboks 330 Bragernes
3001 Drammen
Norway
Tel: +47 32 83 47 09
Email: ragnar.loken@c2i.net
www.n3sport.no/roing/drammenroklubb

Fana Roklubb
Straumevei 18
5152 Bønes
Norway
Tel: +47 55 12 10 79
Email: knut.hordnes@uib.no
www.fana-roklubb.no

Fornebu Sportsklubb
Postboks 80
1325 Lysaker
Norway
Tel: +47 90 95 91 59
Fax: +47 22 52 44 82
Email: Helle.Bye@2wglobal.com
www.fornebu-sportsklubb.no

Fredriksstad Roklub
Postboks 251
1601 Fredrikstad
Norway
Tel: +47 69 36 51 77
Fax: +47 69 34 09 00
Email: kundemottak@motorforum-fredrikstad.no
www.syznett.no/fr

Haldens Roklub
Postboks 140
1751 Halden
Norway
Email: bernhaug@online.no
www.halden.org/roklub

Hamar IL/Rogruppen
Postboks 314
2303 Hamar
Norway
Email: stein@kaser.no

Haugesund og Omegn Roklubb
Haugevegen 78
5515 Haugesund
Norway
Tel: +47 52 72 86 03

Holmen Roklubb
Postboks 129, Laksevåg
5847 Bergen
Norway
Tel: +47 90 53 74 91
Fax: +47 55 55 39 50
Email: holmen.roklubb@c2i.net
www.holmenroklubb.no

Horten Roklubb
Bromsveien 8
3183 Horten
Norway
Tel: +47 33 04 41 64
Fax: +47 33 04 49 35
Email: mail@horten-roklubb.no
www.horten-roklubb.no

Jæren Ro- og Padleklubb
Postboks 97
4358 Kleppe
Norway
Email: arne.sabo@planteforsk.no

Kongsvinger Roklubb
Vingersjøkroken 4
2211 Kongsvinger
Norway
Tel: +47 67 57 72 83
Fax: +47 67 57 99 11
Email: Knut.Strengelsrud@dnv.com

Kristiansand Roklubb
Postboks 523
4665 Kristiansand
Norway
Tel: +47 38 02 49 69
Fax: +47 38 02 25 51
Email: jagars@online.no
www.roklubben.com

Kristiansund Roklubb
Postboks 258
6501 Kristiansund
Norway
Tel: +47 71 67 51 07
Email: krisathe@start.no

Kvinnherad Roklubb
v/Amund Utne
Hidlervn. 8
5460 Husnes
Norway
Tel: +47 53 48 48 65
Email: bh@soral.no

Larvik Roklubb
v/Bent Salvesen
Grønlivegen 12 C
3922 Porsgrunn
Norway
Tel: +47 48 09 48 64
Fax: +47 35 55 40 14
Email: bent.salvesen@c2i.net

Lillehammer Ro- og Kajakklubb
Postboks 422
2603 Lillehammer
Norway
Tel: +47 61 26 17 26
Email: Kai.Gjessing@hil.no
www.lrkk.no

Moss Roklubb
Postboks 208
1501 Moss
Norway
Tel: +47 69 27 22 54
Email: per-ivar.berg@norske-skog.com
www.moss-roklubb.no

Namsos Roklubb
Postboks 164
7801 Namsos
Norway
Tel: +47 74 27 47 29
Email: so-haas@online.no

Nidaros Roklubb
Postboks 2604
7414 Trondheim
Norway
Tel: +47 73 59 63 09
Fax: +47 73 59 63 11
Email: odd.gulseth@bio.ntnu.no

Norges Handelshøgskoles Roklubb
Helleveien 30
5035 Bergen
Norway
Email: nhhcrew@nhhs.nhh.no

Norges Landbrukshøgskoles IL/
Rogruppen
Idrettskontoret
Postboks 1206
1432 ÅS
Norway
nlhstud.nlh.no/~nlhi/

NTNUI-roing
Studpost 222
7491 Trondheim
Norway
Email: roing@stud.ntnu.no
www.stud.ntnu.no/studorg/roing

Norsk Roklub i Berlin e.V.
v/Tom Schumacher
Bautzener Str. 9 A
D-10829 Berlin, Tyskland
Norway
Email: schumachertom@hotmail.com
www.nrb-ev.de

Norske Studenters Roklub
Postboks 552 Skøyen
0214 Oslo
Norway
Tel: +47 90 05 02 68
Fax: +47 22 44 71 39
Email: styret@roklubben.no
www.roklubben.no

Nøklevann Ro- og Padleklubb
Postboks 37, Bogerud
0621 Oslo
Norway
Tel: +47 95 87 91 03
Email: touren@online.no

Ormsund Roklub
Postboks 263 Sentrum
0103 Oslo
Norway
Tel: +47 22 29 77 07
Email: ormsro@frisurf.no

Os Roklubb
Postboks 381
5203 Os
Norway
Tel: +47 56 57 62 36
Email: sisslot@hotmail.com

Oslo Kvinnelige Roklubb
Postboks 3001 Elisenberg
0207 Oslo
Norway
Tel: +47 22 50 94 86
Email: okr@inbox.as

Oslo Roklubb
v/Morten Schjetlein
Eiksveien 56
1359 Eiksmarka
Norway
Tel: +47 67 14 08 64

Porsgrunn Roklubb
Kirstistien 16
3936 Porsgrunn
Norway
Tel: +47 35 55 07 17
Fax: +47 35 57 34 10
Email: sigmund.hansen.1@if.no

Ringsaker Roklubb
Postboks 231
2381 Brumunddal
Norway
Email: j-ar-lu@online.no
www.n3sport.no/roing/ringsaker-roklubb

Risør Ro- og Padleklubb
Øvregata 9
4950 Risør
Norway
Tel/Fax: +47 37 02 21 35
Email: kristgu@online.no
Contact: Kristian Gundersen
Email: kristgu@online.no

Roklubben Terje Viken
Postboks 1551 Kjelvene
4093 Stavanger
Norway
Tel: +47 51 54 00 64
Email: terbergs@online.no

Sandefjord Roklubb
Postboks 386
3201 Sandefjord
Norway
Tel: +47 33 45 36 88
Email: trogun@online.no

Sarpsborg Roklubb
Postboks 1009 Valaskjold
1705 Sarpsborg
Norway
Email: Sarpsborg-roklubb@sensewave.com

Skvetten Roklubb
Grønevikveien 9
5515 Haugesund
Norway
Tel: +47 95 94 07 87
Email: ankv21@hotmail.com
www.angelfire.com/fl/Askeland

Stavanger Roklub
Postboks 652
4003 Stavanger
Norway
Email: ssa@mento.no
www.stavanger-roklub.no

Trondhjems Roklub
Postboks 794
7408 Trondheim
Norway
Email: styret@trondhjems-roklub.org
www.trondhjems-roklub.org

Tønsberg Roklub
Postboks 121
3101 Tønsberg
Norway
Tel: +47 33 31 41 03
Email: tbgro@start.no

Voss Roklubb
v/Arnfinn Halrynjo
Skulestadvegen 120
5710 Skulestadmo
Norway
Tel: +47 95 10 89 05
Email: voss_roklubb@hotmail.com

Aalesunds Roklub
Postboks 724, Sentrum
6001 Ålesund
Norway
Email: akefisk@online.no
www.roklubb.no

Årungen Ro- og Kajakklubb
Postboks 208
1431 Ås
Norway
Tel: +47 64 94 23 29
Fax: +47 64 98 38 01
Email: aamundst@online.no

Pakistan

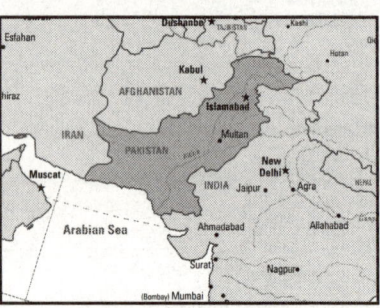

NATIONAL FEDERATION

Pakistan Rowing Federation
25 C Faisal Town
Custom House
Lahore, Pakistan
Tel: +92 42 7725280
Fax: +92 42 7701508
Email: ntc1@paknet2.ptc.pk

Palestine

Palestine Rowing Federation is a FISA and IOC recognized national governing body.

HISTORY

Little is known about the history of Palestinian rowing in Palestine prior to 1948. Part of the work of the Palestinian Rowing Federation is to reconstruct some of that history. What is known about rowing in Palestine seems to be documented primarily by the Israeli Rowing Federation. According to the Israeli Rowing Federation, in the 1930s a group of German Jews fled Nazi persecution with their boats, claiming that they were traveling to a race abroad. They settled in the Tel Aviv area and founded a rowing club on a river near Tel Aviv called the Jerasheh by Palestinians or Yarkon by Israelis. The Ramat Aviv district of Tel Aviv envelopes the river today and the Tel Aviv Rowing Club, which also serves as the headquarters of the Israeli Rowing Federation on Ushisskin Street, is still located in the approximate area of its founding in the 1930s.

Interviews with Palestinians indicate that the sport of rowing was also present in the Haifa and Tiberias districts associated with the British Palestine Police force, but this information has yet to be verified through historical research. For certain we know that rowing as a traditional activity was associated with many of the coastal, fluvial, and lakeside villages and cities as a part of daily life, as many of these villages depended on fishing and shipping as part of their livelihood.

Today, there are no rowing clubs in the West Bank because the Jordan River is an international border with military buffer zones on both sides. Thus, much of the river is inaccessible to the communities that live alongside it. Furthermore, much of the Jordan River has reduced in size and depth due to the pumping of water from the river. The Jordan River dumps into the Dead Sea, part of which is in the West Bank, however, its high mineral and saline content make it unsuitable for rowing due to buoyancy factors, material degeneration, and safety concerns.

In the Gaza Strip there are two rowing clubs that are less than a year old. The Palestinian Rowing Federation was founded in 1998 and became an affiliated member of FISA, the Asian Rowing Federation, and the Arab Rowing Federation in 2000. It sent a women's single scull to the 2002 and 2003 FISA Junior World Championships and began the introduction of rowing into the Gaza Strip in the winter of 2003 with an indoor program at two clubs in Shaati refugee camp with 75,000 residents, to the northwest of Gaza City. The Palestinian Rowing Federation plans to introduce on-the-water, coastal rowing to the community in the summer of 2004 and offer flat water rowing opportunities abroad in the summer of 2005 through sport and cultural exchange programs with other national rowing federations.

Internet Links:
www.palestinerowing.org
www.palestinesports.org
www.palestineolympic.org
www.palsport.org

REGIONS

1948 Territories/Israel (1948 to present): Safad, Acre, Haifa, Nazareth, Tiberias, Bisan, Tel Aviv (Jaffa), Al Ramlah, Ber Sheva. Best time to visit: Depending on the region.

West Bank (post-1993 Oslo Accords): Jenin, Tubas, Tulkarm, Nablus, Salfit, Jericho, Ramallah, Jerusalem (East), Bethlehem, Hebron. Best time to visit: Summer for hot days and cool mountain nights. There is no rowing in the West Bank.

Gaza Strip (post-1993 Oslo Accords): Jabalya, Gaza, Deir Al Balah, Khan Younis, Rafah. Best Time to Visit: Winter for the cooler weather, July through October for the coastal rowing. Temperature: January 11-19.9°C, February 8-18°C, March 10-19°C, April 13-23.1°C, May 17-26°C, June 20-29°C, July 23-31°C, August 22-31°C, September 21-30°C, October 19-28°C, November 15-25°C, December 12-21°C.

Did You Know ?

The earliest Palestinian competitive rower of which the Palestinian Rowing Federation is aware is Abdel Rahman Bushnaq, a graduate of the Arab College of Jerusalem and a rower for Jesus College at Cambridge University in the 1930s. While at Cambridge he studied English literature and subsequently published an Arabic translation of The Splendid Spur by Sir Arthur Thomas Quiller-Couch.

NATIONAL FEDERATION

Palestinian Rowing Federation
c/o Palestine Olympic Committee
PO Box 469
Gaza City, Palestine
Tel: +970 8 282 9222
Fax: +970 8 282 4742
Email: sanhaddad_@hotmail.com

Panama

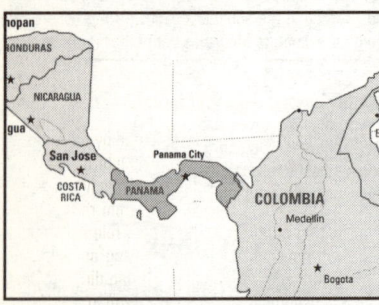

NATIONAL FEDERATION

Unión Panameña de Remo Aficionado
Apartado 2628
Balboa
Ancón, Panama
Tel: (507) 225-3962
Fax: (507) 232-8377
Email: ntc1@paknet2.ptc.pk

Paraguay

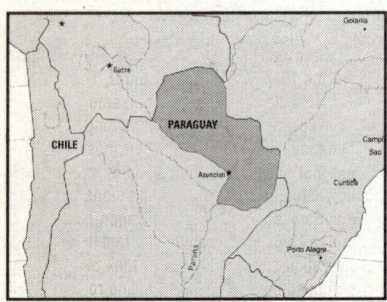

NATIONAL FEDERATION

Federación Paraguaya de Remo
Casilla de Correo de la Fepare No 2244
Asunción, Paraguay
Tel: +595 21 80375
Fax: +595 21 445615
Email: feparemo@hotmail.com

Peru

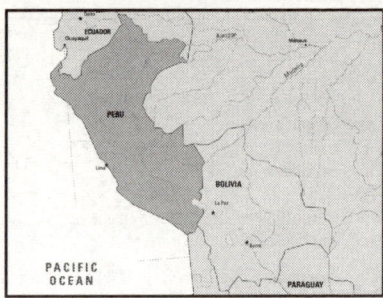

HISTORY

The first rowing club that was established in Peru was the Regatas Club of Lima on April 26, 1875. The earliest regatta was held in 1876 with coxed fours. According to the story, Peru's war hero, Admiral Miguel Grau, at the resort called Chorrillos, refereed it. During subsequent years, more clubs were established; the United Regatas Club in 1890 and the Society of Italian Canottieri in 1907 until the Peruvian Federation of Rowing was established on November 11, 1928.

Peru entered a double at the 1960 Olympics in Rome and the Olympics in Mexico City in 1968. At the Olympics held in Los Angeles, a double and a coxed pair rowed. Peruvian scullers participated in the Junior World Cup in 2000 and 2001 coming in 5th and 6th place respectively, in the finals.

Rowing is located in Lima, the Callao province, the district of La Punta, and on the sea. There are about 200 people between the ages of 11 and 24 who row. Peru participates in masters rowing at the world level and has performed very well in the last 12 years; 15 to 20 rowers practice it.

NATIONAL FEDERATION

Federación Peruana de Remo Amateur
Estadio Nacional Pta N 4 Tribuna Occidente
1er. Piso
Lima, Peru
Tel: +51 1 433 6660
Fax: +51 1433 6660
Email: vapaf@millicom.com.pe

CLUBS

APC Mater Purissima
Av. de la Aviación
445/Calle José Gálvez # 999
Miraflores, Lima
Peru
Tel: +51 (511) 445-6828

Circolo Sportivo Italiano-Societa
Canottieri Italia
Avenida Bolognesi # 865
La Punta - Callao
Peru
Contact: Atilio Cogorno Cogorno, President
Tel: +51 (511) 429-3780

Club de Regatas Lima
Avenida Chachi Dibos # 1201
Chorrillos, Lima
Peru
Contact: Ernesto Flechelle Reppó, President
Tel: +51 (511) 429-2994

Club Universitario de Regatas
Plaza Gálvez S/N
La Punta - Callao
Peru
Contact: Luis Bello, President
Tel: +51 (511) 429-8453

Escuela Naval del Peru
Calle Medina S/N
La Punta - Callao
Peru
Contact: Héctor Soldi Soldi, Director
Tel: +51 (511) 465-3565

Liga Provincial de Remo de Jauja
Jauja, Junín
Contact: Atilio Gutiérrez Ampuero, President
Tel: +51 (064) 36-2149

Philippines

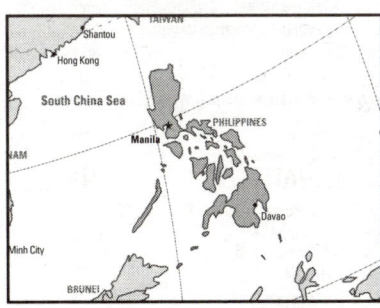

NATIONAL FEDERATION

Amateur Rowing Assn of the Philippines Inc.
2442 Havana Street
PO Box 259 Sta. Ana 1009
Manila, Phillipines
Tel: +63 2 563 3529
Fax: +63 2 816 7441

Poland

HISTORY

The first club in Warsaw was founded by Germans in 1872 and was called Rivers Yacht Club. In 1878, the first Polish sport club was built in Warsaw, Warsaw Rowing Association, which, apart from recreational and sporting activities had a strong role in the fight for Polish nationality. The next rowing associations developed first in cities under Russian direction and then in those under Austrian and German command, KW 04 Poznan in 1904 and PTW "Tryton" Poznan in 1912. There was a very dynamic development of new school clubs in the western part of Poland where many young people had a chance to become familiar with the sport of rowing.

The activity of many rowing clubs in Poland in the first decade of twentieth century led to a need of cooperation between the clubs. In 1908, the Regatta Interclub Commission was founded - it was the forerunner of the Polish Rowing Federation which was founded in 1919. Besides rowing regattas, before World War I, the Regatta Interclub Commission also organized rowing excursions.

In 1939, there were 73 clubs in 41 cities. The strongest clubs came from Warsaw, Bydgoszcz, Poznan and Kraków. This period of time represented dynamic growth in rowing tourism, as well as long and standard distance regattas. Of course, the most important thing at that time was participation in the National Championships, European Championships and Olympic Games. The third stage began after World War II. The 1950's were a very important time when a reorganization of sport structures took place. Many clubs stopped their activities including rowing clubs in schools. From 1945-1999, 64 clubs had been formed; unfortunately, many of them after a few years were forced to end their activity. In 1995, the Pupils Sport Clubs was established. Currently, the Polish Rowing Federation has 36 associations and clubs, 3 sports school and 45 Pupils Sport Clubs.

Internet links:
www.pztw.neostrada.pl

Did You Know ?

The oldest club in Poland, Warsaw Rowing Association, was organized in 1878. The Polish Rowing Association was created in 1919.

PERSONALITIES

Teodor Kocerka: (1927-1999) Two-time Royal Henley Regatta winner; five medals at the European Championships, champion in 1958; two bronze medals at the Olympic Games in Helsinki-1952 and Rome-1960; nineteen times national champion.

Roger Verey: Seven medals at the European Championships, two gold medals in single scull and double sculls in Berlin-1935; bronze medal at the Olympic Games in Berlin-1936.

Kajetan Broniewski: Born in 1963, won a bronze medal at the Olympic Games in Barcelona-1992 and at the World Championships in Vienna-1990.

Robert Sycz: Born in 1973, two-time World Champion in lightweight double scull: Aiguebelette-1997 and Cologne-1998; Olympic Champion in Sydney-2000, Royal Henley Regatta winner.

Tomasz Kucharski: Born in 1975, two-time World Champion in lightweight double scull: Aiguebelette-1997 and Cologne-1998; Olympic Champion in Sydney-2000, Royal Henley Regatta winner.

NATIONAL FEDERATION

Polish Rowing Federation
Ceglowska St. 68/70
Warszawa, 1 809
Poland
Tel: +48 22 669 0991
Fax: +48 22 834 0132
Email: biuropztw@pztw.neostrada.pl
www.pztw.neostrada.pl

CLUBS

AZS-AWF Gdansk
ul. Czyzewskiego 29
80-336 Gdansk-Oliwa
Poland
Tel/Fax: +48 058-5524721
BH: 80-444 Gdansk ul. Siennicka 5
Tel: +48 058-3013922

KS AZS-AWF Gorzow Wielkopolski
ul. Mysliborska 36
66-400 Gorzow Wlkp.
Poland
Tel: +48 095 - 727 92 81
Fax: +48 095 - 727 92 83
Email: azsawf@poczta.onet.pl

AZS-AWF Krakow
ul. Sniadeckich 12b
31-531 Krakow
Poland
Tel: +48 012-4210377
Tel/Fax: +48 012-4211547

AZS-AWF Poznan
ul. sw. Rocha 9
61-135 Poznan 51
Poland
Tel: +48 061-8771557
Tel/Fax: +48 061-8771390
BH: ul. Piastowska 40
61-556 Poznan
Tel: +48 061-8330293

AZS AWF Warszawa
ul. Marymoncka 34
01-868 Warszawa
Poland
Tel: +48 022-8343704
Fax +48 022-8640958

AZS Politechnika Wroclaw
ul. Wybrzeze Wyspianskiego 27
50-370 Wroclaw
Poland
Tel: +48 071-3202609
Fax: +48 071-3203402
BH: ul. Wybrzeze Wyspianskiego 40
50-370 Wroclaw
Tel: +48 071-3203931
www.wioslarstwo.azs.pwr.wroc.pl/

AZS Szczecin
ul. Boh. Warszawy 55
70-070 Szczecin
Poland
Tel: +48 091-4494504
Fax: +48 091-4841800
BH: ul. Hejki 4
70-070 Szczecin
Tel: +48 091-4624927

AZS Torun
ul. Gagarina 35
87-100 Torun
Poland
Tel: +48 056-6542880
Fax: +48 056-6195286
BH: ul. Ks. Popieluszki 1
87-100 Torun
Tel: 056-6228875

Bydgoski Klub Wioslarek
ul. Babia Wies 13
85-024 Bydgoszcz
Poland
Tel: +48 052-3712654/ 052-3712681

Bydgoskie Towarzystwo Wioslarskie
Bydgoszcz 1 skr. poczt. 195
85-030 Bydgoszcz
Poland
Tel/Fax: +48 052-3484357

Chelmzynskie Towarzystwo Wioslarskie 1927
ul. 3 Maja 14
87-140 Chelmza
Poland
Tel: +48 0601-991270

Gdanski Klub Wioslarski "Drakkar"
ul. Sienna 37
80-605 Gdansk
Poland
Tel/Fax: +48 058-3042266

Kaliskie Towarzystwo Wioslarskie
ul. Park Miejski 2
62-800 Kalisz
Poland
Tel/Fax: +48 062-7574669
BH: ul. Wal Piastowski 1
63-800 Kalisz
Tel: +48 062-7573379

Kolejowy Klub Sportowy "Gedania"
ul. Kosciuszki 49
80-445 Gdansk
Poland
Tel: +48 058-3085048-49
Fax: +48 058-3446014
BH: ul. Pastoriusza 1
80-707 Gdansk
Tel: +48 058-3085021

Klub Wioslarski "Wisla"
ul. Portowa 8
86-300 Grudziadz
Poland
Tel: +48 056-6430324/ 056-6430318

Klub Sportowy "Wir"
ul. Kard. Wyszynskiego 12
14-200 Ilawa
Poland
Tel: +48 089-6486499/ 089-6486917

Klub Wioslarski "Goplo"
Polwysep Rzepowskiskr. poczt. 33
88-150 Kruszwica
Poland
Tel/Fax: +48 052-3515230

Klub Sportowy "Sokol"
ul. Slowackiego 40
14-100 Ostroda
Poland
Tel/Fax: +48 089-6463231

Klub Sportowy"Posnania"
ul. Slowianska 78
61-644 Poznan
Poland
Tel: +48 061-8278000
Fax: +48 061-8206101
BH: ul. Wioslarska 72
61-136 Poznan
Tel: +48 061-8770585

Klub Wioslarski z 1904 r.
ul. Piastowska 40
61-556 Poznan
Poland
Tel/Fax: +48 061-8330293

Kolejowy Klub Sportowy "Unia"
ul. Nadbrzezna 15
83-110 Tczew
Poland

Klub Uczelniany Azs Wshe
ul. Okrzei 94
87-800 Wloclawek
Poland
Tel: +48 054-2363755
Fax: +48 054-2368217

Miedzyszkolny Osrodek Sportowy
ul. Grunwaldzka 10
19-300 Elk
Poland
Tel/Fax: +48 087-6104872

Miedzyszkolny Osrodek Sportowy Nr 2
ul. Wal Miedzeszynski 397
03-942 Warszawa
Poland
Tel/Fax: +48 022-617885

Plockie Towarzystwo Wioslarskie
ul. J. Kawieckiego 1a
09-402 Plock
Poland
Tel/Fax: +48 024-2624924
Email: info@ptw.org.pl
www.ptw.org.pl/

Poznanskie Towarzystwo Wioslarzy "Tryton"
ul. Piastowska 38
61-556 Poznan
Poland
Tel: +48 061-8333665
Fax: +48 061-8334287

RTW "Bydgostia - Kabel"
ul. Zupy 4
85-026 Bydgoszcz
Poland
Tel/Fax: +48 052-3712760
www.bydgostia.org.pl/index.php

Szczecinskie Towarzystwo Wioslarskie
ul. Malczewskiego 10/12
41-616 Szczecin
Poland
Tel: +48 091-4240001 w. 340
Tel/Fax: +48 091-4835146

Towarzystwo Wioslarzy "Polonia"
ul. Wioslarska 74
61-136 Poznan
Poland
Tel/Fax: +48 061-8773630

Tomaszowskie Towarzystwo Wioslarskie
Maz. ul. Legionow 25
97-200 Tomaszow
Poland
Tel/Fax: +48 044-7246631

Torunski Klub Sportowo -Turystyczny "Budowlani"
ul. Majdany 1
87-100 Torun
Poland
Tel/Fax: +48 056-6548207

Waleckie Towarzystwo Kajakowe "Orzel"
ul. Chlodna 9
78-600 Walcz
Poland
Tel: +48 067-387 3575

Warszawskie Towarzystwo Wioslarskie
ul. Zaruskiego 12
00-468 Warszawa
Poland
Tel: +48 022-6215976
Fax: +48 022-6285354
BH: ul. Wioslarska 6
Warszawa
Tel: +48 022-6281722

Wojskowy Klub Sportowy "Zawisza"
ul. Gdanska 163
85-915 Bydgoszcz
Poland
Tel/Fax: +48 052-3410224
BH: ul. Mennica 12
85-112 Bydgoszcz
Tel: +48 052-3224777

Wloclawskie Towarzystwo Wioslarskie
ul. Piwna 3
87-800 Wloclawek
Poland
Tel/Fax: +48 054-2363755

Yacht Club Nowa Huta
ul. Grzegorzecka 17
31-532 Krakow
Poland
Fax: +48 012-4221245

Portugal

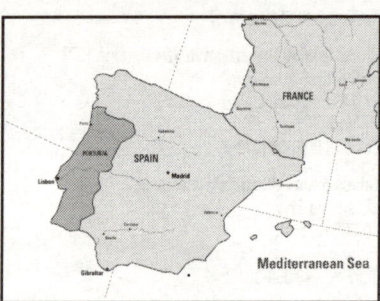

HISTORY

In the year of 1850, the first rowing regatta took place on the Tagus River, near Lisbon. In the south, rowing started under the influence of royalty, and in the north, rowing was started by British influence under the umbrella business of Oporto wine.

Near the end of the nineteenth century, five clubs were active. The races were regionally based; suddenly, in 1904, the Lisbon Cup, a national event took place that shaped Portuguese rowing until today. In the 1920's, the national rowing convention, held in Oporto, created the Portuguese Rowing Federation. A national calendar took shape and the city of Figueira da Foz and the Mondego River become the focus of international events.

A large number of clubs were founded through 1960. Almost all the cities with a river near the Atlantic Ocean had a rowing club with in-rigger boats and out-rigger boats. Due to the national sport policies, rowing became a sport offered to young people in school. So, besides club races, school races were very popular and rowing consistently grew year by year. Railways and trucks transported boats transported all around the country. With strong public investment in dams, new events took place in non-traditional rowing centers. Regular participation in the Olympics has taken place since 1948, mainly in fours and eights due to the competition between two main rowing centers: Aveiro and Caminha.

From 1960 to 1974, sport generally and rowing in particular, suffered. The geography was changing in Africa because of colonial conflicts, but, with a new democratic regime, women's rowing appeared on the agenda. Clubs that were previously part of schools now opened to community and youth rowing. The eighties saw the increase of clubs and rowers. The national team concept brought with it a national development policy for rowing.

Today, rowing is a competitive sport open to the community on a formal and informal basis. In addition to water rowing, indoor rowing is very popular and is offered at leading fitness centres. With this approach and the help of low cost, durable equipment, rowing becomes a sport for all and an option for a life sport. Besides competitive rowing, new forms of rowing are now available for adaptive rowers and groups of rowers with special needs.

INTERNET LINKS
www.remoluso.com

REGIONS

Associacao de Viana do Castelo
Rowing areas: Vila Nova de Cerveira, Caminha, Viana do Castelo; Winter: 10°C;
Summer: 28°C; March, Taça Presidente da Republica (Caminha, long distance, 8+); August, Troféu Nossa Senhora Agonia (Viana Castelo, 2000m, all boats)

Associação do Porto
Rowing areas: Vila do Conde, Porto, Gondomar, Régua, S.João Pesqueira; Winter 12°C; Summer: 30°C; December, Regata do Natal (Porto, long distance, 8+); May (Gondomar, International Regata, 2000m all boats)

Associação da Beira Litoral
Rowing areas: Aveiro, Cacia, Coimbra, Montemor-O-Velho, Figueira da Foz ; Winter
12°C; Summer: 30°C; January, Regata Rota da Luz (Aveiro, long distance, 8+); May (Coimbra, International Queima das Fitas, 1000m/2000m all boats)

Associação de Lisboa
Rowing areas: Lisboa
Winter: 15°C; Summer: 32°C; May (Lisbon, National Regata in rigger-yolle de mer , 2000m 4+ and 8+)

Associação de Setubal
Rowing areas: Barreiro, Setubal, Faro (Algarve)
Winter:15°C; Summer: 35°C; no major rowing events.

Did You Know ?

Associação Naval de Lisboa is the oldest Portuguese rowing club-founded in 1856. "Rowing With No Limits" is a program run by the Portuguese Rowing Federation for promoting alternative rowing for community rowing, adaptive rowing, and rowing for special populations. The Douro Tour is a 110-kilometer tour rowed over a week in fours on the upper part of Douro River and through the vineyards of Oporto

wine. The Portuguese Rowing Federation organizes it every two years.

NATIONAL FEDERATION

Federaçao Portugueasa de Remo
Doca de Sto. Amaro (Alcantara)
1350-353 Lisboa
Portugal
Tel: +351-1-392-9840/6
Fax: +351-1-392-9849
Email: remofp@mail.telepac.pt
Contact: Mr. Fernando Estima

CLUBS

ARCO - Associação de Remadores P/Competicao
R. Padre Antonio Vieira
4900-394 Viana do Castelo
Portugal
Tel: +351 258 822 242
Fax: +351 832 690

Associaçao Academica de Coimbra
R. Padre Antonio Vieira
3000 - 315 Coimbra
Portugal

Tel: +351 239 410 401
Fax: +351 239 410 429
Email: nauticos@aac.uc.pt

Associacao Desportiva Cult. Juv. Cerveira
Apartado 51
4920 Vila Nova de Cerveira
Portugal
Tel: +351 251 794 632
Fax: +351 251 794 632
Email: adcjremo@hotmail.com

Associacao Desportiva Cult. Portus Cale
R. do Cidral de Baixo, 3
4050 - 196 Porto
Portugal
Tel: +351 222 088 830
Fax: +351 222 088 830

Associacao Fernao Mendes Pinto
R. Dr. Jose Galvao, 211
3140 - Montemor-o-Velho
Portugal

Tel: +351 239 687 170
Fax: +351 239 687 175
Email: desporto@afmp.pt

Associacao Naval 1º de Maio
Apartado 2052 Jardim
3080 - 036 Figueira da Foz
Portugal
Tel: +351 233 422 809
Fax: +351 233 428 897

Associacao Naval de Lisboa
Doca de St°. Amaro
1350 - 353 Lisboa
Portugal
Tel: +351 213 960 488
Fax: +351 213 957 252
Email: anlisboa@clix.pt

Centro Desportivo Universitario do Porto
R. da Boa Hora, 20
4050 - 099 Porto
Portugal
Tel: +351 223 393 150
Fax: +351 222 080 089
Email: cdup@aeiou.pt

Clube de Caca e Pesca do Alto Douro
R. Jose Vasques Osorio, 16
5050 Peso da Regua
Portugal
Tel: +351 254 322 523
Fax: +351 254 313 581
Email: ccpad@hotmail.com

Clube dos Galitos
Praca Dr. Melo de Freitas
3800 - 158 Aveiro
Portugal
Tel: +351 234 423 807
Fax: +351 234 423 807

Clube Ferroviario de Portugal
Doca de Sto. Amaro
1350 - 353 Lisboa
Portugal
Tel: +351 213 968 066
Fax: +351 213 968 066

Clube Fluvial Vilacondense
Av³. Jose Regio, 13
4480 - 671 Vila do Conde
Portugal
Tel: +351 252 631 613
Fax: +351 252 645 956

Clube Nautico da Praia de Mira
Apartdao 34
3070 Mira
Portugal
Tel: +351 231 472 204

Clube Nautico de Viana
Lugar da Argacosa
4900 Viana do Castelo
Portugal
Tel: +351 258 842 165
Fax: 258 824 085

Clube Naval Barreirense
Praia Norte
2830 Barreiro
Portugal
Tel: +351 212 073 779
Fax: +351 212 060 974

Clube Naval de Lisboa
Cais do Gás H
1200 Lisboa
Portugal
Tel: +351 213 469 354
Fax: +351 213 429 332

Clube Naval Infante D.Henrique
R. Dr. Joaquim M. da Costa, 511
4420 Valbom gdm
Portugal
Tel: +351 224 833 954
Fax: +351 224 673 860

Clube Naval Setubalense
Praça da Republica
2900 - 587 Setubal
Portugal
Tel: +351 265 523 915
Fax: +351 265 522 756
Email: clubenavalsetubalense@iol.pt

Colectividade Popular de Cacia
R. Dr. Marques da Costa, 120
3800 - 596 Cacia
Portugal
Tel: +351 234 913 992
Fax: +351 234 914 234
Email: colcacia@mega.mail.pt

Ginasio Clube Figueirense
Av³. 1° de Maio
3080 - 011 Figueira da Foz
Portugal
Tel: +351 233 418 765
Fax: +351 233 426 422
Email: ginasiofigueirense@sapo.pt

Ginasio Clube Naval de Faro
Doca de Faro
8000 Faro
Portugal
Tel: +351 289 823 434
Fax: +351 289 807 604
Email: ginasiocnaval@mail.telepac.pt

Grupo Desportivo Ferroviarios do Barreiro
Av³. Batalhao Sapadores dos Caminhos de Ferro
2830-303 Barreiro
Portugal
Tel: +351 212 073 636
Fax: 212 073 860
Email: gdfbarreiro@clix.pt

Grupo Desportivo Fabril do Barreiro
Estadio Alfredo da Silva
2830 Barreiro
Portugal
Tel: +351 212 026 912
Fax: +351 212 046 566

Real Clube Fluvial Portuense
Rua Aleixo da Mota, S/N
4150 - 044 Porto
Portugal
Tel: +351 223 752 486
Fax: 226 172 219
Email: clubefluvialportuense@clix.pt

Sport Club do Porto
Av. Diogo Leite, 290
4400 - 111 Vila Nova de Gaia
Portugal
Tel: +351 223 792 541
Fax: +351 223 792 541
Email: sportremo@hotmail.com

Sporting Club Caminhense
Praca Conselheiro Silva Torres
4910 Caminha
Portugal
Tel: +351 258 921 010
Fax: +351 258 921 010

Puerto Rico

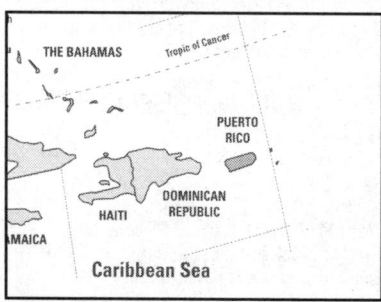

NATIONAL FEDERATION

Puerto Rico Rowing Federation
PO Box 366123
Attn. I.H. Herrero III
San Juan, PR 936
Puerto Rico
Tel: (787) 758 2526
Fax: (787) 754-6698
Email: herreroilll@microjuris.com

Qatar

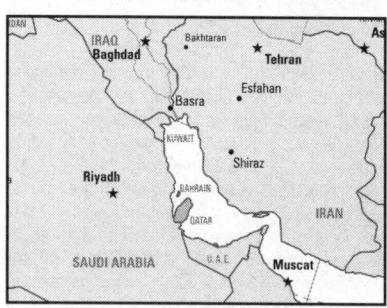

NATIONAL FEDERATION

Qatar Marine Sports Foundation
PO Box 23311
Doha, Qatar
Tel: +974 493 1199
Fax: +974 483 0014
Email: sailing@qatar.net.qa
www.qmsf.org

Romania

HISTORY

History of Romanian rowing dates from the nineteenth century. In 1864, when a group of young students from Timisoara in Western Romania, returned from abroad, they had completed their studies and founded for pleasure the society of little traditional boats, Regatta. Here they practiced rowing as a pastime. In the beginning, the difficulties were many and the rudimentary boats that they had were stored in a wooden shed on the bank of the Bega channel. Between 1910 and 1912, a pavilion was constructed that still hosts the local rowing clubs. In 1879, the Gymnastics Society in Arad was founded and in 1890, the activity of the club expanded to include a rowing section marking the first official rowing club in Romania. In the same year, another club in Arad, Muresul Club, opened its doors to the rowing enthusiasts. World War I interrupted the rowing activity in Romania for several years and resumed again in 1918 as one of the most popular sports among young people.

The first National Rowing Championship was organized by the Muresul Club in 1923 and took place in Arad. The event triggered a national phenomenon and new clubs were created to accommodate the large number of rowing fans. In 1926, one of these clubs, the Hellas Sport Club was the first to welcome women to rowing. In 1925, the Commission for Nautical Sports was founded as a member of the Sport Societies of Romania and in 1927 officially joined FISA. In 1931, the Commission for Nautical Sports was renamed and relocated to Bucharest. The popularization of rowing continued and more then twenty new clubs opened during the period of 1928-1938.

During the World War II, rowing sojourned but quickly resumed in 1945 with the revival of the annual national championships. In 1950, specialized athletic schools started to appear and scouts began nationwide searches for athletic young pupils to enroll in elite development programs. The first Romanian participation in an official international competition was in 1932 at the European Championships in Belgrade, Yugoslavia. Romania took part in the Olympic Games for first time in Helsinki-1952 with its men's eight. The first gold medal was won at the European Championships in Gand-1955 in the men's quadruple sculls with the crew: Stefan Pongracz, Anton Senceac, Stefan Somogyi and Rady Nicolae. In 1962, at the European Championships in Grunay, the four with coxswain comprised of Ana Tamao, Emilia Rigard, Florica Ghiuzelea, Lia Bulugioiu and Stefania Borisov were the first to win a women's gold medal. The first Olympic gold medal was won at the Moscow Games in 1980 and since then the Romanian team has not missed an Olympic Games without a winning a medal. Today, the Romanian team is established as one of the leading powers in the rowing world with strong traditions in the women's events.

REGIONS

Transylvania: Arad, Timisoara, Deva, Tirgu Mures, Oradea. Avg. temp: Winter: 2C-10°C; Spring: 4C- 20°C; Summer: 18C - 28°C; Fall: 12C to 19°C.

Moldova: Iasi, Bacau, Focsani Avg. temp: Winter: -10- 2°C; Spring: 3-16°C; Summer: 18 -25°C; Fall: 9-17°C.

Muntenia: Avg. temp: Winter -9-5°C; Spring: 4-17°C; Summer: 20-26°C; Fall: 14-20°C.

Oltenia: Bucharest, Brasov, Ploiesti Avg. temp: Winter -25°C; Spring 4-16°C; Summer: 19-24°C; Fall: 16-21°C.

Dobrogea: Constanta, Tulcea Avg. temp: Winter: -7- 1°C; Spring: 5-16°C; Summer: 19-27°C; Fall: 13-20C

Did You Know ?

Romania has won 32 Olympic medals-15 gold, 10 silver and 7 bronze-plus 97 medals from World Championships-27 gold, 32 Silver and 28 bronze-making it one of the leading powers in today's rowing world.

PERSONALITIES

Toma Valer and Petre Iosub: The first Romanian men's crew to win Olympic gold at the 1984 games.

Doina Ignat: Romania's modern rowing hero, a world and Olympic champion.

Elizabeta Lipa: The legendary Romanian rower declared "the best female rower of all time" and winner of four gold, two silver and one bronze Olympic medals.

Sanda Toma: An invincible female rower in all competitions during the period of 1979-1981, including gold at the 1980 Olympic Games. She raised to and then retired in full glory.

NATIONAL FEDERATION

Fed. Romana de Canotaj
Str. Maior Coravu 34-36
Sector 2
Bucaresti, Romania
Tel: +40 21 324 5852
Fax: +40 21 324 5800
Email: romanianrowing@yahoo.com
www.frcanotaj.ro

CLUBS

Sportive Club Dinamo Bucharest, Romania
sos. Stefan cel Mare 7-9, sector 2
Bucharest, Romania
Tel: +40 0 21 2103519

Sportive Club Of The Army - Steaua
bd. Ghencea 35, sector 6
Bucharest, Romania
Tel: +40 0 21 4130962

Sportive Club Vointa
sos. Pipera 38 sector 1
Bucharest, Romania
Tel: +40 0 21 2329171

Sportive Club Olimpia
sos Iancului 128A, sector 2
Bucharest, Romania
Tel: +40 0 21 2504031

Sportive Club Muresul
Parcul Sportiv Municipal no.4
Targu Mures, Romania
Tel: +40 0 265 120396

Sportive Club Suceava
Bd. 1 Decembrie 1918, no. 7
Suceava, Romania
Tel: +40 0 230 213127

Sportive Club Triumf
str. Strandului 2, sector 2
Bucharest, Romania
Tel: +40 0 21 2241116

Sportive Club Ceahlaul
sos. Stefan cel Mare 53
Piatra Neamt, Romania
Tel: +40 0 0233 214739

Sportive Club Iasi
str. Smardani 5, Iasi
Romania
Tel: +40 0 0232 218743

Clubul Sportiv Farul Constanta
str Decebal 22, Constanta
Romania
Tel: +40 0 0241615370

Russia

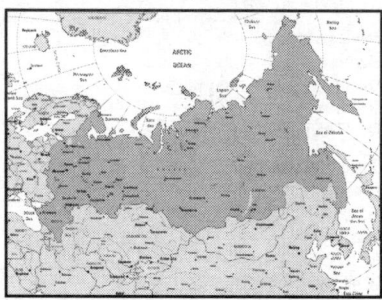

HISTORY

It is believed that the founding of the St. Petersburg Yacht Club on May 21, 1860 marks the beginning of Russia's official rowing history. This was the first organized sport club in Russia, having a charter, an elected president and a board of governors. At this time, St. Petersburg Yacht Club had 183 avid members and 42 rowing shells. On July 12 of the same year, the club initiated the first "Rules for Racing" which defined the various classes of rowing based on the number of rowers and oars per boat. The rules were strict and a special referee committee was appointed to ensure their implementation. Twenty years later, on July 31st, the first national rowing championship open to all rowers was held. All competitors tested their skills over 895 meters and 2,652 meters; results of this regatta are still kept as a historic benchmark.

The establishment of the first rowing club in St. Petersburg and the regular competition attracted many spectators and an increased interest in the sport by vocational rowers. In the next few years, rowing enthusiasts from all corners of Russia, helped establish rowing clubs in Moscow, Riga, Voronezh, Odessa, Saratov and Nikolaev. Three more clubs were established in St. Petersburg and soon the city on the Neva River became the heart of the Russian rowing community. The Moscow River Rowing Club, one of the most prominent clubs in Russia that has left a significant mark on history of the Russian rowing was the founded in 1867. Today Strelka, the modern name of the Moscow River Rowing Club, is a hub for Russia's past and future champions. By 1892, there were twenty-two formal rowing clubs managed by a sophisticated organizational system. In 1872, the first race between the teams of the two largest cities, Moscow and St. Petersburg, was held and it continues to be a major event drawing many fans.

Despite the attempt of the Russian women to receive recognition as athlete rowers and to compete at the open championships in 1886, the by-laws said "women should choose a sport that complies with the norms of social behavior and select only those sports that will leave no impact on their feminine features". Until 1917, rowing gained tremendous popularity and was considered a trendy "gentleman" sport accessible only to some. After the October Revolution, the newly established USSR opened wide the doors of the sports clubs giving many interested young adolescents the opportunity to master the sport. Soon, many young women joined the ranks of the major leagues. Since then, rowing has enjoyed tremendous popularity and Russia has managed to become a powerhouse for elite athletes.

Every September since 1950, Moscow hosts one of the longest and most spectacular regattas in the world, a 25-kilometer challenge on the Moscow River. In preparation for the 1980 Olympic Games, Moscow developed a revolutionary design for an Olympic-size rowing canal in Kryilatskoe that has become a standard for all modern rowing sites.

REGIONS

Russia is the largest country in the world; spread over 11 time zones with diverse geography. Rowing is concentrated mainly in the eastern part of the country.

Moscow: Avg. temp: Winter: December-February -4 to -12°C; Spring: March-May: 6-17°C; Summer: June-August 11-24°C; Fall: September-November -4-14°C.

St. Petersburg: Avg. temp: Winter: December-February -9 to -4°C; Spring: March-May -4-16°C; Summer: June-August 7-25°C; Fall: September-November -2-13°C.

Rostov-na-Don: Avg. temp: Winter: December-February -3 to -14°C; Spring: March-May -4-15°C; Summer: June-August 16-23°C; Fall: September-November -3-16°C.

Krasnodar: Avg. temp: Winter: December-February -3-2°C; Spring: March-May 5- 17°C; Summer: June-August 21-28°C; Fall: September-November 5-20°C.

Saratov: Avg. temp: Winter: December-February -4 to -11°C; Spring: March-May -4-16°C; Summer: June-August 14-27°C; Fall: September-November -1-10°C.

Did You Know ?

Vyacheslav Ivanov is one of the most memorable personalities in the rowing world preceding Steve Redgrave. Ivanov won three consecutive Olympic gold medals in men's single in a dramatic come from behind style, usually in the last 300 meters of the race.

PERSONALITIES

Mikhail Kuzik: The first prominent figure in the Russian rowing. Kuzin raced throughout Europe and won some of the most prestigious prizes in the history of rowing. In 1913, Mikhail Kuzik was the first foreigner ever to win the prestigious Oxford's Blue Rower, an Oxford University regatta that dates back to 1853.

Vyacheslav Ivanov: Three-time Olympic Gold medallist, one of the Russia's most cherished athletes; among the first to be inducted in the FISA Hall of Fame.

NATIONAL FEDERATION

Russian Rowing Federation
Loujnetskaia Nab 8
Moscow, 119871
Russia
Tel: +7 095 201 0465
Fax: +7 095 201 0128
Email: frowrus@cityline.ru

CLUBS

Energy Rowing Club
Deputatskaia ul., 15
S.Petersburg, 197042
Russia
Tel: +7 (812) 235-4617

Krasny Oktiabr
Bolotnaja nab.,d.1
Moscow, 10907
Russia
Tel: +7 (095) 296-3553

Rowing canal, Don
Levy bereg Dona
Rostov-na-Donu, 344007
Russia
Tel: +7 (863) 240-1310
Fax: +7 (863) 405065

Rowing School Pechory
Sennaia square, 2
Nijni Novgorod, 603024
Russia
Tel: +7 (831) 236-8529
Fax: +7 (831) 36 84 00

Rowing School
Tchernychevskogo Str.,184
Saratov, 410002
Russia
Tel: +7 (845) 273-4084

Rowing School
Nutnaia St., 2
V. Novgorod, 173000
Russia
Tel: +7 (816) 223-6294

Rowing School Spartak
Starokubanskaia St., 1/1
Krasnodar, 350058
Russia
Tel: +7 (861) 233-4676

Dinamo Rowing Club
Tamanskaya Str., 1/1
Moscow 123103
Russia
Tel: +7 (095) 968-1433
Email: robosoc@rol.ru

Samoa

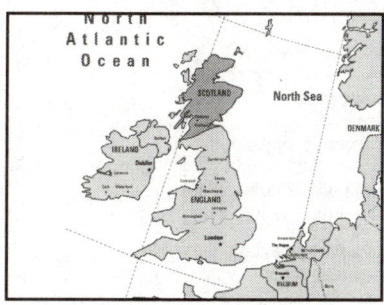

NATIONAL FEDERATION

Samoan Rowing Association
PO Box 1330
Apia, Samoa
Tel: +685 26701
Fax: +685 26366

Scotland

NATIONAL FEDERATION

Scottish Amateur Rowing Association
41 Dumyat Avenue
Cambuspark, Tullibody
Clackmannanshire FK10 2RY
Scotland
Tel: +44 01259 216923
Email: marymassro@aol.com
www.scottish-rowing.org.uk/

CLUBS

Aberdeen Boat Club
New Boathouse, South Esplanade West
Aberdeen AB119AA
Scotland
Tel: +44 01224 871074
Contact: Fiona Insch
Email: fiona.insch@orange.net

Aberdeen Schools Rowing Association
81 Polmuir Road
Aberdeen AB11 2SJ
Scotland
Contact: Bryan Steel
Tel: +44 01224 585552
Email: steel@dircon.co.uk

Aberdeen University Boat Club
AUBC Sec., Butchart Recreation Centre
University Road
Aberdeen AB9 2UW
Scotland
Contact: Fiona Hunter
Email: u01fjh@abdn.ac.uk

Castle Semple Rowing Club
21 Wallace Ave, Bishopton
Renfrewshire, PA7 5ER
Scotland
Contact: Jeffrey Dodgson
Tel: +44 01505-868172
Email: jeffreydodgson@ukonline.co.uk
http://u01fjh@abdn.ac.uk

Clyde Amateur Rowing Club
Boathouse, The Weir
Glasgow Green G1 5Q
Scotland
Contact: John Gildea
Tel: +44 0141-333-0826
Email: johngildea@hotmail.com

Clyde Masters Rowing Club
Boathouse, The Weir
Glasgow Green G1 5Q
Scotland
Contact: Gordon J Day
Tel: +44 0141 772 3756

Clydesdale Amateur Rowing Club
Boathouse, The Weir
Glasgow Green
Scotland
Contact: Ken Diamond
Tel +44 0141-776-5997
Email: ken_diamond@yahoo.co.uk
http://www.ukclubnet.co.uk/members/rowingworld/clydesdale/

Deeside Scullers Club
27 Westbank Park, Oldmeldrum
Inverurie AB51 0DG
Scotland
Contact: Dr Ron Wallace
Tel: +44 01651 872861
Email: r.wallace@connect-2.co.uk

Dundee University Boat Club
Students Union, Airlie Place
Dundee DD 1 4HN
Scotland
Contact: Dave Shea
Tel: +44 07791 889 268
Email: daveshea1@hotmail.com
http://www.sportsunion.dundee.ac.uk/boatclub/

Edinburgh University Boat Club
c/o Sports Union Office
42 The Pleasance
Edinburgh EH8 9TJ
Scotland
Contact: Caroine Stripp
Email: eubc@ed.ac.uk
http://www.ed.ac.uk/~rowing

Fife Rowing Club
The Cottage, Pilessie Road
Bow of Fife KY15 4MJ
Scotland
Contact: Contact: Julie Smullen
Tel: +44 01337 810426
Email: julie_smullen@curtisfinepapers.com

George Heriots School Rowing Club
1 Kirkhill Gardens
Edinburgh EH16 5DF
Scotland
Contact: R H C Neill
Tel: +44 0131 667 5389
Email: rhcn@george-heriots.com

George Watsons College Rowing Club
2 Viewfield Road
Juniper Green
Edinburgh EH14 5 BE
Scotland
Contact: Jim Ferguson
Tel: +44 0131 453 4164
Email: j.ferguson@gwc.org.uk
http://www.gwc.org.uk/rowing

Glasgow Argonauts Boat Club
65 Park Moor
Erskine PA8 7HL
Scotland
Contact: Paul McAllister
Tel: +44 0141 812 0584)
Email: paul@vetloc.freeserve.co.uk

Glasgow Rowing Club
Silverfir Place
Glasgow G5
Scotland
Contact: Fergus Walker
Tel: +44 0141 357 3203
Email: captain@glasgowrowingclub.org
http://www.glasgowrowingclub.org/

Glasgow Schools Rowing Association
7 Skaterigg Gardens
Jordanhill, Glasgow G13 1ST
Scotland
Tel: +44 0141 954 8374

Glasgow University Boat Club
Stevenson Building, 77 Oakfield Avenue
Glasgow G12 8LT
Scotland
Contact: Andrew Dickie
Email: andrew_dickie20@hotmail.com
http://www.gla.ac.uk/Clubs/Boat/

Glasgow University Ladies Boat Club
Stevenson Building, 77 Oakfield Avenue
Glasgow G12 8LT
Scotland
Contact: Alex Lomas
Email: 0002685l@student.gla.ac.uk
http://www.gla.ac.uk/Clubs/BoatL/

Heriot Watt University Boat Club
Sports Union, Riccarton Campus
Edinburgh EH14 4AS
Scotland
Contact: Martin Cowie
Tel: +44 07779163644
Email: M.Cowie@hw.ac.uk
http://www.hwubc.co.uk/

Inverness Rowing Club
Mid Feabuie, Culloden Moor
Inverness-shire, IV2 5EQ
Scotland
Contact: Paddy Walsh
Tel: +44 01463 792534
Email: walsh@feabuie.freeserve.co.uk
http://www.invernessrowingclub.co.uk/

Loch Ard Rowing Club
Renagour House
Aberfoyle FK8 3TF
Scotland
Contact: James Cowderoy
Tel: +44 01877-387291
Email: James@TheGlassert.com
http://www.lochard.net/

Loch Lomond Amateur Rowing Club
Fisher Wood, Alexandria
Dumbartonshire
Scotland
Contact: Ian Butcher
Email: iangbutcher@tiscali.co.uk

Nithsdale Amateur Rowing Club
Drumcraig,Kirkgunzeon
Dumfries, DG2 8LF
Scotland
Contact: Gordon Blandford
Tel: +44 01387 760669
Email: gordon.blandford@btinternet.com

North British Rowing Club
20 Ann St
Edinburgh EH4 1PJ
Scotland
Tel: +44 0131-332-1233
Fax: +44 0131-315-4563
Email kadean@belfast-ni.club24.co.uk

Robert Gordon University Boat Club
Students Association
60 Schoolhill
Aberdeen AB10 1JQ
Scotland
Contact: Andrew Richardson
Email: rgurowing@hotmail.com

Royal West Of Scotland Boat Club
The Esplanade
Greenock PA16 7SE
Scotland
Tel: +44 01475 723260
Email: rwsabc.esplanade@net.ntl.com

Scottish Schools Rowing Council
1 Kirkhill Gardens
Edinburgh EH16 5DF
Scotland
Tel: +44 0131 667 5389

St Andrew Boat Club
13/4 Dorset Place
Edinburgh EH11 1JQ
Scotland
Contact: Jo Wherrett
Tel: +44 0131 221 9608
Email: jo@standrewboatclub.com
http://www.standrewboatclub.com/

St Andrews University Boat Club
P E Centre, St Leonards Road
St Andrews KY16 9AZ
Scotland
Tel: +44 01334 42 2183
Email: boatclub@st-and.ac.uk
http://www.st-andrews.ac.uk

Stirling Rowing Club
Dean Crescent
Stirling FK8 1UL
Scotland
Tel: +44 01786 450221
http://www.rowing.stirling.co.uk/

Stirling University Rowing Club
Gannochy Pavilion
University of Stirling
Stirling FK9 4LA
Scotland
Tel: +44 01786 461029

Strathclyde Park Rowing Club
President: Martin Gechonis
Tel: +44 01698-459202
Email: martingechonis@tiscali.co.uk
http://www.sprc.freeserve.co.uk/

Strathclyde University Boat Club
Sports Union
90 John Street
Glasgow G1 1JR
Scotland
Contact: Fraser Munro
Tel: +44 07973429625
Email: Wonder_munner@yahoo.com
http://www.sportsunion.strath.ac.uk/Rowing/

Senegal

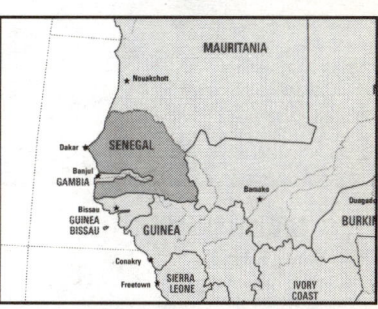

NATIONAL FEDERATION

Fédération Sénégalaise d'Aviron et de Canoé Kayak
BP 11
Dakar, 394
Senegal
Tel: +221 822 1149
Fax: +221 822 1133
Email: adyfall@hotmail.com

Singapore

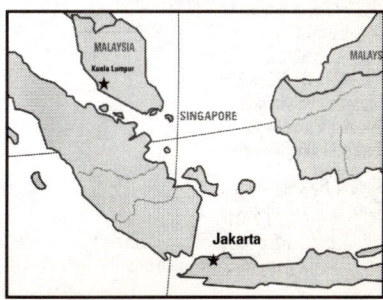

NATIONAL FEDERATION

Singapore Amateur Rowing Association
Blk 113 Serangoon North Ave I
01-579
Singapore, 590113
Tel: 65 281 0537
Fax: 65 281 0538
Email: nicsara@singnet.com.sg
www.sara.org.sg/home01.html

Slovakia

NATIONAL FEDERATION

Slovak Rowing Federation
Junácka 6
Bratislava, 832 80
Slovakia
Tel: +421 749 249 146
Fax: +421 7 49 249 592
Email: denes@veslovanie.sk
www.veslovanie.sk

Piestany Rowing Club
Rekreacná 5, 921 01
Piestany, Slovakia
Tel: +421 (838) 762-4329
Contact: Marián Benedikovic
A. Trajana 10
Bratislava 92101, Slovakia

Slavia Filozof Bratislava
Nevädzová 2/a,
Bratislava 82101, Slovakia
Tel: +421 (07) 433-39810
contact: Lubos Podstupka
Novomestská 44/45
Sered 92600, Slovakia

Sintava Rowing Club
Sintava 92551, Slovakia
Contact: Mr. Michal Lipovsk
Tel: +421 (707) 780-2334

Slavia STU Bratislava
Mokrán záhon 1
Bratislava 82104, Slovakia
Contact: Mr. Alexander Dénes
Tel: +421 (07) 492-4946
Tel: +421 (903) 440 118 cell

Slovak Rowing Club
Viedenská cesta 24,
Bratislava 85105, Slovakia
Tel/Fax: +421 (062) 250-953
Contact: Ing. Matej Vanícek
Astrová 52
Bratislava 82101, Slovakia

Spartak Komarno Rowing Club
Komárno 94501, Slovakia
Contact: Ladislav Lorincz
Hviezdoslavova 1/10
Komárno 94501, Slovakia

Slovenia

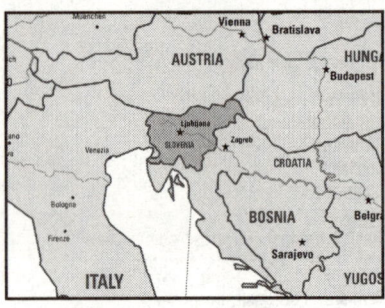

NATIONAL FEDERATION

Rowing Federation of Slovenia
Zupanciceva 9
Bled, 4260
Slovenia
Tel: +386 4 5767 230
Fax: +386 4 574 1017
Email: info@slorowing.com
www.slorowing.com

CLUBS

RC Bled
Zupanciceva 9
4260 Bled
Slovenia
Tel.: +386 4 5767230
Fax: +386 4 5741017
Email: info@vesl-klub-bled.si
www.vesl-klub-bled.si

RC Ljubljanica
Velika colnarska 20
1000 Ljubljana
Slovenia
Fax: +386 1 2523202
Email: info@vesl-klub-ljubljanica.si
www.vesl-klub-ljubljanica.si

RC Dravske elektrarne-Branik of Maribor
Pri motelu 8
2345 Bresternica
Slovenia
Fax: +386 2 6232043

RC Nautilus Koper
Kopalisko nabrezje 3
6000 Koper
Slovenia
Fax: +386 5 6273413

RC Argo Izola
Dantejeva 20
p.p. 18, 6231 Izola
Slovenia
Fax: +386 5 6397976

RC Piran
Seca 115
p.p. 37
Slovenia
6320 Portoroz
Fax: +386 5 6773340
Email: info@vesl-klub-piran.si
Web: www.vesl-klub-piran.si

RC Izola
Tomaziceva 6a
6310 Izola
Slovenia
Fax: +386 5 6605803

South Africa

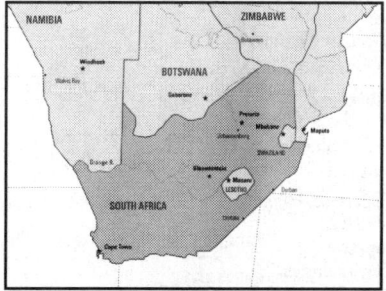

HISTORY

Rowing in South Africa, like cricket and rugby, was an imported pastime of the colonials in the early nine-teenth century. In South Africa, the first formal rowing event dates back to the year 1861. A race between two clubs, the South African Rowing Club and Union Rowing Club, was arranged for six-oared boats over a distance of 4.25 miles. Alfred Rowing Club joined in this competition several years later and the stage was set for annual championships between South Africa's top competitive rowers. South Africa has, in a rather unique manner, distinguished itself by fielding some of the oldest competitors on the international master's rowing circuit. Ernest Gearing, who won the gold medal at the 1996 World Master's Championship, did so just shy of his eightieth birthday.

The Buffalo Grand Challenge Race is South Africa's oldest and most prestigious race. The regatta has been held every year since 1881 with the exception of the war years. In 2004, the regatta will be held for its 117th time. The Buffalo Regatta has been a major highlight on the South African rowing calendar in part due to the two magnificent trophies at stake - the Buffalo Grand Challenge Trophy for senior coxless fours and the Silver Sculls Trophy for senior single sculls. These two cups are commonly regarded as the most valuable rowing trophies in the world. Each is estimated to have a value over $500,000- they are purported to be as tall and weigh as much as a coxswain.

Considering the long regatta history, it is surprising that South Africa's national rowing body took some time to establish. Provincial rowing associations were formed in the early decades of the twentieth century. In 1934, the provincial associations united to establish the South African Amateur Rowing Association in response to the selection requirements for the Olympic Games. The first South African Olympic oarsman was Henry De Kock who rowed at the 1928 Olympic Games. He recently passed away at the age of ninety-two. South Africa regularly fields strong men and women's fours for international competition. Today, rowing enjoys tremendous popularity across South Africa. Rowing in South Africa has come far in recent years with new enthusiasts from diverse backgrounds taking up a common interest in the sport.

REGIONS

Eastern Cape: Port Elizabeth, Rhodes: Avg. temp: Summer: December-February 11-32°C; Fall: March-May 6-31°C; Winter: June-August 3-28°C; Spring: September-November 6-30°C.

Western Cape: Cape Town, Stellenbosch: Avg. temp: Summer: December-February 16-26°C; Fall: March-May 11-24°C; Winter: June-August 9-18°C; Spring September-November 11-22°C.

Gauteng: Johannesburg, Renosterspruit: Avg. temp: Summer: December-February 15-25°C; Fall: March-May 9-23°C; Winter: June-August 6-18°C; Spring: September-November 11-23°C.

Kwazulu Natal: Durban: Avg. temp: Summer: December-February 21-27°C; Fall: March-May: 16-27°C; Winter: June-August 12-22°C; Spring: September-November 17-24°C.

Did You Know ?

The Alfred Rowing Club is the oldest organized sport club in South Africa, established in 1864, and named after Prince Alfred, Duke of Edinburgh who visited Cape Town in 1860.

PERSONALITIES

Henry De Kock: The first South African Olympic oarsman to row at the 1928 Olympic Games.

NATIONAL FEDERATION

Rowing South Africa
PO Box 2563
Parklands, 2121
South Africa
Tel: +27 11 370 3522
Fax: +27 11 836 5509
Email: admin@rowsa.co.za
www.rowsa.co.za

CLUBS (BY REGION)

Alfred RC
South Africa
Contact: Jenni Bowden
Tel: +27 (021) 970-1218
Email: jennibowden@webmail.co.za

Durban RC
PO Box 2384 Durban 4000
South Africa
Contact: Cheryl Smart [Captain]
Tel: +27 (031) 301-4093
Email: cheryl@law.co.za

East London Boating
ELBA Std 050021/08108283501
South Africa
Contact: Rob Myers
Tel: +27 (043) 743-9486

Elgin
PO Box 403 Grabouw 7160
South Africa
Contact: Hans Post
Tel: +27 (021) 859-4334
Email: country@nedclub.co.za

Leander
PO Box 552 East London 5200
South Africa
Contact: Mark Linström
Tel: +27 (043) 740-4556
Email: lindstrom@global.co.za

Old Edwardian
4 Houghton Mansions
South Africa
Contact: Clifford Chaney
Tel: +27 (011) 285-5038
Email: cliffc@hollard.co.za

Boat Club
134 Louis Botha Ave. Yeoville 2198
South Africa
Contact: Jamie Croly

Ravens
PO Box 792 Bedfordview 2008
South Africa
Contact: Heidi Corry (Captain)
Email: heidi@lookandlisten.co.za

Roodeplaat
PO Box 4252 Pretoria 0001
South Africa
Contact: Philip Lutz
Tel: +27 (011) 401-6472
Email: philip.lutz@eu.tenneco-automotive.co.za

Victoria Lake
PO Box 77 Germiston 1400
South Africa
Contact: Peter Glover
Email: pspphg@netactive.co.za

Viking
South Africa
Contact: Bernard Janisch
Tel: +27 (011) 728-1575
Email: brij@global.co.za

Wemmer Pan
PO Box 10440 Johannesburg 2000
South Africa
Contact: Alan Cook
Tel: +27 (011) 781-3474

Zwartkops
60 Glenroy Drive Willowglen PE 6025
South Africa
Contact: Tim Hutton
Tel: +27 (041) 504-3772
Email: thutton@petech.ac.za

Riviera Vaal
PO Box 1868 Parklands 2121
South Africa
Contact: Rod McKinnon
Tel: +27 (011) 880-1623
Email: rod@sdynamics.co.za

Stewards
South Africa
Contact: Nick Hornsby [Secretary]
Tel: +27 (011) 466-2094
Email: nick@betonamit.co.za

UNIVERSITIES

SA Student Sports
Sports Admin. Rondebosch 7700
South Africa
Contact: Hamish Irving
Email: g0210673@campus.ru.ac.za

Union - Rowing
South Africa
Contact: Ramsay Brierley
Email: rbrierley@mech.wits.az.za

University Cape Town
Sports Admin. Rondebosch 7700
South Africa
Contact: Michael Cousins (sec)
Email: CSNMIC003@mail.uct.ac.za

University Port Elizabeth
Sports Admin. PO Box 1600
South Africa
Contact: Collette Aubert
Email: daubert@intekom.co.za

University Natal Durban
South Africa
Contact: Trisha Keenan
Email: pcssys@iafrica.com

University Natal
Sports Union Private Bag X01
South Africa
Contact: Gareth Stobie
Tel: +27 (033) 260-5079
Email: ggs@hilton.kzn.school.za

Pietermaritzburg
Scottsville 3209
South Africa
Contact: Theo Wicks [Sec]
Email: teddywilliamson@yahoo.com

University Rand
PO Box 524 Auckland Park 2006
South Africa
Contact: Matthew Bell
Email: thebells1@freemail.absa.co.za

Rhodes University
PO Box 7426 East London 5200
South Africa
Contact: Grant Parkin
Email: poppyparkin@yahoo.com

University Stellenbosch
Sports Bureau Private Bag X5018
South Africa
Contact: Jess Tyrrell
Email: jesst@hotmail.com

University Witwatersrand
Sports Admin. Private Bag 3
South Africa
Contact: Hilda Kempf
Tel: +27
Email: finzione@hotmail.com

GAUTENG PROVINCE SCHOOLS

Bishop Bavin College
South Africa
Contact: Jean Kelly
Tel: +27 (011) 616-4018
Email: jkelly@bishopbavin.co.za

Crawford College
South Africa
Contact: Linda Malan
Tel: +27 (011) 476-4382
Email: jetim@global.co.za

Florida Park
South Africa
Contact: Ian Parkin
Tel: +27 (011) 672-7925
Email: irparkin@global.co.za

Germiston High School
South Africa
Contact: Warren Laas
Tel: +27 (011) 896-4442
Email: nejewane@mweb.co.za

Gen. Smuts High School
South Africa
Contact: Rod Hughes
Tel: +27 (016) 421-4130
Email: gensmuts@saschools.co.za

Jeppe Boys High School
South Africa
Contact: Steve Hodge
Tel: +27 (011) 614-1938
Email: rowing@jeppeboys.co.za

King Edward VII School
South Africa
Contact: Chris Bam - Chairman
Tel: +27 (011) 786 0130
Email: margeb@xsinet.co.za

Mondeor High School
South Africa
Contact: Tom Price Jnr
Tel: +27 (011) 680-5362
Email:

Parktown Boys High School
South Africa
Contact: Meltz van Zyl
Tel: +27 (011) 642-4531
Email: vanzylm@parktown.za.net

St. Albans School
South Africa
Contact: Andre Vermaerke
Tel: +27 (012) 348-1221
Email: secretary@stalban.pta.school.za

St. Andrews School
South Africa
Contact: Cathy Severin
Tel: +27 (011) 453-9408
Email: cseverin@standrews.co.za

St. Benedits College
South Africa
Contact: Mark Rabie
Tel: +27 (011) 455-1906
Email: rabey@stbenedicts.co.za

St. Dunstan's College
South Africa
Contact: Denise Mantle
Tel: +27 (011) 350-4191
Email: denisem@absa.co.za

St. John's College
South Africa
Contact: Roger Barrow
Tel: +27 (011) 788-5854
Email: rogerb@icon.co.za

St. Mary's School
South Africa
Contact: Mrs Meg Fargher
Tel: +27 (011) 887-8424

St. Stithians College
South Africa
Contact: Luke Hartley
Tel: +27 (011) 787-5618
Email: lhartley@stithian.com

St. Stithian's Girl's
South Africa
Contact: Sue Tasker [Rowing Teacher]
Tel: +27 (011) 781-2976
Email: stasker@stithian.com

Stella Rowing Club
South Africa
Contact: Jean Bailey
Tel: +27 (011) 453-0714
Email: hrssec@netactive.co.za

Willowridge High
South Africa
Contact: Peter Bekker
Tel: +27 (012) 807-3424
Email: peterbekker@yahoo.com

SOUTH AFRICA SCHOOLS

SA College Schools (SACS)
South Africa
Contact: Geoff Olivier
Tel: +27 (021) 689-4164
Email: geoffolivier@hotmail.com

Clarendon Girls High School
South Africa
Contact: Gordon Smith
Tel: +27 (043) 722-4887
Email: pjtruter@iafrica.com

Collegiate
South Africa
Contact: Jeff Smith
Tel: +27 (041) 374-2817
Email: chs@global.co.za

Diocesan College (Bishops)
South Africa
Contact: Kevin Kruger
Tel: +27 (021) 659-1091
Email: kkruger@dc.wcape.school.za

Grassdale
South Africa
Contact: Trevor Payle
Tel: +27 (021) 705-8829

Grey College
South Africa
Contact: George Dock
Tel: +27 (041) 374-3300
Email: greyhs@grey.ecape.schools.za

Herschell School
South Africa
Contact: Lynda Davies
Tel: +27 (021) 674-0357
Email: vavfan@mweb.co.za

Hilton College
South Africa
Contact: Don Whitfield
Tel: +27 (0331) 43-0100
Email: ddw@hilton.kzn.school.za

Maritzburg College
South Africa
Contact: Doug Gow
Tel: +27 (0331) 394-3796
Email: cg@futurenet.co.za

Somerset College
South Africa
Contact: Tanya Jones
Tel: +27 (021) 842-3035
Email: tjones@somcol.co.za

Selborne College
South Africa
Contact: Kevin Taylor
Tel: +27 (043) 722-1822
Email: headselborne@freemail.absa.co.za

Springfield Convent
South Africa
Contact: Jane Passmore
Tel: +27 (013) 235-1933
Email: janiep@yahoo.com

St. Andrews College
South Africa
Contact: John Gearing
Tel: +27 (046) 622-3365
Email: sgeaj@sac.ecape.school.za

South Korea

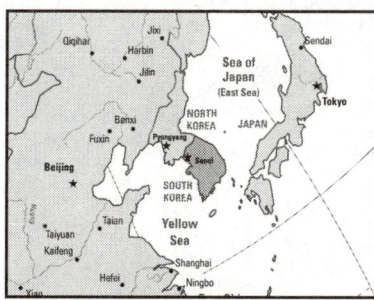

NATIONAL FEDERATION

Korean Rowing Association
Olympic Centre Rm 410
88 Oryun-Dong Songpa-Ku
Seoul, South Korea
Tel: +82 2 423 4510
Fax: +82 2 420 4276
Email: rowing@sports.or.kr

Spain

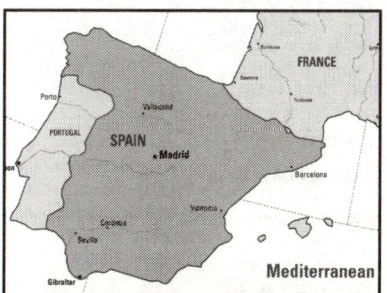

NATIONAL FEDERATION

Federación Español de Remo
Nuñez de Balboa 16 1 Izq.
Madrid, 28001
Spain
Tel: +34 91 4314 709
Fax: +34 91 577 5357
Email: e-mail@federemo.org
www.federemo.org

CLUBS (BY REGION)

LA RIOJA

Club de Remo El Gatón
Plaza Mateo Matute
s/n 26329 Mansilla de la Sierra La Rioja Spain
Spain
Tel: +34 647 229 198
Fax: +34 941 376 001
Web: www.humano.ya.com/7villas

VALENCIA

Club de Remo Gandía
Club deportivo UPV - Sección de Remo
Spain
ttt.epsg.upv.es/~remo/

Club Náutico Port Saplaya
Ronda del Port, s/nº
46128 Port Saplaya (Valencia)
Spain

Club Náutico de Denia
Partida Suertes del Mar, 2
3700 Denia (Alicante) Spain
Spain
Tel: +34 96 5780850

Real Club Regatas Alicante
Muelle de Poniente, 3
03001 Alicante
Spain
Tel: +34 96 5921250
Fax: +34 96 5228542

S.D. Club Náutico Santa Pola
Contradique Puente Pesquero, s/n
03130 Santa Pola (Alicante)
Spain

Club Náutico Altea
Avda. del Puerto, s/n
03590 Altea (Alicante)
Spain
Tel: +34 96 5841591
Fax: +34 96 5841579

Club Náutico Benidorm
Pº de Colón, 2
03500 Benidorm (Alicante)
Spain

Club Náutico Campello
Partida L' Illeta, s/nº
03560 El Campello (Alicante)
Spain
Tel: +34 96 5631748
Fax: +34 96 5631964

Club Náutico Cullera
Avda. del Puerto, 2
46400 Cullera (Valencia)
Spain

Club Náutico Oliva
Alfonso El Magnánimo, s/nº
46780 Oliva (Valencia)
Spain

NAVARRA

Club Náutico Navarra
Plaza Errotazar, s/nº
31014 Pamplona (Navarra)
Spain

Club de Remo Lodosa
San Blas, 10-1º
31580 Lodosa (Navarra)
Spain

MURCIA

Club de Remo Urci
Puerto de Poniente, s/nº
30880 Aguilas (Murcia)
Spain
Tel: +34 968 412310
Fax: +34 968 447363

Club de Remo y Piragüismo Cartagena
Subida San Antonio, 3-2º
30201 Cartagena (Murcia)
Spain
Tel: +34 968 501507
Fax: +34 968 506905

Real Club Regatas Cartagena
Pº Muelle Alfonso XII, s/nº
30201 Cartagena (Murcia)
Spain

Club Náutico Santa Lucia
Dársena del Pescador, s/nº
30202 Cartagena (Murcia)
Spain
Tel: +34 968 501330
Fax: +34 968 501330

Club de Remo Aguilas
Puerto de Poniente, s/nº
30880 Aguilas (Murcia)
Spain
Tel: +34 968 412310
Fax: +34 968 447363

MADRID

C.D. Canal de Isabel II
Cea Bermúdez, 2
28003 Madrid
Spain
Tel: +34 91 5351299

Club de Remo Lago
Francisca Armada, 13
28047 Madrid
Spain
Tel: +34 91 4792858
Fax: +34 91 4792858

Club de Remo Versalles
Berastegui, 54
28017 Madrid
Spain
Tel: +34 91 4074965

Club de Remo Retiro 66
Menéndez Pelayo, 15 - 7º. 1
28009 - Madrid
Spain
Tel: +34 915 74 28 20
Fax: +34 918 90 62 04
Email: info@rcr66.com
www.rcr66.com

GALICIA

Club Náutico Burela
Do Porto, 1
27880 Burela (Lugo)
Spain

Club Náutico Laxe
Puerto, s/nº
15117 Laxe (A Coruña)
Spain

Sporting Club Casino
Real, 83-85
15003 A Coruña
Spain

Club de Remo Cesantes
Cesantes o Penas, 109
36800 Redondela (Pontevedra)
Spain
www.remocesantes.es.fm/

Amegrove Club de Remo
Porto Meloxo, 138
36980 O Grove (Pontevedra)
Spain
Tel: +34 986 731050
Fax: +34 986 732410
www.amegrovecr.com/

Club de Remo Virxen da Guía
Espiñeiro, 2-7 B
36202 Vigo (Pontevedra)
Spain

Club de Remo Y de la Graña
Real Baja, 29 - Graña
15402 Ferrol (A Coruña)
Spain

Club de Remo Cedeira
Crónicas Cordón, 2
15350 Cedeira (A Coruña)
Spain
Tel: +34 981 480440
Fax: +34 981 482893
remocedeira.iespana.es/

Club de Remo Chapela
Praia de Arealonga, 50
36320 Chapela (Pontevedra)
Spain
Tel: +34 986 452976

Club de Remo Muros
Tras Lonja - Apartado Correos, 29
15250 Muros (A Coruña)
Spain

CANTABRIA

S.D.R. Astillero
Crta. Santander-Bilbao, s/nº
39610 Astillero (Cantabria)
Spain

Club de Remo Valle de Camargo
Punta de Parayas
39600 Maliaño (Cantabria)
Spain
Tel: +34 942 254313
Fax: +34 942 254313

Laredo Remo Club
Menéndez Pelayo, 11
39770 Laredo (Cantabria)
Spain
Tel: +34 942 600141

Club de Remo Amigos de la Maruca
Peña Herbosa, 1
39003 Santander (Cantabria)
Spain
Tel: +34 942 362058

Club de Remo Limpias
El Rivero, s/nº
39820 Limpias (Cantabria)
Spain

Club de Remo Ciudad de Santander
Bº Las Mazas, 5-B
39120 Liencres (Cantabria)
Spain
www.geocities.com/crcsantander/

Club de Remo Carasa Voto
El Carmen, 13
39750 Colindres (Cantabria)
Spain
Tel: +34 942 650684

S.D. Remo Pedreña
Apartado Correos, 5
39130 Pedreña (Cantabria)
Spain
Tel: +34 942 740419

Club de Remo Santander
Grupo Fernando Ateca, 9-3º Izqda.
39012 Santander (Cantabria)
Spain

A.D. Remo Castreña
Arturo Duo, s/nº
39700 Castro Urdiales (Cantabria)
Spain

ASTURIAS

Club de Mar de Castropol
Muelle, s/nº
33760 Castropol (Principado de Asturias)
Spain
Tel: +34 985 635035
Fax: +34 985 636298

C.D. Grupo Corvera de Remo
Centro Social Las Vegas
33400 Corvera (Principado de Asturias)
Spain
Tel: +34 985 570644
Fax: +34 985 570644

Club Remeros del EO
Apartado Correos, 30
33770 Vegadeo (Principado de Asturias)
Spain
Tel: +34 985 634046
Fax: +34 985 476023

Esc. Gijonesa de Remo y Piragüismo
Dindurra, 20-4º B
33202 Gijón (Principado de Asturias)
Spain
Fax: +34 985 364460

Club de Remo San Telmo
33125 San Juan de la Arena
(Principado de Asturias)
Spain

Club Castropolense de Remo
Muelle, s/nº
33760 Castropol (Principado de Asturias)
Spain
Tel: +34 985 635035
Fax: +34 985 636298

C.D. Occidental Astur de Remo
Empedrada, 21-1º
33770 Vegadeo (Principado de Asturias)
Spain
Tel: +34 985 634339
Fax: +34 985 476036

C. Náutico de Luanco
Avda. del Gayo, s/nº
33440 Luanco (Principado de Asturias)
Spain
Tel: +34 985 881944
www.mundofree.com/cnluanco/

Club Náutico Remeros Navia
El Muelle s/n
33710 Navia
Spain
Tel: +34 985 630083
members.es.tripod.de/RemoNavia

Club Deportivo Remeros del Nalón
Avda. del Campo
33126 Soto del Barco (Principado Asturias)
Spain

ARAGON

Capri Club de Remo
Ribera Río Segre, s/nº
50170 Mequinenza (Zaragoza)
Spain
Tel: +34 974 464007
Fax: +34 974 465234

C.D. Elemental Aragón Remo
Urb. Torres San Lamberto, 109
50011 Zaragoza
Spain
Tel: +34 976 217288
Fax: +34 976 216291

Centro Natación Helios
Parque Macanaz, s/nº
50015 Zaragoza
Spain
Tel: +34 976 520367
Fax: +34 976 529248
Email: deporte@cnhelios.com
www.cnhelios.com

Club Náutico Zaragoza
Echegaray y Caballero, 101
50002 Zaragoza
Spain
Tel: +34 976 297047
cnzremo.upseros.com

PAIS VASCO

Bermeoko Arraun Elkartea
Hego Kaia, s/nº
48370 Bermeo (Bizkaia)
Spain
Tel: +34 94 6885349
Fax: +34 94 6885349
bermeokue.com/remo.htm

Donibaneko Añares Arraunlariak
San Juan, s/nº
20110 Pasai Donibane (Gipuzkoa)
Spain
Tel: +34 943 526954
Fax: +34 943 526954

Pasai Donibane Koxtape A.E.
Edif. Antihuo - Muelle Pysbe
20110 Pasai Donibane (Gipuzkoa)
Spain
Tel: +34 943 524166
Fax: +34 943 524166

C.R.O. Orio Arraunketa Elkartea
21 Postakutxa 20810 Orio (Gipuzkoa)
Spain
Tel: +34 943 833748
Fax: +34 943 831230
www.oriora.com/paginas/remo/remo.htm

Hernaniko Arraun Elkartea
Ibarluze Industrialdea - Arraun Pabiloia
20120 Hernani (Gipuzkoa)
Spain

Mundakako Arraun Taldea
Bajos Atalaya, s/nº
48360 Mundaka (Bizkaia)
Spain

Club Deportivo Loiolatarra
Loiolatarra, 2 (Bº Loiola)
20014 Donostia (Gipuzkoa)
Spain

Kaiku Arraunaren Kirol Elkartea
Alameda de Kaiku, s/nº
48910 Sestao (Bizkaia)
Spain
Tel: +34 610 462663
Fax: +34 94 4618966

Zierbena Arraun Elkartea
El Puerto, s/nº
48508 Zierbena (Bizkaia)
Spain
Tel: +34 656 778660

Aita Mari Arraun Elkartea
Telmo Deun, 24
20750 Zumaia (Gipuzkoa)
Spain

CATALUNA

Reial Club Maritim Barcelona
Moll d' Espanya, s/nº
08003 Barcelona
Spain
Tel: +34 93 2217394
Fax: +34 93 2215566
www.maritimbarcelona.org/

Club de Rem Tortosa
Pº Moreira, s/nº
43500 Tortosa (Tarragona)
Spain
Tel: +34 977 446058
Fax: +34 977 446058
lupus.worldonline.es/remtorto/

Club Natació Banyoles.
Pº Antoni Gaudí, 3
17820 Banyoles (Girona)
Spain
Tel: +34 972 570859
Fax: +34 972 575017
www.cnbanyoles.es/

G.D. Náutics Roses
Moll Comercial, s/nº
17480 Roses (Girona)
Spain

Club Náutic Vilada
Clotasos, 18
08613 Vilada (Barcelona)
Spain

Club de Rem Portbou
Carrer Mercat, 4
17497 Portbou (Girona)
Spain

Club Náutic Sant Carles de la Rápita
Dársena Port, s/n
43540 Sant Carles de la Rápita (Tarragona)
Spain
Tel: +34 977 741103
Fax: +34 977 741103
come.to/remsantcarles

Club Náutic Lloret de Mar
Torrento, 20)
17310 Lloret de Mar (Girona)
Spain

Club Náutic Cornudella
Conde de Rius, s/nº
43360 Cornudella del Montsat (Tarragona)
Spain

Club Náutico de Amposta
Pº del Riu, 14-16
43870 Amposta (Tarragona)
Spain
Tel: +34 977 706621
Fax: +34 977 706621
www.clubnautic.amposta.org/

ANDALUCIA

Club Náutico Sevilla
Apartado Correos, 1003
41080 Sevilla
Spain
Tel: +34 954 454777
Fax: +34 954 284693
www.nauticosevilla.com

Real Círculo Labradores - Remo
Juan Sebastián Elcano, 1
41011 Sevilla
Spain
Tel: +34 954 270001
Fax: +34 954 275773
www.iespana.es/sevilla-remo/principal/

Real Club Mediterráneo de Málaga
Pº de la Farola, 18
29016 Málaga
Spain
Tel: +34 952 226300
Fax: +34 952 216311
www.realclubmediterraneo.com/

Club de Remo Bahía
Redes Guadarranque
11360 San Roque (Cádiz)
Spain

C.D.R. Guadalquivir "86"
Fedra, 1-2º C
41009 Sevilla
Spain
Tel: +34 954 906014
Fax: +34 954 486805

Club de Remo El Candado
Avda. Principal del Candado, 15
29018 Málaga
Spain
Tel: +34 952 290845

Club de Remo Itucci
Real, 10
41870 Aznalcollar (Sevilla)
Spain
Tel: +34 954 135766

Club de Remo Giraldillo
Pl. de Gomila, 9-P.15
41007 Sevilla

Club Náutico Bélmez
Apartado Correos, 25
14240 Bélmez (Córdoba)
Spain
Tel: +34 957 573419
Fax: +34 957 571125

Sri Lanka

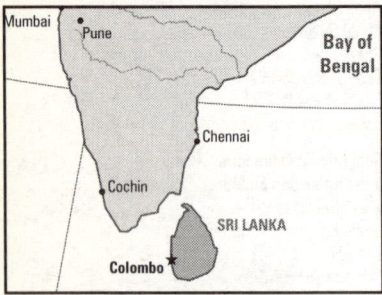

NATIONAL FEDERATION

Amateur Rowing Association of Sri Lanka
c/o Colombo Rowing Club
No.51/1
Colombo 2, Sri Lanka
Tel: +94 1 692945
Fax: +94 1 692946
Email: heladiva@slt.lk

Sudan

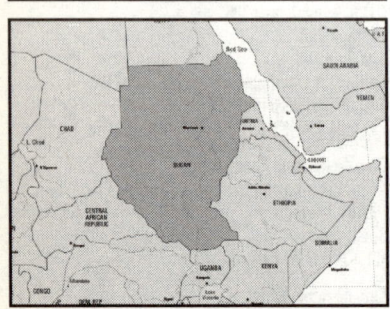

NATIONAL FEDERATION

Sudan Rowing and Canoe Federation
PO Box 3066
Khartoum, 11111
Sudan
Tel: +249 11 78 3422
Fax: +249 11 77 1683

Swaziland

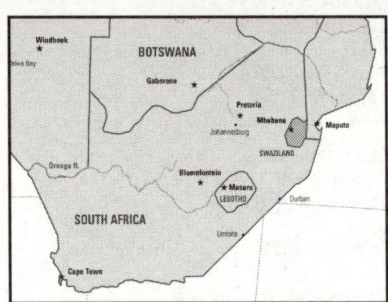

NATIONAL FEDERATION

Swaziland Rowing Association
PO Box 12
Mbabane
Swaziland
Tel: +268 4040 431
Fax: +268 4046 888
Email: brettfoss@hotmail.com

Sweden

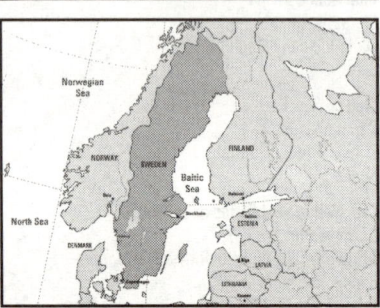

NATIONAL FEDERATION

Svenska Roddförbundet
Idrottens Hus
Farsta, 12387
Sweden
Tel: +46 8 6056 435
Fax: +46 8 947 830
Email: kenth.nordh@rodd.rf.se
www.roddsverige.nu

CLUBS

Akademiska Roddföreningen
Box 19064
10432 Stockholm
Sweden
Email: rodd@akademiskarodd.se
www.akademiskarodd.se/

Arbrå Kyrkbåtsroddare
Lasse Feldtblad
Pl 4034
82011, Vallsta
Sweden
www.helsingerodd.cjb.net/

Avesta Roddklubb
Lindevägen 4 kv
77552, Krylbo
Sweden
Email: avest.roddklubb@euroseek.com
www.algonet.se/~femfas

Bergeforsen Roddklubb
Olle Moberg
Gengränd 7
Sweden
86033, Bergeforsen

Björkö Roddklubb
Västergårdsvägen 42
43094, Bohus Björkö
Sweden
Email: bjorko.roddklubb@bohus-bjorko.net

Borgärdets Roddklubb
Lillemor Andersson
Industrivägen 13
79023, Svärdsjö
Sweden

Borlänge Roddklubb
Box 605
78126, Borlänge
Sweden
Email: strand@borlange.mail.telia.com
217.31.178.69/tunhuken/

Brudpiga Roddklubb
Vivi Anne Börlin
Lappmyrvägen 7
79336, Leksand
Sweden

Donsö Roddförening
Kjell-Inge Malmborg
Bangatan 21
41463, Göteborg
Sweden

Falkenberg Roddklubb
Rönnhagsvägen 9
31144, Falkenberg
Sweden
Email: fbgrodd@mail14.calypso.net
www.falkenbergsroddklubb.nu/

Föreningen Asperö fritid
Asperö 1015
43080, Asperö
Sweden

Föreningen Järvsö Roddare
Hans Lagesson
Bondarväg 2201
82040, Järvsö
Sweden

Göteborgs Roddförening
Anders Hultén
Norra Sextantgatan 5
42676, Västra Frölunda
Sweden
Email: www.come.to/rodd

Göteborgs Roddsällskap
Kjell-Inge Malmborg
Bangatan 21
41463, Göteborg

Götebors Roddklubb
Marie Ahlenvik
Kobergsgatan 5
41671, Göteborg
Sweden
www.grk.nu/

Halmstad Gymnastik & Roddförening
Evert Winnberg
Flaggskeppsvägen 5
30272, Halmstad
Sweden
Email: evert.winnberg@halmstad.se
user.tninet.se/~mnf959d/index.htm

Hammarby Idrottsförening
Bertil Johnsson
Vickertgatan 9 nb
11861, Stockholm
Sweden
Email: bertil.johnsson@gamma.telenordia.se
www.rodd.hammarby-if.se/

Hanebo Segerst kyrkbåtsförening
Sweden
kilafors.nu/kyrkbat/

Helsingborgs Roddkubb
Båthusgatan 11
25267, Helsingborg
Sweden
www.hrk.just.nu/

Henån Roddklubb
Anders Bolinder
Vallmovägen 1
473 32, Henån
Sweden
Email: anders.bolinder@telia.com
hem.passagen.se/hrk

Hjortnäs brygga IF
Åsa Holén
Hjortnäs 180
79390, Leksand

Huskvarna Roddsällskap
Brunnstorpsv 32
56136, Huskvarna
Sweden

Hyple Island Tiohuggarteam
Axelsdotter
Box 47
43096, Hyppeln
Sweden

Härnö Roddklubb
Börje Nygren
Th Hellmansväg 12
87151, Härnösand
Sweden
w1.611.telia.com/~u61112944 / index.html

Höganäs Roddförening
Håkan Östergren
Heimdalsgatan 53
26162, Glumslöv
Sweden
Email: pelle.andersen@hoganas.com
home.bip.net/pelle.andersen/hrf.html

Jönköpings roddsällskap
Box 2111
55002, Jönköping
Sweden

Kalmar Roddklubb
Göran Andersson
Svenborgsväg 2
39354, Kalmar
Sweden
www.kalmarrodd.nu/

Kungälvs Roddklubb
Box 348
44210, Kungälv
Sweden
krk.just.nu

Kälarne IK:s Roddsektion
Box 41
84064, Kälarne
Sweden

Landskrona Roddklubb
Box 241
26123, Landskrona
Sweden
Email: landskrona@winningteam.com
welcome.to/swedishopen

Lidingö Roddklubb
Mats Ensér
Vändstigen 3
18142, Lidingö
Sweden

Lilla Edets Roddare
Åke Wernersson
storgatan 25
45153, Uddevalla
Sweden

Lingheds Roddarklubb
Susanne Englund
Gstavsbergsvägen 2
79025, Linghed
Sweden

Lunds Universitets Roddsektion
Fredsgatan 4A
22220, Lund
Sweden
Email: adam@luna.lu.se
come.to/lurk

Malmö Roddklubb
Slussplan 1
21130, Malmö
Sweden
Email: malmorodd@hotmail.com
www.skanerodd.com/malmo/

Mölndals Roddklubb
Lisbeth Ericsson
Posthornsgatan 3
43166,Mölndal
Sweden
www.mrk.nu

Norrköpings Roddklubb
Fredrick Hjelm
Vilbergsgatan 75
60357, Norrköping
Sweden
Tel: +46 011 237785
www.roddklubben.com

Norrtälje Roddförening
Sune Söderström
Blåbegsvägen 3
761 63, Norrtälje
Sweden

Nusnäs IF Roddsektion
Morängsvägen 10
79277, Nusnäs
Sweden

Nygrannens Roddarklubb
Kristina Ivares
Laknäs 48
79394, Tällberg
Sweden

Orsa If Roddklubb
Hans Lans
Hansjövägen 27
79431, Orsa
Sweden
www.sturfajtn.com

Oskarshamn Roddklubb
Peter Thuresson
trattvägen 16A
57251, Oskarshamn
Sweden

Roddklubben Galären
Göte Westberg
Box 55
43085, Brännö
Sweden

Rättviks Roddklubb
Bernt Zetterström
Box 150
79522, Rättvik
Sweden

Rävens Roddklubb
Kerstin Jansson
Östansjö 13
79023, Svärdsjö
Sweden

Siljansnäs Roddarklubb
Båthusbacken 5
793 60, Siljansnäs
Sweden
Tel: +46 0247-23298

Solleröns IFs Roddsektion
Bernt Hedberg
Gesunda 1285
79290, Sollerön
Tel: +46 0250-21238
Sweden
Email: bernt.hedberg@telia.com

Stockholms roddförening
Anders Franzén
Wargentinsgatan 4
11229, Stockholm
Sweden
Tel: +46 08-6610144
Email: anders.h.franzen@telia.com
www.stockholmsroddforening.se

Stockholmspolisens Roddsektion (SPIF)
Elisabeth Dellacasa
Tvillingarnas gata 315
13663, Hanninge
Sweden
Tel: +46 08-6184519

Strömstad Roddklubb
Box 102
45230, Strömstad
Sweden
Tel: +46 0526-10391
Email: stromstadrk@telia.com

Styrsö Roddare
Kerstin Skantze
Tångenvägen 42
43084, Styrsö
Sweden

Trollhättans Roddsällskap
Stefan Svensson
Kasvägen 16
46155, Trollhättan
Sweden
Tel: +46 0520-16440
Email: stefan.svensson@home.se
hem1.passagen.se/thnrodds

Uddevalla Roddklubb
Box 29
45115, Uddevalla
Sweden
Tel: +46 0522-34435

Uppsala Akademiska Roddarsällskap (UARS)
c/o Beronius
S:t Johannesg. 26
753 12, Uppsala
Sweden
Tel: +46 018-10 65 48
Email: robert.beronius@gmx.net
www.student.uu.se/studorg/uars/

Varbergs Roddklubb
Ann-Sofi Stjernström
Kamelgatan 15
43237, Varberg
Sweden
Tel: +46 0340-18242

Waxholms Roddförening
Sjösportcentrum Eriksö
185 37, Waxholm
Sweden
Tel: +46 08-541 322 82
Email: kenth.nordh@rodd.rf.se
www.svenskidrott.se/a/vaxholmsrf

Westerviks Roddklubb
Wallerius
Stora Trädgårdsgatan 94
59342, Västervik
Sweden
www.mamut.com/rodd

Väggaskolans Roddklubb
www.torget.se/users/a/another/vrk/

Vänersborgs Roddklubb
Box 272
46223, Vänersborg
Sweden
Tel: +46 0521-17330
home1.swipnet.se/~w-17814/VRK.html

Västerås Roddförening
Karl-Erik Lindqvist
Flygplansgatan 17
72348, Västerås
Sweden
www.welcome.to/vrf

Åhus Roddklubb
Hans-Erik Lundqvist
Mistelvägen 24
296 38, Åhus
Sweden
Tel: +46 044-242770
Email: hans@ksab.se
www.skanerodd.com/ahus

Ängelholms Roddklubb
Carl-Sune Ekeroth
Heimdallgatan 12C
26244, Ängelholm
Sweden
Tel: +46 0431-10406

Öckerö Roddförening
Harld Backman
Bankevägen 16
43090, Öckerö
Sweden

Öresjö Seglarsällskap Roddsektion
Skogsrydsvägen 49
50649, Borås
Sweden
Tel: +46 033-247001
www.ossrodd.org

Switzerland

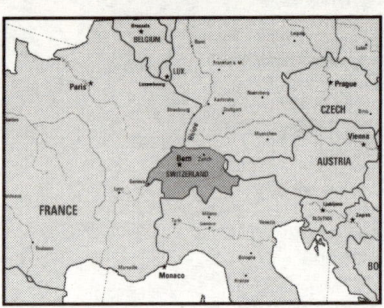

NATIONAL FEDERATION

Fédération Suisse de Sociétés d'Aviron
Brünigstrasse 182a
Sarnen, 6060
Switzerland
Tel: +41 41 660 95 24
Fax: +41 41 660 94 43
Email: info@ruderverband.ch
www.ruderverband.ch

CLUBS

Ruderclub Aarburg
Aarburgerstrasse 96
4618 Boningen
Switzerland
Tel: +41 062 791 60 46
home.datacomm.ch/rcaarburg

Ruderclub Aegeri
Seeplatz
6315 Oberägeri
Switzerland
www.mypage.bluewindow.ch/RCAe

Seeclub Arbon
Wassergasse 2
9320 Arbon
Switzerland
Tel: +41 071 446 81 26
www.seeclub-arbon.ch

Ruderclub Baden
Seestrasse 19
5432 Neuenhof
Switzerland
Tel: +41 056 406 44 20
http://www.rcbaden.ch/

Basler Ruder-Club
Grenzacherstrasse 536
4125 Riehen
Switzerland
Tel: +41 061 601 64 11
www.basler-ruder-club.ch

Ruderclub Blauweiss Basel
Sonnenweg 7
8112 Otelfingen
Switzerland
Tel: +41 061 312 68 68
www.rcblauweiss.ch

Rowing Club Bern
Wohlenstr. 66
3032 Bern
Switzerland
Tel: +41 031 901 10 42
www.rowing.ch

Seeclub Biel
Neuenburgerstrasse 162c
2502 Biel
Switzerland
Tel: +41 032 323 16 36

Société Nautique Etoile Bienne
Route de Neuchatel 156b
2502 Biel/Bienne
Switzerland
www.sneb.ch

Ruderclub Cham
Seestrasse 11
6330 Cham
Switzerland
Tel: +41 041 780 37 10
www.ruderclubcham.ch

Ruderclub Erlenbach
Im Wyden
8703 Erlenbach
Switzerland
Tel: +41 01 910 48 31
www.rudercluberlenbach.ch

Aviron Club Estavayer-le-Lac
Case postale 35
Switzerland
1470 Estavayer-le-Lac

Seeclub Flüelen
Allmend
6454 Flüelen
Switzerland
Tel: +41 041 870 81 91
www.urionline.ch/scf

Société d'Aviron Fribourg
Pensier la Sonnaz
1700 Fribourg
Switzerland
Tel: +41 026 466 23 66
www.safribourg.ch/

Société Nautique Genève, Section Aviron
Port-Noir
1223 Cologny-Genève
Switzerland
Tel: +41 022 707 05 00
www.nautique.org/

Ruderclub Hallwilersee
5616 Meisterschwanden
Switzerland
www.rc-hallwilersee.ch

Ruderclub Greifensee
8606 Greifensee
Switzerland
www.rcgreifensee.ch/

Seeclub Horgen
Hirsackerstrasse
8810 Horgen
Switzerland
Tel: +41 01 725 50 30
seeclub.horgen@bluewin.ch

Seeclub Interlaken
Lanzenen
3800 Interlaken
Switzerland
Tel: +41 033 822 48 06
www.seeclubinterlaken.ch

Ruderclub Kreuzlingen
Promenadenstrasse 50
8280 Kreuzlingen
Switzerland
Tel: +41 071 688 72 71
www.rck.ch.vu

Seeclub Küsnacht
Theodor-Brunner-Weg 4
8700 Küsnacht
Switzerland
Tel: +41 01 910 64 54
www.sc-kuesnacht.ch

Ruderclub Rigi Küssnacht
Strandbad Seeburg
6403 Küssnacht a.R.
Switzerland
www.rcrigi-kuessnacht.ch

Société d'aviron La Rame, La-Tour-de-Peliz
La Poteyla
1814 La-Tour-de-Peliz
Switzerland
Tel: +41 021 944 59 07

Centre Lausannois de l'Aviron
CA Lausannois
Gründung, 2001
Switzerland

Lausanne Sports, Section Aviron
Vidy Lausanne
1000 Lausanne
Switzerland
Tel: +41 021 617 50 47
www.multimania.com/lsaviron

Rowing-Club Lausanne
Case postale 142
1000 Lausanne 6
Switzerland
Tel: +41 021 616 46 46
www.rcl.ch.tt

Società Canottieri Locarno
Via al Lido
6600 Locarno
Switzerland
Tel: +41 091 751 29 97
www.sclocarno.ch

Club Canottieri Lugano
Via Foce
6900 Lugano-Cassarate
Switzerland
Tel: +41 091 971 23 98
www.ticino.com/canottierilugano

Società Canottieri Audax Paradiso
Riva Paradiso 9 / C.P. 310
6902 Paradiso
Switzerland
Tel: +41 091 944 40 66

Società Canottieri Audax Paradiso
Riva Paradiso 9 / C.P. 310
6902 Paradiso
Switzerland
Tel: +41 091 944 40 66

Ruderclub Reuss Luzern
Alpenquai 31
uzern
Switzerland
Tel: +41 041 360 24 25
www.rc-reuss.ch

Ruderclub Rotsee Luzern
Luzern
Switzerland
Tel: +41 041 420 54 40

Seeclub Luzern
Alpenquai 33
6000 Luzern
Switzerland
Tel: +41 041 360 55 05
www.seeclub-luzern.ch

Club Nautique Montreux
Port du Basset
1815 Clarens
Switzerland
Tel: +41 021 964 30 13
www.aviron-montreux.ch/

Forward Rowing Club Morges
Port du Petit-Bois
1110 Morges
Switzerland
Tel: +41 021 801 72 84
www.forwardrowing.ch/

Société Nautique de Neuchâtel
Route de Falaises / C.P.
2002 Neuchâtel 2
Switzerland
Tel: +41 032 724 11 37
www.aviron.ch

Club de l'aviron Nyon
Hotel du Lac, Case postale 168
1260 Nyon 1
Switzerland
Tel: +41 022 361 66 41
www.multimania.com/avironnyon

Ruderclub Olten
Gösgerstrasse 11
4600 Olten
Switzerland
Tel: +41 062 296 24 50

Ruderclub Rapperswil-Jona
8640 Rapperswil
Switzerland
www.rcrj.ch

Seeclub Richterswil
Im Horn
8805 Richterswil
Switzerland
Tel: +41 01 784 98 62
www.seeclub-richterswil.ch

Regattateam Richterswil/Wädenswil
www.seeclub-richterswil.ch/rgt

Le Rosey Rowing-Club Rolle
Institut Le Rosey
1180 Rolle
Switzerland

Seeclub Rorschach
Riedtli
Goldach-Rorschach
Switzerland
Tel: +41 071 841 26 88
www.swix.ch/scr

Ruderclub Sarnen
Kollegimatte
6060 Sarnen

Ruderclub Schaffhausen
Hauptstrasse 100
8246 Langwiesen
Switzerland
Tel: +41 052 659 38 53
www.ruderclub-schaffhausen.ch/

Seeclub Sempach
Am See
6204 Sempach
Switzerland
Tel: +41 041 460 47 07
www.seeclub-sempach.ch

Solothurner Ruderclub
Römerstrasse 29
4500 Solothurn
Switzerland
Tel: +41 032 622 10 14

Seeclub Stäfa
Lattenberg
8712 Stäfa
Switzerland
Tel: +41 01 920 45 08
www.seeclub-staefa.ch

Seeclub Stansstad
Kehrsitenstrasse 17
6362 Stansstad
Switzerland
Tel: +41 041 612 03 44
www.seeclubstansstad.ch

Seeclub Sursee
Trichter am See
6210 Sursee
Switzerland
Tel: +41 041 921 12 04
www.seeclub-sursee.ch

Ruderclub Thalwil
Seestrasse 178
8800 Thalwil
Switzerland
Tel: +41 01 720 29 65
www.rcthalwil.ch

Ruderclub Thun
Am Lachenkanal
3600 Thun
Switzerland
Tel: +41 033 336 36 21
www.ruderclub-thun.ch

Seeclub Thun
Scherzliweg 28
3600 Thun
Switzerland
Tel: +41 033 222 57 09

Ruderclub Uster
Niederuster
8610 Uster
Switzerland
www.ruderclubuster.ch

Club d'Aviron Vésenaz
Pointre-à-la Bise, CP 59
1222 Vésenaz
Switzerland
Tel: +41 022 752 22 98
www.avironvesenaz.ch

Club de l'Aviron Vevey
Quai Ernest Ansermet
1800 Vevey
Switzerland
Tel: +41 021 922 63 18
www.aviron-vevey.ch

Seeclub Wädenswil
Im Giessen
8820 Wädenswil
Switzerland
Tel: +41 01 780 37 14

Ruderclub Wohlensee
Wohleibrücke
3033 Wohlen
Switzerland

Union Nautique Yverdon
Quai de Nogent 6
1400 Yverdon
Switzerland
www.aviron-yverdon.ch/

See-Club Zug
Am Siehbach
6300 Zug
Switzerland
Tel: +41 041 711 16 74
www.scz.ch

Aviron Romand Zürich
Mythenquai 81
Zürich
Switzerland
www.aviron-romand.ch

Belvoir Ruderclub Zürich
Mythenquai 85
Zürich
Switzerland
Tel: +41 01 202 15 98
www.belvoir-rc.ch

Club Nautique Français, Zürich
Mythenquai 83
Zürich
Switzerland
Tel: +41 01 201 10 98
www.cnf.ch

Damen-Ruderclub Zürich
Seestrasse 557
Zürich
Switzerland
Tel: +41 01 482 32 42

Grasshopper Club Zürich
Mythenquai 81
Zürich
Switzerland
Tel: +41 01 201 30 35
www.gcz-rudern.ch

Nordiska Roddföreningen Zürich
Mythenquai 79
Zürich
Switzerland
www.nordiska.ethz.ch

Polytechniker Ruderclub Zürich
Mythenquai 71
Zürich
Switzerland
Tel: +41 01 201 37 63

Ruderclub Kaufleuten Zürich
Mythenquai 83
Zürich
Switzerland
Tel: +41 01 201 10 98

Ruderclub Zürich
Mythenquai 87
Zürich
Switzerland
Tel: +41 01 201 20 03
www.rcz.ch

Rudergesellschaft Zürich
Seestrasse 479
Zürich
Switzerland

Ruderverein Industrieschule Zürich
Mythenquai 81
Zürich
Switzerland

Seeclub Zürich
Mythenquai 75
Zürich
Switzerland
Tel: +41 01 202 23 21
www.seeclub.ch

Syria

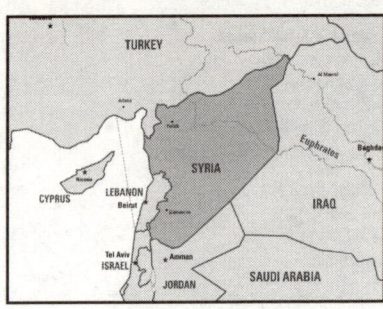

NATIONAL FEDERATION
Syrian Rowing and Open Water Sports Fed.
PO Box 421
Baramke
Damascus, Syria
Tel: +963 11 212 3346
Fax: +963 11 212 3346

Taiwan

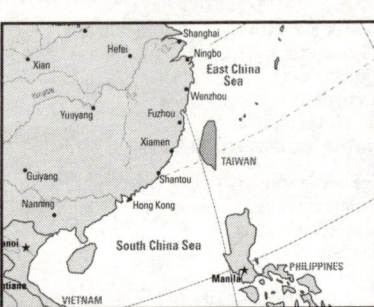

NATIONAL FEDERATION
Chinese Taipei Amateur Rowing Association
707 No. 20 Chu Lun Street
Taipei, Taiwan
Tel: +886 2 773 5755
Fax: +886 2 773 5756
Email: ctara707@ms16.hinet.net

Thailand

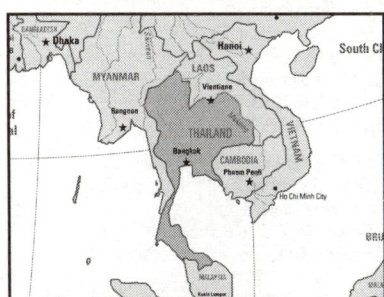

NATIONAL FEDERATION

Rowing and Canoeing Assoc. of Thailand
RM 227 Rajamangala National Stadium
Sports Authority of Thailand 2088 Ramkhamhaeng Road
Bangkok, 10240
Thailand
Tel: +66 2 369 1511
Fax: +66 2 369 1511
Email: rcat11@hotmail.com

Togo

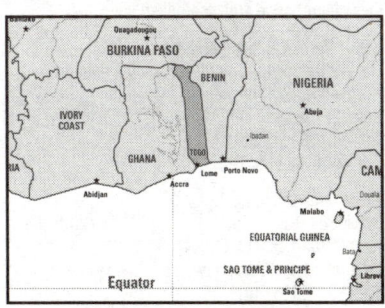

NATIONAL FEDERATION

Fédération Togolaise d'Aviron et Canoë
B.P. 247
Aného, Togo
Tel: +228 2185251
Fax: +228 214546

Tonga

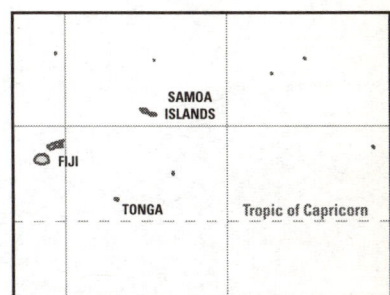

NATIONAL FEDERATION

Tonga Rowing Association
PO Box 1951
Palace Office
Nukualofa, Tonga
Tel: +676 21000
Fax: +676 24102

Tunisia

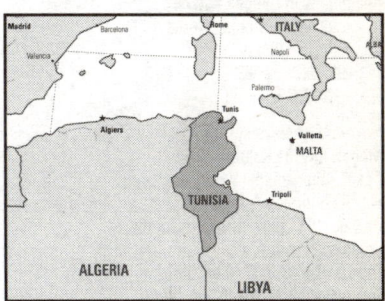

NATIONAL FEDERATION

Fédération Tunisienne d'Aviron et de Canoë
B.P. 284 El Menzah
Tunis, 1004
Tunisia
Tel: +216 71 750 696
Fax: +216 71 750 866
Email: faysal.soula@edunet.tn

Turkey

NATIONAL FEDERATION

Turkish Rowing Federation
Acarkent C 477
Beykoz
Istanbul, Turkey
Tel: +90 216 485 1044
Fax: +90 212 485 1043
www.tkf.org.tr

CLUBS

Anadoluhisari Gençlik Kulübü
Anadolu Hisari-Istanbul, Turkey
Contact: Rifat Togay
Tel: +90 0216 332 5838
Fax: +90 0216 323 5336

Ankara Unyversytesy
Mogan Ihtysas Kulubu
Ankara Universitesi Veteriner
Fakultesi Viroloji Ana Bilim
Daly 06110 Dypkapy Ankara, Turkey
Contact: Yylmaz Akca
Tel: +90 0312 317 33 48 ext. 294
Fax: +90 0312-317 33 48

Besiktas Jimnastik Kulubu
Gezi Boyu Cad. No 7
Pendik Istanbul, Turkey
Contact: Ozgen Korkmazlar
Tel: +90 0216 371 77 74

Bogazici Universitesi Spor Kulubu
Bogazici Universitesi
80815 Bebek Istanbul, Turkey
Contact: Recep Akici
Tel: +90 0212 287 2452
Fax: +90 0212 265 2697

Denizati Spor Kulubu
Yuksel Denizcilik Okulu
Tuzla Istanbul, Turkey
Contact: Aras Bilge Aksuyek
Tel: +90 0216 446 2513

Fax: +90 0216 395 4500

Deniz Kuvvetleri Gucu SPOR Kulubu
Deniz Harp Okulu Kom.
Alay Kom. Askeri Egt. Bapk.
Tuzla Kocaeli, Turkey
Contact: Bülent Ayder
Tel: +90 0216 395 2630 x 2421
Fax: +90 0216 395 2658

Denizcilik Ypletmelery SPOR Kulubu
T. Denizcilik Ipletmeleri Gnl. Md. Spor Tesisleri
Kasimpapa Istanbul, Turkey
2.Baskan Kapt. Saim Oguzulgen
Contact: Ulku Yavuz
Tel: +90 0212 242 2099
Fax: +90 0216 346 7784

Fenerbahce Burnu Kürek
Sube Kaptanligi Kadiköy
Istanbul, Turkey
Contact: Lubo Golev & Ilhami Isseven
Tel: +90 0216 414 4146
Fax: +90 0216 348 3060
www.fenerbahce.org

Galatasaray Spor Kulubu
Hasnun Galip Sok. No:7-9-11
Beyoglu Istanbul, Turkey
Contact: Fatih Gökpen
Tel: +90 0212 263 6373
Fax: +90 0212 251 1212
email: yukselt@superonline.com
www.fenerbahce.org/2spordallari/kurek.asp

Körfez Hereke Sumerspor Kulubu
Hereke Belediyesi Sular Idaresi Müdürlügü
Hereke Kocaeli, Turkey
Contact: Tunay Buker
Tel: +90 0262 511 2600
Fax: +90 0262 511 4025

Moda Spor Kulübü
Sadik Bey Plaji
Heybeliada-Istanbul, Turkey
Contact: Maxim Parvanov
Tel: +90 0216 351 1610
Fax: +90 0212 250 4349

Odtü Spor Kulübü
Odtü Spor Kulübü Kürek Subesi
Odtü Ankara, Turkey
Contact: Aytufan Dogu
Tel: +90 0312 210 2196
Fax: +90 0312 210 1237
www.metu.edu.tr/home/wwwmrow

Sakarya Kurek Yhtysas Kulubu
Atatürk Bulvar_ No 28 Bulvar
Iphany Adapazari, Turkey
Contact: Ismail Ceylan
Tel: +90 0264 277 2717
Fax: +90 0264 275 337

7 Tekel Spor Kulübü
Tekel Ambalaj Fabrikasi
Cevizli-Istanbul, Turkey
Contact: Huseyin Yalinkiliç
Tel: +90 0216 399 1511
Fax: +90 0216 352 0853

Turkmenistan

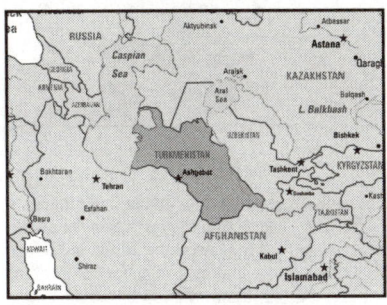

NATIONAL FEDERATION

Rowing Federation of Turkmenistan
Azadi Str. 97
Ashgabat City, 744006
Turkmenistan
Tel: +993 12 253844
Fax: +993 12 474948

Uganda

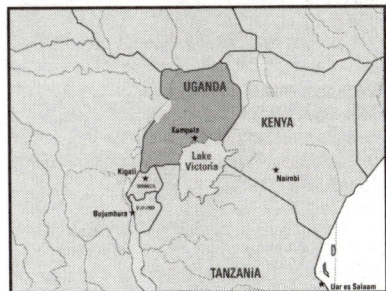

HISTORY

In Uganda, per our emigrations from the Middle East, the center of man's civilization and creation, man learned to use the water in many ways: swim in it, wade across it and cross it in a boat or canoe. In Uganda especially, this includes the areas of the largest lakes in the country, Lake Albert, named after the British explorer and Lake Kabalega, named after the great Bunyoro King Kabalega who fought the

British; resisting their rule until his death. In the Jonam and Alur vernaculars, it is also known as Lake Onek-Bonyo, meaning "a large water which kills swarms of locusts" because the they could not cross its expanse and after flying for hours they became tired and fell in the water to die therefore saving the population's food crops.

The populations along the lakes are Jonam from the Nebbi District of West Nile Region and the Banyoro of Masindi and Hoima Districts in the Midwestern Region of Uganda-both are located in the northern and northwestern axis of Uganda. These populations have suffered terribly as a result of constant drowning in the water due to storms and strong winds because the local boats and canoes were not able to resist when caught in the violent waves. Natural instincts formed and taught them to look for a solution to the tragedy of loosing their loved ones.

A century ago meetings were called by the King of Bunyoro and the Rwodi Caak of Jonam between the elders of the two communities living along the lake to discuss ways of saving themselves and the population from drowning all the time in the lake. A solution came from one of the Paramount Chiefs of Jonam Panyimur, who proposed that a test be carried out on the lake with boats and canoes having longer and heavier oars. The younger, stronger men of the communities carried out the test in two canoes. The end result was that they discovered that the larger and longer oars could withstand the strong gales and indeed propel the canoes much faster and with more comfort.

So from that time, the usage of larger, longer oars became the norm on the entire lake for both transport and fishing. These oars, to this day, are carried in the boats and canoes on reserve for emergencies when storms strike. This method became known as Goyo-Ngai, which is the European word for "rowing". The people of Jonam and Bunyoro are the only populations that are practicing and taking part in rowing competitions in Uganda.

In 1971-1972, a current prominent Ugandan National Sports Administrator was offered the opportunity to go to a German Olympic Committee Coaching Course in Steinbach, Germany. He attended with African English-speaking coaches. He went to study swimming, but the Germans were preparing for the Munich 1972 Olympic Games and he was exposed to many sports. He developed a keen interest in the beauty of handball, archery, rowing, and canoeing, which upon his return, he introduced to Uganda. Today, the four sports have contributed to Uganda's place in international sports and sports history.

The people of Jonam and Bunyoro only need the modern boats and oars for rowing and canoeing in order to challenge the water sports world. Uganda needs international support especially in the areas of equipment and training for our local technical manpower. Uganda is an affiliate of the International Rowing Federation (FISA) and the African Rowing Federation.

NATIONAL FEDERATION

Uganda Rowing Federation
PO Box 11748
Kampala, Uganda
Tel: +256 41 223480
Fax: +256 41 242010
Email: urof2001@yahoo.co.uk

CLUBS

There are several rowing clubs, called "GOYO - NGAI" at fish landing stations along the lake shores of Dei, Singla, Iganda, Munyua, Boro Nyamatagara and Kayonga in the West Nile Region of the Nebbi District. This is the base of the sport of rowing in Uganda.

In addition, there are "GOYO-NGAI" in Wanseko, Butiaba, Kinyoro, Bugoma, Kongo and Kaiso in the Mid-Western Region of Masindi and Hoima Districts. There are also "GOYO-NGAI" in the DRC, which is alongside the banks of Lake Kasenyi, and Lake Mahagi.

Ukraine

NATIONAL FEDERATION

National Rowing Federation of Ukraine
42 Esplanadna Street
Kiev, 1023
Ukraine
Tel: +380 44 220 9576
Fax: +380 44 220 9576

United Kingdom

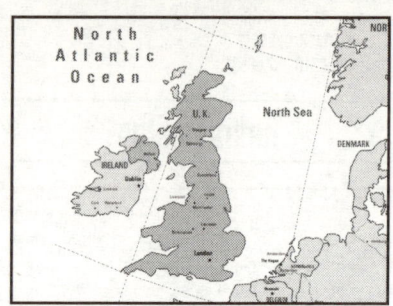

HISTORY

The earliest records tell of the military use of the oar. In 54 BC, Julius Caesar depended largely on oars when crossing the English Channel. In 296 AD, the Roman fleet rowed up the Thames to re-occupy London, and in 893-894 AD, the Danes rowed up the estuaries of the Thames and the Lea.

In England, racing in boats dates from the days when there were few bridges and rivers were crossed by ferry or ford. Passengers were dependent on the watermen who operated ferries or skiffs. In the early 1700's approximately 10,000 watermen were licensed to work on the Thames above London Bridge. These London boatmen wore a special livery and betting developed between the gentry on their speed and skill. The race for "Doggett's Coat and Badge", the foundation of boat racing, was established in 1716 and is still held each summer.

Early amateur oarsmen and scullers were often boxers; some rowing clubs also including boxing sections. Rowing was introduced at Oxford University in the late 1700's and in 1806 the sport arrived at Eton College. The first eight man boats appeared at Brasenose College, Oxford, in 1815. Leander, the oldest club existing, was founded in London at about this time.

The oldest regatta in the rowing calendar is Chester, which dates to before 1814. The first University Boat Race between Oxford and Cambridge was staged at Henley in 1829, and Henley Regatta was established ten years later. The Amateur Rowing Association was established in 1882.

Britain's first international competition was at Henley in 1872, and the first Olympic Regatta was staged in Paris in 1900. Although the European Championships were founded in 1892, British crews did not compete until 1947. The Olympic Regatta was held at Henley in 1908 when British crews won four gold medals — a feat since unsurpassed.

In 1973, Britain opened its first multi-lane international course in Nottingham and the World Championships were staged there in 1975 and 1986. This new facility coincided with a renaissance in British international rowing. The British eight won a silver medal at the 1974 World Championships; the first medal won by a British crew for ten years, and Olympic silvers in the eight and double scull followed at the 1976 Montreal Games.

Since then, Britain has remained amongst the world's leading rowing nations. Successes at World Championships are too many to mention, however, a gold medal in each Olympics since 1984 is a record unrivalled in British sport.

At the Sydney Olympics, rowing's most well-known athlete, Steven Redgrave, won an unbelievable fifth successive Olympic Gold medal, something never achieved by a British Olympian in any sport. No rower, competing over the brutally strength-sapping 2000-meter course, has ever matched it, although Jack Beresford won five medals in successive games from 1920-1936.

Rowing in England is governed by the Amateur Rowing Association, and in Scotland and Wales by the Scottish Amateur Rowing Association and the Welsh Amateur Rowing Association respectively. In England there are 500 clubs and the Amateur Rowing Association has a membership of about 18,000 who compete at the 250 events held throughout the year.

INTERNET LINKS
www.ara-rowing.org
www.scottish-rowing.org.uk
www.rowingservice.co.uk
www.biddulph.org.uk

REGIONS

Northern: Including the counties Cumbria, Durham, Lancashire, The Lake District and Northumberland and well known rowing clubs Durham ARC, Hexham RC, Tees RC; universities and colleges include Newcastle University BC, University College (Durham) BC; and renowned schools include Yarm School Boat Club. **Temp**: about 10°C throughout England but can fall to -4/5°C (winter) and rise to 25°C (summer). **Sites of Interest**: City of Newcastle, Lake District and Peak District, Blackpool and Middlesborough. **Best time to visit**: Spring, summer and autumn.

North West: Including the counties Cheshire, Greater Manchester, Staffordshire, Derbyshire and Nottingham and well known rowing clubs Agecroft RC, Hollingworth Lake RC, Northwich RC; universities: Lancaster University BC, Liverpool University BC, **Manchester University BC**; and recognised schools include Merchant Taylors School BC. **Temp**: Same as most of country but usually slightly colder than the south in winter. Sites of Interest: Chester, Manchester City Centre, Liverpool City Centre and Buxton. **Best time to visit**: Spring, summer and autumn.

Yorkshire and Humberside: Including the counties North, South, East and West Yorkshire and Lincolnshire and well known rowing clubs Doncaster RC, York City RC, City of Sheffield RC; colleges like University of York BC, Sheffield Hallam University RC; and schools like Woodhouse Grove School BC. **Temp**: Much the same as the North West. Sites of Interest: Yorkshire Moors, Scarborough, Leeds. **Best time to visit**: Spring, summer and autumn.

West Midlands: Including the counties Hereford and Worcester, Shropshire, Leicestershire and Buckinghamshire and well known rowing clubs Stourport BC, Pengwern BC, Evesham RC, Bridgnorth RC; universities and colleges such as University of Birmingham BC and University of Warwick BC; and schools like Royal Shrewsbury School BC and The Kings School Worcester BC. Cold and wet in winter and autumn, warmer and drier in spring and summer. **Temp**: about 10°C. Sites of Interest: Birmingham, Shrewsbury, Stratford-upon-Avon. **Best time to visit**: spring, summer and autumn.

East Midlands: Including the counties of Norfolk and Rutland and the well known clubs Loughborough BC, Burton Leander RC, Derby RC, Holme Pierrepont RC as well as colleges like Loughborough Students RC, Nottingham Trent University RC and Leicester University BC; rowing schools are Welbeck College BC and Nottingham Schools' Rowing Association. **Temp**: Same as West Midlands. Sites of Interest: Lincoln, Skegness, Newark and Mablethorpe. **Best time to visit**: Spring, summer and autumn.

Eastern: Including the counties Suffolk, Cambridgeshire, Hertfordshire, Essex and the rowing clubs of Norwich RC, City of Cambridge RC and Bedford RC; universities and colleges include Cambridge University BC, University of East Anglia BC, University of Essex RC and Queens College (Cambridge) BC; and schools include Norwich School BC, Bedford High School RC and The Kings School Ely BC. **Temp**: Wet in spring and autumn, drier in summer and winter. Sites of Interest: Bedford, Cambridge, Ely, Norwich and Chelmsford. **Best time to visit**: Spring, summer and autumn.

Thames Upriver and Downriver: Counties include Greater London, Oxfordshire, Berkshire and Surrey. Rowing clubs which are well known can be found such as Abingdon RC, City of Oxford RC, London RC, Molesey, Thames RC, Twickenham RC and Reading RC; renowned universities include Kingston University RC, Oxford University BC and University of London BC.

There are schools such as Eton, St. Edwards School BC, Headington School Oxford BC, Lady Eleanor Hollis, Westminster and Magdalen College School BC. **Temp**: Warm in summer and reasonably mild throughout the rest of the year. **Sites of Interest**: London, Reading, Oxford and Windsor. **Best time to visit**: Spring, summer and autumn.

South East River: Including the county of Kent and well known rowing clubs include Curlew RC, Poplar and Blackwall RC and The Company of Watermen. Universities and schools include Wye College BC, University of East London BC and Kings School Canterbury BC. **Temp**: Similar to that of Thames Upriver. **Sites of Interest**: Canterbury, Margate, Maidstone and Woking. **Best time to visit**: Spring, summer and autumn.

South East Coast: Counties are East Sussex and West Sussex and well known rowing clubs include Bexhill ARC, Worthing RC, Shoreham RC, Dover RC and Eastbourne RC. **Temp**: Warm in summer mild in winter. **Sites of Interest**: Hastings (the coast), Brighton, Dover, Bognor Regis and Royal Tunbridge Wells. **Best time to visit**: Spring, summer and autumn.

Hampshire and Dorset: Counties are Hampshire and Dorset and rowing clubs are Southampton ARC, Ryde RC, Newport RC and Icena Club; universities include Bournemouth University BC and Southampton University BC, rowing schools are Bryanston School BC, Winchester College BC and Portsmouth Grammar School RC. **Temp**: warm and mild for most of the year but windy and wet in winter. **Sites of Interest**: Southampton, Bournemouth, The Isle of Wight, Salisbury and Winchester. **Best time to visit**: Spring, summer and autumn.

Wilts, Avon, Gloucestershire and Somerset: counties are Wiltshire, Gloucestershire, Avon and Somerset and well known rowing clubs include Avon County RC, City of Bristol RC, Swindon RC and Severn River Rowing Association whilst the well known colleges and universities include Royal Military College of Science BC, University of Bristol BC and Bath University BC. Schools include the Cheltenham Ladies College RC, Clifton College BC and Wycliffe Sculling Centre. **Temp**: Wet in autumn, dry and warm in summer and spring. **Sites of Interest**: Bath, Bristol, Weston-super-Mare, Swindon and Chippenham. **Best time to visit**: Spring, summer and autumn.

Western: Counties are Cornwall and Devon and rowing clubs include Exeter RC, Plymouth RC and Greenbank Falmouth RC; the only rowing university is Exeter University BC. **Temp**: Hot in summer and spring but wet and cold in winter. **Sites of Interest**: The coast of Cornwall (beaches etc.), Penzance, Newquay, Padstow, Newton Abbot and Plymouth. **Best time to visit**: Spring, summer and autumn.

PERSONALITIES

Sir Steven Redgrave: Having won five gold medals at consecutive Olympic Games, Sir Steven has become the greatest British oarsmen ever and the most successful British Olympian in history. He is nine-times world champion and has won countless races at Henley and other famous venues. Having overcome two major illnesses during his rowing career, ulcerative colitis and diabetes, Sir Steven really has performed an amazing feat in achieving all that he has. In doing so, he has deservedly earned the respect of millions of people all over the world. Now retired from the life of rowing, Steven lives in Marlow, London with his family.

Jürgen Grobler: Grobler moved to Britain in 1991 from the former GDR to work as Head Coach for Leander RC, London. The Amateur Rowing Association appointed him Chief Coach of the GB men's squad a year later after the Barcelona Olympics and he has held that position since then. His unique and highly successful methods have been proved effective many times over with the wins by crews such as Steve Redgrave and Matthew Pinsent from 1991 to 1996 and the famous GB coxless four at Sydney. For his contribution to the sport, FISA awarded him the 'Coach of the Year Award 2000'.

Steve Fairbairn: Fairbairn rowed for Cambridge University in the 1880s and went on to become a famous pioneering coach. He was a great innovator having revolutionized both rowing and training methods. He contributed greatly to the establishment of the Head of the River Race - a timed event in which 420 eights row from Mortlake to Putney, it is traditionally held the Saturday before the Boat Race. A memorial has been built at the one-mile point on the course. He died in 1938.

Amy Gentry: Called by many the 'founder of British Women's Rowing', Amy Gentry was a legendary figure in the history of the sport. She started off rowing at Weybridge ARC and did so well with her female teammates that a ladies section was added to the club in 1920, of which Mrs. Gentry became the first captain. This, in turn, stimulated the inclusion of women's boats in many regattas all over the UK. In 1925, Gentry, with her crew, was invited to Brussels to race in a Royal Charity Regatta. Defeating all opposition and becoming the best crew to have competed, the girls were presented to King Albert of the Belgians furthering and promoting international women's rowing. Gentry also won in the first women's eights race in 1927, already renowned for her service to British rowing, being Captain of her club, and responsible for getting Weybridge Ladies RC up on it's feet, she was elected Chairman and held office until her death fifty years later.

Di Ellis: Mrs. Ellis, current chairman of the Amateur Rowing Association, rowed for St. George's Ladies' RC and stroked the GB eight in the 1966 European Championships. She qualified as an umpire in 1978 and has chaired the Amateur Rowing Association Executive Committee since 1989; she also represents the Amateur Rowing Association on the British Olympic Association and in 1997 was elected a Steward of Henley Royal Regatta, the first woman ever to be elected in her own right. Mrs. Ellis' work for the Amateur Rowing Association is voluntary, she has done a great deal for rowing in this country showing dedication and commitment to the sport.

NATIONAL FEDERATION

Amateur Rowing Association
6 Lower Mall
London, W6 9DJ
United Kingdom
Tel: +44 208 237 6700
Fax: +44 208 237 67
Email: sophie@ara-rowing.org
www.ara-rowing.org

CLUBS

A.B. Severn BC
Riverside, 5 King Stephens Mount
Worcester, WR2 5PL
United Kingdom
Contact: Mr. B Griffin
Tel: +44 19 0542 9924

Abingdon RC
57 Anna Pavlova Close, Abingdon
Oxon, OX14 1TF
United Kingdom
Contact: Julian Fowler
Tel: +44 12 3552 4338
Email: julian_fowler_uk@yahoo.co.uk
BH: Wilsham Road, Abingdon
Oxon, OX14 5LD
United Kingdom

Acheronians RC
21a Strathville Road, London
SW18 4QX, United Kingdom
Contact: Mr Alistair Thomas
BH: Thames RC, Embankment
Putney, London, SW15 1LB
United Kingdom
Tel: +44 20 8788 0798

Agecroft RC
5 Wentworth Avenue, Salford
M6 8BG, United Kingdom
Contact: Mr. S Hitchen
Tel: +44 16 1281 7620
Email: hitchen25555@aol.com
BH: The Watersports Centre, Quays Road
Salford Quays, Salford, M5 2SQ
United Kingdom

Alpha Womens ARC
12 Woodville Road, Ealing
London, W5 2SF
United Kingdom
Contact: Mrs. N Padwick
Tel: +44 20 8997 5671
Fax: +44 20 8997 5671
Email: nin@mortlake.net
BH: Mortlake Anglian & Alpha BC, Ibis Lane
Hartington Road, London, W4 3UJ
Tel: +44 20 8994 1628

Ancholme RC
27 St. Francis Grove, Laceby
Grimsby, N.E. Lincs, DN37 7HG
United Kingdom
Contact: Mrs. P Rhoades
Tel: +44 14 7227 6844
Email: patricerhoades@hotmail.com
BH: 14 Manley Gardens, Brigg
N. Lincs, DN20 8LW

Ardingly RC
Melaise, London Road
Sayers Common, W. Sussex, BN6 9HX
United Kingdom
Contact: Mrs. S Taylor
Tel: +44 12 7383 5248
Fax: +44 12 7383 4003
Email: rowcoach@msn.com
BH: Ardingly Activity Centre, College Road
Ardingly Reservoir, Ardingly
Tel: +44 14 4489 2549

Argonaut Club
7 Combe Road, Oxford
OX2 6BL, United Kingdom
Contact: Dr. M. Munafo
Tel: +44 18 6522 6756
Fax: +44 18 6522 7137
Email: argo@coglit.ecs.soton.ac.uk
BH: Christ Church Meadows, Oxford
United Kingdom

Aries BC
17a Weltje Road, Hammersmith
London, W6 9TG
United Kingdom
Contact: Chris Richards
Tel: +44 20 8563 8712
BH: Archbishop Holgate School Boat House
Clifton, York

Army RC
c/o Army Sports Control Board
Block M, Clayton Barracks
Aldershot, GU11 2BG
United Kingdom
Contact: Major M Schofield
Tel: +44 78 8503 8642
Email: armyrowing@army.mod.uk.net
BH: Andrews Boathouse
Dorney Lake, off Cart Lane
Boveney, Windsor, SL4 6QP

Athena/YMCA
1 Kinnerton, Chester
CH4 9AE, United Kingdom
Contact: Mandy Stein-Lear
Tel: +44 12 4466 1346
BH: 22a The Gorves, Chester
CH1 1SD
Tel: +44 12 4431 0865

Auriol Kensington RC
14 Lower Mall, Hammersmith
London, W6 9DJ, United Kingdom
Contact: Mr. P J V Taylor
Tel: +44 20 8840 3925
Email: pjv_taylor@compuserve.com
BH: 14 Lower Mall, Hammersmith
London, W6 9DJ
Tel: +44 20 8748 5352

Avon & Somerset Police PC
Contact: Mrs. N Marsh
Tel: + 44 17 6145 2536
Fax: +44 11 7945 5762
BH: City of Bristol RC
Albion Dockside Estate
Honover Place, Bristol, BS1 6TR
United Kingdom

Avon County RC
Contact: Philippa Sondheimer
Tel: +44 12 2547 1661
Fax: +44 12 2578 0109
Email: philippa@haringtonglass.co.uk
BH: The Shallows, Saltford
Bristol, BA2 4PG
United Kingdom

B.T.C. (Southampton) RC
BH: BTC RC Crosshouse Road, Chapel
Southampton, SO14 1GZ
United Kingdom
Tel: +44 23 8023 1591

Bacon BC
University Boathouse, Trentside
West Bridgford, Nottingham, NG2 5AF
United Kingdom
Contact: Mr. M Chmiel
Tel: +44 11 5951 5516
Fax: +44 11 5951 5525
BH: Nottingham University Boathouse

Bar, The, BC
BH: London RC, Embankment
Putney, London, WC2A 3UA
United Kingdom
Tel: +44 20 8788 0666

Barclays Bank RC
6 Downs Park, Herne Bay
Kent, CT6 6BY
United Kingdom
Contact: Mr. M D Kennedy
Email: midiken@btopenworld.com

Barnes Bridge Ladies RC
BH: Civil Service Boathouse
Dukes Meadows
Chiswick, London, W4 2SH
United Kingdom
Tel: +44 20 8994 0025

Beccles RC
5 The Street, North Cove
Beccles, Suffolk, NR34 7PN
United Kingdom
Contact: James Bartram
Tel: +44 15 0247 6429
Fax: +44 16 0359 1184
Email: j.bartram@uea.ac.uk
BH: Swimming Pool Pontoon
Pudding Moor, Beccles

Bedford Ladies RC
BH: Star Club, Poynters Boathouse, Batts Ford
7 Commercial Road, Bedford, MK40 1RF
United Kingdom
Tel: +44 12 3435 4495

Bedford RC
BH: The Boathouse, Duck Mill Lane
Bedford, MK42 0AX
United Kingdom
Tel: +44 12 3421 8148/event line

Bedford Star RC
BH: Star Club, Poynters Boathouse, Batts Ford
7 Commercial Road, Bedford, MK42 0AX
United Kingdom

Belvoir ARC
BH: Leicester RC, Bede Island
Leicester
United Kingdom
Tel: +44 11 6254 3203

Bentham BC
BH: University of London BC
81 Hartington Road
Chiswick, London, W4 3TU
United Kingdom
Tel: +44 20 8994 5928

Berwick ARC
BH: New Road, Berwick upon Tweed
United Kingdom
Tel: +44 12 8930 8428

Bewdley RC
BH: Severnside North, Wribbenhall
Bewdley, Worcs, DY12 2EE
United Kingdom
Tel: +44 12 9940 2899

Bewl Bridge RC
BH: Bewl Bridge Reservoir
Lamberhurst, Kent
United Kingdom
Tel: +44 18 9253 7959

Bexhill ARC
Contact: Mrs N Gowers
Tel: +44 14 2421 9341
Fax: +44 14 2421 9341
BH: The Colonade, Bexhill-on-Sea
E Sussex, United Kingdom

Bideford Amateur Athletic
BH: The Pill, Kingsley Road
Bideford, Devon, EX39 2PF
United Kingdom
Tel: +44 12 3747 9696

Bideford ARC
Contact: Carole Hadcroft
Tel: +44 12 3747 1344
Fax: +44 12 3747 0221
Email: carol@hadcroft1120.freeserve.co.uk
BH: The Quay, Bideford
Devon, EX39 2EY
United Kingdom

Birmingham RC
BH: c/o Rangers Lodge
115 Reservoir Road
Edgbaston, Birmingham, B16 9EE
United Kingdom
Tel: +44 12 1452 1408

Black Prince BC
BH: 1st & 3rd Trinity BC
Kimberley Road
Cambridge, United Kingdom
Tel: +44 12 2335 6589

Black Sheep RC
51 Greville Road, Cambridge
CB1 3QJ, United Kingdom
Contact: Dom Pickersgill
Tel: +44 12 2369 3941
Email: dom@blacksheepsportingclub.co.uk

Blue Coat BC
Contact: Mr. B Nolan
Tel: +44 77 8662 4904
Fax: +44 11 8976 0119
Email: bnolan1279@aol.com
BH: Reading Blue Coat School, Holme Park
Sonning on Thames, Berks, RG4 6SU
United Kingdom

Blue Star Club
BH: Newcastle University BC
Newburn, Newcastle upon Tyne
United Kingdom
Tel: +44 19 1414 6710

Boar's Head BC
BH: Queens' College Boathouse
Trafalgar Road
Cambridge, CB4 1EU
United Kingdom
Tel: +44 12 2374 0633

Bosporos BC
Contact: Mr. P A J Bridge
Tel: +44 20 8748 0053
Email: peterbridge@freeuk.com
BH: Crabtree Boathouse
Putney Embankment
London, SW15 1LB
United Kingdom

Boston RC
Contact: Mr. J Elms
Tel: +44 12 0536 9289
Email: jeff@elms94.fsnet.co.uk
BH: Carlton Road, Boston
Lincs, PE21 8LL
United Kingdom

Bournemouth University Alumni BC
Contact: Mr.s S L Ayles
Tel: +44 12 0271 8832
Email: kevayles@mcmail.com
BH: Canford School BC, Wimborne
Dorset, NH21 3AD
United Kingdom

Bowbridge BC
Contact: Mr. D G Peill
Tel: +44 20 7585 3994
Email: dpeill@Fpdsavills.co.uk
BH: Reading Road, Cholsey
Wallingford, Oxon, OX10 9HG
United Kingdom

Bradford on Avon RC
BH: Barton Bridge, Pound Lane
Bradford on Avon, BA15 1LF
United Kingdom
Tel: +44 12 2586 2554

Bridgnorth RC
BH: The Maltings, Bandon Lane, Bridgnorth
Shropshire, WV15, United Kingdom
Tel: +44 17 4676 8151

Bristol Ariel RC
Contact: Ms. J Perrins
Tel: +44 14 5461 7262
BH: Birchwood, St. Annes
Bristol, United Kingdom

Bristol, City of, RC
BH: Albion Dockside Estate, Hanover Place
Bristol, BS1 6TR, United Kingdom
Tel: +44 11 7954 4621

British Airways RC
BH: Staines BC, 28 Riverside Drive
Chertsey Lane, Staines, TW18 3JN
United Kingdom
Tel: +44 17 8445 3595

Broxbourne RC
BH: Old Nazeing Road, Broxbourne
Herts, EN10 6QU
United Kingdom
Tel: +44 01 9246 3821

Bryanston Buffaloes BC
BH: Bryanston School BC, River Stour
United Kingdom
Tel: +44 12 5848 4669

Burton Leander RC
BH: Stapenhill Road, Burton on Trent
Staffs, DE15 9AE
United Kingdom
Tel: +44 12 8353 3853

Burway RC
BH: Thameside, Laleham on Thames
United Kingdom
Tel: +44 17 8445 4860

Cambois RC
Contact: Mr. R Brown
Tel: +44 16 7082 8371
BH: Blackclose Bank, Riverside Park
Ashington, Northumberland
United Kingdom

Cambridge 99 RC
BH: Kimberley Road, Cambridge
CB4 1HJ, United Kingdom
Tel: +44 12 2336 7521

Cambridge, City of, RC
Contact: Nicolle McNaughton
Tel: +44 79 8954 2431
Email: nicolle_c_mcnaughton@gsk.com
BH: Riverside, via Kimberley Road
Cambridge, United Kingdom

Canford Crocodiles BC
Contact: Mr. D H Drury
Tel: +44 12 0288 2686
BH: Canford School BC, River Stour Canford
Wimborne, Dorset
United Kingdom

Cantabrigian RC
Contact: Mr. C Dixon
Tel: +44 12 2372 1566
BH: CRA Boathouse, Banhams Middle Yard
Kimberley Road, Cambridge, CB4 1JH
United Kingdom

Canterbury Pilgrims BC
Contact: Mr. A C Rudkin
Tel: +44 13 2783 0965
Fax: +44 13 2787 2728
Email: andrew@canterburypilgrims.com
BH: c/o Kings School Canterbury BC
Westbere Lakes, Fordwich
Canterbury, Kent
United Kingdom

Castle Dore RC
Contact: Mrs. A Cameron
Tel: +44 12 0887 2626
BH: The Boat Shed, Golant, Fowey
Cornwall, United Kingdom

Cerberus BC
Contact: Mr. D E Pinniger
Tel: +44 77 8643 6281
Email: david.pinniger@morganstanley.com
BH: Lady Margaret Hall BC, Oxford
OX2 6QA, United Kingdom

Champion of the Thames (Cambridge) RC
Contact: Mr. P Welton
Tel: +44 12 2344 0317
Email: family@kwelton.fsnet.co.uk
BH: CRA Boathouse, Kimberley Road
Cambridge, CB4 6DA
United Kingdom

Chester Le Street ARC
Contact: Mr. R Heywood
Tel: +44 19 1388 2253
BH: Riverside Sports Complex
Chester Le Street
Co. Durham, United Kingdom

Christchurch RC
BH: River Bank, Wick Lane
Christchurch, Dorset, BH23 1HU
United Kingdom
Tel: +44 12 0248 4964

Colet BC
BH: St. Paul's School BC, Lonsdale Road
London, SW13 9JT
United Kingdom
Tel: +44 20 8748 7184

Combined Services RC
HQ 4 Division, Steeles Road
Aldershot, GU11 2 DP
United Kingdom
Contact: Lt. Col. D J Norton
Tel: +44 12 5261 3129
Fax: +44 12 5234 7010
Email: DCOS.4DIV@gtnet.gov.uk

Crabtree BC
Contact: Theo Brun
Tel: +44 77 6838 4328
Email: mark.davies@betfair.com
BH: Crabtree Boathouse, Embankment
Putney, London, SW15 1LB
United Kingdom

Crane Foundry RC
Contact: Mr. R M Lackner
Tel: +44 13 3255 7757
Fax: +44 13 3254 1364
Email: rogvet@aol.com
BH: Derby RC, Darley Grove
Derby, DE1 3AY
United Kingdom
Tel: +44 13 3246319

Crescent RC
BH: Spring Hill Rowing Centre, Clapton
London, E5 9BL
United Kingdom
Tel: +44 20 8806 8282

Curlew RC
BH: Curlew RC, Trafalgar Centre, Crane Street
London, SE10 9NP
United Kingdom
Tel: +44 79 6872 8555

Cygnet RC
BH: Civil Service Boathouse, Dukes Meadows
Chiswick, London, W4 2SH
United Kingdom
Tel: +44 20 8994 0225

Dacre BC
BH: c/o Emmanuel School BC
Dukes Meadows
Chiswick, London, W4 2SH
United Kingdom
Tel: +44 70 5025 5906

Danesfield (Thames) Club
BH: New Lock, Henley Road, Medmenham
Marlow, Bucks
United Kingdom
Tel: +44 14 9157 1599

Danson RC
BH: Leisure Link, Danson Park, Danson Road
Bexleyheath, Kent, DA16 1TQ
United Kingdom
Tel: +44 20 8303 2828

Dartmouth ARC
BH: Sandquay Road, Dartmouth
Devon, TQ6 9PH
United Kingdom
Tel: +44 18 0383 4149

Dart-Totnes ARC
BH: Long Marsh, Steamer Quay Road
Totnes, Devon, TQ9 5AL
United Kingdom
Tel: +44 18 0386 3772

Deal Walmer and Kingsdown
BH: The Clubhouse
16/18 The Marina, Deal
Kent, CT14 6NG
United Kingdom
Tel: +44 13 0437 3409

Deben RC
Contact: Ms. A. Hedington
Tel: +44 14 7321 4799
Fax: +44 14 7323 1727
Email: anna.hedington@bt.com
BH: The River Wall, Woodbridge
Suffolk, United Kingdom

Derby RC
BH: Darley Grove, Derby
DE1 3AY, United Kingdom
Tel: +44 13 3234 6319

Derwent RC
BH: The White Boathouse
Darley Grove
Derby, DE1 3AY
United Kingdom
Tel: +44 13 3236 7233

Doncaster RC
BH: The Old Boathouse
The Dell, Hexthorpe
Doncaster, United Kingdom
Tel: +44 78 1415 4139

Dorney BC
BH: Boveney Boathouse, Dorney Lake
United Kingdom
Tel: +44 17 5383 2756

Dover RC
BH: The Esplanade
Waterloo Crescent, Dover
Kent, United Kingdom
Tel: +44 13 0421 3566

Drapers, The, RC
Contact: Mr. J E Hasler
Tel: +44 20 7480 3262
BH: University of London
81 Hartington Road
Chiswick, London, W4 3TU
United Kingdom

Durham ARC
BH: City Boathouse, Green Lane
Old Evet, Durham, DH1 3JU
United Kingdom
Tel: +44 19 1386 6431

Eastbourne RC
Contact: Mrs. L Baker
Tel: +44 13 2376 4393
BH: Royal Parade, Eastbourne
East Sussex, BN22 7LD
United Kingdom

Erith RC
BH: Saltford Close, Erith
Kent, DA8 1SA
United Kingdom
Tel: +44 79 3938 7835

Eton Excelsior RC
Contact: Ms. C Davies
Tel: +44 17 5385 7537
Fax: +44 17 5367 1265
Email: ceri.davies@etoncollege.org.uk
BH: Maidenhead Road, Windsor Berks
United Kingdom

Eton Mission RC
Contact: Mr. T Hinchliff
Tel: +44 20 8508 6129
BH: Gilbert Johnson Boathouse
127 Wallis Road
Hackney Wick, London, E9 5LN
United Kingdom

Eton Vikings Club
Contact: Dr. G R Pooley
Tel: +44 17 5367 1095
Fax: +44 17 5367 1159
Email: vikings@etoncollege.org.uk
BH: Eton College BC, Rafts Boathouse
Brocas Street, Eton, Windsor
United Kingdom

Evesham RC
BH: Abbey Park, Evesham
Worcs, WR11 4ST
United Kingdom
Tel: +44 13 8644 6131

Exeter RC
BH: Exe Water Sports Association
62 Haven Road
Exeter, Devon, EX2 8DP
United Kingdom
Tel: +44 13 9225 0740

Exmouth RC
BH: The Esplanade, Exmouth
EX8 2AZ, United Kingdom
Tel: +44 13 9527 2776

Eyre Club
BH: c/o Thames RC, The Embankment
Putney, London, SW15 1LB
United Kingdom
Tel: +44 20 8788 0798

Falcon RC
BH: Meadow Lane (off Iffley Road)
Oxford, United Kingdom
Tel: +44 12 3576 9196

Farmer BC
Magdalen College, Oxford
OX1 4AU, United Kingdom
Contact: Mr. M R Blandford-Baker
Tel: +44 18 6527 6111
Fax: +44 18 6527 6030
Email: mark.blandford-baker@madg.ox.ac.uk
BH: Cambridge

Folkestone RC
BH: The Clubhouse, The Parade, Sandgate
Folkestone, Kent, CT20 3AL
United Kingdom
Tel: +44 13 0324 8228

Free Radical RC
13 Forsells End, Houghton-on-the-Hill
Leics, LE7 9HQ
United Kingdom
Contact: Simon Hughes
Tel: +44 11 6241 6727
Email: simes2002@hotmail.com

Furnivall Sculling Club
BH: 19 Lower Mall, Hammersmith
London, W6 9DJ
United Kingdom
Tel: +44 20 8748 6867

Globe RC
BH: Trafalgar Rowing Centre
11/13 Crane Street, Greenwich
London, SE10 9NP
United Kingdom
Tel: +44 20 8858 2106

Gloucester RC
BH: Gloucester Boathouse
326 Bristol Road
Hempsted, Gloucester, GL2 5DH
United Kingdom
Tel: +44 14 5252 3795

Gonville BC
BH: Caius Boathouse, Ferry Path
Cambridge, CB1
United Kingdom
Tel: +44 12 2333 2400

Goring Gap RC
Contact: Mrs. A F Budesha
Tel: +44 14 9168 0917
BH: Oratory Boathouse, Hardwick Road
Whitchurch-on-Thames, Oxon
United Kingdom

Grafham Water Rowing
Contact: Ms. J Edmunds
Tel: +44 14 8081 0521
Fax: +44 14 8081 3850
Email: judy.edmunds@education.camcnty.gov.uk
BH: Grafham Water Centre, Perry
Huntingdon, PE28 0BX
United Kingdom

Gravesend RC
BH: New Bridge, Gordon Promenade
Gravesend, Kent, DA12 2BS
United Kingdom
Tel: +44 14 7435 2636

Greenbank Falmouth RC
BH: Falmouth Watersports Centre, Grove Place
Falmouth, Cornwall, TR11 4AU
United Kingdom
Tel: +44 13 2621 1223

Griffen, The, BC
BH: Abingdon School BC, Wilsham Road
Abingdon, Oxon
United Kingdom
Tel: +44 12 3552 0145

Grosvenor RC
BH: The Groves, Chester
CH1 1SD, United Kingdom
Tel: +44 12 4431 1231

Guildford RC
BH: The Boathouse, Shalford Road
Guildford, GU1 3XL
United Kingdom
Tel: +44 14 8356 5849

Hastings & St Leonards RC
BH: The Boathouse, Carlisle Parade
Hastings, E. Sussex
United Kingdom
Tel: +44 14 2442 1868

Henley RC
BH: Wargrave Road, Henley Thames
Oxon, RG9 3JD
United Kingdom
Tel: +44 14 9157 3943

Hereford RC
BH: 37 Greyhriars Avenue, Hereford
HR4 0BE, United Kingdom
Tel: +44 14 3227 3915

Herne Bay ARC
BH: Spa Esplanade, Hampton
Herne Bay, CT6 8EP
United Kingdom
Tel: +44 12 2736 4796

Hexham RC
12 Leazes Crescent, Hexham
Northumberland, NE46 3JZ
United Kingdom
Contact: Mrs L Siddle
Tel: +44 14 3460 9864
Email: lucy@the-siddles.fsnet.co.uk
BH: Tyne Green, Hexham

Hinksey Sculling School
The Barn, Thrupp
Kidlington, Oxford, OX5 1JY
United Kingdom
Contact: John C Broadhurst
Tel: +44 18 6584 2552
Fax: +44 18 6584 2551
Email: john@oer.co.uk
BH: South Oxford

Hollingworth Lake RC
BH: The Clubhouse, Lake Bank
Littleborough, Lancs, OL15 0DQ
United Kingdom
Tel: +44 17 0637 7261

Holme Pierrepont RC
60 Green Lane, Ockbrook
Derbyshire, DE72 3SE
United Kingdom
Contact: Mrs M Marshall
Tel: +44 13 3267 3619
BH: National Watersports Centre
Holme Pierrepont
Nottingham, NG12 2LU

Hornet BC
Contact: Mr. P Knights
Tel: +44 12 2374 0633
Fax: +44 12 2374 0633
Email: PMK26@CAM.AC.UK
BH: Queens' College Boathouse
Trafalgar Road
Cambridge, CB4 1EU
United Kingdom

Horseferry RC
BH: Ibis Lane, Hartington Road
London, W4 3UJ
United Kingdom
Tel: +44 20 8994 1628

HSBC RC
BH: Embankment, Putney
London, SW15 1LB
United Kingdom
Tel: +44 20 8788 3055

Huntingdon BC
BH: The Boathouse, Riverside Park
Hartford Road, Huntingdon, PE29 3RP
United Kingdom
Tel: +44 14 8045 6963

Icena Club
Contact: Mr. J Bracey
Tel: +44 19 6282 0217
Fax: +44 19 6262 1106
BH: Winchester College BC
Domun Road, Winchester
United Kingdom

Infantry RC
Le Merchant House
Royal Military Academy Sandhurst
Camberley, Surrey, GU15 4PQ
United Kingdom
Contact: Capt. M Tovell
Tel: +44 12 7641 2422
Fax: +44 12 7641 2105
BH: Eton, Windsor

Infidel, The, BC
2 Horseshoe Cottage, The Street
Greywell, Hook
Hants, RG29 1BY
United Kingdom
Contact: Mr. A Petrie
Tel: +44 12 5670 4669
BH: c/o Girton College BC, Cambridge

Ironbridge RC
BH: Buildwas Road, Coalbrookdale
Telford, TF8 7DW
United Kingdom
Tel: +44 19 5243 2798

ISCA Skullers
25 Higher Warborough Road
Galmpton, Brixham
Devon, TQ5 0PF
United Kingdom
Contact: Mr. R J Davis
Tel: +44 18 0384 4020
Fax: +44 18 0384 3700

Itchen Imperial RC
5 Hounsdown Close, Hounsdown
Totton, Southampton
Hants, SO40 9EW
United Kingdom
Contact: Mr. G S Joyce
Tel: +44 23 8087 1762
Email: gary.joyce2@btopenworld.com
BH: Crosshouse Road, Chapel
Southampton

Juniper Club
BH: Nottingham BC
Middle of 3 Trentside North
West Bridgford, Nottingham, NG2 5FA
United Kingdom
Tel: +44 11 5981 1251

Kingston RC
BH: Canbury Gardens, Lower Ham Road
Kingston on Thames, Surrey, KT2 5AU
United Kingdom
Tel: +44 20 8546 8592

Kingston Grammar Sch. Veterans BC
BH: Kingston Grammar School BC
Aragon Avenue, Thames Ditton, Surrey
United Kingdom
Tel: +44 20 8398 5138

Lancaster John O'Gaunt BC
BH: Halton Road, Skerton
Lancaster, United Kingdom
Tel: +44 15 2484 8285

Lea RC
BH: The Boathouse, Spring Hill
Clapton, London, E5 9BL
United Kingdom
Tel: +44 20 8806 8282

Leander Club
BH: Henley on Thames, Oxon
RG9 2LP, United Kingdom
Tel: +44 19 9157 5782

Leicester RC
BH: The Bede House, Upperton Road
Leicester, LE2 7GR
United Kingdom
Tel: +44 11 6254 3203

Leviathan BC
BH: Trowse Water Sports Centre
Whitlingham Lane
Trowse, Norwich, NR14 8TR
United Kingdom
Tel: +44 16 9258 0447

Lions BC
Contact: Mr. A Whitehorn
Tel: +44 20 8894 5432
BH: The Millenium Boathouse
Lower Sunbury Road
Hampton, Middx
United Kingdom

Liverpool Victoria RC
BH: Wirral Rowing Centre
Poulton Bridge Road
Wallasey, CH62 4UL
United Kingdom
Tel: +44 15 1639 0354

London RC
BH: Embankment, Putney
London, SW15 1LB
United Kingdom
Tel: +44 20 8788 8643

Loughborough BC
BH: County Bridge, Rempstone Road
Hathern, Loughborough, LE12 5JN
United Kingdom
Tel: +44 15 0984 2300

Lowestoft RC
Contact: Mr. N S Lyman, Capt.
Tel: +44 15 0258 5829
BH: Oulton Broad, Lowestoft
Suffolk, United Kingdom

Lymington ARC
90 Samber Close, Lymington
Hants, SO41 9LF
United Kingdom
Contact: Mrs. Suzan Mullins
Tel: +44 77 3486 6492
Email: suzanlarc@yahoo.co.uk
BH: Quay Road, Lymington

Maidenhead RC
BH: The Boathouse, River Road, Taplow
Maidenhead, Berks, SL6 0AT
Tel: +44 16 2862 2664

Maidstone Invicta RC
Contact: Sue Westcott
Tel: +44 16 2281 2786
BH: Maidstone Rowing Centre, James Whatman Way
Maidstone, Kent, ME14 1LQ

Marlow RC
BH: Marlow Bridge, Bisham Road, Marlow
Bucks, SL7 1RH
United Kingdom
Tel: +44 16 2848 2366

Maximum Entropy BC
Cavendish Laboratory, Madingley Road
Cambridge, CB3 0HE
United Kingdom
Contact: Dr. S Gull
Tel: +44 12 2333 7503
BH: Lady Margaret BC, Victoria Bridge
Cambridge

Medway Towns RC
Contact: Ian Wright
Tel: +44 16 8987 6992
BH: Esplanade, Rochester
Kent, ME1 1QL
United Kingdom

Merchants 98 BC
Contact: Mr. G Holden
Tel: +44 15 1924 2770
BH: Merchants Taylors' School Boathouse, Marine
Lake, Promenade
Southport

Mersey RC
Capt. 7 Yelverton Close, Halewood
Liverpool, L26 7NY
United Kingdom
Contact: Mr. M Fogarty
BH: Albert Dock Head, Pier Head
Liverpool

Merton Gannets BC
c/o Merton College, Oxford
OX1 4JD
United Kingdom
Contact: Ms. A L Goodgame
Tel: +44 18 6527 6310
BH: Merton College Boathouse, Oxford

Metropolitan Police RC
BH: Mortlake Anglian & Alpha BC Boathouse, Ibis
Lane
Chiswick, London, W4
United Kingdom
Tel: +44 20 8994 1628

Metropolitan RC
BH: Embankment, Putney
London, SW15 1LB
United Kingdom
Tel: +44 20 8788 8643

Milton Keynes RC
BH: De Montfort Watersports Centre
Caldecote Lake
Caldecote, Milton Keynes
United Kingdom
Tel: +44 19 0826 0223

Minerva Bath RC
Cedar Cottage, Upper Wraxall
Nr Chippenham, Wilts, SN14 7AG
United Kingdom
Contact: Gary John
Tel: +44 12 2589 1370
BH: Batheaston, Bath.

Molesey BC
BH: Barge Walk, Graburn Way
East Molesey, Surrey, KT8 9AJ
United Kingdom
Tel: +44 20 8979 7161

Monkton Bluefriars BC
1 Church Cottages, Monkton Combe
Bath, BA2 7HB
United Kingdom
Contact: Mr. J M Newick
Tel: +44 12 2572 3583
Fax: +44 12 2572 2033
Email: julian@bewick.org
BH: Monkton Combe School BC
Bath, BA2 7HG

Mortlake Anglian & Alpha BC
BH: The Boathouse, Ibis Lane (off Hartington Road)
Chiswick, London, W4 3UJ
United Kingdom
Tel: +44 20 8994 1628

Newark RC
BH: Farndon Road, Newark
Notts, NG24 4SE
United Kingdom
Tel: +44 16 3670 2351

Newport RC
Contact: Mr. R Keats
Tel: +44 19 8355 1261
Email: bobkeats@aol.com
BH: Hurstake, Riverway
Newport, Isle of Wight, PO30 5XH
United Kingdom

North Stafforshire RC
Contact: Mrs. C.A. Hiidhitch
Tel: +44 17 8263 5787
BH: Rudyard Lake, Lake Road
Rudyard, Leek
United Kingdom

Northampton RC
BH: c/o Nene Whitewater Centre, Bedford Rd.
Northampton, NN4 7AA
United Kingdom
Tel: +44 16 0463 4040

Northwich RC
BH: The Crescent, Riverside, Northwich
Chesire, CW9 8AE
United Kingdom
Tel: +44 16 0649 461

Norwich RC
BH: Trowse Water Sports Centre,
Whitlingham Lane
Trowse, Norwich, NR14 8TR
United Kingdom
Tel: +44 16 0362 2540

Norwich Union RC
Jubilee Cottage, 14 Norwich
NR9 5BS, United Kingdom
Contact: Mr. J A Skipper
Tel: +44 16 0388 0720
Email: skip@honingham75.freeserve.co.uk
BH: Thorpe St. Andrew (River Yare)

Nottingham and Union RC
8 Sheraton Drive, Wollaton
Nottingham, NG8 2PR
United Kingdom
Contact: Mr. P S Maxwell
Tel: +44 11 5981 1120
Email: peter@dri-pax.co.uk
BH: Trent Bridge, Nottingham

Nottingham BC
BH: Middle of the Three, Trent Side North
West Bridgford, Nottingham, NG2 5FA
Tel: +44 11 5981 1251

Nottingham Britannica RC
BH: Trentside, Trent Bridge
Nottingham, NG2 5FA
United Kingdom
Tel: +44 11 5981 9291

Nottinghamshire County Rowing Assn
Contact: Mrs. M Marshall
Tel: +44 13 3267 3619
BH: National Watersports Centre, Holme Pierrepont
Nottingham, NG12 2LU
United Kingdom

Orange BC
10 Heathside, Hanger Hill
Weybridge, Surrey, KT13 9YQ
United Kingdom
Contact: Mr. R A Moore
Tel: +44 19 3285 5662

Oratory Cardinals RC
BH: The Oratory School BC
Sheepwash Lane
Whitchurch on Thames
United Kingdom
Tel: +44 11 8984 1092

Orion RC
PO Box 28918, London
SW14 8FL
United Kingdom
Contact: Mr. M Thomson
Tel: +44 20 8878 1676
Email: orion@outriggers.org

Osney Island BC
BH: c/o Captain, 20 East Steet, Osney Island
Oxford, OX2 0AU
United Kingdom
Tel: +44 18 6542 1269

Oundle RC
The Firs, Main Street, Southwick
Oundle, Peterborough, PE8 5BL
United Kingdom
Contact: Mr. R B Davies
Tel: +44 18 3227 4782
Email: oundle.rowing@virgin.net
BH: Oundle BC, The Maltings
Station Road, Oundle

Oxford & District Sculling Centre
The Old Post Office, The Square, Longworth
Oxon, OX13 5DT
United Kingdom
Contact: Mr. F Mascaro
Tel: +44 18 6582 0578
Fax: +44 18 6582 0408
Email: masc96intl@aol.com
BH: Tollgate Road, Culham
Abingdon, Oxon, OX14 1NE

Oxford Adaptive RC
BH: City of Oxford RC
Donnington Bridge
Iffley, Oxford
United Kingdom
Tel: +44 18 6577 1633

Oxford, City of, RC
BH: City Boathouse, Meadow Lane
Oxford, OX4 4BL
United Kingdom
Tel: +44 18 6524 2576

Paignton ARC
Contact: Christine Williams
Tel: +44 18 0386 1842
Email: christine.williams@swdhis.nhs.uk
BH: The Club Bouse
The South Quay, Paignton Harbour
Paignton, Devon, TQ4 6DT
United Kingdom
Tel: +44 18 040 1920

Parr's Priory RC
22 Garrard Road, Banstead
Surrey, SM7 2ER
United Kingdom
Contact: Matthew Wing
Tel: +44 77 9075 7216
Email: msw_fmb@hotmail.com
BH: Barn Elms Boathouse, Queen Elizabeth Walk
Barnes, London, SW13 0DG

Pengwern BC
BH: Kingsland, Shrewsbury
Shropshire, SY3 7BD
United Kingdom
Tel: +44 17 4335 4907

Peterborough City RC
BH: Thorpe Meadows, Thorpe Road
Peterborough, United Kingdom
Tel: +44 17 3334 1333

Phoenix RC
BH: MAABC, Ibis Boathouse
Ibis Lane, Hartington Road
Chiswick, London, W4 3UJ
United Kingdom
Tel: +44 20 8994 1628

Plymouth ARC
BH: Arnolds Point
The Embankment, Plymouth
United Kingdom
Tel: +44 17 5226 0291

Poole ARC
51 Pinewood Road, Upton
Poole, Dorset, BH15 1JD
United Kingdom
Contact: Mrs. L Diffey
Tel: +44 12 0277 6880
BH: 1 West Quay Road, Poole
Dorset, BH15 1JD

Poplar Blackwall & District RC
BH: The Boathouse, Ferry Street
London, E14 3DT
United Kingdom
Tel: +44 20 7987 3071

Prince William School & Oundle Town RC
26 Barnwell, Peterborough
PE8 5PZ, United Kingdom
Contact: Ms. Jemma Shacklock
Tel: +44 18 3227 4172

Putney Town RC
BH: Kew Meadows Path, Kew, Richmond
Surrey, TW9 4EN
United Kingdom
Tel: +44 20 8878 8236

Quintin BC
BH: University Boathouse
Ibis Lane, Hartington Road
London, W4 3UJ
United Kingdom
Tel: +44 20 8994 3715

R.E.M.E RC
HQ REME Trg GP, Box No. H095
Hazebrouck Barracks
Arborfield, Reading, RG2 9NJ
United Kingdom
Contact: Mr. P J Mardsen
Tel: +44 11 8976 3503

R.M.A. Sandhurst BC
Dept. of Defence & Intl. Affairs, RMA Sandhurst
Camberley, Surrey, GU15 4PQ
United Kingdom
Contact: Mr. J. A Higgs
Tel: +44 12 7641 2342
Fax: +44 12 7641 2511
Email: jimhiggs@hotmail.com

Radley Mariners
BH: Radley College BC
Lower Radley, Abingdon
Oxon, United Kingdom
Tel: +44 12 3554 3103

Reading RC
BH: 1 The Boathouse
Thameside Promenade, Reading
Berks, RG1 8EQ
United Kingdom
Tel: +44 11 8956 7091

Rentacrew RC
Spring Cottage, Ibston, High Wycombe
Bucks, HP14 3XT
United Kingdom
Contact: Mr. J D Randall
Tel: +44 14 9163 8577
Fax: +44 20 7404 4472
BH: Henley on Thames, Oxon

Rex BC
24 Hough Green, Chester
CH4 8JG, United Kingdom
Contact: Dr. C J Mackay
Tel: +44 12 4468 2675
BH: King's School Chester RC, Chester

Rhinos RC
52 Kings Road, Kingston upon Thames
Surrey, KT2 5HS
United Kingdom
Contact: Ben Nicholson

Rob Roy BC
c/o Cambridge Rowing Assn. Boathouse, via
Kimberley Road
Cambridge, CB4 1HJ
United Kingdom
Contact: Mr. S J Hames
Tel: +44 12 2350 2742

Ross RC
BH: Brooksmouth, The Ropewalk, Ross on Wye
Herefordshire, United Kingdom
Tel: +44 19 8956 5436

Row Caldecotte
BH: George Amey Centre, 366 Simpson
Milton Keynes, MK6 3AG
United Kingdom
Tel: +4419 0823 2042

Royal Air Force RC
12 The Oval, Ashby de la Launde
Lincoln, LN4 3JE
United Kingdom
Contact: Mr. A Alden Capt/Boats
Tel: +44 15 2632 7428
Email: captain_rafrc@yahoo.com
BH: c/o Danesfield (Thames) Club
Medmenham, Marlow, Bucks

Royal Artillery BC
RHQ RA Artillery House, RA Barracks
Woolwich, London, SE18 4BH
United Kingdom
Contact: Capt. J E H Vigne
Tel: +44 17 5223 6002
Fax: +44 17 5223 6012
Email: gunner_rowing@hotmail.com

Royal Chester RC
BH: The Groves, Chester
CH1 1SD, United Kingdom
Tel: +44 12 4432 2468

Royal Docks RC
Dockside Road, London
E15 2QD
United Kingdom
Contact: Secretary, London Regatta Centre
Tel: +44 20 7511 2211
Fax: +44 20 7474 3333
BH: London Regatta Centre
Tel: +44 20 7511 2211

Royal Engineers RC
c/o RHQ RE, Ravelin Building
Brompton Barracks
Chatnam, Kent, ME4 4UG
United Kingdom
Contact: Secretary Royal Engineers RC
Tel: +44 16 3482 2366

Royal Navy Portsmouth Command Rowing Club
19 Vectic Road, Alverstoke
Gosport, Hants, PO12 2QD
United Kingdom
Contact: Mr. M Young, Chairman
Tel: +44 23 9252 4749
BH: Hornsea Island, Portsmouth

Royal Navy RC
FOTR, Victory Building, HM Naval Base
Portsmouth, PO1 3LS
United Kingdom
Contact: Lt. K M Allsford, Flag Lt.
Tel: +44 02 3972 7602
Email: secretary@navy.rowing.org.uk

Runcorn RC
37 Crosby Road, Birkdale
Southport, PR8 4TE
United Kingdom
Contact: Mr. J E Newcomb
Tel: +44 17 0456 8475
Email: Newcomb@diverseylever.com
BH: The Boathouse, Cholmondeley Road, Clifton
Runcorn, Cheshire, WA7 4XT

Ryde RC
BH: Appley Park, Ryde
PO33 1ND, United Kingdom
Tel: +44 19 8356 2127

Sabre RC
c/o Army Sports Control Board
Block M, Clayton Barracks
Aldershot, GU11 2BG
United Kingdom
Contact: Major M Schofield
Tel: +44 78 8503 8642
Email: armyrowing@army.mod.uk.net
BH: Andrews Boathouse, Dorney Lake, off Cart Lane
Boveney, Windsor, SL4 6QP

Sabrina RC
8 Port Hill Gardens, Shrewsbury
Shropshire, SY3 8SH
United Kingdom
Contact: Mr. S D Baxter, Treasurer
Tel: +44 17 4336 2728
BH: Kingsland, Shrewsbury

Salford Buffalo RC
124 Hoole Road, Chester
CH2 3NU
United Kingdom
Contact: Mr. D Naylor
Tel: +44 12 4431 7889
Fax: +44 12 4434 5180
Email: david.naylor@iee.org

Scarborough ARC
BH: The Boathouse, 29 Foreshore Road
Scarborough, United Kingdom
Tel: +44 17 2336 1857

Sefton RC
36 Fir Street, Southport
Merseyside, PR8 6HP
United Kingdom
Contact: Mrs. J Galloway
BH: Marine Lake, Marine Drive, Southport
Merseyside

Sergeant, The, Club
Downing College, Cambridge
CB2 1DQ
United Kingdom
Contact: Mr. M Corbett
Tel: +44 12 2374 0499
Email: segreants@dow.cam.ac.uk
BH: Downing College Boathouse
Cutter Ferry Lane, Cambridge

Severn River Rowing Association
31 Cowslip Road, Broadstone
Dorset, BH18 9QZ
United Kingdom
Contact: Mr. S C Oxlade
Tel: +44 12 2374 0499
Email: deoxlade@fsmail.net

Shakespeare RC
14 Guild Street, Stratford-upon-Avon
CV37 6RE, United Kingdom
Contact: Linda Kilminster
Tel: +44 77 4877 1434
BH: The Marina, Stratford upon Avon

Shankling Sandown RC
5 Argyle Road, Newport
Isle of Wight, PO30 5SB
United Kingdom
Contact: Mr. G Burch
Tel: +44 19 8352 1607
Email: LLOYDPR@AOL.COM
BH: Esplanade, Shanklin
Tel: +44 19 8386 6246

Sheffield, City of, RC
c/o P Evans, 105 Don Avenue, Wharncliffe Side
Sheffield, S35 0BZ
United Kingdom
Contact: Mr. J Alesbrook
Tel: +44 11 4286 4345
Email: pat@hb1973.fsnet.co.uk
BH: Damflask Reservoir, Low Bradfield
Sheffield
Tel: +44 11 4285 1919

Shiplake Vikings RC
6 Lowes Close, Shiplake
Oxon, RG9 3NG
United Kingdom
Contact: Mrs. C Heath
Tel: +44 11 8940 4076
Fax: +44 11 8940 2568
Email: chris.heath1@virgin.net
BH: Shiplake College BC
River Thames at Shiplake

Shoreham RC
Contact: Ms. D Hills
Tel: +44 12 7344 0960
Fax: +44 12 7346 4880
Email: dh@suscom.demon.co.uk
BH: Kingston Beach
Brighton Road, Shoreham by Sea
W. Sussex, BN43 6RN
United Kingdom

Simoco RC
Contact: Mr. A. Nicol
Tel: +44 77 7192 4380
Email: rowing.committee@cambridge.simoco.com
BH: St. Andrews Road, Cambridge
United Kingdom

Skiff Club, The
BH: Skiff Club Boathouse, Trowlock Way
Teddington, Middx, TW11 9QY
United Kingdom
Tel: +44 20 8977 5254

Sons of the Isis RC
Contact: Mrs. J Wade
Tel: +44 18 6586 2708
Email: jwade@patrol.i-way.co.uk
BH: Christ Church Boathouse
Christ Church Meadows
Oxford, OX1 1DP
United Kingdom

Sons of the Thames RC
BH: Linden House, Upper Mall, Hammersmith
London, W6 9TA
United Kingdom
Tel: +44 20 8748 1841

Southampton ARC
BH: Hazel Road, Woolston
Southampton, Hants, S02 7GA
United Kingdom
Tel: +44 23 8042 1057

Southampton Coalporters ARC
BH: Northam Bridge Road, Northam
Southampton, SO14 0QE
United Kingdom
Tel: +44 23 8063 6521

Southsea RC
BH: Clarence Beach, Southsea
Hants, PO5 3AE
United Kingdom
Tel: +44 23 9273 1305

Spirit of '77 RC
5 Church Gate, Colston, Barnett
Nottingham, NG12 3FP
United Kingdom
Contact: Mr. N Mayglothling
Tel: +44 19 4981 549
BH: Nottingham University, Trentside North
Trent Bridge, Nottingham, NG5

Spitfire BC
Contact: Craig Mynott
Tel: +44 12 2778 1716
Email: craig@cmynott.fsnet.co.uk
BH: Plucks Gutter, Stourmouth
Thanet, Kent, CT2 8JH
United Kingdom

St. Georges Ladies RC
29 Castle Drive, Maiden Head
Berks, SL6 6DB
United Kingdom
Contact: Mrs. M Adams
Tel: +44 16 2877 7550
Fax: +44 16 2862 2997
Email: mmadams@netcomuk.co.uk

St. Ives RC
BH: 25 The Broadway, St. Ives
Huntingdon, Cambs, PE17 4BX
United Kingdom
Tel: +44 14 8049 2384

St. Neots RC
BH: The Priory, Priory Lane, St. Neots
Cambs, PE19 2BH
United Kingdom
Tel: +44 14 8047 2302

Staines BC
Contact: Mr. M L Litvak
Tel: +44 17 8444 9393
Email: murray.litvak.otterproperty.co.uk
BH: 28 Riverside Drive, Chersey Lane
Staines, TW18 3JN
United Kingdom

Star and Arrow Club
BH: Leander Club, Henley on Thames
Oxon, RG9 2LP
United Kingdom
Tel: +44 14 9157 5782

Star Club
BH: Poynters Boathouse, Batts Ford
7 Commercial Road, Bedford, MK40 1RF
United Kingdom
Tel: +44 12 3435 4495

Stoke Rowing Association
Contact: Mr. Graham Jump
Tel: +44 12 7075 0317
Email: G.T.Jump@staffs.ac.uk
BH: Trentham Gardens, Stone Road
Trentham, Stoke on Trent, ST4 8AX
United Kingdom

Stourport BC
BH: Riverside (by bridge), Dunley Road
Stourport on Severn, Worcs, DY13 0AA
United Kingdom
Tel: +44 12 9982 3352

Stratford-Upon-Avon BC
BH: The Clubhouse, Recreation Ground, Swan's Nest
Lane
Stratford-upon-Avon
Warwickshire, CV37 7LS
United Kingdom
Tel: +44 17 8929 7265

Sudbury RC
Contact: Mr. M Arnott
Tel: +44 12 0654 9268
Email: m.arnott@ntworld.com
BH: Quay Lane, Sudbury
Suffolk, CO10 6AN
United Kingdom

Sunderland, City of, RC
BH: Waterside, South Hylton
United Kingdom
Tel: +44 19 1534 4416

Swindon RC
18 Swans Close, Ramsbury
Marlborough, Wilts, SN8 2PH
Contact: Mr. D Ballard
BH: Coatewater Park, Swindon
United Kingdom

Talkin Tarn ARC
BH: Talkin Tarn, Brampton
Cumbria, United Kingdom
Tel: +44 16 977 2525

Taurus BC
Contact: David Peill
Tel: +44 20 7585 3994
Email: dpeill@Fpdsavills.co.uk
BH: Bowbridge Boathouse
Reading Road, Cholsey
Wallingford, OX10 9HG
United Kingdom

Tees RC
Contact: Mrs. Victoria Laing
Tel: +44 13 2536 1684
Fax: +44 16 4235 2741
Email: victorialaing@holmcottage.co.uk
BH: River Tees Watersports Centre, Dugdale Street
Stockton-on-Tees, TS18 2NL
United Kingdom

Thames RC
BH: Embankment, Putney
London, SW15 1LB
United Kingdom
Tel: +44 20 8788 0798
Email: captain@thamesrc.co.uk

Thames Tradesmen's RC
BH: Chiswick Boathouse, Dukes Meadows
Chiswick, London, W4 2SH
United Kingdom
Tel: +44 20 8994 9470

The 1829 BC
Contact: Mr. P Bridge
Tel: +44 77 7556 5152
BH: Crabtree Boathouse, Putney Embankment
London, United Kingdom

Tideway Scullers School
BH: Dukes Meadows, Chiswick Bridge
London, W4 2SH
United Kingdom
Tel: +44 20 8994 3502

Tiffin Parents
BH: Canbury Gardens, Lower Ham Road
Kingston on Thames, Surrey, KT2 5BB
United Kingdom
Tel: +44 20 8546 8592

Torquay RC
Contact: Mr. R E Smith
Tel: +44 18 0340 6855
BH: c/o Royal Torbay Yacht Club, Beacon Hill
Torquay, TQ1 2BQ
United Kingdom

Tortoise Club
c/o 1 Stanley Villas, 35 Guildford Road, Farnham
Surrey, GU9 9PU
United Kingdom
Contact: Mr. N Hirst
Tel: +44 12 5272 6400

Trafford RC
42 Runcorn Road, Barnton, Northwich
Cheshire, CW8 4EL
United Kingdom
Contact: Mr. D J Westwell
Tel: +44 16 0678 2743
Email: ckdjwestwell.@tiscali.co.uk
BH: Walton Park Sports Centre
Raglan Road, Sale

Trent RC
40 Spring Terrace Road, Stapenhill
Burton on Trent, Staffs, DE15 9DU
United Kingdom
Contact: Richard Gipson
Tel: +44 12 8356 8027
Fax: +44 12 8354 8164
Email: rgipson@cix.co.uk
BH: The Boathouse, Stapenhill Road
Burton on Trent

Trireme RC
59 Berkely Court, Oatlands Drive
Weybridge, Surrey, KT13 9HY
United Kingdom
Contact: Mr. A P Ruddle
Tel: +44 19 3222 0401
United Kingdom

Twickenham RC
BH: Eel Pie Island, Twickenham
Middx, TW1 9DY
United Kingdom
Tel: +44 20 8892 5291

Tyne RC
BH: Riverside Boathouse, Water Row, Newburn
Newcastle upon Tyne, NE15 8NL
United Kingdom
Tel: +44 19 1267 3827

Tynemouth RC
Contact: Mr. M Thompson
Tel: +44 19 1296 3763
Email: thompson@tynemouth99.freeserve.uk
BH: Prior's Haven, Tynemouth
North Shields, NE30 4DG
United Kingdom

Tyrian Club (University of London)
BH: University of London BC, 81 Hartington Road
Chiswick, London, W4 3TU
United Kingdom
Tel: +44 20 8994 5928

Upper Thames RC
BH: Remenham Lane, Henley on Thames
Oxon, RG9 3DB
United Kingdom
Tel: +44 14 9157 5745

Upton RC
Contact: Dr. Johnny Birks
Tel: +44 16 8457 5876
Email: johnnybirks@vwt.org.uk
BH: Upton Marina, Upton on Severn
Worcs, United Kingdom

Vesta RC
BH: Embankment, Putney
London, SW15 1LB
United Kingdom
Tel: +44 20 8788 0326

Walbrook & Royal Canoe Club
BH: Royal Canoe Club Boathouse, Trowlock Way
Teddington, Middx, TW11 9QY
United Kingdom
Tel: +44 20 8977 5254

Wallingford RC
BH: Thames Street, Wallingford
Oxon, OX10 0HD
United Kingdom
Tel: +44 14 9182 5985

Walton RC
BH: Sunbury Lane, Walton on Thames
Surrey, KT12 2JA
United Kingdom
Tel: '+44 19 3222 4557

Warrington RC
18 Stanley Avenue, Stockton Heath
Warrington, WA4 2DY
United Kingdom
Contact: Andrew Malins
Tel: +44 19 2526 8824
BH: Howley Lane, Warrington

Warwick BC
BH: 33 Mill Street, Warwick
CV34 4HB, United Kingdom
Tel: +44 19 2649 2043

Watermen, The Company of
Contact: Mr. C C Middlemiss
Tel: +44 19 0858 2718
Fax: +44 20 7283 0477
Email: clerk@watermenshall.org
BH: Watermen's Hall, 16 St. Mary-at-Hill
London, EC3R 8EE
United Kingdom

Wessex RC
Contact: Mr. D Drury
BH: Canford School BC, Wimborne
Dorset, United Kingdom
Tel: +44 12 0284 1254 x416

West Hertfordshire RC
Contact: Mr. J P Neale
Tel: +44 19 2381 7799
BH: Grand Union Canal, Croxley Green
Herts, United Kingdom

West Midlands Rowing Association
Thornbury Cottage, The Upper Gore
Wheathill, Bridgnorth
Shropshire, WV16 6QU
United Kingdom
Contact: David Wright
Tel: +44 15 8482 3689
BH: Pitchcroft, Worcester

West Norfolk RC
BH: c/o Ouse Sailing Club, Saddlebow Road
Kings Lynn, Norfolk
United Kingdom
Tel: +44 14 8552 0257

Westover and Bournemouth RC
BH: The Boathouse, West Beach
Bournemouth, BH2 5AA
United Kingdom
Tel: +44 12 0255 1815

Weybridge Ladies ARC
4 Springfield Lane, Weybridge
Surrey, KT13 8LG
United Kingdom
Contact: Catherin Witt
Tel: +44 19 3284 2993
BH: Walton Lane, Weybridge
Surrey

Weyfarers RC
BH: Weybridge RC, Thames Lock, Jessamy Road
Weybridge, KT13 8LG
United Kingdom
Tel: '+44 19 3284 2993

Whitby Friendship ARC
BH: New Way Ghaut, Church Street
Swhitby, YO22 4DH
United Kingdom
Tel: +44 19 4760 4751

Wimbleball RC
5 Bakers Orchard, Crowcombe Heathfield
Taunton, TA4 4PA
United Kingdom
Contact: Mr. R B Brooks
Tel: +44 19 8461 8400
Email: richard.b.brooks@btopenworld.com
BH: Hills Farm Barn, Brompton Regis
Dulverton

Windsorian, The RC
BH: Stovey Road, Windsor
United Kingdom
Tel: +4417 5386 3882

Worcester RC
BH: The Boathouse, Grandstand Road
Pitchcroft, Worcester, WR1 3EJ
United Kingdom
Tel: +44 19 0522 099

Worthing RC
BH: Splash Point, Marine Parade
Worthing, BN11 3PN
United Kingdom
Tel: +44 19 0323 9779

Wraysbury BC
c/o Wraysbury BC, The Pleasure Grounds, Riverside
Egham, Surrey, TW20 0AA
United Kingdom
Contact: Ms. A Robers
Tel: +44 17 5384 0907
Fax: +44 17 5384 0907
BH: Wraysbury Skiff & Punting Club
Tel: +44 17 8443 7206

X-Press BC
Cambridge Blue, 85 Gwydir Street
Cambridge, CB1 2LG
United Kingdom
Contact: Mrs. D. Lloyd
Tel: +44 12 2350 5110

Yare BC
Fairwinds, 1 Nutfield Close
Norwich, NR4 6PF
United Kingdom
Contact: Mr. A Roper
Tel: +44 16 0350 2390
Email: info@yareboatclub.org.uk
BH: Thorpe Island, Thorpe St. Andrew
Norwich

York City RC
BH: The Boathouse, West Esplanade
Lendal Bridge, York, YO1 6FZ
United Kingdom
Tel: +44 19 0462 3959

UNIVERSITIES AND COLLEGES

Balliol College BC
Oxford
OX1 3BJ, United Kingdom
Contact: c/o Balliol College
Tel: +44 18 6527 7777
BH: Christchurch Meadow, Oxford

Bath Univ. BC
The Univ. of Bath
Claverton Down, Bath, Avon
BA2 7AY, United Kingdom
Contact: c/o Students Union
Tel: +44 12 2582 6607
Fax: +44 12 2544 4061
Email: su6row@bath.ac.uk
BH: Avon County RC
Saltford, Bristol

Birmingham, Univ. of BC
BH: Edgbaston Reservoir
Reservoir Road, Edgbaston, Birmingham
United Kingdom
Tel: +44 12 1471 3443

Bradford, Univ. of RC
BH: Hirst Weir
Saltaire, Shipley
United Kingdom
Tel: +44 12 7453 1859

Brasenose College BC
Oxford
OX1 4AJ, United Kingdom
Contact: c/o Brasenose College
Tel: +44 18 6527 7830

Bristol, Univ. of, BC
Students Union
Queens Road, Bristol
BS8 1LN, United Kingdom
Contact: c/o Univ. of Bristol Athletic Union
Tel: +44 11 7954 5874
Email: AUChair-UBU@bristol.ac.uk
BH: River Avon, Saltford

Brunel Univ. RC
Brunel University
Uxbridge, Middx
UB8 3PH, United Kingdom
Contact: c/o Students Union
Tel: +44 18 9527 4000
Fax: +44 18 9523 2806
Email: rowingclub@hotmail.com
BH: Opposite Magna Carta Island
Runnymede,

C.C.A.T. BC
Anglia Poly. Univ.
East Road, Cambridge
CB1 1PT, United Kingdom
Contact: c/o Students Union
Tel: +44 12 2346 0008
BH: Emmanuel Boathouse
Cutter Ferry Lane, Cambridge

Caius BC
Contact: The Captain, Gonville & Caius College
BH: Pretoria Road
Cambridge, United Kingdom
Tel: +44 12 2331 4733

Cambridge Univ. BC
BH: Goldie Boathouse
Kimberley Road, Cambridge
United Kingdom
Tel: +44 12 2346 7304

Cambridge Univ. LWT RC
Contact: Dr. P D Wothers
Tel: +44 12 2351 1733
Email: pdw12@cam.ac.uk
BH: c/o Cambridge '99 RC
Kimberley Road, Cambridge
CB4 1HJ, United Kingdom

Cambridge Univ. Womens BC
BH: Clare BC
Cutter Ferry Lane, Cambridge
United Kingdom
Tel: +44 12 2335 1137

Christ Church BC
Cambridge
CB2 1TL, United Kingdom
Contact: c/o Christ's College
Tel: +44 12 2333 4900
BH: River Isis, Oxford

Clare BC
United Kingdom
BH: Cutter Ferry Lane
Cambridge
CB2 1TL, United Kingdom
Tel: +44 12 2333 3200

Collingwood College BC
PO Box 158
South Road, Durham
DH1 3YP, United Kingdom
Contact: Captain, Collingwood College
Tel: +44 19 1374 4569
BH: Collingwood Boathouse
Durham
United Kingdom

Corpus Christi College BC (Oxford)
Oxford
OX1 4JF, United Kingdom
Contact: c/o Corpus Christi College
Tel: +44 18 6527 6700
United Kingdom

Corpus Christi College BC (Cambridge)
Cambridge
CB2 1RH, United Kingdom
Contact: c/o Corpus Christi College
Tel: +44 12 2333 8000
BH: Ferry Lane
Cambridge

Darwin College BC
Contact: Dr. C White
Tel: +44 12 2335 6174
Fax: +44 12 2333 5667
BH: c/o Pembroke College Boathouse
Cutter Ferry Lane, Cambridge
United Kingdom

De Montfort Univ. (Leicester)
BH: Leicester RC, The Bede House
Upperton Road, Leicester
LE2 7GR, United Kingdom
Tel: +44 11 6254 3203

Downing College BC
Cambridge
CB2 1DQ, United Kingdom
Contact: The Captain, Downing College
BH: Cutter Ferry Lane, Cambridge
Tel: +44 12 2336 0933

Durham Univ. BC
Dunelm House
New Elvet, Durham
DH1 3AN, United Kingdom
Contact: c/o Athletic Union, Durham Univ.
Tel: +44 19 1374 2196
Fax: +44 19 1374 2199
Email: university.boat-club@durham.ac.uk

East Anglia, Univ. of, BC
Contact: c/o Boat Club, Univ. of East Anglia
Tel: +44 16 0345 6161
BH: Norwich RC, Trowse Water Sports Centre
Whitlingham Lane, Trowse, Norwich
NR14 8TR, United Kingdom

East London, Univ. of, BC
BH: London Regatta Centre
Dockside Road, London
E16 2QD, United Kingdom
Tel: +44 20 7511 2211

Emmanuel BC
Cambridge
CB2 3AP, United Kingdom
Contact: c/o Emmanuel College
BH: Cutter Ferry Lane
Cambridge
Tel: +44 12 2331 6122

Essex, Univ of, RC
Sports Federation, Univ. of Essex
Wivenhoe Park, Cochester
CO4 3SQ, United Kingdom
Contact: c/o The Student Union
Tel: +44 12 0686 3211

Exeter College BC
Exeter College
Oxford, OX1 3DP, United Kingdom
Contact: c/o The Captain
Tel: +44 18 6527 9600
BH: Christchurch Meadow, Oxford

Exeter Univ, BC
Cornwall House
St. Germans Road, Exeter
EX4 6TG, United Kingdom
Contact: c/o Athletic Union
Tel: +44 13 9226 3505
Fax: +44 13 9226 3599
BH: Exeter Canal
Countess Weir Swingbridge, Exeter, Devon

First and Third Trinity BC
Contact: c/o Trinity College
BH: Kimberley Road
Cambridge
United Kingdom
Tel: +44 12 2336 9733

Fitzwilliam College BC
BH: Kimberley Road
Cambridge
CB3 0DG, United Kingdom
Tel: +44 12 2333 2000

Girton College BC
Cambridge
CB3 0JG, United Kingdom
Contact: c/o Girton Gollege
Tel: +44 12 2333 8999
BH: Cutter Ferry Lane, Cambridge

Goldie BC
United Kingdom
BH: Goldie Boathouse
Kimberley Road, Cambridge
CB4 1HG, United Kingdom
Tel: +44 12 2335 4258

Goodenough College London RC
BH: London RC
Embankment, Putney, London
United Kingdom
Tel: +44 20 7837 8888

Graduate Society (Durham) BC
Green Lane, Durham
DH1 3JP, United Kingdom
Contact: c/o Parsons Field House
Tel: +4419 1374 1655
Email: Gradboat.Club@durham.ac.uk
BH: Dunelm House Boathouse
River Wear, Durham

Granta BC
Contact: Dr. P D Wothers
Tel: +44 12 2351 1733
Fax: +44 12 2333 8340
Email: pdw@12@cam.ac.uk
BH: c/o Cambridge '99 RC
Kimberley Road, Cambridge
CB4 1HJ, United Kingdom

Grey College BC
Grey College
South Road, Durham
DH1 3LG, United Kingdom
Contact: The Captain of Boats
Tel: +44 19 1374 2900
BH: Below Dunelm House, Elvet Riverside

Hatfield College BC
North Bailey, Durham
DH1 3RQ, United Kingdom
Contact: C/o Hatfield College
Email: hatfield.boatclub@durham.ac.uk
BH: Hatfield College
River Wear, Durham

Hertford College BC
Catte Street, Oxford
OX1 3BW, United Kingdom
Contact: c/o Hertford College
Tel: +44 18 6527 9400
BH: Longbridges Boathouse
Long Bridges, Oxford

Hertfordshire, Univ. of, RC
United Kingdom
BH: Broxbourne RC
Old Nazeing Road, Broxbourne, Herts
EN10 6QU, United Kingdom
Tel: +44 19 9246 3821

Homerton College BC
Hills Road, Cambridge
CB2 2PH, United Kingdom
Contact: c/o Homerton College
Tel: +44 12 2350 7235
Fax: +44 12 2350 7236
BH: Riverside, Cambridge

Hull Univ. BC
Cottingham Road
Hull, N. Humberside
HU6 7RX, United Kingdom
Contact: c/o Hull Univ. Union
Tel: +44 14 8285 0225
BH: Oak Road, Hull

Imperial College BC
BH: Imperial College Boathouse
Embankment, Putney, London
SW15 1LB, United Kingdom
Tel: +44 20 8788 3563

Imperial College School of Medicine BC
Contact: Harry Boardman
Tel: +44 79 3264 8948
Email: henry.boarman@ic.uk
BH: London Univ. Boathouse
Hartington Road, Chiswick, London
W4, United Kingdom

Isis BC
BH: Oxford Univ. Sports Centre
Iffley Road, Oxford
OX4 1EQ, United Kingdom
Tel: +44 18 6579 0268

Jesus College BC (Cambridge)
BH: River Cam
Cambridge
United Kingdom
Tel: +44 12 2376 6342

Jesus College BC (Oxford)
Oxford
OX1 3PG, United Kingdom
Contact: c/o Jesus College
Tel: +44 18 6527 9700
Fax: +44 18 6527 9687
BH: River Isis, Oxford

Keble College BC
BH: River Isis
Oxford
United Kingdom
Tel: +44 18 6528 2333

Kent, Univ. of , RC
The Univ
Canterbury, Kent
CT2 7NL, United Kingdom
Contact: c/o Sports Hall
Tel: +44 12 2776 8027
Fax: +44 12 2776 8027

Kings College BC
BH: Logan's Way
Cambridge
United Kingdom
Tel: +44 12 2335 7412

Kings College London BC
BH: Tideway Scullers School
Dukes Meadows, Chiswick, London
W4 2SH, United Kingdom
Tel: +44 20 8994 3502

Kingston Univ. RC
BH: Canbury Boathouse
Lower Ham Road, Kingston upon Thames, Surrey
KT2 5AU, United Kingdom
Tel: +44 20 8547 7412

Lady Margaret BC
BH: Victoria Avenue Bridge
Cambridge
CB4 1EH, United Kingdom
Tel: +44 12 2346 4009

Lady Margaret Hall BC
Norham Gardens
Oxford
OX2 6QZ, United Kingdom
Contact: c/o Lady Margaret Hall
Tel: +44 18 6527 4300
Fax: +44 18 6551 1069
BH: River Isis, Oxford

Lancaster Univ. BC
BH: Railway Station
Halton on Lune
United Kingdom
Tel: +44 15 2477 1243

Leeds Univ. BC
Union Building
PO Box 157, Leeds
LS1 1UH, United Kingdom
Contact: c/o LUU BC
Tel: +44 11 3380 1244
BH: Arcbishop Holgates School BC
Clifton, York

Leicester Univ. BC
BH: The Bede House
Upperton Road, Leicester
LE2 7GR, United Kingdom
Tel: +44 11 6254 3203

Linacre BC
Linacre College
St. Cross Road, Oxford
OX1 3JA, United Kingdom
Contact: Captain of Boats
Tel: +44 18 6527 1650
BH: Oxford Univ.
Univ. Boathouse, Oxford

Lincoln College BC
Oxford
OX1 3DR, United Kingdom
Contact: c/o Lincoln College
Tel: +44 18 6527 9800
BH: Christchurch Meadows
Oxford

Liverpool Univ. BC
Contact: c/o Univ. of Liverpool Athletics Union
Tel: +44 15 1794 4126
Fax: +44 15 1794 4174
BH: Runcorn RC
Rocksavage, Runcorn, Cheshire
United Kingdom

London, Univ. of, BC
BH: 81 Hartington Road
Chiswick, London
W4 3TU, United Kingdom
Tel: +44 20 8994 5928

Loughborough Students RC
Ashby Road
Loughborough, Leics
LE11 3TT, United Kingdom
Contact: c/o Students Union Building
BH: Holme Pierrekpont
Nottingham
Tel: +44 15 0963 5054

Magdalen College BC
Oxford
OX1 4AU, United Kingdom
Contact: c/o Magdalen College
Tel: +44 18 6527 6000
Fax: +44 18 6527 6017
BH: River Isis, Oxford

Magdalene BC
Cambridge
CB3 0AG, United Kingdom
Contact: c/o Magdalene College
BH: Victoria Bridge
Cambridge
Tel: +44 12 2350 1522

Manchester Metropolitan
99 Oxford Road
Manchester
M1 7EL, United Kingdom
Contact: c/o Students Union Building
Tel: +44 16 1273 1162
BH: Trafford RC
Walton Park, Sale

Manchester Univ. BC
333 Oxford Road
Manchester
M13 9PG, United Kingdom
Contact: c/o Athletic Union
Tel: +44 16 1275 6977
Fax: +44 16 1275 6992
Email: auchair@man.ac.uk
BH: Bridgewater Canal
Dane Road, Sale

Mansfield College BC
Masfield Road
OX1 3TF, United Kingdom
Contact: c/o Mansfield College
BH: Timms Boathouse, Oxford

Merton College BC
Merton College
Oxford
OX1 4JD, United Kingdom
Contact: c/o The Captain
Tel: +44 18 6527 6310
BH: River Isis, Oxford

Nepthys BC
Iffley Road Sports Complex
Oxford
OX4 1EQ, United Kingdom
Contact: c/o Univ. Rowing Centre
BH: Radley College
Tel: +44 18 6524 7102

New College BC
New College
Oxford
OX1 3BN, United Kingdom
Contact: The Captain
Tel: +44 186527 9555
Fax: +44 18 6527 9590
Email: ncbc@new.ox.ac.uk
BH: River Isis, Oxford

New Hall BC
Hundtingdon Road
Cambridge
CB3 0DP, United Kingdom
Contact: c/o New Hall
Tel: +44 12 2376 2100
BH: Peterhouse College BC
Pretoria Road, Cambridge

Newcastle Univ. BC
Newcastle Univ.
Kings Walk, Newcastle upon Tyne
NE1 8QB, United Kingdom
Contact: c/o The Union Society
Tel: +44 19 123 2455
Fax: +44 19 1222 1876
BH Tel: +44 19 1414 6710

Newnham Collge BC
Newnham College
Cambridge
CB3 9DI, United Kingdom
Contact: BC Captain
Tel: +44 12 2352 4949
BH: Jesus College BC
River Cam, Cambridge

Northumbria Univ. of BC
United Kingdom
BH: c/o Tyne RC
Riverside Boathouse Water Row
Newburn, Newcastle upon Tyne
NE2 3AL, United Kingdom
Tel: +44 19 1227 3217

Nottingham Trent Univ. RC
United Kingdom
BH: NWSC Holme Pierrepont
Adbolton Lane, Nottingham
NG2 5FA, United Kingdom
Tel: +44 11 5952 8800

Nottingham Univ. BC
BH: Trentside
West Bridgford, Nottingham
United Kingdom
Tel: +44 11 5981 1249

Oriel College BC
Oriel College
Oxford, OX1 4EW, United Kingdom
Contact: The Captain
Tel: +44 18 6527 6560
BH: Christchurch Meadow, Oxford

Osiris BC
Contact: Mr. S. Royle
Tel: +44 18 6579 0268
BH: Oxford Univ. Sports Centre
Iffley Road, Oxford
OX4 1EQ, United Kingdom

Osler Green College BC
John Radcliffe Hospital
Oxford, OX3 9DU, United Kingdom
Contact: c/o William Osler House
BH: Timms Towpath, Oxford

Oxford Brookes Univ. BC
BH: Bowbridge Boathouse
Cholsey Road, Wallingford, Oxon
United Kingdom
Tel: +44 14 9165 9018

Oxford Institute of Legal Practice BC
King Charles House
Park End Street, Oxford
OX1 1JD, United Kingdom
Contact: Claudia Haisman
Tel: +44 18 6526 0000
Fax: +44 18 6526 0002
Email: howe@oxilp.ac.uk

Oxford Univ. BC
Oxford Univ. Sports Centre
Iffley Road, Oxford
OX4 1EQ, United Kingdom
Tel: +44 18 6579 0268

Oxford Univ. LWT RC
Contact: c/o Univ. Rowing Centre
BH: Radley College
United Kingdom
Tel: +44 18 6524 7102

Oxford Univ. LWT Womens RC
c/o Mr. S R Royle
Oxford Univ. Sports Centre, Iffley Road, Oxford
OX4 1EQ, United Kingdom
Contact: The Captain, LWTW Rowing Club
Tel: +44 18 6579 0268
Fax: +44 18 6520 4375
BH: Univ. Boathouse
Riverside, Oxford

Oxford Univ. Womens BC
Oxford Univ Sports Complex
Iffley Road, Oxford
OX4 1EQ, United Kingdom
Contact: c/o Steve Royle
Tel: '+44 18 6579 0268
BH: c/o Oxford Univ. Sports Centre
Oxford

Palatine BC
c/o Durham University BC
Athletic Union, Dunelm House
New Elvet, Durham
DH1 3AN, United Kingdom
Contact: The Secretary
Tel: +44 19 1374 2196
Fax: +44 19 1374 2195
BH: Durham University BC
River Wear, Durham

Pembroke College BC (Cambrige)
Pembroke College
Oxford
OX1 1DW, United Kingdom
Contact: The President
Tel: +44 18 6527 6444
Fax: +44 18 6527 6427
Email: president@pembrokerowing.com

Peterhouse BC
BH: Ferry Path
off Chesterton Road, Cambridge
United Kingdom
Tel: +44 12 2333 8200

Queen Mary College BC
Contact: Kieron Walsh
Tel: +44 20 7882 3127
Fax: +44 20 8981 0802
BH: Univ. of London BC
81 Hartington Road, Chiswick, London
W4 3TU, United Kingdom

Queens Campus BC
BH: Tees RC
Boathouse Lane, Stockton-on-Tees
TS18 3AW, United Kingdom

Queens' College BC (Cambridge)
Contact: c/o Queens College
Tel: +44 12 2333 5511
Email: qcbc-secretary@quns.cam.ac.uk
BH: Queens' College, Cambridge
CB3 9ET, United Kingdom

Queens College, The, BC
High Street, Oxford
OX1 4AW, United Kingdom
Contact: c/o The Queen's College
Tel: +44 11 8986 0222
BH: Christchurch Meadows, Oxford

Robinson College BC
Robinson College
Cambridge
CB3 9AN, United Kingdom
Contact: The Captain
Tel: +44 12 2333 9100
BH: Downing College BC
Downing College BC
Cutter Ferry Lane, Cambridge

Roehampton Univ. of Surrey RC
Contact: Matthew Wing
Tel: +44 77 9075 7216
Email: msw_fmb@hotmail.com
BH: Barn Elms Boathouse
Queen Elizabeth Walk, Barnes, London
SW13 0DG, United Kingdom

Royal Holloway (Univ. of London) BC
BH: Strodes College Boat House
Tims Way, Staines, Middx
TW18 3JY, United Kingdom
Tel: +44 17 8448 6320

Royal Univ. Medical Students
BH: Univ. of London BC
81 Hartington Road, Chiswick, London
W4 3TU, United Kingdom
Tel: +44 20 8994 5928

Royal Veterinary College BC
BH: Univ. of London BC
81 Hartington Road, London
W4 3TU, United Kingdom
Tel: +44 20 8994 5928

Salford Univ. BC
BH: Agecroft RC
Littleton Road, Salford, Manchester
M7 0QR, United Kingdom
Tel: +44 16 1736 7811

Selwyn College BC
BH: Logan's Way
Cambridge, United Kingdom
Tel: +44 12 2357 2614

Sheffield Hallam Univ. RC
Athletic Union, Sheffield Hallam Univ
Collegiate Campus, Nelson Mandela Building
Pond Street, Sheffield
S1 2BW, United Kingdom
Contact: c/o Athletic Clubs Officer
Tel: +44 11 4225 2500
Fax: +44 11 4225 4365
Email: au@shu.ac.uk
BH: Dam Flask Reservoir, Low Bradfield

Sheffield Univ. RC
BH: Damflask Reservoir
Low Bradfield
United Kingdom
Tel: +44 11 4285 1919

Shrivenham RC
Univ. of Sheffield Students Union
Western Bank, Sheffield
S10 2TG, United Kingdom
Contact: c/o The Workspace
Tel: +44 11 4222 8524
Fax: +44 11 4276 0566
Email: rowing@sheffield.ac.uk

Sidney Sussex College BC
BH: Cutter Ferry Lane
Cambridge
United Kingdom
Tel: +44 12 2332 8531

Somerville College BC
Somerville College
Oxford, United Kingdom
Contact: The Captain/Secretary
Tel: +44 79 3912 6074
Tel: +44 79 3912 6074

Southampton Institute RC
BH: Southampton Coalporters ARC
Northam Bridge Road, Northam, Southampton
SO2 7GA, United Kingdom
Tel: +44 23 8063 6521

Southampton Univ. BC
Contact: c/o Athletic Union
Tel: +44 23 8059 5203
Fax: +44 23 8059 5234
Email: boatclub@soton.ac.uk
BH: Oliver Road
Swaything, Southampton
United Kingdom

St. Aidans College BC
BH: Univ. College Boathouse
Prebends Bridge, Durham City
United Kingdom
Tel: +44 19 1374 3269

St. Annes College BC
Oxford, OX2 6HS, United Kingdom
Contact: c/o St. Anne's College
Tel: +44 18 6527 4800
BH: River Isis, Oxford

St. Barts & The Royal London Hospitals BC
United Kingdom
BH: Lea RC, The Boathouse
Spring Hill, Clapton, London
E5 9BL, United Kingdom
Tel: +44 20 8806 8282

St. Catharines College BC (Cambs)
Trumpington Street
Cambridge, CB2 1RL, United Kingdom
Contact: c/o St. Catharine's College
Tel: +44 79 6602 9859
Fax: +44 12 2333 8340

St. Catherines College BC (Oxford)
St. Catherine's College
Manor Road, Oxford
OX1 3UJ, United Kingdom
Contact: Captain of Boats
Tel: +44 18 6527 1700
BH: Timms Boathouse
Riverside, Oxford

St. Chads College BC
St. Chad's College
18 North Bailey, Durham
DH1 3RH, United Kingdom
Contact: The Captain
Tel: +44 19 1374 3370
BH: St. Chad's College
Durham

St. Cuthberts Society BC
12 South Bailey, Durham
DH1 3EE, United Kingdom
Contact: The BC Captain
Tel: +44 19 1374 3400
Email: cuthberts.boatclub@durham.ac.uk
BH: Racecourse
Baths Bridge, Durham

St. Edmund Hall BC
St. Edmund Hall
Queens Lane, Oxford
OX1 4AR, United Kingdom
Contact: Captain of Boats
Tel: +44 18 6527 9000
BH: Christchurch Meadows, Oxford

St. Georges Hospital Med. Sch. BC
Contact: c/o St. George's Hospital Medical Sch
Email: stgeorges_boatclub@yahoo.com
BH: Univ. of London BC
81 Hartington Road, Chiswick, London
W4 3TU, United Kingdom

St. Hild & St. Bede College BC
Contact: The Captain in Charge
Tel: +44 19 1374 3000
Email: hb.boatclub@dur.ac.uk
BH: Riverside below college
St. Hild & St. Bede College, Durham
DH1 1SZ, United Kingdom

St. Hildas College BC
St. Hilda's College
Cowley Place, Oxford
OX4 1DY, United Kingdom
Contact: The Captain
Email: shbc@hotmail.com
BH: Timms Boathouse, Oxford

St. Hughs College JCR BC
St. Hugh's College
St. Margaret's Road, Oxford
OX2 6LE, United Kingdom
Contact: BC Vice-President
Tel: +44 18 6527 4900
BH: Isis BC
Univ. Boathouse, Riverside, Oxford

St. Johns College BC (Oxford)
Oxford
OX1 3JP, United Kingdom
Contact: c/o St. John's College
Tel: +44 18 6527 7300
BH: Christchurch Meadows, Oxford

St. Johns College BC (Durham)
3 South Bailey, Durham
DH1 3RJ, United Kingdom
Contact: The Captain of Boats
Tel: +44 19 1374 3579
BH: Riverside, Durham

St. Marys College (JCR)
Elvet Hill Road, Durham
DH1 3LR, United Kingdom
Contact: c/o St. Mary's College
Tel: +44 19 1374 7119
BH: River Wear, County Durham

St. Peter College BC
BH: Oxford Univ. BC
Univ. Boathouse, Riverside, Oxford
United Kingdom
Tel: +44 18 6527 8901

Staffordshire Univ. RC
Students Activities
College Road, Stoke on Trent, Staffs
ST4 2DE, United Kingdom
Contact: c/o Students Union
Tel: +44 17 8229 4117
Fax: +44 17 8229 4322
BH: North Staffordshire RC
Rudyard Lake, Lake Road, Rudyard, Leek

Sunderland, Univ. of, RC
BH: South Hylton RC, Claxheugh Recreation Area
Claxheugh Road, Riverside
South Hylton, Sunderland
United Kingdom
Tel: +44 19 1534 7774

Surrey, Univ. of BC
BH: Walton RC
Sunbury, Walton on Thames, Surrey
KT12 2JA, United Kingdom
Tel: +44 19 3222 4557

Sussex, Univ. of BC
319 Queens Park Road
Brighton
BN2 9XL, United Kingdom
Contact: Karen Goodwin
Tel: +44 12 7368 9849
BH: Shoreham RC
Kingston Beach, Shoreham

Teesside, Univ. of RC
Univ. of Teesside
Middlesbrough
TS1 3BA, United Kingdom
Contact: c/o Recreation Unit
Tel: +44 16 4234 2267
BH: Tees RC
Boathouse Lane, Stockton-on-Tees

Trevelyan College BC
Elvet Hill Road
Durham
DH1 3LN, United Kingdom
Contact: c/o Trevelyan College
Tel: +44 19 1374 3700
Email: Trevelyan_Boat.Club@durham.ac.uk
BH: River Wear, Durham

Trinity College BC
Oxford
OX1 3BH, United Kingdom
Contact: c/o Trinity College
Tel: +44 18 6527 9900
BH: Christchurch Meadows, Oxford

Trinity Hall BC
Cambridge
CB2 1TJ, United Kingdom
Contact: c/o Trinity Hall
Tel: +44 12 2332 7798
BH: Riverside, Cambridge

Umist BC
PO Box 88
Sackville Street, Manchester
M60 1QD, United Kingdom
Contact: c/o Athletic Union
Tel: +44 16 1200 3292
Fax: +44 16 1200 3265
Email: umistrc@mail.com
BH: Bridgewater
Dane Road, Sale

United Hospitals BC
BH: Univ. of London BC
81 Hartington Road, Chiswick, London
W4 3TU, United Kingdom
Tel: +44 20 8994 5928

United Universities Women's BC
BH: Thames RC
Embankment, Putney, London
SW15 1LB, United Kingdom
Tel: +44 20 8788 0676

University College (Durham)
The Castle, Durham
DH1 3RW, United Kingdom
Contact: c/o Univ. College
Tel: +44 19 1386 9446
BH: Near the Old Mill
Prebends Bends, Durham

University College BC (Oxford)
Oxford
OX1 4BH, United Kingdom
Contact: The Captain
Tel: +44 18 6527 6602
BH: Oxford Univ. BC
Univ. Boathouse, Riverside, Oxford

University College Chester
Univ. College Chester Student Union
Cheyney Road, Chester
CH1 4BJ, United Kingdom
Contact: Ms. J Hodson
Tel: +44 12 4439 2740
Fax: +44 12 4439 2866
BH: Grosvenor RC
Tel: +44 12 4439 2740

University College London BC
BH: Univ. of London BC
Hartington Road, Chiswick, London
W4 3TU, United Kingdom
Tel: +44 20 8994 4928

Van Mildert BC
Van Mildert College
Durham
DH1 3LH, United Kingdom
Contact: c/o BC Captain
Tel: +44 19 1374 3900
BH: River Wear, Durham

Wadham College BC
Oxford
OX1 3PN, United Kingdom
Contact: c/o Wadham College
Tel: +44 18 6527 7900
Fax: +44 18 6527 7937
BH: Wadham College BH
Christ Church Meadow, Oxford

Warwick, Univ. of BC
Student's Union
Univ. of Warwick, Gibbet Hill Road, Coventry
CV4 7AL, United Kingdom
Contact: The Captain
Tel: +44 24 7657 2777
Fax: +44 24 7657 2759
BH: Barford on Avon

West of England, Univ. of RC
Coldharbour Lane
Frenchay, Bristol
BS16 1QY, United Kingdom
Contact: c/o Students Uion Building 5F2
Tel: +44 11 7344 2719
Fax: +44 11 7344 2986
Email: rowing@uwe.ac.uk
BH: Albion Dock, Bristol
Tel: +44 11 7344 2719

Wolfson College BC (Cambridge)
Barton Road, Cambridge
CB3 9BB, United Kingdom
Contact: c/o Wolfson College
Tel: +44 12 2333 5930
BH: Camside, Cambridge
Tel: +44 12 2332 8531

Wolfson College BC (Oxford)
Oxford
OX2 6UD, United Kingdom
Contact: c/o Wolfson College
Tel: +44 18 6527 4100
BH: Christ Church Boathouse
Riverside, Oxford

Worcester College BC
Worcester College
Oxford
OX1 2HB, United Kingdom
Contact: The Captain
Tel: +44 18 6527 8300
Fax: +44 18 6527 8369
BH: Christchurch Meadows, Oxford

Wye College BC
University of London
Wye, Ashford, Kent
TN25 5AH, United Kingdom
Contact: Wye College
Email: james.reed@ic.ac.uk
BH: Maidstone Invicta RC
Lower Barracks Road, Maidstone, Kent

York St. John Collge RC
Contact: c/o Students Union
BH: Marygate
York, United Kingdom
Tel: +44 19 0462 9816

York, Univ. of BC
Goodricke College
Univ. of York, Heslington, York
YO10 5DD, United Kingdom
Contact: c/o Athletic Union
Tel: +44 19 0443 3430
Fax: +44 19 0441 3619
BH: Fulford, York

SCHOOLS AND JUNIORS

Abbey School BC
BH: Reading RC, Thameside Promenade
Caversham, Reading, Berks
RG1 8EQ, United Kingdom
Tel: +44 11 8956 7091

Abingdon School BC
BH: Wilsham Road
Abingdon, Oxon
United Kingdom
Tel: +44 12 3552 0145

American School in London BC
BH: Furnivall Sculling Club
19 Lower Mall, Hammersmith, London
W6 9DJ, United Kingdom
Tel: +44 20 8748 6867

Barn Elms RC
BH: Barn Elms
Putney, London
SW13 0DG, United Kingdom
Tel: +44 20 8788 9472

Bedford High School RC
BH: Harpur Trust Boathouse
Bedford
United Kingdom
Tel: +44 12 3435 9076

Bedford Modern School BC
BH: Harpur Trust Boathouse
Longholme, Bedford
United Kingdom
Tel: +44 12 3435 9076

Bedford School BC
BH: Bedford School Boathouse
Longholme
United Kingdom
Tel: +44 12 3435 9076

Blyth Community College RC
BH: Blyth Community College
Blyth, Northumberland
NE24 4LN, United Kingdom
Tel: +44 16 7035 2350

Bradford Grammar School BC
Bradford Grammar School
Keighley Road, Bradford, Yorkshire
BD9 4JP, United Kingdom
Contact: Mr. D Leake, Master I/c Rowing
Tel: +44 12 5845 9213
BH: Hirst Weir
Shipley

Bryanston School BC
Blandford, Dorset
DT11 0PX, United Kingdom
Contact: Mr. G S Elliot, Head of Rowing
Tel: +44 12 5845 9213
Fax: +44 12 5848 4657
Email: gse@bryanston.co.uk
BH: Bryanston School
River Stour, Blandford

Canford School BC
Canford School
Wimborne, Dorset
BH21 3AD, United Kingdom
Contact: Mr. K Ayles, Boathouse Manager
Tel: +44 12 0284 1254
BH: River Stour
Canford, Wimborne, Dorset

Cheltenham College BC
United Kingdom
BH: Lower Lode
Tewkesbury, Glos
GL20 7DP, United Kingdom
Tel: +44 16 8429 2296

Cheltenham Ladies College RC
BH: Lower Lode Lane
Tewkesbury, Glos
GL20 7DP, United Kingdom
Tel: +44 16 8429 2296

Chiswick School BC
BH: Chiswick Boathouse
Barnes Bridge, Chiswick, London
W4 2SH, United Kingdom
Tel: +44 20 8994 8612

Claires Court School BC
BH: Maidenhead RC, Maidenhead Bridge
Bridge Road, Maidenhead
SL6 8DG, United Kingdom
Tel: +4416 2871 2671

Clifton College BC
Clifton College
32 College Road, Clifton, Bristol
BS8 3JH, United Kingdom
Contact: Mr. R Jones, Master i/c Rowing
Tel: +44 11 7942 0132
Fax: +44 11 7315 7101
Email: rjones@clifton-college.avon.sch.uk
BH: Clifton College, Bristol

Dame Alice Harpur School RC
BH: The Schools Boathouse
Longholme, Bedford
United Kingdom
Tel: +44 12 3435 9076

Doncaster Schools' Rowing Association
Contact: Mr. D. Fletcher
Tel: +44 13 0271 0087
Fax: +44 13 0271 0204
Email: Fletch1941@aol.com
BH: The Old Boathouse
The Dell, Hexthorpe, Doncaster
DN4, United Kingdom

Downe House BC
The Bursary
Downe House, Cold Ash, Newbury, Berks
RG18 9JJ, United Kingdom
Contact: Mr. B K Colborne
Tel: +44 18 6585 8438
BH: Pangbourne, Berks

Dragon School BC
Bardwell Road, Oxford
OX2 6SS, United Kingdom
Contact: Mr. M Righton, Sculling Co-ordinator
Tel: +44 18 6531 5400
Fax: +44 18 6531 1664
Email: mar@dragonschool.org
BH: Bardwell Road, Oxford

Dulwich College BC
BH: Dulwich College Boat House
Embankment, Putney, London
SW15 1LB, United Kingdom
Tel: +44 78 3627 2376

Durham High School BC
Durham High School, PE Dept.
Farewell Hall, Durham
DH1 3TB, United Kingdom
Contact: Mrs. J V Slane
Tel: +44 19 1384 3226
BH: The Boathouse
Green Lane, Durham

Durham School BC
Durham
DH1 4SZ, United Kingdom
Contact: Mr. J E Bell, Master I/c Rowing
Tel: +44 19 1386 9350
Fax: +44 19 1383 1025
Email: jebseb@btinternet.com
BH: The Weir, Durham City

Eastbourne College BC
Common Room, Old Wish Road
Eastbourne, East Sussex
BN21 4JY, United Kingdom
Contact: Ms. F E King, Teach I/c Rowing
Tel: +44 13 2364 9104
Email: fek@eastbourne-college.co.uk
BH: Middle Bridge, Pevensey Levels

Emanuel School BC
BH: Dukes Meadows
Chiswick, London
W4 2SH, United Kingdom
Tel: +44 20 8994 5054

Eton College BC
BH: Master's Boathouse
Pococks Lane, Eton, Windsor
United Kingdom
Tel: +44 17 5367 1464

Godolphin & Latymer School BC
BH: Latymer Upper School BC
40 A Upper Mall, Hammersmith, London
W6 9TA, United Kingdom
Tel: +44 20 8741 1854

Grange School (Hartford), the RC
The Grange School
Bradburns Lane, Hartford, Cheshire
CW8 1LU, United Kingdom
Contact: Mr. G. Jump, Master i/c Rowing
Tel: +44 16 0674 0007
Fax: +44 16 0678 4581
Email: G.T.Jump@staffs.ac.uk
BH: Willow Green Lane
Acton Bridge, Northwich, Cheschire

Grange School Rowing Association 2000
BH: The Grange School (Hartford) RC
Willow Green Lane, Acton Bridge, Northwich,
Cheshire
CW8 3AQ, United Kingdom
Tel: +44 16 0675 456

Haileybury RC
BH: Broxbourne RC
Old Nazeing Road, Broxbourne, Herts
EN10 6QU, United Kingdom
Tel: +44 19 9246 2507

Halliford School BC
BH: Walton RC
Sunbury, Walton on Thames, Surrey
United Kingdom
Tel: +44 19 3222 4557

Hampton School BC
BH: The Millenium Boathouse
Lower Sunbury Road, Hampton, Middx
United Kingdom
Tel: +44 20 8941 4393

Harrow School BC
Tutors Flat, The Park
Harrow on the Hill, Middx
HA1 3JB, United Kingdom
Contact: Mr. C J Lee
Tel: +44 20 8872 8351
Email: cjl@harrowschool.org.uk
BH: Marlow RC
Marlow Bridge Lane, Marlow

Headington School Oxford BC
London Road, Oxford
OX3 7TD, United Kingdom
Contact: Ms. S Mitchell, Director of Rowing
Tel: +44 18 6575 9153
Fax: +44 18 6576 4078
Email: mi@headington.oxon.sch.uk
BH: St. Edwards School BC
Wolvercote, Oxford

Henley College BC
BH: Upper Thames RC
Remenham Lane, Henley on Thames
RG9 3DB, United Kingdom
Tel: +44 14 9157 5745

Hereford Cathedral School BC
BH: Hereford BC
37 Greyfriars Avenue, Hereford
HR4 0BE, United Kingdom
Tel: +44 14 3227 3915

King Edward VI School
Contact: Mrs K Bonham
Tel: +44 13 8684 0452
Fax: +44 17 8929 3564
BH: Stratford upon Avon BC
Recreation Ground, Stratford upon Avon
United Kingdom

Kings College School BC
BH: Embankment
Putney, London
SW15 1LB, United Kingdom
Tel: +44 20 8789 6113

Kings School Canterbury, The BC
United Kingdom
BH: Brett Sturry Quarry
Westbere Lakes, Kent
Tel: +44 12 2771 1504

Kings School Chester, The RC
BH: The Groves, Chester
CH1 1SD, United Kingdom
Tel: +44 12 4434 7354

Kings School Ely, The BC
Ely, Cambs
CB7 4DB, United Kingdom
Contact: Mr. E J Davis, Rowing Master
Tel: +44 13 5366 0728
BH: Appleyard & Lincoln's, Ely

Kings School Rochester BC
BH: Allington
Maidstone, Kent
United Kingdom
Tel: +44 16 2268 6763

Kings School Worcester, The BC
Worcester
WR1 2LH, United Kingdom
Contact: Mr. N Maloney, Master i/c Rowing
Tel: +44 19 0573 1398
Fax: +44 19 0572 1710
Email: nmaloney@ksw.org.uk
BH: Severn Street, Worcester

Kingston Grammar School BC
BH: Aragon Avenue
Thames Ditton, Surrey
United Kingdom
Tel: +44 20 8398 5138

Lady Eleanor Holles BC
BH: Millenium Boathouse
Lower Sunbury Road, Hampton, Middx
United Kingdom
Tel: +44 20 8941 4393

Latymer Upper School BC
BH: 40A Upper Mall
Hammersmith, London
W6 9TA, United Kingdom
Tel: +44 20 8741 1851

Leeds Schools BC
Contact: Mrs E Brown
Tel: +44 11 3295 8032
Email: emily@shipweb.plus.uk
BH: The Boathouse
Waterloo Lake, Roundhay Park, Leeds
United Kingdom

Leys School BC
BH: The Combined Boathouses
Logan's Way, Cambridge
CB4 1BL, United Kingdom
Tel: +44 12 2350 8900

London Oratory School BC
BH: Barn Elms BC
Putney, London
United Kingdom
Tel: +44 20 7385 0102

Magdalen College BC
Oxford
OX4 1DZ, United Kingdom
Contact: Mr. S A Spowart, Rowing Master
Tel: +44 14 9467 6642
Fax: +44 18 6524 0379

Merchant Taylors School BC
Merchant Taylors' School
Liverpool Road, Crosby, Liverpool
L23 0QP, United Kingdom
Contact: Mr. P Little, Master I/c Rowing
Tel: +44 77 7027 7586
Fax: +44 15 1949 9300
Email: pl@merchanttaylors.sefton.sch.uk
BH: Marine Lake, Southport

Monkton Combe School BC
Bath
BA2 7HG, United Kingdom
Contact: Mr. D Conington, Rowing Master
Tel: +44 12 2572 3760
Fax: +44 12 2572 1181
Email: coningtond@monkton.org.uk
BH: Monkton Combe School, Bath
Tel: +44 12 2572 3941

Norwich High School RC
Contact: Mr. A Emerson-Moering, Rowing Master
Tel: +44 19 5345 4569
Fax: +44 16 0362 7036
Email: pdgoddard83@hotmail.com
BH: Norwich RC, Trowse Water Sports Centre
Whitlingham Lane, Trowse, Trowse, Norwich
NR14 8TR, United Kingdom

Nottingham Schools' Rowing Association
Contact: Ms. K Gorny
Tel: +44 11 5849 8272
Email: kgorny@hotmail.com
BH: National Water Sports Centre
Holme Pierrepont, Nottingham
NG12 2LO, United Kingdom

Oratory School BC
BH: Sheepwash Lane
Whitchurch on Thames
United Kingdom
Tel: +44 11 8984 1092

Oundle School BC
The School
Church Street, Oundle, Peterborough
PE8 4EE, United Kingdom
Contact: Mr. Edward Oxlade, Master i/c Rowing
Tel: +44 18 3227 4330
Fax: +44 18 3227 3564
Email: eso@oundle.northants.sch.uk
BH: River Nene, Tansor

Pangbourne College BC
BH: Pangbourne College
Bere Court Road, Pangbourne
RG8 8LA, United Kingdom
Tel: +44 11 8984 2997

Ponteland High School RC
BH: Tyne RC, Riverside Boathouse
Water Row, Newburn, Newcastle upon Tyne
NE15 8NL, United Kingdom
Tel: +44 19 1267 3827

Portsmouth Grammar School RC
BH: Southsea RC
Clarence Beach, Southsea, Hants
PO5 3AE, United Kingdom
Tel: +44 23 9282 1893

Putney High School RC
BH: Thames RC
Embankment, Putney, London
SW15 1LB, United Kingdom
Tel: +44 20 8788 0676

Queen Elizabeth High School BC
Whetstone Bridge Road, Hexham
Northumberland
NE46 3JB, United Kingdom
Contact: Mr. C J Grabham, Rowing Master
Tel: +44 14 3460 5706
Fax: +44 3461 0305
BH: Tyne Green, Hexham

Queens Park High School RC
3 Watling Crescent
Handbridge, Chester
CH4 7HD, United Kingdom
Contact: Mrs. A Mohan
BH: River Dee, Queen's Park (meadows side)
Tel: +44 12 4467 5468

Radley College BC
BH: Lower Radley
Abingdon, Oxon
United Kingdom
Tel: +44 12 3552 1114

Reading Blue Coat School BC
BH: Holme Park
Sonning, Reading, Berks
United Kingdom
Tel: +44 11 8944 1005

Reading School BC
Reading, Berks
RG1 8EQ, United Kingdom
Contact: Mr. A P Rothbart, Rowing Master
Tel: +44 11 8901 5600
Fax: +44 11 8935 2755
BH: Thameside Promenade
Reading, Berks

Reading Schools Rowing Association
BH: Reading RC, Thameside Promenade
1 The Boathouse, Thameside Promenade,
Caversham, Reading, Berks
RG1 8EQ, United Kingdom
Tel: +44 11 8956 7091

Royal Grammar Sch. High Wycombe BC
BH: Marlow RC, Marlow Bridge
Bisham Road, Marlow
SL7 1RH, United Kingdom
Tel: +44 16 2848 2366

Royal Grammar School Lancaster BC
The Royal Grammar School
East Road, Lancaster
LA1 3EF, United Kingdom
Contact: Mr. P Jago, Master i/c Rowing
Tel: +44 15 2484 6942
Fax: +44 15 2484 7947
Email: peter_jago@hotmail.com
BH: Caton Road, Lancaster

Royal Grammar School Worcs BC
Royal Grammar School
Upper Tything, Worcester
WR1 1HP, United Kingdom
Contact: Mr. M H Vetch, Master i/c Rowing
Tel: +44 19 0576 4750
Fax: +44 19 0572 6571
BH: Worcester River Sports Centre, Worcester

Royal Shrewsbury School BC
BH: Kingsland
Shrewsbury, , United Kingdom
Tel: +44 17 4335 3068

Shiplake College BC
BH: Shiplake College
Henley on Thames, Oxon
RG9 4BW, United Kingdom
Tel: +44 11 8940 2455

Shrewsbury High School BC
BH: Pengwern BC
Kingsland, Shrewsbury
SY3 7BD, United Kingdom
Tel: +44 17 4336 2196

Sir John Deane's College
The Crescent, Northwich
CW9 8AF, United Kingdom
Contact: Mr. R L Lowrie
Tel: +44 19 2873 3582
Email: lowrierl@aol.com

Sir William Borlase's Gram Sch BC
BH: Marlow RC
Marlow Bridge Lane, Marlow
SL7 1RH, United Kingdom
Tel: +44 16 2848 2366

St. Edwards School BC
BH: 193 Godstow Road
Wovercote, Oxford
OX2 8PJ, United Kingdom
Tel: +44 18 6555 6140

St. Georges College BC
BH: Sunbury Lane
Walton upon Thames
United Kingdom
Tel: +44 19 3225 2678

St. James BC
BH: Twickenham RC
Eel Pie Island, Twickenham, Middx
TW1 3DY, United Kingdom
Tel: +44 14 0325 3564

St. Leonards School BC
BH: Prebends Bridge
Durham
United Kingdom
Tel: +44 19 1386 6614

St. Pauls Girls School BC
BH: St. Paul's School BC
Lonsdale Road, Barnes, London
SW13 9JT, United Kingdom
Tel: +44 20 8748 7184

St. Pauls School BC
BH: St. Paul's School
Lonsdale Road, Barnes, London
SW13 9JT, United Kingdom
Tel: +44 20 8748 7184

St. Peter's School BC
BH: St. Peter's School
Clifton, York
YO30 6AB, United Kingdom
Tel: +44 19 0462 3213

Stowe Sculling Club
Stowe School
Buckingham, Bucks
MD18 5EH, United Kingdom
Contact: The Secretary
Tel: +44 12 8081 3164
BH: Stowe School, Buckingham

Strodes College BC
BH: Cooper's Close
Egham
United Kingdom
Tel: +44 17 8446 9140

Surbiton High School BC
BH: Molesey BC
Barge Walk, East Molesey, Surrey
KT8 9AJ, United Kingdom
Tel: +44 20 8979 6583

Thomas's Prep School Battersea Sculling Club
BH: Westminster School BC
Embankment, London
SW15 1LB, United Kingdom
Tel: +44 20 8788 0669

Tiffin School BC
BH: Canbury Boathouse
Canbury Gardens, Lower Ham Road
Kingston upon Thames, Surrey
KT2 5BB, United Kingdom
Tel: +44 20 8546 8592

Welbeck College BC
Workshop, Notts
S80 3LN, United Kingdom
Contact: Dr. A Morgan, Master i/c Rowing
Tel: +44 19 0947 6326
Fax: +44 19 0953 0447
BH: Welbeck College Workshop

Westminster School BC
BH: Embankment
Putney, London
SW15 1LB, United Kingdom
Tel: +44 20 8788 0669

Wimbledon High School
Mansel Road, London
SW19 4AB, United Kingdom
Contact: Mrs. T Tabor
Tel: +44 20 8948 1375
Fax: +44 20 8971 0901
BH: Thames RC
The Embankment, Putney, London
SW15 1LB, United Kingdom

Winchester College BC
BH: on River Itchen
Donum Road, Winchester
United Kingdom
Tel: +44 19 6282 0217

Windsor Boys School, The BC
BH: Barry Avenue
Windsor, , United Kingdom
Tel: +44 17 5362 1112

Woodhouse Grove School BC
Apperley Bridge, Bradford, W. Yorks
BD10 0NR, United Kingdom
Contact: Mr. J C Cockshott, Master i/c Rowing
Tel: +44 11 3250 0818
Fax: +44 11 3250 5290
BH: Hirst Weir, Shipley

Wycliffe Sculling Centre
Stonehouse, Gloucestershire
GL10 2JQ, United Kingdom
Contact: Mr. T Jones, i/c Rowing
Tel: +44 14 5272 2034
Fax: +44 14 5382 7634
Email: adolo@wycliffe.co.uk
BH: Berkeley Canal
Saul Junction

Yarm School BC
BH: Yarm School
The Friarage, Yarm
TS15 9EL, United Kingdom
Tel: +44 16 4278 6023

United States

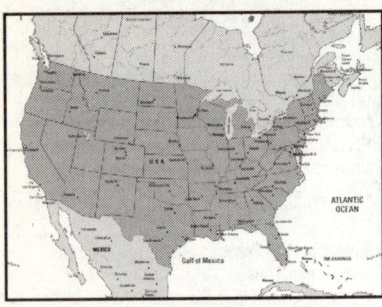

HISTORY

Exported from Great Britain as a "gentleman's" sport, rowing came to the United States in the early to mid 1800's. Professional racing in pairs, fours and single sculls dominated the scene at the time, with single scullers held in the highest regard among athletes and spectators.

Regattas were often sponsored by local railroad lines seeking to attract weekend business. Spectators were transported to the regatta sites, and could purchase a seat on a spectator train running along the bank of the river or lake during the races.

At the same time, amateur boat racing in universities gained prominence with the first Harvard-Yale race in 1852 — the first intercollegiate athletic event in the United States, which is still held to this day every June in New London, Connecticut.

At the end of the 19th Century, betting on professional sculling contests succumbed to acts of sabotage and race fixing, and ultimately saw its demise as a professional sport by the early 20th Century. America's sport was soon replaced by other amateur and professional sports such as baseball, football, and track and field. The outcome of the Harvard-Yale boat race, once front-page news, was buried in the sports section, if covered at all. Despite its disappearance from the headlines, collegiate rowing programs prospered, with U.S. eights winning every gold medal at the Olympics between 1920 and 1956.

Women's rowing, added to the Olympic schedule in 1976, and lightweight rowing, added in 1996 have brought new dimensions to the Games, and a new emphasis on women's and lightweight development programs in the U.S. Title IX has positively impacted women's collegiate rowing, by expanding the sport to state Universities and Colleges, heightening competition levels, and providing scholarship opportunities.

Far from its "gentleman's" roots, today, rowing is a sport enjoyed by ever-expanding segments of the population ranging from juniors (middle and high-school age children), to women, to masters (age 27 and up), the latter of which is perhaps the fastest growing segment of the rowing population.

Many masters rowers are new to the sport; while others are rediscovering it after a hiatus from college. The explosion of masters rowing programs is a testament to the growth and diversification of the sport. Also of significant note is the geographical expansion of rowing from both the east and west coasts to virtually every corner of the country, including the states of North Dakota, Alaska, Idaho, Arizona and Kentucky.

INTERNET LINKS:
www.usrowing.org
www.mastersrowing.org
www.row2k.com

REGIONS

New England States: Connecticut, Maine, Massachusetts, New Hampshire, Rhode Island, Vermont. **Avg. temp**: Winter 0-30°F; Spring 35-50°F; Summer 60-75°F; Fall 45-75°F. **Sites of interest**: Harvard-Yale Race, New London, CT (June); Head of the Charles, Boston, MA (October); Coastal open-water rowing in Maine and Cape Cod, Massachusetts. **Best time to visit**: Summer and fall.

Mid-Atlantic States: Delaware, District of Columbia, Maryland, New Jersey, New York, Pennsylvania. **Avg. temp**: Winter 15-30°F; Spring 40-60°F; Summer 65-80°F; Fall 50-75°F. **Sites of interest**: Boathouse Row, Philadelphia, PA; Independence Day Regatta, Philadelphia, PA (July); Row the Apple, New York, NY; Cherry Blossom Regatta, Washington, DC (Month). **Best time to visit**: Spring, summer or fall.

Southern States: Alabama, Arkansas, Florida, Georgia, Kentucky, Louisiana, Mississippi, North Carolina, South Carolina, Tennessee, Virginia, West Virginia. **Avg. temp**: Winter 30-60°F; Spring 60-75°F; Summer 75-90°F; Fall 50-75°F. **Sites of interest**: Rural Tidewater area of southern Virginia, Mathews County, VA; South Miami Beach, FL; 1996 Olympic Regatta Course, Gainesville, GA. **Best time to visit**: Winter for the mild temperatures. Popular locations or spring break training camps include North Carolina, South Carolina, Florida, Tennessee and Georgia.

Midwest States: Illinois, Indiana, Iowa, Kansas, Michigan, Minnesota, Missouri, Nebraska, North Dakota, Ohio, South Dakota, Wisconsin. **Avg. temp**: Winter 10-30°F; Spring 40-55°F; Summer 60-90°F; Fall 40-60°F. **Best time to visit**: Spring, summer or fall.

Western States: Alaska, California, Colorado, Hawaii, Idaho, Montana, Nevada, Oregon, Utah, Washington, Wyoming. **Avg. temp**: Winter 15-65°F; Spring 40-75°F; Summer 60-90°F; Fall 45-75°F. **Sites of interest**: San Diego Crew Classic, San Diego, CA (April); Opening Day Regatta, Seattle, WA (May). **Best time to visit**: Spring, summer or fall.

Alaska: Winter 15-15°F; Spring 20-55°F; Summer 45-60°F; Fall 35-50°F.
Hawaii: Winter 60-75°F; Spring 70-80°F; Summer 75-90°F; Fall 70-80°F.

Did You Know ?

The Detroit Boat Club is the oldest boat club in the United States and the oldest social club in the state of Michigan. It was organized by oarsman on February 18, 1839, and originally had five clubhouses at several locations in the Detroit area before it built the fireproof boathouse that opened on Belle Isle on August 4, 1902.

PERSONALITIES

John B. Kelly, Sr.: An icon in American rowing, John Kelly won two Olympic gold medals in the single and the double in 1920. Denied an entry to the Royal Henley Regatta because of his blue collar roots, his son, John B. Kelly, Jr. went on to vindicate his father by winning Henley's Diamond Sculls in 1947 and 1949.

Ernestine Bayer: The Pioneer of women's rowing in America. Ernestine married silver Olympic medallist Ernest Bayer in 1928, and she went on to open the doors for women's rowing in the U.S. She founded the Philadelphia Girls Rowing Club in 1938, and still rows and competes in her 90's.

Joseph Burk: Considered a great innovator of sculling technique and racing strategy in the early 20th Century. He won races by rowing high stroke ratings of 38-39 compared to his opponents' cadence of 31-34. Won the Diamond Sculls at Henley in 1938 and 1939.

George Y. Pocock: Grew up in Eton, migrated to Canada, then to Seattle, WA where he built the most innovative and replicated racing boats of the 20th Century. Supplied boats for all countries in the 1952 Olympics. Pocock shells were the mainstays of American rowing through the first three-quarters of the 20th Century.

Harry Parker: A student of Joe Burk, and best known as the Coach of Harvard's Varsity Heavyweight men's program. His "hands-off" style is legendary among the Crimson rowers. Under his watchful eye, Harvard dominated the collegiate and international scene in the 1960's, and continues to be a rowing powerhouse to this day.

NATIONAL FEDERATION

United States Rowing Association
201 S. Capitol Avenue, Ste. 400
Indianapolis, IN 46225, United States
Tel: (800) 314-4769, (317) 237-5656
Fax: (317) 237-5646
Email: members@usrowing.org
www.usrowing.org

CLUBS

Albany Rowing Center
PO Box 857
Albany, NY 12201-0857, United States
Email: info@albanyrowingcenter.org
www.albanyrowingcenter.org

BH: Albany Rowing Center Boathouse
south of intersection of I-90 and I-787, under I-7
Albany, NY
Tel: (518) 446-6282

Colors: Navy blue and orange.
Regatta: Head of the Hudson
History: Albany Rowing Center offers many different programs for its members ranging from a morning competitive program, aJunior and Adult Learn-to-Row, a junior competitive program, and a recreational program.

Alexandria Community Rowing
PO Box 16431
Alexandria, VA 22302, United States
Tel: (703) 836-1151
www.rowalexandria.org

BH: Alexandria Community Boathouse
At the end of Madison Avenue on the Potomac River
Alexandria, VA 22302
Tel: (703) 836-1151

Year est: 1988
Colors: Red, white and black.
Regatta: Blue Plains Sprints
Members: 180
History: In 1988, the Alexandria Schools Rowing Facility was dedicated and Alexandria Crew Boosters created Alexandria Community Rowing as a means of fundraising for the T.C. Williams HS Crew program.

Amenities: Guests, Banquet, Bathroom, Showers, Weights, Ergs

Alte Achter Boat Club
PO Box 812301
Wellesley, MA 02482, United States

Year est: 1972
Colors: Red and white.
Members: 11
History: 1972 Olympic Crew. Club exists solely to row in the Head of the Charles.

American Barge Club
1321 NW 14th Street #400
Miami, FL 33125, United States
Contact: Aldo Berti
Tel: (305) 325-1248
BH: (305) 326-7725

Year est: 1983
Colors: Green and red.
Members: 25
History: Initially founded for disabled rowing and later expanded to include masters and high school rowing.

Amenities: Guests

Amoskeag Rowing Club
c/o YMCA
30 Mechanic Street
Manchester, NH 03101, United States
Tel: (603) 668-2130
Email: AmoskeagRowing@yahoo.com
www.amoskeagrowing.org

Year est: 1982
Colors: Red and blue.
Regatta: Riverfest Rec Boat Regatta
Members: 50
History: Founded in 1984 for the purpose of making the sport available in central New Hampshire. The club has provided a home to 1 prep school and 3 college programs. Host of the NH Championship Head Race, we are dedicated to the concept of community rowing.

Amenities: Guests, Ergs

Anchorage Rowing Association
PO Box 242161
Anchorage, AK 99524-2161, United States
Email: membership@anchoragerowing.com
www.anchoragerowing.com

Year est: 1998
History: Formed in 1998, Anchorage Rowing Association. trains on Sand Lake in West Anchorage. The club rows mostly in the summer months, but Juniors usually attend the Northwest Regionals in May and the Greenlake Summer Regatta in August.

Ancient Mariners Rowing Club
PO Box 95531
Seattle, WA 98145-2531, United States
Contact: Paul Harvey
Tel: (425) 747-3214
Email: marpaul@worldnet.att.net

Year est: 1988
Colors: Red and black.
Members: 50
History: Founded in 1988 by former college oarsmen for rowers over 50 years of age. We compete at all levels of masters rowing. **Other Info:** Guests over 50 years of age are allowed.

Amenities: Guests, Banquet, Bathroom, Showers, Weights, Ergs

Ann Arbor Rowing Club
PO Box 3128
Ann Arbor, MI 48106, United States
Contact: Jennifer Shifferd, President
Email: jenshiff@umich.edu
aarc-board@umich.edu
www.a2crew.com

BH: Ann Arbor Boathouse
1495 Lakeshore Drive
Ann Arbor, MI 48104-1057
Tel: (734) 930-6462

Colors: Red and Blue.
History: The Ann Arbor Rowing Club (AARC) is a non-profit, educational organization that provides a safe and affordable opportunity to anyone who is interested in rowing, regardless of age, gender, physical ability, or rowing experience.

Annapolis Rowing Club
PO Box 4191
Annapolis, MD 21403, United States
Tel: (410) 269-0985
Fax: (410) 216-9324
www.annapolisrowingclub.com

Year est: 1982
Colors: Blue and white.
Regatta: Wye Island Regatta
Members: 150
History: The Annapolis Rowing Club (ARC) is both a recreational and competitive rowing club serving the Annapolis and surrounding area for 17 years. With over 100 members, experience levels range from beginner to advanced. ARC offers programs for both novice and experienced oarsmen. The ARC rowing season starts mid-March and ends in November, weather dependent. ARC is a non-profit, community-based membership organization dedicated to the promotion and advancement of the sport of rowing by providing the widest possible range of opportunities for training and participation.

Amenities: Guests, Bathroom, Ergs

Aqueduct Rowing Club
PO Box 202
Rexford, NY 12148, United States
Email: shobbs@nycap.rr.com
home.nycap.rr.com/rowaqueduct

BH: Aqueduct Rowing Club Boathouse
Aqueduct Park
Niskayuna, NY 12148

Year est: 1973
Colors: Red, black and white.
Regatta: Head of the Mohawk
Members: 130
History: The Aqueduct Rowing Club was founded in 1973 to encourage recreational and competitive rowing on the Mohawk River. **Other Info**: Guests are allowed once a year.

Amenities: Guests

Arlington Rowing Association
PO Box 1171
Pleasant Valley, NY 12569, United States
Tel: (845) 223-7418
Fax: (914) 724-4450
Email: scpdsodcapt@yahoo.com

Colors: Maroon and gold.
Regatta: Mid-Hudson Invitational, Mid-Hudson Triangulars
Members: 300

Amenities: Bathroom, Showers, Ergs

Ashland Rowing Club
Ashland, OR , United States
Contact: Marty Thommes
Tel: (541) 482-3004
Email: ashlandrow@yahoo.com
www.ashlandrowingclub.org

Atlanta Rowing Club
PO Box 500937
Atlanta, GA 31150, United States
Paul Hagan, Communication Contact
Tel: (770) 993-1879
Email: hagancom@speedfactory.net
www.atlantarow.org

BH: Atlanta Rowing Club Boathouse
500 Azalea Drive
Atlanta, GA

Year est: 1974
Colors: Red and white.
Members: 175
History: Atlanta Rowing Club is a non-profit organization formed and maintained to promote the sport of rowing, to teach and train oarsmen and oarswomen without preference to race, creed, religion, or color, to provide the equitable means for both recreational and competitive rowing, locally, regionally, nationally, and internationally, to develop the sport of rowing as a interscholastic and intercollegiate sport in the Atlanta metropolitan area, to maintain the natural beauty and ecological balance of the Chattahoochee river and surrounding area, and finally, to provide a means for community and charitable involvement in the Atlanta metropolitan area. **Other Info**: Guest access allowed for out-of-town memberships for 3 months at a time.

Amenities: Guests, Bathroom, Showers, Ergs

Atlantic County Rowing Association
PO Box 802
Northfield, NJ 08330, United States
Email: RunRow@aol.com
www.eteamz.com/acra

BH: Atlantic County Rowing Association Boathouse
Route 559, Lake Lenape Park
Mays Landing, NJ 8330
Tel/Fax: (609) 344-4104

Year est: 1991
Regatta: The Atlantic City Rowing Championships
Members: 75
History: Our main mission is to teach the proper technique using one-on-one instruction. Located on a beautiful lake, our relaxed atmosphere allows for maximum fun.

Amenities: Guests, Bathroom, Showers, Ergs

Augusta Rowing Club
101 Riverfront Drive
Augusta, GA 30901, United States
Tel: (706) 821-2875
Email: mseanhall@yahoo.com
www.augustarows.com

Year est: 1984
Colors: Oglethorpe red and white.
Regatta: Head of the South, Augusta-Aiken Spring Regatta
Members: 170
History: Located on the Savannah River, Augusta Rowing Club was founded by a handful of rowing enthusiasts. The club has grown to see nationwide recognition for its excellence. It is host to the The Head of The South Regatta and the Augusta-Aiken Spring Regatta.

Amenities: Guests, Banquet, Weights, Ergs

Austin Rowing Club

PO Box 1741
Austin, TX 78767-1741, United States
Tel: (512) 472-0726
Fax: (512) 472-0700
Email: exdir@austinrowing.org
www.austinrowing.org

BH: ARC, 54 Trinity Street
Austin, TX 78701

Year est: 1981
Colors: Red, White and Blue.
Regatta: Heart of Texas, The Pumpkin Regatta
Members: 325
History: First incorporated in 1981 with a membership of 20, the Austin Rowing Club has grown into one of the premier community rowing clubs in Texas. Our first boat, a refurbished, used 8+ was transported on top of a old school bus and stored under the deck of a restaurant on Town Lake! We have grown to a membership of over 200 and a permanent, two bay facility of our own. ARC's membership covers a wide range of ages and abilities. ARC's Junior Program, our pride and joy, has sent competitors to the Junior Championships for the past two years. **Other Info**: Great place for Winter and Spring Break. Boat Rentals available.

Amenities: Guests, Bathroom, Showers, Ergs

Bachelors Barge Club

#6 Boathouse Row
Kelly Drive
Philadelphia, PA 19103, United States
Tel: (215) 236-4328
Email: tchutch@attglobal.net
www.boathouserow.org

Year est: 1853
Colors: Royal blue and red.
Members: 200+
History: Founded in 1853. Oldest operating rowing club in the U.S. and home to many Olympians and world champions.

Amenities: Guests, Banquet, Bathroom, Showers, Weights, Ergs

Bainbridge Island Rowing

PO Box 11168
Bainbridge Island, WA 98110-5168, United States
Email: rowing@bainbridge.net
www.bainbridgerowing.org

Year est: 2001
Members: 20
History: Bainbridge Island Rowing is a community-based, non-profit 501c(3) organization, founded in 2001, whose purpose is to promote all facets of the sport of rowing. BIR activities take place at Waterfront Park on Bainbridge Island and throughout the greater Puget Sound area.

Bair Island Aquatic Center

1450 Maple Street
Redwood City, CA 94063, United States
Contact: Susan Rowinski, BIAC President
Tel: (650) 474-2247
Fax: (650) 474-2247
Email: info@gobair.org
rowinski@earthlink.net
www.gobair.org

Year est: 1985
Colors: Blue, green and black.
Members: 100
History: BIAC is located near the largest remaining restorable wetlands in the South San Francisco Bay, Bair Island of the Edwards San Francisco Bay National Wildlife Refuge. The wetlands is a haven for 126 species of birds, including blue herons, egrets and Caspian terns; 63 types of fish and 13 types of mammals such as seals and sea lions. BIAC offers access to the water channels and sloughs that surround Bair Island. Thus an individual now has a means of experiencing the tranquillity of the wetlands, and the Bay, that cannot be appreciated from the land.

Amenities: Guests, Bathroom, Showers, Weights, Ergs

Baltimore Rowing Club

3301 Waterview AveNUE
Baltimore, MD 21230, United States
Contact: Jeff Rodman, Club President
Tel: (410) 355-5649
Email: brcrowing@yahoo.com
www.baltimorerowing.org

Year est: 1979
Colors: Black and gold.
Regatta: Great Baltimore Burn, Ariel Head of the Patapsco
Members: 100
History: The Ariel and Arundel BC was founded in Baltimore in 1861. Rowing was at its height in Baltimore at the turn of the century with both clubs winning national championships and other prestigious regattas of that time.

Amenities: Guests, Banquet, Bathroom, Showers, Weights, Ergs

Bay Area Rowing Club of Houston
PO Box 580374
Houston, TX 77258-0374, United States
Jeff Tave, Membership Contact
Email: membership@barchouston.org
www.barchouston.org

BH: BARC Boathouse
NASA Road 1
Clear Lake Park, TX 77258-0374
Tel: (281) 326-5995

Year est: 1989
Colors: Red and yellow.
Regatta: Space City Sprints
Members: 115
History: Non-profit club formed in 1989 to promote the sport of rowing in the Houston area. Boathouse was built in 1995. Rice University and Texas A&M — Galveston row out of our boathouse. Motto: "Best little oarhouse in Texas" **Other Info**: Short-term membership available.

Amenities: Guests, Ergs

Bay Area Whaleboat Rowing Association
41 Sutter Street Ste 1620
San Francisco, CA 94104, United States

Year est: 1930
Members: 250-350
History: BAWRA was incorporated in 1984, but has been in existence since the 30's. We row on the Oakland/Alameda Estuary and on the San Francisco Bay. Our longest race is about 6 miles.

Amenities: Guests

Bay City Rowing Club
PO Box 1144
Bay City, MI 48706-1144, United States
Contact: Greg Dickson, BCRC Secretary
Email: support@mmcctech.com
info@baycityrowing.org

BH: BCRC, 350 Lions Club
Bay City, MI 48706
Tel: (989) 892-5769
www.bacityrowing.org

Year est: 1989
Colors: Yellow and Blue
Members: 60
History: The Bay City Rowing Club is a 501(c)3 non-profit community rowing organization with a mission to promote rowing as a healthy and rewarding activity for people of all ages. The club provides a complete rowing opportunity to the entire community including: training, sport rowing, recreational rowing, social activities, competition, boat storage and meeting rooms. Membership is open to anyone. The rowing season begins approximately April 15 of each year. The boathouse remains open until ice forms on the river in the fall. Home for the Bay City Central High School Crew.

Amenities: Guests, Bathroom, Showers, Weights, Ergs

Berkeley Paddling & Rowing Club
1134 Delaware Street, Suite D
Berkeley, CA 94702, United States
Email: jfredds@aol.com

BH: 2851 Bolivar Drive
Berkeley, CA 94710

Year est: 1967
Colors: Blue and white
Members: 100
History: Sculling and kayaking club.

Amenities: Bathroom, Showers, Weights, Ergs

Berkshire Rowing and Sculling Society
PO Box 787
Pittsfield, MA 01201, United States
Contact: Lew Cuyler
Tel/Fax: (413) 496-9160
Email: info@berkshiresculling.com
www.berkshiresculling.com

BH: Cuyler Boathouse
Lakeway Drive, Onota Lake
Pittsfield, MA 1201
Tel: (413) 442-7769

Year est: 1995
Colors: Red and Black
Regatta: Bernie Ryan Regatta
Members: 40
History: Started in 1995 for single scullers. Began school sweep rowing programs in 2000. Acquired boathouse in 2001. **Other Info**: Daily sculling lessons and scull rentals May-September

Amenities: Guests

Bonneville Rowing
3044 E. 3135 Street
Salt Lake City, UT 84109-2116, United States
Contact: Wendy Whitney
Tel: (801) 466-0460
Email: sculling@attbi.com

BH: Bonneville Rowing Boathouse
Great Salt Lake Marina/Beach
Salt Lake City, UT
Tel: (801) 466-0460

Year est: 1990
Colors: Green and white.
Members: 40
History: Rowing on the Great Salt Lake is really a trip! Miles and miles of nothing but water, and only an occasional sculling boat. We teach lessons through the University of Utah.

Amenities: Ergs

Boulder Area Community Rowing
PMB 102
1630-A 30th Street
Boulder, CO 80301, United States
Tel: (303) 443-3487
Email: info@boulderrowing.com
www.boulderrowing.com

Year est: 2000
History: Boulder Community Rowing is a non-profit corporation, founded in 2000, to bring rowing to the Boulder Community. BCR offers rowing opportunities for recreational and competitive rowers. We are close partners with Colorado Crew (the rowing team of the University of Colorado at Boulder) and Rocky Mountain Rowing Club (located at Cherry Creek Reservoir in Denver).

Amenities: Guests

Brigantine Rowing Club
1402 Sheridan Boulevard
Brigantine, NJ 08203, United States
Contact: Tony Molinari
Tel: (609) 266-2025
Fax: (609) 344-3231
Email: brcrowcrew@aol.com
BRCrowcrew@comcast.com
www.brigantinerowingclub.org

History: Brigantine offers a handicap rowing program in the summer, an adult novice rowing program and a competitive rower summer and fall program.

Buffalo Rowing
1021 Mill Road
East Aurora, NY 14052, United States
Contact: Peggy Thrasher
Tel: (716) 652-1467
Fax: (716) 652-1467
Email: buffalorowing@aol.com

Year est: 2000
Colors: Red, white and blue.
Members: 6

Amenities: Guests, Ergs

Burning River Rowing Club
Shaker Heights, OH , United States
Contact: Charlie Braun
Tel: (216) 295-2579
Fax: (216) 391-4761

Year est: 1999
Colors: Red — the color of flames.
Members: 4
History: Named as a commemoration for the memorable fire on the Cuyahoga in the 1970s. **Motto:** Ya gotta row quick or the burning river will get you!

California Adaptive Rowing Programs
PO Box 3879
Long Beach, CA 90803, United States
Contact: Angela Madsen, Adaptive rowing coach
Tel: (562) 434-8334
Email: Msparasurfer@aol.com

BH: Pete Archer Rowing Center
5750 Boathouse Lane
Long Beach, CA
Tel: (562) 438-3352

Amenities: Guests, Bathroom, Showers, Weights,

California Yacht Club
4469 Admiralty Way
Marina del Rey, CA 90292, United States
Contact: Carrie Dair, Program Director
Tel: (310) 823-4567
Email: carrie.dair@calyachtclub.net
caleeds@pacbell.net
www.calyachtclub.com

Year est: 1922
Colors: Blue and White
Regatta: Head of the Marina, Catalina Crossing
Members: 50
History: In 1976, President Charles Hathaway rowed his dory FRITZ from Catalina to the guest dock at California Yacht Club to celebrate his 50th birthday. In 1977, the row from Catalina became known as the "Great Catalina to Marina del Rey Rowing and Paddling Derby." The Derby, coupled with our July Celebration of Henley Regatta, launched new enthusiasm for recreational rowing in the Marina. Our early rowing history would be incomplete without mentioning another member, Stan Mullin. Stan's technical rowing knowledge and charm enabled CYC to develop two rowing houses where the Club's rowing activities are centered. CYC's rowers are consistently top Masters' medal winners in America's leading rowing events.

Amenities: Guests, Banquet, Bathroom, Showers, Ergs

Cambridge Boat Club

7 Meadow Way
Cambridge, MA 02138, United States
Contact: Carmen Garufo, President
Tel: (617) 354-9696
Email: jglcmg@channel1.com
www.cambridge-boat-club.org

Year est: 1909
Colors: Blue and white.
Members: 425
History: Founded in 1909; established Head of the Charles Regatta in 1965 and Community Rowing, Inc., now a separate organization. **Other Info**: Rental Agent, (617) 354-9696

Amenities: Guests, Banquet, Bathroom, Showers, Weights, Ergs

CAMSIS Boat Club Inc.

721 N Overlook Drive
Alexandria, VA 22305, United States
Contact: Lonnie Henley
Tel: (703) 548-7286
Fax: (703) 548-7263
Email: lonnie@henleyhanks.com
www.camsis.org

Year est: 1985
Colors: None
Regatta: Oxford vs. Cambridge alumni boat race
Members: 60
History: An offshoot of the Oxford and Cambridge Universities alumni club of Washington, DC. Formed in 1985 to organize an annual alumni boat race.

Cape Cod Rowing & Sculling Center

30 Harpoon Lane
Yarmouth Port, MA 02675, United States
Contact: Todd P Kennelly, Coach
Tel: (508) 362-OARS
Fax: (508) 362-Row2
Email: CapeCodCrew@usa.com
www.capecodrowing.com

Year est: 1997
Colors: Black/Gold
Regatta: Cape Cod Crew Classic
Members: 30

Amenities: Ergs

Cape Cod Viking Club

121 Sheffield Rd
Brewster, MA 02631, United States
Contact: Jeff McLaughlin
Tel: (508) 896-5363
Fax: (781) 826-1021
www.c4.net/viking

Year est: 1980
Regatta: The Oarsmaster Trials
Members: 30
History: Founded in early 1980s for recreational touring/camping and competitive rowers of traditional oar-on-gunwhale boats. "Home" waters are those surrounding Cape Cod, but Vikings regularly participate in mess-abouts and competitive events all along the Massachusetts coastline. **Other Info**: Guests are always allowed including gigs and other multi-oared boats, and ocean-going boats.

Amenities: Guests

Cape Fear River Rowing Club

PO Box 1586
Wilmington, NC 28402, United States
Contact: Morris Elsen
Tel: (910) 251-5928
Email: melsen@capefear.cc.nc.us

Year est: 1989
Colors: Kelly Green, Gold and Black
Members: 43
History: Over ten years in current incranation. Motto: "If it's green and has teeth, it's not a log!" Host to University of North Carolina at Wilmington and Cape Fear Academy HS.

Amenities: Guests, Banquet, Bathroom, Showers

Capital Rowing Club

1115 O Street SE
Washington, DC 20036, United States
Contact: Sarah Dunham, Club President
Tel: (202) 289-6666
Email: membership@capitalrowing.org
www.capitalrowing.org

Year est: 1988
Colors: Red, White and Blue
Regatta: Capital Sprints
Members: 100
History: Capital has evolved from a club dependent on renting equipment to a club with its own equipment and its own site on the Anacostia River, which helps to fulfill our charter as a community- based club. Much of our competitive success is due to coach Guen.

Amenities: Guests, Bathroom, Ergs

Carnegie Lake Rowing Association

PO Box 330
Princeton, NJ 08542-0330, United States
Contact: Tom Heebink, Membership
Email: info@clra.com
www.clra.com

BH: CLRA Boathouse
Washington Road and Faculty Road
Princeton, NJ
Tel: (609) 683-1618

Year est: 1985
Colors: Orange/Black
Regatta: Carnegie Lake Regatta
Members: 240
History: Founded by a group of scullers in 1985 in conjunction with Princeton University. Developed over 15 years as a "Community Rowing Club". Nickname: "Lakers". **Other Info**: Guests of members allowed. Experienced rowers may join at any time. Beginners may apply for the Learn-to-Row program in September.

Amenities: Guests, Bathroom, Ergs

Carolina Masters Crew Club

7312 Crescent Ridge Drive
Chapel Hill, NC 27516, United States
Contact: Patricia W Hucks
Tel: (919) 968-1182
Fax: (919) 933-1862
Email: pwhucks@intrex.net
www.unc.edu/depts/camprec/Crew

BH: Michael Nicholls Boathouse
University Lake, S. Old Fayetteville Road
Carrboro, NC 27510
Tel: (919) 962-4632

Year est: 1993
Colors: Carolina blue and white
Members: 55
History: Established under the auspices of UNC to provide rowing for a limited number of university faculty, staff, grad students and community members age of 27 and older. **Other Info**: We are a small close-knit group who race on the east coast and also participate in community activities, offer annual sweep lessons and meet regularly for potluck dinners.

Amenities: Guests, Bathroom

Cascade Rowing

3320 Fuhrman Avenue East
Seattle, WA 98102, United States
Tel: (206) 328-0778
Email: cascadewomen@hotmail.com
www.cascadewomen.com

Year est: 1997
Colors: Green and Blue
Members: 100
History: Cascade Rowing is a club in which you can compete nationally and locally, while also having a life outside of crew.

Amenities: Guests, Banquet, Bathroom, Showers, Weights, Ergs

Cascadilla Boat Club Ltd.

PO Box 4032
Ithaca, NY 14852-4032, United States
Email: info@cascadillaboatclub.org
cascadillaboatclub.org

BH: Cascadilla Boathouse
Stewart Park
Ithaca, NY 14852
Tel: (607) 273-1167

Year est: 1977
Colors: Green, White and Black.
Members: 200+
History: A community club which uses part of the city-owned Cascadilla School Boathouse built in 1895. **Other Info**: Masters: Daily individual training, occasional weekend clinics.

Amenities: Guests, Bathroom, Showers, Weights, Ergs

Castle Rowing Club

15 Innis Lane
Old Greenwich, CT 06870, United States
Contact: Larry Muri
Tel: (203) 359-4956
Fax: (203) 353-1949
Email: muril@usmma.edu

Members: 45
History: Currently operate summer sweep programs for competitive college, open and masters rowers and coxswains.

Amenities: Ergs

Catawba Yacht Club

118 E Kingston Avenue
Charlotte, NC 28203, United States
Tel: (704) 332-3032

Year est: 1991
Colors: Red, white and blue.
Members: 70
History: Originally a sailing club from 1940, the rowing program started about 10 years ago. Our club participates in three or four spring races in the spring and summer and three head races in the fall.

Amenities: Banquet, Bathroom, Showers

Cazenovia Rowing Club

PO Box 533
Cazenovia, NY 13035, United States
Contact: Chris Lighthipe
Tel: (315) 682-2183
Fax: (315) 464-2305
www.members.tripod.com/lighthipech

Year est: 1989
Colors: Gray and Green
Regatta: Rowing weekend on Stillwater Reservoir
Members: 62

History: The Cazenovia Rowing Club is a non-profit, volunteer-driven, educationally based, community rowing program that is dedicated to promoting rowing in the Central New York area.

Amenities: Guests

Charles River Rowing Association
Murr Center
65 North Harvard Street
Boston, MA 02163, United States
Contact: Harry Parker
Tel: (617) 495-7775
Fax: (617) 496-4590
Email: harvcrew@hcs.harvard.edu

History: Charles River Rowing Association is an auxiliary club for Harvard University undergraduates and graduates.

Charleston Rowing Club
c/o Commodore C.R. Blyth
1452 Oaklanding Road
Mt Pleasant, SC 29464, United States
Tel: (843) 884-6838,
www.realmaps.com/crc/info.html

BH: Charleston Rowing Club Boathouse
Palmetto Islands County Park
Mt. Pleasant, SC

History: The Charleston Rowing Club is a group of enthusiasts who really mean business when it comes to rowing and sharing their time and expertise. The club membership spans all ages and both genders are well represented. It includes both super meticulous, competitive rowers as well as non-competitive amateurs, who simply enjoy the exercise, the scenery and the camaraderie of a very rewarding sport. The number of rowers has steadily grown since this "official" entity was formed back in 1988. Some of the original founders are still with us and though our mobile society takes its toll, the membership has managed to grow and grow.

Amenities: Guests

Charley McIntyre Rowing Club
710 Cherry Street
Seattle, WA 98104, United States
Contact: John Lundin
Tel: (206) 623-8346
Fax: (206) 623-5951

Year est: 1994
Members: 16

Amenities: Guests, Banquet, Bathroom, Showers, Weights

Chelsea Rowing Club
36 Otis Street
Norwich, CT 06360, United States
Contact: Bob Reed
Tel: (860) 886-5206

BH: Chelsea Rowing Club Boathouse
West Thames Street
Norwich, CA 06360

Year est: 1870
Colors: Blue and White.
Members: 25
History: The Chelsea Club was started in the mid 1870's as the Chelsea Boat Club. The club owned their own boathouse at Norwich Harbor until the 1930's when the club went dark. In 1980, the club started rowing again as Chelsea RC and has a boathouse 1.5 miles south of the original site on the Thames River.

Amenities: Guests

Chester River Rowing Club
300 Washington Avenue
Chestertown, MD 21620, United States
www.chesterriver.org/crrc/index.html

BH: Truslow Boathouse
Quaker Neck Road
Chestertown, MD
Tel: (410) 778-7242

Year est: 1983
Colors: Red and White.
Members: 30-50
Amenities: Guests, Banquet, Bathroom, Showers

Chicago River Rowing & Paddling Center
PO Box 811190
Chicago, IL 60681-1190
Contact: Susan Urbas
Tel: (312) 458-0810
Email: chicagoriverrowing@yahoo.com
http://www.chicagorowing.org

Year est: 1979
Colors: Red, white and blue
Regatta: Iron Oars Marathon
Members: 45-70
History: CRRPC was founded in 1979 for the purpose of demonstrating and promoting the potential of the Chicago River for non-motorized water sports. CRRCP's accomplishments have included hosting the 1980 Women's Olympic Team, the Oxford and Cambridge Universities Boat Race, and the Iron Oars Marathon on the Chicago River.
Other Info: We are located in the heart of the downtown Chicago business district, a stone's throw from many of our members' offices and apartments. We welcome and accommodate all levels of rowing skills and interest.

Amenities: Guests, Bathroom, Showers, Ergs

Chicago Rowing Center
4426 N. Malden St. #1
c/o Katie Leigh
Chicago, IL 60640, United States
Contact: Michael O'Gorman, President
Tel: (312) 593-8040
Email: chicagorowingcenter@yahoo.com
www.rowchicago.org

Year est: 2000
Colors: Black and Red
Members: 30
History: Started in 2000 by a group of 9 rowers who wanted to train and compete on a national level. The team won the Club 4+ at the Head of The Charles Regatta in its first year of organization.

Amenities: Guests

Cincinnati Rowing Club
5460 E. Galbraith Road
Cincinnati, OH 45236, United States
Contact: Howard Meisner, President
Email: hmeisner@acm.org
www.cincinnatirowing.com

BH: Licking River Boathouse
100 Riverboat Row
Newport, KY

Year est: 1990
Colors: Navy Blue, Forest Green and White.
Regatta: Head of the Licking
Members: 100

Coeur d'Alene Rowing Association
Spokane, WA , United States
www.spokanesports.org/org.php

Columbia Rowing Club
9 Old Woodlands Court
Columbia, SC 29209, United States
Contact: Jonathan Fletcher
Tel: (803) 783-7457
Email: jsfletch@ix.netcom.com
crc.netfirms.com
History: Founded in 1997, the Columbia Rowing Club provides an opportunity to promote and develop the sport of rowing in the central South Carolina area.

Amenities: Guests

Commencement Bay Rowing Club
Tacoma, WA , United States
www.ups.edu/athletics/facilities/boathouse

Year est: 1992
Colors: Dark Blue and Maroon
Members: 100
History: A new boathouse was built in 1998 at the Harry Todd Park located on American Lake. American Lake is a beautiful 4-mile long lake lined with evergreen trees and private homes. The lake provides miles of rowable water and magnificent sunrise & sunset views of Mt. Rainier.

Amenities: Guests, Banquet, Bathroom, Showers, Ergs

Community Rowing Inc. of Boston
PO Box 382604
Cambridge, MA 02238-2604, United States
Tel: (617) 964-2455
Fax: (617) 782-3880
Email: office@communityrowing.org
www.communityrowing.org

BH: MDC Daly Skating Rink
Nonatum Road
Newton, MA

Year est: 1985
Colors: Red, White and Black
Regatta: Regatta in Lillies
Members: 1,050

Amenities: Guests, Bathroom, Showers, Ergs

Conibear Rowing Club
3800 Lake Washington Boulevard
Seattle, WA 98118, United States
Contact: Liz Ford
Email: mount.baker@ci.seattle.wa.us
www.conibearrowing.org

BH: Mount Baker Rowing Club Boathouse
3800 Lake Washington Boulevard
Seattle, WA 98118
Tel: (206) 386-1913
Colors: Navy and Yellow.
Members: 50
History: Conibear Rowing Club is a competitive masters rowing club for women age 27 and older. Our members have enjoyed the competition and companionship of the Seattle rowing community since 1984. Our average age is 44, but ages range from 27 to 70.

Amenities: Guests

Connecticut River Oar and Paddle Club

18 Riverside Avenue
Old Saybrook, CT 06475, United States
Contact: Jon Persson
Tel: (860) 388-2343
www.by-the-sea.com/cropc1.html
Colors: Yellow on blue.
Members: 80
History: The Connecticut River Oar and Paddle Club is the Connecticut Chapter of the Traditional Small Craft Association and a founding affiliate of The River School.
Amenities: Guests

Corvallis Rowing Club

3720 NW Boxwood Place
Corvallis, OR 97330, United States
Contact: Steve Rogers
Tel: (541) 753-9134
Email: rogerssnc@aol.com
www.row.corvallis.or.us
Year est: 1992
Colors: Red, Blue and Yellow.
Members: 35
History: The CRC is a non-profit rowing club based in Corvallis, Oregon USA. Club membership is open to all ages and rowing skill levels.
Amenities: Guests, Bathroom, Showers, Weights

Cotuit Rowing Club

PO Box 1664
Cotuit, MA 02635, United States
Contact: Sue Downing
Tel: (508) 428-4484
Fax: (508) 428-1713
Year est: 1990
Colors: Navy, Blue and Yellow.
Members: 20
History: Founded in 1990, the club is dedicated to Masters rowing for men and women.
Amenities: Guests

Crescent Boat Club

#5 Boathouse Row Kelly Drive
Philadelphia, PA 19131, United States
Contact: Clete Graham, Commodore
Tel: (215) 978-9816
Email: clete@netaxs.com
www.boathouserow.org/clubs/crescent.html
Year est: 1867
History: Crescent Boat Club was organized in 1867, incorporated in 1874, and joined the Schuylkill Navy in 1868. The club hosts rowing programs from St. Joseph's University and the Roman Catholic High School.
Amenities: Guests, Banquet, Bathroom, Showers, Weights

Cygnet Rowing Club

6 Ballord Place
Cambridge, MA 02139, United States
Contact: Richard Gonci, Commodore
Tel: (617) 251-6612
Fax: (617) 864-2719
Email: gonci@comcast.net
www.ski-paddle.com

BH: Stoller Boathouse
8 Charles Street
Auburndale, MA 02146
Tel: (617) 964-9302
Year est: 1994
Colors: Blue and Yellow
Members: 65
History: Spin-off of Boston Harbor Rowing Club when harbor became too busy.
Amenities: Guests

D.C. Strokes Rowing Club

PO Box 53019
Washington, DC 20009, United States
Contact: Doug J, President
Tel: (202) 232-1071
Email: president@dcstrokes.org
www.dcstrokes.org
Year est: 1991
Colors: Navy and Pink.
Members: 30
History: DC Strokes Rowing Club was founded in 1991 as the United States' first gay and lesbian rowing club, located in Washington, D.C. and rowing out of Thompson Boat Center on the Potomac River. We are the sponsor club for the Stonewall Regatta.
Amenities: Guests, Bathroom, Showers, Weights, Ergs

Dallas Rowing Club
PO Box 7309
Dallas, TX 75209, United States
Contact: Chuck Ford
Email: chuckford@mindspring.com
www.dallasrowingclub.org

BH: Dallas Rowing Club Boathouse
Shorecrest Drive
Dallas, TX
Tel: (214) 357-0814

Year est: 1980
Colors: Red, White and Blue.
Regatta: The Bachman Lake Autummn
Members: 130
History: Founded in the early 1980's to promote sculling at all levels in the Dallas area. A three-bay boathouse, now home to seventy boats, opened in 1988.

Amenities: Guests, Bathroom, Showers, Weights, Ergs

Des Moines Rowing Club
PO Box 872
Des Moines, IA 50304, United States
Contact: Sue Voegtlin
Tel: (515) 288-4151
Email: dmrowing@aol.com
www.desmoinesrowing.org

BH: Birdland Marina Boathouse, Grays Lake Boathouse

Year est: 1983
Colors: Black, Grey and White.
Members: 180
History: The Des Moines Rowing Club, Inc. was incorporated in its present-day form in 1983. Earlier rowing clubs had competed on the Des Moines River in the late 1880s. With the support of city leaders, local businesses, the Parks and Recreation Department, and a great deal of volunteer effort, the current club has grown into a multi-faceted organization with over 150 members. The club also was instrumental in establishing and fostering the Drake University Crew.

Amenities: Guests, Ergs

Detroit Boat Club
348 Provencal Road
Grosse Pointe Farms, MI 48236, United States
Tel: (313) 642-0555
Fax: (313) 881-2174
Email: lynnesail@aol.com
www.detroitboatclub.com

Year est: 1839
Colors: Light blue, white and red.
Regatta: Detroit Annual Regatta, Michigan HS Champs
Members: 200
History: Organized by oarsman on February 18, 1839, the Detroit Boat Club is the oldest continuous rowing club in the world, the oldest boat club in the United States and the oldest social club in Michigan. The Club had five clubhouses at several locations in the Detroit area before it built the fireproof boathouse that opened on Belle Isle on August 4, 1902.

Amenities: Guests, Bathroom, Showers, Weights, Ergs

Dolphin Rowing Club
502 Jefferson Street Aquatic Park
San Francisco, CA 94109, United States
Tel: (415) 441-9329
Email: webmeister@dolphinclub.org
www.dolphinclub.org

Year est: 1877
Members: 900
History: Dolphin Club members have rowed in the Bay since the Club was founded in 1877.

Amenities: Guests

Dresden Rowing Club
PO Box 419
Hanover, NH 03755, United States
Contact: Laura L Gillespie, Executive Director
Tel: (603) 469-3118
Fax: (603) 643-0606
Email: Dresden@valley.net
www.dresdenrowingclub.com

Year est: 1997
Colors: Blue and green
Members: 425
History: Promote the sport of rowing in the Upper Valley.

Amenities: Guests

Duluth Rowing Club
PO Box 655
Duluth, MN 55801, United States
Contact: Chris Voltzke, President
Tel: (715) 394-9581
www.duluthboatclub.org

BH: Duluth Rowing Club Boathouse
3900 Minnesota Avenue
Duluth, MN 55801
Tel: (218) 727-8689

Year est: 1889
Colors: Maroon and White.
Regatta: Duluth International Regatta

Members: 75
History: The Duluth Boat Club was founded in 1886. The club not only offered rowing, sailing, canoeing, swimming, tennis and other sports, but it also hosted lavish banquets, festivals and dances.

Amenities: Guests, Bathroom, Showers

Durham Boat Club
220 Newmarket Road
Durham, NH 03824, United States
Tel: (603) 659-7575
Email: cfuerst@cris.com
durhamboat.com/CLUB1.HTM

BH: Lamprey River Boathouse
BH: Oyster River Boathouse
Jackson's Landing
Durham, NH 03824

Year est: 1978
Colors: White, red and blue uniforms, black blades
Members: 50
History: Durham Boat Club started in 1978, initially focusing on juniors and was very successful. As the club grew, the focus shifted to developmental, pre-elites, elites and masters rowing. Durham scullers have been sucessful at all levels. Durham-coached athletes have won World Championship titles, and represented the U.S. at the 1992 and 1996 Olympics.

Amenities: Guests, Ergs

Duxbury Bay Maritime School
PO Box 263A
Duxbury, MA 02331, United States
Tel: (781) 934-7555
Fax: (781) 934-7799
Email: dbms@duxbayms.com
www.DuxBayMs.com

Year est: 1999
Colors: Navy blue and white.
Members: 150

Amenities: Guests, Ergs

East Arm Rowing Club
69 Sterling Road
PO Box 301
Greenwood Lake, NY 10925, United States
Tel: (845) 477-3076
Email: info@eastarm.org
eastarm.org

Year est: 1989
Colors: Crimson and white.
Members: 45
History: EARC was founded originally as an extension of a local business selling rowing boats, drawing membership from as far away as New York City. The business closed but our club grows in testimony to the beatiful scenery and hospitable rowing environment. Our small and active membership lends itself to responsive and continually improving programs.

Amenities: Guests, Bathroom, Showers, Ergs

Ecorse Rowing Club
4603 West Jefferson Avenue
Ecorse, MI 48229, United States
Contact: Rod Lively
Tel: (313) 382-4380
Fax: (313) 282-0981
Email: ecorserowingclub@hotmail.com
www.ecorserowingclub.com

Year est: 1930
Colors: Blue and yellow.
Members: 130
History: Ecorse Rowing Club has Henley and U.S. National plaques from every decade since the 1930's.

Amenities: Guests, Bathroom, Showers, Ergs

Embarcadero Rowing Club
San Francisco, CA, United States
Tel: (415) 289-6661
Email: hatblanco@yahoo.com
www.geocities.com/Colosseum/Park/5162/index

History: The Embarcadero Rowing Club is a nonprofit organization, sponsored by the Anchor Brewing Co., offering community residents the opportunity to row on the San Francisco Bay in the Renegade, a 26' whaleboat. Whaleboats, or "Monomoys," were used in life saving and whaling for most of this century. These open water boats weigh about 2 tons with an equipped crew of ten. There is a long tradition of whaleboat rowing in the SF Bay area, and we are proud to carry that tradition forward.

Amenities: Guests

Empire State Rowing Association
14 Emerson Avenue
New Rochelle, NY 10801, United States
Contact: James Sciales
Email: rownewyork@bigfoot.com
www.empirestaterowing.org

BH: Empire State Rowing Association Boathouse
Roberto Clemente State Park
West Tremont Avenue & Matthewson Road
Bronx, NY 10458
Tel: (718) 894-7486

Year est: 1985
Colors: Yellow and red.
Members: 30
History: The mission of the club is to bring recreational and competitive rowing to all New Yorkers. We are building the first boathouse for rowing in New York City in a century and establishing rowing programs for inner-city youth.

Amenities: Bathroom, Showers, Weights

Erie Canal Rowing Club
PO Box 4711
Rome, NY 13442, United States
Contact: Phyllis M Lacy, Secretary
Tel: (315) 337-9609
Fax: (315) 337-9609
Email: glacy@twcny.rr.com
Larscares@AOL.com
www.eriecanalrowingclub.com

Year est: 1995
Colors: Blue and White.
Regatta: Head of The Erie
Members: 30

Amenities: Guests, Ergs

Everett Rowing Association
PO Box 1774
Everett, WA 98206, United States
Tel: (425) 257-8337
Email: everettrowing@mindspring.com
www.everettrowing.com

BH: Everett Rowing Association Boathouse
400 Smith Island Road
Everett, WA
Tel: (425) 257-8337

Fairfax Grays Rowing Club
PO Box 318
Fairfax Station, VA 22039, United States
Contact: William Del Vecchio
Tel: (703) 250-2369
Fax: (703) 249-8991
Email: apache1@ix.netcom.com

Fairmount Rowing Association
#2 Boathouse Row, Kelly Drive
Philadelphia, PA 19130, United States
Contact: Mike Bowers
Tel: (215) 769-9693
Email: mbowers@dealersedge.com
members.bellatlantic.net/~vze27q9e

Year est: 1858
Colors: Royal blue and white.
Members: 250
History: Fairmount Rowing Association is the incorporation of two original rowing clubs, Fairmount at #2 Boathouse Row and Quaker City Barge Club at #3. The facility is on the National Register of Historic Places. Quaker City, (the present entrance), was erected in 1858. This stone building has been in continual use as a rowing club since before the Civil War. The original Fairmount building, dating from 1860, is gone. The current Flemish-bonded brick structure was designed by Walter Smedley and built in 1904. Fairmount and Quaker City, (which merged in 1932), originally attracted the predominately blue-collar Fairmount neighborhood youths. In recent years they have mostly been known as the premiere club for Masters rowing in the mid-Atlantic region. Fairmount is also home to the rowing programs of La Salle University and Episcopal Academy.

Amenities: Guests, Banquet, Bathroom, Showers, Weights, Ergs

Farmington Valley Rowing Association
542 Hopmeadow Street, Suite 101
Simsbury, CT 06070, United States
Contact: Karen Ntajkounakis
Tel: (413) 566-5313
www.fvra.org

Year est: 1982
Colors: Purple and Yellow.
Members: 50
History: The Farmington Valley Rowing Association was founded in 1982 by parents of children who were on the Simsbury High School crew team. The club rents space from Friends of Simsbury Crew at the Paine Boat House on the Farmington River near the Drake Hill Bridge in Simsbury. FVRA's membership consists of adults ranging in age from 18 years on up. The oldest member is in his eighties. Club members compete regularly in regattas and have a medal-winning track record.

Fat Cat Rowing Club
579 Midline Road
Freeville, NY 13068, United States

Floating the Apple
400 West 43rd Street #32R
New York, NY 10036, United States
Contact: Michael Davis
Tel: (212) 564-5412
Fax: (212) 564-5412
Email: Floapple@aol.com
www.floatingtheapple.org

Year est: 1992
Colors: Red, Blue and Green.
Members: 240
History: Floating the Apple was founded as a means of getting people — young and old — back onto New York City's largest public space and richest preserve — its rivers!

Fort Myers Rowing Club
13222 Broadhurst Loop
Fort Myers, FL 33919, United States
Scott Leonard
Tel: (941) 481-9758
Email: sblcrew@aol.com

Fort Worth Rowing Club
2938 5th Avenue
Fort Worth, TX 76110, United States
Contact: David Perez
Tel: (817) 921-0509
Email: oldag87@aol.com
www.fwrc.f2s.com

Year est: 1991
Colors: Yellow
Members: 50
History: The Fort Worth Rowing Club rows in the Trinity River from the main boat house in downtown Fort Worth. While some members of the rowing club train to participate in masters rowing events in Texas and at the national level, others simply enjoy the beauty and seclusion of the Trinity River. The rowing club promotes rowing for recreation and fitness, and is open to members of all ages.

Amenities: Guests

Foster City Sculling
c/o Erik Evensen
1051 Beach Park Blvd #311
Foster City, CA 94404-3456, United States
Email: fcs@californiarowing.org
www.fostercitysculling.org

History: Foster City Sculling has been established as a club to encourage rowing as sporting and recreational activity on the Foster City Lagoon for those residents that live adjacent to the Lagoon, or have access to it.

Fox Valley Rowing Club
229 North Lawe Street
Appleton, WI 54911, United States
Contact: Michael Lokensgard
Tel: (920) 830-2717
Email: mlokensgard@new.rr.com

Year est: 1991
Colors: Blue and White.
Members: 45
History: Club rows from March to November. Originally combined with Lawrence University Rowing Club. Still share boathouse and equipment.

Gainesville Area Rowing
PO Box 2434
Gainesville, FL 32602, United States
Contact: Larry Battoe, President
Tel: (352) 376-5628
Email: battoe@atlantic.net
www.gainesvillearearowing.8m.com

Amenities: Guests

Genesee Waterways Center
149 Elmwood Avenue
PO Box 18609
Rochester, NY 14618, United States
Tel: (585) 328-3960
Email: blake6@frontiernet.net
www.geneseewaterways.org

Year est: 1995
Regatta: Stonehurst Capitol Regatta
Members: 100
History: The purpose of the GWC is to introduce and promote the use of human powered watercraft — whitewater kayaking, sea kayaking, sprint kayaking, rowing, canoeing, and outrigger- to a broad segment of Monroe County. Instructional clinics, training, competitions and other recreational programming will be offered to youth, young adults, master level adults, senior citizens, and the general public.

Grace Harbor Rowing Club
102 Columbia Street
Huntington Manor, NY 11746, United States

Grand Rapids Rowing Club
PO Box 3189
410 N. Park Street
Grand Rapids, MI 49341, United States
Contact: Richard W Anderson, President
Tel: (616) 874-7437, 364-5150

Year est: 1986
Colors: Red, White and Black.
Regatta: Grand Regatta, Grand Rapids HS Invitational
Members: 375
History: A group of rowing enthusiasts brought rowing back to Grand Rapids after an absence of over 40 years when they began rowing out of the remains of the original Grand Rapids Boat & Canoe Club.

Amenities: Guests, Bathroom, Ergs

Great Bay Rowing
Box 846
Durham, NH 03824, United States
Contact: Peter A. Frid, President
Tel: (603) 742-8376
Fax: (603) 868-7552
Email: frid@attbi.com

Year est: 1999
Colors: Blue and white
Members: 35
Amenities: Guests

Great Salt Lake Rowing
1067 East 200 South #2
Salt Lake City, UT 84102, United States
Contact: Mar Janna Dahl, Treasurer
Tel: (801) 366-5260
Email: gslr@xmission.com
www.gslr.org

BH: Great Salt Lake Rowing Boathouse
Great Salt Lake Marina/Beach
Salt Lake City, UT
Tel: (801) 572-6654

Year est: 2000
Colors: Blue and gold.
Regatta: Utah Summer Games, Sail Fest, Antelope Island Row
Members: 40
History: First Utah rowing club formed in 1888. GSLR began as an offshoot of Salt Lake Sculling, Inc.

Amenities: Guests, Banquet, Bathroom, Showers

Greater Columbus Rowing Association
PO Box 218131
Columbus, OH 43221 , United States
Contact: Ryan Briggs
Tel: (614) 777-4003
Email: gcralogistics@hotmail.com
www.columbusrowing.org

Year est: 1982
Colors: Green and Purple.
Regatta: Speakmon Regatta
Members: 110
History: The Greater Columbus RA was formed in 1982 and incorporated in 1984. GCRA is located in a modest former camp lodge building on the Griggs Reservoir on the Scioto River in Columbus, Ohio. GCRA's stated function is to foster interest in the sport by means of organizing regattas for national and international competition.

Amenities: Guests, Bathroom, Showers, Ergs

Greater Dayton Rowing Association
7000 Peters Pike
Dayton, OH 45414, United States
Tel: (937) 222-4769
Fax: (937) 339-6516
Contact: James Wall, President
Tel: (937) 890-5368
Fax: (937) 890-5368
Email: jamesfwall@aol.com
www.daytonrowing.org

BH: Island Park Boathouse
184 E. Helena Street
Dayton, OH 45404

Year est: 1992
Colors: Navy and Red
Regatta: Five Rivers Fall Regatta
Members: 75-100
History: GDRA was begun by five individuals in 1992 to promote the sport of rowing in the Dayton area. Club programs include Adult Rowing and Junior Rowing (high school and junior high ages), and support of the University of Dayton

Amenities: Guests, Bathroom, Showers, Weights, Ergs

Greater Houston Rowing Club
3034 Fairway
Sugar Land, TX 77478, United States
Contact: Dee Connors
Tel: (281) 242-4095
Email: dconnors@introgen.com
www.greaterhoustonrowingclub.com

Amenities: Guests

Greater Lowell Rowing Association
PO Box 1493
Lowell, MA 01853-1493, United States

Greenwich Rowing Club
67 River Road
Greenwich, CT 06807, United States
Contact: Brian Rickauer, Club Manager
Tel: (203) 422-5258
Fax: (203) 422-5813
Email: Brian@greenwichrowing.com
www.greenwichrowing.com

Year est: 2002
Colors: Red, White and Blue
Members: 250
History: The Greenwich Rowing Club (GRC) was founded by RowAmerica, an organization dedicated to providing access to the sport of rowing to young people 12-18 and men and women of all ages. RowAmerica established its reputation with the building and operation of its first and flagship facility, The Saugatuck Rowing Club (SRC) in Westport, CT.

Amenities: Guests, Bathroom, Showers, Weights

Grosse Ile Rowing Club
PO Box 385
Grosse Ile, MI 48138, United States
Dennis J Sitek, Treasurer
Email: oldoar@hotmail.com
Year est: 1989

Halifax Rowing Association
PO Box 1645
101 City Island Parkway
Daytona Beach, FL 32115, United States
Contact: David Bird, Boathouse Manager
Tel: (386) 248-0502
Email: davebirdart@email.msn.com
www.HalifaxRowing.org
Year est: 1994
Colors: Blue and White
Members: 80
History: Founded in 1994 Halifax Rowing Assn has an active, competitive masters and Junior rowing program. HRA rowers have competed successfully at the local and national level. HRA runs a six-week junior sweep rowing summer program, Fall and Spring rowing. HRA rows year round on the Intracoastal waterway.

Amenities: Guests, Bathroom, Showers, Weights, Ergs

Hampton Roads Rowing Club
PO Box 9269
Norfolk, VA 23505, United States
Tom Courtney, Club President
Tel: (757) 233-0311
Email: tlcmd1@cox.net
www.hrrc.net
BH: Hampton Roads Rowing Club Boathouse
760 52nd Street
Norfolk, VA 23508
Year est: 1987
Colors: Red, grey and white.
Regatta: Head of the Licking Regatta
Members: 150
History: The Hampton Roads Rowing Club began in 1987 with a goal to promote area recreational and competitive rowing in Southeastern Virginia. HRRC is comprised of approximately 150 rowers, as well as a Junior division made up currently of crews at Maury High School(Norfolk), Norfolk Catholic, Norfolk Collegiate Upper School, and Cox High School(Virginia Beach). HRRC provides rowing opportunities for novices as well as experienced rowers and participates in local and regional competitive regattas.

Amenities: Guests

Hanover Rowing Club
Dartmouth 301 Alumni Gym
Hanover, NH 03755, United States

Hartford Barge Club
East Hartford, CT 06108, United States
Contact: Frank Garufi
Tel: (860) 659-0474
Year est: 1927
Colors: Red and White.
Members: 50
Amenities: Guests, Bathroom, Showers

Harvard Sculling
60 JFK Street
Cambridge, MA 02138, United States
Contact: Dan Boyne, Head Coach
Tel: (617) 495-2226
Email: boyne@fas.harvard.edu
hcs.harvard.edu/~harvcrew/sculling.html
Members: 20
History: One of the oldest sculling centers in the U.S., Weld Boathouse was built in 1906 to offer sculling and intramural rowing opportunities for the Harvard community. Bathroom, Showers, Weights

Hiawatha Island Boat Club
47 Frederick Drive
Apalachin, NY 13732, United States
Contact: Don Rumrill
Tel: (607) 625-3016
Fax: (607) 770-3561
Email: bg20649@binghamton.edu
www.tier.net/hibccrew
BH: Hiawatha Island Boat Club Boathouse
Route 17C
Owego, NY 13827
History: Hiawatha Island Boat Club is the community rowing association fostering growth in upstate New York's Southern Tier on the waters of the Susquehanna River. Our rowing venue is located between the cities of Binghamton and Elmira, NY, and runs along NYS Route 17(soon to be I86). With more than 5 kilometers of calm, clean water navigable from March through November, HIBC along with Binghamton University Crew have perhaps the most optimal training conditions in upstate New York.

Hocking Valley Rowing Association
17 South Lancaster Street
Athens, OH 45701, United States
oak.cats.ohiou.edu/~rowing/MACRA/cover.html

Hollywood Rowing Club
PO Box 030071
Fort Lauderdale, FL 33303-0071, United States
members.aol.com/bowman2x/index.html
History: Hollywood Rowing Club has facilities just off the Intercoastal Waterway in Hollywood, FL. The water connects to the West Lake, a 2+ mile long estuary completely within the 1,700 acre West Lake Park. Alternatively, rowers can paddle up or down the Intercoastal.

Honolulu Rowing Club
PO Box 1855
Honolulu, HI 96805-1855, United States

Housatonic Rowing Association
574 Amity Road
Woodbridge, CT 06525, United States

Houston Rowing Club
PO Box 292
Seabrook, TX 77586, United States
Contact: James M Orr, Dockmaster
Tel: (281) 337-0268
Email: jmo@asaptt.com
www.houstonrowing.com

BH: Houston Rowing Club Boathouse
Pier 25 Watergate Marina
Clear Lake Shores, TX 77565
Tel: 1-877-rowclub

Year est: 1988
Colors: Red, White and Blue.
Members: 200
History: HRC's floating boathouse is located in Pier 25 in the WYC off of FM2094 (see map on website). This facility is the flagship to launch the club's many and varied rowing craft. Included on this boathouse are several machines used for aerobic workouts including state-of-the-art Concept II rowing machines and a cross country ski machine. Also, the club's seven-place 34-ft. English pilot gigs are launched from here for the club's unique and always pleasurable weekend breakfast rows.

Amenities: Guests, Banquet, Bathroom, Showers, Weights, Ergs

Hudson River Rowing Association
PO Box 506
Poughkeepsie, NY 12602, United States
Contact: Tracy Wright Mauer, Program Director
Tel: (845) 485-4358
Email: tmauer@hvc.rr.com
www.hrrowing.org

Year est: 1998
Colors: Red and Black
Regatta: Mid-Hudson Invit., Hudson Valley Adult Scrimmage
Members: 175
History: HRRA was formed as an umbrella organization to coordinate the resources of 5 high school programs, two university programs and two adult programs. In addition to developing composite crews during the summer and fall seasons we are raising capital to build a five bay boathouse with indoor training facilities to house the local high school and adult rowing programs.

Humboldt Bay Rowing Association
PO Box 750
Trinidad, CA 95570-0750, United States
Contact: Jerome J Simone, President
Tel: (707) 677-3214
Email: rowthebay@humboldt1.com

Year est: 1987
Colors: White
Regatta: Blue Heron Regatta
Members: 40

Amenities: Guests, Bathroom, Showers, Ergs

Huntington Barge & Paddle Club
15 Briarwood Circle
North Easton, MA 02356, United States

Huron Rowing Club
2727 Fuller Road
Ann Arbor, MI 48105, United States

Hyde Park Rowing Association
19 Gilbert Drive
Hyde Park, NY 12538, United States

Illinois River Oarsmen
1227 E Cox
Peoria Heights, IL 61614, United States
Contact: Judy Barlow
Tel: (309) 688-8144
Members: 25

Independence Rowing Club Inc.
PO Box 1412
Nashua, NH 03061-1412, United States
Contact: Tom Mulstay, Secretary
Tel: (603) 598-8887
Email: tom@charlesriveradvisors.com

Year est: 1965
Colors: Golden yellow and white.
Regatta: Head of the Merrimack, Firecracker Sprints
Members: 60
History: Started in 1965 by students at Lowell Technological Institute. Moved to Nashua in 1975 to provide rowing and sculling for men and women at all competitive levels. Sponsor of Bishop Guertin High School Crew Club and the Head of the Merrimack Regatta.
Amenities: Guests, Ergs

Indiana Rowing Association
54923 Shorelane Drive
Elkhart, IN 46514, United States
Dee Ashbaugh, President
Tel: (574) 266-5515
Email: deerowusa@aol.com

Year est: 1989
Regatta: Head of the Elk, Indiana Indoor Rowing Championships
Amenities: Guests

Indianapolis Rowing Center
PO Box 53223
Indianapolis, IN 46253, United States
Contact: Eric Stoll, Director
Tel: (317) 298-9456
Fax: (317) 253-4434
Email: director@rowirc.org
www.rowirc.org

Year est: 1979
Colors: Red and black.
Regatta: Head of the Eagle
Members: 200
History: Founded as the Indianapolis Rowing Club in early 1979. Hosted Pan Am Games, fifteen USRowing National Championships and the 1994 World Championships. FISA certified 2000 meter buoyed course.
Amenities: Guests, Bathroom, Showers, Weights, Ergs

Interlochen Rowing Club
3320 Fuhrman Avenue East
Seattle, WA 98102, United States
Contact: Gail Longhi
Tel: (206) 328-0778

Colors: Purple and red.
Members: 24
History: A group of women, many with previous rowing experience, who row both recreationally and competitively in sweep and some sculling.
Amenities: Guests, Banquet, Bathroom, Showers, Weights

Island Rowing Club Inc
9570 S. Tropical Trail
Merritt Island, FL 32952, United States
Ronald Ingraham
Tel: (407) 777-2578

BH: Island Rowing Club Boathouse
Kiwanis Park Road
Merritt Island, FL

Year est: 1989
Colors: Peach and aqua.
Members: 35
History: Founded in 1988 to promote recreational rowing as a sport in Brevard County. Over 200 people have been introduced to rowing since we began.
Amenities: Guests, Bathroom, Showers, Ergs

Jacksonville Rowing Club
PO Box 8741
Jacksonville, FL 32239, United States
Contact: Barbara Sanchez-Salazar
Tel: (904) 241-1679
fly.to/jaxrowingclub

Year est: 1989
Colors: Navy blue, sky blue and white.
Members: 70
History: Jacksonville RC was started by two rowers in 1988. The membership has grown to over 70 people and the club has started three other rowing programs that now operate independently.
Amenities: Guests

Kansas City Rowing Club
PO Box 025635
Stockyard Station
Kansas City, MO 64102, United States
Tel: (913) 894-UROW
Email: killiat@bcbskc.com
www.kcrowing.com

Year est: 1992
Colors: Green and blue.
Regatta: American Royal Fall Rowing Classic
Members: 70
History: A cooperative of community professionals and philanthropists founded the Kansas City Rowing Club as a non-profit organization in 1992. Since that time, KCRC has made its home in the Old Kansas City Stockyards in the Historic West Bottoms. KCRC is the only rowing club in the Kansas City area.
Amenities: Guests

Kenai Crewsers Rowing Club
PO Box 1313
Sterling, AK 99672, United States
Contact: Lori Landstrom, President
Tel: (907) 260-OARS
Email: lltr@gci.net
Email: sarahcanrow@yahoo.com
www.kenaicrewsers.com

Year est: 1997
Regatta: Head of the Kenai
Members: 75
History: We don't have a boathouse, but we do row on three different lakes in three different communities. Mackey Lake (1+ mile), Soldotna; Kenai Lake (3+ miles), Cooper Landing; Bear Lake (2+ miles), Seward.
Amenities: Guests

Ketos Whale Boat Rowing
2906 San Bruno Ave #2
San Francisco, CA 94134, United States

King's Crown Rowing Association
280 Madison Avenue Ste 1404
New York, NY 10016, United States

Knoxville Rowing Association
PO Box 10440
Knoxville, TN 37939, United States

La Baie Verte Rowing Club
1025 Quincy
Green Bay, WI 54301, United States
Contact: Steve Engelhardt
Tel: (920) 826-7831
Email: engelhardtsteve@netscape.net

BH: Van Den Heuvel Campus Center
St. Norbert College
100 Grant Street
De Pere, WI 54115

Year est: 1987
Colors: Kelly Green, Sky Blue and White
Regatta: Tail of the Fox Regatta
Members: 40
Amenities: Guests, Bathroom, Showers, Ergs

Lake Ewauna Rowing Club
1034 Riverside Drive
Klamath Falls, OR 97601, United States
Contact: Alfred Czerner, Head Coach
Email: freddyrow@juno.com

BH: Lake Ewauna Rowing Club Boathouse
west end of Spring Street
Klamath Falls, OR 97601

Lake Lanier Rowing Club
3105 Clark's Bridge Road
Gainesville, GA 30506, United States
Tel: (770) 287-0077
Fax: (770) 287-0077
Email: llrc@mindspring.com
www.llrc.ws

Year est: 1993
Colors: Navy, white and red.
Members: 100
History: Club was formed in 1993, and was instrumental in bringing the rowing events to Lake Lanier for the 1996 Olympics. Inherited boathouse following the Olympics.
Amenities: Guests, Banquet, Bathroom, Showers, Ergs

Lake Merritt Rowing Club
PO Box 1046
Oakland, CA 94604, United States
Contact: Carole Calvin
Email: wolfwood@mac.com
www.nargis.com/lmrc

History: Originally the lake was a marshy tidal basin that was navigable only at high tide by shallow draft cargo vessels. By 1896, a dam at the southern end of the lake had transformed the marsh into the beautiful lake we now know. There is a bird refuge in the eastern arm of the lake which is an important nesting area in the summer, and a wintering place for several species of migratory birds. In fact, Lake Merritt is home to the nation's oldest bird sanctuary.

Lake Natoma Rowing Club
CSUS Aquatic Center
1901 Hazel Avenue
Rancho Cordova, CA 95670, United States
www.lnra.net

Year est: 1984
Regatta: Head of the American, USRA SW Regatta, Gold Rush Banquet, Weights, Ergs

Lake Oswego Community Rowing
350 Oswego Point Drive
Lake Oswego, OR 97034-3227, United States
Tel: (503) 699-7458
Email: info@lorowing.org
www.lorowing.com

History: Lake Oswego Community Rowing is a nonprofit, volunteer-driven organization offering a full range of rowing classes for beginners to experienced adult and youth rowers.
Amenities: Guests

Lake Stevens Rowing Club
PO Box 159
Lake Stevens, WA 98258-0159, United States
Tel: (425) 337-6614
Email: info@lakestevensrowing.com
www.lakestevensrowing.com/

Lake Union Crew
11 East Allison Street
Seattle, WA 98102, United States
Contact: Rome Ventura, Head Coach
Tel: (206) 860-4199
Fax: (206) 860-7826
Email: raventura@aol.com
www.lakeunioncrew.com

Year est: 1998
Colors: Red and black
Regatta: Seafair Rainbow Regatta
Members: 200

Amenities: Guests, Banquet, Bathroom, Showers, Weights, Ergs

Lake Washington Rowing Club
910 N. Northlake Way
Seattle, WA 98103, United States
Contact: Karyn E Freer, Boathouse Manager
Tel: (206) 547-1583
Fax: (206) 547-3549
Email: lwrcmanager@yahoo.com
www.lakewashingtonrowing.com

BH: LWRC Fremont Boathouse
BH: LWRC Garfield Boathouse
East Garfield Street
Seattle, WA 98103

Year est: 1957
Colors: Blue and white
Regatta: Head of the Lake
Members: 300

Amenities: Guests, Banquet, Bathroom, Showers, Ergs

Lansing Oar and Paddle Club
726 Touraine
East Lansing, MI 48823, United States
Contact: Bruce L Miller, Men's Advisor
Tel: (517) 333-9612
Email: msucrew@msu.edu
www.voyager.net/loapc

Year est: 1989
Colors: Blue and White
Members: 50

Amenities: Guests, Bathroom, Ergs

L'Aviron Rowing Club
904 Lehigh Street
Easton, PA 18042, United States

Lincoln Park Boat Club
2300 North Cannon Drive
Chicago, IL 60614, United States
Tel: (773) 878-8194
Email: rowing@lpbc.net
www.lpbc.net

BH: Lagoon Boathouse
2300 N. Cannon Drive
Chicago, IL
Tel: (773) 549-2628

Year est: 1910
Colors: Blue and white.
Regatta: Chicago Sprints
Members: 340

Amenities: Guests, Bathroom, Showers, Ergs

Lions Rowing Club
One LMU Drive
Gersten Pavilion MS 8235
Los Angeles, CA 90045-2659, United States
Contact: Sara-Mai Conway, Coordinator
Tel: (310) 338-7624
Fax: (310) 338-5915
Email: sconway@lmu.edu
jdenuno.com/Rowing/lmu.htm

Year est: 2002
Colors: Light Blue, Crimson
Members: 50
History: Our mission is to provide coached rowing sessions in which all people are given equal opportunity to row with others at their same age, technique and fitness level. While the recreational experience is respected, the competitive experience is encouraged and members are expected to strive to achieve a personal best in performance. Members are encouraged to work as a team, while personally developing through the challenge of the sport of rowing.

Amenities: Guests, Bathroom, Showers, Weights, Ergs

Litchfield Hills Rowing Club
PO 142
Litchfield, CA 06759, United States
Contact: Stephanie Hyres
Tel: (860) 567-8314
Fax: (860) 567-8598

Long Beach Rowing Association
5750 Boathouse Lane
PO Box 3879
Long Beach, CA 90803, United States
Contact: A.C. duPont
Tel: (562) 438-3352
Email: acdupont4@hotmail.com
www.lbra.org

Year est: 1932
Colors: Red, white and blue.
Regatta: Christmas Regatta, Beach Erg Sprints, Spring Regat
Members: 320
History: LBRA was the rowing site for the 1932 Olympics and LBRA has had a history of nurturing elite rowers since then. Also, LBRA has a strong, long-standing masters groupt that includes former Olympic rowers from teh U.S. and other countries. Long Beach rowers compete in the U.S. and abroad. Bridging the generation gap, LBRA has it all from juniors to collegiate to masters to elite — making up a unique rowing community.
Amenities: Guests, Bathroom, Showers, Weights

Lookout Rowing Club
PO Box 11411
Chattanooga, TN 37401-2411, United States
Contact: Mike Bidderman, President
Tel: (423) 267-2289
Email: lookoutrc@aol.com
members.aol.com/lookoutrc

History: Lookout Rowing Club. LRC is a nonprofit corporation dedicated to the promotion of rowing in the Chattanooga area. Originally founded in 1876, it was dormant until 1974 when it was revived by William G. Raoul and Terry Carney with an initial membership of 15 persons, primarily faculty and students at UTC. The club now comprises over 200 persons from Chattanooga and the surrounding area and takes its name from a rowing club that existed in Chattanooga in the late 19th century.
Amenities: Guests, Bathroom, Showers, Weights

Los Angeles Rowing Club
PO Box 9398
Marina del Rey, CA 90295, United States
Contact: Susan Varga
Tel: (818) 980-9023
Email: susan@larowing.com

Year est: 1985
History: The Los Angeles Rowing Club (LARC) was founded in 1985 by a group of ex-collegiate rowers looking for an outlet to pursue recreational and competitive rowing in Marina del Rey.
Amenities: Guests

Los Gatos Rowing Club
PO Box 188
Los Gatos, CA 95031-0188, United States
Tel: (408) 566-9406
Email: info@lgrc.org
www.lgrc.org/

Year est: 1978
Colors: Navy blue and white.
Members: 220
Amenities: Guests, Weights, Ergs

Louisville Rowing Club
1904 Rutherford Avenue
Louisville, KY 40205, United States
Contact: John Hale
Tel: (502) 895-9871
Fax: (502) 895-5137
Email: louisvillerowing@hotmail.com
www.louisvillerowingclub.org

BH: Harrods Creek Boathouse
6511 Upper River Road
Louisville, KY

BH: Downtown Boathouse
1501 Fulton Street
Louisville, KY

Year est: 1992
Colors: Blue and gold.
Members: 90
History: Started in the mid-1980's. Revitalized with construction of boathouse in 1992. Membership has grown to about 90 active rowers and additional boathouse. Activities include adaptive rowing program, masters rowing, high school programs and University of Louisville.
Amenities: Ergs

Maine Rowing Association
17 Highland Road
Bridgton, ME 04009, United States
Contact: Steve Collins, Secretary
Tel: (207) 647-2196
Email: info@rowmaine.org
www.rowmaine.org

Year est: 1993
Colors: Forest green and white.
Regatta: Somes Sound Rowing Classic
Members: 100
History: MRA is not a club in the sense of having a clubhouse or a given body of water on which we generally row. Rather, we are a group who enjoy the sport of rowing and who want to make available to ourselves and visitors the best in competition and camaraderie.
Amenities: Guests

Malta Boat Club
#9 Boathouse Row, Kelly Drive
Philadelphia, PA 19130, United States
Contact: Fred Duling
Tel: (215) 923-9520
Email: fhduling@aol.com

Year est: 1860
Colors: Blue and white.
Members: 100
History: Founded 1860. Member of Schuylkill Navy located on Philadelphia's historic Boathouse Row. Numerous national champions. Current program consists of intermediate, senior and elite lightweight and heavyweight scullers.

Amenities: Guests, Banquet, Bathroom, Showers, Weights

Marin Rowing Association
50 Drakes Landing Road
Greenbrae, CA 94904, United States
Contact: Sandy Armstrong, Director
Tel: (415) 461-1431
Fax: (415) 461-5520
Email: sandy@marinrowing.org
www.marinrowing.com

Year est: 1969
Colors: Red and white
Members: 350

Amenities: Guests, Weights, Ergs

Martha's Moms
910 N. Northlake Way
Seattle, WA 98103, United States
Contact: Neal Johnson, Captain
Tel: (206) 517-5895
Email: karinrogers@attbi.com

Year est: 1984
Colors: Red, black and white.
History: We began rowing in 1984 with 8 women, coached by Martha Beattie who previously coached the women at Lakeside HS. Some of those parents got interested in rowing and she agreed to coach. As we were old enough to be her mother, we became Martha's Moms. Logo: Apple pie with crossed oars.

Amenities: Guests, Banquet, Bathroom, Showers, Weights

Memmian Rowing Club
31 McAlister Drive
MR 5090
New Orleans, LA 70118, United States
Contact: Geoffrey Parker
Tel: (504) 865-5472
Email: ggparker@alum.mit.edu

Year est: 1992
Members: 15
History: The Memmian Rowing Club was founded in 1992. We don't have any large boats, a boathouse or even a specific geographic home. We've competed at regattas for the past several years, especially U.S. Masters Nationals and the Head of the Charles. It took a while to search for a club name which is obscure, or almost to the point of non-existence. We found it in the wonderful description in Virgil's epic poem, the Aeneid, Book V.

Amenities: Guests

Mendota Rowing Club
PO Box 646
Madison, WI 53701-0646, United States
M B Blanding, Head Coach
Tel: (608) 238-4122
Email: mbbland@spasd.k12.wi.us
info@mendotarowingclub.com
www.mendotarowingclub.com

BH: Mendota Rowing Club Boathouse
622 E Gorham Street
Madison, WI

History: Rowing was made available to the city of Madison as a participant sport with the Mendota Rowing Club. MRC was founded in 1975 by a small group of University of Wisconsin alumni with the primary purpose of fostering national and international rowing competition by developing amateur rowers. The club has since evolved into a non-profit, multifaceted organization of nearly 200 members. It welcomes and encourages men and women of all ages and levels of experience who wish to become involved in the sport of rowing.

Amenities: Guests

Merrimack River Rowing Association
PO Box 1909
Lowell, MA 01853, United States
Email: info@merrimackrowing.org
Tel: (978) 454-4631
www.merrimackrowing.org

BH: Bellegarde Boathouse
Pawtucket Boulevard
Lowell, MA 01853

Regatta: Festival Regatta, Textile River Regatta
Members: 30

Amenities: Bathroom, Showers, Weights, Ergs

Miami Beach Rowing Club
6500 Indian Creek Drive
Miami Beach, FL 33141, United States
Contact: Alex Salas, Head Coach
Tel: (305) 861-8876
Fax: (305) 861-8841
Email: miamibeachrowing@bellsouth.net
www.rowmiamibeach.com

Year est: 1993
Colors: Light blueand darkblue.
Regatta: Head of the Indian Creek, Miami Beach Winter Sprin
Members: 150
History: Miami Beach RC occupies the Ronald W. Shane Watersports Center, a state of the art boathouse, on Indian Creek. Today the club has over 100 members as well as a high school membership of 40 rowers. The University of Miami also rows out of this facility. **Other Info**: Experienced guest rowers are allowed at a rate of $20/day.

Amenities: Guests, Banquet, Bathroom, Showers, Weights, Ergs

Miami Rowing & Watersports Center Inc.
3832 Shipping Avenue
3601 Rickenbacker Causeway
Virginia Key, FL 33149, United States
Contact: Howard Kosowsky, Treasurer
Tel: (305) 444-8520
Fax: (305) 445-1948
Email: kosowsky@sprynet.com
www.mrc.org

Year est: 1974
Colors: Blue and White
Regatta: Miami International Regatta
Members: 120

Amenities: Guests, Banquet, Bathroom, Showers, Weights, Ergs

Michigan Rowing Association
PO Box 7164
Ann Arbor, MI 48104, United States
Contact: Bonnie K Hartsuff, Treasurer
Tel: (734) 998-0365
Fax: (734) 623-8686
Email: bonnie.hartsuff@pfizer.com
www.umich.edu/~umrowing

Year est: 1976
Members: 100

Middletown Rowing Club
831 D Long Hill Road
Middletown, CT 06457, United States
Contact: Elizabeth Milroy
Tel: (860) 685-3148
Email: emilroy@wesleyan.edu

Mid-Hudson Rowing Association
PO Box 683
Poughkeepsie, NY 12603, United States
Contact: Bill Davies
Tel: (845) 452-2970
Email: wdaviesjr@aol.com
home.hvc.rr.com/midhudsonrowing/

BH: Mid Hudson RA Boathouse
Clearwater Road
Poughkeepsie, NY

Year est: 1950
Colors: Red, Green, Yellow and Orange.
Regatta: Mid Hudson Invitational Regatta
Members: 40
History: Home of the original IRA, begun in 1895. Incorporated as a non-profit in 1950, and established scholastic rowing programs in three local high schools when the IRA moved away from the Hudson. Now there are five scholastic rowing programs in the Poughkeepsie area run independently and the MHRA if focused on adult rowing while aiding schools with loan of equipment etc. Motto: Remember the Hudson is tidal!

Amenities: Guests

Milwaukee Rowing Club
3354 N. Gordon Place
Milwaukee, WI 53212, United States
Contact: Gary Ahrens, Club Secretary
Tel: (414) 347-4746
Fax: (414) 277-0656
Email: gaahrens@mbf-law.com
www.milwaukeerowingclub.org

BH: Milwaukee Rowing Club Boathouse
1990 N. Commerce Street
Milwaukee, WI

Year est: 1894
Colors: Royal blue
Regatta: Milwaukee River Challenge
Members: 180

Amenities: Ergs

Minneapolis Rowing Club
PO Box 583102
Minneapolis, MN 55458-3102, United States
Contact: Dave Sheppard, President
Tel: (612) 729-1541
Email: President@mplsrowing.org
www.mplsrowing.org

Year est: 1938
Colors: Green and white
Regatta: Head of the Mississippi
Members: 200
Other Info: New boathouse completed June 2001

Amenities: Guests, Weights, Ergs

Minnesota Boat Club
382 Winslow Avenue
Saint Paul, MN 55107, United States
Email: president@boatclub.org
www.boatclub.org

BH: Minnesota Boat Club Boathouse
1 Wabasha St. S.
St. Paul, MN 55107
Tel: (651) 228-1602

Year est: 1870
Colors: Red and White.
Regatta: Minnesota Classic
Members: 200
History: The Minnesota Boat Club (MBC) is the state's oldest athletic institution. Since 1870, MBC has established a long record of rowing championships in the Midwest. In recent years we have won several national titles and even produced a few Olympians. The club **Other Info**: Learn-To-Row classes available March thru October. Indoor Rowing classes are available in the Winter. Check the website for details. Teams from the MBC compete in regattas across the nation.

Amenities: Guests, Banquet, Bathroom, Showers, Weights, Ergs

Mission Bay Rowing Association
2398 Peacock Valley Road
Chula Vista, CA 91915, United States
Contact: Chris Shannon, Manager
Tel: (619) 307-0018
Email: michaelshann@earthlink.net
www.mbra.net

BH: Mission Bay Aquatic Center Boathouse
1001 Santa Clara Point
San Diego, CA 92109
Tel: (858) 488-1036

Year est: 1978
Colors: Blue and Green.
Members: 65
History: Started as a university/community club house. UCSD, SDSU, and USD share facility with club programs until 1994. Currently, SDSU and MBRA share the facility. We have a strong recreational program with four practices a week using eights, fours, quads, doubles and pairs. Competitive practice are in the mornings. Our teams have competed nationally and internationally, returning with top honors. Our current dues structure is the best in the San Diego area. All new members are encouraged to take advantage of our 2 week free membership.

Amenities: Guests, Banquet, Bathroom, Showers, Ergs

Mobjack Rowing Association
PO Box 14
Ware Neck, VA 23178, United States
Contact: Tim Ulsaker, Director
Tel: (804) 693-5160
Fax: (804) 693-1160
Email: crucoach@inna.net
www.tiercom.com/crew

BH: Mobjack Rowing Association Boathouse
Route 614, Williams Wharf Road
Mathews, VA
Tel: (804) 725-7785

Colors: Yellow and Royal Blue.
Members: 150
History: The initial focus of MRA is to promote rowing in our community area and provide our youth with summer opportunities in novice training, technique, improvement camps,a nd a competitive racing program open to all-comers. With a steady growth in community participation, we now look forward to developing an adult training program for advancing technique and novice level racing. We are also planning to develop living space to give disadvantaged youth and out-of-town guests the opportunity to learn to row in the splendor of rural Tidewater.

Amenities: Guests, Weights, Ergs

Mohawk River Boat Club
5010 St Hwy 30
Amsterdam, NY 12010, United States

BH: Mohawk River BC Boathouse
5010 St. Hwy 30
Amsterdam, NY

Year est: 1985
Colors: Black and silver.
Members: 6

Amenities: Guests

Monongahela Rowing Association
217 Grand Street
Morgantown, WV 26507, United States
Contact: Kim Stearns Dickerson
Tel: (304) 291-5678
Email: boparcjanet@yahoo.com

Year est: 1970
Colors: Blue and gold.
Members: 20
History: We sponsor the WVU rowing team where the women were recently given varsity status.

Amenities: Guests

Moss Bay Rowing and Kayaking Center
1001 Fairview Avenue North #1900
Seattle, WA 98109, United States
Contact: Jim Clark, Director
Fax: (206) 682 0455
Email: mossbay@earthlink.net
www.mossbay.net

Year est: 1986
Colors: Red, white and blue.
Members: varies per season
History: Floating boathouse on South Lake Union, near downtown Seattle **Other Info**: Outstanding sculling instructional program for novices and even younger children. Variety of equipment for novice to elite levels.

Motley Rowing Club
243 McKee Road
Morrisville, VT 05661, United States

Mount Baker Adult Crew
4717 53th Sreet S.
Seattle, WA 98118, United States
Contact: Peggy Tosdal
Tel: (206) 386-1913
Fax: (206) 386-1914
Email: mount.baker@ci.seattle.wa.us

BH: Mount Baker Rowing Club Boathouse
3800 Lake Washington Boulevard
Seattle, WA 98118

Members: 40

Mystic Valley Rowing Association
36 Sawyer Avenue
Tufts University
Medford, MA 02155, United States
Contact: Gary R Caldwell, Director
Tel: (617) 627-5008
Fax: (617) 629-7612
Email: Gary.Caldwell@tufts.edu

Narragansett Boat Club
PO Box 2413
Providence, RI 02906-2413, United States
Contact: Jill Singewald, Program Director
Tel: (401) 351-5295
Email: jill@ids.net
www.rownbc.org

BH: Narragansett Boat Club Boathouse
River Road
Providence, RI
Tel: (401) 272-1838

Year est: 1838
Colors: Navy blue and white.
Regatta: Mayor's Cup, Sweeps & Sculls
Members: 150
History: Founded in 1838, the Narragansett Boat Club is the oldest active rowing club in the U.S. The NBC offers excellent equipment for experienced scullers and sweep rowers, sound instruction for beginners, and competitive regattas for all comers. Motto: Discovering the best way to get into shape is a stroke of genius.

Amenities: Guests, Banquet, Bathroom, Showers, Weights, Ergs

Navesink River Rowing Club
PO Box 6153
Fair Haven, NJ 07704, United States
Tel: (732) 758-6266
Email: mm@crpindustries.com
www.monmouth.com/~nrrc/

Year est: 1983
Colors: Teal and black.
Members: 120
History: Formed in 1983 by a small group of people who love the sport of rowing Rowing is promoted as a recreational sport. Special emphasis on training novices and youth. An active summer youth program. Motto: Coaching for all.

Amenities: Guests, Bathroom, Showers, Weights, Ergs

Navy Masters Rowing Club
1021 Mill Road
East Aurora, NY 14052, United States
Contact: Craig Thrasher
Tel: (716) 652-1467
Fax: (617) 652-1467

Year est: 1990
Colors: Blue and gold.
Members: 52

Amenities: Guests

Nereid Boat Club Inc
350 Riverside Avenue
Rutherford, NJ 07070, United States
Contact: John McEldowney
Tel: (201) 438-3995
Email: drumrocks@prodigy.net
www.nereidbc.org

Year est: 1866
Colors: Forest green and white.
Members: 175
History: Incorporated in 1868, members of Nereid have been rowing on the Passaic River since 1866. Nereid has survived two boathouse fires and is currently in the process of completing renovations on its boathouse.

Amenities: Guests, Banquet, Bathroom, Showers, Weights, Ergs

New Haven Rowing Club
407 Roosevelt Drive
Oxford, CT 06483, United States
Contact: Steve Flagg
Tel: (203) 734-0125
Email: info@newhavenrowingclub.org
www.newhavenrowingclub.org

Year est: 1971
Colors: Royal blue, lime green and white.
Members: 85
History: Motto: Pulsus remorum fit spiritus fortis —
From the rhythm of rowing comes the spirit of life.
Amenities: Guests, Banquet, Bathroom, Showers

New Orleans Rowing Club Ltd
829 Baronne Street #200
New Orleans, LA 70113, United States
Contact: Fred King
Tel: (504) 581-9322
Email: fjking@bellsouth.net
www.neworleansrowingclub.com

BH: New Orleans Rowing Club Boathouse
Marconi Avenue & R.E. Lee on Orleans Canal
New Orleans, LA
Tel: (504) 581-9322

Year est: 1966
Colors: Red, white, blue, yellow and fleur-de-lis.
Members: 20
History: Original boat club was founded in the 1860's,
but suspended existence when the new basin canal
(original rowing venue) was filled in.

Amenities: Guests

New Rochelle Rowing Club
PO Box 7
New Rochelle, NY 10802-0007, United States
Contact: Gary Corwin
Tel: (914) 636-9717

Year est: 1880
Colors: Blue and red.
Members: 50
History: Club founded in 1880. Competed actively until
1965. Silver medal at Tokyo Olympics. Since 1970, primarily recreational rowers. One-half membership
now rows recreational boats and one-half rowing
sculling shells, primarily singles. A few members
compete on the eastern seaboard.

Amenities: Guests, Banquet, Bathroom, Showers

New York Athletic Club
2560 Stedman Place
New York, NY 10469, United States
Contact: Vincent Ventura
Tel: (718) 653-1899
Email: vjvrow@aol.com
www.nyacrowing.net

BH: John J. Sulger Boathouse
Travers Island
Pelham, NY 10803
Tel: (914) 738-9803

Year est: 1868
Colors: Scarlet and white.

Amenities: Guests, Bathroom, Showers, Ergs

Newport Aquatic Center
1 Whitecliffs Drive
Newport Beach, CA 92660, United States
www.newportaquaticcenter.com

Year est: 1987
Colors: Blue and white.
Regatta: Newport Autumn Rowing Festival
Members: 500
History: Built in 1987 to prepare amateur athletes for
1988-1992 Olympic Games and to spark interest in
rowing, canoeing and kayaking in the public sector.

Amenities: Guests, Bathroom, Showers, Weights,
Ergs

Nonesuch Oar and Paddle Club
500 Fowler Road
Cape Elizabeth, ME 04107, United States
Contact: Phin Sprague
Tel: (207) 799-5999
Email: psprague@javanet.com

BH: Nonesuch Oar & Paddle Club Boathouse
Ferry Road
Scarborough, ME

Year est: 1972
History: We operate in the summer months only.

Amenities: Guests

North Bay Rowing Club
Foundry Wharf
PO Box 192
Petaluma, CA 04953, United States
Contact: Win Rumsey, President
Tel: (707) 763-9841
Fax: (707) 938-8558
Email: win@winrumseydds.com
www.northbayrowing.org

Year est: 1980
Colors: Blue and white
Regatta: Petaluma River Regatta, first 6 mile head race
Members: 70

History: The Club has approx 70 Master members, a Junior Program and an Adaptive Rowing component. Masters lessons are offered throughout Santa Rosa Junior College as well as privately. A Summer School Program is also offered for Novice Juniors.

Amenities: Guests, Ergs

North Bay Vikings
San Francisco, CA , United States
members.aol.com/nbvikings

History: The North Bay Vikings Foundation is a non-profit organization dedicated to maintaining Scandinavian maritime heritage. Our members are men and women of the San Francisco Bay Area who participate in whaleboat racing to heighten public awareness of Nordic culture.

Amenities: Guests

Northeast Rowing Center
PO Box 2060
Duxbury, MA 02331, United States

Northern Virginia Rowing Club
7304 Scarlet Oak Court
Fairfax Station, VA 22039-1928, United States

Northwest Sculling Association
3320 Fuhrman Avenue East
Seattle, WA 98102, United States
Contact: Emil Kossev
Tel: (206) 320-8452
Email: emilkossev@cs.com

Year est: 1994
Members: 15
History: Dedicated to the training of elite and development scullers for National Team Trials and selection.

Amenities: Guests

Norwalk River Rowing Association
PO Box 2084
Norwalk, CT 06852, United States
Contact: Greg Barringer, Executive Director
Tel: (203) 299-1546
Fax: (203) 299-1672
Email: gregcrew@sbcglobal.net
www.norwalkriverrowing.org

Year est: 1986
Colors: Blue, red and white.
Regatta: Northeast Regional Jr Championships
Members: 200
History: Founded by area residents in 1986. Has grown to include high school programs involving many local high schools as well as two college pro-

grams (Norwalk Comm. Tech College/Fairfield Univ.) Masters and open race competitively at the local, national and international level.

Amenities: Guests, Bathroom, Ergs

Oak Ridge Rowing Association
PO Box 4384
Oak Ridge, TN 37831-4384, United States
Contact: Randy Cantrell, President
Tel: (865) 482-6538
Email: cantrellhr@aol.com
www.orra.org

Year est: 1978
Colors: Maroon and gray
Regatta: SIRA, Oak Ridge Scholastics, Southeast Region Juniors Championships, NCAA Central and South Region Qualifier
Members: 180
History: The rowing course on Melton Hill Lake opened in 1978. ORRA was founded in 1979. Since that time, it has hosted the Southern Intercollegiate Rowing Association Championships for 23 years. In February 1995, Oak Ridge hosted the trials for the United States' Pan American team. In 1984 and 1988, the Masters Nationals were held on the course. Melton Hill Lake was also the site of the 1997 and 2000 USRowing National Championships. **Other Info:** ORRA hosts spring training during March and April. Please review www.orra.org and Spring Training or call Allen Eubanks at (865) 482-6538 for more information.

Amenities: Guests, Banquet, Bathroom, Weights, Ergs

OARS (Old & Ancient Rowing Society) of R.I.
Kingston, RI , United States
Contact: Robert Ezold
Email: ezolds@earthlink.net

Year est: 1986
Colors: Navy Blue and white
History: Club was created by Bob Gillette, former URI coach.

Occoquan Boat Club
9527 Blackburn Drive
Burke, VA 22015, United States
Contact: Jay Tennent
Tel: (703) 978-3871

BH: Sandy Run Regional Park Facility Boathouse
10450 Van Thompson Road, Boathouse #3
Fairfax Station, VA 22039
Tel: (703) 690-4392

Year est: 1979
Regatta: Head of the Occoquan
Members: 150
History: Located on one of the most beautiful bodies of water in the mid-Atlantic, OBC was founded in 1979 by Rick Evans. The club was established to represent the independent oarsmen rowing on the Occoquan Reservoir. OBC's stated purpose is to recruit new members interested in rowing, sponsor crew races, send teams to regattas, and generally support rowing in Northern Virginia.

Amenities: Guests

Ocean City Rowing & Athletic Association
PO Box 880
Ocean City, NJ 08226, United States
Contact: Vincent Hink
Tel: (609) 814-9070

BH: Ocean City Rowing & Athletic Association Boathouse
The Bayside Center
Ocean City, NJ

History: The Ocean City Rowing & Athletic Association is a New Jersey non-profit organization devoted and dedicated to preserving the rich history of professional ocean lifesaving in Ocean City, NJ. We also provide a venue for rowers to continue or begin their participation in rowing activities, both recreational and competitive. We maintain a Historical Lifesaving Museum as well as a rowing facility on site.

Amenities: Guests

Ohio Athletic Club
PO Box 02033
Columbus, OH 43216-2033, United States
Contact: Michelle LaLonde
Tel: (614) 341-7340
Email: ohiorowing@webtv.net

Year est: 1990
Colors: Navy, blue and white.
Members: 35
History: Enthusiastically born from a rowing league in 1990, the Ohio Athletic Club members pursue their love of rowing through recreational and competitive rowing in downtown Columbus. OAC brings rowing to the community through summer learn-to-row programs and other special events.

Amenities: Guests, Ergs

Ohio Valley Rowing Club
PO Box 2313
Parkersburg, WV 26102-2313, United States
Contact: Les Pritchard
Tel: (304) 485-7613
Email: pritchardles@charter.net

BH: Ohio Valley RC Boathouse
2201 Keefer Street
Parkersburg, WV

Year est: 1960
Colors: Blue and gold.
Members: 250
History: Formed in 1960. Year-round program includes spring season for over 150 high school students from Parkersburg and S. Parkersburg High Schools. Summer and fall for Masters rowers.

Amenities: Guests, Bathroom, Showers, Ergs

Oklahoma City Association for Rowing
601 Eastview Drive
Yukon, OK 73099, United States
Contact: Mike Knopp
Tel: (405) 354-1727
Email: oar@bricktownboathouse.com
www.bricktownboathouse.com

Year est: 1999
Colors: Brick red and white.
Regatta: Bricktown Regatta
Members: 35
History: The Oklahoma City Association for Rowing (OAR) was founded in 1999 to bring the sport of rowing to the community, high school students, and university students. OAR is committed to education the Oklahoma City community about the environmentally-friendly and aesthetically pleasing sport of rowing and its health benefits.

Amenities: Guests, Bathroom, Showers

Old Capitol Rowing Club
Madison Street
Iowa City, IA, United States
Contact: Nora Leonard Ray
Tel: (319) 354-9033
Email: rowiowacity@yahoo.com
www.geocities.com/rowiowacity/

Year est: 1996
Colors: Blue and yellow.
Members: 60
History: Old Capitol Rowing Club (OCRC) in Iowa City, Iowa is a community club devoted to recreational and competitive sweep rowing and sculling. Founded in 1996, it currently has more than 20 adult members and nearly 80 junior members from City High and West High in Iowa City.

Amenities: Guests

Old Glory Boat Club
67 Mystic Road
N. Stonington, CT 06359, United States
Contact: W. Hart Perry
Tel: (860) 535-0634
Fax: (860) 535-0637
Email: NatRowing@NatRowing.org
www.natrowing.org

History: The NRF's purpose in establishing Old Glory is to recognize and celebrate the achievements of the Club's members. In the years ahead, the NRF will be celebrating these achievements in a variety of ways. The NRF defines achievement as having been among the very few in our sport who have been fortunate enough to wear the nation's colors in international competition. Whether someone made a team once or ten times, the NRF wants to recognize that achievement. Old Glory Boat Club is our 35th anniversary gift to all those who have represented the United States at the highest level.

Old Lyme Rowing Association
4 Jean Drive
Old Lyme, CT 06371, United States
Contact: Betsy Buch
Tel: (860) 434-8763
Fax: (860) 434-3265
Email: ebuch34@aol.com
reg18.k12.ct.us/rowassoc.htm

History: Old Lyme organizes a rowing program operating daily in the summer, which enables all community members to use equipment at the Roger Lake Boathouse. It also fosters participation in various competitions, including Canadian Henley, Head of the Connecticut, Head of the Charles and other summer and fall races. It also fundraises for the purchase of equipment, including the fried dough sale at the Memorial Day Fair, the continually successful annual fruit sale and an annual fundraising letter.

Amenities: Guests

Olde Towne Rowing Club
300 North Street
Portsmouth, VA 23704, United States

Olympia Area Rowing
PO Box 7148
Olympia, WA 98507-7148, United States
Email: Wec084@aol.com
www.olympiaarearowing.org/

Omaha Rowing Association
301 South 57th Street
Omaha, NE 68132, United States

Onota Lake Rowing Club
PO Box 411
Williamstown, MA 01267-0411, United States

Open Water Rowing Center
85 Liberty Ship Way #102
Sausalito, CA 94965, United States
Contact: Ellen Braithwaite
Tel: (415) 332-1090
Email: owrc@owrc.com
www.owrc.com

Year est: 1985
Colors: Blue and white.
Regatta: Open Ocean Regatta
Members: 230
History: Formed in 1985 to facilitate sculling on open water — San Francisco Bay. Has grown from 4 shells and 20-30 members to 22 club shells, 85 stored private shells and approximately 230 members. We offer year-round coaching, novice to advanced.

Amenities: Guests, Bathroom, Showers, Ergs

Orcas Island Rowing Club
PO Box 239
Olga, WA 98279, United States
Contact: Mike Reid
Tel: (360) 376-4956
Members: 25
History: Working with the state to get permission to build a boathouse in the State Park. Junior program is Orcas Island High School.

Oregon Association of Rowers
PO Box 11963
Eugene, OR 97440, United States
Contact: Jill Hoyenga
Tel: (541) 484-4557
Fax: (541) 474-5854
Email: oregonrowing@yahoo.com
www.imarcs.com/oar

Year est: 1986
Members: 65
History: Chartered in 1986 as a non-profit corporation. With the help from South Eugene HS crew, and in conjunction with the city of Eugene Outdoor Program, our 2,800 square foot boathouse, built entirely with volunteer labor, opened in May of 1994. The Covered Bridge Regatta, held regularly each spring, attracts junior, collegiate, open and Masters crews from Washington, western Oregon and northern California.

Amenities: Guests, Ergs

Organization of Allderdice Rowing — OAR
PO Box 71
Windermere, FL 34786-0071, United States

Orlando Area Rowing Society (OARS)
PO Box 71
Windermere, FL 34786, United States
Tel: (407) 876-4641
Fax: (407) 876-3578
www.oars-online.com

BH: OARS Boathouse
Main Street
Windermere, FL 34786
Tel: (407) 876-9037

Year est: 1990
Colors: Orange and Blue
Regatta: OARS Invitational — Spring Regatta
Members: 85 juniors
History: Club consists of Olympic HS, Dr. Phillips HS
and West Orange HS and Masters rowers.
Amenities: Guests, Bathroom, Showers, Ergs

Orlando Rowing Association
PO Box 547392
Orlando, FL 32854, United States

Orlando Rowing Club
PO Box 547802
Orlando, FL 32854, United States
Contact: Gary Ehrlich
Email: info@orc-rowing.com
www.orc-rowing.com

BH: Charles Kenneth Corkery Boathouse
2200 Lee Road
Lake Fairview Park
Orlando, FL 32854
Tel: (407) 296-CREW

Year est: 1981
Colors: Forest green
Regatta: Mayor's Cup Regatta, Masters Regatta
Members: 80
History: Founded in the mid-1980's by members of the
Florida Athletic Club wanting to establish a club on
Lake Fairview in Orlando. This dedicated group
enters all area, state and many national regattas,
winning medals too numerous to list. We recently
moved our new boathouse after many years of plan-
ning and effort by all the rowers.
Amenities: Guests, Bathroom, Showers, Ergs

Pacific Rowing Club
PO Box 27548
San Francisco, CA 94127-1548, United States
Tel: (415) 242-0252
Email: olgavsf@aol.com
www.pacificrc.org
History: The Pacific Rowing Club, located at Lake
Merced in San Francisco, CA, offers a seasonal com-
petitive rowing program open to high school students
throughout the Bay Area, as well as recreational
rowing for children and adults of all ages and skill lev-
els at various times of the year.
Amenities: Guests

Pagosa Rowing Club
PO Box 3730
Pagosa Springs, CO 81147, United States
Year est: 1997
Colors: Blue and green.
Members: 20

Palm Beach Rowing Association
1050 Powell Drive
Riviera Beach, FL 33404, United States
Contact: Henry Lumb
Tel: (561) 842-3308

BH: Palm Beach RA Boathouse
2957 N. Australian Avenue
W. Palm Beach, FL
Tel: (561) 848-1767

Year est: 1980
Colors: Blue and white.
Members: 55
Amenities: Guests, Bathroom, Showers, Ergs

Passaic River Rowing Association
PO Box 440
Lyndhurst, NJ 07041, United States
Email: prra.row2@verizon.net
www.prra.org
Year est: 1999
Members: 75
History: The mission of the Passaic River Rowing
Association is to call together and support a commu-
nity of rowers of every age and ability, promote the
highest values of rowing in international, national and
local arenas, promote the stewardship of the Passaic
River environment and to strive for excellence in all
that we do.
Amenities: Guests, Ergs

Peck's Boat Club
PO Box 47
Rowayton, CT 06853, United States
Contact: John Hilts
Tel: (203) 387-1064

Peconic Bay Rowing Club
PO Box 56
Southold, NY 11971, United States

Penn Athletic Club Rowing Association
#12 Boathouse Row Kelly Drive
Philadelphia, PA 19130, United States
www.phillynews.com/packages/boat/pacra

Year est: 1856
Colors: Royal blue and yellow.
Members: 450
History: Penn AC was founded in 1871 as the West Philadelphia BC originally located below the dam. In 1923, the name changed to Penn AC. Penn AC has placed over 100 members on the national team and in national camps. Current and former members of Penn AC include rowing legends Joe Burke, Art Gallagher and Ted Nash to name a few.

Amenities: Guests, Banquet, Bathroom, Showers, Weights

Philadelphia Girls Rowing Club
5035 Pulaski Avenue
Philadelphia, PA 19130, United States
Contact: Elizabeth Bergen
Tel: (215) 978-8824
www.boathouserow.org

Year est: 1938
Colors: Royal blue and white.
Members: 175
History: PGRC was founded in 1938 to develop the sport of rowing for women athletes. The club remains an all-women's rowing club with programs for all levels of competitive and recreational rowers.

Amenities: Guests, Banquet, Bathroom, Showers, Weights, Ergs

Philadelphia Rowing Program for the Disabled
#4 Boathouse Row
Kelly Drive
Philadelphia, PA 19130, United States
Contact: Isabel Bohn, Administrator
Tel: (215) 765-5118
Fax: (215) 765-4504
Email: pacenter@aol.com
www.prpd.net

BH: PRPD Boathouse
1233 West River Drive
Philadelphia, PA 19130
Tel: (215) 877-8906

Year est: 1980
Colors: Blue and white
Regatta: Bayada Regatta, All Disabled Nationals
Members: 150

Amenities: Ergs

Picnic Point Rowing Club
454 Glenway
Madison, WI 53711, United States
Contact: Hal Menendez
Tel: (608) 233-4312
Email: halmen40@chorus.net

Year est: 1998
Members: 30
History: Membership limited to Wisconsin varsity letter winners or Wisconsin alumni.

Piermont Rowing Club
271 Hudson Terrace
Piermont, NY 10968, United States

Pioneer Valley Women's Rowing Club
72 Reservation Road
Sunderland, MA 01375, United States
Contact: MJ Canavan
Tel: (413) 545-6824
Email: mjcanavan@library.umass.edu

Year est: 1994
Colors: Maroon and white.
Members: 35
History: Affiliated with University of Massachusetts in Amherst.

Amenities: Guests

Pocock Boat Club
3320 Fuhrman Avenue East
Seattle, WA 98102, United States
Tel: (206) 328-0778
Email: pocockrow@mindspring.com
www.scn.org/rec/gprf

Year est: 1997
History: Formed in 1997, the club rows from the George Pocock Memorial Rowing Center.

Amenities: Guests, Banquet, Bathroom, Showers, Weights, Ergs

Pocock Rowing Center
3320 Fuhrman Avenue East
Seattle, WA 98102, United States
Tel: (206) 328-7272
Fax: (206) 328-4239
Email: info@pocockrowing.org
www.pocockrowing.org

Year est: 1994
Colors: Green

Members: 300
History: The Pocock Rowing Center opened in May of 1994. A $2.5 million venue, the center is a state-of-the-art rowing facility complete with an indoor weight room, ergometers, locker and shower facilities and boat bays which can accomodate up to 177 shells of various sizes.

Amenities: Guests, Banquet, Bathroom, Showers, Weights, Ergs

Portage Bay Rowing Club
c/o Pocock Rowing Center
3320 Fuhrman Avenue East
Seattle, WA 98102, United States
Year est: 1997
Colors: Navy and white.
Members: 50

Amenities: Guests, Bathroom, Showers, Ergs

Portland Boat Club
PO Box 97
Lake Oswego, OR 97034, United States
Contact: Bernie Thurber
Tel: (503) 778-5202
Email: berniethurber@dwt.com
Year est: 1879
Colors: Light blue, dark blue and white.
Members: 50
History: Formerly Portland Rowing Club. Competitive masters scullers who also get together in sweep boats for racing. Members are all highly self-motivated athletes and are involved in a variety of intense activities. The club functions by group consensus live!

Amenities: Guests, Bathroom, Showers, Ergs

Portland/Vancouver Rowing Association
10223 NW Dick Road
Hillsboro, OR 97124, United States
Tel: (503) 310-1943
Email: oregonrow@hotmail.com

History: Our B.O.D. is made up of representative of all the rowing clubs in the Portland area. Our purpose is to maintain the buoyed course at Vancouver Lake, Vancouver, Washington and manage regattas that are held there. Currently, the NW Junior and Masters Regional Championships are hosted there.

Positive Strokes Rowing
PO Box 2705
Alameda, CA 94501, United States
Contact: Walt Duiron
Tel: (510) 523-9713

BH: Ballena Bat Boathouse
Alameda, CA
BH: Oakland Boathouse
Oakland, CA
Year est: 1989
Members: 60
History: Positive Strokes Rowing was formed in 1989 as a way to generate interest in the sport of rowing and to make recreational rowing easily available to the general public. Members have access to a complete instruction program and a fleet of shells. Two locations are offered: our first facility at Ballena Bat in Alameda, CA, and our new facility at San Leandro Bay, in Oakland, CA. Several rowing events are offered throughout the year.

Amenities: Banquet, Bathroom, Showers, Ergs

Potomac Boat Club
3530 Water Street
Washington, DC 20007, United States
Tel: (202) 347-6084
Email: potomac_boat_club@hotmail.com
www.rowpbc.net
Year est: 1869
Colors: Red and White.
Regatta: Crab Feast Regatta
Members: 400
History: 125 Years Rowing the Potomac.

Amenities: Guests, Ergs

Prince William Rowing Club
Lake Ridge Park
12350 Cotton Mill Drive
Woodbridge, VA 22192, United States
Email: info@pwrc.org
www.pwrc.org
Members: 50

Quad City Rowing Association
PO Box 69
Moline, IA 61265, United States
Contact: Becky Eiting
Tel: (563) 322-4924
Fax: (563) 328-3206
Email: DoggyInn@aol.com

BH: Sylvan Boathouse
1701 1st Avenue
Moline, IL
Tel: (309) 762-6030
www.qcra.org
Year est: 1980
Colors: Red, yellow and black.
Regatta: Quad Classic Head Race
Members: 125

Amenities: Guests

Quinsigamond Rowing Association
PO Box 2461
Worcester, MA 01613-2461, United States
Contact: H.R. Nyce
Tel: (508) 752-5501
Email: rowing@qra.org
Email: membership@qra.org
www.qra.org

Year est: 1950
Colors: Green and blue.
Members: 60
Amenities: Guests, Banquet, Bathroom, Showers, Ergs

Rainier Rowing Club
3708 N 38th Street
Tacoma, WA 98407, United States
Contact: Ted Walkley
Email: twalkley@u.washington.edu

Year est: 1994
Colors: Dark green, red and dark blue.
Members: 55
History: Established as a club for small boats and for unaffiliated rowers. It is also the club of record for special boats from the Northwest.
Amenities: Guests

Raleigh Rowing Center
PO Box 10864
Raleigh, NC 27605, United States
Contact: Shawn Stephenson
Tel: (919) 851-5182

BH: Raleigh RC Boathouse
Lake Wheeler Road
Raleigh, NC

Year est: 1992
Colors: Blue and white.
Members: 75
Amenities: Guests

Raritan Valley Rowing Association
L. Brown Athletic Center
Box 1149
Piscataway, NJ 08855, United States

Red and White Rowing
PO Box 4291
Parkersburg, WV 26104-4291, United States

Riddle Point Rowing
Indiana University Aquatic Center
Bloomington, IN , United States
Email: riddlepointrowing@hotmail.com
Regatta: Lemondhead Regatta

Ring's Island Rowing Club
91 Seven Star Road
Groveland, MA 01834, United States
Contact: Alice Twombly
Tel: (978) 373-7816
Email: rirc99@cs.com

BH: Ring's Island Rowing Club Boathouse
4th Street
Salisbury, MA

Year est: 1990
Colors: Bead yellow.
Members: 17
History: The Ring's Island RC has its headquarterson a rocky knoll called Ring's Island on the Salisbury bank of the Merrimack River. The main purpose of our informal club is to provide young men and women the opportunity to row traditional wooden boats on New England waters and beyond. Though it started as a youth club, people of all ages are welcome to join. Many of the dories were built by Triton High School students.
Amenities: Guests, Banquet,

Rio Abajo Rowing Club
1729 1/2 Agua Fria Street
Santa Fe, NM 87505, United States

Rio Salado Rowing Club
PO Box 1555
Tempe, AZ 85280, United States
www.riosaladorowing.org
Contact: Jake Poinier
Tel: (480) 947-4964
Email: jpoinier@mindspring.com

Year est: 1991
Colors: Green and white.
Members: 140
Amenities: Ergs

Rivanna Rowing Club
PO Box 5797
Charlottesville, VA 22905, United States
Contact: Pamela Murray
Tel: (434) 975-CREW
Email: starboard807@aol.com
info@rivannarowing.org
www.rivannarowing.org

BH: Thomas Temple Allan Boathouse
276 Woodlands Road
Charlottesville, VA 22901
Tel: (434) 975-2739

Year est: 1989
Colors: Light blue.
Members: 100
History: The club was started by Brett Wilson in the summer of 1989. Since then, the club has grown

substantially with over 800 people from the Charlottesville area taking Learn-to-Row classes.

Amenities: Guests, Bathroom, Showers, Ergs

River City Rowing Club
PO Box 980401
West Sacramento, CA 95798, United States
Contact: Mark Dirrim, President
Tel: (916) 428-6282
Email: mark_dirrim@peoplesoft.com
www.rivercityrowing.org

Year est: 1983
Colors: Blue and white.
Members: 150
History: Started as a sculling club and recreational club that paralleled growth of the University of California, Davis. Has expanded into a sweep and sculling program both recreationally and competitively.

Amenities: Guests, Ergs

River Rats Rowing
219 Carver Hawkeye Arena
Iowa City, IA 52242, United States
Tel: (319) 353-5532
Fax: (319) 353-5483
Email: laura-macfarlane@uiowa.edu

Year est: 1999
Colors: Black
Members: 20
History: Offers a summer program in Iowa to develop athletes toward a level on par with pre-elite classification.

Riverfront Recapture Inc.
One Hartford Square West
Ste. 100
Hartford, CT 06106, United States
Contact: Todd Novak, Programs Manager
Tel: (860) 713-3131
Fax: (860) 713-3138
Email: tnovak@riverfront.org
www.riverfront.org

BH: Greater Hartford Jaycees Community Boathouse
Riverside Park, Leibert Road
Hartford, CT 06120

Year est: 1987
Colors: Blue and green.
Regatta: Head to the Riverfront
Members: 150
History: The program, "Go Row Hartford", began 14 years ago with four recreational shells. We will be moving in to our Community Boathouse for the 2002 season.

Amenities: Guests, Banquet, Bathroom, Showers, Weights, Ergs

Riverside Boat Club
769 Memorial Drive
Cambridge, MA 02139, United States
Tel: (617) 492-1869
Email: secretary@riversideboatclub.com
www.riversideboatclub.com

Year est: 1869
Colors: Royal blue and white.
Regatta: Riverside Sprints, Cromwell Cup
Members: 250
History: Founded by workers of the Riverside Press in 1869 to provide a club for the working class in the Boston area.

Amenities: Guests, Bathroom, Showers, Weights, Ergs

Rochester Rowing Club
Box 1072
Rochester, MN 55905, United States
Contact: Phil Greipp, Club President
Tel: (507) 289-0989
Fax: (507) 266-9277
Email: greipp@rrcmn.com
www.rrcmn.com

Year est: 1990
Colors: Forest green and white.
Members: 40
History: The club was founded in 1990 by Bill Pavlicek from Philadelphia with Doug

Amenities: Guests, Ergs

Rocket City Rowing Club
2822 Lafayette Drive
Huntsville, AL 35801, United States
Contact: Forrest Sanders
Email: masterscoach@rocketcityrowing.com
www.rocketcityrowing.org

Year est: 1996
History: The Rocket City Rowing Club is a non-profit organization founded by rowing alumni from the University of Alabama in Huntsville (UAH) in October of 1996. The club rows on the Tennessee River, out of the UAH Boathouse, located just south of the Whitesburg.

Rockford YMCA Rowing Club
200 "Y" Blvd
Rockford, IL 61107, United States
Contact: Jillian Trojniar
Tel: (815) 489-1120
Email: jtrojiniar@rockfordymca.org
www.headoftherock.org

Regatta: Head of the Rock
Members: 55

Amenities: Guests, Bathroom, Showers

Rocky Mountain Rowing Club
PO Box 6242
Denver, CO 80206, United States
Contact: Mark Groshek, President
Tel: (303) 331-2860
Email: president@rockymountainrowing.com
www.rockymountainrowing.com

Year est: 1983
Colors: Red, blue and gold (Colorado Flag).
Members: 120
History: Evolving from mostly sculling to about two-thirds sweep.

Amenities: Guests

Rondout Rowing Club
142 Van Keuren Hwy
Kingston, NY 12401, United States
Contact: Renno Budziak
Tel: (914) 336-4502
Email: rbudziak@aol.com

Row America
500 West Putnam Avenue
Greenwich, CT 06830, United States
Tel: (203) 661-0275
www.rowamerica.com
History: Row America is an non-profit organization that manages two rowing facilities in Connecticut. Row America promotes youth rowing throughout the United States and provides scholarships to under privileged kids.

Rowing Club of the Woodlands
PO Box 8554
The Woodlands, TX 77387, United States
Contact: Heather Mathis
Email: heathermathis@hotmail.com
www.infohwy.com/~jayhawk/rctw/rctw_home

BH: Rowing Club of the Woodlands Boathouse
North Shore Park
The Woodlands, TX

Colors: Dark green and white.
Regatta: The Dragon's Breath Regatta, Slay the Dragon Regat

Amenities: Guests, Ergs

Rowing Dock
PO Box 685162
Austin, TX 78768, United States
Contact: Rachel A Yates, General Manager
Tel: (512) 459-0999
Fax: (512) 452-2788
Email: Rachel@rowingdock.com
www.rowingdock.com

BH: Rowing Dock Boathouse
2418 Stratford Drive
Austin, TX 78703

Year est: 1998
Colors: Red and blue.
Members: 155
Amenities: Bathroom, Showers, Ergs

Rowing Foundation of Oregon
20235 SW Gassner
Beaverton, OR 97007, United States
Contact: Robert F Zagunis, Trustee
Tel: (503) 591-5317

Rude and Smooth Boat Club
19 Wertsville Road
Neshanic, NJ 08853, United States
Contact: Richard Smith
Tel: (908) 369-4645
Fax: (908) 369-6742
Email: richard@porthcawl.com

History: We are a reunion crew, reliving our collegiate rowing experience through on or two head/masters races each year.

Sagamore Rowing Association
PO Box 453
Glenwood Landing, NY 11547, United States
Contact: Richard McLoughlin, Secretary
Tel: (631) 673-8304
Fax: (516) 671-3332
Email: keitum453@aol.com
Email: webmaster@sagamorerowing.org
www.sagamorerowing.org

BH: Coindre Hall Boathouse
101 Brown's Road
Huntington, NY 11743
BH: Oyster Bay Boathouse
Building H, West End Avenue
Oyster Bay, NY
Tel: (516) 624-0054

Year est: 1972
Colors: Green delta and white.
Regatta: Hempstead Lake, Oyster Bay Scholastic, Oyster Bay Frostbite
Members: 400
History: Sagamore Rowing Association (SRA) has trained thousands of rowers since its inception over a quarter century ago. With numerous Olympians, World, National Team members and medalists, Sagamore Rowing Associations is one of the most established and highly regarded rowing clubs in the country. Sagamore Rowing Association has launched a dozen high school and university rowing programs on Long Island, in addition to many adult programs.

Amenities: Guests, Banquet, Bathroom, Showers, Ergs

Saint Louis Rowing Club
PO Box 411094
St. Louis, MO 63141, United States
Contact: Scott Allison
Tel: (314) 965-9456
Fax: (425) 930-6284
Email: swallison@alum.mit.edu
www.slrc.net

BH: St. Louis Rowing Club Boathouse
Marine Avenue
Maryland Heights, MO 63043
Tel: (314) 434-8299

Year est: 1877
Colors: Red, white and blue.
Regatta: St. Louis Sprints, Gateway Regatta
Members: 200
History: The club was incorporated in 1877 and remained active until the 50's when it went dormant. The club was re-established in 1983.

Amenities: Guests, Ergs

Salisbury Boat Club
60 Long Pond Road
Lakeville, CT 06039, United States
Tel: (860) 435-0300
Email: r.bettigole@exodermic.com

Year est: 1977

Sammamish Rowing Association
PO Box 52745
Bellevue, WA 98015-2745, United States
Tel: (425) 895-1704
Email: director@srarowing.com
www.srarowing.com

BH: Sammamish Rowing Association Boathouse
5022 West Lake Sammamish Parkway, NE
Seattle, WA

Year est: 1996
History: The Sammamish Rowing Association is the only rowing club on Seattle's Eastside. Founded in 1996, we moved into our new boathouse just south of Marymoor Park in 1997. Our club is open to everyone. Members range from beginners to advanced rowers, from juniors to veterans.

Amenities: Guests

San Diego Rowing Club
1220 El Carmel Place
San Diego, CA 92109, United States
Tel: (858) 488-1893
Contact: Patricia E Pinkerton
Email: ppinkerton@ucsd.edu
www.sdrc-row.org

San Francisco Bay Blades
PO Box 14185
San Francisco, CA 94114-0185, United States
Contact: Pat Hansen, President
Tel: (510) 653-8107
Fax: (775) 582-6717
Email: sfbbhandson@yahoo.com

Year est: 1996
Members: 20
History: San Francisco Bay Blades is a group of lesbian and gay rowers in the San Francisco Bay area. SFBB is a subgroup within the Lake Merritt Rowing Club in Oakland.

San Francisco Rowing Club
1631 Larkin Street #6
San Francisco, CA 94109, United States

Santa Cruz Rowing Club
PO Box 2544
Santa Cruz, CA 95063, United States
Contact: Terry Joakimides, Treasurer
Tel: (831) 438-1451
Fax: (831) 438-1670
Email: terry@scrowing.org
www.scrowing.org

BH: Santa Cruz small boat harbor
Marine Parade
Santa Cruz, CA 95062-4384

Year est: 1976
Regatta: Monterey Bay Crossing, Lobster Row
Members: 104

Amenities: Guests, Bathroom, Showers

Saratoga Springs Rowing Club
PO Box 1132
Saratoga Springs, NY 12866, United States
Contact: Christopher Grosso
Tel: (518) 584-2600

BH: Saratoga Springs Rowing Club Boathouse
Dyer Switch Road
Saratoga Springs, NY

Year est: 1986
Colors: Cobalt blue and grey.
Members: 20
History: Started by a small group of non-rowers in a local bar in the winter of 1986. At one time as many as 25 members, including females. Club has been represented in national events and Masters Worlds in Ireland, France, Italy and Mexico. We are a club of masters and veteran scullers, hosting various social activities.

Amenities: Guests

Saugatuck Rowing Association
521 Riverside Avenue
Westport, CT 06880, United States
Contact: Nicoleta Mantescu, Director of Rowing
Tel: (203) 221-7475
Fax: (203) 221-1593
Email: nmantescu@saugatuckrowing.com
www.rowamerica.com

Year est: 1990
Colors: Black and white.
Regatta: Connecticut Indoor Rowing Championship
Members: 1,150
History: Operating out of an old freight station with
port-a-john, The Saugatuck Rowing Association was
established in 1990 by James Mangan and developed
a dedicated membership of 100. SRA went out of
existence when the land was sold. Members then
joined The Sauga

Amenities: Guests, Banquet, Bathroom, Showers,
Weights, Ergs

Seattle Yacht Club Rowing Foundation
1807 E. Hamlin Street
Seattle, WA 98112, United States
Contact: MJ Swindley
Tel: (206) 325-1000
Email: mjswindley@aol.com

Year est: 1985
Colors: Red, white and blue.
Regatta: Opening Day Regatta
Members: 60
History: Although Seattle Yacht Club staged sculling
events in the 1920's, it was 1982 when rowing became
an official activity at the club. Honorary SYC member
and ex-UW coach Dick Erickson provided boats and
initial instruction. In 1984, SYC began inviting other
masters clubs to compete prior to the collegiates in
Opening Day. Soon, the more active rowers known as
"Dick's Chicks" began competing year-round. In its
first decade at racing, both its women's and men's
crews have won medals at Nationals as well as at
races in Canada, Scotland, France and Italy.

Amenities: Guests, Banquet, Bathroom, Showers,
Weights, Ergs

Sonoma Sculling Society
937 Ridge View Drive
Healdsburg, CA 95448, United States
Contact: Rebecca La Londe
Tel: (707) 433-1604
Fax: (707) 433-3586

Year est: 1995
Colors: Maroon and white.
Members: 15

Amenities: Bathroom, Showers

Sons of the Beach Rowing
1617 Tigertail Avenue
Coconut Grove, FL 33133, United States
Contact: Andy Parrish
Tel: (305) 285-0137
Fax: (305) 281-1154
Email: Hildog12@aol.com

Year est: 1985
Colors: Pink Flamingos on royal blue.
Regatta: Melbourne Pyms Cup
Members: 12
History: Competitive (always in spirit, sometimes in
body), Florida-based rowers dating form the 60's, 70's
and 80's who occasionally get together to try to go
fast.

Amenities: Guests

Sound Rowers
2318 2nd Ave Box 502
Seattle, WA 98121, United States
www.soundrowers.org

Year est: 1979
Regatta: 15
Members: 120+
History: Formed in 1979 to settle a bet whether it was
possible to row across the Puget Sound in less than
an hour. The club is open to all human powered
watercraft. Special category for home-built boats.
Sound Rowers organizes 15 open water races rang-
ing from 5-25 miles in the Puget Sound region of
Washington.

Amenities: Guests

South Bend Scullers Inc.
3431 South Twylckenham
South Bend, IN 44614, United States
Contact: JR Reineke
Tel: (219) 291-7814
Email: maryanddick@attbi.com

Year est: 1993
Members: 40

Amenities: Guests

South Chicago Rowing Center
c/o Harrison Trading Company
601 South LaSalle Street 2nd floor
Chicago, IL 60605, United States
Tel: (312) 593-8040
Email: chicagorowingcenter@yahoo.com
www.rowchicago.org/

History: Chicago Rowing Center is part of a consor-
tium of rowing clubs comprising the South Chicago
Rowing Center including Chicago Youth Rowing Club,
Northwestern University Crew, St. Ignatius Crew, and
University of Chicago Crew.

Amenities: Guests

South End Rowing Club
500 Jefferson Street
San Francisco, CA 94109, United States
Tel: (415) 776-7372
Email: rowing@south-end.org
www.south-end.org

Year est: 1873
History: The South End boathouse contains over 30 different watercraft ranging from paddle boards and kayaks to decades-old wherries and Viking boats, to sleek 21 and 24-foot fiberglass open water racing shells.

Southern Branch Rowing Club
303 West Road
Portsmouth, VA 23707, United States

Southern California Boat Club
13555 Fiji Way
Marina del Rey, CA 20292, United States
Contact: Buz Tarlow
Tel: (310) 822-0073

Year est: 1992
Members: 180
History: Founded in 1992 to provide a community rowing program with quality coaching. Sliding scale fee.
Amenities: Guests, Bathroom, Showers, Ergs

Station L Rowing Club
PO Box 10875
Portland, OR 97210, United States
Contact: Peter Edwards
Tel: (503) 916-8100
Email: rwarner@pacifier.com
www.aracnet.com/~katemill/Station_L

BH: Station L Rowing Club Boathouse
1466 NW Front Avenue
Portland, OR

Year est: 1973
Colors: Black and turquoise.
Regatta: Row for the Cure
Members: 70
History: Station L, founded in 1973, was originally located adjacent to Portland General Electric's power generating station, "L". First known for teaching rowing to adults, the club began to field competitive masters and open crews in the late 1980's. The club maintains a strong masters program coupled with competitive and recreational opportunities for our members.

Amenities: Guests, Ergs

Steel City Rowing Club
157 James Street
Verona, PA 15147, United States
Mary Zubrow
Tel: (412) 828-5565
Email: scrc@steelcityrowing.org
www.steelcityrowing.org

Year est: 1996
Colors: Black, gold and purple.
Members: 30
History: Founded in 1996 by Ladislau Tompa and Dori Martin to foster competitive rowing in the Pittsburgh area. All ages are welcome to enjoy and learn rowing.

Amenities: Guests, Bathroom, Showers, Weights, Ergs

Stockton Rowing Inc.
4950 Buckley Cove Way
Riverpoint Landing
Stockton, CA 95219, United States
Contact: Ed Kirkpatrick, President
Tel: (209) 943-2950
Email: president@stocktonrowing.com
Tel: (209) 943-2950
Fax: (253) 323-5160
Email: president@stocktonrowing.com
stocktonrowing.com/

Stonington Rowing Club
8 Godfrey Street
Mystic, CT 06355, United States
Contact: Ken Godfrey
Tel: (860) 572-8562
Email: shsrowing@juno.com

Year est: 1998
Colors: Brown/White
Regatta: NA
Members: 90
Amenities: Bathroom, Ergs

Style Drive Rowing Club
145 Pickney Street #134
Boston, MA 02114, United States

Swan Creek Rowing Club
PO Box 153
Lambertville, NJ 08530, United States
Contact: Dorlyn Law, President
Email: dorly@gateway.net
members.aol.com/srplattscrc.html

Members: 150
Amenities: Guests

Syracuse Chargers Rowing Club
PO Box 5643
Syracuse, NY 13220-5643, United States
Tel: (315) 234-0039
www.chargersrow.org

BH: Syracuse Chargers Rowing Club Boathouse
Long Branch Road
Liverpool, NY

Year est: 1972
Members: 300
History: The Syracuse Chargers Rowing Club serves over 300 members by consistently offering outstanding programs at all levels from Learn-to-Row through high school and masters level instruction. Some of our high school athletes have continued beyond the local program to receive scholarships and row at prestigious colleges and universities. The club encourages its experienced members to "give back" to the rowing community.
Amenities: Guests, Ergs

Tampa Rowing Club Inc
PO Box 10148
Tampa, FL 33679-0148, United States

Colors: Red, yellow and blue.
Members: 90
History: Founded in 1972 by Milo Vega with a core group of masters scullers. Lease a bay and outside rack space from the University of Tampa. In 1984, became a FL not-for-profit corporation with an emphasis on masters and community rowing.
Amenities: Guests, Bathroom, Showers

Thames River Sculls
c/o UMass Crew
Boyden Building
Amherst, MA 01003, United States
Contact: Jim Dietz
Tel: (413) 545-9441
Email: jdietz@admin.umass.edu

Year est: 1988
History: TRS was established in 1988 as a step between collegiate rowing and the National Team. It soon expanded to juniors and masters. Its present focus is in women's rowing on the pre-elite level, and both male and female junior rowing.

Thompson Boat Center
2900 Virginia Avenue N.W.
Washington, DC 20037, United States
Contact: Emmanuel Caudron, Manager
Tel: (202) 333-9543
Email: tbc@guestservices.com
www.guestservices.com/tbc

Colors: Blue and white.
History: A Guest Services-owned facility that hosts high school and collegiate rowing in Washington, DC, Virginia and Maryland, as well as recreational, junior, competitive and masters sweep and sculling programs.
Amenities: Guests, Banquet, Bathroom, Showers, Ergs

Three Rivers Rowing Association
300 Waterfront Drive
Pittsburgh, PA 15222, United States
Contact: Michael Lambert
Tel: (412) 231-8772
Fax: (412) 231-5337
Email: mplambert@aol.com
www.ThreeRiversRowing.org

Year est: 1984
Colors: Red, white and blue.
Members: 1,000
History: Three Rivers has 15,000 square feet of boat storage shared by four colleges, twelve high schools, and several programs. We also have a rapidly growing sprint kayaking program. We have summer camps for high school, 10-13 year olds and collegiate athletes.
Amenities: Guests, Banquet, Bathroom, Showers, Weights, Ergs

Tiber Creek Rowing Club
6705 Queens Chapel Road
University Park, MD 20782, United States
www.tibercreekrowingclub.org
Amenities: Guests

Toledo Rowing Club
8 Main Street
Toledo, OH 43605, United States
Contact: Sue Weaver, Membership Director
Tel: (419) 874-5811
Email: sbwpath@yahoo.com
info@toledorowing.org
www.toledorowing.org

Year est: 1981
Colors: Blue and white.
Regatta: Frogtown Indoor, Frogtown Races Fall Regatta
Members: 325
History: Formed in 1981 by 12 men and women who revived a rich rowing tradtion dating back to the latter half of the 19th Century when three rowing clubs were operational along the Maumee River. The club now has 355+ members including students from Central Catholic HS, St. John's Jesuit HS, St. Ursula Academy, Notre Dame Academy, Anthony Way HS, Toledo Metropolitan Rowing Club, TRC Collegiate.
Amenities: Guests, Bathroom, Showers, Weights, Ergs

Topeka Rowing
4336 SE 25th Terrace
Topeka, KS 66605, United States
Contact: Don Craig
Tel: (785) 233-9951
Email: topekarowing@lycos.com
www.topekarowing.com
Year est: 1985
Colors: Blue and white.
Regatta: Great Plains Rowing Championships
Members: 100
Amenities: Guests, Banquet, Bathroom, Showers, Weights, Ergs

Traditional Small Craft Association
70 Hayden Road
Hollis, NH 03049, United States

Treasure Coast Rowing Club
PO Box 1286
Palm City, FL 34990, United States
Contact: George Sharrow
Tel: (561) 286-0808
Year est: 1990
Colors: Yellow and blue.
Regatta: Hutchinson Island Sports Fest — Causeway to Causeway
Members: 50
History: The Treasure Coast Rowing Club is a non-profit club that began in 1991. We are an affiliate of the U.S. Rowing Association, the national organization of amateur rowing. We are primarily aimed at recreational and organized competitive rowing at all skill and age levels. We have club boats for training, instruction and recreational uses.
Amenities: Guests

Triton Rowing Club
9 Lenape Drive
Montville, NJ 07045, United States
Contact: Catherine Comerford
Tel: (973) 263-9240
Year est: 1980
History: BU Alumni who row every year in the Head of the Charles.

Tulsa Rowing Club
715 West 21st Street
Tulsa, OK 74107, United States
Contact: Sarah Dexter
Tel: (918) 599-8115
Email: gpiontak@gbronline.com
www.geocities.com/tulsarowing
Year est: 1983
Colors: Blue and gold.
Members: 75

History: The Tulsa Rowing Club was founded in 1983 and has rowed on several area lakes in Tulsa county. In 1990, a boathouse was constructed on Zink Lake near downtown Tulsa and a permanent rowing site was finally obtained.
Amenities: Guests, Banquet, Bathroom, Showers, Weights, Ergs

Undine Barge Club
PO Box 30236
Philadelphia, PA 19103-8236, United States
Contact: T. Lyons Bradley
Tel: (215) 765-9244
Email: undine@undine.com
www.undine.com
Colors: Blue Chevron inside Yellow Chevron on White Field
Year est: 1856
History: The Undine Barge Club was organized by twelve Philadelphia gentlemen on May 9, 1856 to provide "...healthful exercise, relaxation from business, friendly intercourse and pleasure, having in view to this end the possession of a pleasure barge on the River Schuylkill." Named after the spirit of babbling brooks in the Legend of Undine, the club constructed a simple boathouse in a cove a few hundred yards east of the present boathouse (near the site of Bachelors' Barge Club). Undine also has an "upriver" house, Castle Ringstetten. The Castle, which takes it name from the home of Price Huldbrand in the Legend of Undine, was designed by Frank Furness and constructed in 1875. Originally a goal and rest facility [about 4 miles upstream from the boathouse] for the oarsmen with a floating dock on the river front, Castle Ringstetten marked the social side of the new sport of rowing, at the time. (more about the club can be found http://undine.com/history.html])
Amenities: Guests, Banquet, Bathroom, Showers, Weights, Ergs

Union Bay Rowing Club
Univ of Washington IMA Club Sports
PO Box 354090
Seattle, WA 98195, United States
Contact: Sandi Lindbeck
Tel: (206) 543-9499
Email: ubrc@u.washington.edu
students.washington.edu/ubrc
BH: Waterfront Activities Center
University of Washington Campus
Seattle, WA
Year est: 1980
Colors: Dark green, purple and white.
Members: 40
History: The Waterfront Activities Center (WAC) plays host to the UBRC, offering one of the most famous and scenic rowing sites in the nation.

Through the WAC, the UBRC receives ue of motor launches and boat storage facilities. In trade, members of the UBRC maintain the University's six fiberglass wherries, and abide by the WAC rules and regulations.

Amenities: Guests, Bathroom, Showers

Union Boat Club
144 Chestnut Street
Boston, MA 02108, United States
Tel: (617) 742-1520
Email: info@unionboatclub.org

Colors: Blue and white.
Regatta: Commissioners Cup
Members: 690
History: Second oldest boat club in the U.S. — founded in 1851. Been on the banks of the Charles River for the duration. "New" boathouse built in the 1930's when Storrow Drive was built.

Amenities: Guests, Bathroom, Showers, Ergs

University Barge Club
#7 Boathouse Row Kelly Drive
Philadelphia, PA 19130, United States
Mitch Budman
Tel: (215) 232-2293
www.hosr.org/ubc

Year est: 1854
Colors: Navy blue and white.
Members: 150
History: Ten undergrads of the University of Pennsylvania founded The University Barge Club of Philadelphia on April 25, 1854, as a social, recreational and competitive club for Philadelphia rowers. They built their first boathouse in conjunction with the Naiad Club, whose members joined UBC in 1855. UBC is a charter member of the Schuylkill Navy and organized the first Head of the Schuylkill in 1971 and continues to host the event.

Amenities: Guests, Bathroom, Showers, Weights, Ergs

Upper Merion Boat Club Inc.
738 Hidden Valley Drive
King of Prussia, PA 19046, United States
Contact: Tom Pappanastasiou, President
Tel: (610) 337-3624
Email: tompappanastasiou@netzero.com
www.uppermerionboatclub.com

Year est: 1987
Colors: Teal and black.
Regatta: King's Head Regatta
Members: 120
History: Upper Merion Boat Club is located on the Schuylkill River, in Montgomery County, about 15 miles north and west of the famous Boathouse Row in Philadelphia. The Club was formed in 1986 under the guidance of Tom Pappanastasiou, who still serves as our Commodore and general rowing guru.

Amenities: Guests, Bathroom, Showers, Weights, Ergs

Vashon Island Rowing Club
PO Box 79
Vashon, WA 98070, United States
Contact: Mary Rothermel
Tel: (206) 463-9054
Email: m.rothermel@att.net
home.att.net/~m.rothermel/pages/v1.html
BH: Vashon Island Rowing Club Boathouse
Vashon, WA
Tel: (206) 463-9602

Colors: Blue, turquoise and black.
Regatta: Strawberry Festival Regatta
Members: 35
History: Started in 1989 by a handful of women and a used shell, the Vashon Island Rowing Club has expanded to include a men's and women's adult program and a youth crew that competes on a regional and national level. In the Spring of 2000 the club celebrated the opening of the Jensen Point Boat House, a community rowing center including kayaks and canoes. The club is a non-profit organization that provides the equipment and expertise to run the programs offered to the public.

Amenities: Guests, Banquet, Bathroom, Showers, Ergs

Vesper Boat Club
#10 Boathouse Row Kelly Drive
Philadelphia, PA 19130, United States
Contact: Paul Horvat
Tel: (215) 236-2950
Email: vesper@netaxs.com
www.boathouserow.org

Year est: 1865
Colors: Grey and burgundy.
Members: 170
History: Traditionally, Vesper has been an Elite club with Olympic gold medals in eights in 1900, 1904 and 1964 and numerous world championships up to the present. Over 10% of members have won gold medals at the World Championships and Olympics. First club to run competitive men's and women's program together (1969).

Amenities: Guests, Banquet, Bathroom, Showers, Weights, Ergs

Viking Rowing Foundation
2006 Cornwall Avenue
Northfield, NJ 08225, United States
Contact: Raymond Damico
Tel: (609) 641-8973
Email: rayscull@aol.com
www.vikingcrew.org

Year est: 1950
Colors: Blue and white.
Members: 200
History: Dr. John W. Holland founded the club to teach youth rowing. The Viking Rowing Club is comprised of friends, neighbors, community leaders and crew champions from all parts of South Jersey and surrounding regions. As the pioneer rowing club of South Jersey, Viking has become an integral part of the community by offering unmatched youth athletic programs and by securing a competitive title in the rowing arena. Viking also offers a chance for the new athlete to quickly become a recognized champion through the Novice Program At the team's core is a Men's Master 8 and a Women's Master 8 with medals and titles from some of the most prestigious Universities and Rowing Championships in the World.
Amenities: Guests

Virginia Boat Club
PO Box 26051
Richmond, VA 23260, United States
Contact: Hank C Holswade, President
Tel: (804) 320-2984
Email: hcholswade@aol.com
www.virginiaboatclub.org

Colors: Red and white
Regatta: Virginia Reel
Members: 70
Amenities: Guests, Bathroom, Weights, Ergs

Virginia Rowing Club Inc.
PO Box 9661
Hampton, VA 23670, United States
Contact: Robert E Howard, Jr., President
Tel: (757) 723-0364
Email: thehowards@aol.com
www.varowing.org

BH: Virginia Rowing Club Boathouse
801 Settler's Landing Road
Hampton, VA 23669

Year est: 1989
Colors: Red and white.
Members: 34
History: Started in 1989 as a master's club, we now have a developing junior program. Summer novice classes are offered. Racing is done on an informal basis with other local clubs as well as participating in regattas out of the area.
Amenities: Guests, Bathroom, Showers, Ergs

Water Sports Center
41 Wolfpit Avenue #3K
Norwalk, CT 06851, United States
Tel: (203) 854-5492

Water Street Rowing Club
2900 Virginia Avenue N.W.
Washington, DC , United States
Tel: (319) 291-4361
Email: wrc@cedarnet.org

Waterloo Rowing Club
1101 Campbell
Waterloo, IA 50613, United States
www.cedarnet.org/wrc

Year est: 1980
History: The Waterloo Rowing Club is based in the boathouse in Cedar River Park in Waterloo. The boathouse is owned by the Waterloo Leisure Services who have given the Rowing Club permission to store boats and equipment there and to use it for their activities. The boathouse is large enough to store both four person and eight person boats and is convenient to a dock for launching.
Amenities: Guests

Wayland Weston Rowing Association
6 Pesce Lane
Wayland, MA 01778, United States
Contact: Christopher N Maietta, President
Tel: (508) 358-2102
Fax: (508) 358-2103
Email: president@wwcrew.org
www.wwcrew.org

BH: Wayland-Weston Rowing Association Boathouse
Parkland Drive, Wayland, MA

History: The Wayland-Weston Rowing Association, Inc. is a not-for-profit organization dedicated to bringing the joy of rowing to the greater Wayland-Weston community. Recently established, the WWRA calls beautiful and convenient Lake Cochichuate its home base. Our Mission: The WWRA is dedicated to enhancing our members' lifelong fitness, fun, camaraderie, and well-being through rowing.

West Side Rowing Club of Buffalo Inc
PO Box 506
Buffalo, NY 14213-0506, United States
Tel: (716) 881-9797
Fax: (716) 881-3100
Email: Rowing@wsrc.org
www.wsrc.org

BH: West Side Rowing Club
Foot of Porter Avenue
Buffalo, NY 14201
Tel: (716) 881-9797
History: With the purpose of teaching the sport of

Rowing to the youth of Western New York, the West Side Rowing Club was formed in 1912. In 1921, West Side sponsored public High School Rowing in Buffalo, N.Y.. That same year, The West Side Rowing Club hosted the U.S. National Rowing Championship and won its first U.S. title. Since that time, the men and women wearing the maroon and gray of West Side have won many U.S. and Canadian National Championships. From the 1936 Olympics to present, members from the West Side Rowing Club have represented the United States in the Olympics, Pan Am Games, and Elite and Junior Championships.

Western Reserve Rowing Association
PO Box 5221
Cleveland, OH 44101, United States
Contact: Paul Delbane, Boathouse Manager
Tel: (216) 621-WRRA
Email: pjd61@juno.com
www.clevelandrows.org
BH: Western Reserve Rowing Association Boathouse
1948 Carter Road
Cleveland, OH 44113
Tel: (216) 621-9772
Colors: Purple and forest green.
Regatta: Head of the Cuyahoga
Members: 150
Amenities: Guests

Westerville Rowing Club
PO Box 2187
Westerville, OH 43086, United States
Contact: Matthew Chase
Tel: (614) 565-9199
Fax: (614) 259-2001
Email: mchasemd@medtuity.com
BH: Westerville Rowing Club/JCC
East Walnut Street
Westerville, OH

Whaling City Rowing Club
5 Dover Street
New Bedford, MA 02740, United States
Contact: Lucy Iannotti, Executive Director
Tel: (508) 997-4393
Fax: (508) 993-7988
Email: wcrc@msn.com
www.whalingcityrowing.org/

Wichita Rowing Association
335 W. Lewis
Wichita, KS 67202, United States
Contact: Don Wadsworth
Tel: (316) 685-4535
Email: info@wichitarowing.org
www.wichitarowing.org

BH: Wichita Rowing Association Boathouse
129 S. Erie
Wichita, KS 67211
Tel: (316) 685-4535
Year est: 1974
Regatta: Wichita Frostbite Regatta
Members: 50
History: WRA is a local not-for-profit group that has been active in Wichita for over 25 years. Its membership is made up of individuals, many of whom rowed collegiately, who love the sport and want to see it grow in Wichita.
Amenities: Guests, Banquet, Bathroom, Showers

Wide Load Boat Club
285 Babcock Street
Boston, MA 02215, United States
Contact: Rodney Pratt
Tel: (617) 353-9303 x1
Fax: (617) 353-5286
Email: rspratt@bu.edu
www.bu.edu/crew
Year est: 1937
Colors: Scarlet and white.
Members: 40
Amenities: Guests, Banquet, Bathroom, Showers, Ergs

Wilmington Rowing Center
330 S. Madison Street
Wilmington, DE 19801, United States
Contact: Diane McGrellis, Vice President
Tel: (302) 239-0578
Email: lucydane@aol.com
www.wrcrowing.org
Year est: 1984
Colors: White and blue.
Regatta: Christina River Sprints and Diamond State Masters
Members: 150
History: Built new boathouse in 1988. Added third bay in 1995. New Riverwalk built in 2000. **Other Info:** Novice program and experienced coaching available. Rowing tanks available at neighboring WYRA boathouse.
Amenities: Guests, Bathroom, Showers, Ergs

Wilmington Women's Rowing Club
4 Laetitia Lane
Ladenberg, PA 19350, United States
Contact: Marie Peters
Tel: (610) 255-4520
Email: mlp_crew@yahoo.com
Year est: 1998
Members: 50
Amenities: Guests

Wyandotte Boat Club
PO Box 341
Wyandotte, MI 48192-0341, United States
www.wyandotteboatclub.com

Year est: 1875
Regatta: American Heritage River Fall Classic
Regatta
History: The Wyandotte Boat Club is located on the
Detroit River about fifteen miles "downriver" of
Detroit, in the city of Wyandotte. WBC is the largest
rowing facility in the U.S. The lower level of the club
features two massive indoor tanks, a weight room,
ergometer room, coach's office, men's and women's
locker room, five storage bays that can hold over 100
shells and a workshop for repairs. The second level
of the club features a beautiful bar and dance floor
where members can enjoy each other's company, a
meeting room, outside patio and a balcony overlooking the river.
Amenities: Guests, Banquet, Bathroom, Showers,
Weights

Yankee Rowing Club
c/o UMass Crew Club
416 Student Union
Amherst, MA 01003, United States
Contact: Leslie Smith
Tel: (413) 545-3089
Fax: (413) 545-9419
Email: lesmith@oit.umass.edu
www.yankeerowing.org

BH: Yankee Rowing Club Boathouse
Sportsman's Marina
Route 9
Hadley, MA 01035

Year est: 1986
Colors: Red, white and blue.
Members: 40
History: Founded to provide recreational and com-
petitive rowing to the Pioneer Valley community.
Amenities: Guests

ZLAC
1111 Pacific Beach Hwy
San Diego, CA 92109, United States
Tel: (858) 274-7826
www.zlac.com

Year est: 1892
Colors: Black and yellow.
Members: 400
History: Founded in 1892 by four women whose first
initials form ZLAC. An all-female rowing club with
members ranging from 14 to 90+. Still in its present
location on Sail Bay since 1932.
Amenities: Guests, Banquet, Bathroom, Showers,
Weights, Ergs

COLLEGES AND UNIVESITIES

American University
4400 Massachusetts Ave NW
Washington, DC 20016, United States
www.american.edu
Contact: Ali Samantar
Tel: (202) 885-3050
Email: ayanle@american.edu

Colors: Red white and blue
Mascot: Eagles
Year est: 1990

Amherst College
PO Box 2230
Amherst, MA 01002-5000, United States
Tel: (413) 542-2323
Email: crew@amherst.edu
www.amherst.edu/~crew
Contact: Bill Stekl, Head Coach
Tel: (413) 542-2323
Email: stekl@massed.net

Colors: Purple and white.
Mascot: Lord Jeffs
Year est: 1870 (M), 1967 (W)
Championship Regatta: NE Championships
History: In the past three years Amherst Crew has
emerged as one of the top small college programs in
New England. Every senior on last year's team grad-
uated as a decorated athlete. We train hard, and
expect success; usually, we're pleased with our
results.

Armstrong Atlantic State College
11935 Abercorn
Savannah, GA 31419, United States
www.armstrong.edu
Contact: Mike Johnson
Tel: (912) 441-6623
Email: aasurec@mail.armstrong.edu

Colors: Maroon and gold.
Mascot: Pirates
Championship Regatta: Dad Vail
History: The AASU Crew has been organized since
1995 and attendance has increased each year.
Although we are an intramural club, we travel all over
the southeast and compete in regattas against some
very big programs.

Assumption College
500 Salisbury Street
Worcester, MA 01615, United States
Contact: Steve McKiernen, Men's Head Coach
Contact: Chris Wagner, Women's Head Coach
www.assumption.edu/dept/Athletics/crew/CREW

Colors: Blue and white.
Mascot: Greyhounds
Year est: 1966 (M), 1966 (W)

Auburn University
Recreational Services Office
204 Student Activities Center
Auburn, AL 36849, United States
Contact: Matt Elder
Tel: (334) 502-1344
Email: Solbutte@aol.com
Contact: Paul Howard
Tel: (334) 502-7095
Email: Howarpb@auburn.edu
www.auburn.edu/student_info/rowing

Colors: Burnt orange and navy blue.
Mascot: Tigers
Year est: 1992
History: The Auburn University Rowing Club has been in existence since 1991. The rowing program is a club sport that is growing in popularity. Practices are held on beautiful Lake Sagahatchee, approximately 10 minutes from campus.

Augusta State University
2500 Walton Way
Augusta, GA 30904-2200, United States
www.aug.edu/rowing
Contact: Andy Hauger, Academic Advisor
Tel: (706) 736-3323
BH Augusta Rowing Club Boathouse
101 Riverfront Drive
Augusta, GA 30901
Tel: (706) 821-2875

Colors: Royal blue and white.
Mascot: Jaguars
Year est: 1989
Championship Regatta: SIRA
History: The Augusta State University Rowing Team, organized in 1988, is a collegiate level club sport. Members of the team row for fun and skill development, participating in a variety of collegiate regattas.

Augustana College
639 38th Street
Rock Island, IL 61201-2296, United States
www.augustana.edu/sports/clubsports/crew
Contact: David R Weaver, Head Coach
Email: davidrweaver@hotmail.com

Colors: Blue and gold.
Mascot: Vikings
Year est: 1989
History: Started by a first-year student in the Fall of 1998.

Barry University
11300 NE 2nd Ave
Miami Shores, FL 33161-6695, United States
Tel: (305) 899-3668
www.barry.edu
Contact: Paul Mokha, Women's Head Coach
Tel: (305) 899-3568

Fax: (305) 899-3556
Email: pmokha@mail.barry.edu
Mascot: Buccaneers
Year est: 1993
Scholarships: Women

Bates College
130 Central Avenue
Lewiston, ME 04240, United States
Contact: Andrew G Carter, Head Coach
Tel: (207) 786-6363
Fax: (207) 786-8232
Email: acarter@bates.edu
www.bates.edu/rowing.xml

Colors: Garnet, white, and black
Mascot: Bobcat
Year est: 1982
Championship Regatta: NESCAC, NERC, ECAC

Baylor University
PO Box 97406
Waco, TX 76798, United States
Contact: Nick Seeman, Head Coach
Tel: (254) 723-6547
Email: Nick_Seeman@baylor.edu
www.baylor.edu/rowing

Colors: Green and gold
Mascot: Bears
Year est: 1997

Boston College
Conte Forum
140 Commonwealth Avenue
Chestnut Hill, MA 02467, United States
Contact: MJ Curry, Men's Head Coach
Email: curryma@bc.edu
www.bc.edu/ba_org/svp/st_org/bccrew
Contact: Steve Fiske, Women's Head Coach
Tel: (617) 552-2518
Fax: (617) 552-4930
Email: bc.rowing@bc.edu
bceagles.ocsn.com

Year est: 1987
Colors: Maroon and gold.
Mascot: Eagles

Boston University
285 Babcock Street
Boston, MA 02215, United States

Colors: Scarlet and white
Mascot: Terrier
Contact: Rodney Pratt, Men's Head Coach
Tel: (617) 353-9303 x1
Fax: (617) 353-5286
Email: rspratt@bu.edu
web.bu.edu/crew
Contact: Holly Hatton, Women's Head Coach

Tel: (617) 353-5796
Email: hhatton@bu.edu
bu.edu/athletics/rowing/women/index.html
Year est: 1937 (M), 1974 (W)
Championship Regatta: EARC, Eastern Sprints, NCAA
History: Boston University Men's Crew recruits from high school and junior rowing programs all over the world. We have had rowers/scullers from all 50 states, Canada, Europe, South America, Asia, Africa, and Australia.

Scholarships: Men, Women

Bowdoin College
9000 College Station
Athletic Department
Brunswick, ME 04011, United States
www.bodwoin.edu/athletics
Contact: Gil Birney, Men's and Women's Head Coach
Tel: (207) 829-6256
Fax: (207) 829-2744
Email: gbirney@bowdoin.edu

Colors: Black and white.
Mascot: Polar Bear
Year est: 1985
www.bodwoin.edu/athletics
Championship Regatta: New England Championships, Dad Vail
History: Men's New England Championships: 1999 Bronze, 2000 Gold, 2001 Gold. Women's New England Championships: 1999 Bronze, 2000 Gold, 2001 Gold Medal. Women's Dad Vail: 2000 Gold, 2001 Gold.

Bowling Green State University
Sports and Recreation Office
Bowling Green, OH 43403, United States
Email: nmast@bgnet.bgsu.edu
www.bgsu.edu/studentlife/organizations/crew

Colors: Orange and brown.
Mascot: Falcons
Year est: 1990
Championship Regatta: MACRA
History: Bowling Green State University Rowing Club has been in existence since 1992. During this short period of time, we have grown from a recreational sport to a competitive team.

Brandeis University
MS 007 Gosman Athletic Center
415 South Street
Waltham, MA 02454, United States
www.brandeis.edu/~crew
Contact: Matt Smith, Varsity Head Coach
Tel: (619) 459-3873
Fax: (617) 736-3656
Email: crew@brandeis.edu

Colors: Navy Blue and White
Mascot: Owl
Year est: 1987
Championship Regatta: New England Championship

Brenau University
Gainesville, GA, United States
Contact: Ann Mahefkey
Email: amahefkey@lib.brenau.edu
www.brenau.edu

Brown University
Box 1932
Providence, RI 02912, United States
Contact: Paul Cooke, Men's Head Coach
Tel: (401) 863-1097
Fax: (401) 272-4630
Email: Paul_Cooke@brown.edu
www.browncrew.com
Contact: John Murphy, Women's Head Coach
Tel: (401) 863-1060
Fax: (401) 272-4630
Email: John_Murphy_Jr@brown.edu
www.brownbears.com

BH: Hunter S. Marston Boathouse
258 India Street
Providence, RI 2912
Tel: (401) 863-1097

Colors: Brown and red.
Mascot: Bear
Year est: 1857 (M), 1974 (W)
Championship Regatta: IRA, NCAA

Bryn Mawr College
101 N. Marion Avenue
Bryn Mawr, PA 19010, United States
Contact: Carol Bower, Head Coach
Tel: (610) 526-7307
Fax: (610) 526-7347
Email: cbower@brynmawr.edu
www.brynmawr.edu/athletics

Colors: Black and gold.
Year est: 1999
Championship Regatta: Dad Vail

Bucknell University
Department of Athletics
Lewisburg, PA 17837, United States
Contact: Stephen Kish, Men's and Women's Head Coach
Tel: (570) 577-1770
Email: kish@bucknell.edu
bucknellbison.fansonly.com

Colors: Navy blue and orange.
Mascot: Bison
Year est: 1982 (M), 1984 (W)

Butler University

c/o Butler Crew Club
4600 Sunset Avenue
Indianapolis, IN 46208, United States
Tel: (800) 368-6852
Fax: (317) 940-9930
Email: info@butler.edu
www.butler.edu

BH: Indianapolis Rowing Center Boathouse
Eagle Creek Park
Indianapolis, IN
Tel: (317) 298-9456

California Lutheran University

60 West Olsen Road
Thousand Oaks, CA 91360-, United States
Contact: Scott Flanders
Tel: (805) 493-3153
Fax: (805) 493-3864
Email: flanders@clunet.edu
www.clunet.edu

California Maritime University

200 Maritime Academy Drive
Vallejo, CA 94590, United States
Contact: Chris Walker, Head Coach
Tel: (707) 654-1245
Email: cwalker@csum.edu
www.csum.edu

Colors: Silver, red and black.
Mascot: Keelhaulers
Championship Regatta: California Collegiate Rowing
Champs
History: CMA placed first at the 1999 California State
Championships in the men's varsity lightweight four
with coxswain.
Scholarships: Men, Women

California Polytechnic University

1 Grand Avenue
San Luis Obispo, CA 93407, United States
Contact: Jason Sullivan, Head Coach
Tel: (805) 756-2923
www.calpoly.edu

Colors: Green and gold
Mascot: Mustangs

California State University, Humboldt

Intercollegiate AThletics
Forbes Complex 142
Arcata, CA 95521-8299, United States
Contact: Robin Meiggs
Tel: (707) 826-4531
Email: ram6@axe.humboldt.edu
www.hsujacks.com/html/wr/index.html

California State University, Long Beach

1250 Bellflower Boulevard
Long Beach, CA 90840, United States
Contact: Mike Vescovi, Men's Head Coach
Tel: (562) 985-7351
Fax: (562) 438-5661
Email: jtims@csulb.edu
www.csulb.edu/org/studentlife/studentorgani

Colors: Green and gold.
Mascot: Hornets

California State University, Sacramento

1901 Hazel Avenue
Rancho Cordova, CA 95670, United States
www.csusrowing.com
www.hornetsports.com/sports/wcrew

Colors: Green and gold.
Mascot: Hornets
Contact: Sam Sweitzer, Head Coach
Tel: (916) 985-7239
Fax: (916) 985-7312
Email: coachsweitzer@csusrowing.com
Contact: Bill Zack, Women's Head Coach
Tel: (916) 985-7239
Fax: (916) 985-7312
Email: wmzack@aol.com
www.csusrowing.com
www.hornetsports.com/sports/wcrew
Year est: 1984
Championship Regatta: PCRC, California Collegiate
Rowing Champs
Men's History: The men's club sport program offers a
competitive team for CSUS students. Its aim is to be
one of the best-run and competitive club programs in
the country.
Women's History: The women's team is a Division I,
scholarship, varsity status program. The team is committed to providing a high quality athletic opportunity
to CSUS student athletes. The program continues to
be nationally competitive and recognized.
Scholarships: Women

California State University, San Diego

5500 Campanile Drive
Athletic Department — Crew Office
San Diego, CA 92182, United States
www.sdsu.edu
www.goaztecs.com
Contact: Zach Johnson, Men's Varsity Coach
Tel: (619) 847-6305
Email: sdsumenscrew@aol.com
Contact: Scott F Steckel, Women's Head Coach
Tel: (619) 594-0650
Fax: (619) 582-6541
Email: steckel@mail.sdsu.edu

BH: Mission Bay Aquatic Center Boathouse
1001 Santa Clara Point
San Diego, CA 92109
Tel: (858) 488-1036

Colors: Black and red
Year est: 1955 (M) / 1973 (W)

Carleton College
300 North College Street
Northfield, MN 55057, United States
www.student.carleton.edu/orgs/crew

Colors: Blue and yellow.
Mascot: Knights
Year est: 1994
History: In 1999 the club was restarted by a student. Practices are held on the Zumbro River, through the Rochester Rowing Club.

Carlow College
3333 Fifth Avenue
Pittsburgh, PA 15213, United States
Contact: David A Volpe, Advisor
Tel: (412) 578-8885
Fax: (412) 578-6668
Email: dvolpe@carlow.edu
www.carlow.edu/crew/crewmain.html
Year est: 1991

Colors: Purple and Gold

Carnegie-Mellon University
c/o CMU Crew
300 Waterfront Drive
Pittsburgh, PA 15222, United States
Donald Webber Plank, Head Coach
Tel: (412) 377-5203
Email: dwebberplank@hotmail.com
www.cmu.edu/athletic/index1.html
www.contrib.andrew.cmu.edu/~ur0w

Colors: Cardinal, white and gray.
Mascot: Tartans
Year est: 1987
Championship Regatta: Dad Vail

Case Western Reserve University
10900 Euclid Avenue
Cleveland, OH 44106, United States
Contact: Tim A Marcovy, Head Coach
Tel: (216) 932-2776
Fax: (216) 241-6031
Email: tmarcovy@sbcglobal.com
Chris Sheridan, Women's Head Coach
Tel: (216) 932-2776
Fax: (216) 241-6031
Email: c.sheridan1@worldnet.att.net
crewmaster@cwru.edu
crew.cwru.edu

Colors: Blue and white.
Mascot: Spartans
Year est: 1991
History: CWRU Crew Club is a student run organization, and is a member of the CWRU Sports Club Council. We use the Western Reserve Rowing Association boathouse as our base of operations.

Catholic University
200 University Center West
Washington, DC 20064, United States
Contact: John D Dziedzic, Men's Head Coach
Tel: (703) 920-2150
Email: dziedzij@yahoo.com
Bridgette Stewart, Women's Head Coach
Tel: (703) 920-2150
rowing.cua.edu

Colors: Cardinal Red, Black and White
Mascot: Cardinals
Year est: 1990

Cazenovia College
22 Sullivan Street
Cazenovia, NY 13035, United States
Contact: Brian Burns, Head Coach
Tel: (315) 655-7266
Fax: (315) 655-1099
Email: bburns@cazenovia.edu
www.cazcollege.edu

Colors: Blue and gold.
Mascot: Wildcats
Year est: 1995
History: We strive to make our men and women winners on and off the water.

Centenary College of Louisiana
2911 Centenary Boulevard
PO Box 41188
Shreveport, LA 71134-1188, United States
Contact: Allen Eubanks, Head Coach
Tel: (865) 482-6538
Email: coach@orra.org
www.centenary.edu/students/crew/index.html

Chapman University
One University Drive
Orange, CA 92866, United States
Contact: Paul Wilkins, Women's Head Coach
Tel: (714) 744-7976
Email: swrowing@cs.com
www.chapman.edu

Colors: Cardinal and Gray
Mascot: Panthers

Christopher Newport University
c/o CNU Rowing Club
1 University Place
Newport News, VA 23606-2998, United States
Contact: Clayton Comstock, Head Coach
Tel: (757) 594-7100
Email: rowing@cnu.edu
www.cnu.edu/clubs/rowing

Colors: Blue, white and silver
Mascot: Captain
Year est: 2000
www.cnu.edu/clubs/rowing

Clark University
950 Main Street
Worcester, MA 01610, United States
Contact: Karen Farrell, Assistant Athletic Director
Tel: (508) 793-7161
Fax: (508) 793-7627
Email: kcfarrell@clarku.edu
www.clarku.edu/departments/athletics

Colors: Scarlet and white
Mascot: Cougars
Year est: 1941 (M), 1945 (W)
www.clarku.edu/departments/athletics

Clemson University
PO Box 31
Clemson, SC 29633, United States
Contact: Susie Lueck, Women's Head Coach
Tel: (864) 656-4573
Fax: (864) 656-4576
Email: rowcu@clemson.edu
www.clemsontigers.com

BH: Clemson Rowing Boathouse
1 East Bank Drive
Clemson, SC 29634
Tel: (864) 656-6275

Colors: Orange and Purple
Mascot: Tigers
Year est: 1998
Championship Regatta: ACC Championships, Regional Championships
Scholarships: Women

Cleveland State University
c/o Club Sports
2121 Euclid Avenue
Cleveland, OH 44115, United States
Contact: Dan diAngelo, Men's + Women's Head Coach
www.csuohio.edu

Colby College
4900 Mayflower Hill
Waterville, ME 04901, United States
Stewart Stokes, Men's and Women's Head Coach
Tel: (207) 872-3282
Fax: (207) 872-3420
Email: smstokes@colby.edu
www.colby.edu/athletics/teams/crew

BH: Colby-Hume Center Boathouse
Snow Pond Rd./ Route 23
Sidney, ME 4330
Tel: (207) 872-3282

Colors: Blue, gray and white.
Mascot: White Mule
Year est: 1985

Colgate University
112 Huntington Gym
13 Oak Drive
Hamilton, NY 13346, United States
Contact: Fred Cressman, Head Coach
Email: fcressman@mail.colgate.edu
athletics.colgate.edu

BH: Colgate University Boathouse
Frank Road
Hamilton, NY 13346
Tel: (315) 824-1118

Colors: Maroon and white.
Mascot: Raiders
Year est: 1974

College of Charleston
30 George Street
Charleston, SC 29424, United States
James Maestas, Men's and Women's Head Coach
Tel: (843) 953-5559
Email: crsweb@cofc.edu
www.cofc.edu/~crew

Colors: Maroon and white.
Mascot: Cougars
Year est: 1989
Championship Regatta: SIRA

College of the Holy Cross
One College Street
Worcester, MA 01610-2395, United States
Contact: Patrick Diggins, Director of Rowing
Tel: (508) 793-2571
Email: pdiggins@holycross.edu
Tom Sullivan, Men's Head Coach
Tel: (508) 793-2571
Email: tomsullivan@sgdins.com
www.holycross.edu

BH: Irving James Donahue Rowing Center
267 North Quinsigamond Avenue
Shrewsbury, MA 1545
Tel: (508) 752-5501

Colors: Royal purple.
Mascot: Crusaders

College of the Saint Benedict
37 S. College Avenue
St. Joseph, MN 56374, United States
www.csbsju.edu

Colors: Red and white.
Mascot: Blazers

College of William and Mary
Dept. of Recreational Sports — Crew
PO Box 8795
Williamsburg, VA 23187-8795, United States
Contact: Denny Byrne, Director of Rec Sports
Email: wmrcw@warthog.cc.wm.edu
www.wm.edu/SO/WMRC/

Columbia University/Barnard College
Dodge Fitness Center
119th & Broadway
New York, NY 10027, United States
Contact: Scott McKee, Men's Head Coach
Tel: (212) 854-CREW
Email: sm64@columbia.edu
Contact: Mike Zimmer, Women's Head Coach
Tel: (212) 854-2806
Email: mcz1@columbia.edu
www.columbia.edu/cu/crew

Colors: Blue and white.
Mascot: Lions
Year est: 1877 (M), 1986 (W)
Championship Regatta: EAWRC/NCAA
History: Columbia Crew, dating back to 1857, is the University's oldest intercollegiate sport. The varsity crews have been on the Hudson and Harlem Rivers since 1870, and have developed a proud rowing tradition.

Connecticut College
270 Mohegan Ave.
New London, CT 06320, United States
Contact: Ric Ricci, Head Coach
Contact: Eva Kovach, Women's Head Coach
Tel: (860) 439-2557
Fax: (860) 439-2516
Email: edkov@conncoll.edu
www.conncoll.edu

Colors: Royal Blue and white.
Mascot: Camels
Year est: 1972

Cornell University
Teagle Hall
Campus Road
Ithaca, NY 14853, United States
Contact: Dan Roock, Men's Head Coach
Tel: (607) 255-4017
Email: djr16@cornell.edu
Contact: Melanie Onufrieff, Women's Head Coach
Tel: (607) 255-3631
Email: mmo6@cornell.edu
www.cornellbigred.com

BH: Collyer/Robison Boathouses
Third Street Extension
Ithaca, NY 14853
Tel: (607) 277-1861

Colors: Carnellian red and white.
Mascot: Bear
Year est: 1872 (M), 1975 (W)
Championship Regatta: NCAA
History: Crew is the oldest sport at Cornell, holding twenty-four titles.

Creighton University
2500 California Plaza
Omaha, NE 68178, United States
Daniel Chipps, Men's and Women's Head Coach
Tel: (402) 280-1817
Fax: (402) 280-5596
Email: dchipps@creighton.edu
www.gocreighton.com

Colors: Blue and white.
Mascot: Bluejays
Year est: 1977
Championship Regatta: Midwest Rowing Championships
Scholarships: Women

Dartmouth College
6083 Alumni Gym
Hanover, NH 03755, United States
Contact: Scott Armstrong, Men's Head Coach
Tel: (603) 646-2450
Fax: (603) 646-3348
Email: saa@dartmouth.edu
Contact: Molly McHugh, Women's Head Coach
Tel: (603) 646-2450
Fax: (603) 646-3348
Email: molly.mchugh@dartmouth.edu
www.dartmouth.edu/~crew

Colors: Dartmouth green and white.
Mascot: Big Green
Year est: 1860 (M), 1972 (W)
Championship Regatta: Eastern Sprints/IRA, NCAA
History: Rowing began at Dartmouth in 1833 when the oarsmen rowed their sixes out of an ice house on Lake Mascoma. The crews moved to the Connecticut River on campus in 1937. Lightweight rowing was offered in 1940 and women's rowing started in 1972.

Davidson College
Davidson, NC, United States
www.davidson.edu/student/organizations/crew
Contact: Jamie Causey, Coach
Tel: (704) 894-5193
Email: jacausey@davidson.edu

Colors: Red and black.
Mascot: Wildcats

Denison University
Crew Club Box 1497
Slayter Union
Granville, OH 43023, United States
Contact: Emelie Putnam, Club President
Tel: (419) 563-1062
Fax: (419) 563-1009
Email: putnam_e@denison.edu
crewclub@denison.edu
www.denison.edu/clubs/crew

DePauw University
Lilly Center
Greencastle, IN 46135-1772, United States
www.depauw.edu/student/orgs/listings/crew.htm
Contact: John Carter, Director of Rec Sports
Email: jcarter@depauw.edu

BH: Indianapolis Rowing Center
Eagle Creek Park
Indianapolis, IN
Tel: (317) 298-9456

Colors: Old gold and black.
Mascot: Tigers
Year est: 1987

Dowling College
Idle Hour Boulevard
Oakdale, NY 11769, United States
www.dowling.edu/athletics/intercoll.shtm
Contact: Frank Pizzardi
Tel: (631) 244-3019
Email: pizzardf@dowling.edu

Colors: Blue and gold.
Mascot: Golden Lions
Year est: 1988
Scholarships: Women

Drake University
Drake University c/o Crew Field House
Des Moines, IA 50311, United States
Contact: Charlie DiSilvestro, Head Coach
Tel: (515) 271-4995
Fax: (515) 271-1962
Email: charlie.disilvestro@drake.edu
www.drake.edu

Colors: Royal blue and white.
Mascot: Bulldogs
Year est: 1987
Championship Regatta: Dad Vail

Drexel University
3141 Chestnut Street
Philadelphia, PA 19104, United States
www.Drexel.edu
Contact: Lou Renzulli, Head Coach
Tel: (215) 895-2030
Fax: (215) 895-2037
Email: lr22@drexel.edu

Colors: Blue and gold.
Mascot: Dragon
Year est: 1950 (M), 1983 (W)
Championship Regatta: Dad Vail
Scholarships: Men, Women

Duke University
118 Cameron Stadium
Durham, NC 27708, United States
Contact: Robyn Horner
Email: robyn.horner@duke.edu
www.duke.edu/web/crew/main.html
goduke.ocsn.com

Colors: Royal blue and white.
Mascot: Blue Devils
Year est: 1978
Scholarships: Women

Duquesne University
A.J. Palumbo Center
600 Forbes Avenue
Pittsburgh, PA 15282, United States
goduquesne.ocsn.com
Contact: Katie Kirsten, Head Coach
Tel: (412) 396-6565
Fax: (412) 396-6210
Email: kirsten@duq.edu

Colors: Red white and blue.
Mascot: Dukes
Year est: 1986
Championship Regatta: Dad Vail
Scholarships: Women

Eastern Michigan University
Ypsilanti, MI, United States
Contact: Charley Sullivan, Head Coach
Tel: (734) 487-6690
Email: charley.sullivan@emich.edu
www.emich.edu

Embry-Riddle Aeronautical University
Dept of AeroNautical Engineering
600 Clyde Morris Boulevard
Daytona Beach, FL 32114, United States
students.db.erau.edu/~goodwinj/crew

Year est: 1991

Emory University
1175 North Highland Avenue
Atlanta, GA 30306, United States
www.emorycrew.com
Contact: Quinton Gradek, Men's Head Coach
Email: emory.crew@learnlink.emory.edu
Mike McDonald, Women's Head Coach
Tel: (404) 798-5010
Email: mfxmcd1@aol.com

Colors: Royal blue and gold.
Mascot: Eagles
History: Emory University Crew began its road towards success in 1990. Begun as a small, recreational club sport, Emory has graduated many rowers who compete on the national and international level.

Fairfield University
1073 N. Benson Road
Fairfield, CT 06430, United States
fairfieldstags.ocsn.com
Contact: Andre Albert, Head Coach
Tel: (203) 254-4000
Fax: (203) 254-4270
Email: Aalbert@mail.fairfield.edu

Colors: Cardinal red and black.
Mascot: Stags
Year est: 1990

Florida Institute of Technology
150 West University Blvd.
Melbourne, FL 32901-6975, United States
www.fit.edu/athletics
Contact: Casey J Baker, Director
Tel: (321) 674-8291
Fax: (321) 984-8529
Email: cbaker@fit.edu

BH: Florida Tech Boathouse
1216 E. River Dr.
Melbourne, FL 32901
Tel: (321) 724-1884

Colors: Crimson and gray.
Mascot: Florida Panther
Year est: 1969 (M) / 1975 (W)
Championship Regatta: Dad Vail, NCAA
History: Florida State Points Champions over 20 times since 1974. SIRA Points Champions 14 times, Dad Vail Men's Points Champions 3 times.

Florida State University
Campus Recreation
Talahassee, FL 32306, United States
www.fsu.edu
Conact: Chris Campbell
Tel: (850) 321-1968
Email: fsuchristopher@hotmail.com

Fordham University
Lombardi Centre
Bronx, NY 10458, United States
www.fordham.edu/athletics/rowing/index.htm
Contact: Ted Bonanno, Head Coach
Email: tedbonanno@netscape.net

Colors: Maroon and white.
Mascot: Rams
Year est: 1915 (M), 1972 (W)
Scholarships: Men, Women

Franklin and Marshall College
PO Box 3003
Lancaster, PA 17604-3003, United States
www.fandm.edu/departments/athletics/clubs.htm
Contact: Jay Gallagher, Coach
Tel: (717) 399-4406
Email: J_Gallagher@fandm.edu

Colors: Navy blue and white.
Mascot: Diplomats

Franklin Pierce College
College Road
Rindge, NH 03461, United States

Furman University
3300 Pointsett Highway
Greenville, SC 29613, United States

George Mason University
MSN 3A5 Intercollegiate Athletics
4400 University Drive
Fairfax, VA 22030, United States
Tel: (703) 993-3337
Email: prassam@gmu.edu
www.gmusports.com
Contact: Paul Rassam, Women's Head Coach
Tel: (703) 993-3337
Fax: (703) 993-3591
Email: prassam@gmu.edu

Colors: Green and Gold
Mascot: Patriot
Year est: 1996
Championship Regatta: Dad Vail
Scholarships: Women

George Washington University
Department of Athletics
600 22nd St. NW
Washington, DC 20052, United States
gwsports.fansonly.com
Contact: Matt Boyle, Men's Head Coach
Tel: (202) 994-8603
Fax: (202) 994-2713
Email: mboyle@gwu.edu
Contact: Stephen L Peterson, Director of Rowing
Tel: (202) 994-8603

Fax: (202) 994-2713
Email: spetersn@gwu.edu

Colors: Buff and Blue.
Mascot: Colonials
Year est: 1956 (M), 1972 (W)
Championship Regatta: Dad Vails, IRA/ Eastern Springs, NCAA
Men's History: The men's program was started in 1956. Interestingly enough, the coach and rowers would then go on to help form the Georgetown University rowing program two years later. More recently, the men won a silver medal at the 2000 IRA Championships in the Open 4. Aquil Abdullah '95 is the most recent men's alum to race for the US internationally. He won the prestigious Diamond Sculls event at the Royal Henley Regatta and the US National Championships in the men's 1x in 2000.
Women's History: The women's program was started in 1956 and quickly became and still is the largest team on campus. In 1999, they officially became a member of the Eastern Sprints League. Many alumni have gone on to race with the national team at the World Championships and Olympics, most recently Linda Miller '94, Jen Edwards '97, and Michelle Knox-Zaloom '86. Head Coach Steve Peterson was named the Atlantic 10 Coach of the year in both 2000 and 2001.

Scholarships: Men, Women

Georgetown University
McDonough Gym
Washington, DC 20057, United States
www.guhoyas.com
Contact: Tony Johnson, Men's Head Coach
Tel: (202) 687-2360
Fax: (202) 687-3981
Email: johnsont@gunet.georgetown.edu
Contact: Jimmy King, Women's Head Coach
Tel: (202) 687-3156
Email: kingjim@georgetown.edu

Colors: Blue and gray.
Mascot: Bulldog
Year est: 1958 (M), 1976 (W)
Championship Regatta: EARC, IRA/ EAWRC

Georgia Tech
350285 Ga Tech Station
Atlanta, GA 30332, United States
www.cyberbuzz.gatech.edu/crew
Contact: Rob Canavan, Head Coach
Tel: (770) 594-0400
Fax: (404) 607-8565
Email: robc@thechildrensschool.com

Colors: Black and Gold
Mascot: Yellow Jacket
Year est: 1985
Championship Regatta: IRA/ Dad Vail
History: Many successful years medaling at Dad Vail

Gonzaga University
502 E. Boone Avenue
Spokane, WA 99258-0066, United States
Contact: Shawn Bagnall, Men's Novice Coach
Tel: (509) 323-4045
Fax: (509) 323-5787
Email: bagnall@athletics.gonzaga.edu
www.gozags.com

Colors: Red, white and blue
Mascot: Bulldog
Year est: 1981
Championship Regatta: WCC, ECAC / WCC, NCAA

Scholarships: Women

Grand Valley State University
115 Kirkof Center
1 Campus Drive
Allendale, MI 49401, United States
Contact: Chad Jedlic, Head Coach
Tel: (616) 331-2369
Email: rowing@gvsu.edu
jedlicc@gvsu.edu
www2.gvsu.edu/~crew

Hamilton College
198 College Hill Road
Clinton, NY 13323, United States
Contact: Michael Gilbert, Men's and Women's Head Coach
Tel: (315) 859-4069
Fax: (315) 859-4117
Email: mgilbert@hamilton.edu
students.hamilton.edu/athletics/crew/index.htm

Colors: Buff and Blue
Mascot: Continental
Year est: 1983
Championship Regatta: ECAC

Harvard University/ Radcliffe College
Murr Center
65 N. Harvard Street
Cambridge, MA 02163, United States
hcs.harvard.edu/~harvcrew
Contact: Harry Parker, Men's Head Coach
Tel: (617) 495-7775
Fax: (617) 496-4590
Email: harvcrew@hcs.harvard.edu
Contact: Liz O'Leary, Women's Head Coach
Tel: (617) 495-9249
Fax: (617) 496-2709
Email: eholeary@fas.harvard.edu

Colors: Crimson, black and white.
Mascot: Crimson
Year est: 1852 (M), 1971 (W)

Haverford University
370 Lancaster Avenue
Haverford, PA 19041-1392, United States
Contact: Valeria Gospodinov, Head Coach
Tel: (610) 896-1120
Email: val_row@abv.bg
www.students.haverford.edu/crew

Colors: Black and burgundy
Year est: 1996

Hobart and William Smith College
William Smith Athletic Department
Winn-Seeley Gymnasium
Geneva, NY 14456, United States
www.rowhobart.com
www.hws.edu/herons/crew
Contact: Sandra Chu, Women's Head Coach
Tel: (315) 781-3527
Fax: (315) 781-3503
Email: chu@hws.edu
Contact: Mike Guerreri, Head Coach
Tel: (315) 781-3935
Fax: (315) 781-3503
Email: Guerrieri@hws.edu

Colors: Purple, Navy, Orange / Green and White
Mascot: Great Blue Heron
Year est: 1997 (M), 1983 (W)
Championship Regatta: NY States, ECAC, IRA
Men's History: IRA champions in the pair in 1994,
freshman 4+ in 2003
Women's History: Began as a club program in 1983
though the colleges have rowed since the 1800's. In
1993 the women's program was elevated to varsity.
The team has appeared in all NCAA Championships
since 1997 with the exception of two.

Hofstra University
Rm 242 Student Center
Hempstead, NY 11549, United States
www.hofstracrew.org
Contact: Aaron H Ranstrom, Men's Head Coach
Tel: (631) 664 3234
Fax: (631) 226 0629
Email: aaronr99@hotmail.com

Colors: Blue, Gold and White
Mascot: Pride
Year est: 1988
Championship Regatta: HOCR, NY State
Championships

Indiana University
1001 East 17th Street
Assembly Hall
Bloomington, IN 47408, United States
www.indiana.edu/~iucrew
www.iuhoosiers.com
Contact: Joshua Gray, Men's Head Coach
Tel: (812) 856-4485

Fax: (812) 856-5116
Email: jrgray@indiana.edu
Contact: Mark Wilson, Women's Head Coach
Tel: (812) 856-4485
Fax: (812) 856-5116
Email: wilsonmr@indiana.edu

Colors: Cream and crimson.
Mascot: Hoosier
Year est: 1984 (M), 1999 (W)
www.indiana.edu/~iucrew
Men's History: The Indiana University Rowing Club
was formed in 1984 by a small group of men and
women dedicated to the art of rowing. To this day, the
members of the Indiana University Rowing Club strive
to make a reality the dream of the founding members.
Scholarships: Women

Iona College
715 North Avenue
New Rochelle, NY 10801-1890, United States
Contact: Robert E Novak, Faculty Advisor
Tel: (914) 633-2239
Fax: (914) 633-2240
Email: rnovak@iona.edu
www.iona.edu/gaels

BH: The Castle Boathouse
Glen Island Park
Weyman Avenue
New Rochelle, NY 10805
Tel: (914) 633-2239

Colors: Maroon and gold
Mascot: Gael
Year est: 1947 (M), 1976 (W)
History: One of the first sports on campus. Has been
in continuous existence since its inception. Women's
program was established as a club program in 1976,
and became a full-time varsity program in 1994.

Ithaca College
#3 Hill Center
Ithaca, NY 14850, United States
www.ithaca.edu/crew/
www.ithaca.edu/athletics/wcrew
Contact: Daniel H Robinson, Men's Head Coach
Tel: (607) 274-1266
Fax: (607) 274-1185
Email: iccrew@ithaca.edu
Contact: Becky M Robinson, Women's Head Coach
Tel: (607) 274-3145
Fax: (607) 274-1185
Email: iccrew@ithaca.edu

BH: Haskell Davidson Boathouse
3rd Street Extension
Ithaca, NY 14850
Tel: (607) 273-3104

Colors: Blue and gold
Mascot: Bombers
Year est: 1969 (M), 1975 (W)

Jacksonville University
2800 University Boulevard N.
Jacksonville, FL 32211-3394, United States
Contact: Mark Beckenbach
Tel: (904) 745-7470
Fax: (904) 743-0067
Email: beckenbach@aol.com
Scholarships: Men, Women

John Carroll University
20700 North Park Boulevard
University Heights, OH 44118, United States
Tel: (216) 621-9772
www.jcu.edu/rowing
Contact: Christopher DelaCruz, Men's Head Coach
Tel: (216) 401-6389
Email: delacrch@tremcoinc.com
Contact: Michael Kovacevic, Women's Head Coach
Tel: (216) 321-5629
Email: michael.kovacevic@us.pwcglobal.com

BH: Western Reserve Rowing Association
1948 Carter Road
Cleveland, OH 44113
Tel: (216) 621-9772

Colors: Blue and yellow
Mascot: Blue Streak
Year est: 1992

Johns Hopkins University
3400 N. Charles Street
Baltimore, MD 21218, United States
www.jhu.edu/~jhucrew/crewframe.html
Contact: Steve Perry, Men's Head Coach
Tel: (410) 516-7490
Email: rowperry@aol.com
Contact: Lynn Snyder, Women's Head Coach
Tel: (443) 394-6891
Email: lhsnyder@mindspring.com

Kansas State University
12 Ahearn Field House
Manhattan, KS 66501, United States
kstatesports.ocsn.com
Contact: Jim Barnard, Men's Head Coach
Tel: (785) 532-3595
Fax: (785) 532-5707
Email: jbarnard@kansas.net
Jenny Hale, Women's Head Coach
Tel: (785) 532-7899
Fax: (785) 532-1495
Email: jrawson@ksu.edu
Scholarships: Women

Lafayette College
Recreation Services
#137 Kirby Sports Center
Easton, PA 18042-1771, United States

Contact: Richard Laurance, Head Coach
Tel: (610) 330-5821
Fax: (610) 330-5771
Email: laurancr@lafayette.edu
ww2.lafayette.edu/~crewteam
www.lafayette.edu/~crewteam

Colors: Maroon and white.
Mascot: Leopards
Year est: 1970
Championship Regatta: Dad Vail
History: 2002 Bronze Medal, Frosh/Novice Four, Dad Vail Regatta

LaSalle University
1900 W. Olney Avenue
Box 805
Philadelphia, PA 19141, United States
www.lasalle.edu/athletic
Contact: Matt Bergin, Men's and Women's Head Coach
Tel: (215) 951-5090
Email: bergin@lasalle.edu

Colors: Blue and gold
Mascot: Explorers
Year est: 1932 (M), 1976 (W)
Championship Regatta: Dad Vail

Lasell College
1844 Commonwealth Avenue
Newton, MA 02466, United States
www.lasell.edu
Contact: Kristy Walter
Tel: (617) 243-2000
Email: kwalter@lasell.edu

Lawrence University
Memorial Union
115 S. Drew Street
Appleton, WI 54911, United States
www.lawrence.edu/sorg/crew
Contact: Jeff Billings, President
Tel: 920-832-7271
Email: billingj@lawrence.edu

Colors: Blue and White
Mascot: Viking
Year est: 1990
Championship Regatta: Dad Vail

Lehigh University
Taylor Gym
461 Taylor Street
Bethlehem, PA 18105, United States
Contact: Paul J Savell, Head Coach
Tel: (610) 758-4511
Fax: (610) 758-6629
Email: pjs6@lehigh.edu
www.lehigh.edu/~incrw

Colors: Brown and White
Mascot: Engineers/ Mountain Hawks
Year est: 1988
Championship Regatta: Dad Vail

Lesley University
29 Everett Street
Cambridge, MA 02138, United States
Email: svieira@mail.lesley.edu
www.lesley.edu/news/sports/sports.html
Contact: Dale J Wickenheiser, Head Coach
Tel: (617) 349-6690
Fax: (617) 349-6692
Email: crls_crew@hotmail.com

Colors: Forest Green and Gold
Mascot: Lynx
Year est: 1990
Championship Regatta: New England Championships

Lewis and Clark College
Physical Education & Athletics
0615 SW Palatine Hill Road
Portland, OR 97219, United States
www.lclark.edu/dept/sports
Tessa Spillane, Men's and Women's Coach
Tel: (503) 768-7556
Fax: (503) 768-7058
Email: spillane@lclark.edu

Colors: Black and Orange
Mascot: Pioneers
Championship Regatta: WIRA/ NCAA

Long Island University, CW Post Campus
720 Northern Blvd.
Hillwood Commons Box #191
Brookville, NY 11548, United States
www.cwpostcrew.org

Colors: Green and Gold
Mascot: Ocelot
Year est: 1965
History: The CW Post Crew was founded by its first President, Clifford Chabina, class of 1969. It was re-established by Ken Weydig, class of 1999.

Loyola College
4501 North Charles Avenue
Baltimore, MD 21210, United States
www.loyola.edu
Contact: Albert J Rameriz, Director of Rowing
Tel: (410) 617-5671
Fax: (410) 617-2008
Email: aramirez@loyola.edu

Colors: Green and gray.
Mascot: Greyhound
Year est: 1982
Championship Regatta: Dad Vail
History: Loyola Crew started in 1982 and rows from

the Baltimore Rowing Club boathouse along with Johns Hopkins, University of Maryland, Baltimore and Towson. The program became varsity in 1998 and we compete in regional and national regattas.

Loyola Marymount University
Athletics-Gersten Pavilion
One LMU Drive — MS 8235
Los Angeles, CA 90045-2659, United States
Contact: Patrick Kelly, Head Coach
Tel: (310) 338-7624
Fax: (310) 338-5915
Email: pkelly@lmu.edu
www.lmulions.com

Colors: Crimson and Navy.
Mascot: Lions
Year est: 1960 (M), 1974 (W)
Championship Regatta: WCC Championships
Scholarships: Women

Loyola University, New Orleans
6363 St. Charles Avenue
New Orleans, LA 70118, United States
Contact: Jordan Huc
Email: jdhuck@loyno.edu

Lynn University
Department of Athletics
3601 North Military Trail
Boca Raton, FL 33431, United States
www.lynn.edu
Contact: Karla Ward, Women's Head Coach
Tel: (561) 237-7235
Email: crew@lynn.edu
Year est: 2000

Manhattan College
Athletic Department
Riverdale, NY 10471, United States

Marietta College
215 Fifth Street
Campus Box C-65
Marietta, OH 45759, United States
www.marietta.edu
Contact: John Bancheri, Men's Head Coach
Tel: (740) 376-4515
Fax: (740) 376-4666
Email: bancherj@marietta.edu
Contact: Karen Glowacki, Women's Head Coach
Tel: (740) 376-4671
Fax: (740) 376-4666
Email: glowackk@marietta.edu

BH: Lindamood-Van Voorhis Boathouse
Gilman Avenue
Marietta, OH 45750
Tel: (740) 376-8809

Colors: Navy blue and white.
Year est: 1871 (M), 1971 (W)
History: The second oldest program in the midwest after the University of Wisconsin. Won the inaugural Dad Vail, and one of the winningest schools in Dad Vail history. No cut policy; everyone who trains in the program has a place.
Status: Varsit

Marist College
3399 North Road
Poughkeepsie, NY 12601, United States
goredfoxes.ocsn.com
Contact: Tom Sanford, Director of Rowing
Tel: (845) 575-3828
Email: tom.sanford@marist.edu

Marquette University
PO Box 1881
Milwaukee, WI 53201-1881, United States
Email: mucrew@marquettecrew.com
www.marquettecrew.com
Contact: Jim Peters, Men's Head Coach
Tel: (414) 587-5467
Email: james.peters@marquette.edu

Colors: Blue and gold
Mascot: Golden Eagle
Year est: 1990
Championship Regatta: IRA

Mary Washington College
206 Goolrick Hall
1301 College Avenue
Fredericksburg, VA 22401, United States
Contact: Brad H Holdren, Head Coach
Tel: (540) 654-1884
Fax: (540) 654-1892
Email: bholdren@mwc.edu
www.mwc.edu

Colors: Navy Blue, White and Grey
Mascot: Eagles
Year est: 1998
Championship Regatta: Dad Vail, IRA

Massachusetts Institute of Technology
Box 397404
Cambridge, MA 02139, United States
Contact: Gordon Hamilton, Men's Head Coach
Tel: (617) 253-6246
Fax: (617) 324-3200
Email: gham@mit.edu
Contact: Susan Lindholm, Women's Head Coach
Tel: (617) 258-5299
Email: lindholm@mit.edu

Massachusetts Maritime Academy
101 Academy Drive
Buzzards Bay, MA 02532, United States
Contact: Francis McDonald
Tel: (508) 830-6441
Email: fmcdonald@mma.mass.edu
www.maritime.edu

Mercyhurst College
501 East 38th Street
Erie, PA 16546, United States
Contact: Adrian M Spracklen, Head Coach
Tel: (814) 824-3013
Fax: (814) 824-2204
Email: aspracklen@mercyhurst.edu
www.mercyhurst.edu

Colors: Navy Blue and Kelly Green
Year est: 1971
Championship Regatta: ECAC, IRA/ NCAA
Scholarships: Men, Women

Miami University of Ohio
c/o Miami University Rowing Club
355 Shriver Center
Oxford, OH 45056, United States
Contact: Duck Wadsworth
Email: rwadsworth@cnz.com

Michigan State University
312 A Jenison Fieldhouse
E. Lansing, MI 48824, United States
msuspartans.ocsn.com/sports
Contact: Bebe Bryans, Women's Head Coach
Tel: (517) 432-5661
Email: bryansb@pilot.msu.edu
Contact: Bruce L Miller, Men's Advisor
Tel: (517) 333-9612
Email: msucrew@msu.edu

Colors: Green and white.
Mascot: Spartans
Year est: 1956 (M), 1972 (W)
Scholarships: Women

Middlebury College
Field House
Middlebury, VT 05753, United States
Contact: Alex Machi, Head Coach
Tel: (802) 443-3109
Fax: (802) 443-2091
Email: machi@middlebury.edu
community.middlebury.edu/~crew

BH: Waterhouse
937 West Shore Road
Salisbury, VT 05769

Colors: Deep blue
Mascot: Panther
Year est: 1988
Championship Regatta: New England Championships, ECAC, Dad Vail

Mills College
5000 MacArthur Boulevard
Oakland, CA 94613, United States
Contact: Wendy Franklin, Women's Head Coach
Tel: (510) 430-3256
Email: wfrankli@mills.edu

Mount Holyoke College
Kendall Hall
S. Hadley, MA 01075, United States
www.mtholyoke.edu/athletics/varsity/crew
Contact: Jeanne Friedman, Head Coach
Tel: (413) 538-2851
Fax: (413) 538-2183
Email: jfriedma@mtholyoke.edu

Colors: Blue and White
Mascot: Moose
Year est: 1976
Championship Regatta: New England Champs./ECAC

Murray State University
Stewart Stadium
Murray, KY 42071-3351, United States
www.murraystate.edu
Contact: Jenny Hengehold, Women's Head Coach
Tel: (270) 762-3748
Fax: (270) 762-6814
Email: jenny.hengehold@murraystate.edu

New York University
181 Mercer Street
Coles Sports and Recreation Center
New York, NY 10012, United States
www.nyu.edu/athletics/clubs/crew
Geoff Bickford, Men's and Women's Head Coach
Tel: (212) 998-2019
Fax: (212) 995-4591
Email: nyucrewcoach@hotmail.com

Colors: Purple and White
Mascot: Bobcat
Year est: 1990
Championship Regatta: Dad Vail

North Carolina State University
Intramural-Recreational Sport
1000 Carmichael Gymnasium
Raleigh, NC 27695, United States
Contact: George Murdock, Head Coach
Email: ncsurow@yahoo.com

Northeastern University
219 Cabot Gymnasium
Boston, MA 02115, United States
Contact: John Pojednic, Men's Head Coach
Tel: (617) 373-4468
Fax: (617) 373-8988
Email: jpojedni@aol.com
www.gonu.com/mcrew
Contact: Joe Wilhelm, Women's Head Coach
Tel: (617) 373-5226
Fax: (617) 373-8988
Email: j.wilhelm@neu.edu
www.gonu.com/wcrew

Scholarships: Men, Women

Northern Michigan University
1401 Presque Isle Avenue
PEIF Office
Marquette, MI 49855, United States
Contact: Daryl David, Head Coach/Advisor
Tel: (906) 227-2519
Email: ddavis@nmu.edu

Northwestern State University
Recreational Sports Department
Natchitoches, LA 71497, United States
www.nsula.edu/nsucrew
Contact: Alan C Pasch, Men's Head Coach
Tel: (318) 357-5921
Fax: (318) 357-4232
Email: nsurowingteam@hotmail.com

BH: Wolffe Boathouse
Northwestern State University
Natchitoches, LA 71497
Tel: (318) 357-6516

Colors: Purple and White
Mascot: Demons
Year est: 1988
Championship Regatta: SIRA

Northwestern University
2407 Sheridan Road
Evanston, IL 60208, United States
groups.northwestern.edu/nucrew
Contact: Scott Stambach, Head Coach
Email: sstambach@aol.com

Colors: Purple and white
Mascot: Wildcats
Year est: 1982

Nova Southeastern University
3301 College Avenue
Ft. Lauderdale, FL 33314, United States
Contact: John Gartin, Women's Head Coach
Tel: (954) 262-8273
Fax: (954) 262-3926
Email: gartin@nova.edu
nsuathletics.nova.edu/rowing/

Colors: Navy blue and silver
Mascot: Knights
Year est: 2003
Scholarships: Women

Ohio State University
410 Woody Hayes Drive
Columbus, OH 43210, United States
www.ohiostatebuckeyes.com
Contact: Peter Steenstra, Men's Head Coach
Tel: (614) 286-4010
Email: pjsteenstra@hotmail.com
Contact: Andrew Teitelbaum, Head Coach
Tel: (614) 292-6099
Fax: (614) 292-5668
Email: Teitelbaum.6@osu.edu

Colors: Scarlet and Gray
Mascot: Buckeye
Year est: 1996
Championship Regatta: NCAA

Ohio University
Club Sports Office
Charles J. Ping Center
Athens, OH 45701, United States
Contact: Rick Harrison, Advisor — Men's Crew
Email: rowing@ohiou.edu
www.ohiocrew.com
Contact: Mary Stoertz, Advisor — Women's Crew
Email: ko163102@ohiou.edu
www.ohiou.edu/~wcrew

Colors: Black and green
Mascot: Bobcat
Year est: 1995 (M), 1997 (W)
www.ohiocrew.com

Oklahoma State University
220 Athletic Center
Stillwater, OK 74078, United States
Contact: Ben Fine
Email: osucrewteam@hotmail.com

Old Dominion University
192 H&PE Bldg
Norfolk, VA 23529, United States
Contact: Kathleen McNamee, Head Coach
Email: ODURC@hotmail.com
www.odu.edu

Orange Coast College
1801 West Pacific Coast Highway
Newport Beach, CA 92663, United States
Contact: Jim Jorgenson
Email: jjorgens@occ.cccd.edu

Oregon State University
Athletic Department
103 Gil Coliseum
Corvallis, OR 97331, United States
Contact: Erica Schwab, Women's Novice Coach
Tel: (541) 737-2827
Email: Erica.schwab@orst.edu
Scholarships: Women

Pacific Lutheran University
Department of Athletics — Crew
Tacoma, WA 98447, United States
www.plu.edu/~crew
Contact: John Biddle
Tel: (814) 865-9202
Fax: (814) 863-2851
Email: psucrew@psu.edu
Contact: Sarah Halsted
Tel: (253) 535-8504
Email: coachhalsted@aol.com

Penn State University
Club Sports
146 White Building
University Park, PA 16802-3903, United States
Susan Saint Sing, Head Coach
Tel: (814) 865-9202
Fax: (814) 863-2851
Email: clubsports@psu.edu

Portland State University
PO Box 751 — SD/Crew
Portland, OR 97207-0751, United States
Bryan Dean, Head Coach
Tel: (503) 293-1867

Princeton University
Crew Office
Dillon Gym
Princeton, NJ 08544, United States
www.princeton.edu/~crew
Contact: Curtis Jordan, Men's Head Coach — Hwt
Tel: (609) 258-2490
Email: rcjordan@princeton.edu
Contact: Lori Dauphiny, Women's Head Coach
Tel: (609) 258-6373
Email: dauphiny@princeton.edu

BH: Princeton University Boathouse
Washington Road and Faculty Road
Princeton, NJ
Tel: (609) 683-1618

Colors: Orange and Black
Mascot: Tiger
Year est: 1872 (M), 1972 (W)
Championship Regatta: IRA/ NCAA, Light IRA

Purdue University
1089 RSC
West Lafayette, IN 47907-1089, United States
www.purdue.edu/rowing
Contact: David W Kucik, Head Coach
Tel: (765) 494-3120
Fax: (765) 496-1163
Email: dwk@purdue.edu

Colors: Black and Old Gold
Mascot: Boilermakers, Purdue Pete
Year est: 1949 (M), 1974 (W)
Championship Regatta: Dad Vail

Reed College
Athletics Department
235 Wellesley Street
Weston, MA 02493, United States

Regis College
235 Wellesley Street
Weston, MA 02493, United States
Contact: Anna Pepin
Tel: (781) 768-7141
Fax: (781) 768-7152
Email: athletics@regiscollege.edu
www.regiscollege.edu

Rensselaer Polytechnic Institute
110 8th Street
Mueller Center
Troy, NY 12180, United States
Contact: Todd Rutecki, Head Coach
Tel: (518) 276-8113
Fax: (518) 276-8787
Email: rutect@rpi.edu

BH: Island Creek Boathouse
1 Broadway
South Boathouse
Albany, NY 12202
Tel: (518) 852-3368

Colors: Red and white.
Mascot: Redhawk

Rice University
Facilities & Eng. MS 312
6100 Main Street
Houston, TX 77005-1892, United States
Contact: Hannes Hofer, Head Coach
Tel: (713) 285-5347
Email: crew@rice.edu

Richard Stockton University
PO Box 195
Pomona, NJ 08240, United States

Robert Morris University
Sewall Center 2nd Floor
881 Narrows Run Road
Moon Township, PA 15108-1189, United States
Contact: Elizabeth Jones, Head Coach
Tel: (412) 299-2430
Fax: (412) 262-8573
Email: jonesl@rmu.edu

Rochester Institute of Technology
Center of Intercollegiate Athletics
51 Lomb Memorial Drive
Rochester, NY 14623, United States
Contact: James Bodenstedt, Head Coach
Tel: (585) 475-7360
Fax: (585) 475-5378
Email: jcbatl@ritvax.rit.edu

Roger Williams University
One Old Ferry Road
Bristol, RI 02809, United States
Contact: Megan Gallagher
Tel: (401) 254-3091
Fax: (401) 254-3535
Email: mgallagher@rwu.edu

Colors: Gold and blue
Mascot: Hawk
Year est: 1990

Rollins College
1000 Holt Avenue Box 2730
Winter Park, FL 32789, United States
Contact: Shawn Pistor, Women's Head Coach
Tel: (407) 646-2372
Fax: (407) 647-8088
Email: spistor@rollins.edu
www.rollins.edu/athletics/crew/index.html

Colors: Navy and yellow
Mascot: TARS (Sailor)
Year est: 1903 (M) / 1936 (W)
Championship Regatta: Dad Vails/ NCAA
Scholarships: Men

Russell Sage College
45 Ferry Street
Troy, NY 12180, United States
Email: rscadm@sage.edu

Rutgers University
Crew Office College Avenue Gym
130 College Avenue
New Brunswick, NJ 08903, United States
Contact: Steve Wagner, Head Coach
Email: swagner@rci.rutgers.edu
Scholarships: Men, Women

Sacred Heart University
5151 Park Avenue
Fairfield, CT 06432-1000, United States
Contact: John Turner, Women's Head Coach
Tel: (203) 381-9096
Fax: (888) 295-0551
Email: jpt3621@aol.com
www.sacredheart.edu

Colors: Red and gray.
Mascot: Pioneer
Year est: 1996
Championship Regatta: NERC, ECAC

Saint Anselm College
PO Box 403
Saint Anselm Drive
Manchester, NH 03102, United States
www.anselm.edu

Saint Cloud State University
AMC 117 Rowing Club
St. Cloud, MN 56301, United States
www.scsucrew.com
Andrew Donham, Men's and Women's Head Coach
Tel: (320) 230-4312
Fax: (320) 255-4941
Email: rowing@stcloudstate.edu

Colors: Red, black and white.
Mascot: Husky
Year est: 1972
Championship Regatta: Dad Vail
History: Founded in 1972, the rowing club has survived many events that tested the will of its members. We have come a long way from our beginnings with strong accomplishments both on and off the water.

Saint John's College
Box 2800
Annapolis, MD 21404, United States

Saint Joseph's University
5600 City Avenue
Philadelphia, PA 19131, United States
www.sjuhawks.com
Contact: Gerry Quinlan, Women's Head Coach
Tel: (610) 660-1730
Fax: (610) 660-1716
Email: rowing@sju.edu

Colors: Red and Gray
Mascot: Hawks
Year est: 1954 (M), 1974 (W)
Championship Regatta: IRA, Dad Vail/ NCAA
Scholarships: Men, Women

Saint Lawrence University
Department of Athletics
Canton, NY 13617-1415, United States
Contact : Nick Hughes
Tel: (315) 229-5782
Email: nhughes@stlawu.edu

Saint Louis University
801 Hawbrook Road
St. Louis, MO 63122, United States
Contact: Scott Allison, Head Coach
Tel: (314) 965-9456
Fax: (425) 930-6284
Email: swallison@alum.mit.edu

BH: St. Louis Rowing Club Boathouse
Marine Avenue
Maryland Heights, MO 63043
Tel: (314) 434-8299

Colors: White, blue and black
Mascot: Billiken
Year est: 2000

Saint Mary's College
Department of Recreational Sports — Crew
1928 Saint Mary's Road
Moraga, CA 94575, United States
www.stmarys-ca.edu
Contact: Rich Wendling
Email: Rwendlin@stmarys-ca.edu

Saint Norbert College
5951 Allen Road
Little Suamico, WI 54141, United States
Contact: Paula Engelhardt
Email: leier@stsltd.com

Santa Clara University
500 El Camino Real
Santa Clara, CA 95053, United States
Tel: (408) 554-4636
Fax: (408) 551-6045
Email: sshepherd@scu.edu
www.santaclarabroncos.com
Contact: Jay Farwell, Men's Head Coach
Tel: (408) 554-4627
Email: jfarwell@scu.edu
Contact: Stephanie Shepherd, Women's Head Coach
Tel: (408) 554-4636
Fax: (408) 551-6045
Email: sshepherd@scu.edu

Sarah Lawrence College
1 Mead Way
Bronxville, NY 10708, United States
Contact: Carolyn Miles, Head Coach
Tel: (914) 395-2560
Fax: (914) 395-2564
Email: cmiles@sarahlawrence.edu

Savannah College of Art and Design
235 Habersham Street
Savannah, GA 31402-3146, United States
Contact: Scott Nohejl, Head Coach
Tel: (912) 525-4776
Fax: (912) 525-4818
Email: crew@scad.edu
www.scad.edu

Colors: Black and gold
Mascot: Bee
Year est: 1989
Championship Regatta: ECAC
Men's History: The SCAD Men's team is a full Varsity team showing strong finishes over the years in both eights and fours categories. The team faces a myriad of clubs and varsity programs from Division I, II, and III programs. Varsity and Novice boats travel as far west to San Diego and north as New Jersey.
Women's History: SCAD Women represent the only Varsity team in Georgia. Placing well in fours categories and challenging the Division I's in our eights, our regatta schedule is varied and designed to give bid to a national title. Varsity and Novice boats both travel to regattas as far West as Seattle and North to Boston.
Scholarships: Men, Women

Seattle Pacific University
3307 Third Avenue West
Seattle, WA 98119, United States
Contact: Keith Jefferson, Head Coach
Tel: (206) 281-2931
Fax: (206) 281-2266
Email: kpjeffr@spu.edu
www.spu.edu/depts/crew

Colors: Maroon and white
Mascot: Falcons
Year est: 1973
Championship Regatta: NCRC, WIRA, DVRA, ECAC NIRC
History: Club sport 1973 to 1978, varsity 1978 to present. History of excellence hallmarked by the quality graduates and outstanding results.

Seattle University
Student Union Building — Crew Club
900 Broadway
Seattle, WA 98122, United States
Contact: Carlos Palacian, Head Coach
Email: palacian@yahoo.com
Tel: (206) 296-6150
students.seattleu.edu/clubs/crew

Simmons College
300 The Fenway
Boston, MA 02115, United States
Contact: Nikolay Kurmakov, Head Coach
Email: nkurmakov@simmons.edu

Skidmore College
815 N. Broadway
Saratoga Springs, NY 12866, United States
Contact: Jim Tucci
Tel: (518) 580-5391
Fax: (518) 581-7421
Email: jtucci@skidmore.edu

Smith College
Ainsworth Gym
Northampton, MA 01063, United States
Tel: (413) 585-2717
Fax: (413) 585-2712
www.smith.edu/athletics/sports/crew/home.ht
Contact: Karen C Klinger, Head Coach
Tel: (413) 585-2717
Fax: (413) 585-2712
Email: kklinger@smith.edu

Colors: White with Navy and Yellow
Mascot: Pioneers
Year est: 1972
Championship Regatta: ECAC, NCAA
History: Rowing begun with a four on the pond on campus in 1916. Intercollegiate competition began at Smith in 1972. In the past 6 years averaged 5 eights in the spring with 2 trips to the NCAA's and four conference championships.

Southern Methodist University
PO Box 750216
Dallas, TX 75275-0216, United States
Contact: Tim Moore
Email: dgwright@mail.smu.edu
Scholarships: Women

Stanford University
Ford Center/Burnham Pavilion
Stanford, CA 94305-6150, United States
www.gostanford.com
Contact: Craig Amerkhenian, Men's Head Coach
Tel: (650) 725-0748
Fax: (650) 725-4471
Email: craiga@stanford.edu
Contact: Aimee Baker, Women's Head Coach
Tel: (650) 725-0749
Fax: (650) 725-4471
Email: aimeeb@stanford.edu

BH: Stanford Rowing and Sailing Center
1 Cardinal Way
Redwood City, CA 94063

Colors: Red and white
Mascot: Cardinal
Year est: 1896 (M) / 1972 (W)
Championship Regatta: Pac 10/ NCAA
History: The program is centered around student athletes who take pride in their work on the water and in the classroom.
Scholarships: Women

State University of New York at Albany
Campus Center 116
Albany, NY 12222, United States
Tel: (518) 489-0836
Fax: (518) 235-6856
Email: ualbanycrew@yahoo.com

State University of New York at Binghamton
PO Box 6000
Club Sports East Gym
Binghamton, NY 13902, United States
Tel: (607) 777-4883
Email: clubsprt@binghamton.edu
www.binghamtoncrew.com

BH: Hiawatha Island Boat Club Boathouse
Route 17C
Owego, NY 13827

Colors: Green and Black
Mascot: Bearcat
Year est: 1989
Championship Regatta: NY State Championships, Dad Vail

State University of New York at Buffalo
18 Alumni Arena
68C Alumni Arena
Buffalo, NY 14260-5000, United States
www.ubathletics.buffalo.edu/recreation/sports
www.buffalobulls.com
Contact: Margaret Barnes, Women's Head Coach
Tel: (716) 645-7941
Fax: (716) 645-3756
Email: mmbarnes@buffalo.edu

Colors: Royal blue and white.
Mascot: Bulls
Year est: 1999
Championship Regatta: Dad Vail
Scholarships: Women

State University of New York at Geneseo
SUNY Geneseo Crew Club
179 MacVittie College Union
Geneseo, NY 14454, United States

State University of New York at Maritime College
6 Pennyfield Ave Fort Schuyler
Throggs Neck, NY 10465, United States
Contact: Martin Glieco
Email: crew@geneseo.edu

State University of New York at Stony Brook
Stony Brook, NY 11794, United States
Contact: Peter Lee, Club President
Tel: (631) 632-6000
Email: petey3231@aol.com

Stetson University
421 N. Woodland Boulevard, # 8359
DeLand, FL 32723, United States
www.stetson.edu/offices/athletics/crew/index.htm
Contact: Charles Huthmaker, Director of Rowing
Tel: (904) 822-8102
Fax: (904) 822-8148
Email: chuthmak@stetson.edu

Colors: Forest Green and white
Mascot: Hatter
Year est: 1988
Championship Regatta: Dad Vail, ECAC Championships
History: Stetson Crew was started as a club in 1988 and was elevated to Varsity status in 1993.

Susquehanna University
Athletic Department
514 University Ave.
Selinsgrove, PA 17870, United States
Contact: Brian Tomko, Head Coach
Tel: (570) 372-4274
Fax: (570) 372-2758
Email: TomkoB@susqu.edu
www.susqu.edu

Colors: Orange and Maroon
Mascot: Crusader

Syracuse University
Archbold Gym
Syracuse, NY 13244, United States
www.suathletics.com
Contact: Dave Reischman, Men's Head Coach
Tel: (315) 443-4798
Email: dreischm@syr.edu

Contact: Kris Sanford, Women's Head Coach
Tel: (315) 443-2454
Fax: (315) 443-4454
Email: kmsanfor@syr.edu
www.suathletics.com

BH: Ten Eyck Boathouse
Longbranch Road
Liverpool, NY 13090
Tel: (315) 451-1809

Colors: Orange and blue.
Mascot: Otto the Orange.
Year est: 1873 (M) / 1972 (W)
Championship Regatta: Eastern Sprints, IRA/ NCAA
History: Crew started in 1873 and is the oldest sport on campus. Syracuse is one of the oldest schools in the IRA. Now a steward of the IRA with Penn, Navy, Columbia and Cornell. Women's crew started in 1972 and became a varsity sport in 1977.

Scholarships: Men, Women

Temple University
McGonigle Hall — Room 106
Broad & Montgomery Streets
Philadelphia, PA 19122, United States
Contact: Christine Deatrick, Women's Head Coach
Tel: (215) 204-3692
Fax: (215) 204-5254
Email: deatrick@temple.edu
Contact: Gavin White, Men's Head Coach
Tel: (215) 663-8180
Email: grwhite73@hotmail.com
www.owlsports.com

Colors: Cherry and white
Mascot: Owls
Championship Regatta: Dad Vail, IRA/ NCAA
Scholarships: Men, Women

Texas A&M Galveston
PO Box 1675
Galveston, TX 77553-1675, United States
www.tamu.edu
Contact: Marilyn Hughes, Staff Sponsor
Tel: (409) 740-4857
Email: hughesm@tamug.tamu.edu

The Citadel
171 Moultrie Street
Charleston, SC 29409, United States
citadel.edu/icra/clubsports/
Contact: Mary Ellen Huddleston, Dir. Club Sports
Tel: (843) 953-7955
Fax: (843) 953-6798
Email: Mary.Huddleston@citadel.edu

Colors: Light blue and white.
Mascot: Bulldogs/Cadets

Trinity College (CT)
Ferris Athletic Center
Hartford, CT 06106, United States
Contact: Steven Fluhr
Email: steve.fluhr@mail.trincoll.edu

Trinity College (DC)
Athletic Department
125 Michigan Avenue
Washington, DC 20017-1094, United States
www.trinitydc.edu/athletics
Contact: Brad Smith, Head Coach
Tel: (202) 884-9606
Fax: (202) 884-9607

Tufts University
36 Sawyer Avenue
Tufts University
Medford, MA 02155, United States
ase.tufts.edu/athletics
Contact: Gary R Caldwell, Director
Tel: (617) 627-5008
Fax: (617) 629-7612
Email: Gary.Caldwell@tufts.edu

BH: Combined Properties Tufts Boathouse Site
Boathouse
378R Commercial Street
Malden, MA 2148
Tel: (857) 257-3728

Colors: Brown, Light Blue, and White
Mascot: Jumbo
Year est: 1981

Tulane University
Tulane Department of Campus Recreation
New Orleans, LA 70118, United States
Tel: (504) 952-0023
Fax: (504) 862-8211
Email: row2lan@tulane.edu
www.tulane.edu/~sports/Rowing/html
Contact: Bob Jaugstetter, Head Coach
Tel: (504) 952-0023
Fax: (504) 862-8211
Email: ROW2LAN@tulane.edu

Colors: Olive Green and Sky Blue
Mascot: Green Wave
Year est: 1985
Championship Regatta: SIRA, ECAC

U.S. Coast Guard Academy
15 Mohegan Avenue
New London, CT 06320-8104, United States

Union College
Department of Sports
Schenectady, NY 12308-3107, United States
Tel: (518) 388-6483
www.union.edu
Contact: Tom White, Head Coach
Tel: (518) 388-6483
Email: whitet@union.edu

Merchant Marine Academy
USMMA Crew Team
Yocum Family Sailing Center
Kings Point, NY 11024, United States
www.usmma.edu/waterfront/default.htm
Contact: Larry Muri, Men's Head Coach
Tel: (203) 359-4956
Fax: (203) 353-1949
Email: muril@usmma.edu

Colors: Blue and Gray
Mascot: Mariner
Year est: 1970 (M), 1990 (W)
Championship Regatta: Dad Vail

United States Military Academy
Caufield Boathouse
Building 806
West Point, NY 10996, United States
Tel: (845) 938-2177
Fax: (845) 938-5956
www.usma.edu/uscc/dca/clubs/crew
Contact: Stas Preczewski, Men's Varsity Coach
Tel: (845) 938-5811
Email: zs0169@usma.edu

BH: Caufield Rowing Center Boathouse
South Dock
West Point, NY 10996

Colors: Black and Gold
Mascot: Black Knight
Year est: 1985
Championship Regatta: Dad Vail
History: Army started rowing in 1985 with lightweight men and won their first Patriot League Championship in 1991. Varsity Men and Women were added in 1989 and the team has won numerous medals at the New York State Championships and the Dad Vail Regatta since.

United States Naval Academy
USNA Hubbard Hall
Annapolis, MD 21402, United States
www.navysports.com/sports/mcrew
www.navywomenscrew.org
Contact: Rick Clothier, Men's Heavyweight Coach
Tel: (410) 293-3636
Email: clothier@usna.edu
Contact: Mike Hughes, Women's Head Coach
Tel: (410) 293-2419
Fax: (410) 293-5010
Email: mhughes@usna.edu

BH: Naval Academy Boathouse
60 College Avenue at King George St.
Annapolis, MD
Tel: (410) 269-0985
Year est: 1869 (M), 1978 (W)
Men's History: Navy Crew began over 125 years ago when intramural crews raced in craft similar to whale boats. Navy's crews started out with awkward whale boats, but by 1869, the Midshipmen had progressed to what was considered then "standard" four-oared racing gigs which enabled them for the first time to race against outside competition.
Women's History: The sport made its initial appearance at Navy in the spring of 1978 during the second year that women were allowed to attend the Naval Academy.
Scholarships: Men, Women

University of Alabama
PO Box 866964
Ferguson Student Center
Tuscaloosa, AL 35487, United States
www.ua.edu
Larry Davis
Tel: (205) 348-6010
Men's Information

University of Buffalo
Division of Athletics
18 Alumni Arena
Buffalo, NY 14260, United States

University of California at Berkeley
Strawberry Canyon Center
Berkeley, CA 94720-4428, United States
www.calbears.com
Contact: Steve Gladstone, Men's Head Coach
Tel: (510) 642-6196
Fax: (510) 643-1116
Email: grbond@uclink4.berkeley.edu
Contact: Dave O'Neill, Women's Head Coach
Email: dmoneill@uclink4.berkeley.edu

BH: Ky Ebright Boathouse
2909 Glascock Street
Oakland, CA
Tel: (510) 261-4648

Colors: Blue and Gold
Mascot: Golden Bears
Year est: 1868 (M), 1974 (W)
Championship Regatta: Pac-10, IRA
Scholarships: Women

University of California at Davis
140 Recreation Hall
Davis, CA 95616, United States
ucdavisaggies.ocsn.com
Contact: Emily Plesser, Women's Head Coach
Tel: (530) 754-7814
Fax: (530) 752-6681
Email: eplesser@pacbell.net

University of California at Irvine
Crawford Hall
Irvine, CA 92697, United States
Contact: Duvall Hecht, Men's Head Coach
Tel: (949) 683-5152
Contact: Carrie Chamberlain-Parsons, Women's Head Coach
Tel: (949) 824-1377
Email: cachambe@uci.edu

University of California at Los Angeles
PO Box 24044
Los Angeles, CA 90024-0044, United States
Contact: Erinn McMahan, Men's Head Coach
Tel: (310) 305-1637
Fax: (310) 305-1587
Email: emcmahan@ucla.edu
Contact: Amy Fuller, Women's Head Coach
Tel: (310) 206-6828
Fax: (310) 784-2143
Email: afuller@athletics.ucla.edu
www.ucla.edu

Colors: Blue and gold.
Mascot: Bruins
Championship Regatta: Pac-10 Championships
Scholarships: Women

University of California at San Diego
Intercollegiate Athletics ICA 0531
9500 Gilman Drive
La Jolla, CA 92093-0531, United States
crew.ucsd.edu
Contact: Michael Fillipone, Men's Head Coach
Tel: (858) 822-2671
Email: mfilippone@ucsd.edu
Contact: Patricia E Pinkerton, Women's Head Coach
Tel: (858) 534-8452
Fax: (858) 534-8172
Email: ppinkerton@ucsd.edu

BH: Coggeshall Rowing Center Boathouse
1220 El Carmel Place
San Diego, CA 92109-4384
Tel: (858) 488-1893

Colors: Blue and Gold
Mascot: Triton
Year est: 1963 (M) 1976 (W)
Championship Regatta: WIRA
Women's History: Women's program was established in 1976, with a long history of successful lightweight programs. Moved from D-III to D-II in 2001, and the program upgraded to full-time coaching staff, establishing successful heavyweight and lightweight programs, consistant medalists in WIRA Championships.

University of California at Santa Barbara
Student Recreation Center #1110
Santa Barbara, CA 93106-5200, United States
www.par.ucsb.edu/recsports/sportclubs/rowing/
Contact: Rick Brown, Men's Head Coach
Tel: (805) 893-3674
Fax: (805) 893-5973
Email: rowing@par.ucsb.edu
Contact: Mike Homes, Program Director
Tel: (805) 893-3674
Fax: (805) 893-5973
Email: rowing@par.ucsb.edu

Colors: Blue and gold
Mascot: Gauchos
Year est: 1965 (M), 1970 (W)
Championship Regatta: WIRA, Dad Vail, ECAC

University of Central Florida
4000 Central Florida Blvd
Orlando, FL 32816-3555, United States
www.ucfathletics.com
Dennis Kamrad, Head Coach
Tel: (407) UCF-3559
Fax: (407) UCF-4634
Email: dkamrad@mail.ucf.edu

Colors: Black and Gold
Mascot: Golden Knight
Year est: 1972
Championship Regatta: Dad Vail, IRA
Scholarships: Men, Women

University of Charleston
2300 MacCorkle Ave SE
Charleston, WV 25304, United States
Contact: Kevin Gruber, Head Coach
Tel: (304) 357-4829
Fax: (304) 357-4989
Email: kevingruber@cc.ucwv.edu
www.ucwv.edu/eagle/index.cfm

Colors: Maroon and gold
Mascot: Golden Eagles
Year est: 1969 (M) / 1978 (W)
Championship Regatta: WVIAC
Scholarships: Men, Women

University of Chicago
Crew Club
5734A S. Ellis Avenue
Chicago, IL 60637, United States
Contact: Chris Stanek, Head Coach
Email: kris13@uchicago.edu

University of Cincinnati
PO Box 210021
Cincinnati, OH 45221, United States
www.ucbearcats.com
Contact: Tim Royalty, Women's Head Coach
Tel: (513) 556-9799
Fax: (513) 556-2209
Email: tim.royalty@uc.edu

Colors: Black and Red
Mascot: Bearcat
Year est: 1983
Championship Regatta: NCAA
Scholarships: Women

University of Colorado at Boulder
Student Rec Center c/o Colorado Crew
Campus Box 355
Boulder, CO 80309-0355, United States
Tel: (303) 522-6367
Email: programdirector@coloradocrew.org
www.coloradocrew.org/
Contact: Kurt Najork, Men's Head Coach
Tel: (303) 522-6367
Email: knajork@aol.com
Contact: Jessica Terry,Women's Head Coach
Tel: 303) 522-6367
Email: vwomen@coloradocrew.org

Colors: Silver, gold and black.
Mascot: Buffalos
Year est: 1992
History: Colorado Crew is a club rowing program, affiliated with the University of Colorado, Boulder. From late August through mid-May, we practice mornings on Boulder Reservoir and compete in both the Midwest and Pacific Coast regions.

University of Connecticut
2095 Hillside Road, U-78
Storrs, CT 06269, United States
www.uconnhuskies.edu
Email: president@uconnmenscrew.com
Contact: Jennifer Sanford-Wendry, Women's Head Coach
Tel: (860) 486-3848
Fax: (860) 486-1212
Email: jennifer.sanford@uconn.edu

Colors: Blue and White
Mascot: Husky
Year est: 1997
Championship Regatta: Dad Vail
Scholarships: Women

University of Dayton
300 College Park
Dayton, OH 45469, United States
www.udayton.edu/~udcrew
www.daytonflyers.com
Contact: Jim Anthony, Men's Head Coach
Email: udcrew@udayton.edu
Contact: Mike Miles, Women's Head Coach
Tel: (937) 297-0487
Fax: (937) 229-4461
Email: mikemiles@erinet.com

BH: Island Park Boathouse
184 E. Helena Street
Dayton, OH 45404
Tel: (937) 222-4769

Colors: Red and blue.
Mascot: Flyers
Year est: 1991
Championship Regatta: Dad Vail
History: Started in 1991 as a club. Women went varsity in 1999, men remained club, but we still share facilities and some equipment and have done a pretty good job of managing the transition. Both men and women's light eights have been ranked in the top 15.

University of Delaware
Delaware Fieldhouse
Newark, DE 19716, United States
Contact: Amanda Kukla
Tel: (302) 831-0882
Fax: (302) 831-4058
Email: akukla@udel.edu
www.udel.edu/sportsinfo/womens_crew/
gpdl.home.mindspring.com/Index.html
Year est: 1991

University of Florida
Southwest Recreation Center UFL
Gainesville, FL 32604, United States
www.ufl.edu
Contact: Ryan Ludick, Head Coach
Tel: (352) 392-9181
Email: UFCrew@aol.com

University of Georgia
Recreational Sports
201 Ramsey Center
Athens, GA 30609, United States
Contact: Ryan Santurri, Head Coach
Tel: (706) 542-5060
Email: rsanturri@hotmail.com

University of Iowa
219 Carver-Hawkeye Arena
Iowa City, IA 52242, United States
Contact: Kristopher Muhl, Men's Head Coach
PO Box 2111, Iowa City, IA 52244-2111
Tel: (319) 331-2ROW
Email: kristopher-muhl@uiowa.edu
www.uiowa.edu/~uimenrow
Contact: Mandi Kowal, Women's Head Coach
Tel: (319) 335-9259
Fax: (319) 353-5483
Email: mandi-kowal@uiowa.edu
www.hawkeyesports.com

Colors: Black and gold.
Mascot: Herky
Year est: 1977
Championship Regatta: Big Ten, ECAC, IRA
History: Originally Men's & Women's Club Team
beginning in 1977, Women were taken Varsity in 1993
after V4+ took first at Dad Vail.

Scholarships: Women

University of Kansas
115 Allen Fieldhouse
1651 Naismith Dr.
Lawrence, KS 66045, United States
www.kuathletics.com
Contact: Robert Catloth, Head Coach
Tel: (785) 864-3557
Fax: (785) 864-5802
Email: kurowing@ku.edu

Colors: Crimson and Blue
Mascot: Jayhawk
Year est: 1995
Championship Regatta: NCAA

University of Louisville
Athletics @ KFEC
Louisville, KY 40292, United States
www.louisville.edu
Contact: Richard Ruggieri, Women's Head Coach
Tel: (502) 852-7933
Email: rjrugg01@louisville.edu

Scholarships: Women

University of Maryland
1115 Campus Recreation Center
University of Maryland
College Park, MD 20742, United States
www.marylandcrew.org
Contact: John Phillips, Head Coach
Tel: (301) 779-2574
Email: dgc@wam.umd.edu

BH: Bladensburg Waterfront Park
4601 Annapolis Road
Bladensburg, MD 20710
Tel: (301) 699-6204

Mascot: Terrapin
Year est: 1999

University of Maryland — Baltimore County
UMBC Crew Mailbox UMBC
Fieldhouse
Baltimore, MD 21228, United States
Contact: Lou Cantori, Director of Rowing
Email: cantori@umbc.edu

BH: Baltimore Rowing Club
3301 Waterview Ave
Baltimore, MD 21230
Tel: (410) 355-5649

University of Massachusetts at Amherst
416 Student Union Building
Amherst, MA 01003, United States
Contact: Tony Cronin, Men's Head Coach
Tel: (413) 545-0487
Email: info@umasscrew.com
www.umasscrew.com
Contact: Jim Dietz, Women's Head Coach
Tel: (413) 545-9441
Email: jdietz@admin.umass.edu
Tel: (413)-545-0487
www.umassathletics.com

Colors: Maroon, black and white.
Mascot: Minuteman
Year est: 1871 (M), 1972 (W)
Championship Regatta: IRA / NCAA
Men's History: Our club today carries on the long and
successful heritage established by the Aggies of
years gone by. Like those champions of 1871, we
bring to bear the same spirit and dedication to the
Connecticut River.
Women's History: Our goal is to have our women
race at the highest level of our sport.

Scholarships: Women

University of Massachusetts at Lowell
Department of Athletics
One University Avenue
Lowell, MA 01854, United States
Contact: William McGowan
Email: william_mcgowan@uml.edu

University of Miami
Hecht Athletic Center
5821 San Amaro Drive
Coral Gables, FL 33146, United States
Contact: Debra Morgan, Head Coach
Tel: (305) 284-3811
Fax: (305) 284-2703
Email: dmorgan@miami.edu
www.miami.edu

BH: Ronald W. Shane Watersports Center
6500 Indian Creek Drive
Miami Beach, FL 33141
Tel: (305) 861-8876

Scholarships: Men, Women

University of Michigan
PO Box 7164
Ann Arbor, MI 48107, United States
www.umich.edu/~umrowing
Contact: Gregg A Hartsuff, Head Coach
Tel: (734) 604-5611
Fax: (734) 623-8686
Email: uofmcrew@umich.edu

BH: Michigan Rowing Association
1315 Lakeshore Drive
Ann Arbor, MI 48107

Colors: Maize and Blue
Mascot: Wolverines
Year est: 1976
Championship Regatta: IRA/ NCAA
Men's History: Formed in 1976 by 5 people, the program has developed into the most competitive men's intercollegiate club program in the US.

Scholarships: Women

University of Minnesota
Cooke Hall, 1900 University Avenue SE
Minneapolis, MN 55455, United States
www.tc.umn.edu/~umcrew/
www.gophersports.com
Contact: Tom Altnehofen, Men's Head Coach
Tel: (612) 288-0166
Fax: (612) 288-0161
Email: talten@altkie.com
Contact: Wendy Davis, Women's Head Coach
Tel: (612) 625-5588
Email: davis194@umn.edu

Colors: Maroon and gold.
Mascot: Golden Gopher
Year est: 1951 (M), 1974 (W)
Championship Regatta: IRA/ NCAA
Men's History: Established in 1951, the Minnesota men's crew competes throughout the country including: Head of the Charles, Head of the Chattahoochee, Midwest Championships, Dad Vail Regatta, and the IRA's.

Year est: 1974
Women's History: The University of Minnesota women's crew became a varsity sport in 2000.
Scholarships: Women

University of Nebraska
55 Campus Rec Drive
Lincoln, NE 68588, United States
Contact: Frank Dolezal
Tel: (402) 472-1220
Fax: (402) 472-4040
Email: frankd@inetnebr.com
nebcrew@frontier.unl.edu

BH: Campus Boathouse
1000 N 16th Street
Lincoln, NE 68508
Tel: (402) 472-1220
www.unl.edu/nebcrew

Colors: Red and white
Mascot: Cornhusker
Year est: 1969 (M) 1978 (W)
www.unl.edu/nebcrew
Championship Regatta: Great Plains Sprints

University of New Hampshire
Whittemore Center
128 Main Street
Durham, NH 03824, United States
Tel: (603) 862-3902
www.unhwildcats.com
Contact: Brian Mehr, Men's Head Coach
Tel: (603) 862-2074
Email: bmehr@cisunix.unh.edu
Contact: Sue Taylor, Women's Head Coach
Tel: (603) 862-3902
Email: sdtaylor@cisunix.unh.edu

BH: UNH Boathouse
Jackson's Landing
Durham, NH 3824
Tel: (603) 868-2088

Colors: Blue and white.
Mascot: Wildcat
Year est: 1973
Championship Regatta: ECAC

University of North Carolina at Chapel Hill
Box 2126
Chapel Hill, NC 27515, United States
www.tarheelblue.com
Contact: Steve Condrin, Men's Head Coach
Tel: (919) 962-4632
Email: condrin@unc.edu
Contact: Sarah Haney, Women's Head Coach
Tel: (919) 962-8278
Fax: (919) 843-8175
Email: skhaney@email.unc.edu

Colors: Carolina blue and white.
Mascot: Ram
Year est: 1999
Championship Regatta: ACC
Scholarships: Women

University of North Carolina at Wilmington
601 South College Road
Wilmington, NC 28403-3297, United States
www.uncwil.edu

University of Notre Dame
Joyce Center
Notre Dame, IN 46556, United States
www.nd.edu/~ndcrew
Contact: Kurt E Butler, Men's Head Coach
Tel: (219) 283-0708
Fax: (219) 631-4818
Email: Kurt.E.Butler.40@nd.edu
Contact: Martin Stone, Head Women's Coach
Tel: (219) 631-3071
Fax: (219) 631-9690
Email: Stone.14@nd.edu

Colors: Blue and Gold
Mascot: Leprechaun
Year est: 1965 (M) 1997 (W)
Championship Regatta: Dad Vail/ Central Regional
Championships
Scholarships: Women

University of Oregon
Club Sports Crew EMU
Eugene, OR 97403, United States
www.uoregon.edu/~uocrew
Contact: Eric Koenig, Head Coach
Tel: (541) 346-3733
Email: ekoenig15@yahoo.com

University of Pennsylvania
Dunning Coaches Center
235 S. 33rd St.
Philadelphia, PA 19104, United States
www.pennathletics.com
Stan Bergman, Men's Head Coach
Email: lcc@pobox.upenn.edu
Contact: Barbara Kirch, Head Coach
Tel: (215) 898-6283
Fax: (215) 573-6030
Email: kirch@pobox.upenn.edu

Colors: Red and Blue
Mascot: Quakers
Championship Regatta: EARC, IRA/ EAWRC

University of Pittsburgh
140 William Pitt Union
Pittsburgh, PA 15260, United States
Contact: Mark F Bellinger, Head Coach
Tel: (412) 781-3392
Fax: (412) 687-5545
Email: bellinger@peduro.com
www.pitt.edu

Colors: Blue and gold
Mascot: Panther

University of Portland
5000 N. Willamette Boulevard
Portland, OR 97203-5798, United States
Contact: Phil Busse, Head Coach
Tel: (503) 943-7911
Email: pwbusse@yahoo.com
Year est: 2000
Championship Regatta: WIRA, WCC

University of Puget Sound
Department of Athletics
1500 North Warner Street
Tacoma, WA 98416, United States
Contact: Sam Taylor, Program Director
Tel: (253) 879-3538
Fax: (253) 879-3634
Email: upscrewcoach@juno.com
www.ups.edu/athletics/crew

Colors: Maroon and White
Mascot: Logger
Year est: 1964 (M), 1997 (W)
Championship Regatta: WIRA/ NCAA

University of Rhode Island
Department of Athletics
Kingston, RI 02881, United States
gorhody.ocsn.com
Contact: Julia Chilicki, Women's Head Coach
Tel: (401) 874-7895
Fax: (401) 874-5354
Email: rhodyrowing@uri.edu

University of Richmond
c/o Campus Recreation
Richmond, VA 23173, United States
www.richmond.edu
Contact: Chuck Kelly, Club Advisor
Tel: (804) 662-3572
Email: ckelly2@richmond.edu

University of Rochester
Goergen Athletic Center
Rochester, NY 14627-0296, United States
sa.rochester.edu/urcrew
Contact: Bill McLean, Men's and Women's Head
Coach
Tel: (585) 275-5596
Fax: (585) 461-5081
Email: bmcl_urcrew@yahoo.com

Colors: Navy and yellow.
Mascot: Yellowjacket
Year est: 1981
Championship Regatta: IRA, Dad Vail

University of Saint Thomas
2115 Summit Avenue
St. Paul, MN 55105-1096, United States

University of San Diego
5998 Alcala Park
San Diego, CA 92110-2492, United States
www.usdtoreros.com
Contact: Brooks Dagman, Men's Head Coach
Tel: (619) 260-2261
Email: bdagman@sandiego.edu
Contact: Leeanne Crain, Women's Head Coach
Tel: (619) 260-5923
Fax: (619) 269-2213
Email: lcrain@sandiego.edu

Colors: Columbia blue, navy and white.
Mascot: Toreros
Year est: 1978
Championship Regatta: WCC, WIRA
History: Founded in 1978. We aim to teach student-
athletes how to strive for and achieve excellence.

University of South Dakota
Student Recreation and Athletics
414 E. Clark Street
Vermillion, SD 57069, United States

University of Southern California
3501 Watt Way
203A Heritage Hall
Los Angeles, CA 90089-0602, United States
Zenon B Babraj, Director of Rowing
Tel: (213) 740-3830
Fax: (213) 740-1306
Email: zbabraj@usc.edu www.usctrojans.com
usctrojans.ocsn.com

Colors: Cardinal and Gold
Mascot: Trojans
Year est: 1976
Championship Regatta: NCAA, Pac-10
Scholarships: Women

University of Tampa
401 West Kennedy Boulevard
Tampa, FL 33606, United States

University of Tennessee at Chattanooga
EHLS Department #6606
615 McCallie Avenue
Chattanooga, TN 37403, United States
Robert D Espeseth, Rowing Coordinator
Tel: (423) 755-5333
Fax: (423) 755-4457
Email: robert-espeseth@utc.edu www.utc.edu

Colors: Blue and gold.
Mascot: Mocking Bird
Year est: 1984
Championship Regatta: SIRA, Dad Vail
History: UTC is a club sport open to any UTC students.
There are no fees or dues.

University of Tennessee at Knoxville
117 Stokely Athletic Center
Knoxville, TN 37996-3110, United States
Tel: (865) 974-8192
Fax: (865) 974-8914
www.utladyvols.com
Lisa Glenn, Head Coach
Tel: (865) 974-8192
Fax: (865) 974-8914
Email: lglenn@utk.edu

BH: Lady Vol Boathouse
900 Neyland Drive
Knoxville, TN 37916
Tel: (865) 544-1954

Colors: Orange and White.
Mascot: Volunteers/Smokey
Year est: 1995
Championship Regatta: NCAA
Scholarships: Women

University of Texas at Austin
324 Bellmont Hall
Austin, TX 78712, United States
Carie Graves, Women's Head Coach
Tel: (512) 232-2585
Fax: (512) 232-5467
Email: cgraves@athletics.utexas.edu
www.utexas.edu
www.utexas.edu/students/txcrew

Colors: Burnt Orange
Mascot: Longhorns
Year est: 1986
Championship Regatta: NCAA
Scholarships: Women

University of the South
735 University Avenue
Sewanee, TN 37383, United States

University of Tulsa
600 S. College Avenue
Tulsa, OK 74104, United States
www.tulsahurricane.com
Contact: Kevin Harris, Women's Head Coach
Tel: (918) 631-2971
Fax: (918) 631-2127
Email: kevin-harris@utulsa.edu

BH: Tulsa Rowing Club Boathouse
715 W 21st Street
Tulsa, OK 74107
Tel: (918) 599-8115

Colors: Royal blue and old gold.
Mascot: Golden Hurricane
Year est: 1997
Scholarships: Women

University of Vermont
SGA — Billings Student Center
Burlington, VT 05405, United States
Tel: (802) 656-2056
Email: crew@zoo.uvm.edu
www.uvm.edu
Contact: Stephen dePasquale, Men's Head Coach
Tel: (401) 294-2938
Email: stephend@engelberth.com
Contact: Rick Kelliher, Women's Head Coach
Tel: (802) 656-2056
Email: crew@zoo.uvm.edu

University of Virginia
PO Box 400852
Mccue Center
Charlottesville, VA 22904-4852, United States
www.virginiasports.com
www.virginiarowing.org
Contact: Anthony Kilbridge, Men's Head Coach
Tel: (434) 982-5681
Email: aek3f@virginia.edu
Contact: Kevin A Sauer, Women's Head Coach
Tel: (434) 982-5827
Fax: (434) 982-4926
Email: sauer@virginia.edu

BH: Thomas Temple Allan Boathouse
276 Woodlands Road
Charlottesville, VA 22901
Tel: (434) 975-2739

Colors: Navy blue and orange
Mascot: Cavaliers
Year est: 1967
Championship Regatta: Dad Vail/EAWRC
Scholarships: Women

University of Washington
Box 354080
Seattle, WA 98195, United States
Tel: (206) 543-2136
Fax: (206) 616-3082
Email: ernrow@u.washington.edu
www.gohuskies.com
Bob Ernst, Director of Rowing
Tel: (206) 543-2136
Fax: (206) 616-3082
Email: ernrow@u.washington.edu

Colors: Blue and white.
Mascot: Husky
Year est: 1903 (M) / 1975 (W)
Championship Regatta: IRA/ NCAA
History: IRA Varsity Eight in the top four for the past ten years. In 1997 won the Varsity, JV and Freshman eights at IRA. The women have won more national championships in the last 25 years than any other school.
Scholarships: Women

University of Wisconsin at Madison
1440 Monroe Street
Madison, WI 53711, United States
www.uwbadgers.com
Contact: Chris Clark, Men's Head Coach
Tel: (608) 262-8521
Email: chc@athletics.wisc.edu
Contact: Mary L Browning, Women's Head Coach
Tel: (608) 263-6422
Fax: (608) 263-7849
Email: mlb@athletics.wisc.edu

Colors: Red
Mascot: Badger
Championship Regatta: IRA/ NCAA
Scholarships: Women

Vanderbilt University
PO Box 7083 Station B
Nashville, TN 37235, United States
www.vanderbilt.edu/Crew

Vassar College
Box 750
124 Raymond Avenue
Poughkeepsie, NY 12604, United States

Villanova University
Jake Nevin Field House
800 Lancaster Avenue
Villanova, PA 19085, United States
www.villanovarowing.com
Contact: Jack F St. Clair, Women's Head Coach
Tel: (610) 519-4568
Email: jack.stclair@villanova.edu

BH: Villanova University Boathouse
601 Washington Avenue
Conshohocken, PA 19428
Tel: (484) 530-0849

Colors: Blue and White
Mascot: Wildcat
Year est: 1964 (M), 1978 (W)
Championship Regatta: Dad Vail

Virginia Polytechnic Inst. and State Univ.
142 McComas Hall
Blacksburg, VA 24061, United States
Contact: Dave Shuster
Tel: (540) 552-0736
Email: vtcrew@vt.edu

Wabash College
PO Box 352
Crawfordsville, IN 47933, United States
Michael Molde, Club Contact
Email: moldem@wabash.edu

BH: Indianapolis Rowing Center Boathouse
Eagle Creek Park
Indianapolis, IN
Tel: (317) 298-9456

Washington College
Athletic Department
300 Washington Ave
Chestertown, MD 21620, United States
Michael L Davenport, Head Coach
Tel: (410) 778-7226
Fax: (410) 778-7741
Email: mdavenport2@washcoll.edu
athletics.washcoll.edu/mrowing
athletics.washcoll.edu/wrowing

Colors: Red, black and white
Mascot: Sho'men
Year est: 1968 (M), 1972 (W)
Championship Regatta: Dad Vail/ NCAA

Washington State University
Bohler Gym, Colorado Avenue
PO Box 641602
Pullman, WA 99164-1602, United States
Jane LaRiviere, Women's Head Coach
Tel: (509) 335-0320
Fax: (509) 335-0328
wsucougars.ocsn.com

Colors: Crimson and Gray
Mascot: Cougar
Year est: 1974
Championship Regatta: PAC-10
Scholarships: Women

Washington University, St Louis
One Brookings Dr. box 1067
330 Big Bend
St. Louis, MO 63130, United States
Contact: Cameron Carter, Head Coach
Tel: (314) 935-4496
Email: carter@athletics.wustl.edu

Colors: Red and Green.
Mascot: Bears
Year est: 1983
Championship Regatta: Dad Vail

Wellesley College
Keohane Sports Center
Wellesley, MA 02181, United States
www.wellesley.edu/Athletics/athletics/crew.
Abby Peck, Women's Head Coach
Email: apeck@wellesley.edu
History: Wellesley was the first college in the country to establish a women's crew team. Since the late 1800's, rowing has been a Wellesley tradition. Both varsity and novice teams compete in fall and spring regattas. The Wellesley campus has a 1000-meter lake where the novices begin rowing. Once they gain experience, the novices join the varsity on the Charles River.

Wesleyan University
Freeman A.C.
161 Cross Street
Middletown, CT 06459, United States
Contact: Phil Carney
Email: pcarney@wesleyan.edu
Contact: Beth Emery, Women's Head Coach
Email: eemery@wesleyan.edu

West Virginia University
PO Box 0877
Morgantown, WV 26507-0877, United States
Contact: Nancy LaRoque, Women's Head Coach
Tel: (304) 293-2300 x5366
Fax: (304) 293-2525
Email: Nancy.LaRocque@mail.wvu.edu
www.wvu.edu

Colors: Blue and gold
Mascot: Mountaineer
Year est: 2000
Scholarships: Women

Western Washington University
Department of Athletics MS 9066
516 High Street
Bellingham, WA 98225-9066, United States
wwuvikings.ocsn.com
John Fuchs, Rowing Coordinator
Tel: (360) 650-7336
Email: john.fuchs@wwu.edu

Wheaton College
501 College Avenue
Wheaton, IL 60187-5593, United States
Contact: Tim P Lindquist, Head Coach
Tel: (630) 752-6196
Email: tim.p.lindquist@wheaton.edu
www.wheaton.edu/Athletics/clubsports/crew.html

Wichita State University
#126 Heskett Center
1845 North Fairmount
Wichita, KS 76260-0126, United States
www.wichita.edu
Contact: Calvin Cupp, Men's and Women's Head Coach
Tel: (316) 978-5285
Fax: (316) 978-3071
Email: calvin.cupp@wichita.edu

BH: Part of BG Products, Inc. complex
701 S. Wichita
Wichita, KS
Tel: (316) 371-7513

Colors: Black and gold.
Mascot: Shocker
Year est: 1974
Championship Regatta: Dad Vail
History: Started in 1974 and lead the first years by Mike Vespoli, the team quickly became a force in the Mid-West. A victory over Yale in a 1976 home meet solidified the competitiveness of the program. The men's team has been a competitive team over the three decades of its existence.
Women's History: Started as an equal sport with men's rowing from the beginning, WSU has a strong history of women's rowing. Highlights include Dad Vail placing: 1982-Gold WV4+, 1992-Silver WV4+, 1994-Bronze WJV8+, 1995-5th WV8+, 2001-4th WLt4+.
Scholarships: Men, Women

Willamette University
900 State Street
Salem, OR 97301, United States
Rodney B Mott, Head Crew Coach
Tel: (503) 370-6655
Fax: (503) 370-6379
Email: rmott@willamette.edu
www.willamette.edu/athletics/rowing

Colors: Cardinal and Old Gold
Mascot: Bearcat
Year est: 1994
www.willamette.edu/athletics/rowing
Championship Regatta: WIRA/ NCAA
History: Began as Club by students in 1992, became varsity in 1994.

Williams College
PO Box 411 Athletic Dept
22 Spring Street
Williamstown, MA 01267, United States
Contact: Peter Justin, Men's Head Coach
Tel: (413) 597-2480
Fax: (413) 597-4440
Email: pwells@williams.edu

Mascot: Ephmen/Ephwomen — Purple Cow
Year est: 1869 (M), 1971 (W)
Championship Regatta: New Englands/ NCAA

Wittenberg University
Springfield, OH, United States
www.wittenberg.edu
Contact: Suzanne Arnold, Men's Head Coach
Tel: (614) 421-1230
Email: arnold.169@osu.edu
Contact: Steve Lopez, Women's Head Coach
Tel: (614) 246-7900
Email: slopez@columbus.rr.com

Colors: White and red.
Mascot: Tigers
Year est: 2000

Worcester Polytechnic Institute (WPI)
1000 Institute Road
Box 2565
Worcester, MA 01609-2280, United States
Contact: Larry Noble, Director of Rowing
Tel: (508) 831-6119
Fax: (508) 831-5775
Email: lnoble@wpi.edu www.wpi.edu
www.wpi.edu

Colors: Gray and Maroon
Year est: 1999
Championship Regatta: New England Championships

Worcester State College
Student Center
486 Chandler Street
Worcester, MA 01602, United States
Tel: (508) 929-8566
www.worcester.edu

Year est: 1971

Xavier University
3800 Victory Parkway
Cincinnati, OH 45207, United States

Yale University
Yale University Athletics
PO Box 208216
New Haven, CT 06520-8216, United States
www.yale.edu/rowing
Contact: John Pescatore, Men's Head Coach
Tel: (203) 432-1413
Fax: (203) 432-7772
Email: john.pescatore@yale.edu
Contact: Will Porter, Women's Head Coach
Tel: (203) 432-1412
Fax: (203) 432-7772
Email: william.porter@yale.edu

Colors: Blue and White
Mascot: Bulldog
Year est: 1843 (M), 1972 (W)
Championship Regatta: EARC/ NCAA

HIGH SCHOOLS/JUNIORS

Agnes Irwin School
Ithan Avenue and Conestoga Road
Rosemont, PA 19010-1042, United States
Contact: Liesel Hud, Women's Head Coach
Tel: (610) 525-8400
Fax: (610) 525-8908
Email: kdaulerio@agnesirwin.org
www.agnesirwin.org

Colors: Blue and yellow
Mascot: Owls

Albany Rowing Center for Juniors
PO Box 857
Albany, NY 12201-0857, United States
Tel: (518) 446-6282
Email: info@albanyrowingcenter.org
Contact: Mary K Hart, Junior Contact
Tel: (518) 446-6282
Email: hartmar@hvcc.edu
www.albanyrowingcenter.org

Alexandria Crew Boosters Inc.
PO Box 3202
Alexandria, VA 22302, United States
Contact: Skip Bea
Tel: (703) 549-7040
Fax: (703) 887-0282
Email: phbea@comcast.net

Annapolis Rowing Club for Juniors
PO Box 4191
Annapolis, MD 21403, United States
Contact: Lisa Van Citters
Tel: (410) 269-0985
Fax: (410) 216-9324
Email: Vancitters@aol.com
www.annapolisrowingclub.com

Year est: 1989
History: ARC began its Junior Rowing Program in 1989. The objective is to provide area high school students with training and experience in competitive rowing before college and as a life sport

Anthony Wayne High School
5967 Finzel Road
Whitehouse, OH 43571-9661, United States
Contact: David Cusano, Men's Head Coach
Tel: (419) 877-0927
Fax: (419) 877-5028

Colors: Royal blue and white
Mascot: Generals

Archbishop Prendergast
401 North Lansdowne Avenue
Drexel Hill, PA 19026, United States
Tel: (610) 259-0265
Fax: (610) 259-3676
www.prendie.com/

Colors: Maroon and gray
Mascot: Pandas

Arlington Rowing Association for Juniors
PO Box 1171
Pleasant Valley, NY 12569, United States
Contact: Paul A Stasaitis, Head Coach
Tel: (845) 223-7418
Fax: (845) 223-3918
Email: wcpdsodcapt@yahoo.com

Colors: Maroon and Gold
Year est: 1955
History: The Arlington RA exists to support the Arlington HS rowing program. ARA provides equipment, coaching and repair services for the high school program along with running a fall and summer program under the Hudson River RA.

Atlanta Junior Rowing Association
PO Box 435
Atlanta, GA 30239, United States
Contact: Hadley Brandt, Co-BoosterPresident
Tel: (770) 751-0701, 667-5522
Email: aebrandt@nuepoint.com
www.ajracrew.com

Atlantic City High School
1400 N Albany Avenue
Atlantic City, NJ 08401-1208, United States
Contact: Dan Daley, Head Coach
Tel: (609) 266-0576
Fax: (609) 264-9256
Email: daleywaves@aol.com
www.acboe.org/acschools/achs/achs.html
alpha1.acboe.org/crew/coaches.html

Colors: Blue and white.
Mascot: Viking
Year est: 1965 (M)/ 1974 (W)

Augusta Rowing Club for Juniors
101 Riverfront Drive
Augusta, GA 30901, United States
Contact: Donna Jannik, President
Tel: (803) 278-0003
Email: donnaarj@aol.com
www.augustarows.com

Austin Rowing Club for Juniors
PO Box 1741
Austin, TX 78767, United States
Tel: (512) 472-0726
Fax: (512) 472-0700
Email: Arcjuniors@aol.com
Contact: Jennifer deHaas, Women's Head Coach
Email: epfoster@uts.cc.utexas.edu
Contact: Frank Sclafani, Men's Head Coach
Email: fsclafani@aol.com
row.cc.utexas.edu/juniors/index.html

Barnstable Rowing Club for Juniors
PO Box 1024
Centerville, MA 02632, United States
Email: junior.women@barnstablerowing.org
www.barnstablerowing.org

Bay City Central High School
PO Box 1144
Bay City, MI 48706, United States
Contact: Scott Hardy, Head Coach
Tel: (989) 893-9116
Email: Advntr2006@aol.com, info@baycityrowing.org
www.baycityrowing.org/crew/crew-001.htm
Year est: 1993

Bay Shore High School
155 3rd Avenue
Bay Shore, MI 11706, United States
Contact: Bill Blackman, Men's Head Coach
Tel: (516) 665-2543
Email: wblackman1@juno.com
Contact: Bridget Burke, Women's Head Coach
Tel: (516) 472-2842
Fax: (516) 968-1270
Email: sunfun516@aol.com

Colors: Maroon and white
Mascot: Marauders
Year est: 1998
Championship Regatta: NYSSRA
History: The team started in the spring of 1998 as a club level program of 20 athletes. In 1999 the sport was recognized by the school district as a varsity level program with a combined boys and girls team of 40 athletes.

Baylor School
PO Box 1337
Chattanooga, TN 37401, United States
Contact: Jack Batt
Tel: (423) 267-8505
Fax: (423) 265-4276
Email: jack_batt@baylor.chattanooga.net
www.baylorschool.org/bs_home.asp

Colors: Red and grey
Mascot: Red Raiders

Beach Channel High School
10000 Beach Channel Drive
Rockaway, NY 11694, United States
Tel: (718) 945-6900
Fax: (718) 474-7682
Email: spock360@aol.com
www.beachchannel.net

Colors: Blue and gold
Mascot: Dolphins

Beaumont School for Girls
3301 North Park Boulevard
Cleveland, OH 44118, United States
Tel: (216) 321-2954
Fax: (216) 321-3947
Contact: Gail Fadel, Head Coach
Tel: (216) 932-3881
Email: gfadel1@aol.com
www.beaumontschool.org

Colors: Blue and gold
Mascot: Blue streaks

Beaver Country Day
791 Hammond Road
Chestnut Hill, MA 02167, United States
Tel: (617) 734-6950
Fax: (617) 566-6628
www.beavercds.org

Belen Jesuit Prep
500 S.W. 127th Avenue
Miami, FL 33184, United States
Tel: (305) 223-8600
Fax: (305) 227-2565
Contact: Rolo DeLeon, Director
Tel: (305) 854-2899
Email: Jfmdeleon@aol.com
www.belenjesuit.org

Colors: Navy, blue and gold
Mascot: Wolverines

Belleville School
100 Passaic Avenue
Belleville, NJ 07109, United States
Tel: (973) 450-3465
Fax: (973) 844-0604
www.belleville.k12.nj.us

Colors: Blue and gold
Mascot: Buccaneers

Belmont Hill School
221 Concord Avenue
Belmont, MA 02478-3026, United States
Tel: (617) 484-1361
Fax: (617) 489-7705

Colors: Maroon and blue
Mascot: Marauders

Berkeley High School
2223 Martin Luther King Way
Berkeley, CA 94704, United States
Contact: Molly Brannigan, Women's Head Coach
Email: mollybrannigan@hotmail.com
Contact: Chris Dadd, Men's Head Coach
Tel: (925) 676-8025
www.berkeleyhighcrew.org

Berkeley Preparatory School
4811 Kelly Road
Tampa, FL 33615, United States
Contact: David D Schumacher, Head Coach
Tel: (813) 885-1673 x491
Fax: (813) 884-4553
Email: schumdav@berkeleyprep.org
www.berkeleyprep.org

Colors: Columbia blue and white.
Mascot: Buccaneer
Year est: 1998
Championship Regatta: FSRA Championships

Berkshire School
245 N. Undermountain Road
Sheffield, MA 01257, United States
Tel: (413) 229-8511
Contact: Steven Orova
Tel: (413) 229-1291
Fax: (413) 229-1034
www.berkshireschool.org

Bethesda-Chevy Chase High School
4525 North Chelsea Lane
Bethesda, MD 20814, United States
Contact: Chris Graves, Head Coach
Tel: (301) 526-4835
Email: cgrave1@yahoo.com
www.bccrowing.net

Colors: Blue and yellow.
Mascot: Barons
Year est: 1996

Bishop Eustace Prep
5552 Route 70 East
Pennsauken, NJ 08109-4798, United States
Tel: (856) 662-2160
Fax: (856) 662-0802
www.eustace.org

Colors: Black and white
Mascot: Crusaders

Bishop Guertin High School
194 Lund Road
Nashua, NH 02061, United States
Contact: Tom Mulstay, Secretary
Tel: (603) 598-8887
Email: tom@charlesriveradvisors.com
www.bghs.org

Colors: Kelly green and gold
Mascot: Cardinals

Bishop Ireton
201 Cambridge Road
Alexandria, VA 22314, United States
Tel: (703) 751-7608
Fax: (703) 751-7948
www.bishopireton.org

Colors: Cardinal and gold
Mascot: Cardinals

Bishop Moore High School
3901 Edgewater Drive
Orlando, FL 32804-2834, United States
Tel: (407) 293-7561
Fax: (407) 295-2012
Contact: Scott Fulkerson, Men's Head Coach
Tel: (407) 332-9173
Email: scott.fulkerson@ci.orlando.fl.us
Contact: Amy Robinson, Women's Head Coach
Tel: (407) 677-4007
Email: ucface@aol.com
www.eteamz.com/bishopmoorecrew/

Colors: Black and gold
Mascot: Hornets

Bishop OConnell High School
6600 Little Falls Road
Arlington, VA 22213, United States
Email: Info@djocrew.org
www.djocrew.org
Contact: Elliott Lane, Head Coach
Email: coachlane@hotmail.com

Colors: Silver and Blue
Mascot: Knights
Year est: 1996 (M)/ 1997 (W)
Championship Regatta: NVASRA

Bishop Verot High School
5598 Sunrise Drive
Fort Myers, FL 33919-1716, United States
Tel: (941) 274-6751
Fax: (941) 936-1753

Colors: Black and gold
Mascot: Vikings

Bladensburg High School
5610 Tilden Road
Bladensburg, MD 20710-1500, United States
Tel: (301) 985-1482
Fax: (301) 985-1479
Contact: Jim Connolly
Tel: (703) 812-5797
Email: jim@anacostiaws.org

Colors: Maroon and white

Blair Academy
Post Office Box 600
2 Park Street
Blairstown, NJ 07825-0600, United States
Tel: (908) 362-6121
Fax: (908) 362-5157
www.blair.edu

Colors: Blue and white
Mascot: Bucaneers

Brewster Academy
80 Academy Drive
Wolfeboro, NH 03894, United States
Tel: (603) 569-7115
Fax: (603) 569-7180
Contact: Seth Ahlborn, Head Coach
Email: seth_ahlborn@brewsternet.com
www.brewsteracademy.org

Colors: Cardinal and navy
Mascot: Bobcats

Brigantine Rowing Club for Juniors
1402 Sheridan Boulevard
Brigantine, NJ 08203, United States
Tel: (609) 266-0576
Fax: (609) 264-9256
Email: BRCrowcrew@comcast.com
Contact: Dan Daley, Head Coach
Tel: (609) 266-0576
Fax: (609) 264-9256
Email: daleywaves@aol.com
www.brigantinerowingclub.org

Brighton High School
1150 Winton Rd S
Rochester, NY 14618-2244, United States
Tel: (716) 461-9670
Fax: (716) 242-5060
Contact: Jeffrey Swing

Tel: (585) 422-4414
Email: jswing1@rochester.rr.com

Colors: Navy and white
Mascot: Barons

Brookline High School
115 Grenough Street
Brookline, MA 02445, United States
Tel: (617) 713-5289
Fax: (617) 713-5287

Colors: Red and blue
Mascot: Warriors

Brooks School
1160 Great Pond Road
North Andover, MA 01845-1298, United States
Tel: (978) 725-6210
Fax: (978) 683-0808
Email: athletics@brooksschool.org
www.brooksschool.org

Buckingham Browne & Nichols School
80 Gerry's Landing Road
Cambridge, MA 02138, United States
Contact: Joe Gill
Tel: (617) 800-2140
Fax: (617) 547-7841
Email: joe_gill@bbns.org
www.bbns.org

Colors: Navy and gold
Mascot: Knights

Buffalo City Honors
186 East North Street
Buffalo, NY 14204, United States
Contact: Dennis Call
Tel: (716) 886-0133
Email: ssdcall@aol.com
cityhonors.buffalo.k12.ny.us/default.html

Buffalo Seminary
205 Bidwell Parkway
Buffalo, NY 14222, United States
Contact: Robert Becht, Coach
Tel: (716) 881-6712
Fax: (716) 885-6785
Email: rjbecht@hotmail.com
www.buffaloseminary.org

Colors: Red and white
Mascot: Sirens

Burnt Hills Rowing Association for Juniors
PO Box 248
Burnt Hills, NY 12027, United States
Contact: Matthew Palitsch, President
Tel: (518) 399-2254

Fax: (518) 399-2254
Email: president@burnthillsrowing.com
www.burnthillsrowing.com/

Colors: Maroon and White
Mascot: Spartans
Year est: 1993

Cambridge Rindge and Latin School
CRLS Athletics — Crew
459 Broadway
Cambridge, MA 02138, United States
Contact: Dale J Wickenheiser, Head Coach
Tel: (617) 349-6690
Fax: (617) 349-6692
Email: crls_crew@hotmail.com
www.cambridge-boat-club.org/crls/index.html

Colors: Black and Silver
Mascot: Falcon
Year est: 2000
Championship Regatta: Massachusetts Public
School State Championships

Camden Catholic High School
Route 38 & Cuthbert Boulevard
Cherry Hill, NJ 08002, United States
Tel: (609) 663-2247
Fax: (609) 663-2247
Email: mikekeough@comcast.net
www.camdencatholicrowing.org

Colors: Kelly green and white
Mascot: Irish

Canisius High School
1180 Delaware Avenue
Buffalo, NY 14209, United States
Tel: (716) 882-0466
Fax: (716) 883-1870
www.canisiushigh.org

Colors: Blue and gold
Mascot: Crusaders

Cape Cod Academy
PO Box 469
Osterville, MA 02655-0469, United States
Tel: (508) 428-5400
Fax: (508) 428-5400

Cape Cod Crew
PO Box 831
Barnstable, MA 02630, United States
Contact: Todd P Kennelly, Coach
Tel: (508) 362-OARS
Fax: (508) 362-Row2
Email: CapeCodCrew@usa.com
info@CapeCodRowing.com
www.CapeCodRowing.com

Colors: Black & Gold
Year est: 1997

Cape Fear Academy
3900 South College Road
Wilmington, NC 28412, United States
Tel: (910) 791-0287
Fax: (910) 791-0290
www.capefearacademy.org

Capital Crew
CSUS Aquatic Center
1901 Hazel Avenue
Rancho Cordova, CA 95670, United States
Contact: Sam Sweitzer, Head Coach
Tel: (916) 985-7239
Fax: (916) 985-7312
Email: coachsweitzer@csusrowing.com
Contact: Dave Hayashi, Women's Varsity Coach
Tel: (916) 985-7239
Email: hayashd@scc.losrios.cc.ca.us
www.capitalcrew.cc

History: Capital Crew is a competitive junior rowing
program based out of the California State University,
Sacramento Aquatic Center on Lake Natoma in
Rancho Cordova, California. Capital Crew is run by
Associated Students Inc. of California State
University, Sacramento.

Carlson High School
30550 W Jefferson Avenue
Rockwood, MI 48173-9780, United States
Tel: (734) 379-9617

Colors: Blue and white
Mascot: Marauders

Cascadilla Boat Club for Juniors
PO Box 4032
Ithaca, NY 14852, United States
Tel: (607) 273-1167
Email: info@cascadillaboatclub.org
cascadillaboatclub.org

CD Hylton High School
14051 Springs Road
Woodbridge, VA 22193, United States
Tel: (703) 580-4076
Fax: (703) 580-4299
Contact: Brian Tassi, Women's Head Coach
Tel: (703) 490-3557
Email: btassi@erols.com
Contact: Michael Heisey, Men's Head Coach
Tel: (703) 491-2207
Email: lightweights@aol.com
www.hyltoncrew.org

Colors: Blue and gold
Mascot: Bulldog

Central Catholic High School
2550 Cherry Street
Toledo, OH 43608, United States
Tel: (419) 255-2280
Contact: Sue Weaver, Membership Director
Tel: (419) 874-5811
Email: sbwpath@yahoo.com
www.centralcatholic.org

Colors: Scarlet and gray
Mascot: Fightin' Irish

Central High School
Ogontz & Olney Avenues
Philadelphia, PA 19141, United States
Tel: (215) 276-5262
Fax: (215) 276-4721
www.centralhigh.net

Colors: Red and gold
Mascot: Lancers

Chaminade High School
340 Jackson Avenue
Mineola, NY 11501-2448, United States
Tel: (516) 742-5733
Fax: (516) 742-1989
Contact: John Callinan
Tel: (516) 742-5555
Email: jcallinan@chaminade-hs.org
www.chaminade-hs.org

Colors: Crimson and gold
Mascot: Flyers

Charles W. Baker High School
29 E. Oneida Street
Baldwinsville, NY 13027, United States
Tel: (315) 638-6001
Contact: Bob Garofalo, Head Coach
Tel: (315) 455-2000
Email: bobbyg24@twcny.rr.com
www.bville.org

Colors: Red and white
Mascot: Bees

Charles Wright Academy
7723 Chambers Creek Road
University Place, WA 98467-2099, United States
Tel: (253) 620-8300
Fax: (253) 620-8431
www.charleswright.com/

Colors: Green, White
Mascot: Tarriar

Chattanooga Junior Rowing
PO Box 11286
Chattanooga, TN 37401, United States
Tel: (423) 622-6846

Contact: John H Fish, Director
Tel: (423) 267-7059
Email: jwilkins@chattrowing.org
www.chattrowing.org

Chattanooga School for Arts & Sciences
865 East Third Street
Chattanooga, TN 37403, United States
Tel: (423) 209-5812
Fax: (423) 209-5817
hcschools.org/csas/

Chestnut Hill Academy
500 W Willow Grove Avenue
Philadelphia, PA 19118, United States
Tel: (215) 247-4700
www.chestnuthillacademy.org

Chicago Youth Rowing Club
601 S. LaSalle, #200
Chicago, IL 60605, United States
Tel: (312) 593-8040
Email: chicagorowingcenter@yahoo.com
Contact: Tim Field
Tel: (312) 656-4497
Email: cyrc01@hotmail.com
www.rowchicago.org

Year est: 1999

Choate Rosemary Hall
333 Christian Street
Wallingford, CT 06492-3800, United States
Tel: (203) 697-2000
Fax: (203) 697-2601
Contact: Tom White, Head Coach
Tel: (518) 388-6483
Email: whitet@union.edu
Contact: Joseph Scanio, Women's Head Coach
Tel: (203) 269-7722
Email: jscanio@choate.edu
www.choate.edu

Colors: Blue and gold.
Mascot: Wild Boars

Christchurch School
Route 33
Christchurch, VA 23031, United States
Tel: (804) 758-2306
Fax: (804) 758-0721
Contact: Timothy M O'Keeffe, Head Coach
Tel: (804) 758-2306
Fax: (804) 758-0721
Email: tokeeffe@christchurchschool.org
www.christchurchschool.org

Colors: Orange and navy.
Mascot: Fighting Seahourses
Year est: 1995

Championship Regatta: SRA Nationals, NCASRA
History: 2000 and 2001 State Team Champions, 2001 NCASRA Team Champions.

Cincinnati Country Day School
6905 Given Road
Cincinnati, OH 45243, United States
Contact: Theresa Hirschaeur, Athletic Director
Tel: (513) 561-7298
Fax: (513) 527-7600
Email: hirschaut@countryday.net
www.countryday.net

Colors: Blue and white.
Mascot: Indians
Year est: 1982

Cincinnati Junior Rowing Club
15 West Central Parkway
Cincinnati, OH 45202, United States
Contact: Todd Jesdale
Tel: (513) 248-8521
Email: tjesdale@cjrc.net
www.cjrc.net

Year est: 1992

Clarkstown High School South
31 Demarest Mill Road
West Nyack, NY 10994, United States
Contact: Mr. Louther
Tel: (914) 624-3448
Fax: (914) 624-2640
Email: vlouther@ccsd.edu
www.ccsd.edu/south/

Clermont High School
6169 Dogwood Ridge
Milford, OH 45150, United States
Contact: Bill Engeman
Tel: (513) 575-3149
Email: engeman@choicemail.com

Year est: 2001

Cleveland Scholastic Rowing Association
PO Box 451462
Westlake, OH 44115, United States
Contact: Tim A Marcovy, Head Coach
Tel: (216) 932-2776
Fax: (216) 241-6031
Email: tmarcovy@sbcglobal.com
www.clevelandrowing.org

Year est: 2000
History: Our club consists of female scholastic age rowers (14-18). We are located in the heart of Cleveland, Ohio and we row on the Cuyahoga River. Our club consists of high school age rowers from several schools, such as, Beaumont High School (Cleveland Hts.), Bay Village High School (Bay Village), Magnificat (Rocky River), Padua Franciscan (Parma), and Hathaway Brown (Shaker Hts.).

Clinton Rowing Club for Juniors
PO Box 1213
Clinton, TN 37717-1213, United States
Contact: Jerry Riley
Tel: (865) 457-9403
Fax: (865) 457-2941
Email: JRiley5131@aol.com

Year est: 1973
History: Several club names since establishment in 1973. Renamed Clinton Rowing Club in 1998, built new boathouse and moved club to Clinton. Boathouse is located in downtown Clinton.

Cold Spring Hrbr Jr-Sr High School
82 Turkey Lane
Cold Spring Harbor, NY 11724, United States
Tel: (516) 692-8796
Fax: (516) 692-8083
Contact: Al Borghard, Head Coach
Tel: (631) 427-6884
Email: joalborghard@yahoo.com
www.csh.k12.ny.us/

Colors: Red, white and blue
Mascot: Seahawk

Community Rowing Inc. for Juniors
PO Box 382604
Cambridge, MA 02238, United States
Tel: (617) 964-2455
Fax: (617) 782-3880
Email: office@communityrowing.org
www.communityrowing.org

Concord High School
2501 Ebright Road
Wilmington, DE 19350, United States
Contact: Marie Peters, Coach
Tel: (610) 255-4520
Email: mlp_crew@yahoo.com

Colors: Maroon and white
Mascot: Raider
Year est: 2002

Conestoga High School
200 Irish Road
Berwyn, PA 19312-1260, United States
Contact: David Grace, Advisor
Tel: (610) 240-1026
Email: graced@tesd.k12.pa.us
www.conestogacrew.org

Colors: Maroon and gray
Mascot: Pioneers
www.conestogacrew.org

Country Day School of the Sacred Heart
480 S Bryn Mawr Avenue
Bryn Mawr, PA 19010-2101, United States
Tel: (610) 623-6551
Fax: (610) 527-0942
Contact: Joe Sullivan, Women's Head Coach
Email: mjdavis1@voicenet.com
www.users.voicenet.com/~mjdavis1/SHRA/

Colors: Red and white
Mascot: Lions

Cranbrook-Kingswood Upper School
PO Box 801
39221 Woodward Avenue
Bloomfield Hills, MI 48303-0801, United States
Tel: (248) 645-3638
Fax: (248) 645-3086

Colors: Navy and Kelly
Mascot: Cranes

Culver Academies
1300 Academy Rd #2
Culver, IN 46511-1234, United States
Tel: (219) 842-8216
Fax: (219) 842-8066
Contact: Guy Weaser, Head Coach
Tel: (574) 842-7042
Fax: (574) 842-8390
Email: weaserg@culver.org
www.culver.org/students/sports/crew

Colors: Maroon, gold and white.
Mascot: Eagle
Year est: 1921 (M)/ 1978 (W)
Championship Regatta: Midwest Scholastic

Deerfield Academy
Main Street
Deerfield, MA 01342, United States
Contact: Joe Harvey, Coach
Tel: (413) 772-0241
Fax: (413) 772-0241
Email: harvey@deerfield.edu

DeMatha Catholic High School
4313 Madison Street
Hyattsville, MD 20781-1692, United States
Tel: (301) 864-2755
Fax: (301) 864-0248

Colors: Red, white and blue

Detroit Boat Club for Juniors
348 Provencal Road
Grosse Pointe Farms, MI 48236, United States
Tel: (313) 642-0555
Fax: (313) 881-2174
Email: lynnesail@aol.com
Contact: Chris Dorman

Tel: (586) 598-1540
Email: dorman@comcast.net
www.detroitboatclub.com/

Dr. Phillips High School
6500 Turkey Lane Road
Orlando, FL 32819, United States
Tel: (407) 352-4040
Fax: (407) 352-4040

Colors: Light blue and dark blue
Mascot: Panthers

Dryden High School
PO Box 88
Dryden, NY 13053, United States
Tel: (607) 844-8694
Fax: (607) 844-9004
www.drydenschools.org

Colors: Purple and white
Mascot: Lions

Dublin Crew
PO Box 764
Dublin, OH 43017, United States
Contact: Greg Harvie, Women's Varsity Coach
Email: gregharvie@dublincrew.org
dcboard@dublincrew.org
Contact: Russ Merritt, Men's Varsity Coach
Email: russmerritt@dublincrew.org
www.dublincrew.org

Colors: Green and white.
Year est: 1991
History: Dublin Crew is established to provide competitive, amateur rowing opportunities — in terms of organization, events, coaching and equipment — for high school age students.

Durham Boat Club for Juniors
20 Newmarket Road
Durham, NH 03824, United States
Tel: (603) 659-7575
Email: info@durhamboat.com
www.durhamboat.com

East Grand Rapids High School
2211 Lake Drive SE
East Grand Rapids, MI 49506, United States
Tel: (616) 235-7593
Fax: (616) 235-8855

Colors: Blue and gold
Mascot: Pioneers

East Lyme High School
PO Box 210
30 Chesterfield Road
East Lyme, CT 06357, United States

Tel: (860) 739-6946
Fax: (860) 739-1241
Contact: Teresa Tucchio
Email: therower@aol.com

Colors: Maroon and white.
Mascot: Vikings

Eastside High School
1201 SE 45th Terrace
Gainesville, FL 32641-7647, United States
Tel: (352) 371-4303
Fax: (352) 955-7291

Colors: Orange and green
Mascot: Rams

Eau Gallie High School
1400 Commodore Boulevard
Melbourne, FL 32935, United States
Tel: (407) 242-6415
Fax: (407) 242-6427
www.spacecoastcrew.org

Colors: Navy Blue
Mascot: Commodores

Edgewater High School
3100 Edgewater Drive
Orlando, FL 32804, United States
Tel: (407) 849-0130
Fax: (407) 849-0130
Contact: Phil and Judy Weaver, co-Booster President
Tel: (407) 859-1321
Email: weaverpjjd@aol.com
www.edgewatercrew.org

Colors: Red and white
Mascot: Fighting Eagles

Edwin O. Smith High School
1235 Storrs Road
Storrs, CT 06268-2287, United States
Tel: (860) 487-0877
Fax: (860) 429-0085

Colors: Red and black.
Mascot: Panthers

Elizabeth Seton High School
5715 Emerson Street
Bladensburg, MD 20710, United States
Tel: (301) 864-4532
Fax: (301) 864-4532
www.setonhs.org

Colors: Red, Yellow and gold
Mascot: Roadrunner
Year est: 1997

Ellis School
6425 5th Avenue
Pittsburgh, PA 15206-4499, United States
Tel: (412) 661-5992
Fax: (412) 661-3979
www.theellisschool.org

Colors: Hunter green and white
Mascot: Tigers

Emma Willard School
285 Pawling Avenue
Troy, NY 12180, United States
Tel: (518) 274-4440
Fax: (518) 274-0923
Contact: Stacy Apfelbaum, Women's Head Coach
Email: sapfelba@emma.troy.ny.us
www.emma.troy.ny.us/

Episcopal Academy
376 N. Latches Lane
Merion Station, PA 19066, United States
Tel: (610) 667-9612
www.ea.pvt.k12.pa.us/

Episcopal High School
1200 N. Quaker Lane
Alexandria, VA 22302, United States
Tel: (703) 933-4043
Fax: (703) 933-3015
Contact: Ashton Richards, Women's Head Coach
Email: AWR@episcopalhighschool.org
www.episcopalhighschool.org

Colors: Maroon and black
Mascot: The Maroon

Episcopal High School of Jacksonville
4455 Atlantic Boulevard
Jacksonville, FL 32207, United States
Tel: (904) 396-7133
Fax: (904) 396-7209
Contact: Cristi Peterson, Women's Head Coach
Tel: (904) 396-5751
Fax: (904) 399-1983
Email: cristipeterson@hotmail.com

Colors: Maroon and Gold
Mascot: Eagles
Year est: 1971
Championship Regatta: Florida State Championships
History: Episcopal Crew is one of the oldest programs in Florida and boasts around 100 participants a year. Episcopal High School is a private school in Jacksonville, FL with about 850 students.

Episcopal School of Dallas
4100 Merrell Road
Dallas, TX 75229, United States
Tel: (214) 358-4368
Fax: (214) 357-1232
Troy Howell, Coach
Tel: (214) 358-4368
Email: howellt@esdallas.org
www.esdallas.org/esd/

Colors: Maroon and gray
Mascot: Eagles

Erie Canal Rowing Club for Juniors
PO Box 4711
Rome, NY 13442, United States
Contact: Gerald Lacy, Head Coach
Email: Larscares@AOL.com
ecrc@borg.com
www.eriecanalrowingclub.com/

Ethel Walker School
230 Bushy Hill Road
Simsbury, CT 06070, United States
Contact: Karen Kromak, Coach
Email: karen_cromack@ethelwalker.org
Tel: (860) 408-4290
Fax: (860) 658-6763

Colors: Purple and gold
Mascot: Sundials

Evans High School
PO Box 130
Evans, GA 30809-0130, United States
Tel: (706) 855-8540
Fax: (706) 868-3720

Colors: Black and gold
Mascot: Knights

Everett Rowing Association for Juniors
PO Box 1774
Everett, WA 98206, United States
Contact: Marty Beyer
Tel: (425) 257-8337
Email: everettrowing@mindspring.com
www.everettrowing.com

F.D. Roosevelt High School
South Cross Road
PO Box 2032
Hyde Park, NY 12538, United States
Contact: Harry Harrington
Tel: (845) 889-4049
Email: hbharri@attglobal.net

Fairfax High School
PO Box 318
Fairfax Station, VA 22039, United States
Contact: William Del Vecchio, Head Coach
Tel: (703) 250-2369
Fax: (703) 249-8991
Email: apache1@ix.netcom.com
www.fairfaxcrew.com

Colors: Blue and gray
Mascot: Rebel
Year est: 1998

Fairport Central High School
1358 Ayrault Road
Fairport, NY 14450, United States
Tel: (716) 421-2112
Fax: (716) 421-2135
Email: fairportrowing@hotmail.com
Contact: Bruce D Weick, Booster President
Tel: (585) 377-0099
Fax: (585) 377-8213
Email: bruceweick@hotmail.com
www.fairportcrew.org

Colors: Red and blue
Mascot: Red Raiders

Father Judge High School
3301 Solly Avenue
Philadelphia, PA 19136-2340, United States
Tel: (215) 331-8831
Fax: (215) 338-0250
Contact: Phil Roche
Tel: (215) 338-9494
Email: proche@fjquest.com
fjquest.com/crew.htm

First Colonial High School
1272 Mill Dam Road
Virginia Beach, VA 23454, United States
Tel: (757) 496-6711
Fax: (757) 496-6719
www.firstcolonialhs.vbcps.k12.va.us/

Colors: Blue, gold and white
Mascot: Patriots

Florida Air Academy
1950 South Academy Drive
Melbourne, FL 32901, United States
Tel: (312) 723-3211
www.flair.com

Forest Hills Central High School
5901 Hall ST. SE
Grand Rapids, MI 49506, United States
Email: crewcoach21@aol.com
www.FHCCREW.org

Colors: Forest Green, White and Black
Mascot: Rangers
Year est: 1995 (M)/1996 (W)
Championship Regatta: Midwest Scholastic Championships
History: The program started in 1995 with 7 boys as a club sport, granted Varsity Status in 2001. The program currently has 33 boys in 2003. Rowed out of the Grand Rapids Rowing Club until 2002 when school district partially financed a new boathouse closely located to the school. There are 2 coaches for the woman's program. Women added to program in second year with approximately 10 girls. Club sport until 2001 when granted Varsity Status. The program has seen continued growth with 65 women in 2003. Rowed out of the Grand Rapids Rowing Club until 2002 when school district partially financed a new boathouse closely located to the school. The woman's program has won the Hebda Cup (Michigan State Champions) in 2000 and 2002, winners of Wyandotte Regatta in 2003 and two medal winners in 2003 CSSRA regatta. There are 6 coaches for the woman's program. Head coach and founder of the team is Don LeBlanc.

Forest Hills Northern High School
3801 Leonard Street
Grand Rapids, MI 49525, United States
Tel: (616) 493-8659
Fax: (616) 493-8626

Colors: Blue, black and silver
Mascot: Huskies

Forest Park High School
15721 Spринggs Road
Woodbridge, VA 22193, United States
Tel: (703) 583-3200
Contact: Eddie Barnette, Booster President
Tel: (703) 441-1743
Fax: (703) 221-3828
Email: fpcrudad@aol.com
www.pwcs.edu/forestpark/crew.htm

Colors: Green and blue
Mascot: Bruins

Fort Myers High School
2635 Cortez Boulevard
Fort Myers, FL 33901-5839, United States
Tel: (941) 334-2167
Fax: (941) 334-3095
Contact: Herb Leonard, Men's Head Coach
Tel: (941) 481-9758

Fox Chapel High School
c/o Three Rivers Rowing Association
90 Riverfront Drive
Millvale, PA 15209, United States
Tel: (412) 231-8772
Contact: Mark F Bellinger, Head Coach
Tel: (412) 781-3392
Fax: (412) 687-5545
Email: bellinger@peduro.com
www.foxchapelcrew.com

Colors: Red, white and black
Mascot: fox
Year est: 1985

Frank W. Cox High School
2425 Shorehaven Drive
Virginia Beach, VA 23454, United States
Tel: (757) 496-6746
Fax: (757) 496-6731
Contact: Coach Evens, Head Coach
Tel: (757) 496-6767
Email: crkstrk@aol.com
www.coxhs.vbcps.k12.va.us/

Colors: Green and gold
Mascot: Falcons

Friends Academy
270 Duck Pond Road
Locust Valley, NY 11560, United States
Contact: Peter Bisek, Head Coach
Tel: (516) 393-4225
Fax: (516) 465-1713
www.fa.org/default.cfm

Colors: Red and black
Mascot: Quakers

Friends Select
17th & The Parkway
Philadelphia, PA 19103, United States
Tel: (215) 261-5900
Fax: (215) 864-2979
www.friends-select.org

Colors: Brown and gold
Mascot: Falcons

Gainesville High School
1900 NW 13th Street
Gainesville, FL 32609, United States
Tel: (352) 955-6707
Fax: (352) 955-7283

Colors: Purple and white
Mascot: Purple Hurricanes

GarField High School
PO Box 1926
Woodbridge, VA 22192, United States
Tel: (703) 730-7137
Fax: (703) 730-7197
Contact: Angela Hart, Women's Head Coach
Tel: (703) 490-1276
Email: ahart@gwu.edu
gar-field.org/sports/crew/

Colors: Royal blue and red
Mascot: Indians
Year est: 1984
Championship Regatta: NVASRA, SRA

George C. Marshall High School
7731 Leesburg Pike
Falls Church, VA 22043, United States
Tel: (703) 714-5409
Fax: (703) 714-5490
www.fcps.k12.va.us/MarshallHS/

Mascot: Statesmen

Georgetown Day School
4200 Davenport Street N.W.
Washington, DC 20016-4560, United States
Contact: Meredith Alexander, Head Coach
Tel: (202) 274-3232
Fax: (202) 364-9603
Email: malexander@gds.org
www.gds.org/athletics/crew/

Colors: Green and white
Mascot: Mighty hoppers
Year est: 1995
Championship Regatta: Stotesbury
History: The Georgetown Day High School crew program was launched in 1995 by a small group of enthusiastic parents, and interested students, relying on rented equipment and the goodwill of the local rowing fraternity. In the intervening six seasons, the team has grown to approximately forty members and has become a full GDS Varsity/Novice sport.

Georgetown Visitation Preparatory School
1524 35th Street NW
Washington, DC 20007, United States
Contact: Eileen Hudson, Athletic Director
Tel: (202) 337-3350
Email: ehudson@visi.org
www.visi.org

Colors: Gold and white
Mascot: Cubs

Germantown Academy
PO Box 287
Fort Washington, PA 19034-0287, United States
Tel: (215) 646-3300
Fax: (215) 646-1216
www.germantownacademy.org

Colors: Black, blue and red
Mascot: Patriots

Girls Preparatory School (GPS)
PO Box 4736
Chattanooga, TN 37405-0736, United States
Tel: (423) 634-7617
Fax: (423) 634-5430
Contact: Rachel McCallie, Head Coach
Tel: (423) 634-7600
Fax: (423) 634-7682
Email: RachelM@gps.edu
www.gps.edu

Colors: Black and Royal Blue
Mascot: Bruisers

Gloucester High School
6680 Short Lane
Gloucester, VA 23061, United States
Tel: (804) 693-2526
Fax: (804) 693-7685
www.ghs.gc.k12.va.us/

Colors: Scarlet, white and gold
Mascot: Dukes

Gonzaga College High School
19 Eye Street NW
Washington, DC 20001, United States
Tel: (202) 336-7111
Fax: (202) 336-7112
Email: gonzagacrw@aol.com
Contact: David Foley, Men's Head Coach
Tel: (202) 336-7411
Email: dfoley@gonzaga.org
www.crewgonzaga.com

Colors: Purple and White
Mascot: Eagles
Year est: 1996

Grand Rapids City League Crew
1550 Mackinaw Road SE
Grand Rapids, MI 49506, United States
Contact: Dustin Ordway
Tel: (616) 241-6111
Email: grcityleaguecrew@aol.com

Year est: 1999

Great Bridge High School
301 West Hanbury Road
Chesapeake, VA 23322-4228, United States
Tel: (757) 482-5191
Fax: (757) 482-5559
eclipse.cps.k12.va.us/Schools/GBH/

Colors: Green and gold
Mascot: Wildcats

Great Valley High School
225 N Phoenixville Pike
Malvern, PA 19355, United States
Tel: (610) 889-1922
Fax: (610) 889-2166
www.great-valley.k12.pa.us/gvhs/

Colors: Royal and white
Mascot: Patriots

Green Hill Academic School
375 SW 11th Street
Chehalis, WA 98532, United States
www.chehalis.k12.wa.us/ghas/

Green Lake High School
5900 W. Green Lake Way N.
Seattle, WA 98103, United States
Contact: Jason Frisk, Coach
Tel: (206) 684-4074
Fax: (206) 684-4042
Email: glrowing@aol.com

Grosse Ile High School
7800 Grays Drive
Grosse Ile, MI 48138, United States
Tel: (734) 362-2400
Contact: Patrick Hickey, Women's Head Coach
Tel: (313) 388-7785
Email: phickeypm@aol.com
Contact: Scott D Sitek, Men's Head Coach
Email: rowhard00@hotmail.com
www.gischools.org/high.htm

Colors: Scarlet and Gray
Mascot: Red Devil
Year est: 1989

Grosse Pointe-South High School
11 Grosse Pointe Boulevard
Grosse Pointe, MI 48236, United States
Tel: (313) 343-2181
Fax: (313) 343-2474

Colors: Blue and gold
Mascot: Blue Devils

Groton School
PO Box 991
Groton, MA 01450, United States

Contact: Wayne Berger, Men's Head Coach
Tel: (978) 448-7533
Fax: (978) 448-3100
Email: wberger@groton.org
www.groton.org

Colors: Black and white
Mascot: Zebras

Gunnery School
99 Greenhill Road
Washington, CT 06793, United States
Tel: (860) 868-7751
Fax: (860) 868-7205

Colors: Maroon and gray
Mascot: Highlanders

H.B. Plant High School
2415 South Himes Avenue
Tampa, FL 33629, United States
Tel: (813) 272-3033
Fax: (813) 272-0624
Contact: Mike Smith, Head Coach
Email: smit33@hotmail.com
www.planthigh.org

Colors: Black and gold
Mascot: Panthers

Harriton High School
600 N Ithan Avenue
Rosemont, PA 19010, United States
Contact: Antoinette Calimag, Head Coach
Email: coachc@irow.com
hcrewpa.tripod.com/friends.html

Colors: Red, white and black
Mascot: Rams

Hartford Public High School
55 Forest Street
Hartford, CT 06105, United States
Tel: (860) 278-5920
Fax: (860) 722-8779

Colors: Blue and white.
Mascot: Owls

Haverford School
450 Lancaster Avenue
Haverford, PA 19041, United States
Tel: (610) 642-3020
Fax: (610) 645-9784
Email: crew@haverford.edu
Contact: Valeria Gospodinov, Head Coach
Tel: (610) 896-1120
Email: val_row@abv.bg
www.haverford.org

Colors: Maroon and gold
Mascot: Fords

Henninger High School
600 Robinson Street
Syracuse, NY 13206, United States
Tel: (315) 435-4395
Fax: (315) 435-4350
Contact: Joe Bufano, Head Coach
Tel: (315) 424-0890
Email: jjbufano@syr.edu
henninger.syracuseschools.net

Colors: Black and gold
Mascot: Black Knights

Hickory High School
1996 Hawk Boulevard
Chesapeake, VA 23322, United States
Tel: (757) 421-HAWK
Fax: (757) 421-2190
eclipse.cps.k12.va.us/Schools/HHS/

Highland Park High School
433 Vine Avenue
Highland Park, IL 60035, United States
Tel: (847) 926-9212
Fax: (847) 432-7827

Colors: Blue and white
Mascot: Giants

Hilliard Davidson High School
5100 Davidson Road
Hilliard, OH 43026, United States
Tel: (614) 771-2273
Fax: (614) 529-7448
www.hilliard.k12.oh.us/schools/HSDavidson.asp

Colors: Royal and white
Mascot: Wildcats

Hillsborough High School
5000 N Central Avenue
Tampa, FL 33603-2214, United States
Tel: (813) 276-5620
Fax: (813) 276-5629
Contact: Meg Wolfe, Head Coach
Tel: (813) 870-3745
Email: crewwolfe@aol.com

Colors: Red and black
Mascot: Terriers

Hilton Head High School
70 Wilborn Road
Hilton Head Island, SC 29926-1627, United States
Tel: (843) 689-7565
Fax: (843) 689-7552

Colors: Columbia blue and navy
Mascot: Seahawks

Hockaday School
11600 Welch Road
Dallas, TX 75229-2913, United States
Tel: (214) 365-6660
Fax: (214) 365-6634
Contact: Jennifer Sharez, Women's Head Coach
Email: bellyjen@hotmail.com
www.hockaday.org

Colors: Forest green and white
Mascot: Daisy

Holton-Arms School
7303 River Road
Bethesda, MD 20817, United States
Tel: (301) 365-6044
Fax: (301) 365-6023

Holy Angels Academy
24 Shoshone Street
Buffalo, NY 14214, United States
Tel: (716) 834-7120
Contact: John P Dorn, Head Coach
Tel: (716) 446-0512
Email: john.dorn@ingrammicro.com
www.holyangelsacademy.org

Colors: Navy and White
Mascot: Angel
Year est: 1994
Championship Regatta: SRA, CSSRA

Holy Names Academy
c/o Lake Union Crew
11 East Allison
Seattle, WA 98102, United States
Contact: Rome Ventura, Head Coach
Tel: (206) 860-4199
Fax: (206) 860-7826
Email: raventura@aol.com
www.holynames-sea.org

Colors: Maroon and gray
Mascot: Cougars
Year est: 1993

Holy Spirit High School
500 S New Road
Absecon, NJ 08201, United States
Tel: (609) 646-3000
Email: spiritcrew@hotmail.com
Contact: Joe Welsh, Women's Head Coach
Email: hshs-girls-crew@angelfire.com
www.angelfire.com/sports/spiritcrew/

Holy Trinity Episcopal Academy
5625 Holy Trinity Drive
Melbourne, FL 32940, United States
Tel: (407) 723-8323
Fax: (407) 723-2553
www.htacademy.org

Horace Mann-Barnard Upper School
231 West 246th Street
Riverdale, NY 10471, United States
Tel: (718) 432-3810
Fax: (718) 796-6271

Colors: Maroon and white
Mascot: Lions

Hudson County Vo-Tech High School
525 Montgomery Street
Jersey City, NJ 07032, United States
Tel: (201) 413-5954
www.hcst.tec.nj.us/

Huntington High School
Mckay & Oakwood Rds
Huntington, NY 11743, United States
Contact: Robert Polizzo, Head Coach
Tel: (631) 757-5736
Email: rpolizzo1@hotmail.com
www.huntingtoncrew.org

Colors: Blue and white
Mascot: Blue Devil

Huron High School
32044 Huron River Drive
New Boston, MI 48164-9282, United States
Contact: David Morrison, Coach
Tel: (734) 994-2075
Fax: (734) 994-2069
Email: coachdave@email.com

Hyde School
616 High Street
Bath, ME 04530, United States
Tel: (207) 443-5584
Fax: (207) 443-1450
Contact: Walter H Gregg, Head Coach
Tel: (207) 443-7137
Fax: (207) 443-1450
Email: wgregg@hyde.edu
www.hyde.edu

Colors: Gold and Blue
Mascot: Phoenix
Year est: 1989 (M)/2000 (W)

Indianapolis Rowing Center for Juniors
PO Box 53223
Indianapolis, IN 46253, United States
Contact: Eric Stoll, Director
Tel: (317) 298-9456
Fax: (317) 253-4434
Email: director@rowirc.org
www.rowirc.org

Ithaca High School
1401 N Cayuga Street
Ithaca, NY 14850-2101, United States
Tel: (607) 274-2155
Fax: (607) 274-6821
www.icsd.k12.ny.us/highschool/

Colors: Red and gold
Mascot: Lil Red

James Madison High School
2500 James Madison Drive
Vienna, VA 22181, United States
Tel: (703) 319-2360
Fax: (703) 319-2384
Contact: Glen Hoptman, Booster President
Tel: (703) 281-5863
Fax: (703) 281-5923
Email: ghoptman@cox.net
www.fcps.k12.va.us/MadisonHS/

Colors: Red, White and Black
Mascot: Warhawks
Year est: 2002

James River High School
3700 James River Road
Midlothian, VA 23113-3717, United States
Tel: (804) 378-2420

Colors: Green, White and Purple
Mascot: Rapids

JEB Stuart High School
3301 Peace Valley Lane
Falls Church, VA 22044-1508, United States
Tel: (703) 824-3960
Fax: (703) 820-8968
Contact: Terry Jemison, Booster President
Tel: (703) 578-0152
Email: tmjemison@aol.com
www.fcps.k12.va.us/StuartHS/

Colors: Blue and red
Mascot: Raiders
Year est: 1966 (M)/ 1986 (W)
Championship Regatta: NCASRA

JR Robinson High School
Robinson Crew Boosters Club Inc.
PO Box 7086
Fairfax Station, VA 22039, United States
Email: crewgjem@hotmail.com
Contact: Jim Scanlon, Booster President
Email: jhscanlon@aol.com
www.robinsoncrew.com

Kearny High School
336 Devon Street
Kearny, NJ 07032, United States
Tel: (201) 955-5000
Fax: (201) 955-5070

Colors: Red and black
Mascot: Cardinals

Kent School
Rte. 341
Kent, CT 06757, United States
Contact: Eric L Houston, Men's Head Coach
Tel: (860) 927-6096
Fax: (860) 927-5397
Email: houston@kent-school.edu
www.Kent School .com

Colors: Gray and blue
Mascot: Fighting Lions
Year est: 1922 (M)/ 1982 (W)
Championship Regatta: NEIRA

Kenwood High School
5015 S Blackstone Avenue
Chicago, IL 60615-3005, United States
Tel: (773) 535-1350
Fax: (773) 535-1360

Colors: Robin blue and red
Mascot: Broncos

Lake Braddock High School
c/o Lake Braddock Crew Boosters Club
PO Box 10458
Burke, VA 22009-0458, United States
Contact: Bob Linn, Booster President
Tel: (703) 455-4712
Fax: (703) 455-5990
Email: boblinn@worldnet.att.net
www.bruincrew.com/

Colors: Purple and gold
Mascot: Bruins
Year est: 1999

Lake Brantley High School
991 Sand Lake Road
Altamonte Springs, FL 32714-7705, United States
Tel: (407) 862-1776
Fax: (407) 788-2366
Email: coach@lakebrantleycrew.com
Contact: Matt Schlichenmaier, Women's Head Coach
Tel: (407) 399-2448
Email: keckard1@cfl.rr.com
www.LakeBrantleyCrew.com

Colors: Red, blue and white
Mascot: Patriots

Lake Ewauna Rowing Club for Juniors
1034 Riverside Drive
Klamath Falls, OR 97601, United States
Contact: Jay Schindler
Tel: (541) 882-7589
Email: jayschin@cvc.net

Lake Lanier Rowing Club for Juniors
3105 Clarks Bridge Road
Gainesville, GA 30506, United States
Tel: (770) 287-0077
Fax: (770) 287-0077
Email: llrc@mindspring.com
www.llrc.ws

Lake Merritt Rowing Club for Juniors
PO Box 1046
Oakland, CA 94604, United States

Lakeside High School (GA)
3801 Briarcliff Rd NE
Atlanta, GA 30345-3856, United States
Tel: (404) 633-2632
Fax: (770) 633-2631

Colors: Purple and gold
Mascot: Vikings

Lakeside School (WA)
14050 1st Avenue NE
Seattle, WA 98125, United States
Tel: (206) 440-2745
Fax: (206) 368-3638
Contact: Susan Parkman, Coach
Email: susanparkman@msn.com
www.lakesideschool.org

Colors: Maroon and gold
Mascot: Lions

Landsdale Catholic
700 Lansdale Avenue
Landsdale, PA 19446-2995, United States
Tel: (215) 362-6160
Fax: (215) 362-5746
www.lansdalecatholic.com/

Colors: Green and gold
Mascot: Crusaders

Langley High School
PO Box 804
McLean, VA 22101, United States
Email: saxoncrew@aol.com
Contact: Robert Ittig
Email: ittigrc@erols.com
www.langleycrew.com/

Colors: Dark green and old gold
Mascot: Saxons

Lansing High School
300 Ridge Road
Lansing, NY 14882, United States
Tel: (607) 533-4868
Fax: (607) 533-3602
Contact: Stephen Lahr
Tel: (607) 257-3717
Email: lahr@clarityconnect.com
www.lansingschools.org/lhs/

Colors: Royal blue and gold
Mascot: Bobcats

LaSalle College High School
8605 Cheltenham Avenue
Wyndmoor, PA 19128, United States
Tel: (215) 233-2911
Fax: (215) 233-1418
www.lschs.org

Colors: Navy and gold
Mascot: Explorers

Lawrenceville School
Box 6008
Lawrenceville, NJ 08648, United States
Contact: Mark Schoeffel, Head Coach
Tel: (609) 896-0400
Fax: (609) 895-2158
Email: mschoef@lawrenceville.org
www.lawrenceville.org
www.geocities.com/lvillecrew/

Colors: Red and black.

Leon High School
550 E Tennessee Street
Tallahassee, FL 32308-4938, United States
Contact: Tom Morgan, Head Coach
Tel: (850) 488-1971 x1150
Fax: (850) 644-0481
Email: tjmorganjr@hotmail.com
Ginger and Jerome Cox, Booster Presidents
Tel: (850) 422-0814
Email: jgcox@nettally.com
www.leon.k12.fl.us

Colors: Red and white
Mascot: Lions

Lincoln Park Juniors
4045 N. Kimball Avenue #2
Chicago, IL 60618, United States
Tel: (773) 913-9110
Email: rowing@lpbc.net
Contact: Rachel Waterson, Head Coach
Tel: (772) 750-7212
Email: drwaterman@hotmail.com
www.lpbc.net

Colors: Navy blue and white
Year est: 1998
www.rowchicago.com
Championship Regatta: Midwest Junior Rowing
Championships
History: LPJ is a competitive junior rowing program.
We are very proud to host 1/3 of our junior athletes
with financial scholarships. The United States
Olympic Committee and Friends of Lincoln Park Boat
Club started our program with a seed grant in 1998.

Litchfield High School
14 Plumb Hill Road
PO Box 110
Litchfield, CT 06759, United States
Tel: (860) 567-7536
Fax: (860) 567-7538

Colors: Royal blue and white
Mascot: Cowboys

Liverpool High School
4338 Wetzel Road
Liverpool, NY 13090, United States
Tel: (315) 453-0220
Fax: (315) 453-1246
Contact: Jason Boyce, Head Coach
Tel: (315) 427-1685
Email: wisco98@hotmail.com
www.lhs.liverpool.k12.ny.us/crew/

Colors: Navy and orange
Mascot: Warriors
www.lhs.liverpool.k12.ny.us/crew/

Long Beach Junior Crew
PMB 366
5318 E. Second Street
Long Beach, CA 90803, United States
Tel: (562) 438-3352
Fax: (562) 438-3444
Contact: Ian Simpson, Head Coach
Tel: (562) 438-3352
Email: longbeachrowing@hotmail.com
www.lbra.org
www.longbeachrowing.org

Colors: Blue and white
Year est: 1987
Championship Regatta: USRowing Southwest
Regionals

Los Gatos Rowing Club for Juniors
PO Box 188
Los Gatos, CA 95031-0188, United States
Contact: Wieslaw Kujda, Program Director
Tel: (650) 738-9229
Email: tovees@yahoo.com
info@lgrc.org
www.lgrc.org

Colors: Navy blue and white
Year est: 1979
Championship Regatta: Southwest Regionals

Louisiana School for Math Science and the Arts
715 College Avenue
Natchitoches, LA 71457, United States
Tel: (318) 357-3174
Contact: Alan C Pasch, Men's Head Coach
Tel: (318) 357-5921
Fax: (318) 357-4232
Email: nsurowingteam@hotmail.com
www.lsmsa.edu

Louisville Rowing Club for Juniors
1904 Rutherford Avenue
Louisville, KY 40205, United States
Email: louisvillerowing@hotmail.com
Contact: Sharon Heckel, Coach
Email: heckel@kyma.org
www.louisvillerowingclub.org

Year est: 1997

Lourdes Rowing Association
11 Meyer Avenue
Poughkeepsie, NY 12603, United States
Contact: Coach Mauer
Tel: (845) 485-4358
Email: ajmauer@hvc.rr.com
www.hrrowing.org/Scholastic/OLL/index.shtml

Lowell High School
50 Fr. Morissette Boulevard
Lowell, MA 01852, United States
Tel: (978) 937-8951
Fax: (978) 446-7445

Colors: Red and gray
Mascot: Raiders

Lower Merion High School
245 E Montgomery Avenue
Ardmore, PA 19003, United States
Tel: (610) 645-1821
Fax: (610) 645-1821
schools.lmsd.org/lowermerion/

Colors: Maroon and white
Mascot: Aces

Loyola Academy
1100 Laramie Avenue
Wilmette, IL 60091, United States
Contact: Martin Crotty, Head Coach
Tel: (773) 456-1148
Email: mcrotty@loy.org
www.goramblers.org
www.loyolaacademycrew.com/

Colors: Maroon and gold
Mascot: Ramblers
Year est: 1984

Lyme-Old Lyme High School
69 Lyme Street
Old Lyme, CT 06371-2335, United States
Tel: (860) 434-1651
Fax: (860) 434-8234

Colors: Blue and white
Mascot: Wildcats

Maclay School
3737 N Meridian Road
Tallahassee, FL 32312-1110, United States
Tel: (850) 668-2373
Fax: (850) 893-7434
Contact: Ed McIlvaine, Head Coach
Tel: (850) 933-0458
Email: cayuco@mindspring.com

Colors: Navy and white
Mascot: Marauders

Malvern Preparatory School
418 S Warren Avenue
Malvern, PA 19355-2707, United States
Tel: (610) 640-5942
Fax: (610) 640-5951
malvernprep.com/malvern/index.html

Colors: Blue and gray
Mascot: Friars

Marietta High School
208 Davis Avenue
Marietta, OH 45750, United States
Tel: (740) 374-6542
mariettacityschools.k12.oh.us/

Colors: Orange and black
Mascot: Tigers

Marin Rowing Association for Juniors
50 Drakes Landing Road
Greenbrae, CA 94904, United States
Contact: Sandy Armstrong, Director/Coach
Tel: (415) 461-1431
Fax: (415) 461-5520
Email: sandy@marinrowing.org
www.marinrowing.org

Marina Aquatic Center Junior Rowing
14001 Fiji Way
Marina del Rey, CA 90292, United States
Contact: Zohar Abramovitz, Head Coach
Tel: (310) 577-9756
Fax: (310) 305-1587
Email: zoey@ucla.edu
www.macrowing.org

Colors: Maroon and blue.
Year est: 1995

Maritime & Science Tech Academy
3979 Rickenbacker Causeway
Key Biscayne, FL 33149, United States
Tel: (305) 365-6278
Fax: (305) 361-0996
mast.dade.k12.fl.us/

Mathews High School
PO Box 14
Ware Neck, VA 23178, United States
Contact: Tim Ulsaker, Director
Tel: (804) 693-5160
Fax: (804) 693-1160
Email: crucoach@inna.net
crucoach@aol.com
www.tiercom.com/crew/

Colors: Blue and gold
Mascot: Blue Devils

Maury High School
322 Shirley Avenue
Norfolk, VA 23517, United States
Tel: (757) 628-3344
Fax: (757) 628-3359
www.nps.k12.va.us/schools/mauryhs/

Colors: Burnt Orange, Navy Blue
Mascot: Commodores

McCallie High School
500 Dodds Avenue
Chattanooga, TN 37404, United States
Tel: (423) 493-5539
Fax: (423) 493-5578
Contact: Richard A Swanson
Tel: (423) 624-8300
Email: dswanson@mccallie.com

Colors: Blue and white
Mascot: Blue Tornado

McLean High School
PO Box 7104
McLean, VA 22106-7104, United States
Contact: Chris Gordon, Head Coach
Tel: (703) 237-7654
Email: chris.gordon@mcleancrew.org
www.mcleancrew.org

Colors: Red and silver
Mascot: Highlander
Year est: 1995

Melbourne Central Catholic High School
100 East Florida Avenue
Melbourne, FL 32901, United States
Tel: (321) 727-0793
Fax: (321) 727-1134
www.spacecoastcrew.org

Melbourne High School
74 Bulldog Boulevard
Melbourne, FL 32901-3151, United States
Tel: (321) 952-5891
Fax: (321) 952-5898
Contact: Karen Sukolsky, Booster President
Email: rsukolsky@cfl.rr.com

Colors: Dark green and white
Mascot: Bulldogs

Mendota Rowing Club for Juniors
PO Box 646
Madison, WI 53701, United States
Email: info@mendotarowingclub.com
Contact: M B Blanding, Head Coach
Tel: (608) 238-4122
Email: mbbland@spasd.k12.wi.us
www.mendotarowingclub.com
Year est: 1980

Mercyhurst Preparatory School
538 E Grandview Boulevard
Erie, PA 16504-2260, United States
Tel: (814) 824-2068
Fax: (814) 824-2116
www.mpshome.com/

Colors: Green and white
Mascot: Lakers

Merion Mercy Academy
511 Montgomery Avenue
Merion Station, PA 19066, United States
Tel: (610) 664-6655
Fax: (610) 664-6322
www.merion-mercy.com/

Colors: Blue and gold
Mascot: Golden Bears

Merrimac River Rowing Association for Juniors
PO Box 686
Lowell, MA 01853, United States
Tel: (978) 454-4631
Email: info@merrimackrowing.org
www.merrimackrowing.org

Miami Beach High School
2231 Prairie Avenue
Miami Beach, FL 33139, United States
Tel: (305) 535-6601
Fax: (305) 535-6601

Miami Beach Rowing Club for Juniors
6500 Indian Creek Drive
Miami Beach, FL 33141, United States
Contact: Elaine Roden, Director
Tel: (305) 861-8876
Email: Elaine_mbrowing@bellsouth.net
www.rowmiamibeach.com

Michael M. Krop High School
1410 County Line Road
Miami, FL 33179, United States
mkhs.dadeschools.net

Middlesex School
1400 Lowell Road
Concord, MA 01742, United States
Contact: Michael E Porrazzo, Head Coach
Tel: (978) 371-6921
Email: mporrazzo@middlesex.edu
www.middlesex.edu

Colors: cardinal/white
Mascot: Zebra
Year est: 1903 (M)/ 1974 (W)
Championship Regatta: NEIRA

Middleton High School
370 Hunting Hill Avenue
Middletown, CT 06457, United States
Tel: (860) 704-4558
Fax: (860) 704-4512

Colors: Navy and columbia
Mascot: Blue Dragons

Mid-Hudson Rowing Association for Juniors
PO Box 683
Poughkeepsie, NY 12603, United States
Email: kquackenbush@hvc.rr.com
home.hvc.rr.com/midhudsonrowing/

Milwaukee Rowing Club for Juniors
3354 N. Gordon Place
Milwaukee, WI 53212, United States
www.milwaukeerowingclub.org

Minnesota Boat Club for Juniors
382 Winslow Avenue
Saint Paul, MN 55107, United States
Tel: (651) 228-1602
Contact: Annie Lux
Tel: (612) 821-9102
Email: annielux2002@yahoo.com
president@boatclub.org
www.boatclub.org
Year est: 1997

Miss Porters School
60 Main Street
Farmington, CT 06032, United States
Tel: (860) 409-3711
Fax: (860) 409-3525
Contact: Brad Choyt, Head Coach

Colors: Hunter green and white

Monsignor Bonner High School
#12 Boathouse Row
Kelly Drive
Philadelphia, PA 19130, United States
Contact: Dave Krmpotich, Men's Head Coach
Email: chip@nni.com
www.delcodirectory.com/bonnercrew/

Colors: Green and white
Mascot: Friars

Moorestown Rowing Club
PO Box 184
Moorestown, NJ 08057, United States
Contact: Jennifer Wesson, Head Coach
Email: CoachJen@moorestownrowing.org
www.moorestownrowing.org
History: MRC is a non-profit parent-sponsored organization founded to provide training and competition in the sport of rowing for secondary school students in the Moorestown, New Jersey area. Schools include: Cinnaminson High School, Haddonfield Memorial High School, Lenape Regional High School, Moorestown Friends School, and Moorestown High School.

Moss Bay Rowing Club for Juniors
1001 Fairview Avenue N. #1900
Seattle, WA 98109, United States
Contact: Jim Clark, Director
Fax: (206) 682 0455
Email: mossbay@earthlink.net
www.mossbay.net

Mount Baker High School
3800 Lake Washington Boulevard S.
Seattle, WA 98118, United States
www.mtbaker.wednet.edu/mbhs/

Colors: Red and black
Mascot: Mountaineers

Mount Carmel High School
6410 S Dante Avenue
Chicago, IL 60637, United States
Tel: (773) 324-2834
Fax: (773) 324-9235

Colors: Brown and white
Mascot: Caravan

Mount Lebanon High School
155 Cochran Road
Pittsburgh, PA 15228-1319, United States
Contact: Sean T Nangle, Head Coach
Tel: (412) 319-6102
Email: sjnangle@attbi.com
www.MTLRowing.org

Colors: Blue and Gold
Mascot: Blue Devil
Championship Regatta: Midwest Scholastic
Championships

Mount Saint Joseph Academy
120 West Wissahickon Avenue
Flourtown, PA 19031, United States
Tel: (215) 233-3177
Fax: (215) 233-4734

Colors: Purple and gold
Mascot: Magic

Nardin Academy
135 Cleveland Avenue
Buffalo, NY 14222, United States
Tel: (716) 881-9797
Fax: (716) 881-3100
Email: Rowing@wsrc.org
www.nardin.org

Narragansett Boat Club for Juniors
PO Box 2413
Providence, RI 02906-2413, United States
Tel: (401) 272-1838
Contact: Jill Singewald, Program Director
Tel: (401) 351-5295
Email: jill@ids.net
www.rownbc.org

National Cathedral School
Mount Saint Alban's
Washington, DC 20016, United States
Tel: (202) 537-6331
Fax: (202) 537-2170

Contact: Allison Kornet, Women's Head Coach
Tel: (703) 836-0793
Email: allison.kornet@alum.dartmouth.org
www.ncs-sta-crew.org

Colors: Red, white and blue.
Mascot: Eagles
Year est: 1993

Navesink River Rowing Club for Juniors
PO Box 6153
Fair Haven, NJ 07704, United States
Tel: (732) 758-6266
Email: mm@crpindustries.com
www.monmouth.com/~nrrc/

Nazareth Academy High School
4001 Grant Avenue
Philadelphia, PA 19114, United States
Tel: (215) 637-1116
www.nazarethacademyhs.org

Colors: Blue and gold
Mascot: Fighting Pandas

New Canaan High School
11 Farm Road
New Canaan, CT 06840, United States
Tel: (203) 972-4444
Fax: (203) 966-8037
Contact: Yan Vengerovskiy, Head Coach
Tel: (203) 849-8113
Email: MaritimeRowing@aol.com
newcanaancrew.com/

Newburgh Free Academy
201 Fullerton Avenue
Newburgh, NY 12550-3718, United States
Tel: (914) 563-7557
Fax: (914) 563-7559
Contact: Ed Kennedy
Tel: (845) 563-7373
Email: coachkennedy60@aol.com
www.newburghschools.org

Newburgh Rowing Club for Juniors
109 Holly Drive
New Windsor, NY 12553, United States
Tel: (845) 561-7901
www.newburgh-ny.com/rebuild/wards.htm
History: The Newburgh Rowing Club is incorporated
in New York State as a not-for-profit corporation. It is
comprised of students, both girls and boys, from
grades 7-12 in the Newburgh school district and surrounding areas.

Newport Aquatic Center for Juniors
1 Whitecliffs Drive
Newport Beach, CA 92660, United States

Tel: (949) 646-7725
Email: rowing@pacbell.net
www.newportaquaticcenter.com/rowing.htm

Nichols School
1250 Amherst Street
Buffalo, NY 14216, United States
Contact: Beth Wood
Tel: (716) 875-8212
Fax: (716) 877-2053
Email: ewood@nicholsschool.org
www.nicholsschool.org

Colors: Dark green and white
Mascot: Vikings

Niskayuna High School
1626 Balltown Road
Niskayuna, NY 12309-2304, United States
Tel: (518) 382-2531
Fax: (518) 382-2524
Contact: Matt Hopkins
Tel: (518) 384-1955
Email: mattmhop@aol.com
www.nisk.k12.ny.us/nhs

Colors: Silver and red
Mascot: Silver Warriors

Noble and Greenough School
10 Campus Drive
Dedham, MA 02026, United States
Tel: (781) 326-3700
www.nobles.edu

Norfolk Collegiate School
7336 Granby Street
Norfolk, VA 23505, United States
Tel: (757) 480-1411
Fax: (757) 480-1411
oak.ncs.pvt.k12.va.us/index.html

Colors: Royal and white
Mascot: Oaks

North Allegheny High School
10375 Perry Highway
Wexford, PA 15090-9209, United States
Contact: Don Heckenstaller, Women's Head Coach
Tel: (724) 843-0756
Email: DHeckenstaller@gianteagle.com
www.narowing.org

Colors: Black and yellow
Mascot: Tiger
Year est: 1989
Championship Regatta: Midwest Scholastic Championships

North Catholic High School
1400 Troy Hill Road
Pittsburgh, PA 15212-5124, United States
Contact: Frank Sands
Tel: (412) 367-0236
Fax: (412) 321-8981
Email: coachsands@attbi.com
www.northcatholic.com/

Colors: Red and gold
Mascot: Trojans

North Suburban/Woodlands
760 E Westleigh Road
Lake Forest, IL 60045, United States
Contact: Dick Burgess, President
Tel: (847) 795-7677
Email: dickburgess@earthlink.net
Year est: 1995

Northampton High School
380 Elm Street
Northampton, MA 01060, United States
Tel: (413) 587-1356
Fax: (413) 587-1374

Colors: Blue and gold
Mascot: Bluedevils

Northeast Catholic High School
1842 Torresdale Avenue
Philadelphia, PA 19124, United States
Tel: (215) 831-5220

Colors: Red and white
Mascot: Falcons

Northfield Mount Hermon School
PO Box 4075
206 Main Street
Northfield, MA 01360, United States
Contact: Peter Jenkins, Coach
Tel: (413) 498-3000
Fax: (413) 498-3368
Email: Peter_Jenkins@nmhschool.org
www.nmhschool.org

Colors: Cardinal and Columbia blue
Mascot: Hoggers

Norwalk River Rowing Association for Juniors
PO Box 2084
Norwalk, CT 06852, United States
Contact: Greg Barringer, Executive Director
Tel: (203) 299-1546
Fax: (203) 299-1672
Email: gregcrew@sbcglobal.net
www.norwalkriverrowing.com

Colors: Red and navy blue.
Year est: 1986

Notre Dame Academy
3535 West Sylvania Avenue
Toledo, OH 43623, United States
Tel: (419) 475-9359
Fax: (419) 724-2640
www.nda.org

Colors: Navy blue and gold
Mascot: Eagles

Notre Dame High School
1540 Ralston Avenue
Belmont, CA 94002, United States
Tel: (650) 595-1913
Fax: (650) 595-2116
Contact: Monica Hilcu, Coach
Tel: (858) 496-8342
Fax: (858) 571-3457
Email: mhilcu@earthlink.net

Colors: Navy, gold and white.
Mascot: Tigers

Nottingham High School
3100 E Genesee Street
Syracuse, NY 13224-1647, United States
Tel: (315) 435-4390
Contact: Joe Bufano, Head Coach
Tel: (315) 424-0890
Email: jjbufano@syr.edu

Colors: Orange and royal
Mascot: Bulldogs

Nutley High School
300 Franklin Avenue
Nutley, NJ 07110, United States
Tel: (973) 661-8849
Fax: (973) 661-3664
www.nutleyschools.org

Colors: Maroon and gray
Mascot: Raiders

Oak Ridge Rowing Association for Juniors
PO Box 4384
Oak Ridge, TN 37831-4384, United States
Contact: Allen Eubanks, Head Coach
Tel: (865) 482-6538
Email: coach@orra.org
www.orra.org

Oakland Catholic High School
144 North Craig Street
Pittsburgh, PA 15213, United States
Tel: (412) 682-6633
Fax: (412) 682-2496

Colors: Maroon and silver
Mascot: Eagles

Oakland Strokes Inc.
4096 Piedmont Avenue
PMB 308
Piedmont, CA 94611, United States
Contact: Will King, Board Chairman
Tel: (510) 893-6877
Email: WillKing@aol.com
www.oaklandstrokes.org

Colors: Green and orange
Year est: 1976 (M)/ 1974 (W)
Championship Regatta: 2003 USRowing Youth Invitational
History: Oakland Strokes is a junior rowing club founded in 1974. Approximately 140 women and 60 men from 40 high schools in Alameda and Contra Costa counties. Co-sponsor with Jack London Aquatic Center of the Head of the Estuary race in late October, 25th anniversary in 2004. Many members have served on the USRowing Junior National Team and some on the Senior National Team. Our alumni go on to compete in Division I (Cal, Washington, Yale, Dartmouth, Penn, Cornell, Princeton, Rutgers) as well as Division II and III.

Olympia High School
4301 S Apopka Vineland Road
Orlando, FL 32835, United States
Tel: (407) 905-6400
Fax: (407) 905-6465

Orchard Park High School
4040 Baker Rd
Orchard Park, NY 14127-2205, United States
Tel: (716) 209-6243
Fax: (716) 209-6353
Contact: Frank Becht
Tel: (716) 839-1280
Email: fbecht80@aol.com
www.opschools.org/highschool/

Colors: Maroon and white
Mascot: Quakers\

Oregon Rowing Unlimited for Juniors
PMB 322
333 South State Street Suite V
Lake Oswego, OR 97034, United States
Tel: (503) 233-9426
Email: oregonrow@hotmail.com
Contact: Nick Haley, Program Director
Tel: (503) 233-9426
Email: nickhaley@hotmail.com
www.oregonrowing.org

Orlando Area Rowing Society for Juniors
PO Box 71
Windermere, FL 34786, United States
www.oars-online.com/

History: Orlando Area Rowing Society (OARS) is a not for profit corporation created to promote rowing as a sport at all levels of interest. To date, our crew is comprised of high school students, both men and women, grades 9 through 12. Our student athletes represent Dr. Phillips High School, West Orange High School, Olympia High School, and a variety of private high schools in the area.

Our Lady of Lourdes High School
131 Boardman Road
Poughkeepsie, NY 12603-4821, United States
Tel: (845) 436-0400
Fax: (845) 463-0191
Contact: Coach Mauer, Head Coach
Tel: (845) 485-4358
Email: tmauer@hvc.rr.com
www.ladyoflourdes.org/
www.hrrowing.org/Scholastic/OLL/index.shtml

Colors: Blue and gold
Mascot: Warriors

Our Lady of Mercy Academy
815 Convent Road
Syosset, NY 11791, United States
Tel: (516) 921-1047
Fax: (516) 921-3634
Contact: Ellen Hughes
Tel: (516) 624-7599
Email: hughesem@ix.netcom.com
www.olma.org

Colors: Navy and columbia blue
Mascot: Mustangs

Pacific Rowing Club for Juniors
PO Box 27548
San Francisco, CA 94127-0548, United States
Tel: (415) 242-0252
Contact: Paul Berger, Men's Head Coach
Tel: (415) 407-3132
Email: paulberge@hotmail.com
Contact: Wayne Rickert, Women's Varsity Coach
Tel: (415) 643-5036
Email: wrickert@pvsd.net
www.pacificrc.org

Palo Alto High School
50 Embarcadero Road
Palo Alto, CA 94301, United States
Tel: (650) 329-3710
Fax: (650) 329-3753
Contact: Lynn Gardner, Program Director
Tel: (415) 990-0604
Email: loragrion@aol.com
www.geocities.com/pahsrc

Colors: Hunter green and white.
Mascot: Vikings
Year est: 2002

Parkersburg High School
2101 Dudley Avenue
Parkersburg, WV 26101, United States
Email: phscrew@hotmail.com
www.phsrowing.org

Colors: Red and white.
Mascot: Big Red Indians
Year est: 1970

Parkersburg South High School
1511 Blizard Drive
Parkersburg, WV 26101, United States
Email: phscrew@hotmail.com
www.phsrowing.org

Passaic River Rowing Association for Juniors
PO Box 440
Lyndhurst, NJ 07071-0440, United States
Email: prra.row2@verizon.net
www.prra.org

Peabody High School
515 North Highland Avenue
Pittsburgh, PA 15206, United States
Tel: (412) 665-2063
Fax: (412) 665-2097

Colors: Maroon and white
Mascot: Highlanders

Peninsula Aquatic Center Junior Crew
PO Box 669
Redwood City, CA 94064, United States
Contact: Monica Hilcu, Coach
Tel: (858) 496-8342
Fax: (858) 571-3457
Email: mhilcu@earthlink.net
www.peninsulajuniorcrew.org

Philadelphia Girls Rowing Club for Juniors
#14 Boathouse Row Kelly Drive
Philadelphia, PA 19130, United States

Phillips Academy
180 Main Street
Andover, MA 01810-4166, United States
Tel: (978) 749-4080
Fax: (978) 749-4098
Contact: Kathryn Lucier Green
Email: kgreen@andover.edu
www.andover.edu

Colors: Blue and white
Mascot: Big Blue

Phillips Exeter Academy
20 Main Street
Exeter, NH 03833, United States
Tel: (603) 772-4311
Fax: (603) 778-4384
Contact: Becky Moore, Women's Head Coach
Email: bmoore@exeter.edu
Contact: Lawrence Smith, Men's Head Coach
Email: lsmith@exeter.edu
www.exeter.edu

Colors: Red and gray
Year est: 1864 (M)/ 1974 (W)
Championship Regatta: NEIRA

Pine Crest Preparatory School
1501 NE 62nd Street
Ft. Lauderdale, FL 33334, United States
Tel: (954) 492-4562
Fax: (954) 492-4167
Contact: Josh Fien-Helfman, Head Coach
Tel: (954) 351-4651
Email: josh@irow.com
www.ftl.pinecrest.edu

Colors: Green and white
Mascot: Panthers
Year est: 1994
Championship Regatta: FSRA Championships

Pioneer High School
601 W Stadium Boulevard
Ann Arbor, MI 48103-5812, United States
Tel: (734) 994-2151
Fax: (734) 994-2172

Colors: Purple and white
Mascot: Pioneers

Pittsford Crew
Friends of Pittsford Rowing Inc.
33 Summit Oaks
Pittsford, NY 14534, United States
Tel: (585) 234-7463
Contact: Richard Yochum, Men's Head Coach
Tel: (585) 872-7197
Email: yochumrc@hotmail.com
Contact: Ryan Bernfield, Women's Head Coach
Tel: (585) 235-7171
Email: jazzsculler@hotmail.com
www.pittsfordcrew.org

Pomfret School
398 Pomfret Street
PO Box 128
Pomfret, CT 06258, United States
Contact: Bruce Paro, Athletic Director
Tel: (860) 963-6135
Fax: (860) 963-2086
Email: beparo@pomfretschool.org
www.pomfretschool.org

Colors: Red and black
Mascot: Griffins
Year est: 1900 (M)/ 1970 (W)
Championship Regatta: NEIRA

Potomac High School
PO Box 924
Dumfries, VA 22026-0924, United States
Contact: Ted Phoenix, Treasurer
Tel: (703) 670-6077
Fax: (703) 848-0299
Email: tedphoenix@aol.com
www.angelfire.com/sports/pnthrcrw/

Colors: Navy Blue, Carolina Blue, and White
Mascot: Panthers
Year est: 1982
Championship Regatta: VSRC, NCASRA

Poughkeepsie High School
70 Forbus Street
Poughkeepsie, NY 12603, United States
Tel: (845) 451-4896
Fax: (845) 451-4807
Email: phscrew@pcsd.k12.ny.us
Contact: Mike Smith
Tel: (845) 229-7032
Email: dmlsmith@aol.com
www.pcsd.k12.ny.us/phs/

Colors: Blue and white
Mascot: Pioneers

Putney School
Elm Lea Farm
Putney, VT 05346, United States
Tel: (802) 387-5566
Fax: (802) 387-6219
Contact: Joe Holland, Coach
Email: Joe_Holland@pegasus.putney.com
www.putney.com/

Quad City Juniors
PO Box 69
Moline, IA 61265, United States
Contact: Nancy denBesten
Tel: (319) 355-0886
Email: rdenbesten@aol.com
www.qcra.org

Year est: 1993
History: The Junior Program of the Quad Cities began in the fall of 1993 under the direction of Nancy Den Besten with 17 students from the St Katharine's St. Mark's Preparatory School. In 1995, the high school program invited other students from area schools to join the sculling program. Since 1995, hundreds of young people from the Quad City metropolitan area have been introduced to the sport of rowing.

Raleigh Charter High School
1111 Haynes Street
Raleigh, NC 27604-1454, United States
Tel: (919) 715-1155
Fax: (919) 839-1766
Email: coach@rchsrowing.com
www.raleighcharterhs.org
www.rchsrowing.com/

Randolph Macon Academy
200 Academy Drive
Front Royal, VA 22630, United States
Tel: (540) 636-5200
www.rma.edu

Red and White Rowing
PO Box 4291
Parkersburg, WV 26104-4291, United States

Rhinebeck High School
PO Box 351
Rhinebeck, NY 12572-0351, United States
Tel: (845) 871-5500
Fax: (845) 876-8755
Contact: Pat Coon, Chairman
Tel: (845) 876-5940
Email: pcoon@ulster.net
www.rhinebeckcsd.org/rcsdhigh/

River City Rowing Club for Juniors
PO Box 980401
West Sacramento, CA 95798, United States
Contact: Jacob Hatch, Men's Head Coach
Tel: (916) 429-1226
Email: jacobhatch@hotmail.com
www.rivercityrowing.org

Year est: 1995

Scholarships: Men, Women

Riverside Military Academy
2001 Riverside Drive
Gainesville, GA 30501, United States
Contact: Ken Basinger, Head Coach
Tel: (770) 532-6251
Fax: (678) 291-3374
www.cadet.com/

Colors: Royal blue and white
Mascot: Eagles

Riverview Community High School
12431 Longsdorf Street
Riverview, MI 48192, United States
Contact: Paul Orto
Tel: (734) 285-5067
Fax: (734) 675-6325
Email: yukondon@driveinc.com

Colors: Maroon and gold
Mascot: Pirates

Robinson Secondary School
5035 Sideburn Road
Fairfax, VA 22032, United States
Email: rowrams@hotmail.com
Contact: John David, Men's Head Coach
Tel: (703) 690-4392
Fax: (703) 273-0905
Email: rowrams@hotmail.com
www.fcps.k12.va.us/RobinsonSS/

Colors: Blue and gold
Mascot: Ram

Rocket City Rowing Club for Juniors
2822 Lafayette Drive
Huntsville, AL 35801, United States

Rocky Mountain Rowing Club for Juniors
PO Box 6242
Denver, CO 80206, United States

Roman Catholic High School
301 North Broad Street
Philadelphia, PA 19107, United States
Contact: Tom Henwood, Head Coach
Tel: (215) 627-1270
www.cahillite.com/Athletics/crew.htm

Colors: Purple and gold
Mascot: Roman Gladiator
Year est: 1894

Roosevelt T. High School
540 Eureka Road
Wyandotte, MI 48192, United States
Tel: (734) 246-1008
Fax: (734) 284-1782

Colors: Navy and gold
Mascot: Bears

Rumsey Hall School
201 Romford Road
Washington Depot, CT 06794, United States
Tel: (860) 868-0535
Fax: (860) 868-7907

Sagamore Rowing Association for Juniors
PO Box 453
Glenwood Landing, NY 11547, United States
Tel: (631) 673-8304
Email: webmaster@sagamorerowing.org
www.sagamorerowing.org

Saint Albans School
Mount Saint Albans
Washington, DC 20016, United States
Contact: Ted Haley, Men's Head Coach
Tel: (703) 967-4265
www.ncs-sta-crew.org

Colors: Blue and white.
Mascot: Bulldog
Year est: 1993

Saint Andrew's Rowing Club
PO Box 500065
Atlanta, GA 31105, United States
Contact: Craig Webster, Program Director
Tel: (770) 417-CREW
Fax: (810) 958-8302
Email: coach@standrewrowing.com
www.standrewrowing.com/

Saint Andrew's School (DE)
350 Noxontown Road
Middletown, DE 19709-1605, United States
Tel: (302) 378-4209
Fax: (302) 378-7120
Email: mhyde@standrews-de.org
www.standrews-de.org

Colors: Red and white
Mascot: Cardinals

Saint Anthony's High School
275 Wolf Hill Road
South Huntington, NY 11747-1394, United States
Tel: (516) 271-2020
Fax: (516) 549-0620
Contact: Boban Rankovic, Head Coach
Email: rank4812@dowling.edu
www.stanthonycrew.org

Colors: Black and Gold
Mascot: Friars
Year est: 1991
Championship Regatta: NYSSRA Championships
Year est: 1991

Saint Augustine Prep
PO Box 279
Richland, NJ 08350, United States
Tel: (609) 697-2600
www.hermits.com/

Colors: Blue and white
Mascot: Hermits

Saint Ignatius College Prep (CA)
2001 37th Avenue
San Francisco, CA 94116, United States
Tel: (415) 566-3814
Email: sirowing@yahoo.com
Contact: Gwyeth Blevins, Women's Head Coach

Tel: (415) 285-5658
Tom O'Connell, Men's Head Coach
Tel: (415) 333-9235
Email: oc448@aol.com
Email: gwynethb@mindspring.com
www.sirowing.org

Saint Ignatius College Prep (IL)
910 West Van Buren Street #124
Chicago, IL 60607, United States
Contact: Bob Weber, Booster President
Tel: (312) 269-8961
Email: rweber@seyfarth.com
www.ignatiuschicagocrew.org

Year est: 1996

Saint Ignatius High School (OH)
1911 W 30th Street
Cleveland, OH 44113, United States
Contact: Bob Valerian, Head Coach
Tel: (216) 651-0222
Fax: (216) 651-6313
Email: crewcoach@aol.com
rvalerian@kkya.com
www.ignatiuscrew.com/

Colors: Blue and gold
Mascot: Wildcats

Saint John's Country Day
3100 Doctors Lake Drive
Orange Park, FL 32073, United States
Tel: (904) 264-9572
Fax: (904) 264-0375
Contact: Debra Huling
Email: debra_huling@stjohnscds.com
www.stjohnscds.com/

Saint John's High School
378 Main Street
Shrewsbury, MA 01545, United States
Contact: John Ermilio
Tel: (508) 842-8934
Fax: (508) 842-3670
Email: erjcrew@famtree.com
www.stjohnshigh.org

Colors: Red and white.
Mascot: Pioneer
Year est: 1962
Championship Regatta: NEIRA

Saint John's Jesuit
5901 Airport Highway
Toledo, OH 43615, United States
Tel: (419) 865-5743
Fax: (419) 867-9695
Contact: Rod McElroy, Men's Head Coach
Tel: (419) 893-8406

Fax: (419) 893-5608
Email: rmcelroy@businessvoice.com
www.stjohns.toledo.oh.us/
www.sjjtitans.edu

Colors: Blue and gold.
Year est: 1986
Championship Regatta: MSRA

Saint Joseph's Collegiate Institute
845 Kenmore Avenue
Buffalo, NY 14223, United States
Tel: (716) 874-4024
Contact: Joseph Wolf, Athletic Director
Tel: (716) 874-2224
Email: jwolf@sjci.com
www.sjci.com/

Colors: Maroon, white and silver
Mascot: Marauders

Saint Joseph's Prep
1733 W Girard Avenue
Philadelphia, PA 19130, United States
Contact: Bill Lamb, Men's Head Coach
Tel: (215) 242-3619
Fax: (215) 242-2161
Email: lambieiii@aol.com
www.sjprep.org

Colors: Crimson and gray
Mascot: Hawks

Saint Katharine's/Saint Mark's College Prep
1821 Sunset Drive
Bettendorf, IA 52722, United States
Tel: (319) 359-1366
Fax: (319) 359-7576

Colors: Red and white
Mascot: Lions

Saint Louis Rowing Club for Juniors
PO Box 411094
St. Louis, MO 63141, United States
Tel: (314) 434-8299
Contact: Scott Allison, Head Coach
Tel: (314) 965-9456
Fax: (425) 930-6284
Email: swallison@alum.mit.edu
www.slrc.net

Colors: Red, white and blue
Year est: 1993

Saint Margaret's School
444 Water Lane
PO Box 158
Tappahannock, VA 22560-0158, United States
Tel: (804) 443-3357
Fax: (804) 443-1832

Contact: Skye Elliott, Head Coach
Email: selliott@sms.org
www.sms.org

Colors: Blue and gray
Mascot: Scotties

Saint Mark's School
25 Marlborough Road
Southborough, MA 01772, United States
Tel: (508) 786-6141
Fax: (508) 786-6139
Contact: Guy Gregoire, Head Coach
Tel: (508) 486-9292
Email: Guy_Gregoire@hoenig.com
www.stmarksschool.org

Colors: Blue and white
Mascot: Lions

Saint Mark's School of Texas
10600 Preston Road
Dallas, TX 75230, United States
Tel: (214) 363-6491
Fax: (214) 750-6859
Contact: David Hirsch, Men's Head Coach
Tel: (214) 346-8000
Fax: (214) 346-8002
Email: aafcor@aol.com
www.smtexas.org

Colors: Blue and gold
Mascot: Lions

Saint Mary's Hall
PO Box 33430
San Antonio, TX 78265-3430, United States
Tel: (210) 655-7721
Fax: (210) 655-6276
www.smhall.org

Colors: Purple and white
Mascot: Barons

Saint Mary's Preparatory
3535 Indian Trail
Orchard Lake, MI 48324, United States
Tel: (248) 683-0530
Fax: (248) 683-1740
Contact: Michael J German, Head Coach
Tel: (248) 738-6728
Email: mikegerman@worldnet.att.net

Colors: Red, white and black.
Mascot: Eaglets
Year est: 1976
Championship Regatta: Midwest Scholastics, SRAA, CSSRA

Saint Paul's School
325 Pleasant Street
Concord, NH 03301-2591, United States
Contact: Richard F Davis, Head Coach
Tel: (603) 224-4451
Fax: (603) 229-4878
Email: rdavis@sps.edu
www.sps.edu

Colors: Red
Mascot: Pelican
Year est: 1871/ 1971 (W)
Championship Regatta: NEIRA
Men's History: Won the Princess Elizabeth Cup at the Henley Royal Regatta in 1980 and 1994. Won the NEIRA First Eights Championship in 1974-1976, 1978, 1982, 1986, 1989, 1991, 1992, 1994 (standing course record), 1995 and 2000.
Women's History: Won the Peabody Cup for School/Junior Eights at the Henley Women's Regatta in 1996, 1998 and 2001, setting the course record in 1998 and matching the course record in 2001. Won the NEIRA First Eights Championship in 1974-79, 1981, 1998, 1999 and 2001.

Saint Paul's School (Baltimore)
11152 Falls Road
Brooklandville, MD 21022, United States
Contact: Judd Anderson, Head Coach
Tel: (410) 825-4400
Fax: (410) 427-0392
Email: janderson@stpaulsschool.org
www.stpaulsschool.org

Colors: Blue and gold.
Mascot: Crusader
Year est: 2001

Saint Paul's School for Girls (Baltimore)
11232 Falls Road
Brooklandville, MD 21022, United States
Contact: Judd Anderson, Head Coach
Tel: (410) 825-4400
Fax: (410) 427-0392
Email: janderson@stpaulsschool.org
www.stpaulsschoolforgirls.org

Colors: Green and white
Mascot: Gators
Year est: 2000

Saint Stephen's Episcopal School
PO Box 1868
Austin, TX 78767-1868, United States
Tel: (512) 327-1213
Fax: (512) 327-1311
Contact: David Bonomi, Head Coach
Email: dbonomi@sss.austin.tx.us
www.sss.austin.tx.us

Colors: Scarlet and purple
Mascot: Spartans

Saint Ursula Academy
4025 Indian Road
Toledo, OH 43606-2226, United States
Tel: (419) 531-1693
Fax: (419) 534-5777
www.saintursula.org

Salisbury School
21 Canaan Road
Salisbury, CT 06068, United States
Contact: Matt Fitzgerald, Head Coach
Tel: (860) 435-5811
Fax: (860) 435-5750
Email: mfitzgerald@salisburyschool.org
www.salisburyschool.org

Colors: Crimson and white
Mascot: Crimson Knights

Sanford High School
PO Box 888
6900 Lancaster Pike
Hockessin, DE 19707, United States
Tel: (302) 239-5263
Fax: (302) 239-3182
www.sanfordschool.org

Colors: Navy, gold and white
Mascot: Warriors

Sarasota Scullers Youth Rowing Program Inc.
125 Bayview Drive
Osprey, FL 34229, United States
Tel: (941) 966-2244
Fax: (941) 966-4830
Email: ssyrp@aol.com
Contact: Aida Bloomquist, Director
Tel: (941) 966-2244
Email: sarasotascullers@yahoo.com
www.sarasotascullers.com

Saratoga Springs High School
186 West Avenue
Saratoga Springs, NY 12866-5902, United States
Tel: (518) 587-4360
Fax: (518) 587-1597
Contact: Christopher Chase
Tel: (518) 587-6697
Email: chaserow@nycap.rr.com
www.saratogaschools.org/hs/

Colors: Blue and white
Mascot: Streaks

Satellite High School
300 Scorpion Court
Satellite Beach, FL 32937-2949, United States
Tel: (321) 779-2000
Fax: (321) 773-0703
www.spacecoastcrew.org

Colors: Scarlet and silver
Mascot: Scorpion

Savannah Country Day
824 Stillwood Drive
Savannah, GA 31419, United States
Tel: (912) 925-8800
Fax: (912) 920-7800

Colors: Green and gold
Mascot: Hornets

Schenectady High School
1401 The Plaza
Schenectedy, NY 12308-2639, United States
Tel: (518) 370-8185
Fax: (518) 370-8169
Contact: Leigh Butler
Tel: (518) 581-2590
Email: leigh_butler@hotmail.com
www.schenectady.k12.ny.us/SchenectadyHighScho
ol.htm

Colors: Red, white and blue
Mascot: Patriots

Schenley High School
4101 Bigelow Boulevard
Pittsburgh, PA 15213, United States
Tel: (412) 622-8200
Fax: (412) 622-8238
Contact: Michael Nowak, Head Coach
Tel: (860) 599-5781
Fax: (860) 572-9808
Email: SHSRowing@juno.com

Colors: Red and black
Mascot: Spartans

Scotia-Glenville Rowing Association
8 Red Coach Drive
Scotia, NY 12302, United States
Contact: Dan Elliott
Tel: (518) 381-4617
Email: delliott@sgcsd.neric.org

Serra High School
5156 Santo Road
San Diego, CA 92124, United States
Tel: (619) 496-8342
Fax: (619) 571-3457

Colors: Brown, gold and white.
Mascot: Conquistadors

Shaker Heights High School
15911 Aldersyde Drive
Shaker Heights, OH 44120-2250, United States
Tel: (216) 295-4263
Fax: (216) 295-4260
www.shaker.org/schools/high.htm

Colors: Red and white
Mascot: Raiders

Shaker Rowing Association
PO Box 11212
Loudonville, NY 12211, United States
Contact: Rossi Maldonado, Head Coach
Tel: (518) 482-7344
home.nycap.rr.com/shakercrew

Colors: Blue and white.
Year est: 1998
History: Shaker Crew was formed in 1989. In May of
1998, Shaker Rowing Assn was formed to support
Shaker Crew because rowing is not part of the formal
sports program offered at Shaker HS.

Shenendehowa High School
970 Rte 146
Clifton Park, NY 12065, United States
Tel: (518) 371-1123
Fax: (518) 383-1670
Contact: William Egan
Tel: (518) 881-0310
Email: william.egan@wcb.state.ny.us
www.shenet.org/high/high.htm

Colors: Green and white

Shipley School
814 Yarrow Street
Bryn Mawr, PA 19010, United States
Tel: (610) 525-4300
Fax: (610) 525-5082
Contact: John Galloway, Men's Head Coach
www.shipleyschool.org

Colors: Forest green and columbia
Mascot: Gators

Shrewsbury High School
45 Oak Street
Shrewsbury, MA 01545, United States
Contact: Justin Ladnar, Men's Head Coach
Tel: (508) 769-5769
Email: JLednar@hotmail.com

Colors: Navy and gold
Mascot: Colonials

Sidwell Friends School
3825 Wisconsin Ave NW
Washington, DC 20016, United States
Tel: (202) 537-8190
Fax: (202) 537-8191
Contact: Laura R Handman, President
Tel: (202) 508-6624
Fax: (202) 508-6699
Email: laurahandman@dwt.com
www.sidwell.edu

Colors: Maroon and black
Mascot: Quakers
Year est: 1995

Silicon Valley High School
1285 Oakmead Parkway
Sunnyvale, CA 94085, United States
Email: svcrew@aol.com
Contact: Mike Still, Head Coach
Tel: (650) 322-9888
Fax: (208) 248-3009
Email: power10@sbcglobal.net
www.svcrew.com/
Year est: 2000

Simsbury High School
34 Farms Village Road
Simsbury, CT 06070, United States
Tel: (860) 408-4617
Fax: (860) 658-2439
Contact: Betsy Collins, Women's Head Coach
Tel: (860) 658-0451
Email: betsycollins@home.com
Contact: Ann Carabillo, Men's Head Coach
Tel: (860) 651-7862
www.simsbury.k12.ct.us/shs/

Colors: Blue and gold
Mascot: Trojans

South Eugene High School
400 E 19th Avenue
Eugene, OR 97401-4162, United States
Tel: (541) 687-3190
Fax: (541) 687-3693
Contact: Craig Gerlach, Coach
Tel: (541) 302-6748
Email: kepler@pond.net
www.sehs.lane.edu

Colors: Purple and white
Mascot: Axemen

South Kent School
40 Bulls Bridge Road
S. Kent, CT 06785, United States
Contact: Dan Calore
Tel: (860) 927-3539
Fax: (860) 927-1161
Email: hannent@southkentschool.net
www.southkentschool.net

Space Coast Crew Boosters
PO Box 372252
Satellite Beach, FL 32937-0252, United States
Tel: (321) 779-0533
Email: President@spacecoastcrew.org
www.spacecoastcrew.org

History: Space Coast Crew is a non-profit organization established during the summer of 1996 to promote the sport of rowing among Brevard County Scholastic students, grades 9-12. Current high schools include: Satellite High Scorpions, Eau Gallie Commodores, Melbourne Central Catholic Hustlers, West Shore Wildcats, and Florida Air Academy,

Spackenkill High School
112 Spackenkill Road
Poughkeepsie, NY 12603, United States
Tel: (914) 463-7810
Fax: (914) 463-7820

Colors: Green and white
Mascot: Spartans

Springside School
8000 Cherokee Street
Philadelphia, PA 19118, United States
Tel: (215) 247-7184
Fax: (215) 248-9039
www.springside.org

Colors: Blue and gold
Mascot: Lions

Stanton College Preparatory School
1149 W 13th Street
Jacksonville, FL 32209, United States
Tel: (904) 630-6760
Fax: (904) 630-6758
Contact: Steve Hitchcock, Head Rigger
Tel: (904) 630-6760
Fax: (904) 630-6758
Email: tessdurant@hotmail.com
www.stantoncollegeprep.org

Colors: Blue and white
Mascot: Blue Devil
Year est: 1990

Stonington High School
176 S Broad Street
Pawcatuck, CT 06379-1924, United States
Contact: Michael Nowak, Head Coach
Tel: (860) 599-5781
Fax: (860) 572-9808
Email: SHSRowing@juno.com
www.stoningtonhigh.org/athletics/

Colors: Brown and white
Mascot: Bears
Year est: 1999 (M), 1998 (W)
Championship Regatta: CPSRA, NEIRA Championships
Men's History: While smaller than the women's team, men's crew at Stonington High has attracted some outstanding athletes and continues to field a competitive varsity 8 each spring.
Women's History: Program started in 1998 as a club sport. Two years later, it received varsity status and after one year as a varsity sport it became the largest sport offering at Stonington HS.

Syracuse Chargers Rowing Association for Juniors
PO Box 5643
Syracuse, NY 13220-5643, United States
Tel: (315) 234-0039
www.chargersrow.org

T.C. Williams High School
3330 King Street
Alexandria, VA 22302, United States
Contact: Steve Weir, Women's Head Coach
Tel: (703) 836-8968
Email: sweir@wba-arch.com
Contact: Ed Cannon, Men's Head Coach
Tel: (703) 212-7252
Email: ecannon@acps.k12.va.us
www.tcwcrew.org

Colors: Red, Blue & White
Mascot: Titans
Year est: 1947 (M)/ 1975 (W)
Championship Regatta: Virginia Scholastic Rowing Championship

Tabor Academy
66 Spring Street
Marion, MA 02738, United States
Contact: Hank Osborn, Head Coach
Tel: (508) 748-2000
Fax: (508) 291-6666
Email: hosborn@taboracademy.org
www.taboracademy.org

Colors: Red/Maroon and Black
Mascot: Seawolf
Year est: 1919 (M), 1986 (W)
History: Won Henley Royal Regatta 1936, 1937, 1939, 1965.

Taft School
110 Woodbury Road
Watertown, CT 06795, United States
Contact: Michael Spencer, Women's Head Coach
Tel: (860) 945-7803
Email: SpencerM@taftschool.org
Contact: Garrison W Smith, Men's Head Coach
Tel: (860) 945-7831
Fax: (860) 945-7922
Email: smithgarrison@taftschool.org
www.taftschool.org

Colors: Cardinal, Blue and White
Mascot: Rhino

Talahassee Area Crew
PO Box 13941
Tallahassee, FL 32317-3941, United States
Contact: Terry Kellogg, Head Coach
Email: coach@tacrowing.org
www.tacrowing.org

History: Tallahassee Area Crew is an organization for youth rowing in the Tallahassee area. TAC is currently made up of rowers from Lincoln High School and Chiles High School, though students from other schools are welcome to participate.

Tampa Catholic High School
4630 N. Rome Avenue
Tampa, FL 33625, United States
Contact: Patrick Huey, Director
Tel: (813) 870-0860
Fax: (813) 877-9136
Email: huey@gate.net
www.tampacatholic.com

Colors: Green and white
Mascot: Crusaders

Tampa Preparatory School
625 North Boulevard
Tampa, FL 33606, United States
Contact: Kim Brabson, Head Coach
Tel: (813) 251-8481
Fax: (813) 361-4166
Email: kbrabson@tampaprep.org
www.tampaprep.org

Colors: Red, gold and black
Mascot: Terrapins

Taylor-Allderdice High School
2409 Shady Avenue
Pittsburgh, PA 15217, United States
Tel: (412) 422-4800
allderdicehs.pghboe.net

Tempe Junior Crew
PO Box 1555
Tempe, AZ 85280, United States
Contact: Daniel Duxbury, Head Coach
Tel: (480) 706-9040
Email: dan_duxbury@hotmail.com
www.tempejuniorcrew.com/

The Baldwin School
701 Montgomery Avenue
Bryn Mawr, PA 19010-3505, United States
Tel: (610) 525-2700
Fax: (610) 525-7534
www.baldwinschool.org

Colors: Navy and grey

The Bolles School
7400 San Jose Boulevard
Jacksonville, FL 32217, United States
Contact: Ted Riedeburg, Head Coach
Tel: (904) 733-9292 ext. 371
Fax: (904) 739-9929
Email: riedeburg@yahoo.com
www.Bolles.org

Colors: Navy Blue and Orange
Mascot: Bulldog
Year est: 1994
www.Bolles.org
Championship Regatta: Florida Scholastic Championship Regatta

The Bullis School
10601 Falls Road
Potomac, MD 20854-4404, United States
Tel: (301) 983-5747
Fax: (301) 634-3652

Colors: Gold and navy
Mascot: Bulldogs

The Bush School
3400 E. Harrison Street
Seattle, WA 98112, United States
Tel: (206) 322-7978
Fax: (206) 323-1403
www.bush.edu

Colors: Blue and white
Mascot: Blazers

The Gow School
2491 Emery Road
South Wales, NY 14139, United States
Tel: (716) 687-2296
Fax: (716) 652-3457
Contact: Douglas B Cotter, Head Coach
Tel: (716) 639-0735
www.gow.org

Colors: Navy and Crimson
Mascot: Raven
Year est: 1994
Championship Regatta: U.S and Canadian Schoolboys
History: Program was founded in 1994, we are a small school with high quality local competition. We have raced in the Head of the Ohio and Mother's Day regattas . Most of our races are in the Buffalo area.

The Hun School
176 Edgerstoune Road
Princeton, NJ 08540, United States
Tel: (609) 921-7600
www.hunschool.org

Colors: Red and black
Mascot: Raiders

The Peddie School
PO Box A
Hightstown, NJ 08520, United States
Tel: (609) 921-7600
Fax: (609) 921-0573
Contact: Tim J Giordano, Head Coach
Tel: (609) 490-7539
Fax: (609) 490-0551

Email: tgiordan@peddie.org
www.peddie.org

Colors: Blue and Gold
Mascot: Falcon
Year est: 1988
Championship Regatta: Stotesbury, SRA

The Woodlands Senior High School
6101 Research Forest Drive
The Woodlands, TX 77381, United States
Tel: (936) 273-8596
Fax: (936) 273-8593
www.conroe.isd.tenet.edu/schools/twhs.htm

Colors: Red, White and Forest Green
Mascot: Highlanders

Thomas Jefferson HS for Science and Technology
6560 Braddock Road
Alexandria, VA 22312, United States
Contact: Matt Shoop
Email: row4lif@prodigy.net
www.tjhsst.edu/crew/

Thompson Boat Center for Juniors
2900 Virginia Ave NW
Washington, DC 22037, United States
Tel: (202) 333-9543
Email: tbc@guestservices.com
www.guestservices.com/tbc

Toledo Metropolitan Rowing Club
8 Main Street
Toledo, OH 43605, United States
Email: info@toledorowing.org
www.toledorowing.org

Colors: Royal blue and white.
Year est: 2000
History: A compilation of rowers from several area high schools including Sylvania Northview, Sylvania Southview, St. Francis HS, Perrysburg HS, Maumee Valley Country Day, and Toledo Academy of the Performing Arts.

Treasure Coast Junior Rowing Association
c/o Maritime & Yachting Museum
3250 S. Kanner Highway
Stuart, FL 34994, United States
Contact: Denise Velinsky, Club President
Tel: (772) 287-9985
Fax: (772) 225-2305
Email: Denise@velinsky.com
Tel: (772) 692-1234

Colors: Blue and Yellow
Year est: 2000
History: An intentionally small juniors only club formed to instruct local youth in recreational and competitive sculling and sweep rowing

Tulsa Rowing Club for Juniors
715 W. 21st Street
Tulsa, OK 74107, United States
Contact: Neil Bergenroth, Head Coach
Tel: (918) 523-5106
Email: bergenrothn@cox.net
www.tulsajuniorsrowing.org

Undine Barge Club for Juniors
#13 Kelly Drive
Philadelphia, PA 19130, United States
Contact: Joe Quaid, Coach
Tel: (215) 897-1571
Email: quaidjp@nswccd.navy.mil
undine@undine.com
www.undine.com

University High School
11550 Lokanotosa Terrace
Orlando, FL 32817, United States
Tel: (407) 482-8706
Fax: (407) 737-1455

Colors: Blue and gold
Mascot: Cougars

Upper Arlington High School
1650 Ridgeview Road
Upper Arlington, OH 43221, United States
Tel: (614) 487-5200
www.uaschools.org/uahshme.htm
www.uacrew.org

Colors: Black and gold
Mascot: Golden Bears

Upper Merion High School
435 Crossfield Road
King of Prussia, PA 19406, United States
Tel: (610) 337-6042
Fax: (610) 962-1059
www.umasd.org

Colors: Navy and gold
Mascot: Vikings

Upper Saint Clair High School
1825 McLaughlin Run Road
Pittsburgh, PA 15241, United States
Tel: (412) 833-1600
Fax: (412) 833-4889
Contact: Don LeClair, Head Coach
Tel: (412) 818-7512
Email: leclairdon@hotmail.com

Colors: Black and white
Mascot: Panthers

Ursuline Academy of Dallas
4900 Walnut Hill Lane
Dallas, TX 75229, United States
Tel: (469) 232-1819
Fax: (469) 232-3975
www.ursuline.pvt.k12.tx.us/

Colors: Red and white
Mascot: Bears

Viking Rowing Foundation for Juniors
2006 Cornwall Avenue
Northfield, NJ 08225, United States
www.vikingcrew.org

Wakefield High School
4901 S. Chesterfield Road
Arlington, VA 22203, United States
Tel: (703) 228-6733
Fax: (703) 575-8832
Contact: Noel Deskins, Coach
Email: Ndeskins@arlington.k12.va.us
www.arlington.k12.va.us/schools/wakefield.html

Colors: Kelly Green, White
Mascot: Warriors

Walt Whitman High School
7100 Whittier Blvd
Bethesda, MD 20817, United States
Contact: Matt Russell, Head Coach
Tel: (202) 333-9543
Email: mrussell567@hotmail.com
www.whitmancrew.org

Colors: Black, White, Columbia blue
Mascot: Vikings
Year est: 1987 (M)/ 1988 (W)
Championship Regatta: NCASRA
Status: Varsity Club

Washington-Lee High School
1300 N. Quincy Street
Arlington, VA 22201, United States
Contact: Derek C Parsons, Head Coach
Tel: (703) 273-7553
Email: crewcoach@hotmail.com
www.w-lcrew.org

Colors: Blue and Grey
Mascot: Generals
Year est: 1949 (M)/ 1975 (W)

Wayland-Weston Crew
6 Pesce Lane
Wayland, MA 01778-1032, United States
Contact: Christopher N Maietta, President
Tel: (508) 358-2102
Fax: (508) 358-2103
Email: president@wwcrew.org, highschool@wwcrew.org
www.wwcrew.org

Colors: Orange and crimson
Year est: 2000
History: Wayland-Weston Crew's umbrella entity, Wayland-Weston Rowing Association, Inc., was incorporated in August of 2000 by Rob & Sandy Dupcak, Ken Green, Cecily & Tom Kiefer, Eric & Amelia Kuhn, Barbara & Chris Maietta, Kelly Pierce, Stu Schmill, and Barbara & Eric Sheffels. WWRA is a not-for-profit, 501(c)(3) educational organization whose mission is to provide an outstanding rowing program for local high school student-athletes. We compete in fall and spring seasons. We have developed rapidly, thanks to the hands-on involvement of many parents and to our dedicated coaches led by Program Director and Boys Varsity Coach Andy Sacchetti. In 2003 we captured the third place trophy for team points at the Massachusetts Public High School Championships.

Wellington High School
629 N Main Street
Wellington, OH 44090-1081, United States
Tel: (440) 647-3734
Fax: (440) 647-7318

Colors: Maroon and white
Mascot: Dukes

West Orange High School
51 Conforti Avenue
West Orange, NJ 07052, United States
Tel: (973) 669-5301
Fax: (973) 669-8605

Colors: Navy, white
Mascot: Mountaineers

West Orange High School (FL)
1625 Beulah Road
Winter Garden, FL 34787-4407, United States
Tel: (407) 656-2424
Fax: (407) 656-4970

Colors: Blue and orange
Mascot: Warriors

West Potomac High School
6500 Quander Road
Alexandria, VA 22307, United States
Contact: Malcolm Doldron, Women's Head Coach
Tel: (703) 768-5574
Email: doldronm@aol.com
www.wpcrew.org

West Shore High School
250 Wildcat Alley
Melbourne, FL 32935-6466, United States
Tel: (321) 242-4730
westshore.hs.brevard.k12.fl.us/

West Side Rowing Club of Buffalo Inc. for Juniors
PO Box 506
Buffalo, NY 14213-0506, United States
Tel: (716) 881-9797
Fax: (716) 881-3100
Email: rowing@wsrc.org
www.wsrc.org

West Springfield High School
PO Box 2473
Springfield, VA 22152, United States
Contact: Chuck Geyer
Tel: (703) 451-6681
Email: cegeyer@compuserve.com
www.spartancrew.com

Colors: Orange and blue
Mascot: Spartans
Year est: 1988
History: Active since 1988, Spartan Crew has grown into one of the premiere high school rowing clubs in Northern Virginia. We offer a popular fall novice program, a comprehensive winter workout regimen and an array of spring rowing opportunities to enable students.

Westerville Crew
4111 Executive Parkway
Ste 305
Westerville, OH 43081, United States
Contact: Matthew Chase, Head Coach
Tel: (614) 565-9199
Fax: (614) 259-2001
Email: mchasemd@medtuity.com
www.westervillecrew.org

Colors: Navy and white
Year est: 1995
History: Westerville Crew incorporated in 1996 for the purpose of promoting competitive rowing among Westerville-area high school students. It has grown from 18 members to approximately 95 members since then.

Westside High School
1002 Patriots Way
Augusta, GA 30907, United States
Tel: (706) 868-4002
Fax: (706) 868-4005

Colors: Red, blue and white
Mascot: Patriots

William Penn Charter High School
3000 West Schoolhouse Lane
Philadelphia, PA 19144, United States
Tel: (215) 844-3460
Fax: (215) 844-5537
www.penncharter.com/

Colors: Blue and yellow
Mascot: Quakers

William R. Boone HS/S.O.R.A.
2000 S. Mills Avenue
Orlando, FL 32806, United States
Tel: (407) 893-7200
Fax: (407) 897-2466
Contact: Bob Reynolds, President
Tel: (407) 381-4122
Email: reynolr@aol.com
www.rowfl.com/boone

Colors: Orange and white
Mascot: Braves
Year est: 1989

Wilmington Youth Rowing Association
206 Hoiland Drive
Wilmington, DE 19806, United States
Contact: Gordon Pizor, Head Coach
Tel: (302) 762-2445
Fax: (302) 622-8189
Email: power10@aol.com
www.wyra.org

Year est: 1989

Winchester Thurston High School
555 Morewood Avenue
Pittsburgh, PA 15213, United States
Tel: (412) 578-7503
Fax: (412) 578-7504

Colors: Black, yellow and purple
Mascot: Bears

Winsor School
Pilgrim Road
Boston, MA 02215, United States
Tel: (617) 735-9500
www.winsor.edu

Winter Park High School
PO Box 1003
Winter Park, FL 32790, United States
Contact: Johnathan and Beth Rich, Co-Booster
President
Email: jrich@hklaw.com
Mike Vertullo, Women's Head Coach
Tel: (407) 622-3200
Fax: (407) 975-2434
Email: vertulm@ocps.k12.fl.us
www.wpcrew.com

Colors: Orange and black
Mascot: Wildcats

Woodbridge High School
3001 Old Bridge Road
Woodbridge, VA 22192, United States
Contact: Tom Land, President
Email: eagles1950@aol.com
Tom Moulen, Head Coach

Email: aanrows@aol.com
www.woodbridgecrew.org

Colors: Green, Gold, White
Mascot: Vikings

Woodrow Wilson High School
Nebraska Ave & Chesapeake Street NW
Washington, DC 20016, United States
Tel: (202) 282-0120
Fax: (202) 282-0120
Contact: Derry Allen, Booster President
Tel: (202) 244-5991
Email: derryallen@aol.com
www.wilsonhs.org/sports/crew/

Colors: Green and white
Mascot: Tiger
Year est: 1985

Worcester Public Schools
Foley Stadium
305 Chandler Street
Worcester, MA 01602-3439, United States
Tel: (508) 799-3081
www.staruks.net/WorcesterCrew.html

WT Woodson High School
PO Box 2881
Fairfax, VA 22031, United States
Contact: John Morris, Booster President
Email: jtsmgb@aol.com
www.wtwoodsoncrew.org

Colors: Blue and white
Mascot: Cavaliers
Year est: 1984

Yorktown High School
Crew Boosters
5201 N. 28th Street
Arlington, VA 22207, United States
hometown.aol.com/mplanb/yhscrew.html

Colors: Columbia Blue, White
Mascot: Patriots

ZLAC Rowing Club for Juniors
1111 Pacific Beach Drive
San Diego, CA 92109, United States
Contact: Tom Evans, Program Director
Email: tnevans@san.rr.com
Paul Johnson, Head Coach
Tel: (619) 269-6770
Email: pablosd@cox.net
Tel: (858) 274-7826
Email: juniors@zlac.com
www.zlac.com

Uruguay

NATIONAL FEDERATION

Federación Uruguaya de Remo
Canelones 982
1er Piso
Montevideo
Uruguay
Tel: +598 2 913689
Fax: +598 2 9009435
Email: obertijuan@hotmail.com

Uzbekistan

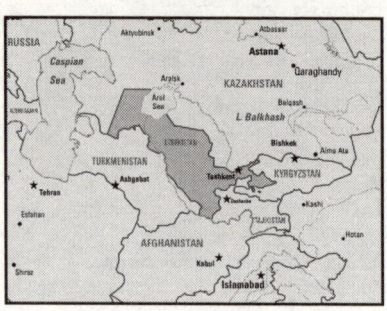

NATIONAL FEDERATION

The Rowing Fed. of The Republic of Uzbekistan
Furkat Street 1
Tashkent, 700027
Uzbekistan
Tel: +998 7 3712 452 262
Fax: +998 7 3712 450 852

Venezuela

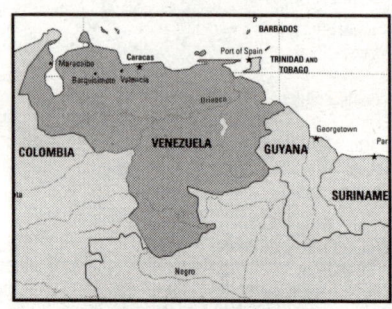

NATIONAL FEDERATION

Federación Venezolana de Remo
Instituto Nacional de Deportes
Velodromo Teo Capriles Ofic n32
Caracas, Venezuela
Tel: +58 414 389 18 29
Email: fevederem@hotmail.com

Vietnam

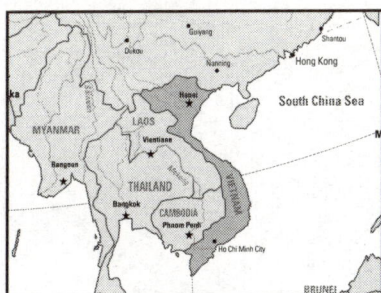

NATIONAL FEDERATION

Rowing Federation of Vietnam
10 Trinh Hoai Duc Street
Hanoi, Vietnam
Tel: +84 4 8452 987
Fax: +84 4 8234 557

Yugoslavia

NATIONAL FEDERATION

Yugoslav Rowing Federation
Ada Ciganlija 1
Beograd, 11030
Yugoslavia
Tel: +381 11 553 124
Fax: +381 11 361 3106
Email: yrf@eunet.yu
www.yurowing.org.yu

CLUBS

Begej 1883
Obala Milosa Velikog BB
23000 Zrenjanin
Yugoslavia
Tel: +381 023/562-073
www.begej1883.org.yu

Crvena Zvezda
Ada Ciganlija 5
11030 Beograd
Yugoslavia
Tel/Fax: +381 011-554-652

Danubius 1885
Suncani Kej 13
21000 Novi Sad
Yugoslavia
Tel/Fax: +381 021/450-853

Djerdap 1999
Porecki Put BB
18300 Donji Milanovac
Tel: +381 030/86-877

Galeb
Kej Oslobodilaca 73
11080 Zemun
Yugoslavia
Tel: +381 011/618-501

Graficar
Ada Ciganlija 7
11030 Beograd
Yugoslavia
Tel: +381 011/553-010

Partizan
Ada Ciganlija 3
11030 Beograd
Yugoslavia
Tel/Fax: +381 011/553-124
http://www.vkpartizan.net

Palic
Gavrila Principa 9
24413 Palic
Yugoslavia
Tel: +381 024/546-239

Smederevo
Despota Djurdja 4
11300 Smederevo
Yugoslavia
Tel: +381 026/223-027

Tamis
Postanski Fah 1
26000 Pancevo
Yugoslavia
013/351-543

Tisa 2001
Trg Oslobodjenja 7
Titel, Yugoslavia
Tel: +381 021/862-101

Zrenex 1995
Zarka Zrenjanina 68
23000 Zrenjanin
Yugoslavia
Tel/Fax: +381 023/534-536
Email: zrenex@mgnet.co.yu
www.zrenex.org.yu

Zimbabwe

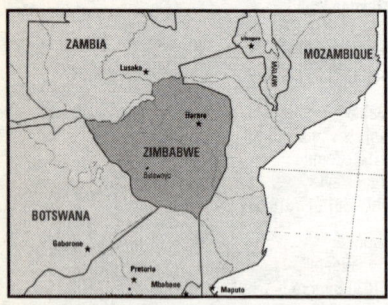

NATIONAL FEDERATION

Rowing Association of Zimbabwe
PO Box CY 285
Causeway
Harare, Zimbabwe
Tel: +263 4 497 525
Fax: +263 4 668 250
Email: lombard@africaonline.co.zw

Buyer's Guide ★ Rowing Schools and Camps

Buyer's Guide ★ Rowing Schools and Camps

CALM WATERS ROWING INC.

All-inclusive rowing vacations for 3, 4 or 7 days. We offer small classes, excellent coaching, optimum rowing conditions, delicious meals and elegant accommodations — all catered toward the Masters rower.

10155 Mary Ball Road, Lancaster, VA 22503
Tel: (804) 435-6887 or (800) 238-5578
www.calmwatersrowing.com

DBC SCULLING SCHOOL

Located on scenic Lamprey River. Provide on the water coaching with video taping. Also have an Indoor Rowing Facility and CARE Rowperfect Rowing Simulator to help teach proper sculling technique.

Durham Boat Company
220 Newmarket Road
Durham, NH 03824
Tel: (603) 659-7575
info@durhamboat.com
www.durhamboat.com

CRAFTSBURY

For nearly 30 seasons the Craftsbury Sculling Center has been the definitive sculling camp vacation. Its week, weekend, and four-day camps run May through September. Coaches include Olympic medallists and world champions. The Center offers a unique demo boat program that gives scullers an opportunity to test a variety of boats and oars from top manufacturers. Craftsbury also offers its campers and their families a walkable campus, great food, a swimming beach, massage, nature trails, and mountain biking. Learn to scull or tune your technique. Park your car and enjoy the best of the Vermont summer.

PO Box 31, 535 Lost Nation Road, Craftsbury Common, VT 05827
Tel: (802) 586-7767   Fax: (802) 586-7768
stay@craftsbury.com   www.craftsbury.com

Buyer's Guide ★ Rowing Schools and Camps

Buyer's Guide ★ Rowing Schools and Camps

Buyer's Guide ★ Racing Boats

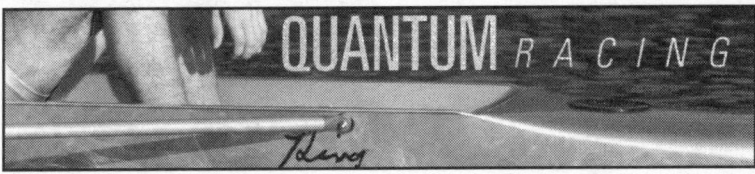

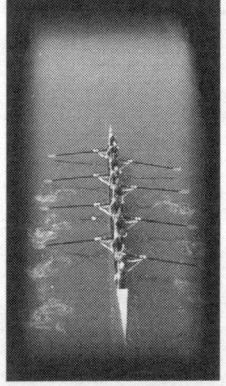

Buyer's Guide ★ Racing Boats

PEINERT

Peinert single sculls are built with the best materials to have the speed and feel of an elite boat while being durable and easy to row.

P26: 26', 33 lbs. $3,250.
X25: 25', 31 lbs. $3,850.

PO Box 1029, 46 Marion Road
Mattapoisett, MA 02739

Tel: (508) 758-3020

info@sculling.com
www.sculling.com

LevatorRACER

Since its debut in 1995 the LevatorRACER continues to be the best value. Levator offers the best materials, most adjustments, and choice for the money. Available for scullers 135-215 lbs. Quality and performance/guaranteed 5 yrs.

767 Industrial Road,
London, ONT N5V 4J5 Canada

Tel: (877) LEVATOR or (519) 659-2317

row@levator.com
www.levator.com

DURHAM BOAT COMPANY

Dreher Carbon Seats, Foot Stretchers and Riggers, Rowing Hardware and Accessories, NK and FC Cadence Electronics, Yakima Racks, CARE Rowperfect Rowing Simulators.

Durham Boat Company
220 Newmarket Road
Durham, NH 03824

Tel: (603) 659-7575

info@durhamboat.com
www.durhamboat.com

Buyer's Guide ★ Racing/Open Water and Recreational Boats

MAAS SINGLE

A flat water club racer with the stiffness and adjustability of the best elite boats.

Length: 27' 1"
Beam at washbox: 16.5"
Beam at waterline: 12"

Weight fully rigged: 35lbs.
(Carbon series only)

To locate a dealer nearest you visit our web site at www.maasboats.com

VIRUS
YOLE CLUB — DOUBLE/SINGLE

The Yole for clubs, families and serious open water rowing. Polyethylene rotomolded, robust, stable, 100% self bailing. Gratis video *Introduction to Rowing a Virus Scull* with each boat.

Length: 14.10" (4m 50cm) Width: 38" (96cm)
Weight: 130 lbs. (63kg)

Virus Sculls — RUM International, Inc.
Tel: (941) 387-7773 or (888) 767-8824
info@rowvirusboats.com
www.rowvirusboats.com

ALDEN ROWING SHELLS
#1 IN RECREATIONAL ROWING FOR OVER THIRTY YEARS.

We have a shell for everyone.
Full line of oars, gear and accessories.

Alden Rowing Shells
PO Box 368, Eliot, ME 03903

Tel: (207) 439-5277
Fax: (207) 439-0762

rjarvis@rowalden.com
www.rowalden.com

Buyer's Guide ★ Open Water and Recreational Boats

MAAS AERO

The shell that set the standard for design and construction of modern recreational and open water shells — forgiving enough for a novice, fast enough to win a race.

Length: 21' 3"
Beam on deck: 25"
Beam at waterline: 19"
Weight fully rigged: 39 lbs.
Carbon series: 35 lbs.
Maximum rower weight: 240 lbs.

To locate a dealer nearest you visit our web site at www.maasboats.com

PEINERT ZEPHYR

Stable, rugged novice or open water single.
Length: 19'
Weight: 41 lbs. Kevlar/Glass/Core
$2,900

PO Box 1029, 46 Marion Road, Mattapoisett, MA 02739
Tel: (508) 758-3020
info@sculling.com
www.sculling.com

ADIRONDACK ROWING

46 Meadow Lane,
Queensbury, NY 12804
Tel: (518) 745-7691
adkrowing@adelphia.net
www.adirondackrowing.com

Proudly offering the finest MAAS, Alden, Adirondack Series Sliding Seat Wherries and Guideboats, Little River Marine, Bay Shells and Drew Harrison Rowing Shells along with full availability on Piantedosi and Latanzo parts. For the best price and customer service guaranteed since 1971, no one treats their customers better than Adirondack Rowing.

Buyer's Guide ★ Open Water and Recreational Boats

RON RANTILLA ROWING SYSTEMS
HARBOR CRUISER 17

Designed for pleasure rowing using one or two Frontrower drop-in rowing stations. Same power and exercise quality as sculling, but with a comfortable forward facing position. Can be rowed as a single, a double, or single with passenger.

Length: 17'2"   Beam: 36"   Weight: 65 lbs. + 25 lbs. per drop-in rowing station. Construction: Wood with fiberglass exterior.

30 Cutler Street, Warren, RI 02885

Tel: (401) 247-1482   www.FrontRower.com

ROSSITER
DISCOVER THE BENEFITS OF ROWING

Rowing is a safe, quiet and healthy way to enjoy the water. Consider our high quality, low maintenance rowboats. From 12' to 26' we carry the largest selection of new and used fixed and sliding seat rowboats in Ontario. The full line of Alden Ocean Shells, Laser, Paluski and Hudson Shells as well as our own traditional designs are available. We want to help you discover the benefits of rowing this summer.

R.R. #2, Ravenna, Ontario, N0H 2E0, Canada
Tel: (705) 445-2908   www.rossiterboats.com

MAAS 24

For the serious open water racer or advanced recreational rower.

The ideal training tool for competitive single scullers.

Length: 24'
Beam on deck: 20"
Beam at waterline: 14"
Weight fully rigged: 39 lbs.
Carbon Series: 36 lbs.
Maximum rower weight: 240 lbs.

To locate a dealer nearest you visit our web site at www.maasboats.com

Buyer's Guide ★ Open Water and Recreational Boats

PIANTEDOSI OARS
THE FIRST CHOICE FOR BOAT BUILDERS

Drop-In Rigs, Canoe Conversions, OEM & Custom Rigging,
Wing Riggers, Sliding Riggers, Sculls

Piantedosi Oars
P.O. Box 643
West Acton, MA 01720 USA

Tel: (978) 263-1814
Fax: (978) 263-5940

info@rowingrigs.com
www.rowingrigs.com

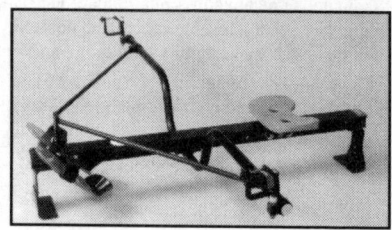

ECHO ROWING SHELL

Spirited and lively, yet very stable, the ECHO is fun for any skill level. Pushed hard in flat water or in surfing conditions it rises and skims like a power boat. With no removable parts, the light hull and unique folding rigger system make for quick rigging and easy handling.

Length: 18'   Beam at waterline: 21"   Beam on deck: 26"

Rigged weight: 48 lbs.   Capacity: Children to Large Adults

141 Rte 236, PO Box 68, Eliot, ME 03903   www.echorowing.com

PEINERT DOLPHIN
THE FASTEST OPEN WATER RACER

A Perennial Blackburn Challenge winner.

Length: 24'
Weight: 38 lbs Kevlar/Carbon
$3,250

PO Box 1029, 46 Marion Road,
Mattapoisett, MA 02739

Tel: (508) 758-3020

info@sculling.com   www.sculling.com

Buyer's Guide ★ Open Water and Recreational Boats

MAAS FLYWEIGHT

For the serious open water racer or advanced recreational rower under 140 lbs. Here's a shell that fits!

Length: 24'1"   Beam at washbox: 16.5"   Beam at waterline: 12"
Weight fully rigged: 35 lbs.   Carbon Series: 32 lbs.   Max rower weight: 140 lbs.

To locate a dealer nearest you visit our web site at www.maasboats.com

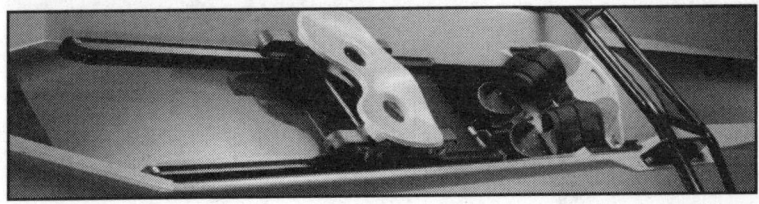

Website:www.whitehallrow.com   Phone:1-800-663-748

Whitehall Spirit 17 ----- Double position rowing boat

Length 17   Beam 51   Weight 280lbs.

MIDDLE PATH BOATS

This elegant design's dominance of the open water racing circuit sparked the modern fixed seat performance revolution.

LOA: 16'2" LWL: 15'8" Beam: 38"
WLB 32" Weight: 95 lbs.

$3,250.00

Middle Path Boats
PO Box 314, Edinburg, PA 16116
Tel: (724) 652-4448
www.by-the-sea.com/middlepathboats

Buyer's Guide ★ Open Water and Recreation Boats

MAAS DOUBLE

Designed for Intermediate to advanced open
water rowers. Fast enough to
compete with flat water boats. Stable
enough for open water.

Length: 31'
Beam at washbox: 22.5"
Beam at waterline: 14.75"
Weight fully rigged: 65 lbs.
(Carbon series only)
Maximum rower weight: 480 lbs.

To locate a dealer nearest you visit our web
site at www.maasboats.com

NEWFOUND WOODWORKS

The Newfound Woodworks of Bristol, New
Hampshire manufactures cedar strip/epoxy
canoe, kayak, and rowing boat kits. The
current crop of rowing boat designs include
the Rangeley Lake Boat, a 17' Whitehall, a 16'
Adirondack Guideboat, a Wherry and a pulling boat named Liz (designed by Ken Bassett).
The cedar strip construction method allows home builders to complete lightweight, beautiful, maintenance free boats. Go to the website to request our free color catalog.

The Newfound Woodworks, Inc.
67 Danforth Brook Road, Bristol, NH 03222
Tel: (603) 744-6872   Fax: (603) 744-6892
info@newfound.com   www.newfound.com

★ Business Listings ★

Art, Prints and Photographs

Amy Wilton — Photographer
458 Camden Road
Hope, ME 04847
United States
Tel: (207) 542-5497
Email: info@laughingdogphotography.com
www.laughingdogphotography.com
please see our color ad.

Chris Milliman — Photographer
PO Box 831
Hanover, NH 03755
United States
Tel: (603) 643-0606
Email: chris@chrismilliman.com
www.chrismilliman.com

Digital Future Photography
900 North Stafford Street, Ste 1914
Arlington, VA 22203, United States
Tel: (703) 812-5069
Email: byron@digitalfuturephotography.com
www.digitalfuturephotography.com

Dominik Keller — Photographer
Weineggstrasse 32
8008 Zurich, Switzerland
Tel: +41 1 422 2440
Fax: +41 1 383 4646
Email: dckeller@bluewin.ch

EC & BC Shot' em — Photographers
Busken Huetstraat 14
GV Utrect, 3532
Netherlands
Tel: +31 3029 38538
Fax: +31 0624 609756
Email: treffers@sybrand.nl
www.nlroei.nl/ecbc

Eric G. Jennens
1978 McDougall Street
Kelowna, BC V1Y 1A3
Canada
Tel: (604) 763-2273
Fax: (604) 762-5242

FISA Souvenir Shop
Postfach 4822
Talstrasse 65
8022 Zurich
Switzerland
Tel: +41 121 14773
Fax: +41 121 14528

Frederic Haslin — Photographer
8 Square du Mal Lyautey
60200, France
Tel: +33 344 868032
perso.wanadoo.fr/haslin.photos.sports

Middle Path Boats
PO Box 314
Edinburg, PA 16116
United States

Tel: (724) 652-4448

middlepath@aol.com
www.by-the-sea.com/middlepathboats

Gold Medal Photos

19 Strathmore Road
St. Catharines, ON L2T 2CR
Canada

Tel: (905) 685-9404

slapinsk@vaxxine.com
www.rowersalmanac.com/photos/

Photographing champions at the
Royal Canadian Henley Regatta
and the Canadian Secondary
Schools Rowing Championships
since 1982. Call or visit
www.rowersalmanac.com
to order your photograph!

Art, Prints and Photographs

Gold Medal Photos
19 Strathmore Road
St. Catharines, ON L2T 2CR
Canada
Tel: (905) 685-9404
Email: slapinsk@vaxxine.com
www.rowersalmanac.com/photos/
please see our ad page 418.

Hebfotos Sports Photography
PO Box 7261, Hutt Str
Adelaide, 5000, Australia
Tel: +61 8 8232 4477
Fax: +61 8 8233 7770
Email: hebfotos@hebfotos.com
www.hebfotos.com

House Portraits by John Maxwell
838 Knapp Road
Lansdale, PA 19446, United States
Tel: (215) 855-6716
Email: maxwellhouse@netcarrier.com
www.maxwellhouseportraits.com/

Igor Meijer — Photographer
c/o FFSA
17 boulevard de la Marne
94736, Nogent sur Marne
France
Tel: +33 6 8090 3706

Jean Pierre Surault — Photographer
26 avenue de Landshut
60200, Compiegne
France

JET Photographics
Unit 30, Dry Drayton Ind. Estate
Cambridge, CB3 8AT
United Kingdom
Tel: +44 1954 211007
Fax: +44 1954 211007
Email: info@jetphotographic.demon.co.uk
www.jetphotographic.com

Joel Rogers — Photographer
8324 19th Avenue NW
Seattle, WA 98117
United States
Tel: (206) 789-3108
Fax: (206) 789-3204
Email: stock@joelrogers.com
www.joelrogers.com/
please see our ad page 419.

John H. Shore — Photography
11 Jessamy Road
Weybridge
Surrey, KT13 8LB
United Kingdom

Art, Prints and Photographs

Kit Raymond
619 Cherry Valley Road
Princeton, NJ 08540
United States
Tel: (609) 924-0145
www.kitraymond.artspan.com

Mimmo Perna — Photographer
Via G.B. Vela 231
80147, Napoli
Italy
Tel: +39 081 572 6846
Fax: +39 338 251 1558
Email: mimmoperna@interfree.it

Nors Gear
PO Box 143
Woolrich, ME 04579
United States
Fax: (207) 442-8904
Email: nors@norsgear.com
www.norsgear.com

Paolo Genovesi
Via Cesarea 165
48100, Ravenna
Italy
Tel: +39 335 693 9808
Email: pgenovesi@libero.it

Peter Spurrier — Photographer
58 South Avenue
Egham
Surrey, TW20 8HQ
United Kingdom
Tel: +44 1784 440771
Fax: +44 1784 440771
Email: spurrier@moose.co.uk

Quester Gallery
On The Green, PO Box 32U
Stonington, CT 06378 United States
Tel: (860) 535-3860
Fax: (860) 535-3533
Email: info@questergallery.com
www.questergallery.com/

Rainier Empacher — Photographer
Rockenauer Strasse 7
69412, Eberbach A.N.
Germany
Tel: +49 6271 80000
Fax: +49 6271 800079
Email: empacher.boats@t-online.de

Art, Prints and Photographs

River & Rowing Museum
Mill Meadows
Henley-on-Thames
Oxon, RG9 1BF
United Kingdom
Tel: +44 1491 415600
Fax: +44 1491 415601
Email: museum@rrm.co.uk
www.rrm.co.uk

Sports Graphics
110 Great Road
Maynard, MA 01754
United States
Tel: (978) 897-1748
Fax: (978) 897-5609

The Art of Rowing
1 Oak Hill Road, 2nd floor
Fitchburg, MA 01420
United States
Tel: (978) 342-8333
Fax: (978) 349-6200
Email: info@ArtofRowing.com
www.ArtofRowing.com
please see our color ad.

The Coaching Resource
1381 Mecklenburg Road
Ithaca, NY 14850
United States
Tel: (607) 277-4471
Email: info@coachingresource.com
www.coachingresource.com

The Cooley Gallery
25 Lyme Street
Old Lyme, CT 06371
United States
Tel: (860) 434-8807
Fax: (860) 434-7526
Email: cooleygallery@snet.net
www.cooleygallery.com

Trailing Fire, LLC
1 Winding Lane
Westport, CT 06880
United States
Tel: (203) 222-1230
Fax: (203) 221-1211
Email: mljuran@yahoo.com

Camps and Schools

Augusta Training Center
PO Box 3752
966 Heard Avenue
Augusta, GA 30914
United States
Email: mseanhall@yahoo.com

Australian Institute of Sport
PO Box 176
Belconnen ACT, 2616
Australia
Tel: +61 6285 2756
Fax: +61 6285 2813

Base d'aviron d'Aiguebelette
Lieu dit "Le Bouvent"
73470, Novalaise
France
Tel: +33 4793 60634
Fax: +33 4794 41024

Calm Waters Rowing Inc.
10155 Mary Ball Road
Lancaster, VA 22503
United States
Tel: (804) 435-6887 or (800) 238-5578
Email: info@calmwatersrowing.com
www.calmwatersrowing.com

Camp Bob Cooper
Spring Training Center
8001 MW Rickenbaker
Summerton, SC 29148
United States
Tel: (803) 478-2090
Fax: (803) 478-2179
Email: bdeming@clemson.edu
www.clemson.edu/yli/cooper
please see our color ad.

Camp Randall Rowing Club Inc.
15 North Butler
Suite 404
Madison, WI 53703
United States
Tel: (608) 256-3636
Fax: (608) 661-9200
Email: schaefelaw@aol.com

Canyon Sports and Rowing Tours
Box 4787
Smithers, BC V0J 2N0
Canada
Tel: (250) 847 6103
Fax: (250) 847 6103
Email: info@rowingtours.com
www.rowingtours.com/

Casco Bay Rowing Center Inc.
5 Lupine Court
Yarmouth, ME 04096
United States
Tel: (207) 846-3277
Email: info@cascobayrowing.com
www.cascobayrowing.com/

Centro de Alto Rendimiento de Remo
Isla de la Cartuja
41092, Seville, Spain
Tel: +34 95 4461 400
Fax: +34 95 4461 456
Email: secretaria.car@deporteanduluz.com

Charles River Rowing Camps
Murr Center, 65 N. Harvard Street
Cambridge, MA 02163
United States
Tel: (617) 495-9249
Fax: (617) 496-2709
Email: eholeary@fas.harvard.edu

Club Natacio de Banyoles
Passeig Gaudi 3
17820, Banyoles, Spain
Tel: +34 972 570 859
Fax: +34 972 575 017
Email: info@banyoles-agenda.com

Camps and Schools

Craftsbury Sculling Center Inc.
Box 31 RA
Craftsbury Common, VT 05827
United States
Tel: (802) 586-7767 or 800-729-7751
Fax: (802) 586-7768
Email: stay@craftsbury.com
www.craftsbury.com
please see our color ad & page 406.

CRC Sculling Camps
13 Marlborough Crescent
Sevenoaks, Kent, England TN13 2HH
Tel: +44 (0) 1732 469670
Email: cooksonpd@hotmail.com
www.rowingcamps.com

DBC Sculling School Inc.
220 Newmarket Road
Durham, NH 03824
United States
Tel: (603) 659-7575
Fax: (603) 659-2548
Email: info@durhamboat.com
www.durhamboat.com
please see our ad page 406.

Deep Cove Rowing Centre
2156 Banbury Road
North Vancouver, BC V8Y 2L3
Canada
Tel: (604) 980-6766
www.f2000p.org/deepcove

Florida Rowing Center LLC
11924 Forest Hill Boulevard
Ste 22-326
Wellington, FL 33414
United States
Tel: (800) 996-0021
Email: postmaster@floridarowingcenter.com
www.floridarowingcenter.com
please see our ad page 407.

Frisco Bay Rowing Center
PO Box 220
Frisco, CO 80443
United States
Tel: (800) 766-1477
Fax: (970) 668-3748
Email: info@themanagers.com
www.themanagers.com/rowingcenter
please see our ad page 407.

Camps and Schools

GMS Rowing Center
The Bleachery — Unit X
143 West Street
New Milford, CT 06776
United States
Tel: (860) 350-4004
Fax: (860) 350-4004
Email: supersculler@hotmail.com

Henry Hamilton's
Vermont Sculling School
PO Box 98
Craftsbury Common, VT 05827
United States
Tel: (802) 586-9621
Email: sculling@ix.netcom.com
pw1.netcom.com/~sculling/school.html
please see our ad page 424.

Hartmut Buschbacher Rowing
Chattanooga, TN
Tel: (423) 503-5903
Email: info@hbrowing.com
www.hbrowing.com

HomePond Rowing
Email: marniemc2@cs.com
www.homepondrowing.com/

Joint-Stock Company "STEMP Ltd"
Krylatskoye Rowing Chanal
Krylatskaya Street 2
112552, Moscow
Russia
Tel: +7 095 140 1335
Fax: +7 095 190 2923

Kelowna Rowing and Paddling Centre
4220 Hobson Road
Kelowna, BC V1W 1Y3
Canada
Tel: (250) 764-0992
Email: info@f2000p.org
www.f2000p.org/kelowna

Leistungszentrum Munchen fur Rudern
Dachauer Strasse 35
85764, Oberschleissheim
Germany
Tel: +49 89 315 85200
Fax: +49 89 315 2990

Miami Beach Watersports Center
6500 Indian Creek Drive
Miami, FL 33141
United States
Tel: (305) 861-8876
Fax: (305) 861-8841
Email: elaine6500@aol.com
www.rowmiamibeach.com

Camps and Schools

Minnedosa Rowing Centre
PO Box 5000
Minnedosa, MB R0J 1E0, Canada
Tel: (204) 867-5320
Fax: (204) 253-9131

Navy Rowing Camp for Girls
50-I Sandstone Court
Annapolis, MD 21403, United States
Tel: (410) 263-4655
Email: info@navyrowingcamp.com
www.navyrowingcamp.com

Nike Rowing Camps
4470 Redwood Highway
San Rafael, CA 94903, United States
Tel: (800) 645-3226
Email: crew@ussportscamps.com
www.ussportscamps.com

Northeast Sculling & Rowing Center

PO Box 2060
Duxbury, MA 02331
United States
Tel: (781) 934-6192
Fax: (781) 934-5354
Email: email@RowCamp.com
www.rowcamp.com
please see our ad page 408.

Pocock Rowing Center Inc.
3320 Fuhrman Avenue East
Seattle, WA 98102
United States
Tel: (206) 328-0778
Fax: (206) 328 4239
Email: pocockrow@mindspring.com
www.pocockrowing.org

Port Moody Rowing Centre
2715 Esplanade Street
Port Moody, BC V3H 3P4
Canada
Tel: (604) 936-1155
www.f2000p.org/portmoody

Raritan Valley Rowing Camp
PO Box 1149
Lewis Brown Athletic Center
Piscataway, NY 08855
United States
Tel: (908) 445-4226
Fax: (908) 445-4226

Camps and Schools

Row As One
PO Box 55
Newton, MA 02456
United States
Tel: (617) 924-2120
Fax: (617) 924-2126
Email: info@rowasone.org
www.rowasone.org/
  please see our ad page 407.

Ruderakademie Ratzeburg
Domhof 37
23909, Ratzeburg
Germany
Tel: +49 454 1 86430
Fax: +49 454 1 864310

Ruderzentrum Berlin
Jungfernheideweg 80
13629, Berlin
Germany
Tel: +49 30 381 7061
Fax: +49 30 381 9437

Summer Camps on the River
Christchurch School
Christchurch, VA 23031
United States
Tel: (800) 296-2306
www.christchurchschool.org

Vernon Rowing Centre
115-2940 Jutland Road
Victoria, BC V8T 5K6
Canada
Tel: (250) 542-ROW1
www.f2000p.org/vernon

West Coast Rowing
81 Caton Place
Victoria, BC V9B 1L2
Canada
Tel: (250) 727-0966
Fax: (250) 727-2393
Email: coach@westcoastrowing.com
www.westcoastrowing.com

Willebroek
Bloso Sportcentrum "Hazewinkel"
Beenhouwersstraat 28
2830, Willebroek, Belgium
Tel: +32 3 886 6464
Fax: +32 3 886 2297
Email: hazewinkel@bloso.be

WPI Crew Camp
WPI Athletic Department
Worcester, MA 01609
United States
Tel: (508) 831-6119
Fax: (508) 831-5775
Email: lnoble@wpi.edu

Clothing and Accessories

AE Clothier
5A Pembroke Street
Cambridge, CB2 3QY
United Kingdom
Tel: +44 1223 354339
Fax: +44 1223 441710
Email: sales@aeclothier.co.uk
www.aeclothier.co.uk/

ARA Shop
The Priory
6 Lower Mall
London, W6 9DJ
United Kingdom
Tel: +44 181 7483632
Fax: +44 181 7414658

Astonetower
Amazonon 17
167 77, Elliniko
Greece
Tel: +30 210 9641211
Fax: +30 210 9641211
Email: sales@astonetower.com
www.astonetower.com

Boathouse Sports
425 E Hunting Park Avenue
Philadelphia, PA 19124
United States
Tel: (800) 875-1883, (215) 425-4300
Fax: (215) 425-2068
Email: info@boathouse.com
www.boathouse.com
please see our ad page 428.

BodyMIND
Busestrasse 33
28213, Bremen
Germany
Tel: +49 421 21 76 94
Fax: +49 421 22 37 38 9
Email: info@bm-sportswear.de
www.bm-sportswear.de

Catch 2 Finish
PO Box 380968
Cambridge, MA 02238-0968
United States
www.catch2finish.com

Charnwood Ties Ltd
91 Farndale Drive
Loughborough
Leics, LE1 2RG
United Kingdom
Tel: +44 (0) 1509 231448
Fax: +44 (0) 1509 215378
Email: mail@charnwoodties.co.uk
www.charnwoodties.co.uk

Clobber Rowing Apparel
PO Box 743
Wanganui, New Zealand
Tel: +64 6 344 5300
Fax: +64 6 344 5454
Email: info@clobber.co.nz
www.clobber.co.nz

Crew Line
Le Gojat — Lac D'Aiguebelette
F-73470 Novalaise
France
Tel: +33 04 79 44 12 16
Fax: +33 04 79 44 12 16
Email: crewline@free.fr

Clothing and Accessories

DesignerShoes.com
125 Newbury Street
Boston, MA 02116
United States
Tel: (617) 247-0202, (888) 371-SHOE
Email: info@designershoes.com
www.DesignerShoes.com

Durham Boat Co/Dreher
220 Newmarket Road
Durham, NH 03824
Tel:(603) 569-7575
Email: info@durhamboat.com
www.durhamboat.com
please see our color ad.

Eel Pie Rowing Supplies
PO Box 426
Godalming, GU7 1JF
United Kingdom
Tel: +44 1483 429074
Fax: +44 1483 429074
Email: eelpie-rowing@btconnect.com
www.eelpie-rowing.co.uk/

Godfrey Sports Ltd.
Mundella Works, Mundella Road
The Meadows
Nottingham, NG2 2EQ
United Kingdom
Tel: +44 115 9864600
Fax: +44 115 9862018
Email: sales@godfrey.co.uk
www.godfrey.co.uk

JL Design Enterprises, Inc.
1821 E. Newport Circle
Santa Ana, CA 92705
United States
Tel: (800) 831-3305, (714) 479-0240
Fax: (714) 479-0152
Email: info@jlracing.com
www.jlracing.com

JL Designs, UK
The Crew Room
34 Lower Richmond Road Putney
London, SW15 1JP
United Kingdom
Tel: +44 20 8788 1505
Fax: +44 87 0127 3881
Email: info@jlracing.com
www.jlracing.com

Clothing and Accessories

Judy's Enterprises
58 Savona Walk
Long Beach, CA 90803
United States
Tel: (562) 439-7912
Email: judysenterprises@aol.com

maax
300 Bedford Street
Manchester, NH 03101
United States
Tel: (603) 623-6268
Fax: (603) 622-2966
Email: info@bluefishriver.com
www.bluefishriver.com

New Wave Sportswear Handels GmbH
Schmidt-Knobelsdorf-Str.31/ Hs.40
13581, Berlin
Germany
Tel: +49 18056399283
Fax: +49 700 63919283
Email: office@newwave.de
www.newwave.de

Oarsman Shop
PO Box 1535
Maidenhead, SL6 5AS
United Kingdom
Tel: +44 1628 788515
Email: threemens@aol.com
www.oarsmansshop.com

Potomac Rowing
29908 South Stockton
Farmington Hills, MI 48336
United States
Tel: (800) 477-0440
Fax: (248) 471-1026
Email: info@potomacrowing.com
www.potomacrowing.com
please see our ad – Inside Front Cover.

Power 10 Apparel Inc.
5 Sleepy Hollow Cove
Longwood, FL 32750
United States
Tel: (888) 830-9759, (407) 830-9759
Fax: (407) 645-1480
Email: info@power10.com
www.power10.com

Power 10 Designs
1017 El Camino Real
PMB #315
Redwood City, CA 94063
United States
Tel: (650) 780-0679
www.cramton.com/power10/

Powerhouse Clothing Company
The Barns 18 Aughnatrisk Road
Hillsborough
Down, BT26 6JJ
United Kingdom
Tel: +44 184 6689890
Fax: +44 189 6689895
Email: rowing@powerhouseclothing.co.uk
www.powerhouseclothing.co.uk

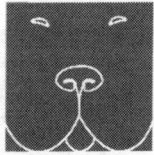

Clothing and Accessories

Redhead Clothing Ltd
2 Olympia House
36/38 Beaconsfield Rd Street George
Bristol, BS5 8ER
United Kingdom
Tel: +44 117 955 2226
Fax: +44 117 855 2033
Email: enquiries@redhead.co.uk
www.redhead.co.uk/

Regatta Northwest Inc.
6428 NE 185th Street
Kenmore, WA 98028
United States
Tel: (425) 482-1070
Fax: (425) 398-5588
Email: regattanw@aol.com
www.regattanorthwest.com

RegattaSport
50 Lakeport Road, #202
St. Catharines, ON L2N 4P7
Canada
Tel: (905) 937-5130
Fax: (905) 937-4941
Email: teams@regattasport.com
www.regattasport.ca
please see our color ad.

Rock the Boat
PO Box 157
Abingdon Oxfordshire
Oxon, OX14 3YU
United Kingdom
Tel: +44 1235 554457
Fax: +44 1235 554457
Email: enquiries@rock-the-boat.co.uk
www.rock-the-boat.co.uk
please see our ad page 426.

Sew Sporty
2215 La Mirada Drive
Vista, CA 92083
United States
Tel: (800) 765-6277, (760) 599-0585
Fax: (760) 599-0814
Email: sewsporty@aol.com
www.sewsporty.com

Silverstone Rowing
74 Clifton Downs Road
Hamilton, ON L9C 2P3
Canada
Tel: (905) 383-9952
Fax: (905) 389-0984
Email: silver@interlynx.net
www.silverstonerowing.com

Clothing and Accessories

SouthBay Rowing
2949A Summerall Circle
Ft. Eustis, VA 23604
United States
Tel: (757) 820-0653
Email: jessrcrane@aol.com
www.rowhard.com

Spartan Clothing Ltd
Unit 12 Sixways Trading Estate
Barnards Green
Malvern, WR14 3LY
United Kingdom
Tel: +44 1684 568208
Fax: +44 1684 572808
Email: info@spartan-clothing.co.uk
www.spartan-clothing.co.uk/

Sub Zero Technology Ltd
35 Churchill Way
Fleckney
Leicester, LE8 8UD
United Kingdom
Tel: +44 116 2402634
Fax: +44 116 2404099
Email: sales@subzero.co.uk

Wave One Sports Inc.
1992 Butler Pike
Conshohocken, PA 19428
United States
Tel: (800) 779-2831 or (610) 238-4770
Fax: (610) 238-9098
Email: info@waveonesports.com
www.waveonesports.com

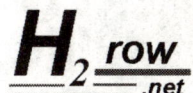

Docks and Floats

Atlantic Floating Docks
202 Talbot Avenue
Cambridge, MD 21613
United States
Tel: (866) 230-0099
Fax: (410) 228-0187
Email: choltz@bluecrab.org
www.atlanticfloatingdocks.com
please see our color ad.

CanDOCK
9441, Boul, Borque
Deauville QC J1N3G1
Canada
Email: candock@abacom.com
www.candock.com
please see our color ad.

Connect-A-Dock
1000 Flag Road
Adair, IA 50002
United States
Tel: (877) 742-3071, (641) 742-3071
Fax: (641) 742-3624
Email: steve@ssi-ia.com
www.connectadock.com
please see our color ad.

Connect-A-Dock — UK
Wave Seven Marine Ltd.
46 Ellesfield Road, West Parley
Ferndown, Dorset, BH22 8QN, UK
Email: sales@wseven.com
www.wseven.com

Merco Marine
60 Merco Road
Wellsburg, WV 26070, United States
Tel: (800) 39MERCO, (304) 737-3006
Fax: (304) 737-3008
Email: merco@mercomarine.com
www.mercomarine.com

Mylos B.V.
J. van Lennepkade 24
1053 MK Amste, The Netherlands
Tel: +31 20 6832903
Fax: +31 20 6169196
www.mylos.nl/

Sullivan Flotation System
PO Box 639
Warwick, NY 10990, United States
Tel: (800) 232-3625
Fax: (845) 986-8531
Email: docks@sullfloat.com
www.sullfloat.com
please see our color ad.

Equipment and Electronics

Accusport
Sports Resource Group
210 Belmont Road
Hawthorne, NY 10532
United States
Tel: (914) 747-8572, (800) 462-2876
Fax: (914) 741-5623
Email: accusport@lactate.com
www.lactate.com

AeRoWingRiggers
Carl Douglas Racing Shells
The Boathouse Timsway, Chertsey Lane
Staines, Middlesex, TW18 3JZ
United Kingdom
Tel: +44 1784 456344
Fax: +44 1784 466550
Email: aerowing@rowing-cdrs.demon.co.uk

Allegheny Trailers
739 E 140th Street
Cleveland, OH 44110
United States
Tel: (216) 541-0300
Fax: (216) 541-6092
Email: alleghenytrailers@henrywright.com
www.alleghenytrailers.com/boat.htm

Ankaa Shoes
A27/16, DLF City I
Gurgaon 122002
India
Tel: +91 124 256 0102
Fax: +91 124 256 0102
Email: apslamba@hotmail.com
please see our ad page 431.

Bootbouwerij J.A. Busman
Ysseldijk Noord 273
2935 Br Ouderkerk Ad Yssel
Netherlands
Tel: +31 180 683257
Fax: +31 180 683243
Email: cees.busman@wxs.nl
www.etrade.nl/etrade/klant/16406/

Cadence Rowing
PO Box 380064
Cambridge, MA 02238
United States
Tel: (320) 215-9231
Email: info@CadenceRowing.com
cadencerowing.com/

Crewsaver Ltd.
Mumby Road, Gosport
Hants, PO12 1AQ
United Kingdom
Tel: +44 23 9252 8261
Fax: +44 23 9252 0905
Email: sales@crewsaver.co.uk
www.crewsaver.co.uk/

Custom Carbon UK
29 Oakmere Drive
Great Broughton
Chester, CH3 5SD
United Kingdom
Tel: +44 124 4317650

Davies Row Tech
The Firs' Main Street
Southwick
Peterborough, PE8 5BL
United Kingdom
Tel: +44 1832 274782
Email: davies.rowtech@virgin.net
www.davies.rowtech.btinternet.co.uk

Equipment and Electronics

De Graaff Trailers
Langshot Stud Gracious Pond Road
Chobham
Surrey, GU24 8HJ
United Kingdom
Tel: +44 1276 855566
Fax: +44 1276 855577
Email: sales@degraafftrailers.co.uk
www.degraafftrailers.co.uk

Eton Rowing Courses
Eton College, Windsor
Berkshire, SL4 6BW
United Kingdom
Tel: +44 1753 671124
Fax: +44 1753 671265
Email: ceri.davies@etoncollege.co.uk

FM Baretta
PO Box 57
Cold Spring Harbor, NY 11724
United States
Tel: (516) 365-4932

Focus Boat Racks
United States
Tel: (269) 945-2173
Email: psmithfocus@tm.net
www.focusracks.com

H2row.net
2131 Trenton Drive S.
Trenton, MI 48183
United States
Tel: (734) 552-2663
Fax: (734) 675-6325
Email: yukondon@comcast.net
www.h2row.net
  please see our ad page 431.

Healthcare Technology Ltd
York House
City Fields Business Park Tangmere
W. Sussex, PO20 6FR
United Kingdom
Tel: +44 12 43528800
Fax: +44 12 43774728

Hill Boat Racks
Fred Hill and Son Company
2101 Hornig Road
Philadelphia, PA 19116-4202
United States
Tel: (800) 523-0112
Fax: (215) 698-4539
Email: kshaw@fredhillandsonco.com
www.fredhillandsonco.com

JoRow (Jorg Santen)
Valkenkamp 758
3607 MX Maarssen
Netherlands
Tel: +31 34 6579233
Fax: +31 65 5712289
Email:

Len Neville
The Boathouse
Tims Way Staines
Middlesex, Middlesex TW18 3JY
United Kingdom
Tel: +44 1784 463900
Fax: +44 1784 469965

Equipment and Electronics

Lou Lindsey's Movable Shell Racks
9900 Starfly Road
Las Cruces, NM 88011-9555
United States
Tel: (505) 642-9435
Email: plindsey@zianet.com
please see our ad page 451.

Martinoli
Via Ceriana, 12A
21051 Arcisate
Italy
Tel: +39 0332 471110
Email: info@martinoli.it
www.martinoli.it

Neaves Rowing Fittings
Unit 2 Currendon Farm Building
Swanage
Dorset, BH19 3AA
United Kingdom
Tel: +44 1929 450018
Fax: +44 1929 450019
Email: david.neaves@btinternet.com

Nielsen-Kellerman
104 West 15th Street
Chester, PA 19013
United States
Tel: (610) 447-1555
Fax: (610) 447-1577
Email: info@nkhome.com
www.nkhome.com

Nutrition Education Services
PO Box 33
West Chester, PA 19381
United States
Tel: (800) 692-5579
Fax: (610) 918-9835

Partez
2041 N. Kensington Street
Arlington, VA 22205
United States
Tel: (703) 534-9256
Email: jdwhiteii@aol.com

Piantedosi Oars Inc
PO Box 643
West Acton, MA 01720
United States
Tel: (978) 263-1814
Fax: (978) 263-5940
Email: gary@rowingrigs.com
www.rowingrigs.com/

Power Lung Inc. — U.S.
10690 Shadow Wood Drive, #100
Houston, TX 77043
United States
Tel: (713) 465-1180
Fax: (713) 465-5742
Email: cmorse@powerlung.com
www.powerlung.com

PowerLung Inc. — Australia
Divers Supplies Australia Pty Ltd
PO Box 643, Braeside
Australia
Tel: +61 3 9580 5666
Fax: +61 3 9587 1244
Email: john@diverssupplies.com.au
www.diverssupplies.com.au

PowerLung Inc. — Bermuda
Filter Queen Bermuda
PO Box 1316, Hamilton
Bermuda
Tel: (441) 292-9232
Fax: (441) 292-9233

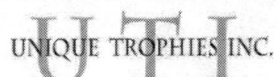

Equipment and Electronics

PowerLung Inc. — Canada
Peak Centre for Human Performance
24-3570 Canotek Road
Ottawa, ON K1J 9E8
Canada
Tel: (613) 737-7325
Fax: (613) 569-7661
Email: info@peakcentre.ca
www.peakcentre.ca

PowerLung Inc. — New Zealand
Sport Divers Supplies, Ltd
19 Regency Place
Mairangi Bay, Auckland
New Zealand
Tel: +64 9 479 4826
Fax: +64 9 479 1109
Email: info@sportdive.co.nz
www.sportdive.co.nz

PowerLung Inc. — Switzerland
Sun for Fun GmbH Sportartikel
Seerosenstrasse 20
6362, Stansstad
Switzerland
Tel: +44 41 610 30 21
Fax: +41 41 610 30 20
Email: waser@buyit.ch
www.powerlung.ch

PowerLung Inc. — The Netherlands
Duikcentrum SubLub/Duikschool SubLub
Frits Ruysstraat 18-20
3061 ME Rotterdam
Netherlands
Tel: +31 10 244 0111
Email: duiken@sublub.nl
www.sublub.nl

PowerLung Inc. — U.K.
Raymond Sims Ltd.
Trentside North, West Bridgford
Notts, NG2 5FA
United Kingdom
Tel: +44 115 981 7477
Fax: +44 115 982 1110
Email: sales@sims-sport.co.uk
www.sims-sport.co.uk

PS Sport
23 157th Ave SE
Bellevue, WA 98008
United States
Tel: (425) 373-3379
Email: paul@ps-sport.net
www.ps-sport.net
Home of the CBreeze, Personal Training, and
Performance Optimization for Rowing.

Raymond Sims Rowing Supplies
Trentside North
West Bridgford
Nottingham, NG2 5FA
United Kingdom
Tel: +44 1159 817477
Fax: +44 1159 821110
Email: simssupplies@compuserve.com
www.rowing.co.uk

Rigging Tools
20 Brookwood Ct
Princeton, NJ 08540
United States
Tel: (908) 274-2628

Round Rowing Tanks
2156 Route 67
Galway, NY 12074
United States
Tel: (518) 882-9372
Email: roundrowingtank@webtv.net
www.usewebdesign.com/rowingtank

Equipment and Electronics

Rudy Project — Italy
Via Benedetto Marcello
44-31100 Treviso
Italy
Tel: +39 422 43 30 11
Fax: +39 422 43 19 78
Email: info@rudyproject.com
www.rudyproject.com

Rudy Project — North America
971 Calle Amanecer
San Clemente, CA 92673
United States
Tel: (888) 860-7597
Fax: (800) 316-8733
Email: info@rudyprojectusa.com
www.rudyproject.com

Streamline Technology
12 Old Coach Road, Kelsall
Cheshire, CW6 0QJ
United Kingdom
Tel: +44 18 29752100
Fax: +44 18 29752100
Email: John.Streamline@btinternet.com
www.btinternet.com/~streamline/#Tips

Thiemann Equipment
760A Saxony Road
Encinitas, CA 92024
Tel: (760) 479-9876
Email: doug@ThiemannEquipment.com
www.ThiemannEquipment.com

Trailers & Components
Stoneacre Shrewsbury Road
Craven Arms
Shropshire, SY7 8BX
United Kingdom
Tel: +44 1588 673345
www.rowingboattrailers.co.uk

Verschoor Riggerbouw
Haringkade 12a
Ijmuiden, 1976 CP
Netherlands
Tel: +31 255 540550
Fax: +31 255 515635
Email: info@riggerbouw.nl
www.riggerbouw.nl

X-iser
PO Box 504
Boston, MA 02134
United States
Tel: (617) 782-1734
Fax: (617) 787-1570
Email: x-iser@x-iser.com
www.x-iser.com

Health and Nutrition

Evolution Sports Science
840 Winter Street
Waltham, MA 02451
United States
Tel: (781) 768-0940
Fax: (781) 768-0943
Email: info@evolutionsportsscience.com
www.evolutionsportsscience.com

RowersRehab
Deirdre McLoughlin — MSPT
2214 Jefferson Avenue
Berkeley, CA 94703
United States
Tel: (510) 548-5408
Email: Deirdre@Rowersrehab.com
www.rowersrehab.com
  please see our ad page 432.

RoyleRow
Performance Training Programs
PO Box 21
Craftsbury Common, VT 05827
United States
Tel: (802) 793-9195
Email: roylerow@sover.net
www.Roylerow.com
  please see our color ad.

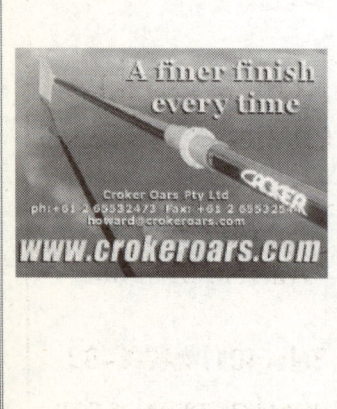

Jewelry, Medals and Awards

Blades Galore
19 Elm Way, Melbourn
Royston, SG8 6UH
United Kingdom
Tel: +44 7973 616404
Fax: +44 1763 222363
Email: info@bladesgalore.com
www.BladesGalore.com

Celebration Crystal Co. Ltd
Montford Bridge
Shrewsbury, SY4 1BR
United Kingdom
Tel: +44 800 616335
Fax: +44 1743 850146
Email: info@celebrationcrystal.co.uk
www.celebrationcrystal.co.uk

Crown Awards
9 Skyline Drive
Hawthorne, NY 10532
United States
Tel: (800) 227-1557
Fax: (914) 347-7008
Email: crowninfo@crowntrophy.com
www.crownawards.com

Fco Otero
20 East 68 Street # 11F
New York, NY 10021
United States
Tel: (917) 353-7742
Email: cs@e925.com
www.fcootero.com
Hand crafted Sterling silver rowing jewelry.

First Coast Promotions Rowing Jewelry
3948 Sunbeam Road, Suite 5
Jacksonville, FL 32257
United States
Tel: (800) 762-4653, (904) 262-9155
Fax: (904) 262-2992
Email: promonorm@aol.com
www.sportsgifts4u.com
please see our ad page 434.

Hanne Ruiter
Raam 5
8032 ET Zwolle
Netherlands
Tel: +31 38 4548526

Jewelry, Medals and Awards

Mason Designs
Wimbledon Art Studios
Riverside Road
Wimbledon, SW17 0BA
United Kingdom
Tel: +44 771 325 5870
Email: masondesignsmail@aol.com
www.mason-designs.com

Rubini Jewelers
632 N Washington Street
Alexandria, VA 22314
United States
Tel: (703) 548-5509
Email: srubini@aol.com
www.rubinijewelers.com

Sparhawk Model Oars
2299 Porters Point Road
Colchester, VT 05446
United States
Tel: (802) 638-4799
Fax: (802) 658-1115
www.sparhawkmodeloars.com

Unique Trophies Inc.
14502 115 Avenue
Edmonton, AB T5M 3B9
Canada
Tel: (780) 434-6593
Fax: (780) 433-5600
Email: sales@uniquetrophies.ca
www.uniquetrophies.ca/

Whirling Girl Rowing Jewelry
1215 N. 43rd Street
Seattle, WA 98103
United States
Tel: (206) 355-4567
Fax: (206) 374-8227
Email: info@whirlinggirl.com
www.whirlinggirl.com
please see our ad page 436.

Media, Publications, Software

Airo Rowing Magazine
Kotipolku 2
55120, Imatra
Finland
Tel: +358 5 4317 224
Fax: +358 5 4317 226

Alek.org — Graphic Design
3801 S. Alaska St. #105
Seattle, WA 98118
United States
Tel: (206) 769-2913
Email: alek@alek.org
www.alek.org

Cotting Companies
145 Pinckney Street #134
Boston, MA 02114
United States
Tel: (617) 723-4274
www.cottingco.com

Coxswain's Locker
PO Box 1167
Washington, DC 20013
United States
Tel: (703) 237-COXN (2696)
Email: joethecoxn@aol.com
www.coxing.com

Danish Rowing Magazine
Skovalleen 38A
Postboks 74
2880, Bagsvaerd
Denmark
Tel: +45 4444 0633
Fax: +45 4444 0449
Email: roning@roning.dk
www.roning.dk

L'Aviron
Fed. Francaise des Societes d'Aviron
17 Boulevard de la Marne
94736, Nogent sur Marne Cedex
France
Tel: +33 1 45 14 26 40
Fax: +33 1 45 75 78 75
Email: ffsa@@avironfrance.asso.fr
www.avironfrance.asso.fr

Messing About in Boats
29 Burley Street
Wenham, MA 01984-1943
United States
Tel: (508) 774-0906
www.messingaboutinboats.com/

OeRV Ruder Report
Oesterreichischer Ruderverband
Blattgasse 4
1030, Vienna
Austria
Tel: +43 1 7120 878
Fax: +43 1 7120 8784
Email: orv@asn.or.at
www.rudern.at

RaceDay
206 Duncan Avenue
Wilmington, DE 19803
United States
Tel: (215) 851-0406
Fax: (215) 851-0791

Media, Publications, Software

Regatta Magazine
The Priory 6 Lower Mall
Hammersmith
London, W6 9DJ
United Kingdom
Tel: +44 20 8237 6700
Fax: +44 20 8237 6749
Email: regatta@ara-rowing.org
www.ara-rowing.org

Regatta Master
PO Box 230836
Portland, OR 97281-0836
United States
Tel: (503) 968-5888
Fax: (503) 670-9249
Email: Stevej@jenisys.net
www.jenisys.net

Remo Magazine
Apartado de Correos n29
33770 Vegadeo
Principado de Asturias
Spain
Tel: +34 98 563 4339
Fax: +34 98 547 6036

Roeien Redactie
Bosbaan 6
1182, AG Amstelveen, The Netherlands
Tel: +31 20 646 2740
Fax: +31 20 646 3881
Email: info@knrb.nl
www.knrb.nl

Row Canada Aviron
NOTC Venture
PO Box 17 000 STN Forces
Victoria, BC V9A 7N2, Canada
Tel: 1-877-RCA-GROW (722-4769)
Email: comm@rowingcanada.org
www.rowingcanada.org

Rowing Magazine Monthly
Rowing Centre
Bessborough Works, 7 Molesey Road
West Molesey, Surrey
United Kingdom
Tel: +44 19 798249
Fax: +44 19 796754

Rowing News
PO Box 831
Hanover, NH 03755, United States
Tel: (603) 643-0059
Fax: (603) 643-0606
Email: rowingnews@aol.com
www.rowingnews.com

Media, Publications, Software

Rowing Sport Magazine
Russian Rowing Federation
119871, Moscow
Russia
Tel: +7 095 725 4698
Fax: +7 095 201 0128

Rudern Schweiz
SRV Geschaftsstelle
Brunigstrasse 182a
6060, Sarnen
Switzerland
Tel: +41 41 6607 557
Fax: +41 41 6609 443
Email: info@ruderverband.ch
www.ruderverband.ch

Rudersport
Deutscher Ruderverband e.V.
Geschaftsstelle: Maschstr. 20
30169, HannoverGermany
Tel: +49 0511 980 94 0
Fax: +49 0511 980 94 25
Email: info@rudern.de
www.rudern.de/

Scull Magazine
Emedia srl
Via Germanico 109
192, Rome
Italy
Tel: +39 06 3250 7855

Sports Book Publisher
278 Robert Street
Toronto, ON M56 2K8
Canada
Tel: (416) 922-0860
Fax: (416) 966-9022

Svensk Rodd
Box 131
275 23, Sjobo
Sweden
Email: per.ekstrom@fhnet.net
www.roddsverige.nu

The Rowing Library
309 Washington Street
Duxbury, MA 02332
United States
Tel: (617) 934-6192
Fax: (617) 934-5350

USRowing Magazine
201 S Capitol Avenue, Suite 400
Indianapolis, IN 46225
United States
Tel: (800) 314-4769
Fax: (317) 237-5656
Email: brett@usrowing.org
www.usrowing.org

Veslanje Rowing Magazine
Remetinec Laniste 14/B
Grvatska
10020, Zagreb
Croatia

Way's Bookshop
54 Friday Street
Henley-on-Thames, RG9 1AH
United Kingdom
Tel: +44 1491 576663

www.irow.com
375 Clinton Ave
New Haven, CT 06513
United States
Email: webmaster@irow.com
www.irow.com

Oars and Ergs

Braca-Sport — Hungary
Commercial Division
Torokesz ut 16/A
1022 Budapest, Hungary
Tel: +36 1 326 8853
Fax: +36 1 3265350
Email: Braca-Hu@Braca-sport.com
www.braca-sport.com

Braca-Sport — Lithuania
Taikos Pr. 159/A
LT3023, Kaunas
Lithuania
Tel: +370 37 474 033
Fax: +370 37 474 035
Email: braca-@braca-sport.com
www.braca-sport.com

CARE Rowperfect B.V.
Baalder Esch 8
7772 JV Hardenberg, The Netherlands
Tel: +31 523 270184
Fax: +31 523 270185
Email: care@rowperfect.com
www.rowperfect.com

Concept2
105 Industrial Park Drive
Morrisville, VT 05661
United States
Tel: (800) 245-5676
Fax: (802) 888-4791
Email: rowing@concept2.com
www.concept2.com
  please see our color ad.

Concept2 — Australia
45-53 Riversdale Road
Newton, Victoria, 3220, Australia
Tel: +61 3 5221 3450
Fax: +61 3 5221 2596
Email: info@concept2.com.au
www.concept2.com.au
  please see our color ad.

Croker Oars Pty Ltd
206 Cowans Lane
Oxley Island, NSW 2430
Australia
Tel: +61 2 65 532 473
Fax: +61 2 65 532 544
Email: howard@crokeroars.com
www.crokeroars.com
  please see our ad page 438.

Custom Carbon Ltd.
PO Box 12-101
Penrose, Auckland
New Zealand
Tel: +64 9 634 9285
Fax: +64 9 634 9019
Email: custom.carbon@xtra.co.nz
www.rowingnz.org.nz

Durham Boat Co/Dreher
220 Newmarket Road
Durham, NH 03824
Tel:(603) 569-7575
Email: info@durhamboat.com
www.durhamboat.com
  please see our color ad.

J Sutton Racing Oars & Sculls
Romney Lock
Riverside Walk Windsor
Berkshire, Berks SL4 6HU
United Kingdom
Tel: +44 1753 855540
Fax: +44 1753 856982
Email: steve.bryan@suttonblades.co.uk
www.suttonblades.co.uk

Joel Jullien
Croix des Chenes
30650, Saze
France
Tel: +33 49 03 17245

Oars and Ergs

Mupiro Rowing Services
Westerley House
Tellisford
Bath, BA3 6RL
United Kingdom
Tel: +44 1373 830920
Fax: +44 1225 722033
Email: info@mupiro.co.uk
www.mupiro.co.uk

Oarsmaker Ziegler
Nikolausstr. 9
D 8700, Wuerzburg
Germany
Tel: +49 931 86725

Oarsport Ltd
Vermont House Unit 5
Nottingham South & Wilford Ind Estate
Ruddington Lane, Wilford
Nottingham, NG11 7HQ
United Kingdom
Tel: +44 115 981 8183
Fax: +44 115 981 8184
Email: oarsport@oarsport.co.uk
www.oarsport.co.uk

Waterline Equipment
Oegstgeeststraat 83
5045 TZ Tilburg
Netherlands
Tel: +31 13 572 0851
Fax: +31 13 572 0852
Email: info@waterline.nl
www.waterline.nl

WaterRower — Australia
Unit E2, 27-29 Fariola Street
Silverwater, NSW 2128
Australia
Tel: +61 (0)2 9748 0591
Fax: +61 (0)2 9748 0593
Email: peter_murphy@waterrower.com
www.waterrower.com.au

WaterRower — U.K.
25 Acton Park Estate
The Vale
London, W3 7QE
Tel:+44 (0)20 8749 8400
Fax:+44 (0)20 8749 8600
Email: support@waterrower.co.uk
www.waterrower.co.uk

WaterRower — U.S.
560 Metacom Avenue,
Warren, RI, 02885
Tel:(401) 247 7742
Fax: (401) 247 7743
Email: support@waterrower.com
www.waterrower.com

Xcell Oars & Sculls Ltd
Tom Jones Boatyard Romney Lock
Riverside Walk Windsor
Berks, SL4 6HU
United Kingdom
Tel: +44 1753 855540
Fax: +44 1753 856982
Email: info@xcell.uk.com
www.xcell.uk.com

Open Water and Recreational Boats

Adirondack Goodboat
HC01 Box 44
Long Lake, NY 12847
United States
Tel: (518) 624-6398
Fax: (518) 624-6398
Email: mason@telenet.net
www.adirondackgoodboat.com

Adirondack Guideboat Inc.
PO Box 144
Charlotte, VT 05445
United States
Tel: (802) 425-3926
Email: guidebot@together.net
www.adirondack-guide-boat.com

Adirondack Rowing Inc.
46 Meadow Lane
Queensbury, NY 12804
Tel: (518) 745-7691
Email: adkrowing@adelphia.net
www.adirondackrowing.com
please see our ad page 412.

Al Borghard Inc.
14 Windham Drive
Huntington Station, NY 11476
United States
Tel: (516) 437-6884
Email: joalborghard@yahoo.com

Alden Rowing Shells
PO Box 368
Eliot, ME 03903
United States
Tel: (207) 439-5277
Fax: (207) 439-0762
Email: rjarvis@rowalden.com
www.rowalden.com
please see our color ad & page 411.

Arch Davis Design
37 Doak Road
Box 39
Belfast, ME 04915
United States
Tel: (207) 930-9873
Fax: (207) 338-1103
www.by-the-sea.com/archdavisdesign

Arne Hasle Boats A/S
Postboks 464
Vestre Ringvei 1
1831, Askim
Norway
Tel: +47 69 88 23 66
Fax: +47 69 88 54 58
Email: behasle@online.no
www.arnehasle.no

Atkin & Company
PO Box 3005
Noroton, CT 06820
United States
Tel: (203) 655-0886
Email: apatkin@aol.com
www.by-the-sea.com/atkin&co/

Bay Shells Inc.
PO Box 3392
Kirkland, WA 98083-3392
United States
Tel: (425) 746-7148
Fax: (425) 649-1291
Email: marpaulh@worldnet.att.net
www.pocock.com/recshells.html

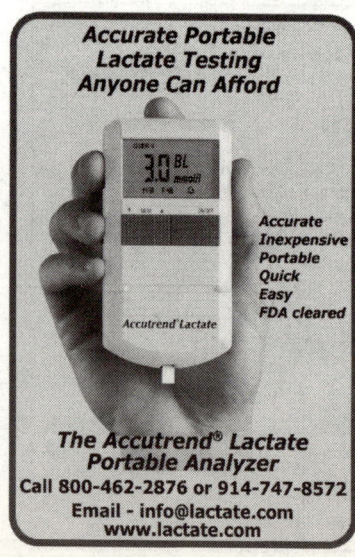

Open Water and Recreational Boats

Blue Grouse Boats
3352 Ridge Drive
McCall, ID 83638-5408
United States
Tel: (208) 634-8711
Email: woodboat@bluegrouseboats.com
www.bluegrouseboats.com

Blue Heron Boatworks
47332 Westminster Park
Wellesley Island, NY 13640
United States
Tel: (315) 482-4934
Fax: (315) 482-3537

Boathouse Woodworks
Jim Cameron — Master Builder
PO Box 317
Lake Clear, NY 12945
United States
Tel: (518) 327-3470
Email: info@adkguideboat.com
www.adkguideboat.com

Brooks Boats
PO Box 101
Mount Desert, ME 04660
United States
Tel: (207) 288-9761
Email: brooksboats@acadia.net

Chesapeake Light Craft Inc.
1805 Georgia Avenue
Annapolis, MD 21401
United States
Tel: (410) 267-0137
Fax: (301) 858-6335
Email: kayaks@clcinc.cm
www.clcboats.com

Chesapeake Rowing
7280 Swan Creek Road
Rock Hall, MD 21661
United States
Tel: (800) 400-7172, (410) 639-7172
Fax: (410) 639-7688
Email: rowing@dmv.com
www.maasrowing.com

Chippendale Craft Ltd.
Unit One
Rock Channel, Rye
East Sussex, TN31 7HJ
United Kingdom
Tel: +44 1797 227707
Fax: +44 1797 227707
Email: chipebird@compuserve.com

D.H. Kurylko Yacht Design
317 Gore Street
Nelson, BC V1L 5B8
Canada
Tel: (250) 352-2750
Email: dkurylko@netidea.com
www.dhkurylko-yachtdesign.com/

David Nutt — Boatbuilder
PO Box 320
648 Hendricks Hill Road
Southport, ME 04576
United States
Tel: (207) 633-6009
Fax: (207) 633-9947
Email: nutt@lincoln.midcoast.com
www.lincoln.midcoast.com/~nutt

Echo Rowing
141 Rte 236, PO Box 68
Eliot, ME 03903
United States
Tel: (207) 439-9620
Fax: (207) 439-5028
Email: ewboats@comcast.com
www.echorowing.com
please see our ad page 414.

Eric Dow Boatshop
PO Box 7
Brooklin, ME 04616
United States
Tel: (207) 359-2277
Email: dowboats@hypernet.com

Evergreen Rowing LLC
875 Pear Court NE
Olympia, WA 98506
United States
Tel: (360) 357-6588
Fax: (360) 375-6111
Email: steve@evergreenrowing.com
www.evergreenrowing.com
please see our ad page 442.

Flounder Bay Boat Lumber Co
1019 Third Street
Anacortes, WA 98221-1503
United States
Tel: (800) 228-4691
Fax: (360) 293-4749
Email: boatkit@flounderbay.com
www.flounderbay.com

Open Water and Recreational Boats

Gig Harbor Boatworks LLC
9905 Peacock Hill Avenue NW
Gig Harbor, WA 98332
United States
Tel: (253) 851-2126
Fax: (253) 851-2156
Email: boatshop@ghboats.com
www.ghboats.com

Grand Mesa Boatworks LLC
Route 1, Box 75
Collbran, CO 81624
United States
Tel: (970) 487-3088

Great Lakes Boat Building Co.
7066 103rd Avenue
South Haven, MI 49090
United States
Tel: (269) 637-6805
Email: mjk@i2k.com
www.greatwoodboats.com/

Indian Point Boat Company
493 Engle Road
Industry, PA 05052
United States
Tel: (724) 643-6001
Fax: (724) 643-5457
www.by-the-sea.com/indianpointboat/

Lambrechtsen & Meijer
H. Bulhuisweg 23
8606 KB Sneek
Netherlands
Tel: +31 515 411244
Email: info@lambrechtsen-meijer.nl
www.lambrechtsen-meijer.nl

Little Boat Shop
88 Hatch Street
New Bedford, MA 02745
United States
Tel: (508) 992-1846
Fax: (508) 471-5686
Email: shopboat@aol.com
www.thelittleboatshop.com/

Little River Marine
PO Box 986
Gainesville, FL 32602
United States
Tel: (800) 247-4591, (352) 378-5025
Email: info@littlerivermarine.com
www.littlerivermarine.com

Maas Boat Company
11319 Canal Boulevard
Richmond, CA 94804
United States
Tel: (510) 232-1612
Fax: (510) 232-6164
Email: maasboats@earthlink.net
www.maasboats.com
please see our ad page 411-416.

Maine Coast Boathouse
1275 Atlantic Highway
Northport, ME 04849
United States
Tel: (207) 338-0100
Email: dhux@mainecoastboats.com
www.mainecoastboats.com

Middle Path Boats
PO Box 314
Edinburg, PA 16116
United States
Tel: (724) 652-4448
Email: middlepath@aol.com
www.by-the-sea.com/middlepathboats
please see our ad page 415.

Open Water and Recreational Boats

Monfort Associates
50 Haskell Road
Westport, ME 04578
United States
Tel: (207) 882-5504
Fax: (207) 882-6232
Email: pmonfort@ime.net
www.geodesicairoliteboats.com

Muskoka Canoe & Rowing Shop
RR #2
Port Carling, ON POB 1J0
Canada
Tel: (800) 952-8414
Fax: (705) 765-6282
www.heritageboats.com

Mystic River Boathouse
55 Spicer Avenue
Noank, CT 06340
United States
Tel: (860) 536-6930
Email: mrbh@ctol.net
www.mysticriverboathouse.com

Off-Course Rowing Boats
135 George Street
Newcastle, ON L1B 1J5
Canada
Tel: (905) 987-1549

Ogdensburg Boat Works
52 East River Street
Ogdensburg, NY 13669
United States
Tel: (315) 393-8553
Fax: (315) 393-6766
Email: duffy2@compuserve.com
www.northnet.org/tduffy

Old Wharf Dory Company
170 Old Chequessett Neck Road
Wellfleet, MA 02667
United States
Tel: (508) 349-2383
Email: info@oldwharf.com
www.oldwharf.com/

Paul Gartside Ltd.
10305 West Saanich Road
Sidney, BC V8L 5T7
Canada
Tel: (250) 656-2048
Fax: (250) 656-2048

Pearson Unlimited Inc.
PO Box 545
Manhattan Beach, CA 90266
United States
Tel: (310) 545-7659
Fax: (310) 545-5929
Email: oardealer@aol.com
www.pearsonsurfcraft.com

Peinert Boat Works
PO Box 1029
46 Marion Road (Route 6)
Mattapoisett, MA 02739
United States
Tel: (508) 758-3020
Fax: (508) 758-3020
Email: info@sculling.com
www.sculling.com
please see our ad page 412 & 416.

Prairie Rowing
6600 NW 110th Street
Oklahoma City, OK 73162
United States
Tel: (405) 822-4347
Fax: (405) 728-4447
Email: dave@prairierowing.com
www.prairierowing.com
please see our ad page 423.

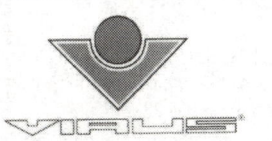

Open Water and Recreational Boats

Quarrier Boats
PO Box 125
Alstead, NH 03602
United States
Tel: (603) 835-6985
Email: kquarrier@aol.com
www.home.attbi.com/~qboats

Ron Rontilla Rowing Systems
30 Cutler Street
Warren, RI 02885
United States
Tel: (401) 247-1482
Fax: (401) 247-1582
Email: aquamotion@juno.com
www.frontrower.com
please see our ad page 413.

Rossiter Boats
RR #2
Ravenna, ON N0H 2E0
Canada
Tel: (705) 445-2908
Email: rossiter@bmts.com
www.rossiterboats.com
please see our ad page 413.

Seth Persson Boat Builders
18 Riverside Avenue
Old Saybrook, CT 06475
United States
Tel: (860) 388-2343
Email: perssonmfg@abac.com
www.perssonmfg.com/

Solitaire Boats, LLC
2421 Bass Bay Drive
Tallahassee, FL 32312
United States
Tel: (850) 228-3528
Fax: (850) 894-3480
Email: lampman@newact.com
solitaire.newact.com

Spindrift Boats by Gledhill
507 Stewart Avenue
Nanaimo, BC V9S 4C8
Canada
Tel: (250) 753-8590

Still Water Design
1 Winnisimet Street
Chelsea, MA 02150
United States
Tel: (781) 608-3079
Email: dick@stillwaterdesign.com
www.stillwaterdesign.com

Swan Boat Design
PO Box 267
Hubbard, OR 97032
United States
Tel: (503) 982-5062
Email: aswan@swanboatdesign.com
www.swanboatdesign.com

The Newfound Woodworks Inc.
67 Danforth Brook Road
Bristol, NH 03222
United States
Tel: (603) 744-6872
Fax: (603) 644-6892
Email: info@newfound.com
www.newfound.com
please see our ad page 416.

Cucchietti Racing Shells

USA
632 N Washington Street
Alexandria, VA 22314
United States

Tel: (703) 548-5509
rubiniboats@aol.com

Argentina
Posadas 465CP 1643 San Isidro
Buenos Aires
Argentina

Tel: +54 114 744 8302
Fax: +54 114 743 4904
cucchietti@arnet.com.ar

Open Water and Recreational Boats

Virus — Europe
ZI du Biconte
56680 Plouhinec
France
Tel: +33 29736 6233
Fax: +33 29736 6906
Email: sales@virusuk.demon.co.uk
www.virusboats.com

**Virus Rowing Boats —
No. & So. America & Caribbean**
RUM row International Inc.
4134 Gulf of Mexico Drive Suite 206
Long Boat Key, FL 34228
United States
Tel: (888) 767-8824, (941) 387-7773
Fax: (941) 387-7774
Email: info@rowvirusboats.com
www.rowvirusboats.com
   please see our color ad & page 411.

Whitehall Rowing and Sail
Box 1141
Victoria, BC V8W 2T6
Canada
Tel: (250) 384-6574
Fax: (250) 384-6506
Email: whitehall@whitehallrow.com
www.whitehallrow.com
   please see our ad page 415.

Woods Designs
Foss Quay
Millbrook Torpoint
Cornwall, PL10 1AN
United Kingdom
Tel: +44 1752 823301
Fax: +44 1752 823301
Email: rwoods@telinco.co.uk

Racing Boats

Ballast sagl
Via Bressanella 6a
6828, Balerna
Switzerland
Tel: +41 76 562 04 62
Email: ballast@freesurf.ch
www.ballast.ch

BBG Bootsbau Berlin GmbH
Mueggelseedamm 70
12587, Berlin
Germany
Tel: +44 30 6455374
Fax: +44 30 6455251
Email: info@bbg-bootsbau.de
www.bbg-bootsbau.de

Behr Bootshandel — Euro Racing Boats
Siegburger Strafle 130
53639, Koenigswinter
Germany
Tel: +49 2244 81240
Fax: +49 2244 81428
Email: info@behr-bootshandel.de
www.behr-bootshandel.de

Bootswerft Max Schellenbacher
Am Winterhafen 15
A-4020, Linz/Donau
Austria
Tel: +43 732 784686
Fax: +43 732 784696

Browns Boat House Ltd.
The Boat House
Elvet Bridge
Durham, DH1 3AF
United Kingdom
Tel: +44 191 386 3779

Burgashell
67a The Row
Sutton, Ely
Cambs, CB6 2PB
United Kingdom
Tel: +44 1353 777184
Fax: +44 1353 777184
Email: info@burgashellrowing.co.uk
www.burgashellrowing.co.uk

Carl Douglas Racing Shells
The Boathouse Timsway
Chertsey Lane
Staines Middlesex, TW18 3JZ
United Kingdom
Tel: +44 1784 456344
Fax: +44 1784 466550
Email: fitting@carldouglas.co.uk
www.carldouglas.co.uk

Cat Boat Company
c/o VK Partizan
Ada Ciganliga 3
Belgrade, 11030
Yugoslavia
Tel: +381 11 436 642
Fax: +381 11 305 5347
Email: neba-row@eunet.yu
www.catboatco.com/

Cucchietti Racing Shells — USA
632 N Washington Street
Alexandria, VA 22314
United States
Tel: (703) 548-5509
Email: rubiniboats@aol.com
please see our ad page 450.

Cucchietti Racing Shells — Argentina
Posadas 465
CP 1643 San Isidro
Buenos Aires
Argentina
Tel: +54 114 744 8302
Fax: +54 114 743 4904
Email: cucchietti@arnet.com.ar
please see our ad page 450.

Dinamo — UK
10 Gazelle Glade
Riverside Park Gravesend
Kent, DA12 4PU
United Kingdom
Tel: +44 474 363480
Fax: +44 474 363480

Dirigo/Schoenbrod
496 Elm Street
Biddeford, ME 04005
United States
Tel: (207) 283-3026
Fax: (207) 985-6814
Email: charlie@dirigousa.com
www.dirigousa.com

Racing Boats

Drew Harrison Racing Shells
2501 Skyline Crescent
Saanichton, BC V8M 1M6
Canada
Tel: (250) 652-8543
Fax: (250) 652-8543
Email: info@drewharrisonracingshells.com
www.drewharrisonracingshells.com

Durham Boat Company Inc.
220 Newmarket Road
Durham, NH 03824
United States
Tel: (603) 659-7575
Fax: (603) 659-2548
Email: info@durhamboat.com
www.durhamboat.com
please see our color ad.

Empacher Racing Shells
Post Box 1541
69412, Eberbach
Germany
Tel: +49 6271 8000
Fax: +49 6271 800099
Email: info@empacher-usa.com
www.empacher-usa.com

220 Newmarket Road
Durham, NH 03824
United States

Tel: (603) 659-7575

info@durhamboat.com
www.durhamboat.com/school.htm

*Dreher Carbon Seats, Foot Stretchers
and Riggers, Rowing Hardware and
Accessories, NK and FC Cadence
Electronics, Yakima Racks, CARE
Rowperfect Rowing Simulators.*

Empacher Racing Shells — US
4306 Mountain Creek Road
Chattanooga, TN 37415
United States
Tel: (423) 503-5903
Fax: (423) 876-8178
Email: info@hbrowing.com
www.hbrowing.com

Eton Racing Boats
Brocast Street, Eton
Windsor Berkshire, SL4 6BW
United Kingdom
Tel: +44 1753 671294
Fax: +44 1753 671293
Email: etonracingboats@etoncollege.org.uk
www.etonracingboats.co.uk

Euro-Fun-Boat
Hajo Keldenich
Winkelstrasse 5
D-53639, Konigswinter
Germany
Tel: +49 22 4481250
Fax: +49 22 4481250
Email: info@behr-bootshandel.de
www.euro-fun-boat.de

Felker Boat Company
12501 Mixson Drive
Austin, TX 78732
United States
Tel: (512) 266-3558
Fax: (512) 266-9485

Filippi Shells
Via Matteotti 113
57024, Donoratico
Italy
Tel: +39 565 777311
Fax: +39 565 777483
Email: info@filippiboat_ings.it
www.FilippiBoats.it

FISO-Werft
Goerlitzer Ring 24
D-2410 Moelin
Germany
Tel: +49 454 22219

Racing Boats

Fluidesign Composite Inc.
175 Exeter Road, Unit C
London, ON N6L 1A4, Canada
Tel: (519) 652-2272
Fax: (519) 652-3972
Email: fluidesign@rowfluidesign.com
www.rowfluidesign.com
please see our ad page 455.

George Sims Racing Boats
PO Box 3042, Goring
West Sussex, BN12 6RT
United Kingdom
Tel: +44 1903 248044
Fax: +44 1903 248009
Email: georgesims@racingboats.demon.co.uk
www.racingboats.demon.co.uk

HangZhou Flying Eagle Boat Co Ltd
Lushan Fuyang Road XiShan 148#
Zhejiang Province 311401, China
Tel: (541) 488-4457
Email: wudi@wudiboat.com
www.wudiboat.com

Harald Richter
Westerholz 87
D-4600, Dortmund 1
Germany
Tel: +49 231 859101

Harris Racing Boats
ISIS Boathouse, Iffley
Oxford, OX1 4UW
United Kingdom
Tel: +44 1865 243870
Email: info@harrisracing.co.uk
www.harrisracing.co.uk

Hudson Boat Works Inc.
1930 Mallard Road
London, ON N6H 5M1, Canada
Tel: (519) 473-9864
Fax: (519) 473-2861
Email: hugh@hudsonboatworks.com
www.hudsonboatworks.com
please see our ad page 456.

Jan Klerks
Rijnen Schiekade 1/1
2311 AJ Leiden, The Netherlands
Tel: +31 71 5131527

Janousek Racing Boats
1A Abbots Close, Byfleet
Surrey, KT14 7JN, United Kingdom
Tel: +44 1932 353421
Fax: +44 1932 336381
Email: boats@janousek.co.uk
www.janousek.co.uk

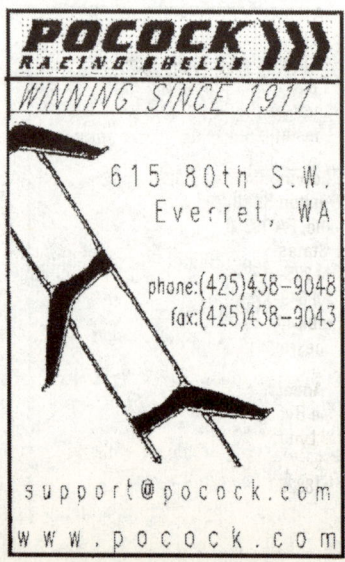

Racing Boats

Jeff Sykes and Associates Pty Ltd.
Riversdale Road
Newton Geelong 3220
Victoria
Australia
Tel: +61 35221 3655
Fax: +61 352212596
Email: sales@sykes.com.au
www.sykes.com.au

Jennings Racing Shells
124 Night Owl Court
Longwood, FL 32779
United States
Tel: (321) 356-7682
Fax: (407) 862-4651
Email: info@jrshells.com
www.jrshells.com

JMF Boats
Ateliers Essais sur la Seine
26, quai du Pdt Paul Doumer
92400, Courbevoie
France
Tel: +33 20 8788 1542
Fax: +33 87 0127 3881
Email: jmf@jmf-yole.com
www.jmf-yole.com

Johnston Racing Pty Ltd.
43 Ninth Avenue
Woodville
North SA, 5012
Australia
Tel: +61 8 8244 0949
Fax: +61 8 8373 7475
Email: enquiries@johnstonracing.com
www.johnstonracing.com/

Jones Rowing Company
1619 Winston Road
Gladwyne, PA 19350
United States
Tel: (215) 205-9148
Fax: (610) 649-7954
Email: robin@jonesrowing.com
www.jonesrowing.com

Jorgen Andersen
Uggelose Bygade 148
DK-3540 Lynge
Denmark
Tel: +42 188289

Kaschper Racing Shells Ltd.
33972 Saintsbury Line
PO Box 40
Lucan, ON N0M 2J0
Canada
Tel: (519) 227-4652
Fax: (519) 227-4247
Email: info@kaschper.com
www.kaschper.com

Levator Boatworks Ltd.
767 Industrial Road
London, ON N5V 4J5
Canada
Tel: (877) LEVATOR, (519) 659-2317
Email: row@levator.com
www.levator.com
  please see our ad page 410.

Lola-Aylings
Lola House Glebe Road
St. Peters Road
Huntington Cambs, PE29 7DS
United Kingdom
Tel: +44 8451 304046
Fax: +44 1487 711777
www.lola-aylings.com

Racing Boats

MPS Composites
groupe MC2
47470, Beauville
France
Tel: +33 553 954556
Fax: +33 553 954126
Email: nick@scull.com.au
mps.composites.free.fr

Neczypor
100 DeKalb Pike
PO Box 214
Bridgeport, PA 19405-0214
United States
Tel: (610) 275-5638
Fax: (610) 275-5839
Email: neczypor@op.net
www.neczypor.com

Pocock Racing Shells
615 80th Street SW
Everett, WA 98203
United States
Tel: (425) 438-9048
Fax: (425) 438-9043
Email: mail@pocock.com
www.pocock.com
   please see our ad page 454.

Quantum Racing
PO Box 370
Topsham, ME 04086-0370
United States
Tel: (207) 725-0463
Fax: (207) 725-8692
Email: raz@quantumracingshells.com
www.quantumracingshells.com
   please see our ad page 409.

Resolute Racing Shells
PO Box 1109
Bristol, RI 02809-1109
United States
Sue Hinckley, Manager of Service and Sales
Tel: (401) 253-7384
Fax: (401) 253-5898
Email: sales@resoluteracing.com
www.resoluteracing.com
   please see our color ad & page 409.

Rowland
Hortensialaan 6
8400 Oostende
Belgium
Tel: +32 59 268145

Spartan Racing Boats
Herriard Old Station Near Basingstroke
Hampshire, RG24 9EJ
United Kingdom
Tel: +44 1256 415354
Fax: +44 1256 415354
Email: sales@spartanclothing.demon.co.uk

Stampfli International
14 Wintersells Road
Byfleet
Surrey, KT14 7LF
United Kingdom
Tel: +44 1932 400568
Fax: +44 1932 336381
Email: boats@stampfli.co.uk
www.stampfli.co.uk

Stampfli Racing Boats AG
Seestrasse 497
8038, Zurich
Switzerland
Tel: +41 1482 9944
Fax: +41 1482 0503
Email: kontakt@staempfli-boats.ch
www.staempfli-boats.ch

Racing Boats

Starline Racing Boats LLC
Unit 1002 10/F New Trend Centre
704 Prince Edward Road
Kowloon
Hong Kong — China
Tel: +852 2558 8677
Fax: +852 2558 2864
Email: kennethrowing@hotmail.com

Sykes Racing North America
PO Box 3165
Tempe, AZ 85280-3165
United States
Tel: (480) 234-4912
Fax: (602) 495-3793
Email: tom@sykes.com.au
www.sykes.com.au

Tjasco B.V.
Snoek 12
1275 AW Huizen
Netherlands
Tel: +31 355 241199
Fax: +31 653 931523
Email: tjasco@euronet.nl

TS Bootshandel
Rodenkirchener Str 12
Berlin, 12524
Germany
Tel: +49 30 67803112
Fax: +49 30 6724752
Email: TSBootshandel@rudern-kann-jeder.de
www.rudern-kann-jeder.de

Van Dusen Racing Boats
Divison of Composite Engineering
277 Baker Avenue
Concord, MA 01742
United States
Tel: (978) 371-3132
Fax: (978) 369-3162
Email: vandusen@tiac.net
www.vandusenracingboats.com

Vega R.C.
113 rte des Argos
F-74940
Annecy-le-Vieux
France
Tel: +33 4500 98050
Fax: +33 4506 61557
Email: pascual@magic.fr
www.vega-realisations-composites

Racing Boats

Vespoli USA
385 Clinton Avenue
New Haven, CT 06513
United States
Tel: (203) 773-0311
Fax: (203) 562-1891
Email: talk@vespoli.com
www.vespoli.com
please see our color ad & page 409.

Wayland Marine Ltd.
817 Harris Avenue
PO Box 4330
Bellingham, WA 98227
United States
Tel: (800) 700-8059, (360) 738-8059
Email: wayland@merrywherry.com
www.merrywherry.com

Welau BvBa
Blauwe Paal 2
B 9230 Wetteren
Belgium
Tel: +32 9369 4304
Fax: +32 9366 1128

Werner Kahl — Die Ruderwerkstatt
Henri-Duffaut — Str 17
D-35578 Wetzlar
Germany
Tel: +49 644 17777
Fax: +49 641 975277
Email: info@ruderwerkstatt.com
www.ruderwerkstatt.com

Win Racing Boats
101 Alshion Toda Koen Building
5-2-20 Honcho Toda-shi
Saitama-ken, 335-0023
Japan
Email: gareth@rowingcenter.com
www.rowingcenter.com

Services — Insurance

Amilcroft Insurance Management Ltd.
Heathervale House
Vale Avenue — Royal Tunbridge Wells
Kent, TN1 1DJ
United Kingdom
Tel: +44 1892 509011
Fax: +44 1892 509020
Email: chris.moon@amilcroft.net
www.amilcroft.co.uk

Leonard Insurance Group Inc
2103 E. Darby Road
Havertown, PA 19083
United States
Tel: (800) - SCULLER
Fax: (610) 789-5757
Email: scullerjon@aol.com
www.LeonardInsuranceGroup.com
  please see our color ad.

Mariner Insurance Group, Inc.
15 Garrett Avenue
Rosemont, PA 19010-1452
United States
Tel: (888) 752-9616, (610) 520-9611
Fax: (610) 525-4390
Email: jhogan@marinerins.com
www.marinerins.com
  please see our color ad.

Noble Marine Insurance Ltd
Clinton House
Lombard Street, Newark
Nottinghamshire, NG24 1XB
United Kingdom
Tel: +44 16 36707606
Fax: +44 1636 707632
Email: rowing@noblemarine.co.uk
www.noblemarine.co.uk

Partners Indemnity
10 Adelaide St. E., Suite 400
Toronto, ON M5C 1J3
Canada
Tel: (416) 366-5243, 1-877-427-8683
Fax: (416) 862-2416
Email: info@partnersindemnity.com
www.partnersindemnity.com/
Insurance brokerage firm providing insurance
coverage for the Canadian rowing community.
  please see our color ad.

Perkin Slade Sports Insurance
3 Broadway, Broad Street
Birmingham B15 1BQ
United Kingdom
Tel: +44 1216 988000
Fax: +44 1216 431360

Services — Miscellaneous

Architectural Resources Cambridge Inc.
140 Mount Auburn Street
Cambridge, MA 02138
United States
Tel: (617) 547-2200
Fax: (617) 547-7222
Email: ARCMail@arcusa.com
www.arcusa.com

Artisan Racing Shell Restoration
United States
Tel: (703) 593-2487

Comprehensive Rowing Services
2123 102nd Ave NE
Bellevue, WA 98004
United States
Tel: (425) 455-1012

Engineering Consulting Services
PO Box 844
Livermore, CA 94551-0844
United States
Tel: (925) 960-1603
Fax: (209) 396-3726
Email: aszolnay@yahoo.com
www.hydrosoar.com

Gentle Giant Moving Company
29 Harding Street
Sommerville, MA 02143
United States
Tel: (800) 466-8844, (617) 806-1008
Email: dlister@gentlegiant.com

Joy of Sculling
PO Box 567
Geneva, NY 14456
United States
Tel: (315) 781-2383
Fax: (315) 781-5308
Email: joyofsculling@aol.com
please see our color ad.

Meeuwisse Botentransport
De Oude Bleijk 82
2266 CL Leidschendam
Netherlands
Tel: +31 70 3277126
Fax: +31 70 3177330
Email: info@keesmeeuwisse.nl

Services — Miscellaneous

Masters Rowing Association
National Headquarters
#4 Boathouse Row Kelly Drive
Philadelphia, PA 19103
Tel: (877) Rowing4
Email: mra@mastersrowing.org
www.mastersrowing.org
please see our color ad.

National Rowing Foundation
67 Mystic Road
N. Stonington, CT 06359
United States
Tel: (860) 535-0634
Fax: (860) 535-0637
Email: natrowing@natrowing.org
www.NatRowing.org
please see our ad page 461.

New Zealand Rowing Institute Ltd
PO Box 12-101
Penrose, Auckland
New Zealand
Tel: +64 9 634 9285
Fax: +64 9 634 9019
Email: custom.carbon@xtra.co.nz
www.customcarbon.co.nz/nzri_main.htm

North Country Racing Shells
PO Box 82
Norwich, VT 05055
United States
Tel: (802) 649-2919
Fax: (802) 649-2919
Email: irow@dartmouth.edu

Peterson Architects
1132 Massachusetts Avenue
Cambridge, MA 02138
United States
Tel: (617) 354-2268
Fax: (617) 354-2825
Email: info@peterson-architects.com/
www.peterson-architects.com

RegattaCentral
1414 Crisfield Drive
Columbus, OH 43204
United States
Tel: (877) 376-4359
Email: steve@regattacentral.com
www.regattacentral.com
please see our ad — Inside Back Cover.

Services — Miscellaneous

Rowing Repair Center
374 Warehouse Road
Oak Ridge, TN 37830
United States
Tel: (865) 482-1808
Email: rowingrepair@earthlink.net
www.rowingrepair.com
please see our — Back Cover.

Schuylkill Navy
6470 Drexel Road
Philadelphia, PA 19151
United States
Email: clete@netaxs.com
www.boathouserow.org

Shell Transport Service
2910 W. Garry Avenue
Santa Ana, CA 92704
United States
Tel: (877) 262-8273

Stanley & Thomas
United Kingdom
Tel: +44 1753 833 166
Email: info@stanleyandthomas.co.uk
www.stanleyandthomas.co.uk

Team Concepts Inc.
PO Box 8625
Collingswood, NJ 08108
United States
Tel: (800) 630-3252
Fax: (856) 858-0689
Email: RMahoney@TeamConceptsInc.com
www.teamconceptsinc.com/

WPR Racing Shell Repair, Est
Bruce G. La Londe
243 Righters Ferry Road
Bala Cynwyd, PA 19004
United States
Tel: (215) 765-1898

United States ★ State by State Directory
Presented alphabetically by state, then city.

ALASKA
Kenai Crewsers RC, Sterling

ALABAMA
Rocket City RC, Huntsville
Auburn University, Auburn
University of Alabama at Huntsville, Huntsville
University of Alabama, Tuscaloosa
Rocket City RC for Juniors, Huntsville

ARIZONA
Rio Salado RC, Tempe
Tempe Junior Crew, Tempe

CALIFORNIA
Positive Strokes Rowing, Alameda
Berkeley Paddling & RC, Berkeley
Mission Bay RA, Chula Vista
Foster City Sculling, Foster City
Marin RA, Greenbrae
Sonoma Sculling Society, Healdsburg
California Adaptive Rowing Programs, Long Beach
Long Beach RA, Long Beach
Lions RC, Los Angeles
Los Gatos RC, Los Gatos
California Yacht Club, Marina del Rey
Los Angeles RC, Marina del Rey
Southern California BC, Marina del Rey
Newport Aquatic Center, Newport Beach
Lake Merritt RC, Oakland
North Bay RC, Petaluma
Lake Natoma RC, Rancho Cordova
Bair Island Aquatic Center, Redwood City
San Diego RC, San Diego
ZLAC, San Diego
Bay Area Whaleboat RA, San Francisco
Dolphin RC, San Francisco
Embarcadero RC, San Francisco
Ketos Whale Boat Rowing, San Francisco
Pacific RC, San Francisco
San Francisco Bay Blades, San Francisco
San Francisco RC, San Francisco
South End RC, San Francisco
Santa Cruz RC, Santa Cruz
Open Water Rowing Center, Sausalito
Stockton Rowing Inc., Stockton
Humboldt Bay RA, Trinidad
River City RC, West Sacramento
North Bay Vikings
California State University Humboldt, Arcata
University of California at Berkeley, Berkeley
University of California at Davis, Davis

University of California at Irvine, Irvine
University of California at San Diego, La Jolla
California State University Long Beach, Long Beach
Loyola Marymount University, Los Angeles
University of California at Los Angeles, Los Angeles
University of Southern California, Los Angeles
Saint Mary's College, Moraga
Orange Coast College, Newport Beach
Mills College, Oakland
Chapman University, Orange
California State University Sacramento, Rancho Cordova
California State University San Diego, San Diego
University of San Diego, San Diego
California Polytechnic University, San Luis Obispo
University of California at Santa Barbara, Santa Barbara
Santa Clara University, Santa Clara
Stanford University, Stanford
California Lutheran University, Thousand Oaks
California Maritime University, Vallejo
Notre Dame High School, Belmont
Berkeley High School, Berkeley
Marin RA for Juniors, Greenbrae
Long Beach Junior Crew, Long Beach
Los Gatos RC for Juniors, Los Gatos
Marina Aquatic Center Junior Rowing, Marina del Rey
Newport Aquatic Center for Juniors, Newport Beach
Lake Merritt RC for Juniors, Oakland
Palo Alto High School, Palo Alto
Oakland Strokes Inc., Piedmont
Capital Crew, Rancho Cordova
Peninsula Aquatic Center Junior Crew, Redwood City
Serra High School, San Diego
ZLAC RC for Juniors, San Diego
Pacific RC for Juniors, San Francisco
Saint Ignatius College Prep, San Francisco
Silicon Valley High School, Sunnyvale
River City RC for Juniors, West Sacramento

COLORADO
Boulder Area Community Rowing, Boulder
Rocky Mountain RC, Denver
Pagosa RC, Pagosa Springs
University of Colorado at Boulder, Boulder
Rocky Mountain RC for Juniors, Denver

CONNECTICUT
Hartford Barge Club, East Hartford
Greenwich RC, Greenwich
Row America, Greenwich
Riverfront Recapture Inc., Hartford
Salisbury BC, Lakeville

Litchfield Hills RC, Litchfield
Middletown RC, Middletown
Stonington RC, Mystic
Old Glory BC, N. Stonington
Norwalk River RA, Norwalk
Water Sports Center, Norwalk
Chelsea RC, Norwich
Castle RC, Old Greenwich
Old Lyme RA, Old Lyme
Connecticut River Oar and Paddle Club, Old Saybrook
New Haven RC, Oxford
Peck's BC, Rowayton
Farmington Valley RA, Simsbury
Saugatuck RA, Westport
Housatonic RA, Woodbridge
Charlottesville Postal Workers RC,
Fairfield University, Fairfield
Sacred Heart University, Fairfield
Trinity College (CT), Hartford
Wesleyan University, Middletown
Yale University, New Haven
Connecticut College, New London
U.S. Coast Guard Academy, New London
University of Connecticut, Storrs
East Lyme High School, East Lyme
Miss Porters School, Farmington
Hartford Public High School, Hartford
Kent School, Kent
Litchfield High School, Litchfield
Middleton High School, Middletown
New Canaan High School, New Canaan
Norwalk River RA for Juniors, Norwalk
Lyme-Old Lyme High School, Old Lyme
Stonington High School, Pawcatuck
Pomfret School, Pomfret
South Kent School, S. Kent
Salisbury School, Salisbury
Ethel Walker School, Simsbury
Simsbury High School, Simsbury
Edwin O. Smith High School, Storrs
Choate Rosemary Hall, Wallingford
Gunnery School, Washington
Rumsey Hall School, Washington Depot
Taft School, Watertown

DISTRICT OF COLUMBIA

Capital RC, Washington
Combined Cathedral Crews RC, Washington
D.C. Strokes RC, Washington
Potomac BC, Washington
Thompson Boat Center, Washington
Water Street RC, Washington
American University, Washington
Catholic University, Washington

George Washington University, Washington
Georgetown University, Washington
Trinity College (DC), Washington
Friends of Catholic University, Washington, DC
Georgetown Day School, Washington
Georgetown Visitation Preparatory School, Washington
Gonzaga College High School, Washington
National Cathedral School, Washington
Saint Albans School, Washington
Sidwell Friends School, Washington
Thompson Boat Center for Juniors, Washington
Woodrow Wilson High School, Washington

DELAWARE

Wilmington Rowing Center, Wilmington
University of Delaware, Newark
Sanford High School, Hockessin
Saint Andrew's School, Middletown
Concord High School, Wilmington
Wilmington Youth RA, Wilmington

FLORIDA

Sons of the Beach Rowing, Coconut Grove
Halifax RA, Daytona Beach
Hollywood RC, Fort Lauderdale
Fort Myers RC, Fort Myers
Gainesville Area Rowing, Gainesville
Jacksonville RC, Jacksonville
Island RC Inc, Merritt Island
American Barge Club, Miami
Miami Beach RC, Miami Beach
Orlando RA, Orlando
Orlando RC, Orlando
Treasure Coast RC, Palm City
Palm Beach RA, Riviera Beach
Tampa RC Inc, Tampa
Miami Rowing & Watersports Center Inc., Virginia Key
Organization of Allderdice Rowing - OAR, Windermere
Orlando Area Rowing Society (OARS), Windermere
Lynn University, Boca Raton
University of Miami, Coral Gables
Embry-Riddle Aeronautical University, Daytona Beach
Stetson University, DeLand
Nova Southeastern University, Ft. Lauderdale
University of Florida, Gainesville
Jacksonville University, Jacksonville
Florida Institute of Technology, Melbourne
Barry University, Miami Shores
University of Central Florida, Orlando
Florida State University, Talahassee
University of Tampa, Tampa
Rollins College, Winter Park
Lake Brantley High School, Altamonte Springs
Bishop Verot High School, Fort Myers
Fort Myers High School, Fort Myers

Pine Crest Preparatory School, Ft. Lauderdale
Eastside High School, Gainesville
Gainesville High School, Gainesville
Episcopal High School of Jacksonville, Jacksonville
Stanton College Preparatory School, Jacksonville
The Bolles School, Jacksonville
Maritime & Science Tech Academy, Key Biscayne
Eau Gallie High School, Melbourne
Florida Air Academy, Melbourne
Holy Trinity Episcopal Academy, Melbourne
Melbourne Central Catholic High School, Melbourne
Melbourne High School, Melbourne
West Shore High School, Melbourne
Belen Jesuit Prep, Miami
Michael M. Krop High School, Miami
Miami Beach High School, Miami Beach
Miami Beach RC for Juniors, Miami Beach
Saint John's Country Day, Orange Park
Bishop Moore High School, Orlando
Dr. Phillips High School, Orlando
Edgewater High School, Orlando
Olympia High School, Orlando
University High School, Orlando
William R. Boone HS/S.O.R.A., Orlando
Sarasota Scullers Youth Rowing Program Inc., Osprey
Satellite High School, Satellite Beach
Space Coast Crew Boosters, Satellite Beach
Treasure Coast Junior RA, Stuart
Leon High School, Tallahassee
Maclay School, Tallahassee
Talahassee Area Crew, Tallahassee
Berkeley Preparatory School, Tampa
H.B. Plant High School, Tampa
Hillsborough High School, Tampa
Tampa Catholic High School, Tampa
Tampa Preparatory School, Tampa
Orlando Area Rowing Society for Juniors, Windermere
West Orange High School (FL), Winter Garden
Winter Park High School, Winter Park

GEORGIA

Atlanta RC, Atlanta
Augusta RC, Augusta
Lake Lanier RC, Gainesville
Middle Georgia RC
University of Georgia, Athens
Emory University, Atlanta
Georgia Tech, Atlanta
Augusta State University, Augusta
Armstrong Atlantic State College, Savannah
Savannah College of Art and Design, Savannah
Brenau University
Atlanta Junior RA, Atlanta
Lakeside High School (GA), Atlanta

Saint Andrew's RC, Atlanta
Augusta RC for Juniors, Augusta
Westside High School, Augusta
Evans High School, Evans
Lake Lanier RC for Juniors, Gainesville
Riverside Military Academy, Gainesville
Savannah Country Day, Savannah

HAWAII

Honolulu RC, Honolulu

IOWA

Des Moines RC, Des Moines
Old Capitol RC, Iowa City
River Rats Rowing, Iowa City
Quad City RA, Moline
Waterloo RC, Waterloo
Drake University, Des Moines
University of Iowa, Iowa City
Saint Katharine's/Saint Mark's College Prep, Bettendorf
Quad City Juniors, Moline

ILLINIOS

Chicago River Rowing & Paddling Center, Chicago
Chicago Rowing Center, Chicago
Lincoln Park BC, Chicago
South Chicago Rowing Center, Chicago
Zog RC, Hinsdale
Illinois River Oarsmen, Peoria Heights
Rockford YMCA RC, Rockford
University of Chicago, Chicago
Northwestern University, Evanston
Augustana College, Rock Island
Wheaton College, Wheaton
Chicago Youth RC, Chicago
Kenwood High School, Chicago
Lincoln Park Juniors, Chicago
Mount Carmel High School, Chicago
Saint Ignatius College Prep (IL), Chicago
Highland Park High School, Highland Park
North Suburban/Woodlands, Lake Forest
Loyola Academy, Wilmette

INDIANA

Riddle Point Rowing, Bloomington
Indiana RA, Elkhart
Indianapolis Rowing Center, Indianapolis
South Bend Scullers Inc., South Bend
Indiana University, Bloomington
Wabash College, Crawfordsville
DePauw University, Greencastle
Butler University, Indianapolis
University of Notre Dame, Notre Dame
Purdue University, West Lafayette
Culver Academies, Culver
Indianapolis Rowing Center for Juniors, Indianapolis

KANSAS

Topeka Rowing, Topeka
Wichita RA, Wichita
University of Kansas, Lawrence
Kansas State University, Manhattan
Wichita State University, Wichita

KENTUCKY

Louisville RC, Louisville
University of Louisville, Louisville
Murray State University, Murray
Louisville RC for Juniors, Louisville

LOUISIANA

Memmian RC, New Orleans
New Orleans RC Ltd, New Orleans
Northwestern State University, Natchitoches
Loyola University New Orleans, New Orleans
Tulane University, New Orleans
Centenary College of Louisiana, Shreveport
Louisiana School for Math Science and the Arts,
Natchitoches

MASSACHUSETTS

Thames River Sculls, Amherst
Yankee RC, Amherst
Charles River RA, Boston
Style Drive RC, Boston
Union BC, Boston
Wide Load BC, Boston
Cape Cod Viking Club, Brewster
Cambridge BC, Cambridge
Community Rowing Inc. of Boston, Cambridge
Cygnet RC, Cambridge
Harvard Sculling, Cambridge
Riverside BC, Cambridge
Cotuit RC, Cotuit
Duxbury Bay Maritime School, Duxbury
Northeast Rowing Center, Duxbury
Ring's Island RC, Groveland
Greater Lowell RA, Lowell
Merrimack River RA, Lowell
Mystic Valley RA, Medford
Whaling City RC, New Bedford
Huntington Barge & Paddle Club, North Easton
Berkshire Rowing and Sculling Society, Pittsfield
Pioneer Valley Women's RC, Sunderland
Wayland Weston RA, Wayland
Alte Achter BC, Wellesley
Onota Lake RC, Williamstown
Quinsigamond RA, Worcester
Cape Cod Rowing & Sculling Center, Yarmouth Port
Amherst College, Amherst
University of Massachusetts at Amherst, Amherst
Boston University, Boston

Northeastern University, Boston
Simmons College, Boston
Massachusetts Maritime Academy, Buzzards Bay
Harvard University/ Radcliffe College, Cambridge
Lesley University, Cambridge
Massachusetts Institute of Technology, Cambridge
Boston College, Chestnut Hill
University of Massachusetts at Lowell, Lowell
Tufts University, Medford
Lasell College, Newton
Smith College, Northampton
Mount Holyoke College, S. Hadley
Brandeis University, Waltham
Wellesley College, Wellesley
Reed College, Weston
Regis College, Weston
Williams College, Williamstown
Assumption College, Worcester
Clark University, Worcester
College of the Holy Cross, Worcester
Worcester Polytechnic Institute (WPI), Worcester
Worcester State College, Worcester
Phillips Academy, Andover
Cade Cod Academy, Barnstable
Cape Cod Crew, Barnstable
Belmont Hill School, Belmont
Winsor School, Boston
Brookline High School, Brookline
Buckingham Browne & Nichols School, Cambridge
Cambridge Rindge and Latin School, Cambridge
Community Rowing Inc. for Juniors, Cambridge
Barnstable RC for Juniors, Centerville
Beaver Country Day, Chestnut Hill
Middlesex School, Concord
Noble and Greenough School, Dedham
Deerfield Academy, Deerfield
Groton School, Groton
Lowell High School, Lowell
Merrimac River RA for Juniors, Lowell
Tabor Academy, Marion
Brooks School, North Andover
Northampton High School, Northampton
Northfield Mount Hermon School, Northfield
Cape Cod Academy, Osterville
Berkshire School, Sheffield
Saint John's High School, Shrewsbury
Shrewsbury High School, Shrewsbury
Saint Mark's School, Southborough
Wayland-Weston Crew, Wayland
Worcester Public Schools, Worcester

MARYLAND

Annapolis RC, Annapolis
Baltimore RC, Baltimore

Chester River RC, Chestertown
Tiber Creek RC, University Park
Saint John's College, Annapolis
United States Naval Academy, Annapolis
Johns Hopkins University, Baltimore
Loyola College, Baltimore
University of Maryland - Baltimore County, Baltimore
Washington College, Chestertown
University of Maryland, College Park
Annapolis RC for Juniors, Annapolis
Bethesda-Chevy Chase High School, Bethesda
Holton-Arms School, Bethesda
Walt Whitman High School, Bethesda
Bladensburg High School, Bladensburg
Elizabeth Seton High School, Bladensburg
Saint Paul's School (Baltimore), Brooklandville
Saint Paul's School for Girls (Baltimore), Brooklandville
DeMatha Catholic High School, Hyattsville
The Bullis School, Potomac

MAINE

Maine RA, Bridgton
Nonesuch Oar and Paddle Club, Cape Elizabeth
Bowdoin College, Brunswick
Bates College, Lewiston
Colby College, Waterville
Hyde School, Bath
MICHIGAN
Ann Arbor RC, Ann Arbor
Huron RC, Ann Arbor
Michigan RA, Ann Arbor
Bay City RC, Bay City
Lansing Oar and Paddle Club, East Lansing
Ecorse RC, Ecorse
Grand Rapids RC, Grand Rapids
Grosse Ile RC, Grosse Ile
Detroit BC, Grosse Pointe Farms
Wyandotte BC, Wyandotte
Grand Valley State University, Allendale
University of Michigan, Ann Arbor
Michigan State University, E. Lansing
Northern Michigan University, Marquette
Eastern Michigan University
Pioneer High School, Ann Arbor
Bay City Central High School, Bay City
Bay Shore High School, Bay Shore
Cranbrook-Kingswood Upper School, Bloomfield Hills
East Grand Rapids High School, East Grand Rapids
Forest Hills Central High School, Grand Rapids
Forest Hills Northern High School, Grand Rapids
Grand Rapids City League Crew, Grand Rapids
Grosse Ile High School, Grosse Ile
Grosse Pointe-South High School, Grosse Pointe
Detroit BC for Juniors, Grosse Pointe Farms

Huron High School, New Boston
Saint Mary's Preparatory, Orchard Lake
Riverview Community High School, Riverview
Carlson High School, Rockwood
Roosevelt T. High School, Wyandotte

MINNESOTA

Duluth RC, Duluth
Minneapolis RC, Minneapolis
Rochester RC, Rochester
Minnesota BC, Saint Paul
University of Minnesota, Minneapolis
Carleton College, Northfield
Saint Cloud State University, St. Cloud
College of the Saint Benedict, St. Joseph
University of Saint Thomas, St. Paul
Minnesota BC for Juniors, Saint Paul

MISSOURI

Kansas City RC, Kansas City
Saint Louis RC, St. Louis
Saint Louis University, St. Louis
Washington University St Louis, St. Louis
Saint Louis RC for Juniors, St. Louis

NORTH CAROLINA

Carolina Masters Crew Club, Chapel Hill
Catawba Yacht Club, Charlotte
Raleigh Rowing Center, Raleigh
Cape Fear River RC, Wilmington
University of North Carolina at Chapel Hill, Chapel Hill
Duke University, Durham
North Carolina State University, Raleigh
University of North Carolina at Wilmington, Wilmington
Davidson College,
Raleigh Charter High School, Raleigh
Cape Fear Academy, Wilmington

NEBRASKA

Omaha RA, Omaha
University of Nebraska, Lincoln
Creighton University, Omaha

NEW HAMPSHIRE

Durham BC, Durham
Great Bay Rowing, Durham
Dresden RC, Hanover
Hanover RC, Hanover
Traditional Small Craft Association, Hollis
Amoskeag RC, Manchester
Independence RC Inc., Nashua
University of New Hampshire, Durham
Dartmouth College, Hanover
Saint Anselm College, Manchester
Franklin Pierce College, Rindge
Saint Paul's School, Concord

Durham BC for Juniors, Durham
Phillips Exeter Academy, Exeter
Bishop Guertin High School, Nashua
Brewster Academy, Wolfeboro

NEW JERSEY

Brigantine RC, Brigantine
Navesink River RC, Fair Haven
Swan Creek RC, Lambertville
Passaic River RA, Lyndhurst
Triton RC, Montville
Rude and Smooth BC, Neshanic
Atlantic County RA, Northfield
Viking Rowing Foundation, Northfield
Ocean City Rowing & Athletic Association, Ocean City
Raritan Valley RA, Piscataway
Carnegie Lake RA, Princeton
Nereid BC Inc, Rutherford
Rutgers University, New Brunswick
Richard Stockton University, Pomona
Princeton University, Princeton
Holy Spirit High School, Absecon
Atlantic City High School, Atlantic City
Belleville School, Belleville
Blair Academy, Blairstown
Brigantine RC for Juniors, Brigantine
Camden Catholic High School, Cherry Hill
Navesink River RC for Juniors, Fair Haven
The Peddie School, Hightstown
Hudson County Vo-Tech High School, Jersey City
Kearny High School, Kearny
Lawrenceville School, Lawrenceville
Passaic River RA for Juniors, Lyndhurst
Moorestown RC, Moorestown
Viking Rowing Foundation for Juniors, Northfield
Nutley High School, Nutley
Bishop Eustace Prep, Pennsauken
The Hun School, Princeton
Saint Augustine Prep, Richland
West Orange High School, West Orange

NEW MEXICO

Rio Abajo RC, Santa Fe

NEW YORK

Albany Rowing Center, Albany
Mohawk River BC, Amsterdam
Hiawatha Island BC, Apalachin
West Side RC of Buffalo Inc, Buffalo
Cazenovia RC, Cazenovia
Buffalo Rowing, East Aurora
Navy Masters RC, East Aurora
Fat Cat RC, Freeville
Sagamore RA, Glenwood Landing
East Arm RC, Greenwood Lake

Grace Harbor RC, Huntington Manor
Hyde Park RA, Hyde Park
Cascadilla BC Ltd., Ithaca
Rondout RC, Kingston
Empire State RA, New Rochelle
New Rochelle RC, New Rochelle
Floating the Apple, New York
King's Crown RA, New York
New York Athletic Club, New York
Piermont RC, Piermont
Arlington RA, Pleasant Valley
Hudson River RA, Poughkeepsie
Mid-Hudson RA, Poughkeepsie
Aqueduct RC, Rexford
Genesee Waterways Center, Rochester
Erie Canal RC, Rome
Saratoga Springs RC, Saratoga Springs
Peconic Bay RC, Southold
Syracuse Chargers RC, Syracuse
State University of New York at Albany, Albany
State University of New York at Binghamton, Binghamton
Fordham University, Bronx
Sarah Lawrence College, Bronxville
Long Island University, Brookville
State University of New York at Buffalo, Buffalo
University of Buffalo, Buffalo
Saint Lawrence University, Canton
Cazenovia College, Cazenovia
Hamilton College, Clinton
State University of New York at Geneseo, Geneseo
Hobart and William Smith College, Geneva
Colgate University, Hamilton
Hofstra University, Hempstead
Cornell University, Ithaca
Ithaca College, Ithaca
United States Merchant Marine Academy, Kings Point
Iona College, New Rochelle
Columbia University/Barnard College, New York
New York University, New York
Dowling College, Oakdale
Marist College, Poughkeepsie
Vassar College, Poughkeepsie
Manhattan College, Riverdale
Rochester Institute of Technology, Rochester
University of Rochester, Rochester
Skidmore College, Saratoga Springs
Union College, Schenectady
State University of New York at Stony Brook, Stony Brook
Syracuse University, Syracuse
State University of New York at Maritime College, Throggs Neck
Rensselaer Polytechnic Institute, Troy
Russell Sage College, Troy
United States Military Academy, West Point

Albany Rowing Center for Juniors, Albany
Charles W. Baker High School, Baldwinsville
Buffalo City Honors, Buffalo
Buffalo Seminary, Buffalo
Canisius High School, Buffalo
Holy Angels Academy, Buffalo
Nardin Academy, Buffalo
Nichols School, Buffalo
Saint Joseph's Collegiate Institute, Buffalo
West Side RC of Buffalo Inc. for Juniors, Buffalo
Burnt Hills RA for Juniors, Burnt Hills
Shenendehowa High School, Clifton Park
Cold Spring Hrbr Jr-Sr High School, Cold Spring Harbor
Dryden High School, Dryden
Fairport Central High School, Fairport
Fairport Crew Club Inc., Fairport
Sagamore RA for Juniors, Glenwood Landing
Huntington High School, Huntington
F.D. Roosevelt High School, Hyde Park
Cascadilla BC for Juniors, Ithaca
Ithaca High School, Ithaca
Lansing High School, Lansing
Shaker High School, Latham
Liverpool High School, Liverpool
Friends Academy, Locust Valley
Shaker RA, Loudonville
Chaminade High School, Mineola
Newburgh RC for Juniors, New Windsor
Newburgh Free Academy, Newburgh
Niskayuna High School, Niskayuna
Orchard Park High School, Orchard Park
Pittsford Crew, Pittsford
Arlington RA for Juniors, Pleasant Valley
Lourdes RA, Poughkeepsie
Mid-Hudson RA for Juniors, Poughkeepsie
Our Lady of Lourdes High School, Poughkeepsie
Poughkeepsie High School, Poughkeepsie
Spackenkill High School, Poughkeepsie
Rhinebeck High School, Rhinebeck
Horace Mann-Barnard Upper School, Riverdale
Brighton High School, Rochester
Beach Channel High School, Rockaway
Erie Canal RC for Juniors, Rome
Saratoga Springs High School, Saratoga Springs
Schenectady High School, Schenectedy
Scotia-Glenville RA, Scotia
Saint Anthony's High School, South Huntington
The Gow School, South Wales
Our Lady of Mercy Academy, Syosset
Henninger High School, Syracuse
Nottingham High School, Syracuse
Syracuse Chargers RA for Juniors, Syracuse
Emma Willard School, Troy
Clarkstown High School South, West Nyack

OHIO

Hocking Valley RA, Athens
Cincinnati RC, Cincinnati
Western Reserve RA, Cleveland
Ohio Athletic Club, Columbua
Greater Columbus RA, Columbus
Greater Dayton RA, Dayton
Toledo RC, Toledo
Westerville RC, Westerville
Burning River RC,
Ohio University, Athens
Bowling Green State University, Bowling Green
University of Cincinnati, Cincinnati
Xavier University, Cincinnati
Case Western Reserve University, Cleveland
Cleveland State University, Cleveland
Ohio State University, Columbus
University of Dayton, Dayton
Denison University, Granville
Marietta College, Marietta
Miami University of Ohio, Oxford
Wittenberg University, Springfield
John Carroll University, University Heights
Cincinnati Country Day School, Cincinnati
Cincinnati Junior RC, Cincinnati
Beaumont School for Girls, Cleveland
Saint Ignatius High School (OH), Cleveland
Dublin Crew, Dublin
Hilliard Davidson High School, Hilliard
Marietta High School, Marietta
Clermont High School, Milford
Shaker Heights High School, Shaker Heights
Central Catholic High School, Toledo
Notre Dame Academy, Toledo
Saint John's Jesuit, Toledo
Saint Ursula Academy, Toledo
Toledo Metropolitan RC, Toledo
Upper Arlington High School, Upper Arlington
Wellington High School, Wellington
Westerville Crew, Westerville
Cleveland Scholastic RA, Westlake
Anthony Wayne High School, Whitehouse
Oklahoma City RC, Oklahoma City
Tulsa RC, Tulsa
Oklahoma City Association for Rowing, Yukon
Oklahoma State University, Stillwater
University of Tulsa, Tulsa
Tulsa RC for Juniors, Tulsa

OREGON

Ashland RC, Ashland
Rowing Foundation of Oregon, Beaverton
Corvallis RC, Corvallis
Oregon Association of Rowers, Eugene

Portland/Vancouver RA, Hillsboro
Lake Ewauna RC, Klamath Falls
Lake Oswego Community Rowing, Lake Oswego
Portland BC, Lake Oswego
Station L RC, Portland
Oregon State University, Corvallis
University of Oregon, Eugene
Lewis and Clark College, Portland
Portland State University, Portland
University of Portland, Portland
Willamette University, Salem
South Eugene High School, Eugene
Lake Ewauna RC for Juniors, Klamath Falls
Oregon Rowing Unlimited for Juniors, Lake Oswego

PENNSYLVANIA
L'Aviron RC, Easton
Upper Merion BC Inc., King of Prussia
Wilmington Women's RC, Ladenberg
Bachelors Barge Club, Philadelphia
Crescent BC, Philadelphia
Fairmount RA, Philadelphia
Malta BC, Philadelphia
Penn Athletic Club RA, Philadelphia
Philadelphia Girls RC, Philadelphia
Philadelphia Rowing Program for the Disabled, Philadelphia
Undine Barge Club, Philadelphia
University Barge Club, Philadelphia
Vesper BC, Philadelphia
Three Rivers RA, Pittsburgh
Steel City RC, Verona
Central Pennsylvania RA,
Lehigh University, Bethlehem
Bryn Mawr College, Bryn Mawr
Lafayette College, Easton
Mercyhurst College, Erie
Haverford University, Haverford
Franklin and Marshall College, Lancaster
Bucknell University, Lewisburg
Robert Morris University, Moon Township
Drexel University, Philadelphia
LaSalle University, Philadelphia
Saint Joseph's University, Philadelphia
Temple University, Philadelphia
University of Pennsylvania, Philadelphia
Carlow College, Pittsburgh
Carnegie-Mellon University, Pittsburgh
Duquesne University, Pittsburgh
University of Pittsburgh, Pittsburgh
Susquehanna University, Selinsgrove
Penn State University, University Park
Villanova University, Villanova
Lower Merion High School, Ardmore
Conestoga High School, Berwyn

Country Day School of the Sacred Heart, Bryn Mawr
Shipley School, Bryn Mawr
The Baldwin School, Bryn Mawr
Archbishop Prendergast, Drexel Hill
Mercyhurst Preparatory School, Erie
Mount Saint Joseph Academy, Flourtown
Germantown Academy, Fort Washington
Haverford School, Haverford
Upper Merion High School, King of Prussia
Landsdale Catholic, Landsdale
Great Valley High School, Malvern
Malvern Preparatory School, Malvern
Episcopal Academy, Merion Station
Merion Mercy Academy, Merion Station
Fox Chapel High School, Millvale
Central High School, Philadelphia
Chestnut Hill Academy, Philadelphia
Father Judge High School, Philadelphia
Friends Select, Philadelphia
Monsignor Bonner High School, Philadelphia
Nazareth Academy High School, Philadelphia
Northeast Catholic High School, Philadelphia
Philadelphia Girls RC for Juniors, Philadelphia
Roman Catholic High School, Philadelphia
Saint Joseph's Prep, Philadelphia
Springside School, Philadelphia
Undine Barge Club for Juniors, Philadelphia
William Penn Charter High School, Philadelphia
Ellis School, Pittsburgh
Mount Lebanon High School, Pittsburgh
North Catholic High School, Pittsburgh
Oakland Catholic High School, Pittsburgh
Peabody High School, Pittsburgh
Schenley High School, Pittsburgh
Taylor-Allderdice High School, Pittsburgh
Upper Saint Clair High School, Pittsburgh
Winchester Thurston High School, Pittsburgh
Agnes Irwin School, Rosemont
Harriton High School, Rosemont
North Allegheny High School, Wexford
LaSalle College High School, Wyndmoor

RHODE ISLAND
OARS (Old & Ancient Rowing Society) of R.I., Kingston
Narragansett BC, Providence
Roger Williams University, Bristol
University of Rhode Island, Kingston
Brown University, Providence
Narragansett BC for Juniors, Providence

SOUTH CAROLINA
Columbia RC, Columbia
Charleston RC, Mt Pleasant
College of Charleston, Charleston
The Citadel, Charleston

Clemson University, Clemson
Furman University, Greenville
Hilton Head High School, Hilton Head Island

SOUTH DAKOTA
University of South Dakota, Vermillion

TENNESSEE
Lookout RC, Chattanooga
Knoxville RA, Knoxville
Oak Ridge RA, Oak Ridge
University of Tennessee at Chattanooga, Chattanooga
University of Tennessee at Knoxville, Knoxville
Vanderbilt University, Nashville
University of the South, Sewanee
Baylor School, Chattanooga
Chattanooga Junior Rowing, Chattanooga
Chattanooga School for Arts & Sciences, Chattanooga
Girls Preparatory School (GPS), Chattanooga
McCallie High School, Chattanooga
Clinton RC for Juniors, Clinton
Oak Ridge RA for Juniors, Oak Ridge

TEXAS
Austin RC, Austin
Rowing Dock, Austin
Dallas RC, Dallas
Fort Worth RC, Fort Worth
Bay Area RC of Houston, Houston
Houston RC, Seabrook
Greater Houston RC, Sugar Land
Rowing Club of the Woodlands, The Woodlands
University of Texas at Austin, Austin
Southern Methodist University, Dallas
Texas A&M Galveston, Galveston
Rice University, Houston
Baylor University, Waco
Austin RC for Juniors, Austin
Saint Stephen's Episcopal School, Austin
Episcopal School of Dallas, Dallas
Hockaday School, Dallas
Saint Mark's School of Texas, Dallas
Ursuline Academy of Dallas, Dallas
Saint Mary's Hall, San Antonio
The Woodlands Senior High School, The Woodlands

UTAH
Bonneville Rowing, Salt Lake City
Great Salt Lake Rowing, Salt Lake City

VIRGINIA
Alexandria Community Rowing, Alexandria
CAMSIS BC Inc., Alexandria
Occoquan BC, Burke
Rivanna RC, Charlottesville
Fairfax Grays RC, Fairfax Station
Northern Virginia RC, Fairfax Station

Virginia RC Inc., Hampton
Hampton Roads RC, Norfolk
Olde Towne RC, Portsmouth
Southern Branch RC, Portsmouth
Virginia BC, Richmond
Mobjack RA, Ware Neck
Prince William RC, Woodbridge
Virginia Polytechnic Inst. and State Univ., Blacksburg
University of Virginia, Charlottesville
George Mason University, Fairfax
Mary Washington College, Fredericksburg
Christopher Newport University, Newport News
Old Dominion University, Norfolk
University of Richmond, Richmond
College of William and Mary, Williamsburg
Alexandria Crew Boosters Inc., Alexandria
Bishop Ireton, Alexandria
Episcopal High School, Alexandria
T.C. Williams High School, Alexandria
Thomas Jefferson HS for Science and Technology, Alexandria
West Potomac High School, Alexandria
Bishop OConnell High School, Arlington
Wakefield High School, Arlington
Washington-Lee High School, Arlington
Yorktown High School, Arlington
Lake Braddock High School, Burke
Great Bridge High School, Chesapeake
Hickory High School, Chesapeake
Christchurch School, Christchurch
Potomac High School, Dumfries
Robinson Secondary School, Fairfax
WT Woodson High School, Fairfax
Fairfax High School, Fairfax Station
JR Robinson High School, Fairfax Station
George C. Marshall High School, Falls Church
JEB Stuart High School, Falls Church
Randolph Macon Academy, Front Royal
Gloucester High School, Gloucester
Langley High School, McLean
McLean High School, McLean
James River High School, Midlothian
Maury High School, Norfolk
Norfolk Collegiate School, Norfolk
West Springfield High School, Springfield
Saint Margaret's School, Tappahannock
James Madison High School, Vienna
First Colonial High School, Virginia Beach
Frank W. Cox High School, Virginia Beach
Mathews High School, Ware Neck
CD Hylton High School, Woodbridge
Forest Park High School, Woodbridge
Gar-Field High School, Woodbridge
Woodbridge High School, Woodbridge

VERMONT
Motley RC, Morrisville
University of Vermont, Burlington
Middlebury College, Middlebury
Putney School, Putney

WASHINGTON
Bainbridge Island Rowing, Bainbridge Island
Sammamish RA, Bellevue
Everett RA, Everett
Lake Stevens RC, Lake Stevens
Orcas Island RC, Olga
Olympia Area Rowing, Olympia
Ancient Mariners RC, Seattle
Cascade Rowing, Seattle
Charley McIntyre RC, Seattle
Conibear RC, Seattle
Interlochen RC, Seattle
Lake Union Crew, Seattle
Lake Washington RC, Seattle
Martha's Moms, Seattle
Moss Bay Rowing and Kayaking Center, Seattle
Mount Baker Adult Crew, Seattle
Northwest Sculling Association, Seattle
Pocock BC, Seattle
Pocock Rowing Center, Seattle
Portage Bay RC, Seattle
Seattle Yacht Club Rowing Foundation, Seattle
Sound Rowers, Seattle
Union Bay RC, Seattle
Coeur d'Alene RA, Spokane
Rainier RC, Tacoma
Vashon Island RC, Vashon
Commencement Bay RC,
Western Washington University, Bellingham
Washington State University, Pullman
Seattle Pacific University, Seattle
Seattle University, Seattle
University of Washington, Seattle
Gonzaga University, Spokane
Pacific Lutheran University, Tacoma
University of Puget Sound, Tacoma
Green Hill Academic School, Chehalis
Everett RA for Juniors, Everett
Green Lake High School, Seattle
Holy Names Academy, Seattle
Lakeside School (WA), Seattle
Moss Bay RC for Juniors, Seattle
Mount Baker High School, Seattle
The Bush School, Seattle
Charles Wright Academy, University Place

WISCONSIN
Fox Valley RC, Appleton
La Baie Verte RC, Green Bay
Mendota RC, Madison
Picnic Point RC, Madison
Milwaukee RC, Milwaukee
Lawrence University, Appleton
Saint Norbert College, Little Suamico
University of Wisconsin at Madison, Madison
Marquette University, Milwaukee
Mendota RC for Juniors, Madison
Milwaukee RC for Juniors, Milwaukee

WEST VIRGINIA
Monongahela RA, Morgantown
Ohio Valley RC, Parkersburg
Red and White Rowing, Parkersburg
University of Charleston, Charleston
West Virginia University, Morgantown
Parkersburg High School, Parkersburg
Parkersburg South High School, Parkersburg
Red and White Rowing, Parkersburg